# TURBO PASCAL®

## Owner's Handbook

## Version 4.0

Borland International
4585 Scotts Valley Drive
Scotts Valley, CA 95066

**This manual was produced in its entirety with Sprint:® The Professional Word Processor, available from Borland.**

# Table of Contents

## Part 3

Welcome to version 4.0 of Turbo Pascal! Turbo Pascal is designed to meet the needs of all types of users of IBM PCs and compatibles. It's a structured, high-level language you can use to write programs for any type or size application.

The current version of Turbo Pascal is the fourth generation of Borland's flagship language product. With Turbo Pascal 1.0, Borland pioneered the high-speed microcomputer language compiler; version 4.0 strengthens Turbo Pascal in its role as a serious development language. With 4.0, you'll get

- two to three times faster compilation speed (lines per minute) than version 3.0 (on an 8MHz IBM AT).

- much improved code generation, producing faster execution.

- a smart built-in linker that removes unused code at link time, producing smaller code.

- .EXE files that allow programs larger than 64K.

- the ability to perform separate compilation using units.

- built-in project management that performs automatic recompilation of dependent source files (including units).

- several standard units, including *System, Dos, Crt,* and *Graph*.

- a more powerful assembly language interface and inline assembly options.

- the ability to nest Include files to eight levels deep.

- several new data types, including longint, shortint, word, and IEEE floating-point types (single, double, extended, and comp) if you're using an 8087 chip.

- several new built-in procedures and functions, including *Inc()* and *Dec()*.

- ANSI standard compatibility.

- built-in 8087/80287 coprocessor support.

- short-circuit Boolean expression evaluation.

- conditional compilation directives.

- a high degree of compatibility with version 3.0, and utilities and units to aid in converting 3.0 programs to 4.0.
- command-line and integrated environment versions of the compiler.

# Understanding 4.0

As you're reading through this manual, several major concepts will be introduced. To help clarify these ideas, here's a summary of some of 4.0's highlights.

## Integrated Environment and Command-Line Compilers

The Turbo Pascal compiler is actually two compilers: a command-line compiler and an integrated environment version. The traditional command-line or batch mode compiler allows you to use your own editor to create and modify program source code. You then run the compiler from either the command line or a batch file, giving the file name and any other compiler options. This compiler is the TPC.EXE file on your disk.

There is also a Borland-style integrated environment that combines a text editor and compiler. The environment provides pull-down menus, windows, input boxes, configuration control, and context-sensitive help. This compiler is the TURBO.EXE file on your disk.

## Separate Compilation

Separate compilation lets you break programs into parts and compile them. That way you can test each part to make sure it works. You can then link all the parts together to build a program. This is useful, since you don't have to recompile everything that makes up a program each time you use it. In addition, this feature lets you build up a toolbox of precompiled, tested code that you can use in all your programs.

## Programs and Units

A program is the main piece of Pascal source code that you write and execute. In order to provide for separate compilation and still maintain Pascal's strict checking among program parts, units are used. A *unit* is a piece of source code that can be compiled as a stand-alone entity. You can think of units as a library of data and program code. They provide a description of the interface between the unit's code and data and other programs that will use that unit. Programs and other units can use units; units don't use programs.

## Compile, Make, and Build

It's probable that you may change the source code of several of the units you're using without recompiling them; however, you'll definitely want your main program to use the absolute latest units. How do you make sure you're using the most recently modified units? We've provided two ways for you to make sure the unit files are brought up to date.

The **Make** option tells the compiler to go and look at the date and time of any source and compiled unit file used by your main program (or another unit, since units can use units). If the source file was modified since the unit was compiled, the compiler will recompile the unit to bring it up to date.

The **Build** option is similar to **Make** except that it will recompile all of the units used by your main program (or unit) *without* checking date and time. Use this option if you want to make absolutely sure you have all the latest compiled units.

## Pick File List

The pick file contains the state of the integrated environment so that when you leave TURBO.EXE and return to it later, you are placed at the spot in the file where you left off previously. The pick file list also offers you easy access to files when you are editing multiple files. The last eight file names and the state of each respective file that you've edited are kept in the pick list. When you select a file from the pick list, the file is loaded and the cursor is placed at the point in the file where you were when you left it. You can enable or disable pick file (TURBO.PCK) generation.

## File Extensions

There are all kinds of file name extensions used in the DOS world; most are usually application- or program-specific. (Remember that a file name consists of up to eight characters with an optional three-character extension.) Turbo Pascal uses several different file name extensions:

- **.EXE:** an executable file. The two compilers themselves are .EXE files. The compiled programs you'll build with the compilers will be .EXE files. (Turbo Pascal 3.0 created .COM files that were also executable files.)

- **.TPU:** a precompiled unit file. When you compile a Pascal unit, the compiler generates a .TPU file with the same first eight characters of the source file. A .TPU file contains the symbol information and compiled code for the unit.

- **.TPL:** a Turbo Pascal library file. You can use only one of these at a time. The standard library file on the disk is called TURBO.TPL. You can modify TURBO.TPL to suit your needs.

- **.TP and .CFG:** configuration files for the two compilers. These files allow you to override default settings in the compilers and customize compiler default values to your own needs.

  A .TP file is a binary file containing the options you set for the integrated environment. You can have multiple .TP files for different settings.

  TPC.CFG is the configuration file for the command-line version of the compiler. There can be only one TPC.CFG file. It is a text file that contains directories to the compiler, command-line switches, etc.

- **.TPM:** a Turbo MAP file. This file is generated if you use the {$T+} compiler option. It contains information about your program that can be useful for finding runtime errors and doing source-level debugging. The TPMAP.EXE utility on the disk will convert the .TPM file to a MAP file that can be used with most standard symbolic debuggers.

- **.PAS:** Use this for your Pascal source code files. You can use other file name extensions, but traditionally .PAS is used.

- **.BAK:** backup source file extension. The editor in the integrated environment renames the existing file on disk to a .BAK file when you save a modified version of the file. You can enable or disable .BAK file generation.

- **.PCK:** the Turbo Pascal pick file extension. The pick file contains the state of the integrated environment so that when you leave TURBO.EXE and return later on, you are placed at the spot in the file where you were last working. You can enable or disable pick file generation.

## About This Manual

This manual walks you through writing, compiling, and saving Turbo Pascal programs. It explains in detail the many new features and how to use them. It also teaches you how to take existing version 3.0 programs and convert them to run under Turbo Pascal version 4.0.

Sample programs are provided on your distribution disks for you to study. You can also tailor these sample exercises to your particular needs.

Before you get started, you should be somewhat familiar with the basics of operating an IBM PC (or compatible) under MS-DOS (or PC-DOS). You'll need to know how to run programs, copy and delete files, and how to use other basic DOS commands. If you're not sure about how to do these things, spend some time playing with your PC and reviewing the MS-DOS user's manual that came with it; you can also look at Appendix G, "A DOS Primer," to learn some basics. Appendix H lists many of the terms introduced in this manual.

This manual is divided into three main sections: "The User's Guide" (Part 1), "The Reference Section" (Part 2), and "The Appendices" (Part 3).

## *The User's Guide*

"The User's Guide" introduces you to Turbo Pascal, shows you how to use it, and includes chapters that focus on such specific features as units and debugging. Here's a breakdown of the chapters:

- **Chapter 1: Getting Started** explains how to make backup copies of your Turbo Pascal disks, describes the different files on the disks, and tells you how to set up Turbo Pascal for your particular system.

- **Chapter 2: Beginning Turbo Pascal** leads you directly from loading Turbo Pascal into writing simple programs, and then on to compiling and running them. A discussion of a few common programming errors and how to avoid them is also presented. You'll learn some basics about getting around in the integrated environment. We then suggest how to go about reading the rest of the manual, depending on your familiarity with Pascal.

- **Chapter 3: Programming in Turbo Pascal** introduces you to the Pascal programming language.

- **Chapter 4: Units and Related Mysteries** tells you what a unit is, how it's used, what predefined units (libraries) Turbo Pascal provides, and how to write your own. It also describes the general structure of a unit and its interface and implementation portions, as well as how to initialize and compile a unit.

- **Chapter 5: Getting the Most from Your PC** describes how to use units and the built-in Turbo Pascal extensions, and also explains how to use inline and external assembly language.

- **Chapter 6: Project Management** tells how to develop large programs using multiple source files and libraries, and discusses conditional compilation.
- **Chapter 7: Using the Unit Mover** explains the use of TPUMOVER for copying units from file to file.
- **Chapter 8: Converting from Turbo Pascal 3.0** provides guidelines for converting Turbo Pascal 3.0 programs to Turbo Pascal 4.0.
- **Chapter 9: Debugging Your Turbo Pascal Programs** gives suggestions on how to track down and eliminate errors in your programs, and also tells how to use Periscope, a symbolic debugger.
- **Chapter 10: The Turbo Pascal Menu Reference** is a complete guide to the menu commands in Turbo Pascal's integrated environment.
- **Chapter 11: Using The Editor** explains how to use the built-in editor to open, edit, change, save a file, and more.
- **Chapter 12: The Command-Line Reference** is a complete guide to the command-line version of Turbo Pascal.

## *The Reference Manual*

Part 2 of the manual offers technical information on the following features:

- **Chapter 13: Tokens and Constants**
- **Chapter 14: Blocks, Locality, and Scope**
- **Chapter 15: Types**
- **Chapter 16: Variables**
- **Chapter 17: Typed Constants**
- **Chapter 18: Expressions**
- **Chapter 19: Statements**
- **Chapter 20: Procedures and Functions**
- **Chapter 21: Programs and Units**
- **Chapter 22: Input and Output**
- **Chapter 23: Standard Procedures and Functions**
- **Chapter 24: Standard Units**
- **Chapter 25: Using the 8087**
- **Chapter 26: Inside Turbo Pascal**
- **Chapter 27: Turbo Pascal Reference Lookup**

## *Appendices*

Finally, Part 3 of this manual contains nine appendices that deal with the following topics:

- **Appendix A: Differences Between Version 3.0 and 4.0**
- **Appendix B: Comparing Turbo Pascal 4.0 with ANSI Pascal**
- **Appendix C: Compiler Directives**
- **Appendix D: The Turbo Pascal Utilities**
- **Appendix E: Reference Materials**
- **Appendix F: Customizing Turbo Pascal**
- **Appendix G: A DOS Primer**
- **Appendix H: A Glossary**
- **Appendix I: Error Messages and Codes**

# Typography

This manual was produced entirely by Borland's Sprint: The Professional Word Processor, on an Apple LaserWriter Plus. The different typefaces displayed are used for the following purposes:

| | |
|---|---|
| *Italics* | In text, this typeface represents constant identifiers, field identifiers, and formal parameter identifiers, as well as unit names, labels, types, variables, procedures, and functions. |
| **Boldface** | Turbo Pascal's reserved words are set in this typeface. |
| `Monospace` | This type represents text that appears on your screen. |
| *Keycaps* | This typeface indicates a key on your keyboard. It is often used when describing a key you have to press to perform a particular function; for example, "Press *Esc* to exit from a menu." |

# How to Contact Borland

If, after reading this manual and using Turbo Pascal, you would like to contact Borland with comments or suggestions, we suggest the following procedures:

- The best way is to log on to Borland's forum on CompuServe: Type GO BORPRO at the main CompuServe menu and follow the menus to section 4. Leave your questions or comments here for the support staff to process.

- If you prefer, write a letter detailing your problem and send it to Technical Support Department, Borland International, 4585 Scotts Valley Drive, Scotts Valley, CA 95066 U.S.

- As a last resort, you can telephone our Technical Support department. To help us handle your problem as quickly as possible have these items handy before you call: product name and version number, product serial number, computer make and model number, and operating system and version number.

If you're not familiar with Borland's No-Nonsense License statement, now's the time to read the agreement at the front of this manual and mail in your completed product registration card.

P A R T

**1**

# 1

# Getting Started

In this chapter, we'll get you started using Turbo Pascal by providing instructions for loading it on systems with floppy disk or hard disk drives. We'll also offer some guidance on how to go about reading this manual, based on your programming experience.

The three distribution disks that accompany this manual are formatted for standard 5 1/4-inch disks, 360K disk drives, and can be read by IBM PCs and compatibles (those with 3 1/2-inch disk, 720K disk drives will receive two distribution disks). Now, before you do anything else, we want you to make backup copies of these three disks and then put the originals away. Since there's a replacement charge if you erase or damage the original disks, take heed and use your originals only to make work or backup copies. Here's how:

- Get three new (or unused) floppy disks.

- Boot up your computer.

- At the system prompt, type `diskcopy A: B:` and press *Enter*. The message `Insert source diskette in drive A:` will be displayed on your screen. Remove your system disk from drive *A* and put distribution disk 1 into drive *A*.

- If your system has two floppy disk drives, your screen will also say `Insert destination diskette into drive B`. In that case you'll need to remove any disk in drive *B*, replacing it with a blank disk. If your system only has one floppy drive, then you'll be swapping disks in drive *A*. Just remember that the distribution disk is the *source* disk, the blank disk is the *destination* disk.

- If you haven't done it already, press *Enter*. The computer will start reading from the source disk in drive *A*.

- If you have a two-drive system, it will then write out to the destination disk in drive *B* and continue reading from *A* and writing to *B* until copying is complete. If you have a one-drive system, you'll be asked to put the destination disk in *A*, then the source disk, then the destination disk, and so on and so forth until it's finished.

- When copying is completed, remove the distribution (source) disk from drive *A*, and put it away. Remove the copy (destination) disk from drive *B* and label it "Disk #1."

- Repeat the preceding process with the second and third distribution disks and the other blank floppies.

Now that you've made your backup copies, we can get on to the meat of this chapter.

# What's On Your Disks

The two distribution disks that come with this manual include two different versions of the Pascal compiler: an integrated environment version and a stand-alone, command-line version.

You won't need to put all the files on your distribution disks onto your Turbo Pascal system disk—in fact, you'll probably only need TURBO.TPL (the resident library) and either TURBO.EXE (the integrated environment) or TPC.EXE (the command-line compiler), depending on which compiler you prefer to use. For your reference, here's a summary of most of the files on disks and how to determine which ones to retain:

| | |
|---|---|
| TURBO.EXE | This is the integrated (menu-driven) environment version of Turbo Pascal. If you want to use the development environment of Turbo Pascal to edit, compile, and run your program, be sure to copy this. |
| TURBO.TPL | This contains the units (program libraries) that come with Turbo Pascal, including *System*, *Crt*, *Dos*, *Printer*, *Turbo3*, and *Graph3*—this is a must! |
| TINST.EXE | This utility allows you to customize certain features of TURBO.EXE. If you're using TURBO.EXE, copy this file. You can delete it once you've modified TURBO.EXE to your liking. |
| GRAPH.TPU | This contains the *Graph* unit (the Borland Graphics Interface unit). |

| | |
|---|---|
| TPC.EXE | This is the command-line version of Turbo Pascal. If you use a separate editor, make heavy use of batch files, and so on, you'll probably want to copy this. |
| TPMAP.EXE | This utility creates a symbolic debugger-compatible .MAP file from a .TPM file. TPMAP also creates a .DEP file, which is a comprehensive list of all the unit, include, and .OBJ file dependencies. If you aren't using a symbolic debugger, then you don't need this file. |
| TPUMOVER.EXE | This utility allows you to move units between .TPL files; more specifically, you can use it to add units (that you write) to TURBO.TPL or to remove units from that file. Copy it if you plan to modify TURBO.TPL. |
| README.COM | This is the program to display the README file. Once you've read the README, you can delete this. |
| README | To see any updated information, run this file by typing README at the system prompt. (If you have a printer, you can print it out.) Once you review this material, you can delete this. |
| UPGRADE.EXE | This utility does a quick upgrade of Turbo Pascal version 3.0 source files, modifying them for compatibility with Turbo Pascal version 4.0. If you don't have 3.0 programs to convert, don't copy it. |
| TPCONFIG.EXE | This utility takes your integrated environment configuration file and converts it to work with the command-line compiler (as TPC.CFG). It's helpful if you want to use the integrated environment to set all your options, but want to compile with the command-line version. This utility will also convert a TPC.CFG file to a .TP file. |
| MAKE.EXE | This is an intelligent program manager that allows you to automatically update files (via assembly and compilation) you've modified. It only works with the command-line compiler (TPC.EXE). |
| TOUCH.COM | This utility changes the date and time of one or more files to the current date and time, making it "newer" than the files that depend on it. |
| GREP.COM | This is a powerful search utility that can look for several files at once. |

| | |
|---|---|
| *.PAS files | These include the MicroCalc source files, as well as other sample programs. You can ignore these unless you want to read or experiment with them. |
| BINOBJ.EXE | Use this utility to convert a binary file to an .OBJ file. |
| *.DOC files | These include the interface section listings for all the standard units. |
| *.BGI files | BGI graphics device drivers. |
| *.CHR files | BGI graphics stroked character fonts. |

# Installing Turbo Pascal On Your System

Your Turbo Pascal package includes all the files and programs necessary to run both the integrated environment and command-line versions of the compiler. The files you copy depend on which version of the compiler you want to use.

## *Setting Up On a Floppy Disk System*

The basic files you need for Turbo Pascal are small enough to be easily run from a one-floppy system; though, you may want to use only one version of the compiler (TURBO.EXE or TPC.EXE), rather than have both on disk.

First, you're going to create a bootable (system) disk. Get yourself another blank disk and at the DOS prompt, type

```
format b:/s
```

Your system will ask you to insert a DOS disk into drive *A*; just insert your regular system boot disk. If you have a two-drive system, place a blank disk into drive *B* and press *Enter* when prompted. If you have a one-drive system, place your blank disk into the drive whenever you are asked to insert a blank disk into drive *B*, and place your original boot disk into the drive whenever you are asked to insert a DOS disk into drive *A*.

When you're finished, your blank disk will be formatted and will contain a copy of MS-DOS (the operating system). Label it as your Turbo Pascal system disk and continue to the next step.

Put your Turbo Pascal system disk into drive *A*. If you have a second drive, put your Turbo Pascal distribution disk 1 into drive *B* and type

```
A>dir b:
```

That will list all the files on the first distribution disk. You can copy them one at a time from your Turbo Pascal distribution disk onto your system disk by typing

```
A>copy b:filename a:
```

where *filename* is the name of the file you wish to copy. As mentioned, the two files you absolutely must copy are TURBO.TPL, and either TURBO.EXE or TPC.EXE (or both).

## Setting Up On a Hard Disk

The first thing you want to do is to create a subdirectory called TP (or whatever you choose) off of your root directory. Assuming that your hard disk is designated as drive *C*, use the following commands:

```
c:
cd c:\
mkdir tp
```

Now place each Turbo Pascal distribution disk into drive *A* and type the following command:

```
copy a:*.* c:\tp
```

Now put your distribution disks in a safe place. If you'd like, you can delete from your hard disk any of the files you don't need. (Refer to the preceding section for which files you might not need.)

# Choosing From Two Compilers

Believe it or not, you've bought two complete versions of the Turbo Pascal compiler. The first, TURBO.EXE, is known as the *integrated environment*. It provides a pull-down menu- and keystroke-driven multiwindow environment. You can load, edit, save, compile, and run your programs without ever leaving it. Most of the chapters that follow this one are devoted to using the integrated environment.

The second version, TPC.EXE, is known as the *command-line compiler*. It presumes that you have created your Pascal program with some other editor (MicroStar, BRIEF, EDLIN, even the integrated environment). You run it from the MS-DOS system prompt; for example, if your program is in a file named MYFIRST.PAS, you would type at the prompt

```
tpc myfirst
```

and then press *Enter*. TPC.EXE compiles and links your program, producing an .EXE file (just like TURBO.EXE). Command-line options allow you to specify a number of things, such as where the system library (TURBO.TPL) resides and whether to recompile any files upon which MYFIRST.PAS depends.

Which version should you use? Chances are you'll find the integrated environment best suits your needs. It provides a complete development system in which you can quickly build and debug programs. On the other hand, if you are currently using a command-line Pascal compiler, if you have another editor that you prefer, or if you are making heavy use of an assembler (for external subroutines), you may want to use the command-line compiler in conjunction with a batch file or Make utility.

# Using This Manual

Now that you've loaded the Turbo Pascal files and libraries onto the appropriate floppy disks or hard disk directories, you can start digesting this manual and using Turbo Pascal. But, since this user's guide is written for three different types of users, certain chapters are written with your particular Turbo Pascal programming needs in mind. Take a few moments to read the following, then take off programming.

- **Programmers Learning Pascal:** If you're a beginning Pascal programmer, you will want to read Chapters 2 through 7. These are written in tutorial fashion and take you through creating and compiling your first Pascal programs. Along the way, they teach you how to use the integrated environment. (You may want to also look at the *Turbo Pascal Tutor* manual.)

- **Experienced Pascal Programmers:** If you're an experienced Pascal programmer, you should have little difficulty porting your programs to this implementation. You'll want to skim Chapters 10 and 11 to get familiar with the integrated environment, and take some time to read Chapter 4 to understand the role of units. You'll also want to study "Part 2: The Reference Section," and note the differences between Turbo Pascal 4.0 and your Pascal compiler. Appendix B, "Comparing Turbo Pascal 4.0 With ANSI Pascal," will offer you some additional insights.

- **Turbo Pascal Programmers:** Chapter 8, "Converting from 3.0 Programs," is written specifically for you; here's where we provide guidelines on the things you'll need to convert your 3.0-produced programs to version 4.0. (Appendix A highlights the differences between 3.0 and 4.0.) You'll also need to glance at Chapter 10 to get familiar with the integrated environment and Chapter 12 to learn the command-line version.

Whatever your approach, welcome to the world of Turbo Pascal 4.0!

C   H   A   P   T   E   R

# 2

# Beginning Turbo Pascal

Turbo Pascal is more than just a fast Pascal compiler; it is an efficient Pascal compiler with an easy-to-learn and easy-to-use integrated development environment. With Turbo Pascal, you don't need to use a separate editor, compiler, and linker in order to create and run your Pascal programs (although, you can use the command-line version). All these features are built into Turbo Pascal, and they are all accessible from the Turbo Pascal integrated environment.

Now that you're set up, you can begin writing your first Turbo Pascal program using the integrated environment compiler. By the end of this chapter, you'll have learned the basics of this development environment, written three small programs, saved them, and learned a few basic programming skills.

## Using the Integrated Environment

In this section, we describe the components of the Turbo Pascal main screen, and explain briefly how to move around in the environment. For greater detail, refer to Chapter 10, "The Turbo Pascal Menu Reference"; for more on the editor, refer to Chapter 11.

Turbo Pascal provides context-sensitive onscreen help at the touch of a single key. You can get help at any point (except when executing a program) by pressing *F1*. The Help window details the functions of the item on which you're currently positioned. Any Help screen can contain one or more *keywords* (a highlighted item) on which you can get more information. Use the arrow keys to move to any keyword, and press *Enter* to get more detailed help on the selected item. You can use the *Home* and *End* keys to go to the first and last keywords on the screen, respectively.

To get to the Help index, press *F1* again once you're in the Help system. The Help index lets you access both language and environment help. While you're in the editor, you can also get help on a particular procedure, function, variable, constant, type, or unit by positioning the cursor on the item and pressing *Ctrl-F1*. (**Note:** *Ctrl-F1* is an editor command that can be redefined using TINST described in Appendix F.)

If you want to return to a previous Help screen while either in or out of the Help system, press *Alt-F1*. (You can back up through 20 previous Help screens.) Within a help group (a series of related help screens), *Alt-F1* remembers the group as one screen viewed rather than remembering each screen individually. In a help group, wherever *PgUp* and *PgDn* occur, *PgUp* takes you back a screen, and *PgDn* takes you forward. To exit from Help and return to your menu selection, press *Esc* (or any of the hotkeys described in the next section).

When you load Turbo Pascal (type `turbo` and press *Enter* at the DOS prompt), the program's first screen includes the main screen and product version information (pressing *Alt-F10* any time will bring up this information). When you press any key, the version information disappears, but the main screen remains.

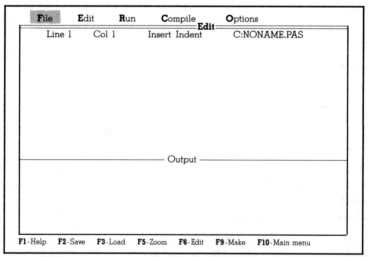

Look closely at the main screen; it consists of four parts: the main menu, the Edit window, the Output window, and the *bottom* line (which indicates which keys do what at that particular instance).

To get familiar with the Turbo Pascal system, here are some navigating basics.

**From within a menu:**

- Use the highlighted capital letter to select a menu item or use the arrow keys to move to the item and press *Enter*.

- Press *Esc* to leave a menu.

- Press *Esc* when in the main menu to go to the previously active window. (When active, the window will have a double bar at its top, and its name will be highlighted.)

- Press *F6* to get from any menu level to the previously active window.

- Use the *Right* and *Left arrow* keys to move from one pull-down menu to another.

**From anywhere in Turbo Pascal:**

- Press *F1* to get information about your current position (help on running, compiling, and so on).

- Press *F10* to invoke the main menu.

- Pressing *Alt* plus the first letter of any main menu command (*F, E, R, C, O*) invokes the command specified. For example, from anywhere in the system, pressing *Alt-E* will take you to the Edit window; *Alt-F* takes you to the File menu.

**From within the Edit or Output window:**

- Press *F5* to zoom/unzoom the active window.

- Press *F6* to switch windows.

**Note:** To exit Turbo Pascal and return to DOS, press *Alt-X* or go to the File menu and select **Quit** (press *Q* or move the selection bar to **Quit** and press *Enter*). If you select **Quit** without saving your current work file, the editor will query whether you want to save it.

## Using Hotkeys

There are a number of hotkeys (shortcuts) you can use. *Hotkeys* are keys set up to perform a certain function. For example, as discussed previously, pressing *Alt* and the first letter of a main menu command will take you to the specified option's menu or perform an action (see Figure 2.1 for a graphic example); these are all considered hotkeys. The only other *Alt*/first-letter command is *Alt-X*, which is really just a shortcut for File/**Quit**.

In general, hotkeys work from anywhere; but there are two exceptions.

One is that hotkeys are disabled in error boxes and verify boxes. In these cases, you are required to press the key specified.

The second exception is in the editor. If you use TINST to install editor key commands, you can define hotkeys as edit commands. This means that while you are in the editor, the hotkey will behave as an edit command, and when you are not in the editor, the hotkey will work as originally defined. For example, if you define *Alt-R* to be *PgUp* in the editor, it will not run your programs from the editor. So you must somehow exit the editor (*F10* or *F6*) before *Alt-R* will run your program. This gives you the flexibility to define the keys you prefer to use when editing. (Refer to Appendix F for a complete discussion of redefining the editor keys.)

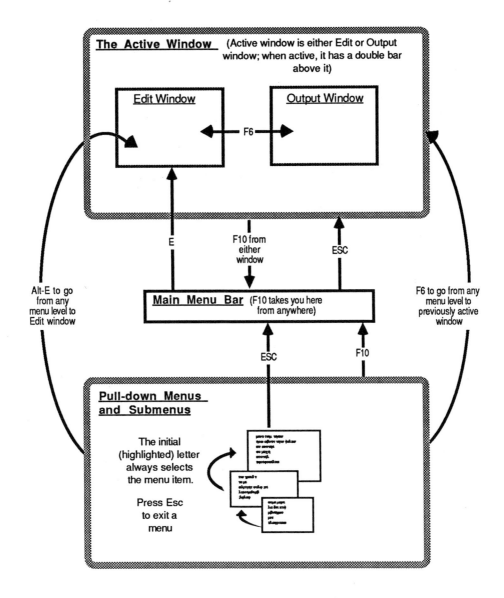

The Active Window   (Active window is either Edit or Output window; when active, it has a double bar above it)

Edit Window

Output Window

F6

E

F10 from either window

ESC

Alt-E to go from any menu level to Edit window

Main Menu Bar  (F10 takes you here from anywhere)

F6 to go from any menu level to previously active window

ESC

F10

Pull-down Menus and Submenus

The initial (highlighted) letter always selects the menu item.

Press Esc to exit a menu

From anywhere in Turbo Pascal, Alt plus the first letter of any main menu command (F, E, R, C, or O) invokes that command, and F1 calls up context-sensitive help information. Press Alt and hold for a list of Alt-key shortcuts.

Figure 2.1: A Sample Use of Hotkeys

Table 2.1 lists all the hotkeys you can use while in Turbo Pascal. Remember that when these keys are pressed, their specific function is carried out no matter where you are in the Turbo Pascal environment.

Table 2.1: Turbo Pascal's Hotkeys

| Key(s) | Function |
| --- | --- |
| F1 | Brings up a Help window with information about your current position |
| F2 | Saves the file currently in the editor |
| F3 | Lets you load a file (an input box will appear) |
| F5 | Zooms and unzooms the active window |
| F6 | Switches to the active window |
| F9 | Performs a "Make" |
| F10 | Invokes the main menu |
| Alt-F1 | Brings up the last Help screen you referenced |
| Alt-F3 | Lets you pick a file to load |
| Alt-F5 | Takes you to the saved screen |
| Alt-F9 | Compiles your program |
| Alt-F10 | Displays the version screen |
| Alt-C | Takes you to the Compile menu |
| Alt-E | Puts you in the editor |
| Alt-F | Takes you to the File menu |
| Alt-O | Takes you to the Options menu |
| Alt-R | Runs your program |
| Alt-X | Quits Turbo Pascal and takes you to DOS |
| Ctrl-F6 | Next window |

In this book, we will refer to all menu items by an abbreviated name. The abbreviated name for a given menu item is represented by the sequence of letters you type to get to that item from the main menu. For example:

■ At the main menu, the menu offering compile-time options related to memory sizes is the **Options/Compiler/Memory** sizes; we'll tell you to select **O/C/Memory** (press *O C M*).

■ At the main menu, the menu for specifying the name of the Include directories is the **Options/Directories/Include** directories; we'll tell you to select **O/D/Include** (press *O D I*).

If you feel like you need more help using the integrated environment, look at Chapter 10. If you're comfortable with what you've learned to date, let's get on to actually writing some programs in Turbo Pascal.

# Loading Turbo Pascal

If you're using a floppy disk drive, put your Turbo Pascal system disk into drive A: and type the following command at the system prompt:

```
A>turbo
```

and press *Enter*. This runs the program TURBO.EXE, which brings up the integrated environment, placing you in the main menu.

If you're using a hard disk, get into the Turbo Pascal subdirectory you created in the previous chapter and run TURBO.EXE by typing the following:

```
C>cd tp
C:\TP>turbo
```

You're now ready to write your first Turbo Pascal program.

# Creating Your First Program

When you first get into Turbo Pascal, you're placed at the main menu. Press *E* to get to the Edit window (or you can use the arrow keys and press *Enter* when positioned at the Edit command). You'll be placed in the editor with the cursor in the upper left-hand corner. You can start typing in the following program, pressing *Enter* at the end of each line:

```
program MyFirst;
var
  A,B   : integer;
  Ratio : real;
begin
  Write('Enter two numbers: ');
  Readln(A,B);
  Ratio := A / B;
  Writeln('The ratio is ',Ratio)
end.
```

To move around in the Edit window, you can use the arrow keys. (If you're unfamiliar with editing commands, Chapter 11 discusses all the editing commands you have at your disposal.) Note the semicolon at the end of most lines, as well as the period at the end of the last line—these are necessary. If you make any errors, you can use the arrows keys on the keyboard to move around; you can use the *Backspace* key to make deletions; and you can simply type new text to make insertions.

## Analyzing Your First Program

You can type in and run this program without ever knowing how it works, but here's a brief explanation. The first line gives the program the name *MyFirst*. This is an optional statement, but it's a good practice to include it.

The next three lines declare some *variables*, with the word **var** signaling the start of variable declarations. *A* and *B* are declared to be of type integer; that is, they can contain whole numbers, such as 52, –421, 0, 32283, and so on. *Ratio* is declared to be of type real, which means it can hold fractional numbers such as 423.328, –0.032, and so on (in addition to all integer values as well).

The rest of the program contains the *statements* to be executed. The word **begin** signals the start of the program. The statements are separated by semicolons and contain instructions to write to the screen (*Write* and *Writeln*), to read from the keyboard (*Readln*), and to perform calculations (*Ratio := A / B*). Execution starts with the first instruction after **begin** and continues until **end.** is encountered.

## Saving Your First Program

Having entered your first program, it's a good idea to save it to disk. To do this, press *F2* while you're still in the Edit window. By default, your file will have been been given the name NONAME.PAS. You can rename it now by typing in MYFIRST.PAS, and then pressing *Enter*. Any time you press *F2* after that, your program will be saved as MYFIRST.PAS.

An alternate method of saving your program uses the File menu. Press *F10* (or *Ctrl-K D*) to get out of the Edit window and invoke the main menu. Then press *F* to bring up the File menu and *S* to select the **S**ave command. Like pressing *F2*, you'll be queried whether you want to save this file as NONAME.PAS. Again, enter in the name MYFIRST.PAS as your file name.

## Compiling Your First Program

To compile your first program, get back to the main menu; if you're still in the Edit window, press *F10* (or *Ctrl-K D*) to do so. Press *C* to bring up the Compile menu, then press *C* again to select the **C**ompile command from that menu; otherwise press *F9*. (The Compile menu has several options; see Chapter 10.)

Turbo Pascal compiles your program, changing it from Pascal (which you can read) to 8086 machine code for the microprocessor (which your PC can execute). You don't see the 8086 machine code; it's stored in memory somewhere (or on disk).

When you start compiling, a box appears in the middle of the screen, giving information about the compilation taking place. A message flashes across the box to press *Ctrl-Break* to quit compilation. If compilation is successful, the message `Success: Press any key` flashes across the box. The box remains visible until you press a key. See how fast that went?

If an error occurs during compilation, Turbo Pascal stops, positions the cursor at the point of error in the editor, and displays an error message at the top of the editor. Press any key to clear the error message. (Note: The keystroke you select is used by the editor.) Then make the correction, save the updated file, compile it again.

## *Running Your First Program*

After you've fixed any errors that might have occurred, go to the main menu and select **Run** to run it.

The Output window is displayed full screen, and the message

```
Enter two numbers:
```

appears on the screen. Type in any two integers (whole numbers), with a space between them, and press *Enter*. The following message will appear:

```
The ratio is
```

followed by the ratio of the first number to the second.

Once your program has finished running, the prompt

```
Press any key to return to Turbo Pascal
```

appears at the bottom of the screen. Notice that your program output is displayed in the Output window so you can refer to it while looking at your program.

If an error occurs while your program is executing, you'll get a message on the screen that looks like this:

```
Runtime error <errnum> at <segment>:<offset>
```

where *<errnum>* is the appropriate error number (see Appendix I), and *:<offset>* is the memory address where the error occurred.(If you need this number later, look for it in the Ouptput window.) The rest of the program is skipped over, and you'll be asked to press any key to return to

Turbo Pascal. Once you're there, Turbo Pascal automatically finds the location of the error and displays it to you. If you need to find the error location again, select the **F**ind error command from the **C**ompile menu.

When your program has finished executing, you press any key and the PC returns control to Turbo Pascal, and you're back where you started. You can now modify your program if so desired. If you select the **R**un command before you make any changes to your program, Turbo Pascal immediately executes it, without recompiling.

## *Checking the Files You've Created*

If you exit Turbo Pascal (select **Q**uit from the **F**ile menu), you can see a listing of the source (Pascal) file you've created. Press *O* for **O**S shell in the **F**ile menu or, alternatively, press *Q* and type the following command at the DOS prompt:

```
dir myfirst.*
```

You'll get a listing that looks something like this:

```
MYFIRST     PAS     171  7-10-87   11:07a
```

The file MYFIRST.PAS contains the Pascal program you just wrote.

(**Note:** You'll only see the executable file if you've changed your default **D**estination setting in the **C**ompile menu to Disk. You would then get a file called MYFIRST.EXE, which would contain the machine code that Turbo Pascal generated from your program. You could then execute that program by typing MYFIRST followed by *Enter* at the DOS system prompt.)

# Stepping Up: Your Second Program

Now you're going to write a second program, building upon the first. If you've exited from Turbo Pascal, return to the integrated environment by typing the following command at the prompt:

```
turbo myfirst.pas
```

This will place you directly into the editor. Now, modify your MYFIRST.PAS program to look like this:

```
program MySecond;
var
  A,B     : integer;
  Ratio   : real;
  Ans     : char;
begin
```

```
  repeat
    Write('Enter two numbers:  ');
    Readln(A,B);
    if B = 0 then
      Writeln('Division by zero is not allowed.')
    else
    begin
      Ratio := A / B;
      Writeln('The ratio is ',Ratio:8:2)
    end;
    Write('Are you done? ');
    Readln(Ans)
  until UpCase(Ans) = 'Y'
end.
```

You want to save this as a separate program, so go to the main menu (press *F10*), select the File menu (press *F*), and then **Write** to (press *W*). When prompted for a new name, type MYSECOND.PAS and press *Enter*. Exit from the File menu by pressing *Esc*.

Now here's a shortcut: To compile and run your second program, just press *R* for **Run** (at the main menu). This tells Turbo Pascal to run your updated program. And since you've made changes to the program, Turbo Pascal knows to compile the program before running it.

Two major changes have been made to the program. First, most of the program has been enclosed in the **repeat..until** loop. This causes all the statements between **repeat** and **until** to be executed until the expression following **until** is True. Also, a test is made to see if *B* has a value of zero or not. If *B* has a value of zero, then the message

```
Division by zero is not allowed
```

appears; otherwise, the ratio is calculated and displayed. Note that the ratio has a more readable format now; it looks like this:

```
The ratio is 2.43
```

rather than this:

```
The ratio is 2.4338539929E+00
```

If you enter *Y* to the `Are you done?` message, you'll get the `Press any key to return to Turbo Pascal` message at the bottom of the screen. Press any key and you'll be returned to Turbo's main menu.

# Programming Pizazz: Your Third Program

For the last program, let's get a little fancy and dabble in graphics. This program assumes that you have some type of graphics card or adapter for your system, and that you are currently set up to use that card or adapter. If in doubt, try the program and see what happens. If an error message appears, then you probably don't have a graphics adapter (or you have one that's not supported by our *Graph* unit). In any case, pressing *Enter* twice should get you back to the integrated environment.

At the main menu, press File/Load. Enter the program MYTHIRD.PAS at the prompt, and you'll be placed in the editor. Here's the program to enter:

```pascal
program MyThird;
uses
  Graph;
const
  Start  =  25;
  Finish = 175;
  Step   =   2;
var
  GraphDriver : integer;                    { Stores graphics driver number }
  GraphMode   : integer;               { Stores graphics mode for the driver }
  ErrorCode   : integer;                        { Reports an error condition }
  X1,Y1,X2,Y2 : integer;
begin
  GraphDriver := Detect;                      { Try to autodetect Graphics card }
  InitGraph(GraphDriver, GraphMode, '');
  ErrorCode := GraphResult;
  if ErrorCode <> grOk then                                          { Error? }
  begin
    Writeln('Graphics error: ', GraphErrorMsg(ErrorCode));
    Writeln('(You probably don''t have a graphics card!)');
    Writeln('Program aborted...');
    Halt(1);
  end;
  Y1 := Start;
  Y2 := Finish;
  X1 := Start;
  while X1 <= Finish do
  begin
    X2 := (Start+Finish) - X1;
    Line(X1, Y1, X2, Y2);
    X1 := X1 + Step;
  end;
  X1 := Start;
  X2 := Finish;
  Y1 := Start;
  while Y1 <= Finish do
  begin
    Y2 := (Start+Finish) - Y1;
    Line(X1, Y1, X2, Y2);
    Y1 := Y1 + Step;
  end;
  OutText('Press <RETURN> to quit:');
  Readln;
  CloseGraph;
end. { MyThird }
```

After you finish entering this program, press *F2* to save it and then *C* to compile. If you have no errors during compilation, press *R* to run it. This program produces a square with some wavy patterns along the edges. When execution is over, you'll get the message `Press any key to return to Turbo Pascal` at the bottom of your screen. Let's look at how it works.

The **uses** statement says that the program uses a unit named *Graph*. A *unit* is a library, or collection, of subroutines (procedures and functions) and other declarations. In this case, the unit *Graph* contains the routines you want to use: *InitGraph*, *Line*, *CloseGraph*.

The section labeled **const** defines three numeric constants—*Start*, *Finish*, and *Step*—that affect the size, location, and appearance of the square. By changing their values, you can change how the square looks.

**Warning:** Don't set *Step* to anything less than 1; if you do, the program will get stuck in what is known as an *infinite loop* (a loop that circles endlessly). You won't be able to exit except by pressing *Ctrl-Alt-Del* or by turning your PC off.

The variables *X1*, *Y1*, *X2*, and *Y2* hold the values of locations along opposite sides of the square. The square itself is drawn by drawing a straight line from *X1,Y1* to *X2,Y2*. The coordinates are then changed, and the next line drawn. The coordinates always start out in opposite corners: The first line drawn goes from (25,25) to (175,175).

The program itself consists primarily of two loops. The first loop draws a line from (25,25,) to (175,175). It then moves the *X* (horizontal) coordinates by two, so that the next line goes from (27,25) to (173,175). This continues until the loop draws a line from (175,25) to (25,175).

The program then goes into its second loop, which pursues a similar course, changing the *Y* (vertical) coordinates by two each time. The routine *Line* is from the *Graph* unit and draws a line between the endpoints given.

The final *Readln* statement causes the program to wait for you to press a key before it goes back into text mode and exits to the integrated environment.

## The Turbo Pascal Compiler

You now know how to enter, compile, and run your programs. And because of Turbo Pascal's method of locating errors and high compilation speed, the cycle of entering, testing, and correcting your program takes little time. Let's look at the different aspects of that cycle in more detail.

## So, What's a Compiler Anyway?

Your PC, like most microcomputers, has a central processing unit (CPU) that is the workhorse of the machine. On your PC, the CPU is a single chip from a "family" of chips: the iAPx86, a series of microprocessors designed by Intel. The actual chip in your machine could be an 8088, an 8086, an 80186, an 80286, or even an 80386; it doesn't matter, since the code Turbo Pascal produces will run on all of them.

The iAPx86 family has a set of binary-coded instructions that all the chips can execute. By giving the iAPx86 the right set of instructions, you can make it put text on the screen, perform math, move text and data around, draw pictures—in short, do all the things that you want it to do. These instructions are known collectively as *machine code*.

Since machine code consists of pure binary information, it's neither easy to write nor easy to read. You can use a program known as an *assembler* to write machine-level instructions in a form that you can read, which means you would then be programming in assembly language. However, you still have to understand how the iAPx86 microprocessors work. You'll also find that to perform simple operations—such as printing out a number—often requires a large number of instructions.

If you don't want to deal with machine code or assembly language, you use a high-level language such as Pascal. You can easily read and write programs in Pascal because it is designed for humans, not computers. Still, the PC understands only machine code. The Turbo Pascal compiler translates (or compiles) your Pascal program into instructions that the computer can understand. The compiler is just another program that moves data around; in this case, it reads in your program text and writes out the corresponding machine code.

## What Gets Compiled?

You can only edit one Turbo Pascal program at a time, and under normal circumstances that's the only program that would be compiled. So when you select the **Compile**, **Make**, or **Build** commands from the **Compile** menu, or the **Run** command from the main menu, Turbo Pascal compiles the program you're currently editing, producing an .EXE file, a .TPU file, or code in memory.

There are two exceptions to this rule. First, you can specify a *primary file*, using the **Primary file** command in the **Compile** menu. Once you've done that, then the primary file will be compiled for **Makes** and **Builds**, but the edit file will be compiled for **Compiles**.

Second, you can ask Turbo Pascal to recompile any units that the program you're compiling might use. You actually have two options here:

1. You can tell Turbo Pascal to recompile any units that have been changed since the last time you compiled your program. This is called a "make."
2. You can tell Turbo Pascal to recompile all units that your program uses. This is called a "build."

## Where's the Code?

When you use the **R**un command, Turbo Pascal (by default) saves the resulting machine code in memory (RAM). This has several advantages. First, the compiler runs much faster because it takes less time to write the machine code out to RAM than out to a floppy or hard disk. Second, since your program is already loaded into RAM, Turbo Pascal tells the PC to execute your code. Third, the PC more easily returns to Turbo Pascal once your program stops executing, since Turbo Pascal also stays in RAM the whole time.

If compiling to RAM is so wonderful, why wouldn't you want to do it every time? Two reasons. First, because the resulting machine code is never saved on disk, you could only run your programs from Turbo Pascal. There would be no way to execute your program from MS-DOS, nor would you be able to copy your program.

The second problem is memory—you might not have enough. This could happen if your system doesn't have much memory, if your program is very large, or if your program uses a lot of memory for dynamic data allocation.

It's easy to produce an .EXE file (application) you can run from outside Turbo Pascal: Select the **D**estination option from the **C**ompile menu. This option allows you to toggle between Disk and Memory for your destination. If you select Disk and then recompile, Turbo Pascal produces a code file that you can run from MS-DOS by typing its name at the prompt.

The file produced has the same name as your source file but with the extension .EXE; for example, the resulting code file of a program named MYFIRST.PAS would be MYFIRST.EXE.

Regardless of whether you are compiling to disk or to memory, the **R**un command still executes the resulting program once the compilation is done.

## Compile, Make, and Build

The **Compile** menu has many options, three of which are compilation commands: **Compile**, **Make**, and **Build**. All three take a source file and produce an .EXE file (if **Destination** is set to Disk) or a .TPU file. Let's look at the differences between them.

The **Compile** command compiles the file in the editor.

The **Make** command checks to see whether you have specified a primary file. Once it has determined that, it checks the time and date of the .PAS and .TPU (precompiled unit files) files for every unit referenced in the **uses** statement (if there is one) in the program being compiled. (A *unit* is a collection of constants, data types, variables, and procedures and functions; see Chapter 4 for more information.) If the .PAS file has been modified since the corresponding .TPU file was created, then Turbo Pascal will automatically recompile that unit's .PAS file, creating a new .TPU file. Turbo also recompiles any unit that uses a unit whose interface has changed, whose include files have been changed, or any unit that links an .OBJ file that has been modified since the unit's .TPU file was built. In short, Turbo Pascal ensures that all units your program depends on are up to date. Once it's done that, Turbo Pascal compiles and links your program, producing an .EXE file.

The **Build** command acts just like the **Make** command but with one important exception: It recompiles all units used by your program (and all units used by those units, and so on), regardless of whether they are current.

Here are some notes you should know about using **Make** and **Build**:

- If **Make** or **Build** cannot find the .PAS file corresponding to a given unit, then the unit is considered valid. That way, if your program uses any of the standard units, Turbo Pascal won't try to recompile them.

- When Turbo looks for a unit called *unitname*, it assumes that it is located in a file called *unitname*.PAS. However, you can store the unit in a file with another name by using the {$U *othername*} compiler directive in your code. For example, if your program uses a unit called *UtilityRoutines*, but you store it in a file called MYUTILS.PAS, then you would put the following in your program (assuming that your program also uses *Dos* and *Crt*):

  ```
  uses Dos, Crt, {$U MYUTILS.PAS} UtilityRoutines;
  ```

  Note that the $U directive comes right before the corresponding unit name.

## Compile-Time Errors

Like English, Pascal has rules of grammar you must follow. However, unlike English, Pascal's structure isn't lenient enough to allow for slang or poor syntax—the compiler won't understand what you want. In Pascal, when you don't use the appropriate words or symbols in a statement or when you organize them incorrectly, it results in a compile-time (syntax) error.

What compile-time errors are you likely to get? Probably the most common error novice Pascal programmers will get is `Unknown identifier` or `';' expected`. Pascal requires that you declare all variables, data types, constants, and subroutines—in short, all identifiers—before using them. If you refer to an undeclared identifier or if you misspell it, you'll get this error. Other common errors are unmatched **begin..end** pairs, assignment of incompatible data types (such as assigning reals to integers), parameter count and type mismatches in procedure and function calls, and so on.

## Runtime Errors

In programming, sometimes just following the rules governing correct syntax isn't enough. For example, suppose you write a simple program that prompts you for two integer values, adds them together, then prints out the result. The entire program might look something like this:

```
program AddSum;
var
  A,B,Sum  : integer;
begin
  Write('Enter two integer values: ');
  Readln(A,B);
  Sum := A + B;
  Writeln('The sum is ',Sum,'.')
end.
```

In response to the prompt, `Enter two integer values:`, say you type in real numbers (numbers with decimal points), integer values that are too large, or even character strings instead of numbers. What happens? You'll get a message that looks something like this:

```
Runtime error 106 at 1F9C:0062
```

and your program will halt.

If you are running from within Turbo Pascal, you'll get the `Press any key to return to Turbo Pascal` prompt; after pressing any key, you'll be returned to Turbo Pascal's integrated environment, which will then automatically locate the error for you in the Edit window.

What if the runtime error occurred in a unit used by your program? Turbo Pascal can still locate the error if the unit was compiled with the *$D+* compiler option. (This is the **D**ebug info toggle in the **O**ptions/**C**ompile menu; it is on by default.)

In either case, Turbo Pascal loads that source code file into the editor and positions the cursor at the appropriate spot. (You may be prompted to save the current edit file.) You can then make the appropriate changes, recompile, and run it again.

If you need to relocate the error after having moved to another section of your file, use the *Ctrl-Q W* command. If you change files, you can find the error again by loading the main program and using the **F**ind error command in the **C**ompile menu. It will ask you for the segment and offset values displayed when the error occurred, but will default to the last error address that was found.

# 3

# Programming in Turbo Pascal

The Pascal language was designed by Niklaus Wirth in the early 1970s to teach programming. Because of that, it's particularly well-suited as a first programming language. And if you've already programmed in other languages, you'll find it easy to pick up Pascal.

To get you started on the road to Pascal programming, in this chapter we'll teach you the basic elements of the Pascal language, and show you how to use them in your programs. Of course, we won't cover everything about programming in Pascal in this chapter. So if you're a Pascal novice, your best bet would be to pick up a copy of the *Turbo Pascal Tutor*, a complete book-plus-disk tutorial about programming in Pascal and using version 4.0 of Turbo Pascal.

Before you work through this chapter, you might want to read Chapters 10 and 11 to learn how to use the menus and text editor in Turbo Pascal. You should have installed Turbo Pascal (made a working copy of your Turbo Pascal disk or copied the files onto your hard disk) as described in Chapter 1. Make sure that you've created the file TURBO.TP or installed the .EXE file using TINST.EXE (see Appendix F); otherwise, Turbo Pascal won't know the location of the standard units in TURBO.TPL and the configuration file. (Unless you happen to own MS-DOS 3.x and you have those files in the same directory as TURBO.EXE.)

Once you've done all that, get ready to learn about programming in Turbo Pascal.

# The Seven Basic Elements of Programming

Most programs are designed to solve a problem. They solve problems by manipulating information or data. What you as the programmer have to do is

- get the information into the program—input.
- have a place to keep it—data.
- give the right instructions to manipulate the data—operations.
- be able to get the data back out of the program to the user (you, usually)—output.

You can organize your instructions so that

- some are executed only when a specific condition (or set of conditions) is True—conditional execution.
- others are repeated a number of times—loops.
- others are broken off into chunks that can be executed at different locations in your program—subroutines.

We've just described the seven basic elements of programming: *input, data, operations, output, conditional execution, loops,* and *subroutines.* This list is not comprehensive, but it does describe those elements that programs (and programming languages) usually have in common.

Many programming languages, including Pascal, have additional features as well. And when you want to learn a new language quickly, you can find out how that language implements these seven elements, then build from there. Here's a brief description of each element:

**Input**
This means reading values in from the keyboard, from a disk, or from an I/O port.

**Data**
These are constants, variables, and structures that contain numbers (integer and real), text (characters and strings), or addresses (of variables and structures).

**Operations**
These assign one value to another, combine values (add, divide, and so forth), and compare values (equal, not equal, and so on).

**Output**
This means writing information to the screen, to a disk, or to an I/O port.

**Conditional Execution**

This refers to executing a set of instructions if a specified condition is True (and skipping them or executing a different set if it is False) or if a data item has a specified value or range of values.

**Loops**

These execute a set of instructions some fixed number of times, while some condition is True or until some condition is True.

**Subroutines**

These are separately named sets of instructions that can be executed any-where in the program just by referencing the name.

Now we'll take a look at how to use these elements in Turbo Pascal.

## Data Types

When you write a program, you're working with information that generally falls into one of five basic types: *integers*, *real numbers*, *characters* and *strings*, *boolean*, and *pointers*.

**Integers** are the whole numbers you learned to count with (1, 5, –21, and 752, for example).

**Real numbers** have fractional portions (3.14159) and exponents ($2.579 \times 10^{24}$). These are also sometimes known as *floating-point* numbers.

**Characters** are any of the letters of the alphabet, symbols, and the numbers 0-9. They can be used individually (*a*, *Z*, !, 3) or combined into character strings ('This is only a test.').

**Boolean** expressions have one of two possible values: True or False. They are used in conditional expressions, which we'll discuss later.

**Pointers** hold the address of some location in the computer's memory, which in turn holds information.

## Integer Data Types

Standard Pascal defines the data type integer as consisting of the values ranging from –*MaxInt* through 0 to *MaxInt*, where *MaxInt* is the largest possible integer value allowed by the compiler you're using. Turbo Pascal supports type integer, defines *MaxInt* as equal to 32767, and allows the value –32768 as well. A variable of type integer occupies 2 bytes.

Turbo Pascal also defines a long integer constant, *MaxLongInt*, with a value of 2,147,483,647.

Turbo Pascal also supports four other integer data types, each of which has a different range of values. Table 3.1 shows all five integer types.

Table 3.1: Integer Data Types

| Type | Range | Size in Bytes |
|------|-------|---------------|
| byte | 0..255 | 1 |
| shortint | −128..127 | 1 |
| integer | −32768..32767 | 2 |
| word | 0..65535 | 2 |
| longint | −2147483648..2147483647 | 4 |

**A final note:** Turbo Pascal allows you to use hexadecimal (base-16) integer values. To specify a constant value as hexadecimal, place a dollar sign ($) in front of it; for example, $27 = 39 decimal.

## Real Data Types

Standard Pascal defines the data type real as representing floating-point values consisting of a significand (fractional portion) multiplied by an exponent (power of 10). The number of digits (known as *significant digits*) in the significand and the range of values of the exponent are compiler-dependent. Turbo Pascal defines the type real as being 6 bytes in size, with 11 significant digits and an exponent range of $10^{-38}$ to $10^{38}$.

In addition, if you have an 8087 math coprocessor and enable the numeric support compiler directive or environment option ({$N+}), Turbo Pascal also supports the IEEE Standard 754 for binary floating-point arithmetic. This includes the data types single, double, extended, and comp. Single uses 4 bytes, with 7 significant digits and an exponent range of $10^{-38}$ to $10^{38}$; double uses 8 bytes, with 15 significant digits and an exponent range of $10^{-38}$ to $10^{38}$; and extended uses 10 bytes, with 19 significant digits and an exponent range of $10^{-4931}$ to $10^{4931}$.

Table 3.2: Real Data Types

| Type | Range | Significant Digits | Size in Bytes |
|------|-------|--------------------|---------------|
| real | $2.9 \times 10E\text{-}39 .. 1.7 \times 10E38$ | 11-12 | 6 |
| single | $1.5 \times 10E\text{-}45 .. 3.4 \times 10E38$ | 7- 8 | 4 |
| double | $5.0 \times 10E\text{-}324 .. 1.7 \times 10E308$ | 15-16 | 8 |
| extended | $1.9 \times 10E\text{-}4951 .. 1.1 \times 10E4932$ | 19-20 | 10 |
| comp* | −2E+63+1..2E+63-1 | 19-20 | 8 |

* comp only holds integer values.

Get into the Turbo Pascal editor and enter the following program:

```
program DoRatio;
var
  A,B   : integer;
  Ratio : real;
begin
  Write('Enter two numbers:  ');
  Readln(A,B);
  Ratio := A div B;
  Writeln('The ratio is ',Ratio)
end.
```

Save this as DORATIO.PAS by bringing up the main menu and selecting the **File/Write to** command. Then press *R* to compile and run the program. Enter two values (such as 10 and 3) and note the result (3.000000).

You were probably expecting an answer of 3.3333333333, and instead you received a 3. That's because you used the **div** operator, which performs integer division. Now go back and change the div statement to read as follows:

```
  Ratio := A / B;
```

Save the code (press *F2*), then compile and run. The result is now 3.3333333333, as you expected. Using the division operator (/) gives you the most precise result—a real number.

## Character and String Data Types

You've learned how to store numbers in Pascal, now how about characters and strings? Pascal offers a predefined data type char that is 1 byte in size and holds exactly one character. Character constants are represented by surrounding the character with single quotes (for example, 'A', 'e', '?', '2'). Note that '2' means the *character* 2, while 2 means the *integer* 2 (and 2.0 means the *real number* 2).

Here's a modification of DORATIO that allows you to repeat it several times (this also uses a **repeat..until** loop, which we'll discuss a little later):

```
program DoRatio;
var
  A,B   : integer;
  Ratio : real;
  Ans   : char;
begin
  repeat
    Write('Enter two numbers:  ');
    Readln(A,B);
    Ratio := A / B;
    Writeln('The ratio is ',Ratio);
```

```
    Write('Do it again? (Y/N)  ');
    Readln(Ans)
  until UpCase(Ans) = 'N'
end.
```

After calculating the ratio once, the program writes the message

```
Do it again? (Y/N)
```

and waits for you to type in a single character, followed by pressing *Enter*. If you type in a lowercase *n* or an uppercase *N*, the **until** condition is met and the loop ends; otherwise, the program goes back to the **repeat** statement and starts over again.

Note that *n* is *not* the same as *N*. This is because they have different ASCII code values. Characters are represented by the ASCII code: Each character has its own 8-bit number (characters take up 1 byte, remember). Appendix E lists the ASCII codes for all characters.

Turbo Pascal gives you two additional ways of representing character constants: with a caret (^) or a number symbol (#). First, the characters with codes 0 through 31 are known as *control characters* (because historically they were used to control teletype operations). They are referred to by their abbreviations (CR for carriage return, LF for linefeed, ESC for escape, and so on) or by the word *Ctrl* followed by a corresponding letter (meaning the letter produced by adding 64 to the control code). For example, the control character with ASCII code 7 is known as BEL or *Ctrl-G*. Turbo Pascal lets you represent these characters using the caret (^), followed by the corresponding letter (or character). Thus, *^G* is a legal representation in your program of *Ctrl-G*, and you could write statements such as *Writeln(^G)*, causing your computer to beep at you. This method, however, only works for the control characters.

You can also represent *any* character using the number symbol (#), followed by the character's ASCII code. Thus, #7 would be the same as *^G*, #65 would be the same as '*A*', and #233 would represent one of the special IBM PC graphics characters.

## *Defining a String*

Individual characters are nice, but what about strings of characters? After all, that's how you will most often use them. Standard Pascal does not support a separate string data type, but Turbo Pascal does. Take a look at this program:

```
program Hello;
var
  Name  : string[30];
begin
  Write('What is your name?  ');
  Readln(Name);
  Writeln('Hello, ',Name)
end.
```

This declares the variable *Name* to be of type **string**, with space set aside to hold 30 characters. One more byte is set aside internally by Turbo Pascal to hold the current length of the string. That way, no matter how long or short the name is you enter at the prompt, that is exactly how much is printed out in the *Writeln* statement. Unless, of course, you enter a name more than 30 characters long, in which case only the first 30 characters are used, and the rest are ignored.

When you declare a string variable, you can specify how many characters (up to 255) it can hold. Or you can declare a variable (or parameter) to be of type **string** with no length mentioned, in which case the default size of 255 characters is assumed.

Turbo Pascal offers a number of predefined procedures and functions to use with strings; they can be found in Chapter 27.

## Boolean Data Type

Pascal's predefined data type boolean has two possible values: True and False. You can declare variables to be of type boolean, then assign the variable either a True or False value or (more importantly) an expression that resolves to one of those two values.

A *Boolean expression* is simply an expression that is either True or False. It is made up of relational expressions, Boolean operators, Boolean variables, and/or other Boolean expressions. For example, the following **while** statement contains a Boolean expression:

```
while (Index <= Limit) and not Done do ...
```

The Boolean expression consists of everything between the keywords **while** and **do**, and presumes that *Done* is a variable (or possibly a function) of type boolean.

# Pointer Data Type

All the data types we've discussed until now hold just that—data. A *pointer* holds a different type of information—addresses. A pointer is a variable that contains the address in memory (RAM) where some data is stored, rather than the data itself. In other words, it *points* to the data, like an address book or an index.

A pointer is usually (but not necesarily) specific to some other data type. Consider the following declarations:

```
type
  Buffer  = string[255];
  BufPtr  = ^Buffer;
var
  Buf1    : Buffer;
  Buf2    : BufPtr;
```

The data type *Buffer* is now just another name for **string**[255], while the type *BufPtr* defines a pointer to a *Buffer*. The variable *Buf1* is of type *Buffer*; it takes up 256 bytes of memory. The variable *Buf2* is of type *BufPtr*; it contains a 32-bit address and only takes up 4 bytes of memory.

Where does *Buf2* point to? Nowhere, currently. Before you can use *BufPtr*, you need to set aside (allocate) some memory and store its address in *Buf2*. You do that using the *New* procedure:

```
New(Buf2);
```

Since *Buf2* points to the type *Buffer*, this statement creates a 256-byte buffer somewhere in memory, then puts its address into *Buf2*.

How do you use the data pointed to by *Buf2*? Via the indirection operator ^. For example, suppose you want to store a string in both *Buf1* and the buffer pointed to by *Buf2*. Here's what the statements would look like:

```
Buf1 := 'This string gets stored in Buf1.'
Buf2^ := 'This string gets stored where Buf2 points.'
```

Note the difference between *Buf2* and *Buf2^*. *Buf2* refers to a 4-byte pointer variable; *Buf2^* refers to a 256-byte string variable whose address is stored in *Buf2*.

How do you free up the memory pointed to by *Buf2*? Using the *Dispose* procedure. *Dispose* makes the memory available for other uses. After you use *Dispose* on a pointer, it's good practice to assign the (predefined) value **nil** to that pointer. That lets you know that the pointer no longer points to anything:

```
Dispose(Buf2);
Buf2 := nil;
```

Note that you assign **nil** to *Buf2*, not to *Buf2*^.

This ends our brief discussion on pointers; a good Pascal text will tell you how and when they're useful.

## *Identifiers*

Up until now, we've given names to variables without worrying about what restrictions there might be. Let's talk about those restrictions now.

The names you give to constants, data types, variables, and functions are known as *identifiers*. Some of the identifiers used so far include

| | |
|---|---|
| *integer, real, string* | Predefined data types |
| *Hello,DoSum,DoRatio* | Main function of program |
| *Name, A, B, Sum, Ratio* | User-defined variables |
| *Write,Writeln,Readln* | Predeclared procedures |

Turbo Pascal has a few rules about identifiers; here's a quick summary:

- All identifiers must start with a letter (*a...z* or *A...Z*). The rest of an identifier can consist of letters, underscores, and/or digits (0...9); no other characters are allowed.

- Identifiers are *case-insensitive*, which means that lowercase letters (*a...z*) are considered the same as uppercase letters (*A...Z*). For example, the identifiers *indx*, *Indx*, and *INDX* are identical.

- Identifiers can be of any length, but only the first 63 characters are significant.

## *Operators*

Once you get that data into the program (and into your variables), you'll probably want to manipulate it somehow, using the operators available to you. There are eight types: assignment, unary/binary, bitwise, relational, logical, address, set, and string.

Most Pascal operators are *binary*, taking two operands; the rest are *unary*, taking only one operand. Binary operators use the usual algebraic form, for example, *a* + *b*. A unary operator always precedes its operand, for example, *–b*.

In more complex expressions, rules of precedence clarify the order in which operations are performed (see Table 3.3).

Table 3.3: Precedence of Operators

| Operators | Precedence | Categories |
|---|---|---|
| @, not | First (high) | Unary operators |
| *, /, div, mod, and, shl, shr | Second | Multiplying operators |
| +,-, or, xor | Third | Adding operators |
| =, <>, <, >, <=, >=, in | Fourth (low) | Relational operators |

Operations with equal precedence are normally performed from left to right, although the compiler may at times rearrange the operands to generate optimum code.

Sequences of operators of the same precedence are evaluated from left to right. Expressions within parentheses are evaluated first and independently of preceding or succeeding operators.

## Assignment Operators

The most basic operation is *assignment*, as in *Ratio := A / B*. In Pascal, the assignment symbol is a colon followed by an equal sign (:=). In the example given, the value of *A / B* on the right of the assignment symbol is assigned to the variable *Ratio* on the left.

## Unary and Binary Operators

Pascal supports the usual set of binary arithmetic operators—they work with type integer and real values:

- Multiplication (*)
- Integer division (**div**)
- Real division (/)
- Modulus (**mod**)
- Addition (+)
- Subtraction (–)

Also, Turbo Pascal supports both *unary minus* (*a* + (*-b*)), which performs a *two's complement* evaluation, and *unary plus* (*a* + (*+b*)), which does nothing at all but is there for completeness.

## Bitwise Operators

For bit-level operations, Pascal has the following operators:

- **shl** (shift left)      Shifts the bits left the indicated number of bits, filling at the right with 0's.
- **shr** (shift right)     Shifts the bits right the indicated number of bits, filling at the left with 0's.
- **and**                   Performs a logical **and** on each corresponding pair of bits, returning 1 if both bits are 1, and 0 otherwise.
- **or**                    Performs a logical **or** on each corresponding pair of bits, returning 0 if both bits are 0, and 1 otherwise.
- **xor**                   Performs a logical, exclusive **or** on each corresponding pair of bits, returning 1 if the two bits are different from one another, and 0 otherwise.
- **not**                   Performs a logical complement on each bit, changing each 0 to a 1, and vice versa.

These allow you to perform very low-level operations on type integer values.

## Relational Operators

Relational operators allow you to compare two values, yielding a Boolean result of True or False. Here are the relational operators in Pascal:

| | |
|---|---|
| > | greater than |
| >= | greater than or equal to |
| < | less than |
| <= | less than or equal to |
| = | equal to |
| <> | not equal to |
| **in** | is a member of |

So why would you want to know if something were True or False? Enter the following program:

```
program TestGreater;
var
  A,B  : integer;
  Test : boolean;
```

```
begin
  Write('Enter two numbers:  ');
  Readln(A,B);
  Test := A > B;
  Writeln('A is greater than B', Test);
end.
```

This will print True if *A* is greater than *B* or False if *A* is less than or equal to *B*.

## Logical Operators

There are four logical operators—**and**, **xor**, **or**, and **not**—which are similar to but not identical with the bitwise operators. These logical operators work with logical values (True and False), allowing you to combine relational expressions, Boolean variables, and Boolean expressions.

They differ from the corresponding bitwise operators in this manner:

- Logical operators always produce a result of either True or False (a Boolean value), while the bitwise operators do bit-by-bit operations on type integer values.

- You cannot combine boolean and integer-type expressions with these operators; in other words, the expression `Flag` **and** `Indx` is illegal if *Flag* is of type boolean, and *Indx* is of type integer (or vice versa).

- The logical operators **and** and **or** will short-circuit by default; **xor** and **not** will not. Suppose you have the expression `exp1` **and** `exp2`. If *exp1* is False, then the entire expression is False, so *exp2* will never be evaluated. Likewise, given the expression `exp1` **or** `exp2`, *exp2* will never be evaluated if *exp1* is True. You can force full Boolean expression using the {$B+} compiler directive or environment option.

## Address Operators

Pascal supports two special address operators: the *address-of* operator (@) and the *indirection* operator (^).

The @ operator returns the address of a given variable; if *Sum* is a variable of type integer, then @Sum is the address (memory location) of that variable. Likewise, if *ChrPtr* is a pointer to type char, then *ChrPtr*^ is the character to which *ChrPtr* points.

## Set Operators

Set operators perform according to the rules of set logic. The set operators and operations include:

+    union
−    difference
*    multiplication

## String Operators

The only string operation is the + operator, which is used to concatenate two strings.

## *Output*

It may seem funny to talk about output before input, but a program that doesn't output information isn't of much use. That output usually takes the form of information written to the screen (words and pictures), to a storage device (floppy or hard disk), or to an I/O port (serial or printer ports).

## The Writeln Procedure

You've already used the most common output function in Pascal, the *Writeln* routine. The purpose of *Writeln* is to write information to the screen. Its format is both simple and flexible:

```
Writeln(item,item,...);
```

where each *item* is something you want to print to the screen. *item* can be a literal value, such as an integer or a real number (3, 42, −1732.3), a character ('a', 'Z'), a string ('Hello, world'), or a Boolean value (True). It can also be a named constant, a variable, a dereferenced pointer, or a function call, as long as it yields a value that is of type integer, real, char, string, or boolean. All the items are printed on one line, in the order given. The cursor is then moved to the start of the next line. If you wish to leave the cursor after the last item on the same line, then use the statement

```
Write(item,item,...);
```

When the items in a *Writeln* statement are printed, blanks are *not* automatically inserted; if you want spaces between items, you'll have to put them there yourself, like this:

```
Writeln(item,' ',item,' ',...);
```

So, for example, the following statements produce the indicated output:

```
A := 1; B := 2; C := 3;
Name := 'Frank';
Writeln(A,B,C);                    123
Writeln(A,' ',B,' ',C);            1 2 3
Writeln('Hi',Name);               HiFrank
Writeln('Hi, ',Name,'.');         Hi, Frank.
```

You can also use *field-width specifiers* to define a field width for a given item. The format for this is

```
Writeln(item:width,...);
```

where *width* is an integer expression (literal, constant, variable, function call, or combination thereof) specifying the total width of the field in which *item* is written. For example, consider the following code and resulting output:

```
A := 10; B := 2; C := 100;
Writeln(A,B,C);                    102100
Writeln(A:2,B:2,C:2);              10 2100
Writeln(A:3,B:3,C:3);               10   2100
Writeln(A,B:2,C:4);                10 2 100
```

Note that the item is padded with leading blanks on the left to make it equal to the field width. The actual value is right-justified.

What if the field width is less than what is needed? In the second *Writeln* statement given earlier, C has a field width of 2 but has a value of 100 and needs a width of 3. As you can see by the output, Pascal simply expands the width to the minimum size needed.

This method works for all allowable items: integers, reals, characters, strings, and booleans. However, real numbers printed with the field-width specifier (or with none at all) come out in exponential form:

```
X := 421.53;
Writeln(X);                        4.2153000000E+02
Writeln(X:8);                      4.2E+02
```

Because of this, Pascal allows you to append a second field-width specifier: *item:width:digits*. This second value forces the real number to be printed out in fixed-point format and tells how many digits to place after the decimal point:

```
X := 421.53;
Writeln(X:6:2);                      421.53
Writeln(X:8:2);                        421.53
Writeln(X:8:4);                      421.5300
```

## Input

Standard Pascal has two basic input functions, *Read* and *Readln*, which are used to read data from the keyboard. The general syntax is

```
Read(item,item,...);
```

or

```
Readln(item,item,...);
```

where each *item* is a variable of any integer, real, char, or string type. Numbers must be separated from other values by spaces or by pressing *Enter*.

## Conditional Statements

There are times when you want to execute some portion of your program when a given condition is True or not, or when a particular value of a given expression is reached. Let's look at how to do this in Pascal.

## The If Statement

Look again at the **if** statement in the previous examples; note that it can take the following generic format:

```
if expr
   then statement1
   else statement2
```

where *expr* is any Boolean expression (resolving to True or False), and *statement1* and *statement2* are legal Pascal statements. If *expr* is True, then *statement1* is executed; otherwise, *statement2* is executed.

We must explain two important points about **if/then/else** statements:

First, **else** *statement2* is optional; in other words, this is a valid **if** statement:

```
if expr
   then statement1
```

In this case, *statement1* is executed if and only if *expr* is True. If *expr* is False, then *statement1* is skipped, and the program continues.

Second, what if you want to execute more than one statement if a particular expression is True or False? You would use a compound statement. A *compound statement* consists of the keyword **begin**, some number of statements separated by semicolons (;), and the keyword **end**.

The ratio example uses a single statement for the **if** clause

```
if B = 0.0 then
   Writeln('Division by zero is not allowed.')
```

and a compound statement for the **else** clause

```
else
begin
  Ratio = A / B;
  Writeln('The ratio is ',Ratio)
end;
```

You might also notice that the body of each program you've written is simply a compound statement followed by a period.

## The Case Statement

This statement gives your program the power to choose between alternatives without having to specify lots of **if** statements.

The **case** statement consists of an expression (the selector) and a list of statements, each preceded by a **case** label of the same type as the selector. It specifies that the one statement be executed whose **case** label is equal to the current value of the selector. If none of the **case** labels contain the value of the selector, then either no statement is executed or, optionally, the statements following the reserved word **else** are executed. (**else** is an extension to standard Pascal.)

A **case** label consists of any number of constants or subranges, separated by commas and followed by a colon; for example:

```
case BirdSight of
  'C', 'c' : Curlews := Curlews + 1;
  'H', 'h' : Herons  := Herons + 1;
  'E', 'e' : Egrets  := Egrets + 1;
  'T', 't' : Terns   := Terns + 1;
end;  { case }
```

A subrange is written as two constants separated by the subrange delimiter '..'. The constant type must match the selector type. The statement that follows the **case** label is executed if the selector's value equals one of the constants or if it lies within one of the subranges.

## Loops

Just as there are statements (or groups of statements) that you want to execute conditionally, there are other statements that you may want to execute repeatedly. This kind of construct is known as a *loop*.

There are three basic kinds of loops: the **while** loop, the **repeat** loop, and the **for** loop. We'll cover them in that order.

## The While Loop

You can use the **while** loop to test for something at the beginning of your loop. Enter the following program:

```
program Hello;
var
  Count : integer;
begin
  Count := 1;
  while Count <= 10 do
  begin
    Writeln('Hello and goodbye!');
    Inc(Count)
  end;
  Writeln('This is the end!')
end.
```

The first thing that happens when you run this program is that *Count* is set equal to 1, then you enter the **while** loop. This tests to see if *Count* is less then or equal to 10. *Count* is, so the loop's body (**begin..end**) is executed. This prints the message Hello and goodbye! to the screen, then increments *Count* by 1. *Count* is again tested, and the loop's body is executed once more. This continues as long as *Count* is less than or equal to 10 when it is tested. Once *Count* reaches 11, the loop exits, and the string This is the end! is printed on the screen.

The format of the **while** statement is

```
while expr do statement
```

where *expr* is a Boolean expression, and *statement* is either a single or a compound statement.

The **while** loop evaluates *expr*. If it's True, then *statement* is executed, and *expr* is evaluated again. If *expr* is False, the **while** loop is finished and the program continues.

## The Repeat..Until Loop

The second loop is the **repeat..until** loop, which we've seen in the program DORATIO.PAS:

```
program DoRatio;
var
  A,B   : integer;
  Ratio : real;
  Ans   : char;
begin
  repeat
    Write('Enter two numbers:  ');
    Readln(A,B);
    Ratio := A / B;
    Writeln('The ratio is ',Ratio);
    Write('Do it again? (Y/N)  ');
    Readln(Ans)
  until UpCase(Ans) = 'N'
end.
```

As described before, this program repeats until you answer *n* or *N* to the question Do it again? (Y/N). In other words, everything between **repeat** and **until** is repeated until the expression following **until** is True.

Here's the generic format for the **repeat..until** loop:

```
  repeat
    statement;
    statement;
    ...
    statement
  until expr
```

There are three major differences between the **while** loop and the **repeat** loop. First, the statements in the **repeat** loop always execute at least once, because the test on *expr* is not made until after the **repeat** occurs. By contrast, the **while** loop will skip over its body if the expression is initially False.

Next, the **repeat** loop executes *until* the expression is True, where the **while** loop executes *while* the expression is True. This means that care must be taken in translating from one type of loop to the other. For example, here's the HELLO program rewritten using a **repeat** loop:

```
program Hello;
var
  Count : integer;
begin
  Count := 1;
  repeat
    Writeln('Hello and goodbye!');
    Inc(Count)
  until Count > 10;
  Writeln('This is the end!')
end.
```

Note that the test is now *Count > 10*, where for the *while* loop it was *Count <= 10*.

Finally, the **repeat** loop can hold multiple statements without using a compound statement. Notice that you didn't have to use **begin..end** in the preceding program, but you did for the earlier version using a **while** loop.

Again, be careful to note that the **repeat** loop will always execute at least once. A **while** loop may never execute depending on the expression.

## The For Loop

The **for** loop is the one found in most major programming languages, including Pascal. However, the Pascal version is simultaneously limited and powerful.

Basically, you execute a set of statements some fixed number of times while a variable (known as the *index variable*) steps through a range of values. For example, modify the earlier HELLO program to read as follows:

```
program Hello;
var
  Count : integer;
begin
  for Count := 1 to 10 do
    Writeln('Hello and goodbye!');
  Writeln('This is the end!')
end.
```

When you run this program, you can see that the loop works the same as the **while** and **repeat** loops already shown and, in fact, is precisely equivalent to the **while** loop. Here's the generic format of the **for** loop statement:

```
for index := expr1 to expr2 do statement
```

where *index* is a variable of some scalar type (any integer type, char, boolean, any enumerated type), *expr1* and *expr2* are expressions of some type compatible with *index*, and *statement* is a single or compound statement. *Index* is incremented by one after each time through the loop.

You can also decrement the index variable instead of incrementing it by replacing the keyword **to** with the keyword **downto**.

The **for** loop is equivalent to the following code:

```
index := expr1;
while index <= expr2 do
begin
  statement;
  Inc(index)
end;
```

The main drawback of the **for** loop is that it only allows you to increment or decrement by one. Its main advantages are conciseness and the ability to use char and enumerated types in the range of values.

## Procedures and Functions

You've learned how to execute code *conditionally* and *iteratively*. Now, what if you want to perform the same set of instructions on different sets of data or at different locations in your program? Well, you simply put those statements into a *subroutine*, which you can then call as needed.

In Pascal, there are two types of subroutines: *procedures* and *functions*. The main difference between the two is that a function returns a value and can be used in expressions, like this:

```
X := Sin(A);
```

while a procedure is called to perform one or more tasks:

```
Writeln('This is a test');
```

However, before you learn any more about procedures and functions, you need to understand Pascal program structure.

## Program Structure

In Standard Pascal, programs adhere to a rigid format:

```
program ProgName;
label
  labels;
const
  constant declarations;
type
  data type definitions;
var
  variable declarations;
procedures and functions;
begin
  main body of program
end.
```

The five declaration sections—**label**, **const**, **type**, **var**, and **procedures** and **functions**—do not all have to be in every program. But in standard Pascal, if they do appear, they must be in that order, and each section can appear only once. The declaration section is followed by any procedures and functions you might have, then finally the main body of the program, consisting of some number of statements.

Turbo Pascal gives you tremendous flexibility in your program structure. All it requires is that your program statement (if you have one) be first and that your main program body be last. Between those two, you can have as many declaration sections as you want, in any order you want, with procedures and functions freely mixed in. But things must be defined before they are used, or else a compile-time error will occur.

## Procedure and Function Structure

As mentioned earlier, procedures and functions—known collectively as *subprograms*—appear anywhere before the main body of the program. Procedures use this format:

```
procedure ProcName(parameters);
label
  labels;
const
  constant declarations;
type
  data type definitions;
var
  variable declarations;
procedures and functions;
begin
  main body of procedure;
end;
```

Functions look just like procedures except that they start with a **function** header and end with a data type for the return value of the function:

```
function FuncName(parameters) : data type;
```

As you can see, there are only two differences between this and regular program structure: Procedures or functions start with a **procedure** or **function** header instead of a **program** header, and they end with a semi-colon instead of a period. A procedure or function can have its own constants, data types, and variables, and even its own procedures and functions. What's more, all these items can only be used with the procedure or function in which they are declared.

## Sample Program

Here's a version of the DORATIO program that uses a procedure to get the two values, then uses a function to calculate the ratio:

```
program DoRatio;
var
  A,B   : integer;
  Ratio : real;
procedure GetData(var X,Y : integer);
begin
  Write('Enter two numbers:  ');
  Readln(X,Y)
end;

function GetRatio(I,J : integer) : real;
begin
  GetRatio := I/J
end;

begin
  GetData(A,B);
  Ratio := GetRatio(A,B);
  Writeln('The ratio is ',Ratio)
end.
```

This isn't exactly an improvement on the original program, being both larger and slower, but it does illustrate how procedures and functions work.

When you compile and run this program, execution starts with the first statement in the main body of the program: `GetData(A,B)`. This type of statement is known as a *procedure call*. Your program handles this call by executing the statements in *GetData*, replacing *X* and *Y* (known as *formal parameters*) with *A* and *B* (known as *actual parameters*). The keyword **var** in front of *X* and *Y* in *GetData*'s procedure statement says that the actual parameters must be variables and that the variable values can be changed and passed back to the caller. So you can't pass literals, constants, expressions, and so on to *GetData*. Once *GetData* is finished, execution returns to the main body of the program and continues with the statement following the call to *GetData*.

That next statement is a function call to *GetRatio*. Note that there are some key differences here. First, *GetRatio* returns a value, which must then be used somehow; in this case, it's assigned to *Ratio*. Second, a value is assigned to *GetRatio* in its main body; this is how a function determines what value to return. Third, there is no **var** keyword in front of the formal parameters *I* and *J*. This means that the actual parameters could be any two integer expressions, such as *Ratio := GetRatio(A + B,300)*; and that even if you change the values of the formal parameters in the **function** body, the new values will not be passed back to the caller. This, by the way, is *not* a distinction between procedures and functions; you can use both types of parameters with either type of subprogram.

## Program Comments

Sometimes you want to insert notes into your program to remind you (or inform someone else) of what certain variables mean, what certain functions or statements do, and so on. These notes are known as *comments*. Pascal, like most other programming languages, lets you put as many comments as you want into your program.

You can start a comment with the left curly brace ({), which signals to the compiler to ignore everything until after it sees the right curly brace (}).

Comments can even extend across multiple lines, like this:

```
{ This is a long
  comment, extending
  over several lines. }
```

Pascal also allows an alternative form of comment, beginning with a left parenthesis and an asterisk, (*, and ending with a right parenthesis and an asterisk, *). This allows for a limited form of comment nesting, because a comment beginning with (* ignores all curly braces, and vice versa.

Now that we've gotten you off to a fine start, we recommend that you buy a good tutorial on Turbo Pascal (for instance, *Turbo Pascal Tutor*).

C H A P T E R

# 4

# Units and Related Mysteries

In Chapter 3, you learned how to write standard Pascal programs. What about non-standard programming—more specifically, PC-style programming, with screen control, DOS calls, and graphics? To write such programs, you have to understand units or understand the PC hardware enough to do the work yourself. This chapter explains what a unit is, how you use it, what predefined units are available, how to go about writing your own units, and how to compile them.

## What's a Unit, Anyway?

Turbo Pascal gives you access to a large number of predefined constants, data types, variables, procedures, and functions. Some are specific to Turbo Pascal; others are specific to the IBM PC (and compatibles) or to MS-DOS. There are dozens of them, but you seldom use them all in a given program. Because of this, they are split into related groups called *units*. You can then use only the units your program needs.

A *unit* is a collection of constants, data types, variables, procedures, and functions. Each unit is almost like a separate Pascal program: It can have a main body that is called before your program starts and does whatever initialization is necessary. In short, a unit is a library of declarations you can pull into your program that allows your program to be split up and separately compiled.

All the declarations within a unit are usually related to one another. For example, the *Crt* unit contains all the declarations for screen-oriented routines on your PC.

Turbo Pascal provides seven standard units for your use. Five of them—*System*, *Graph*, *Dos*, *Crt*, and *Printer*—provide support for your regular Turbo Pascal programs. The other two—*Turbo3* and *Graph3* are designed to help maintain compatibility with programs and data files created under version 3.0 of Turbo Pascal. All but *Graph* are stored in the file TURBO.TPL. Some of these are explained more fully in Chapter 5, but we'll look at each one here and explain its general function.

## A Unit's Structure

A unit provides a set of capabilities through procedures and functions—with supporting constants, data types, and variables—but it hides how those capabilities are actually implemented by separating the unit into two sections: the *interface* and the *implementation*. When a program uses a unit, all the unit's declarations become available, as if they had been defined within the program itself.

A unit's structure is not unlike that of a program, but with some significant differences. Here's a unit, for example:

```
unit <identifier>;
interface
uses <list of units>;   { Optional }
  { public declarations }
implementation
  { private declarations }
  { procedures and functions }
begin
  { initialization code }
end.
```

The unit header starts with the reserved word **unit**, followed by the unit's name (an identifier), exactly like a program has a name. The next item in a unit is the keyword **interface**. This signals the start of the interface section of the unit—the section visible to any other units or programs that use this unit.

A unit can use other units by specifying them in a **uses** clause. If present, the **uses** clause appears immediately after the keyword **interface**.

## Interface Section

The interface portion—the "public" part—of a unit starts at the reserved word **interface**, which appears after the unit header and ends when the reserved word **implementation** is encountered. The interface determines what is "visible" to any program (or other unit) using that unit; any program using the unit has access to these "visible" items.

In the unit interface, you can declare constants, data types, variables, procedures, and functions. As with a program, these can be arranged in any order, and sections can repeat themselves (for example, **type** ... **var** ... *<procs>* ... **const** ... **type** ... **const** ... **var**).

The procedures and functions visible to any program using the unit are declared here, but their actual bodies—implementations—are found in the implementation section. **forward** declarations are neither necessary nor allowed. The bodies of all the regular procedures and functions are held in the implementation section after all the procedure and function headers have been listed in the interface section.

## Implementation Section

The implementation section—the "private" part—starts at the reserved word **implementation**. Everything declared in the interface portion is visible in the implementation: constants, types, variables, procedures, and functions. Furthermore, the implementation can have additional declarations of its own, although these are not visible to any programs using the unit. The program doesn't know they exist and can't reference or call them. However, these hidden items can be (and usually are) used by the "visible" procedures and functions—those routines whose headers appear in the interface section.

If any procedures have been declared external, one or more {$L *filename*} directive(s) should appear anywhere in the source file before the final **end** of the unit.

The normal procedures and functions declared in the interface—those that are not inline—must reappear in the implementation. The **procedure/function** header that appears in the implementation should either be identical to that which appears in the interface or should be in the short form. For the short form, type in the keyword (**procedure** or **function**), followed by the routine's name (identifier). The routine will then contain all its local declarations (labels, constants, types, variables, and nested procedures and functions), followed by the main body of the routine itself. Say the following declarations appear in the interface of your unit:

```
procedure ISwap(var V1,V2 : integer);
function IMax(V1,V2 : integer) : integer;
```

The implementation could look like this:

```
procedure ISwap;
var
  Temp : integer;
begin
   Temp := V1; V1 := V2; V2 := Temp
end;   { of proc ISwap }
function IMax(V1,V2 : integer) : integer;
begin
  if V1 > V2 then
    IMax := V1
  else IMax := V2
end;   { of func IMax }
```

Routines local to the implementation (that is, not declared in the interface section) must have their complete **procedure/function** header intact.

## Initialization Section

The entire implementation portion of the unit is normally bracketed within the reserved words **implementation** and **end**. However, if you put the reserved word **begin** before **end**, with statements between the two, the resulting compound statement—looking very much like the main body of a program—becomes the *initialization* section of the unit.

The initialization section is where you initialize any data structures (variables) that the unit uses or makes available (through the interface) to the program using it. You can use it to open files for the program to use later. For example, the standard unit *Printer* uses its initialization section to make all the calls to open (for output) the text file *Lst*, which you can then use in your program's *Write* and *Writeln* statements.

When a program using that unit is executed, the unit's initialization section is called before the program's main body is run. If the program uses more than one unit, each unit's initialization section is called (in the order specified in the program's **uses** statement) before the program's main body is executed.

## How Are Units Used?

The units your program uses have already been compiled, stored as machine code not Pascal source code; they are not Include files. Even the interface section is stored in the special binary symbol table format that Turbo Pascal uses. Furthermore, certain standard units are stored in a special file (TURBO.TPL) and are automatically loaded into memory along with Turbo Pascal itself.

As a result, using a unit or several units adds very little time (typically less than a second) to the length of your program's compilation. If the units are being loaded in from a separate disk file, a few additional seconds may be required because of the time it takes to read from the disk.

As stated earlier, to use a specific unit or collection of units, you must place a **uses** clause at the start of your program, followed by a list of the unit names you want to use, separated by commas:

```
program MyProg;
uses thisUnit,thatUnit,theOtherUnit;
```

When the compiler sees this **uses** clause, it adds the interface information in each unit to the symbol table and links the machine code that is the implementation to the program itself.

The ordering of units in the **uses** clause is not important. If *thisUnit* uses *thatUnit* or vice versa, you can declare them in either order, and the compiler will determine which unit must be linked into MyProg first. In fact, if *thisUnit* uses *thatUnit* but MyProg doesn't need to directly call any of the routines in *thatUnit*, you can "hide" the routines in *thatUnit* by omitting it from the **uses** clause:

```
unit thisUnit;
uses thatUnit;
...
program MyProg;
uses thisUnit, theOtherUnit;
...
```

In this example, *thisUnit* can call any of the routines in *thatUnit*, and MyProg can call any of the routines in *thisUnit* or *theOtherUnit*. MyProg cannot, however, call any of the routines in *thatUnit* because *thatUnit* does not appear in MyProg's **uses** clause.

If you don't put a **uses** clause in your program, Turbo Pascal links in the *System* standard unit anyway. This unit provides some of the standard Pascal routines as well as a number of Turbo Pascal-specific routines.

## *Referencing Unit Declarations*

Once you include a unit in your program, all the constants, data types, variables, procedures, and functions declared in that unit's interface become available to you. For example, suppose the following unit existed:

```
unit MyStuff;
interface
  const
    MyValue  = 915;
  type
    MyStars  = (Deneb,Antares,Betelgeuse);
  var
    MyWord  : string[20];
  procedure SetMyWord(Star : MyStars);
  function  TheAnswer : integer;
```

What you see here is the unit's interface, the portion that is visible to (and used by) your program. Given this, you might write the following program:

```
program TestStuff;
uses MyStuff;
var
  I     : integer;
  AStar : MyStars;
begin
  Writeln(MyValue);
  AStar := Deneb;
  SetMyWord(AStar);
  Writeln(MyWord);
  I := TheAnswer;
  Writeln(I)
end.
```

Now that you have included the statement **uses** *MyStuff* in your program, you can refer to all the identifiers declared in the interface section in the interface of *MyStuff* (*MyWord*, *MyValue*, and so on). However, consider the following situation:

```
program TestStuff;
uses MyStuff;
const
  MyValue  = 22;
var
  I      : integer;
  AStar  : MyStars;
function TheAnswer : integer;
begin
  TheAnswer := -1
end;

begin
  Writeln(MyValue);
  AStar := Deneb;
  SetMyWord(AStar);
  Writeln(MyWord);
  I := TheAnswer;
  Writeln(I)
end.
```

This program redefines some of the identifiers declared in *MyStuff*. It will compile and run, but will use its own definitions for *MyValue* and *TheAnswer*, since those were declared more recently than the ones in *MyStuff*.

You're probably wondering whether there's some way in this situation to still refer to the identifiers in *MyStuff*? Yes, preface each one with the identifier *MyStuff* and a period (.). For example, here's yet another version of the earlier program:

```
program TestStuff;
uses MyStuff;
const
  MyValue = 22;
var
  I     : integer;
  AStar : MyStars;
function TheAnswer : integer;
begin
  TheAnswer := -1;
end;

begin
  Writeln(MyStuff.MyValue);
  AStar := Deneb;
  SetMyWord(AStar);
  Writeln(MyWord);
  I := MyStuff.TheAnswer
  Writeln(I)
end.
```

This program will give you the same answers as the first one, even though you've redefined *MyValue* and *TheAnswer*. Indeed, it would have been perfectly legal (although rather wordy) to write the first program as follows:

```
program TestStuff;
uses MyStuff;
var
  I     : integer;
  AStar : MyStuff.MyStars;
begin
  Writeln(MyStuff.MyValue);
  AStar := MyStuff.Deneb;
  MyStuff.SetMyWord(AStar);
  Writeln(MyStuff.MyWord);
  I := MyStuff.TheAnswer;
  Writeln(I)
end.
```

Note that you can preface any identifier—constant, data type, variable, or subprogram—with the unit name.

# TURBO.TPL

The file TURBO.TPL contains all the standard units except *Graph*: *System*, *Crt*, *Dos*, *Printer*, *Turbo3*, and *Graph3*. These are the units loaded into memory with Turbo Pascal; they're always readily available to you. You will normally keep the file TURBO.TPL in the same directory as TURBO.EXE (or TPC.EXE). However, you can keep it somewhere else, as long as that "somewhere else" is defined as the Turbo directory. That's done using TINST.EXE to install the Turbo directory directly in the TURBO.EXE file.

### System          Units used: none

*System* contains all the standard and built-in procedures and functions of Turbo Pascal. Every Turbo Pascal routine that is *not* part of standard Pascal and that is *not* in one of the other units is in *System*. This unit is always linked into every program.

### Dos          Units used: none

*Dos* defines numerous Pascal procedures and functions that are equivalent to the most commonly used DOS calls, such as *GetTime*, *SetTime*, *DiskSize*, and so on. It also defines two low-level routines, *MsDos* and *Intr*, which allow you to directly invoke any MS-DOS call or system interrupt. *Registers* is the data type for the parameter to *MsDos* and *Intr*. Some other constants and data types are also defined.

### Crt          Units used: none

*Crt* provides a set of PC-specific declarations for input and output: constants, variables, and routines. You can use these to manipulate your text screen (do windowing, direct cursor addressing, text color and background). You can also do "raw" input from the keyboard and control the PC's sound chip. This unit provides a lot of routines that were standard in version 3.0.

**Printer**                                                        **Units used:** *none*

*Printer* declares the text-file variable *Lst* and connects it to a device driver that (you guessed it) allows you to send standard Pascal output to the printer using *Write* and *Writeln*. For example, once you include *Printer* in your program, you could do the following:

```
Write(Lst,'The sum of ',A:4,' and ',B:4,' is ');
C := A + B;
Writeln(Lst,C:8);
```

**Graph3**                                                          **Units used:** *Crt*

*Graph3* supports the full set of graphics routines—basic, advanced, and turtlegraphics—from version 3.0. They are identical in name, parameters, and function to those in version 3.0.

**Turbo3**                                                          **Units used:** *Crt*

This unit contains two variables and several procedures that are no longer supported by Turbo Pascal. These include the predefined file variable *Kbd*, the Boolean variable *CBreak*, and the original integer versions of *MemAvail* and *MaxAvail* (which return paragraphs free instead of bytes free, as do the current versions).

**Graph**                                                          **Units used:** *none*

The *Graph* unit is not built into TURBO.TPL, but instead resides on the same disk with the .BGI and .CHR support files. Place GRAPH.TPU in the current directory or use the unit directory to specify the full path to GRAPH.TPU.

*Graph* supplies a set of fast, powerful graphics routines that allow you to make full use of the graphics capabilities of your PC. It implements the device-independent Borland graphics handler, allowing support of CGA, EGA, Hercules, AT &T 400, MCGA, 3270 PC, and VGA graphics.

Now that you've been introduced to units, let's see about writing your own.

# Writing Your Own Units

Say you've written a unit called *IntLib*, stored it in a file called INTLIB.PAS, and compiled it to disk; the resulting code file will be called INTLIB.TPU. To use it in your program, you must include a **uses** statement to tell the compiler you're using that unit. Your program might look like this:

```
program MyProg;
uses IntLib;
```

Note that Turbo Pascal expects the unit code file to have the same name (up to eight characters) of the unit itself. If your unit name is *MyUtilities*, then Turbo is going to look for a file called MYUTILIT.PAS. You can override that assumption with the $*U* compiler directive. This directive is passed the name of the .PAS file and must appear just before the unit's name in the **uses** statement. For example, if your program uses *Dos*, *Crt*, and *MyUtilities*, and the last one is stored in a file called UTIL.PAS, then you would write

```
uses Dos, Crt, {$U UTIL.PAS} MyUtilities;
```

## *Compiling a Unit*

You compile a unit exactly like you'd compile a program:  Write it using the editor and select the Compile/Compile command (or press *Alt-C*). However, instead of creating an .EXE file, Turbo Pascal will create a .TPU (Turbo Pascal Unit) file. You can then leave this file as is or merge it into TURBO.TPL using TPUMOVER.EXE (see Chapter 7).

In any case, you probably want to move your .TPU files (along with their source) to the unit directory you specified with the **O/D/Unit** directories command. That way, you can reference those files without having to give a {$*U*} directive (The **U**nit directories command lets you give multiple directories for the compiler to search for in unit files.)

You can only have one unit in a given source file; compilation stops when the final **end** statement is encountered.

## *An Example*

Okay, now let's write a small unit. We'll call it *IntLib* and put in two simple integer routines—a procedure and a function:

```
unit IntLib;
interface
procedure ISwap(var I,J : integer);
function  IMax(I,J : integer) : integer;
implementation
procedure ISwap;
var
  Temp  : integer;
begin
  Temp := I; I := J; J := Temp
end;  { of proc ISwap }

function IMax;
begin
  if I > J then
    IMax := I
  else IMax := J
end;  { of func IMax }
end.  { of unit IntLib }
```

Type this in, save it as the file INTLIB.PAS, then compile it to disk. The resulting unit code file is INTLIB.TPU. Move it to your unit directory (whatever that might happen to be).

This next program uses the unit *IntLib*:

```
program IntTest;
uses IntLib;
var
  A,B  : integer;
begin
  Write('Enter two integer values:  ');
  Readln(A,B);
  ISwap(A,B);
  Writeln('A = ',A,' B = ',B);
  Writeln('The max is ',IMax(A,B));
end.  { of program IntTest }
```

Congratulations! You've just created your first unit!

## *Units and Large Programs*

Up until now, you've probably thought of units only as libraries—-collections of useful routines to be shared by several programs. Another function of a unit, however, is to break up a large program into modules.

Two aspects of Turbo Pascal make this modular functionality of units work: (1) its tremendous speed in compiling and linking and (2) its ability to manage several code files simultaneously, such as a program and several units.

Typically, a large program is divided into units that group procedures by their function. For instance, an editor application could be divided into initialization, printing, reading and writing files, formatting, and so on. Also, there could be a "global" unit—one used by all other units, as well as the main program—that defines global constants, data types, variables, procedures, and functions.

The skeleton of a large program might look like this:

```
program Editor;
uses
  Dos,Crt,Printer                        { Standard units from TURBO.TPL }
  EditGlobals,                                    { User-written units }
  EditInit,
  EditPrint,
  EditRead,EditWrite,
  EditFormat;

{ Program's declarations, procedures, and functions }
begin   { main program }
end.   { of program Editor }
```

Note that the units in this program could either be in TURBO.TPL or in their own individual .TPU files. If the latter is true, then Turbo Pascal will manage your project for you. This means when you recompile the program Editor, Turbo Pascal will check the last update for each of the .TPU files and recompile them if necessary.

Another reason to use units in large programs has to do with code segment limitations. The 8086 (and related) processors limit the size of a given chunk, or segment, of code to 64K. This means that the main program and any given segment cannot exceed a 64K size. Turbo Pascal handles this by making each unit a separate code segment. Your upper limit is the amount of memory the machine and operating system can support—640K on most PCs. Without units, you're limited to 64K of code for your program. (See Chapter 6, "Project Management," for more information about how to deal with large programs.)

## *TPUMOVER*

You don't have to use a {$U <*filename*>} directive when using the standard runtime units (*System*, *Dos*, and so on). That's because all those units have been moved into the Turbo Pascal unit file (TURBO.TPL). When you compile, those units are always ready to be used when you want them.

Suppose you want to add a well-designed and thoroughly debugged unit to the standard units so that it's automatically loaded into memory when you run the compiler. Is there any way to move it into the Turbo Pascal standard unit library file? Yes, by using the TPUMOVER.EXE utility.

You can also use TPUMOVER to remove units from the Turbo Pascal standard unit library file, reducing its size and the amount of memory it takes up when loaded. (More details on using TPUMOVER can be found in Chapter 7.)

As you've seen, it's really quite simple to write your own units. A well-designed, well-implemented unit simplifies program development; you solve the problems only once, not for each new program. Best of all, a unit provides a clean, simple mechanism for writing very large programs.

# 5

# Getting the Most from Your PC

Now that you've learned about Pascal and units, it's time to see how to put it all together.

In this chapter, you'll start off learning about writing "textbook" programs in Turbo Pascal, then move on to some of the extensions that Turbo Pascal offers over standard Pascal. After that, we'll look at the standard units, giving some sample programs of how to use the routines in them. Finally, we'll touch on how to access machine and assembly language in your Pascal program.

## Writing Textbook Programs

Turbo Pascal supports most aspects of ANSI standard Pascal (refer to Appendix B, "Comparing Turbo Pascal 4.0 With ANSI Pascal"). As a result, it's easy for you to use Turbo Pascal with most Pascal textbooks. All you need to do is type in the program found in your textbook, compile it, and run it.

The only major difference between Turbo Pascal and standard Pascal you are likely to encounter is in *reading from* and *writing to* typed files. Turbo Pascal does not support the original *Get* and *Put* procedures, nor does it support file window variables. It does fully support (as defined in standard Pascal) *Read* and *Write* for typed file I/O.

Another area of clarification also deals with file I/O. Standard Pascal does not define any mechanism for associating a file variable (of any type) with an actual disk file. As a result, every Pascal compiler has its own means of performing this task. In Turbo Pascal, you use the *Assign* procedure, which has the format

```
Assign(filevar,filestr);
```

where *filevar* is a file variable of any type, and *filestr* any string expression containing the name of a disk file (including its path name if desired or necessary).

# Turbo Pascal Extensions

Turbo Pascal offers a large number of built-in extensions to standard Pascal. Here's a quick look at some of them.

## *Data-Type Extensions*

Turbo Pascal 4.0 has some significant data-type extensions to standard Pascal. These consist of new integer and floating-point data types that give you greater control over variable precision and size.

In addition to the standard type integer (-32768..32767), Turbo Pascal supports shortint (-128..127), byte (0..255), word (0..65535), and longint (-2147483648..2147483647). This variety of integer types allows you to precisely define the variables and data structures you need, rather than having to fit everything into the type integer.

Turbo Pascal 4.0 now has an option to support the 8087/80287/80387 math coprocessor. When you enable the {$N+} compiler directive or environment option, you then have access to four new data types: single (4-byte real), double (8-byte real), extended (10-byte real), and comp (8-byte integer). All floating-point operations are compiled as calls to the 8087 coprocessor, so that a program compiled using the {$N+} option can run only on a computer equipped with that processor.

## *Built-In Procedures and Functions*

Besides supporting all the defined procedures and functions in standard Pascal, Turbo Pascal 4.0 offers many additional built-in procedures and functions for your use. These are documented in Chapter 24. Also, note that many of the procedures and functions that were "standard" in version 3.0 are now in the various units found in TURBO.TPL.

# Using MS-DOS Calls

One of the units found in TURBO.TPL is *Dos*, which contains definitions, procedures, and functions designed to help you make greater use of MS-DOS. To use this unit, place the statement

```
uses Dos;
```

at the start of your program, after your program statement but before any of your declarations. If you are using more than this one unit, you can list all the units in this **uses** statement, separated by commas.

Let's start by writing a directory program. Here's the initial main body:

```
program GetDirectory;
uses Dos;
var
  Path  : string;
  SRec  : SearchRec;

{ Rest of program }
begin
  repeat
    Write('Enter path name: '); Readln(Path);
    if Path <> '' then
    begin
      FindFirst(Path,AnyFile,SRec);
      while DosError = 0 do
      begin
        PutSRec(SRec);
        FindNext(SRec)
      end;
      Writeln
    end
  until Path = ''
end. { of proc GetDirectory }
```

Note that the **uses** Dos statement is after the **program** statement, and also that the global variables *Path* and *SRec* are declared. In this program fragment, you are using five items from *Dos*: *SearchRec, AnyFile, FindFirst, DosError,* and *FindNext*.

The procedure *PutSRec* is user-defined; it'll go right where the Rest of program comment is. Let's look at that procedure:

```
procedure PutSRec(SRec : SearchRec);
var
  DT  : DateTime;
begin
  with SRec do
  begin
    PutName(Name);
```

```
    if (Attr and Directory) <> 0 then
      Write(' <DIR>')
    else
    begin
      Write(Size:10,'   ');
      UnpackTime(Time,DT);
      PutDateTime(DT)
    end;
    Writeln
  end
end; { of proc PutSRec }
```

Again, you borrow from *Dos*: the data types *SearchRec* and *DateTime*, the constant *Directory*, and the procedure *UnpackTime*. *Name*, *Attr*, *Size*, and *Time* are all fields of *SRec*.

*PutName* and *PutDateTime* are both user-defined procedures. They, and their support routines, all go in front of *PutSRec* and look like this:

```
procedure PutLead(I : integer);
begin
  if I >= 10 then
    Write(I:2)
  else Write('0',I:1)
end;  { of proc PutLead }

procedure PutDateTime(DT : DateTime);
var
  H   : integer;
  Ch  : char;
begin
  with DT do
  begin
    Write(Month:2,'-');
    PutLead(Day); Write('-');
    PutLead(Year mod 100); Write('  ');
    if Hour >= 12 then
      Ch := 'p'
      else Ch := 'a';
    H := Hour mod 12;
    if H = 0 then
      H := 12;
    Write(H:2,':');
    PutLead(Min); Write(Ch);
  end
end; { of proc PutDateTime }

procedure PutName(Name : string);
var
  DotPos  : integer;
  Ext     : string[3];
begin
  DotPos := Pos('.',Name);
```

```
  if DotPos <> 0 then
  begin
    Ext := Copy(Name,DotPos+1,Length(Name)-DotPos);
    Delete(Name,DotPos,1+Length(Name)-DotPos)
  end
  else Ext := '';
  Write(Name,' ':(10-Length(Name)),Ext,' ':(5-Length(Ext)))
end;
```

*PutLead* writes out an integer with a leading zero if it's less than 10.
*PutDateTime* prints out the date and time in the same format used by the
*Dir* command. Likewise, *PutName* writes out the file (or directory) name
using a *Dir*-like format.

This is just a small sample of what Turbo Pascal allows you to do with the
*Dos* unit. In addition to the file and clock manipulation routines, *Dos* offers
two general routines that let you make any DOS call or system software
interrupt: *MsDos* and *Intr*. Full details on this unit are found in Chapter 24.

# Screen Routines

Another unit, *Crt*, gives you full control over your text display. It contains
many of the routines offered in version 3.0, but adds a number of new,
powerful routines. As with other features of Turbo Pascal, the emphasis is
on flexibility and user control. For example, you can now enable (or disable) program abort on *Ctrl-Break*, end-of-file recognition of *Ctrl-Z*, direct
output to video RAM (as opposed to using BIOS calls), and limiting direct
video RAM output to the period during horizontal retrace to avoid "snow"
onscreen.

To show you what you can do with the *Crt* unit, here's a simple "editing"
program that brings up a window on the screen and lets you type in text,
including some very simple editing commands. The main body of the program looks like this:

```
program Edit;
uses Crt;
const
  X1   = 50;
  Y1   =  5;
  X2   = 75;
  Y2   = 22;
var
  Ch  : char;

{ More code goes here }
begin
  CheckBreak  := False;
  CheckEOF    := False;
  DirectVideo := True;
```

```
  SetWindow(X1,Y1,X2,Y2);
  GoToXY(1,1);
  repeat
    Ch := ReadKey;
    if Ch <> #0 then
      HandleKey(Ch)
    else HandleFuncKey(ReadKey)
  until Ch = ^Z;                              { End of file character }
  Window(1,1,80,25);
  ClrScr
end.
```

First, you turn off *CheckBreak* and *CheckEOF* and turn on *DirectVideo*. You then set up your own window (*SetWindow* is a user-defined routine) and enter an input/output loop. This consists of reading in a character straight from the keyboard (using *ReadKey*), checking to see if it's a function key or not, then handling it appropriately. Note that if *ReadKey* returns a #0 (NUL character), it means the user has pressed a function key, and the next call to *ReadKey* gives the scan code. This loop continues until the user types a *Ctrl-Z*, at which point the program resets the screen.

The *SetWindow* procedure (which follows) uses the special line-drawing characters of the IBM PC to draw a border around the requested window area. It clears that window and then sets the cursor in the upper left-hand corner of the actual text area.

Note that once you've called *Window*, GotoXY(1,1) always goes to the upper left screen. Here's the code:

```
procedure SetWindow(X1,Y1,X2,Y2 : integer);
const
  UpLeftCorner   = #201;
  HorzBar        = #205;
  UpRightCorner  = #187;
  VertBar        = #186;
  LowLeftCorner  = #200;
  LowRightCorner = #188;
var
  I  : integer;
begin
  Window(X1-1,Y1-1,X2+1,Y2+1);
  ClrScr;
  Window(1,1,80,25);
  GotoXY(X1-1,Y1-1);
  Write(UpLeftCorner);
  for I := X1 to X2 do
    Write(HorzBar);
  Write(UpRightCorner);
  for I := Y1 to Y2 do
  begin
    GoToXY(X1-1,I);  Write(VertBar);
    GoToXY(X2+1,I);  Write(VertBar)
  end;
```

```
  GoToXY(X1-1,Y2+1);
  Write(LowLeftCorner);
  for I := X1 to X2 do
    Write(HorzBar);
  Write(LowRightCorner);
  Window(X1,Y1,X2,Y2)
end; { of proc SetWindow }
```

The last two procedures called in the main program are *HandleKey* and *HandleFuncKey*. These execute an action based on the character value or scan code. Note that only the arrow keys are used for *HandleFuncKey,* and the user-defined routines *SetXY* and *Condition* limit the movement of the cursor. These routines appear before the main body of the program.

```
procedure HandleKey(Ch : char);
const
  BEL =  #7;                                                    { Bell }
  BS  =  #8;                                               { Backspace }
  CR  = #13;                                                  { Enter }
  SP  = #32;                                              { Space bar }
begin
  if Ch = BS
    then Write(BS,SP,BS)
    else if Ch = CR                                            { Enter }
    then Writeln
    else if Ch >= SP
    then Write(Ch)
    else if Ch <> ^Z
    then Write(BEL)
end; { of proc HandleKey }

procedure Condition(Low : integer; var X : integer; High : integer);
begin
  if X < Low then
    X := Low
  else if X > High then
    X := High
end; { of proc Condition }

procedure SetXY(NewX,NewY : integer);
begin
  Condition(1,NewX,(1+X2-X1));
  Condition(1,NewY,(1+Y2-Y1));
  GotoXY(NewX,NewY)
end; { of proc SetXY }

procedure HandleFuncKey(Ch : char);
const
  UpArrow     = #72;
  LeftArrow   = #75;
  RightArrow  = #77;
  DownArrow   = #80;
```

```
begin
  case Ch of
    UpArrow    : SetXY(WhereX,WhereY-1);
    LeftArrow  : SetXY(WhereX-1,WhereY);
    RightArrow : SetXY(WhereX+1,WhereY);
    DownArrow  : SetXY(WhereX,WhereY+1)
  end
end; { of proc HandleFuncKey }
```

Again, this is only a sample of what you can achieve using the *Crt* unit. For full documentation, see Chapter 24.

# Graphics Routines

Turbo Pascal 4.0 contains the *Graph* unit, which supports the new Borland device-independent standard for graphics devices; *Graph* implements more than 50 graphics procedures and functions.

For an example of the use of graphics, take a look at the sample program with *Graph* in Chapter 2. Also, several example programs are given on your distribution disks; full documentation can be found in Chapter 24.

# Getting Down to Assembly Language

Turbo Pascal is a powerful, flexible language, but for those times when you want to perform very low-level operations with direct control of the machine's hardware, the answer is to write them in assembly language. That way you can give small, precise instructions to the computer's microprocessor. Turbo Pascal, of course, allows you to do just that, and in fact gives you three ways to do it: inline statements, inline directives, and external procedures and functions. Full details on these methods are given in Chapter 26, but here's a quick discussion of each.

## *The Inline Statement*

The **inline** statement lets you put machine instructions into your program. You can use the **inline** statement anywhere you can use a regular statement—in the main body of your program or inside any procedure or function.

The format of the **inline** statement is

```
inline(item/item/item/.../item);
```

where *item* is an expression that resolves to either an 8-bit (byte) or 16-bit (word) value. Each *item* is composed of the following:

- An optional size specifier, either < or >. < means only the least-significant byte of the expression's value is in use; > means the expression is always treated as a word, with 0 in the most-significant byte if necessary.

- A constant *or* a variable identifier. A constant can be either decimal or hexadecimal—the latter is usually more convenient—and resolves to either a byte or word value. A variable identifier is the name of any global variable, typed constant, or local variable, and resolves to the offset (within the appropriate segment) of that variable.

- Zero or more offset specifiers, which consist of either + or – followed by a constant.

See Chapter 26 for more details and examples.

## *The Inline Directive*

Turbo Pascal 4.0 allows a new use of the **inline** keyword: to create inline directives. These are like procedures and functions that consist entirely of an **inline** statement; they have no local declarations, and no **begin..end** block. They consist only of the procedure (or function) header, followed by an **inline** statement:

```
procedure procname(parms);
inline(item/.../item);

function funcname(parms) : ftype;
inline(item/.../item);
```

You can then use these procedures and functions as you would any others. However, you are not actually calling subroutines. Instead, the Turbo Pascal compiler replaces each call with the given inline code. Because of that, inline directives are typically not very large. See Chapter 26 for more details and examples.

# External Procedures and Functions

Yes, Turbo Pascal now lets you link in external subroutines written in 8086 assembly language. The full details, including how to pass parameters and return function values, can be found in Chapter 26. Here's a quick explanation of how to call assembly language routines.

Before using an external procedure or function in a program, you must define it by writing its procedure or function header, followed by the keyword **external**:

```
procedure LowToUp(var Str : string); external;
function RotLeft(var L : longint; D : integer) : longint; external;
```

Note that there is no body to the procedure or function, only the header statement.

The **procedure/function** headers go wherever a regular procedure or function can go. If they're in a program, you can place them anywhere (as long as you define them before you use them). If they're in a unit, they can go either in the interface (if you want the user to be able to call them) or in the implementation (if you don't) section.

Next, write the appropriate routines using an assembler that generates standard .OBJ files. Two assemblers that Turbo Pascal works with are A86 and MASM. (A86 is a shareware assembler available from Eric Isaacson of Bloomington, Indiana. A86 is downloadable from CompuServe and many bulletin board systems. MASM is Microsoft's macro-assembler.) Refer to Chapter 26 for details on how Turbo Pascal passes parameters to external routines, and how external functions should pass values back.

Finally, you must tell the compiler what file to link to it, using the {$L} compiler directive. If you had assembled your assembly language routines into a file called MYSTUFF.OBJ, then you'd put the following directive somewhere in your program:

```
{$L MyStuff}
```

This directive can appear anywhere before the **begin** of the main body of your program or the **begin** of the initialization section in your unit (if you're writing your own unit).

When you compile your program, Turbo Pascal goes to MYSTUFF.OBJ, copies the machine code into your application file, and creates the necessary links.

This chapter gave you an idea of the kinds of programs you can write for the IBM PC; what you actually decide to write is limited only by your system memory and your imagination. There are more examples on the distribution disks and in Chapter 27.

C H A P T E R

# 6

# Project Management

So far, you've learned how to write Turbo Pascal programs, how to use the predefined units, and how to write your own units. At this point, your program has the capability of becoming large and separated into multiple source files. How do you manage such a program? This chapter suggests how to organize your program into units, how to take advantage of the built-in **M**ake and **B**uild options, how to use the stand-alone Make utility, how to use conditional compilation within a source code file, and how to optimize your code for speed.

## Program Organization

Turbo Pascal 4.0 allows you to divide your program into code segments. Your main program is a single code segment, which means that after compilation, it can have no more than 64K of machine code. However, you can exceed this limit by breaking your program up into units. Each unit can also contain up to 64K of machine code when compiled. The question is how should you organize your program into units?

The first step is to collect all your global definitions—constants, data types, and variables—into a single unit; let's call it *MyGlobals*. This is necessary if your other units reference those definitions. Unlike include files, units can't "see" any definitions made in your main program; they can only see what's in the interface section of their own unit and other units they use. Your units can use *MyGlobals* and thus reference all your global declarations.

A second possible unit is *MyUtils*. In this unit you could collect all the utility routines used by the rest of your program. These would have to be routines that don't depend on any others (except possibly other routines in *MyUtils*).

Beyond that, you should collect procedures and functions into logical groups. In each group, you'll often find a few procedures and functions that are called by the rest of the program, and then several (or many) procedures/functions that are called by those few. A group like that makes a wonderful unit. Here's how to convert it over:

- Copy all those procedures and functions into a separate file and delete them from your main program.
- Open that file for editing.
- Type the following lines in front of those procedures and functions:

```
unit unitname;
interface
uses MyGlobals;
implementation
```

where *unitname* is the name of your unit (and also the name of the file you're editing).

- Type **end.** at the very end of the file.
- Into the space between **interface** and **implementation**, copy the procedure and function headers of those routines called by the rest of the program. Those headers are simply the first line of each routine, the one that starts with **procedure** (or **function**).
- If this unit needs to use any others, type their names (separated by commas) between *MyGlobals* and the semicolon in the **uses** statement.
- Compile the unit you've created.
- Go back to your main program and add the unit's name to the **uses** statement at the start of the program.

Ideally, you want your program organized so that when you are working on a particular aspect of it, you are modifying and recompiling a single segment (unit or main program). This minimizes compile time; more importantly, it lets you work with smaller, more manageable chunks of code.

## *Initialization*

Remember in all this that each unit can (optionally) have its own initialization code. This code is automatically executed when the program is first loaded. If your program uses several units, then the initialization code for each unit is executed. The order of execution follows in which the units are listed in your program's **uses** statement; thus, if your program had the statement

```
uses MyGlobals,MyUtils,EditLib,GraphLib;
```

then the initialization section (if any) of *MyGlobals* would be called first, followed by that of *MyUtils*, then *EditLib*, then *GraphLib*.

To create an initialization section for a unit, put the keyword **begin** above the **end** that ends the implementation section. This defines the initialization section of your unit, much as the **begin..end** pair defines the main body of a program, a procedure, or a function. You can then put any Pascal code you want in here. It can reference everything declared in that unit, in both the public (interface) and private (implementation) sections; it can also reference anything from the interface portions of any units that this unit uses.

# The Build and Make Options

Turbo Pascal has an important feature to aid you in project management: a built-in Make utility. To discuss its significance, let's look at the previous example again.

Suppose you have a program, MYAPP.PAS, which uses four units: *MyGlobals*, *MyUtils*, *EditLib*, and *GraphLib*. Those four units are contained in the four text files MYGLOBAL.PAS, MYUTILS.PAS, EDITLIB.PAS, and GRAPHLIB.PAS, respectively. Furthermore, *MyUtils* uses *MyGlobals*, and *EditLib* and *GraphLib* use both *MyGlobals* and *MyUtils*.

When you compile MYAPP.PAS, it looks for the files MYGLOBAL.TPU, MYUTILS.TPU, EDITLIB.TPU, and GRAPHLIB.TPU, loads them into memory, links them with the code produced by compiling MYAPP.PAS, and writes everything out to MYAPP.EXE (if you're compiling to disk). So far, so good.

Suppose now you make some modifications to EDITLIB.PAS. In order to recreate MYAPP.EXE, you need to recompile both EDITLIB.PAS and MYAPP.PAS. A little tedious, but no big problem.

Now, let's suppose you modify the interface section of MYGLOBAL.PAS. To update MYAPP.EXE, you have to recompile all four units, as well as MYAPP.PAS. That means five separate compilations each time you make a change to MYGLOBAL.PAS—which could be enough to discourage you from using units to any great extent. But wait…

# The Make Option

As you probably guessed, Turbo Pascal offers a solution. By using the **Make** option (in the **Compile** menu), you can get Turbo Pascal to do all the work for you. The process is simple: After making any changes to any units and/or the main program, just recompile the main program.

Turbo Pascal then makes three kinds of checks.

■ First, it checks and compares the date and time of the .TPU file for each unit used by the main program against the unit's corresponding .PAS file. If the .PAS file has been modified since the .TPU file was created, Turbo Pascal recompiles the .PAS file, creating an updated .TPU file. So, as in the first example, if you modified EDITLIB.PAS and then recompiled MYAPP.PAS (using the **Make** option), Turbo Pascal would automatically recompile EDITLIB.PAS before compiling MYAPP.PAS.

■ The second check is to see if you changed the interface portion of the modified unit. If you did, then Turbo Pascal recompiles all other units using that unit.

Like in the second example, if you modified the interface portion of MYGLOBAL.PAS and then recompiled MYAPP.PAS, Turbo Pascal would automatically recompile MYGLOBAL.PAS, MYUTILS.PAS, EDITLIB.PAS, and GRAPHLIB.PAS (in that order) before compiling MYAPP.PAS. However, if you only modified the implementation portion, then the other dependent units don't need to be recompiled, since (as far as they're concerned) you didn't change that unit.

■ The third check is to see if you changed any Include or .OBJ files (containing assembly language routines) used by any units. If a given .TPU file is older than any of the Include or .OBJ files it links in, then that unit is recompiled. That way, if you modify and assemble some routines used by a unit, that unit is automatically recompiled the next time you compile a program using that unit.

To use the **Make** option under the integrated environment, either select the **Make** command from the **Compile** menu, or press *F9*. To invoke it with the command-line compiler, use the option */M*. Note that the **Make** option does not apply to any units found in TURBO.TPL.

# The Build Option

The **Build** option is a special case of the **Make** option. When you compile a program using **Build**, it automatically recompiles *all* units used by that program (except, of course, those units in TURBO.TPL). This is an easy way of ensuring everything is up to date.

To use the **B**uild option under the integrated environment, select the **B**uild command from the **C**ompile menu. To invoke it with the command-line compiler, use the option /*B*.

# The Stand-Alone Make Utility

Turbo Pascal places a great deal of power and flexibility at your fingertips. You can use it to manage large, complex programs that are built from numerous unit, source, and object files. And it can automatically perform a Build or a Make operation, recompiling units as needed. Understandably, though, Turbo Pascal has no mechanism for recreating .OBJ files from assembly code routines (.ASM files) that have changed. To do that, you need to use a separate assembler. The question then becomes, how do you keep your .ASM and .OBJ files updated?

The answer is simple: You use the MAKE utility that's included on the disk. MAKE is an intelligent program manager that—given the proper instructions—does all the work necessary to keep your program up to date. In fact, MAKE can do far more than that. It can make backups, pull files out of different subdirectories, and even automatically run your programs should the data files that they use be modified. As you use MAKE more and more, you'll see new and different ways it can help you to manage your program development.

MAKE is a stand-alone utility; it is different from the **M**ake and **B**uild options that are part of both the integrated environment and the command-line compiler. Full documentation of MAKE is given in Appendix D, but we'll give an example here to show how you might use it.

## *A Quick Example*

Suppose you're writing some programs to help you display information about nearby star systems. You have one program—GETSTARS.PAS—that reads in a text file listing star systems, does some processing on it, then produces a binary data file with the resulting information in it.

GETSTARS.PAS uses three units: STARDEFS.TPU, which contains the global definitions; STARLIB.TPU, which has certain utility routines; and STARPROC.TPU, which does the bulk of the processing. The source code for these units are found in STARDEFS.PAS, STARLIB.PAS, and STARPROC.PAS, respectively.

The next issue is dependencies. STARDEFS.PAS doesn't use any other units; STARLIB.PAS uses STARDEFS; STARPROC.PAS uses STARDEFS and STARLIB; and GETSTARS.PAS uses STARDEFS, STARLIB, and STARPROC.

Given that, to produce GETSTARS.EXE you would simply compile GETSTARS.PAS. Turbo Pascal (in either the integrated environment or the command-line version) would recompile the units as needed.

Suppose now that you convert a number of the routines in STARLIB.PAS into assembly language, creating the files SLIB1.ASM and SLIB2.ASM. When you assemble these files, you create SLIB1.OBJ and SLIB2.OBJ. Each time STARLIB.PAS is compiled, it links in those .OBJ files. And, in fact, Turbo Pascal is smart enough to recompile STARLIB.PAS if STARLIB.TPU is older than either of those .OBJ files.

However, what if either .OBJ file is older than the .ASM file upon which it depends? That means that the particular .ASM file needs to be re-assembled. Turbo Pascal can't assemble those files for you, so what do you do?

You create a *make file* and let MAKE do the work for you. A make file consists of *dependencies* and *commands*. The dependencies tell MAKE which files a given file depends upon; the commands tell MAKE how to create that given file from the other ones.

## Creating a Makefile

Your makefile for this project might look like this:

```
getstars.exe: getstars.pas stardefs.pas starlib.pas slib1.asm \
              slib2.asm slib1.obj slib2.obj
  tpc getstars /m

slib1.obj: slib1.asm
  A86 slib1.asm slib1.obj

slib2.obj: slib2.asm
      A86 slib2.asm slib2.obj
```

Okay, so this looks a bit cryptic. Here's an explanation:

■ The first two lines tell MAKE that GETSTARS.EXE depends on three Pascal, two assembly language, and two .OBJ files (the backslash at the end of line 1 tells MAKE to ignore the line break and continue the dependency definition on the next line).

- The third line tells MAKE how to build a new GETSTARS.EXE. Notice that it simply invokes the command-line compiler on GETSTARS.PAS and uses the built-in Turbo Pascal **Make** facility (/*M* option).
- The next two lines (ignoring the blank line) tell MAKE that SLIB1.OBJ depends on SLIB1.ASM and show MAKE how to build a new SLIB1.OBJ.
- Similarly, the last two lines define the dependencies (only one file, actually) and MAKE procedures for the file SLIB2.OBJ.

## Using MAKE

Let's suppose you've created this file using the Turbo Pascal integrated environment editor (or any other ASCII editor) and saved it as the file STARS.MAK. You would then use it by issuing the command

```
make -fstars.mak
```

where -f is an option telling MAKE which file to use. MAKE works from the bottom of the file to the top. First, it checks to see if SLIB2.OBJ is older than SLIB2.ASM. If it is, then MAKE issues the command

```
A86 SLIB2.asm SLIB2.obj
```

which assembles SLIB2.ASM, creating a new version of SLIB2.OBJ. It then makes the same check on SLIB1.ASM and issues the same command if needed. Finally, it checks all of the dependencies for GETSTARS.EXE and, if necessary, issues the command

```
tpc getstars /m
```

The /*M* option tells Turbo Pascal to use its own internal MAKE routines, which will then resolve all unit dependencies, including recompiling STARLIB.PAS if either SLIB1.OBJ or SLIB2.OBJ is newer than STARLIB.TPU.

This is only a simple example using MAKE; more complete documentation can be found in Appendix D.

# Conditional Compilation

To make your job easier, Turbo Pascal version 4.0 offers conditional compilation. This means that you can now decide what portions of your program to compile based on options or defined symbols.

The conditional directives are similar in format to the compiler directives that you're accustomed to; in other words, they take the format

```
{$directive arg}
```

where *directive* is the directive (such as DEFINE, IFDEF, and so on), and *arg* is the argument, if any. Note that there *must* be a separator (blank, tab) between *directive* and *arg*. Table 6.1 lists all the conditional directives, with their meanings.

Table 6.1: Summary of Compiler Directives

| | |
|---|---|
| {$DEFINE symbol} | Defines symbol for other directives |
| {$UNDEF symbol} | Removes definition of symbol |
| {$IFDEF symbol} | Compiles following code if symbol is defined |
| {$IFNDEF symbol} | Compiles following code if symbol is not defined |
| {$IFOPT x+} | Compiles following code if directive *x* is enabled |
| {$IFOPT x-} | Compiles following code if directive *x* is disabled |
| {$ELSE} | Compiles following code if previous IF*xxx* is not True |
| {$ENDIF} | Marks end of IF*xxx* or ELSE section |

## *The DEFINE and UNDEF Directives*

The IFDEF and IFNDEF directives test to see if a given symbol is defined. These symbols are defined using the DEFINE directive and undefined UNDEF directives. (You can also define symbols on the command line and in the integrated environment.)

To define a symbol, insert the directive

```
{$DEFINE symbol}
```

into your program. *symbol* follows the usual rules for identifiers as far as length, characters allowed, and other specifications. For example, you might write

```
{$DEFINE debug}
```

This defines the symbol *debug* for the remainder of the program, or until the statement

```
{$UNDEF debug}
```

is encountered. As you might guess, UNDEF "undefines" a symbol. If the symbol isn't defined, then UNDEF has no effect at all.

## Defining at the Command Line

If you're using the command-line version of Turbo Pascal (TPC.EXE), you can define conditional symbols on the command line itself. TPC accepts a */D* option, followed by a list of symbols separated by semicolons:

```
tpc myprog /Ddebug;test;dump
```

This would define the symbols *debug, test*, and *dump* for the program MYPROG.PAS. Note that the */D* option is cumulative, so that the following command line is equivalent to the previous one:

```
tpc myprog /Ddebug /Dtest /Ddump
```

# Defining in the Integrated Environment

Conditional symbols can be defined by using the **O/C/Conditional** defines option. Multiple symbols can be defined by entering them in the input box, separated by semicolons. The syntax is the same as that of the command-line version.

# Predefined Symbols

In addition to any symbols you define, you also can test certain symbols that Turbo Pascal has defined. Table 6.2 lists these symbols; let's look at each in a little more detail.

Table 6.2: Predefined Conditional Symbols

| | |
|---|---|
| VER40 | Always defined (TP 4.1 will define VER41, etc.) |
| MSDOS | Always defined |
| CPU86 | Always defined |
| CPU87 | Defined if an 8087 is present at compile time |

## The VER40 Symbol

The symbol *VER40* is always defined (at least for Turbo Pascal version 4.0). Each successive version will have a corresponding predefined symbol; for example, version 4.1 would have *VER41* defined, version 5.0 would have *VER50* defined, and so on. This will allow you to create source code files that can use future enhancements while maintaining compatibility with version 4.0.

## The MSDOS and CPU86 Symbols

These symbols are always defined (at least for Turbo Pascal version 4.0 running under MS-DOS). The *MSDOS* symbol indicates you are compiling under the MS-DOS operating system. The *CPU86* symbol means you are compiling on a computer using an Intel iAPx86 (8088, 8086, 80186, 80286, 80386) processor.

As future versions of Turbo Pascal for other operating systems and processors become available, they will have similar symbols indicating which operating system and/or processor is being used. Using these symbols, you can create a single source code file for more than one operating system or hardware configuration.

## The CPU87 Symbol

Turbo Pascal 4.0 supports floating-point operations in two ways: hardware and software. If you have an 80x87 math coprocessor installed in your computer system, you can use the IEEE floating-point types (single, double, extended, comp), and Turbo Pascal will produce direct calls to the math chip. If you don't, then you can use the floating-point type real (6 bytes in size), and Turbo Pascal will support all your operations with software routines. You can use the $N directive to indicate which you wish to use.

When you load the Turbo Pascal compiler, it checks to see if an 80x87 chip is installed. If it is, then the *CPU87* symbol is defined; otherwise, it's undefined. You might then have the following code at the start of your program:

```
{$IFDEF CPU87}                          { If there's an 80x87 present }
{$N+}                                   { Then use the inline 8087 code }
{$ELSE}
{$N-}                                   { Else use the software library }
{$ENDIF}
```

You can use a similar construct to define variables, or you could use the {$IFOPT N+} directive to handle those.

## The IFxxx, ELSE, and ENDIF Symbols

The idea behind conditional directives is that you want to select some amount of source code to be compiled if a particular symbol is (or is not) defined or if a particular option is (or is not) enabled. The general format follows:

```
{$IFxxx}
   source code
{$ENDIF}
```

where *IFxxx* is IFDEF, IFNDEF, or IFOPT, followed by the appropriate argument, and *source code* is any amount of Turbo Pascal source code. If the expression in the IF*xxx* directive is True, then *source code* is compiled; otherwise, it is ignored as if it had been commented out of your program.

Quite often you have alternate chunks of source code. If the expression is True, you want one chunk compiled, and if it's False, you want the other one compiled. Turbo Pascal lets you do this with the $ELSE directive:

```
{$IFxxx}
   source code A
{$ELSE}
   source code B
{$ENDIF}
```

If the expression in *IFxxx* is True, then *source code A* is compiled, else *source code B* is compiled.

Note that all IF*xxx* directives must be completed within the same source file, which means they cannot start in one source file and end in another. However, an IF*xxx* directive can encompass an include file:

```
{$IFxxx}
{$I file1.pas}
{$ELSE}
{$I file2.pas}
{$ENDIF}
```

That way, you can select alternate include files based on some condition.

You can nest *IFxxx..ENDIF* constructs so that you can have something like this:

```
{$IFxxx}                              { First IF directive }
...
{$IFxxx}                              { Second IF directive }
...
{$ENDIF}                    { Terminates second IF directive }
...
{$ENDIF}                     { Terminates first IF directive }
```

Let's look at each of the *IFxxx* directives in more detail.

## The IFDEF and IFNDEF Directives

You've learned how to define a symbol, and also that there are some pre-defined symbols. The IFDEF and IFNDEF directives let you conditionally compile code based on whether those symbols are defined or undefined. You saw this example earlier:

```
{$IFDEF CPU87}                        { If there's an 80x87 present }
```

```
{$N+}                              { Then use the inline 8087 code }
{$ELSE}
{$N-}                              { Else use the software library }
{$ENDIF}
```

By putting this in your program, you can automatically select the $N option if an 8087 math coprocessor is present when your program is compiled. That's an important point: This is a compile-time option. If there is an 8087 coprocessor in your machine when you compile, then your program will be compiled with the $N+ compiler directive or environment option, selecting direct calls to the 8087 and allowing you to use only the IEEE floating-point types. Otherwise, it will be compiled with the $N- directive or option, using the software floating-point package and allowing you to use only the usual Turbo Pascal 6-byte real data type. If you compile this program on a machine with an 8087, you can't run the resulting .EXE file on a machine without an 8087.

Another typical use of the IFDEF and IFNDEF directives is debugging. For example, you could put the following code at the start of each procedure:

```
{$IFDEF debug}
  Writeln('Now entering proc name');
  Readln;                          { Pause until user presses Enter }
{$ENDIF}
```

where *proc name* is the name of that procedure. If you put the following directive at the start of your program:

```
{$DEFINE debug}
```

and compile your program, then those statements will be included at the start of each procedure. If you remove the DEFINE directive or follow it with an UNDEF directive, then those statements at the start of each procedure won't be compiled. In a similar fashion, you may have sections of code that you want compiled only if you are not debugging; in that case, you would write

```
{$IFNDEF debug}
  source code
{$ENDIF}
```

where *source code* will be compiled only if *debug* is not defined at that point.

## The IFOPT Directive

You may want to include or exclude code, depending upon which compiler options (range-checking, I/O-checking, numeric processing, and so on) have been selected. Turbo Pascal lets you do that with the IFOPT directive, which takes two forms:

```
{$IFOPT x+}
```

and

```
{$IFOPT x-}
```

where *x* is one of the compiler options: *B, D, F, I, L, N, R, S, T,* or *V* (see Appendix C for a complete description). With the first form, the following code is compiled if the compiler option is currently enabled; with the second, the code is compiled if the option is currently disabled. So, as an example, you could have the following:

```
var
  {$IFOPT N+}
    Radius,Circ,Area  : double;
  {$ELSE}
    Radius,Circ,Area  : real;
  {$ENDIF}
```

This selects the data type for the listed variables based on whether or not 8087 support is desired. If you combine this with the {$IFDEF CPU87} example given earlier, then your source code will automatically select the proper compiler option and data type(s) based on whether there's an 8087 coprocessor in the machine on which you're compiling.

An alternate example might be

```
Assign(F,Filename);
Reset(F);
{$IFOPT I-}
IOCheck;
{$ENDIF}
```

where *IOCheck* is a user-written procedure that gets the value of *IOResult*, and prints out an error message as needed. There's no sense calling *IOCheck* if you've selected the *$I+* option since, if there's an error, your program will halt before it ever calls *IOCheck*.

# Optimizing Code

A number of compiler options influence both the size and the speed of the code. This is because they insert error-checking and error-handling code into your program. They are best left enabled while you are developing your program, but you may want to disable them for your final version. Here are those options, with their settings for optimization:

- {$B-} uses short-circuit Boolean evaluation. This produces code that can run faster, depending upon how you set up your Boolean expressions. The default equals *B-*.

- {$I-} turns off I/O error-checking. By calling the predefined function *IOResult*, you can handle I/O errors yourself. The default equals *I+*.

- {$R-} turns off range-checking. This prevents code generation to check for array subscripting errors and assignment of out-of-range values. The default equals *R-*.

- {$S-} turns off stack-checking. This prevents code generation to ensure that there is enough space on the stack for each procedure or function call. The default equals *S+*.

- {$V-} turns off checking of var parameters that are strings. This lets you pass actual parameters strings that are of a different length than the type defined for the formal **var** parameter. The default equals *V+*.

Disabling each of these options has two advantages. First, it usually makes your code smaller and faster. Second, it allows you to get away with something that you couldn't normally. However, they all have corresponding risks as well, so use them carefully, and reenable them if your program starts behaving strangely.

Note that besides embedding the compiler options in your source code directly, you can also set them using the **O**ptions/**C**ompiler menu in the integrated environment or the /$*x* option in the command-line compiler (where *x* represents a letter for a compiler directive).

C  H  A  P  T  E  R

# 7

# Using the Unit Mover

When you write units, you want to make them easily available to any programs that you develop. Chapter 4 explains what a unit is and tells how to create your own units. This chapter shows you how to use TPUMOVER to *remove* seldom-used units from TURBO.TPL, and how to *insert* often-used units into TURBO.TPL.

## A Review of Unit Files

There are two types of unit files: .TPU files and .TPL files. When you compile a unit, Turbo Pascal puts the resulting object code in a .TPU (**Turbo Pascal Unit**) file, which always contains exactly one unit.

A .TPL (**Turbo Pascal Library**) file, on the other hand, can contain multiple units. For example, all the units that come on your Turbo Pascal disk are in the file TURBO.TPL. The file TURBO.TPL is currently the only library file Turbo Pascal will load units from.

The naming distinction becomes important during compilation. If a particular unit used is not found in TURBO.TPL, then Turbo Pascal looks for the file *unitname*.TPU; if that file is not found, then compilation halts with an error. If you are using the **Build** option, then Turbo Pascal first looks for *unitname*.PAS and recompiles it, using the resulting .TPU file. If you are using the **Make** option, then Turbo Pascal looks for both *unitname*.PAS and *unitname*.TPU, compares their latest modification dates and times, and recompiles the .PAS file if it has been modified since the .TPU file was created.

Normally, when you write your own unit, it gets saved to a .TPU file; to use that unit, you must tell Turbo Pascal where to find it. If you're using the integrated environment, you must set the **U**nit directories option in the **O**ptions/**D**irectories menu. (TURBO.TPL is loaded from the **T**urbo directory in the same menu.) If you're using the command-line environment, you must use the /U option. (Use the /T option to load the Turbo library from another subdirectory in the command-line compiler.)

You may have noticed, though, that you can use the standard Turbo Pascal units without giving a file name. That's because these units are stored in the Turbo Pascal standard unit file—TURBO.TPL on your distribution disk. Because the units are in that file, any program can use them without "knowing" their location.

Suppose you have a unit called TOOLS.TPU, and you use it in many different programs. Though adding *Tools* to TURBO.TPL takes up memory (TURBO.TPL is automatically loaded into memory by the compiler), adding it to the resident library makes "using" *Tools* faster because the unit is in memory instead of on disk.

There are six standard units already in TURBO.TPL: *System, Printer, Crt, Dos, Turbo3,* and *Graph3*.

You probably won't ever use *Turbo3* or *Graph3* unless you have a lot of programs written with version 3.0 and haven't yet converted them. So, you might as well use TPUMOVER to remove them from TURBO.TPL and recover about 10K of memory.

# Using TPUMOVER

TPUMOVER is a display-oriented program, much like the integrated environment. It shows you the units contained in two different files and allows you to copy units back and forth between them or to delete units from a given file. It's primarily used for moving files in and out of TURBO.TPL, but it has other useful functions.

Note that the TPUMOVER display consists of two side-by-side windows. The name of the file appears at the top of the window, followed by a list of the units in that file. Each line in a window gives information for a single unit: unit name, code size, data size, symbol table size, and the name(s) of any unit(s) that this unit uses. The sizes are all in bytes, and the unit names are all truncated to seven characters. If the list of units being used is too long to fit, it ends with three dots; press *F4* to see a pop-up window to see the names of the other unit dependencies. Finally, two lines of information appear in that window, giving (in bytes) the current size of that file and the amount of free space on the disk drive containing that file.

At any time, one of the two windows is the "active" window. This is indicated by a double line around the active window. Also, only the active window contains a highlighted bar that appears within the list of units in that file; the bar can be moved up or down using the arrow keys All commands apply to the active window; pressing *F6* switches back and forth between the two windows.

To use TPUMOVER, simply type

```
TPUMOVER file1 file2
```

where *file1* and *file2* are .TPL or .TPU files. The extension .TPU is assumed, so you must explicitly add .TPL for .TPL files.

TPUMOVER loads and displays two windows—with *file1* in the left window of the display and *file2* in the right window. Note that both *file1* and *file2* are optional. If you only specify *file1*, then the right window has the default name NONAME.TPU. If you don't specify either file, TPUMOVER will attempt to load TURBO.TPL (in the left window with nothing in the right window). If that file cannot be found, TPUMOVER will display a directory of all files on the current disk that end in .TPL.

## *TPUMOVER Commands*

The basic commands are listed at the bottom of the screen. Here's a brief description of each:

- *F1* brings up a help screen.
- *F2* saves the current file (the file associated with the active window) to disk.
- *F3* lets you select a new file for the active window.
- *F4* displays a pop-up window showing you all the unit dependencies for that unit. Only the first unit dependency is shown in the main window. If there are three dots following it, there are additional ones to be found by pressing *F4*.
- *F6* allows you to switch between the two windows, making the inactive window the active window (and vice versa).
- + (plus sign) marks a unit (for copying or deletion). You can have multiple units marked simultaneously; also, you can unmark a marked unit by pressing the + key again.

- *Ins* copies all marked units from the active window to the inactive window.

- *Del* deletes all marked units from the active window.

- *Esc* lets you exit from TPUMOVER. Note that this does not automatically save any changes that were made; you must explicitly use *F2* to save modifications before leaving TPUMOVER.

## Moving Units into TURBO.TPL

Let's suppose you've created a unit *Tools*, which you've compiled into a file named TOOLS.TPU. You like this unit so much you want to put it into TURBO.TPL. How do you do this? To start, type the command

```
A>tpumover turbo tools
```

This will bring up the TPUMOVER display with TURBO.TPL in the left window (the active one) and TOOLS.TPU in the right window. Note that this example assumes that TURBO.TPL and TOOLS.TPU are both in the current directory; if they are not, then you need to supply the appropriate path name for each.

Now perform the following steps:

1. Press *F6* to make the right window (TOOLS.TPU) active.
2. Press + to mark *IntLib* (the only unit in the right-hand window).
3. Press *Ins* to copy *IntLib* into TURBO.TPL.
4. Press *F6* to make the left window (TURBO.TPL) active.
5. Press *F2* to save the changes in TURBO.TPL to disk.
6. Press *Esc* to exit TPUMOVER.

The unit *Tools* is now part of TURBO.TPL and will be automatically loaded whenever you use Turbo Pascal.

If you want to add other units to TURBO.TPL, you can do so without exiting TPUMOVER. After pressing *F2* to save TURBO.TPL to disk, perform the following steps:

1. Press *F6* to make the right window active.
2. Press *F3* to select a new file for the right window.
3. Repeat the preceding steps two through five to mark the appropriate unit, copy it into TURBO.TPL, make the left window active, and save TURBO.TPL to disk.

You can repeat this as many times as desired in order to build up your library.

## *Deleting Units from TURBO.TPL*

Now let's remove those unused units from TURBO.TPL: *Turbo3* and *Graph3*. To do this, first type

```
tpumover turbo
```

This brings up TPUMOVER with TURBO.TPL in the left window and NONAME.TPU (the default name) in the right. The left window is the active one, so do the following:

■ Use the *Down arrow* key to move the highlighted bar over *Turbo3*.

■ Press + to select *Turbo3*.

■ Press *Del* to delete *Turbo3*.

■ Press *F2* to save the changes to TURBO.TPL.

■ Press *Esc* to exit TPUMOVER.

You can repeat this procedure to remove *Graph3*.

## *Moving Units Between .TPL Files*

Suppose a friend has written a number of units and has given you the file (MYSTUFF.TPL) containing them. You want to copy only the units *GameStuff* and *RandStuff* into TURBO.TPL. How do you do this? Your command line would read like this:

```
tpumover mystuff.tpl turbo.tpl
```

This brings up TPUMOVER with MYSTUFF.TPL in the left (active) window and TURBO.TPL in the right window. Now use the following commands:

■ Use the *Up arrow* and *Down arrow* keys to move the highlighted bar to *GameStuff*.

■ Press + to select *GameStuff*.

■ Use the *Up arrow* or the *Down arrow* key to move the highlighted bar to *RandStuff*.

■ Press + to select *RandStuff*.

■ Press *Ins* to copy *GameStuff* and *RandStuff* to TURBO.TPL.

■ Press *F6* to make the TURBO.TPL window active.

- Press *F2* to save the changes made to TURBO.TPL.
- Press *Esc* to exit TPUMOVER.

## Command-Line Shortcuts

You can use several command-line parameters that let you manipulate units quickly. The format for these parameters is

```
TPUMOVER TURBO /parameter unitname
```

where *parameter* is either +, –, or *.

These commands perform the following functions without displaying the side-by-side windows of the TPUMOVER program:

/+    Adds the named unit to TURBO.TPL

/-    Deletes the named unit from TURBO.TPL

/*    Extracts (copies) the named unit from TURBO.TPL and saves it in a file named *unitname*.TPU

/?    Displays a small help window

# 8

# Converting from Turbo Pascal 3.0

Turbo Pascal 4.0 contains some exciting new features. This chapter discusses the tools we've provided to help you convert your 3.0 programs to 4.0. Note that in some cases, changes in your source code may be necessary.

We've provided a few upgrading tools: UPGRADE.EXE and two compatibility units, *Turbo3* and *Graph3*.

UPGRADE reads in a version 3.0 source code file and makes a series of changes to convert it for compilation under version 4.0. Some of these changes include commenting out obsolete buffer sizes, inserting appropriate **uses** statements, and optionally splitting large applications into separate units.

*Turbo3* offers several predefined identifiers from version 3.0 that version 4.0 no longer supports. *Graph3* supports the full set of graphics calls (basic, extended, turtlegraphics) from version 3.0.

In this chapter, we've also provided a checklist of conversion tasks that you may need to perform in addition to using these utilities. If you have a lot of code, don't worry—conversion usually goes very quickly, and the high speed of the version 4.0 compiler helps that along. (Appendix A has more information on converting.)

## Using UPGRADE

The UPGRADE program will aid in converting Turbo Pascal programs written for earlier versions of the compiler. UPGRADE scans the source code of an existing program, and performs the following actions:

- Places warnings in the source where Turbo Pascal 4.0 differs in syntax or runtime behavior from earlier versions of the compiler.

- Automatically fixes some constructions that have new syntactic requirements.

- Optionally writes a journal file that contains detailed warnings and advice for upgrading a program to 4.0.

- Automatically inserts a **uses** statement to pull in needed routines from the standard units.

- Optionally divides large programs into multiple units, to remove overlays or take advantage of separate compilation.

In order to use UPGRADE, you must access two files from your Turbo Pascal distribution disk. Copy the files UPGRADE.EXE and UP-GRADE.DTA into your working drive and directory, or copy them into a subdirectory that is listed in the MS-DOS path.

UPGRADE is command-line driven; its format from the DOS prompt is

```
UPGRADE [options] filename
```

*filename* specifies the name of an existing Pascal source file, which should be present in the current drive and directory. If no extension is specified, UPGRADE assumes '.PAS' as the file's extension.

If UPGRADE is executed with no command-line parameters (that is, with no options and no file name), it will write a brief help message and then halt.

The specified file must contain a complete Pascal program, not just a fragment. If the file contains include directives, the specified include files must also be present, either in the current directory or in another directory specified by the include directive.

The specified file must be a syntactically correct program, as determined by Turbo Pascal 3.0 or 2.0. UPGRADE does not perform a complete syntax check of source code—syntax errors in its input will cause unpredictable results. If you are uncertain whether a program contains syntax errors, compile it first with an earlier version of Turbo Pascal before proceeding with UPGRADE.

By default, UPGRADE will write a new version of the source code, overwriting the old version but saving it under a new name. Each old version saved will have the same name as the original, but with the extension '.3TP' attached. In the event that the extension '.3TP' would cause UPGRADE to overwrite an existing file, UPGRADE will try using the extensions '.4TP', '.5TP', and so on, until it finds a safe extension.

UPGRADE, by default, inserts comments into the source program; an example follows:

```
TextMode;
{! 20. ^ TextMode requires a parameter (Mode:integer) in Turbo Pascal 4.0.}
```

In this example, *TextMode;* is a statement found in the program being upgraded. UPGRADE's comments always begin with *{!*, which makes it easy to find UPGRADE's warnings. UPGRADE numbers each comment with a sequential value, *20* in this example, which corresponds to the comments found in the optional journal file (described later). UPGRADE's comments contain a short statement describing the upgrade issue. UPGRADE inserts into the comment a caret (^) pointing to the exact location that triggered the warning in the preceding line of source code.

In a few cases, UPGRADE will make active changes to the source code; for example:

```
var
  f:text{[$1000]};
  {! 6. Us^e the new standard procedure SetTextBuf to set Text buffer size.}
```

This comment refers to the fact that Turbo Pascal 4.0 uses a new syntax to specify buffering of text files. Instead of the optional bracketed buffer size in the data declaration, Turbo Pascal 4.0 provides a new standard procedure *SetTextBuf*, which should be called to specify a buffer area and buffer size. Note that in this case UPGRADE automatically comments out the obsolete buffer size, and inserts a comment notifying you to call the *SetTextBuf* procedure at the appropriate location in your program.

UPGRADE accepts the following options on the command line:

| | |
|---|---|
| /3 | Use *Turbo3* compatibility unit when needed |
| /J | Write a detailed journal file |
| /N | No descriptive markup in source code |
| /O [*d:*][*path*] | Send output to *d:path* |
| /U | Unitize the program based on .*U* switches in source |

A description of each option follows.

## /3 Activate Turbo3 Unit

A special unit, *Turbo3*, is provided with the new compiler. This unit defines several variables and routines that cause new programs to mimic the behavior of Turbo Pascal 3.0 programs. The following identifiers defined within the *Turbo3* unit result in special handling by UPGRADE:

- *Kbd*
- *CBreak*
- *MemAvail*
- *MaxAvail*
- *LongFileSize*
- *LongFilePos*
- *LongSeek*

If your program uses any of these identifiers and you specify the /3 option, UPGRADE will insert the *Turbo3* unit name into the **uses** statement generated for the program.

Although the *Turbo3* unit and the /3 option can minimize the time required to convert an existing application, in the long run it may be better to make the (small) additional effort to use Turbo Pascal 4.0's new facilities. If you don't specify the /3 option, you will cause UPGRADE to generate warnings for each instance of the identifiers. With these warnings and the journal file (described next), you can achieve a complete upgrade in a short time.

## /J  Activate Journal File

When you specify the /J option, UPGRADE writes an additional file called the journal file. This file has the same name as your main program file but has the extension .JNL.

The journal file contains detailed descriptions of each warning UPGRADE produces, along with advice on how to go about upgrading your program. Here's an excerpt from a typical journal file:

```
4. MYPROG.PAS(6)
   s:byte absolute Cseg:$80;
                  ^
Cseg and Dseg can no longer be used in absolute statements.

Variables in Turbo Pascal 4.0 may be made absolute to other variables or typed
constants (for example, StrLen : byte absolute String1), or to a fixed location in
memory (for example, KeyBoardFlag : byte absolute $40:$17).

Given the action of Turbo Pascal 4.0's separate compilation and smart linker, it is
unlikely that variables absolute to Cseg or Dseg would have the intended effect.
(See Chapter 16 for more details.)
```

Each journal entry begins with a numeric identifier, corresponding to the numbered comment inserted by UPGRADE into the actual source code. The journal file number is followed by the name of the original source file and the line number (within the original source file) of the statement that caused the warning. Note that the line number reported may be different than the line number in a marked-up or unitized source file. UPGRADE also inserts the actual source line and a pointer to the problem to make identification complete.

## /N  No Source Markup

Use this option is you don't want UPGRADE's comments inserted into your source code. UPGRADE will still perform any automatic fixes: the **uses** statement, Turbo Pascal 3.0 default compiler directives, mapping of compiler directives to Turbo Pascal 4.0 standards, and deactivation of *Overlay*, *Ovrpath*, and text buffer sizes.

Generally, you should use the */N* option in combination with the */J* (journal file) or */U* (unitize) option.

## /O [d:][path]  Output Destination

Use this option to send UPGRADE's output to another drive or directory. When you activate this option, UPGRADE will not overwrite existing source files, nor will it rename them after processing. All UPGRADE output, including the journal file if activated, will go to the drive and directory specified.

## /U  Unitize

The */U* option activates a second major function of UPGRADE. In combination with directives you place into your existing source code, UPGRADE will automatically split a large application into separate units.

You should use the */U* option only if your program is large enough to require overlays in Turbo Pascal 3.0, or if compilation times are long enough to be bothersome.

Before using the */U* option, you must make minor additions to your existing source program. These additions take the form of special comments that serve as directives to the UPGRADE utility. Each directive must have the following form:

```
{.U unitname}
```

*unitname* is a name that meets the following requirements:

■ It is a legal Pascal identifier.

- It is a legal MS-DOS file name.
- It does not match the name of any existing global identifier in the program being upgraded.

It should begin with an alphabetic character and be limited to eight characters. Here are some examples of legal unit name directives:

```
{.U UNIT1}
(*.U ScrnUnit *)
{.u  heapstuf}
```

Wherever UPGRADE encounters a unit name directive in your program's source code, it will route source code following that directive to the unit named. UPGRADE performs all necessary steps to prepare the unit source code for compilation, including

- Inserting the **unit** and **uses** statements
- Interfacing all global routines and data declarations
- Implementing the source code
- Generating an empty initialization block

In order to make the unitized program fit the structure of Turbo Pascal 4.0's units, certain restrictions apply to the placement and use of unit name directives:

- Unit name directives can be placed only in the main file of a program, not within any include file. This restriction avoids the need to split existing Include files into parts. In any case, Include files generally contain related routines that should reside within the same unit.
- Each unit name can be specified at most once. This restriction avoids the generation of mutual dependencies between units, something that the Turbo Pascal 4.0 compiler does not allow.
- A unit name directive must be placed outside of the scope of any procedure or function, that is, it must be placed at the global level of the program. This restriction enforces Turbo Pascal 4.0's definition of units as global entities.
- UPGRADE predefines one unit name, *Initial*. UPGRADE will automatically route to *Initial* any declarations or routines that precede the first unit name directive you place into your source code. UPGRADE defines the *Initial* unit so that later units will have access to any global identifiers defined prior to the first unit name. If you specify a unit name directive prior to any global declarations, *Initial* will be empty, and UPGRADE will delete it automatically.
- Each Turbo Pascal 4.0 unit is limited to at most 64K of code. You must place unit name directives so that this restriction is met.

- UPGRADE cannot deal effectively with global forward declarations, placing a warning into the source code whenever it encounters one. You must determine how to treat forwards and manually modify the source code after UPGRADE is finished. The best strategy is to absolutely minimize the use of forwards in the original program.

The /U option automatically deletes all **overlay** keywords that may have appeared in the original source code.

After UPGRADE has unitized a program, the main unit will be in the simplest possible form. It will contain the **program** statement and a **uses** statement that lists required system units as well as units you defined via unit name directives, and the original main block of code. All other procedures, functions, and data declarations will have been routed to other units.

UPGRADE interfaces user identifiers to the maximum extent possible. This means that all global procedures and functions will appear in the interface section of a unit, and that all global types, variables, and constants will appear in the interface. After your program is converted to the unit structure of Turbo Pascal 4.0, you may wish to hide selected global identifiers within the implementation sections of their units.

Although the /U option of UPGRADE cannot deal with the more subtle issues of breaking a program into well-structured units, it does automate the otherwise time-consuming process of generating syntactically correct unit files.

## *What UPGRADE Can Detect*

Here is a full list of the short warnings that UPGRADE generates:

- Use the new standard procedure *SetTextBuf* to set the text buffer size.
- New stack conventions require that many inlines be rewritten.
- Assure that *Cseg* refers to the intended segment.
- *Cseg* and *Dseg* no longer can be used in **absolute** statements.
- Restructure Chain and Execute programs to use units or *Exec*.
- Convert BIN files to .OBJ files or convert them to typed constants.
- Use the new *ExitProc* facility to replace *ErrorPtr* references.
- Use new textfile device drivers to replace I/O *Ptr* references.
- Use units and/or the DOS *Exec* procedure to remove overlays.
- *OvrPath* is not needed when overlays are not used.

- The *Form* function (and BCD arithmetic) are not supported in Turbo Pascal 4.0.
- *BufLen* (for restricting *Readln*) is not supported in Turbo Pascal 4.0.
- The *TextMode* procedure requires a parameter (*Mode:integer*) in Turbo Pascal 4.0.
- **interrupt, unit, interface, implementation**, and **uses** are now reserved words.
- *System, Dos,* and *Crt* are standard unit names in Turbo Pascal 4.0.
- Special file names INP:, OUT:, ERR: are not supported in Turbo Pascal 4.0.
- Assign unsigned values of $8000 or larger only to word or longint types.
- Use *Turbo3* unit in order for *MemAvail* and *MaxAvail* to return paragraphs.
- Use *Turbo3* unit to perform *LongFile* operations.
- *Cbreak* has been renamed to *CheckBreak* in Turbo Pascal 4.0.
- *IOResult* now returns different values corresponding to DOS error codes.
- Use *Turbo3* unit for access to *Kbd*, or instead use *Crt* and *ReadKey*.
- The $I include file directive must now be followed by a space.
- Directives *A, B, C, D, F, G, P, U, W,* and *X* are obsolete or changed in meaning.
- Stack-checking directive *K* has been changed to *S* in Turbo Pascal 4.0.
- The effects of *HighVideo, LowVideo,* and *NormVideo* are different in Turbo Pascal 4.0.
- Special file name LST: is not supported now. Use *Printer Lst* file.
- Special file name KBD: is not supported now. Use *Turbo3 Kbd* file.
- Special file names CON:, TRM:, AUX:, USR: are not supported in Turbo Pascal 4.0.
- Special devices Con, Trm, Aux, Usr are not supported in Turbo Pascal 4.0.
- An identifier duplicating a program/unit name is not allowed in Turbo Pascal 4.0; instead use the *Registers* type from the Turbo Pascal 4.0 *Dos* unit.
- **forward**s will require manual modification after unitizing.
- Include directives cannot be located within an executable block.
- The *CrtInit* and *CrtExit* procedures are not supported in Turbo Pascal 4.0.
- **for** loop counter variables must be pure locals or globals in Turbo Pascal 4.0.
- All defined labels within the current routine must be used.

## What UPGRADE Cannot Detect

Here are descriptions of the various types of things that UPGRADE cannot detect in your source file:

■ Mixing of String and char types in a way not allowed by Turbo Pascal 4.0; for example:

```
Ch:=Copy(S,1,1)
```

■ Type mismatches due to Turbo Pascal 4.0's more stringent checking; for example:

```
var
  a : ^integer;
  b : ^integer;
begin
  a := b;                                    { Invalid assignment }
end.
```

■ Unexpected runtime behavior due to side-effects of short-circuited Boolean expressions; for example:

```
{$B-}
if HaltOnError and (IoResult <> 0) then
  Halt;
```

Turbo Pascal 3.0 would have always called the built-in *IOResult* function, and thus cleared it to zero when the Boolean expression was evaluated. With short-circuiting activated in Turbo Pascal 4.0, the *IOResult* function would not be called if *HaltOnError* were False, and thus *IOResult* would potentially be left holding an error code from the previous I/O operation.

Note that UPGRADE automatically inserts compiler directives that deactivate Boolean short-circuiting, thus avoiding problems such as that just described. Use caution before changing the Boolean evaluation directive.

## An UPGRADE Checklist

Here is a summary of the basic steps for using UPGRADE:

1. Copy the files UPGRADE.EXE and UPGRADE.DTA from the compiler distribution disk to your current directory or to a directory in the DOS path.

2. If necessary, go to the directory where the Pascal source files for the program you wish to upgrade are located.

3. Decide which UPGRADE options, if any, you wish to use.

4. If you decide to unitize the program, you must first edit the main source file to insert *{.U unitname}* directives, subject to the restrictions outlined previously.

5. From the DOS command line, enter the appropriate UPGRADE command, using the following syntax:

```
UPGRADE [options] filename
```

Examples of acceptable command lines follow:

```
upgrade MYPROG.PAS /J /3
UPGRADE bigprog /n /u /o c:\turbo4
```

6. UPGRADE will make two passes through the source code: one pass to detect areas of the program that may require modification, and a second pass to insert the appropriate **uses** statement, and optionally complete the process of unitization. At the end of the second pass, it will report the number of warnings that it generated.

7. When UPGRADE is finished, change to the directory where output was sent (if other than the current directory). If you specified the /J option, you may wish to browse through the journal file first to see the detailed explanations of UPGRADE's warnings. After doing so, use the Turbo Pascal editor to edit each source file that UPGRADE produced. Search for the string *{!*. Each match will display a warning produced by UPGRADE. In many cases, you will be able to change the source code immediately—when you do so, you may wish to delete UPGRADE's warning.

8. Once you have looked at all of UPGRADE's warnings and made changes to your source code as appropriate, you are ready to compile with Turbo Pascal 4.0.

# Using Turbo3 and Graph3

*Turbo3* and *Graph3* were designed to help you support programs written for version 3.0. These units contain constants, data types, variables, and procedures and functions that were supported in version 3.0 but have changed or no longer exist in version 4.0. If your programs rely on them heavily, you may want to continue to use them.

Both units are already in TURBO.TPL; if you plan on using one or both, place the statement

```
uses unitname;
```

at the start of your program, following your program header (if you have one). If you use more than one unit, then the unit names should be separated by commas, like this:

```
uses Crt,Turbo3,Graph3;
```

## *The Turbo3 Unit*

The *Turbo3* unit restores some low-level I/O and system items found in version 3.0 but not found in version 4.0. (Chapter 27 contains more details on all these items.) These include the following:

- *Kbd*: Version 4.0 doesn't have the predefined file variable *Kbd*; instead, it provides the function *ReadKey*. However, for those of you who don't want to change your program, you can use *Kbd* instead.

- *CBreak*: This was an undocumented Boolean variable in version 3.0. It is named *CheckBreak* in version 4.0 and is documented in Chapter 24. *Turbo3* declares *CBreak* to be at the same address so that you can use it instead.

- *MemAvail*: Version 4.0 has *MemAvail*, but it is a function of type longint and returns the memory available in bytes. The *Turbo3* version returns the amount available in paragraphs (groups of 16 bytes), as version 3.0 did. Note that if you use *Turbo3*, this will now be the default version of *MemAvail*; to access the version 4.0 *MemAvail*, you must refer to *System.MemAvail*.

- *MaxAvail*: returns the size of the largest chunk of available memory in paragraphs, while version 4.0 returns it in bytes. Again, if you use *Turbo3*, you'll need to refer to *System.MaxAvail* to get the one in version 4.0.

- *LongFileSize*: The *FileSize* function in version 4.0 is of type longint and can handle any file. *Turbo3* supports this function (of type real) for version 3.0 compatibility.

- *LongFilePos*: The *LongFilePos* function in version 4.0 is of type longint and can handle any file. *Turbo3* supports this function (of type real) for version 3.0 compatibility.

- *LongSeek*: The *LongSeek* function in version 4.0 is of type longint and can handle any file. *Turbo3* supports this function (of type real) for version 3.0 compatibility.

- *IOResult*: The 4.0 *IOResult* returns different error codes. *Turbo3*'s *IOResult* simply calls *System.IOResult*, and re-maps the 4.0 error codes in the same way Turbo Pascal 3.0 did (wherever possible).

- *NormVideo, LowVideo, and HighVideo*: By using the *Turbo3* unit, these three routines will set the foreground and background colors to the same as 3.0:

|  | Mono/B&W | Color |
|---|---|---|
| *LowVideo* | light gray | light gray |
| *NormVideo* | white | yellow |
| *HighVideo* | white | yellow |

- These same three routines are implemented differently in 4.0 (see Chapter 27).

## *The Graph3 Unit*

This unit provides the basic, advanced, and turtlegraphics support routines, which are too lengthy to list here. If you use *Graph3*, however, you have full access to all the constants, types, variables, procedures, and functions described in Chapter 19 of the *Turbo Pascal Owner's Handbook*, version 3.0.

Note that a powerful new library of device-independent graphics routines is contained in the *Graph* standard unit. Unless you have programs that make extensive use of 3.0 graphics, you should use the new *Graph* unit instead.

# Primary Conversion Tasks

Even with UPGRADE and *Turbo3* and *Graph3*, you may still need to make changes in your source code. This section will look at what those changes are, how you might go about making them, and how vital they are to your program. When tasks are listed, they'll be flagged as one of these three types:

- **HELPFUL:** These take advantage of some feature in version 4.0 that makes life easier; they are discretionary.

- **RECOMMENDED:** These really should be done, though you may be able to get by without doing so; ignore these at your own risk.

- **ESSENTIAL:** No two ways about it; these must be done or your program won't correctly compile and run under version 4.0.

# Predefined Identifiers

Version 4.0 doesn't support all the predefined identifiers (constants, types, variables, procedures, functions) that version 3.0 did. Some have been dropped; others have been superseded by new identifiers; still others have been moved into the units found in TURBO.TPL.

■ Use *Crt* as needed.

■ Use *Turbo3* and/or *Graph3* as needed. This is a great stop-gap measure, but ultimately you may want to completely convert to version 4.0 identifiers. (HELPFUL)

■ Take advantage of the new routines found in the standard units, such as *ReadKey* (returns a scan code). (HELPFUL)

■ Use the appropriate units for certain data types, variables, procedures, and functions that were "built-in" in version 3.0. For example, the procedures *Intr* and *MsDos* are no longer predeclared; instead, they are found in the *Dos* unit. Similarly, the *Lst* device (text file associated with the printer) is defined in the *Printer* unit. (ESSENTIAL)

# Data Types

Version 4.0 introduces a number of new data types and language functions involving data types. Many of these will help you to drop some of the "kludges" you've had to use in the past.

■ Use typecasting in place of the *Move()* routine to copy the contents of one variable into the space of another variable of an incompatible type. For example, use

```
RealVar := real(BuffPtr^);
```

instead of

```
Move(BufferPtr^,RealVar,SizeOf(RealVar));
```

With extended typecasting, you can handle most such transfers as long as the destination is the exact same size as the source. (HELPFUL)

■ Convert to new data types where appropriate and practical. These include longint and word (to replace integer); pointer as a generic pointer type; and string, with an assumed maximum length of 255 characters. (RECOMMENDED)

■ Be aware that hexadecimal (base 16) constants are considered to be of type word rather than type integer, so that the hex constant $FFFF represents 65535 instead of –1. You should consider converting any variables that are assigned hex constants to type word. (RE-COMMENDED)

- Likewise, be aware that version 4.0 now allows you to assign –32768 to a variable of type integer. Previously, the only way you could do that was by assigning it the hex constant $8000. However, that hex constant now represents the value 32768 (which is of type word), and assigning it to an integer variable will cause a compile-time error, convert the constant to –32768, convert the constant to $FFFF8000, or convert the variable to type word. (RECOMMENDED)

- Use string library routines (such as *Length* and *Copy*) instead of directly accessing the internal string structure (such as *Ord(SVar[0])* or absolute-addressed byte variables on top of strings). (RECOMMENDED)

- Be aware that version 4.0 has stricter type-checking on strings, characters, and arrays of characters. The assignment

```
CharVar := StringVar
```

is no longer acceptable, even if *StringVar* is declared as **string[1]**. The assignment

```
StringVar := ArrayVar
```

is still acceptable, but

```
ArrayVar := StringVar
```

is not. (ESSENTIAL)

- Version 4.0 enforces stricter type-checking on derived types, which means that variables must have identically named types or be declared together in order to be assignment compatible. For example, given

```
var
  A : ^integer;
  B : ^integer;
```

then *A* and *B* are not assignment-compatible (that is, the statement `A := B` will cause a compile-time error) because they are separately derived types. In order to be assignment compatible, they must be declared together:

```
var
  A,B : ^integer;
```

or they must be of the the same named data type:

```
type
  IntPtr = ^integer;
var
  A : IntPtr;
  B : IntPtr;
```

Either of these solutions will work just fine; the second one is more general and is preferred (allowing other variables, parameters, and functions to be of the same data type). (ESSENTIAL)

■ The BCD data type (and the *Form* routine) are not supported in this version. Consider using the longint data type; if you have a math coprocessor, then use the {$N+} directive and use the IEEE type comp (8-byte integer). (See the sample program on disk, BCD.PAS.) (ESSENTIAL)

## *Language Features*

Version 4.0 introduces some restrictions and some enhancements. The restrictions are geared to help it conform to the ANSI standard definition of Pascal, while the enhancements are there to make your life as a programmer easier.

■ Version 4.0 assumes *short-circuit Boolean evaluation*. This means that evaluation of Boolean expressions is halted as soon as possible. For example, consider the expression

```
if expr1 and expr2 ...
```

If *expr1* is False, then the entire expression will be False, regardless of the value of *expr2*. If Boolean expression evaluation is short-circuit, then if *expr1* is False, *expr2* won't be evaluated. This means, for example, if *expr2* contains a function call, then that function won't be called if *expr1* is False. You can enable complete (nonshort-circuit) Boolean evaluation with the {$B+} compiler directive or the environment option in the Options/Compiler menu. Be aware of the implications of enabling short-circuit evaluation. (HELPFUL)

■ Keeping in line with the ANSI standard, Turbo Pascal version 4.0 allows you to use only global and local variables as **for** loop control variables. For example, if the statement

```
for Indx := Start to Finish ...
```

appears in a procedure (or function), then *Indx* must be declared either globally or within that procedure. *Indx* cannot be a formal parameter of that procedure, nor can it be declared within an enclosing procedure. (ESSENTIAL)

## *Input and Output*

Turbo Pascal version 4.0 has made some significant changes in I/O handling, many of which are intended to increase ANSI compatibility.

- *Read(IntVar)* now waits for an integer value to be entered; pressing *Enter* will no longer cause the program to continue, leaving *IntVar* unchanged. Revise your program appropriately. (RECOMMENDED)

- If you are reading and writing real values with data files, be aware of the differences between the standard type real (6 bytes, compatible with version 3.0) and the IEEE floating-point types supported by the {$N+} directive (single, double, extended and comp). Use the latter types only if you are sure that your program and any resulting data files will be used exclusively on systems equipped with a math coprocessor. (RECOMMENDED)

- In version 3.0, you could call the procedure *Close* on a file that was already closed with no results. In version 4.0, it produces an I/O error, which you can trap by using {$I-} and testing the value returned by *IOResult*.

- You can no longer directly declare variable-length buffers for text files in the format **var** *F : text[length]*; instead, you must use the predefined procedure *SetTextBuf* (see Chapter 27).

## *Program and Memory Organization*

One significant change in version 4.0 is the introduction of *units*. (If you aren't clear what units are, go back and read Chapter 4.) Units give you four important capabilities:

- They allow you to create tools that you can use in many different programs.

- They allow you to break up a large program into manageable chunks by collecting related declarations and subprograms (procedures and functions) together.

- They allow you to "hide" declarations and subprograms that you don't need (or want) to be "visible" to the rest of the program.

- They allow you to break the 64K code barrier, since each unit can contain up to 64K of code.

As a consequence, significant changes have been made in memory organization as well. Chapter 26 explains more of the details; here are some of the tasks you need to consider.

- Convert your libraries from include files to units. This is by no means necessary, but it has several advantages. For one, you don't have to recompile the routines in the unit each time; for another, you can distribute your library routines without distributing source code. The UPGRADE program can help you with this conversion. (HELPFUL)

- Version 4.0 has a new compiler directive, {$M}, that allows you to set the stack and heap sizes within your program. The format is as follows:

```
{$M stacksize,heapmin,heapmax}
```

where all three values are in bytes. The default values are {$M 16384,0,655360}. You can also set the default values in the integrated environment (O/C/Memory sizes) and use the command-line compiler (/$M). (HELPFUL)

- Convert large programs from overlays to units. You must do this, because version 4.0 does not support overlays. If you have been using overlays to get around the 64K code limit, then you won't have to worry anymore: The main program and each unit can be up to 64K in size. If you've been using overlays because all your code wouldn't fit into memory at once anyway, then you'll have to do some rewriting—the main program and all units must fit into memory at the same time. (ESSENTIAL)

- Be aware that *MemAvail* and *MaxAvail* are now of type longint and return their values in bytes instead of paragraphs. You should make the appropriate changes to your program (or use *Turbo3*, which supplies the original versions of *MemAvail* and *MaxAvail*). (ESSENTIAL)

## Compiler Directives and Error-Checking

Version 4.0's compiler directives and error codes have been extensively redefined. UPGRADE helps to modify the compiler directives, but you have to be sure you've caught all of them, and that you've also changed over to the new error codes.

- If an existing program doesn't work correctly, try setting Boolean evaluation to "complete" with the {$B+} directive; the default is {$B-}. (HELPFUL)

- Range-checking is now off by default; if you want it on, place the {$R+} directive at the start of your program. If you're unsure, leave it off for now. If your program is halting with range-checking errors, turn it on and figure out the problems or turn it off. (RECOMMENDED)

- Review *all* use of error codes (for example, I/O error codes), especially when the check is more than simply zero or nonzero. Define all error codes as constants in a global location so you can deal more easily with future changes. (RECOMMENDED)

- Review *all* compiler directives. Of special note are {$B}, {$D}, and {$F}, since they are still valid but now have different meanings. Appendix C details all the directives. (ESSENTIAL)

- *ErrorPtr* is gone; you should now use *ExitProc*. User-written error handlers must be modified; refer to Chapter 26 for more details. (ESSENTIAL)

- The {$I} include file directive is no longer allowed between a **begin**/**end** pair. In addition, an include file directive must always have a space between the *I* and the file name.

## Assembly Language Usage

We still support inline in assembly language; it now includes the inline directive for procedure and function definitions, which defines an inline macro rather than a separate, callable routine.

- For short assembly language code, consider using the inline directive (which differs from the **inline** statement). This generates actual inline macros in the resulting object code. (See Chapter 26 for more details.) (HELPFUL)

- Convert from inline to external subroutines where appropriate and practical; use inline only when necessary. (RECOMMENDED)

- The **inline** statement (within a subroutine) no longer allows references to the location counter (*), nor does it allow references to procedure and function identifiers. In order to refer to a procedure identifier, for example, declare a local pointer variable, assign it the address of the procedure (a procedure name), and refer to the pointer in the **inline** statement.(ESSENTIAL)

- External subroutines must be reassembled and incorporated in .OBJ format. (ESSENTIAL)

- Typed constants now reside in the data segment (DS) and so must be accessed differently by any external subroutines. (ESSENTIAL)

- **Inline/external** procedures and functions that used byte value parameters in version 3.0 often took advantage of the fact that the high byte of the word pushed on the stack was initialized to 0. This initialization is not done in version 4.0, so you'll need to make sure inline/external routines don't assume that the high byte is 0.

There are many changes to the conventions for passing parameters and function results on the stack; see Chapter 26 for more details.

This list is not exhaustive. Many of your programs will run with little or no modification; others will work fine with the processing UPGRADE performs. Likewise, this list doesn't cover all possible compatibility issues, since many Turbo Pascal programs take advantage of undocumented or unsupported features of version 3.0. Be sure to check the README file on your Turbo Pascal verion 4.0 distribution disk for any additional conversion notes.

C H A P T E R

# 9

# Debugging Your Turbo Pascal Programs

The term *debugging* comes from the early days of computers, when actual bugs (moths and the like) sometimes clogged up the machinery. Nowadays, it means correcting errors in a program.

You'll undoubtedly have bugs to contend with—errors of syntax, semantics, and logic within your program—and you'll have to fix them by trial and error. However, there are tools and methods to make it less of a trial and to cut down on the errors. In this chapter, we'll look at common errors and the different ways to debug them.

## Compile-Time Errors

A compile-time, or syntax, error occurs when you forget to declare a variable, you pass the wrong number of parameters to a procedure, or you assign a real value to an integer variable. What it really means is that you're writing Pascal statements that don't follow the rules of Pascal.

Pascal has strict rules, especially compared to other languages, so once you've cleaned up your syntax errors, much of your debugging will be done.

Turbo Pascal won't compile your program (generate machine code) until all your syntax errors are gone. If Turbo Pascal finds a syntax error while compiling your program, it stops compiling, goes into your program, locates the error, positions the cursor there, and prints what the error message was in the Edit window. Once you've corrected it, you can start compiling again.

# Runtime Errors

Another type of error that can occur is a runtime (or semantic) error. This happens when you compile a legal program but then try to do something illegal while executing it, such as open a nonexistent file for input or divide an integer by 0. In that case, Turbo Pascal prints an error message to the screen that looks like this:

```
Runtime error ## at seg:ofs
```

and halts your program. If you ran your program from the MS-DOS prompt, you'll be returned to MS-DOS. If you ran it under Turbo Pascal, you'll get the usual `Press any key...` message.

If you're running under the integrated environment, then Turbo Pascal automatically finds the location of the runtime error, pulling in the appropriate source file. You'll also notice that the output from your program appears in the Output window at the bottom of the screen.

If you're running under the command-line environment (TPC), you can find the error using the */F* option. (See Chapter 12 for a complete explanation and tour of finding runtime errors by using TPC.EXE when running an .EXE program.)

## *Input/Output Error-Checking*

Let's look again at a program given in an previous chapter:

```
program DoSum;
var
  A,B,Sum  : integer;

begin
  Write('Enter two numbers:  ');
  Readln(A,B);
  Sum := A + B;
  Writeln('The sum is ',Sum)
end.
```

Suppose you ran this program and entered the following values:

```
Enter two numbers: 45  8x
```

then pressed *Enter*. What would happen? You'd get a runtime error (106, in fact) like we described in the previous section. And if you used the Find error command, you'd discover that it occurred at the statement

```
Readln(A,B);
```

What happened? You entered non-numeric data—*8x*—when the program was expecting an integer value, which generated the appropriate runtime error.

In a short program like this, such an error isn't a big bother. But what if you were entering a long list of numbers and had gotten through most of it before making this mistake? You'd be forced to start all over again. Worse yet, what if you wrote the program for someone else to use, and *they* slipped up?

Turbo Pascal allows you to disable automatic I/O error-checking and test for it yourself within the program. To turn off I/O error-checking at some point in your program, include the compiler directive {$*I*-} in your program (or the **O/C/I/O** error-checking option). This instructs the compiler not to produce code that checks for I/O errors.

Let's revise the preceding program so that it does its own I/O checking:

```
program DoSum;
var
  A,B,Sum  : integer;
  IOCode   : integer;

begin
  repeat
    Write('Enter two numbers:  ');
    {$I-}                                    { Disable automatic I/O error-checking }
    Readln(A,B);
    {$I+}                                    { Enable automatic I/O error-checking }
    IOCode := IOResult;
    if IOCode <> 0 then
      Writeln('Bad data:  please enter again')
  until IOCode = 0;
  Sum := A + B;
  Writeln('The sum is ',Sum)
end.
```

First, you disable automatic I/O error-checking with the {$*I*-} compiler directive. Then you put the input code into a **repeat..until** loop, because you're going to repeat the input until the user gets it right. The *Write* and *Readln* statements are the same, but after them comes the statement

```
    IOCode := IOResult;
```

You've declared *IOCode* as a global variable, but what's *IOResult*? It's a predefined function that returns the error code from the last I/O operation, in this case, *Readln*. If no error occurred, then the value returned is 0; otherwise, a nonzero value is returned, indicating what happened. Once you've called *IOResult*, it "clears" itself and will return 0 until another I/O error occurs. This is why you assign *IOResult* to *IOCode*—so that you can test the result in both the **if** statement and the **until** clause.

A similar structure can be used for error-checking while opening files for input. Look at the following code sample:

```
var
  FileName  : string[40];
  F         : text;

begin
  Write('Enter file name: ');
  Readln(FileName);
  Assign(F,Filename);
  Reset(F);
  ...
```

This code fragment asks you to enter a file name, then tries to open that file for input. If the file you name doesn't exist, the program will halt with a runtime error (02). However, you can rewrite the code like this:

```
var
  FileName  : string[40];
  F         : text;
  IOCode    : integer;

begin
  {$I-}
  repeat
    Write('Enter file name: ');
    Readln(FileName);
    Assign(F,Filename);
    Reset(F);
    IOCode := IOResult;
    if IOCode <> 0 then
      Writeln('File', FileName, 'does not exist, try again')
  until IOCode = 0;
  {$I+}
  ...
```

Using these and similar techniques, you can create a crash-proof program that lets you make mistakes without halting your program.

## Range-Checking

Another common class of semantic errors involves out-of-range or out-of-bounds values. Some examples of how these can occcur include assigning too large a value to an integer variable or trying to index an array beyond its bounds. If you want it to, Turbo Pascal will generate code to check for range errors. It makes your program larger and slower, but it can be invaluable in tracking down any range errors in your program.

Suppose you had the following program:

```
program RangeTest;
var
  List : array[1..10] of integer;
  Indx : integer;

begin
  for Indx := 1 to 10 do
    List[Indx] := Indx;
  Indx := 0;
  while (Indx < 11) do
  begin
    Indx := Indx + 1;
    if List[Indx] > 0 then
      List[Indx] := -List[Indx]
  end;
  for Indx := 1 to 10 do
    Writeln(List[Indx])
end.
```

If you type in this program, it will compile and run. And run. And run. It will, in fact, get stuck in an infinite loop. Look carefully at this code: The **while** loop executes 11 times, not 10, and the variable *Indx* has a value of 11 the last time through the loop. Since the array *List* only has 10 elements in it, *List[11]* points to some memory location outside of *List*. Because of the way variables are allocated, *List[11]* happens to occupy the same space in memory as the variable *Indx*. This means that when *Indx* = 11, the statement

```
List[Indx] := -List[Indx]
```

is equivalent to

```
Indx := -Indx
```

Since *Indx* equals 11, this statement sets *Indx* to –11, which starts the program through the loop again. That loop now changes additional bytes elsewhere, at the locations corresponding to *List[-11..0]*.

In other words, this program can really mess itself up. And because *Indx* never ends the loop at a value greater than or equal to 11, the loop never ends. Period.

How do you check for things like this? You can insert {$R+} at the start of the program to turn range-checking on. Now when you run it, the program will halt with runtime error 201 (out of range error, because the array index is out of bounds) as soon as you hit the statement *if List[Indx] > 0* with *Indx* = 11. If you were running under the integrated environment, it will automatically take you to that statement and display the error. (Range-checking is off by default; turning range-checking on makes your program larger and slower.)

There are some situations—usually in advanced programming—in which you might want or need to violate range bounds, most notably when working with dynamically allocated arrays, or when using *Succ* and *Pred* with enumerated data types.

You can selectively implement range-checking by placing the {$R-} directive at the start of your program. For each section of code that needs range checking, place the {$R+} directive at the start of it, then place the {$R-} directive at the end of the code. For example, you could write the preceding loop like this:

```
while Indx < 11 do
begin
  Indx := Indx + 1;
  {$R+}                                   { Enable range-checking }
  if List[Indx] > 0 then
    List[Indx] := -List[Indx]
  {$R-}                                   { Disable range-checking }
end;
```

Range-checking will be performed only in the **if..then** statement and nowhere else. Unless, of course, you have other {$R+} directives elsewhere.

# Tracing Errors

A tried-and-true debugging practice is to insert trace statements within your program. A *trace statement* is usually a statement that writes variable values to the screen, telling you where you are and listing some current values. Often a trace is set up to execute only if a global Boolean variable has been set to True (so that you can turn tracing on or off).

Suppose you have a large program in which some variables are set to incorrect (but not necessarily illegal) values. The program consists of several procedures, but you haven't figured out which one is causing the problem. You might do something like this for each procedure:

```
procedure ThisOne({any parameters});
{ any declarations }
begin
  if Trace then
    Writeln('entering ThisOne: A = ',A,' B = ',B);
  { rest of procedure ThisOne }
  if Trace then
    Writeln('exiting ThisOne:   A = ',A,' B = ',B)
end;  { of proc ThisOne }
```

This code assumes that *Trace* is a global variable of type boolean, and that you set it to True or False at the start of the program. It also assumes that *A* and *B* are parameters to *ThisOne* or global variables of some sort.

If *Trace* is True, then each time *ThisOne* is called, it writes out the values of *A* and *B* after it is called and again just before it returns to where it was called from. By putting similar statements in other procedures, you can trace the values of *A* and *B* and find out where and when they change to undesired values.

Once the wrong values of *A* and *B* come out in a trace statement, you know that the changes occurred somewhere before that statement but after the previously executed one. You can then start moving those two trace statements closer together, or you can insert additional trace statements between the two. By doing this, you can eventually pinpoint where the error is and take appropriate steps.

As another example of tracing, you could have modified the program listed in the previous section to look like this:

```pascal
program RangeTest;
var
  List : array[1..10] of integer;
  Indx : integer;

begin
  for Indx := 1 to 10 do
    List[Indx] := Indx;
  Indx := 0;
  while (Indx < 11) do
  begin
    Indx := Indx + 1;
    Writeln('Indx = ',Indx:2);               { <-- TRACING STATEMENT }
    if List[Indx] > 0 then
      List[Indx] := -List[Indx]
  end;
  for Indx := 1 to 10 do
    Writeln(List[Indx])
end.
```

The addition of the `Writeln('Indx = ',Indx:2)` statement in the loop does two things. First, it shows you that *Indx* is acting crazy: It gets up to 11 and then suddenly jumps back down to –10 (yes, *Indx* was –11, but it had 1 added to it before the *Writeln* statement). Second, Turbo Pascal will (by default) allow you to interrupt an infinite loop with a *Ctrl-C* or *Ctrl-Break* if you are doing input or output.

# Using .TPM and .MAP Files

When you compile a Turbo Pascal program, the resulting .EXE file has information in it about line numbers, procedure names, variable names, and so on. This is because the {$D+} directive is on by default. If you enable the option to generate a .TPM file (using the **O/C/Turbo** pascal map file toggle or the /$T+ command-line option), you can have the compiler generate a .TPM (**T**urbo **P**ascal **M**ap) file for your program if you're compiling it to disk. This is a specially encoded file that contains information about the addresses within the .EXE file of procedures and functions, and about the data segment offsets of global variables.

Note, however, that in order to get information about the entire .EXE file, you must compile all the units used by your program with the {$D+} directive enabled. The easiest way to do that is to turn it on (via a menu option or a command-line switch), then do a **B**uild, which forces all units to be recompiled.

To get this into human- and program-readable form, you must run the program TPMAP.EXE (included on your Turbo Pascal distribution disk). The result is a .MAP file that shows the memory layout (or map) of your program.

Suppose you had the following program, saved as MAPTEST.PAS:

```
{$T+}                                         { Generate .TPM file }
{$D+}                                   { Put line numbers in .TPM }

program MapTest;
var
  A, B, C : integer;
procedure Test;
begin
  Writeln('Enter two values: ');
  Readln(A, B);
  C := A div B;
  Writeln('The answer is ', C);
end;
begin
  Test;
end.
```

When you compile this program to disk, it produces the file TEST.TPM. You can then generate a .MAP file with the following command:

```
tpmap Maptest
```

Note that you need not put *test.tpm* after *tpmap*. This is because TPMAP always assumes the .TPM extension.

The result of this command is an ASCII file named MAPTEST.MAP. If you then look at it (using the Turbo editor), you'll see something like this:

```
Start  Stop   Length Name               Class

00000H 000B2H 000B3H MAPTEST            CODE
000C0H 00995H 008D6H SYSTEM             CODE
009A0H 00BEEH 0024FH DATA               DATA
00BF0H 04BEFH 04000H STACK              STACK
04BF0H 04BF0H 00000H HEAP               HEAP

Address            Publics by Value

0000:0022          TEST
0000:00A0          @
000C:0000          @
009A:0000          A
009A:0002          B
009A:0004          C
009A:0006          INPUT
009A:0106          OUTPUT
009A:0206          PREFIXSEG
009A:0208          HEAPORG
009A:020C          HEAPPTR
009A:0210          FREEPTR
009A:0214          FREEMIN
009A:0216          HEAPERROR
009A:021A          EXITPROC
009A:021E          EXITCODE
009A:0220          ERRORADDR
009A:0224          RANDSEED
009A:0228          SAVEINT00
009A:022C          SAVEINT02
009A:0230          SAVEINT23
009A:0234          SAVEINT24
009A:0238          SAVEINT75
009A:023C          FILEMODE

Line numbers for MAPTEST(MAPTEST.PAS) segment MAPTEST

    9 0000:0022    10 0000:002C   11 0000:0048   12 0000:0067
   13 0000:0072    14 0000:009C   16 0000:00A0   17 0000:00A7
   18 0000:00AA

Program entry point at 0000:00A0
```

The first section of the .MAP file shows the memory map for the entire .EXE file, with all addresses and values shown in hexadecimal (base 16). First comes the code for the program MapTest itself, 179 bytes long. This is followed by whatever routines have been linked in from the unit *System* (2262 bytes). Next comes the data segment, which takes up 591 bytes. That is followed by the stack, which is 16K in size. After that comes the heap, which occupies (in theory) all the rest of memory.

The second part of the .MAP file lists all the public (global) symbols: procedures, functions, and variables. All values are given in hexadecimal. The first three records refer to code entry points, the remaining references are addresses for variables.

The first code record describes procedure *Test*, which resides at offset 34 in MapTest's code segment. Next, the two @ symbols represent the beginning of the initialization code for each program module in this program (in this case, program MapTest and the *System* unit). The first @ record points to the main program of MapTest, the second points to the beginning of the *System* unit's code segment.

There are three publics variables in MapTest: *A*, *B*, and *C*. The rest of the publics are variables in the *System* unit. All the variables reside in the DATA segment, which begins 2464 bytes from the start of the code.

The third section correlates line numbers in the source code with the machine code in the .EXE file. There is one line number record for each line of code in each program file. (In this simple example, MAPTEST.PAS is the only source code module.) Each record consists of the line number of a source code statement, and the segment and offset of the corresponding machine code.

The last line in the .MAP file tells you that program execution starts at address 0000:00A0, or 160 bytes from the start of the code segment.

In addition to converting a .TPM file to a .MAP file, the TPMAP program now also produces a text file that contains a complete list of all dependencies (units, Include and .OBJ files) in the Turbo Pascal program.

For example, given a file named TEST.PAS:

```
program Test;
uses Crt;
begin
  ClrScr;
  Write('Turbo Pascal');
end.
```

then the commands

```
tpc test /$t+
tpmap test
```

will (1) compile TEST.EXE and produce a TEST.TPM file and (2) convert TEST.TPM to TEST.MAP and produce TEST.DEP.

Here's a dump of TEST.DEP:

```
program TEST in TEST.PAS;
```

```
uses
  Crt;

unit Crt in CRT.PAS;
Links
  CRT.OBJ;
```

As you can see, the listing contains the module names (TEST, Crt), the corresponding file names (TEST.PAS and CRT.PAS), and a list of .OBJ files linked in using the {$L} compiler directive (CRT.OBJ). TPMAP will produce a .MAP file only if you use the /M command-line option. Similarly, the /D option will only produce a .DEP file.

# Using a Debugger

Sometimes none of the traditional Pascal language-based approaches work. The nature of the problem is such that either you can't track down where the errors are or, having located them, you can't figure out why they're occurring or what's causing them. Then it's time to call in the heavy artillery: a debugger.

A *debugger* is a program designed to allow you to trace the execution of your program step by step, one instruction at a time. There are many varieties of debuggers, but most require some familiarity with assembly language (machine code) instructions and with the architecture (registers, memory map, and so on) of your computer's microprocessor.

One such debugger, Periscope, is described in the next section. (Periscope is published by The Periscope Company, Inc., of Atlanta, Georgia.)

## *Preparing to Use Periscope*

Periscope is especially well suited for debugging programs written in Turbo Pascal and is also a symbolic debugger. Periscope allows you to view your source code while debugging, and to limit the amount of machine code that is displayed. Full instructions on how to use Periscope can be found in its accompanying manual. This section simply describes how to prepare your Turbo Pascal programs for use with Periscope, as well as a few of the debugger's basic instructions.

In order to use Periscope, you must first generate a .MAP file by doing the following:

- Turn on both the {$D+} and {$T+} compiler directives via the **O**ptions menu, a command-line switch, or by inserting the directives at the start of your program.
- Compile your program to disk, which will create .EXE and .TPM files.
- Run the TPMAP utility (as described previously) to create a .MAP file.

For example, if your program were named TEST.PAS, you would now have three other files: TEST.EXE, TEST.TPM, and TEST.MAP.

You are now ready to debug your program with Periscope.

## *Starting Periscope*

Periscope is a memory-resident program, much like SideKick and SuperKey. If you have these or other memory-resident programs installed in your system, you will need to exercise some caution when loading the debugger. Consult the Periscope manual for more details on how to configure the debugger for your computer, as well as how to load it safely when other memory-resident programs are present. In the simplest case, however, you can load Periscope simply by entering

```
ps
```

at the DOS prompt.

Once Periscope is loaded into memory, you can debug a program such as TEST.PAS by typing

```
run test.exe
```

As explained in the Periscope manual, RUN.COM is a "program loader." It loads a program into memory, finds and loads the contents of the corresponding .MAP file, and ultimately passes control to the debugger itself. Once control has been passed, you'll see something like this on your screen:

```
AX=0000  BX=0000  CX=08C0  DX=0000  SP=2000  BP=0000  SI=0000 DI=0000
DS=46AA  ES=46AA  SS=476A  CS=46BA  IP=0031  FL=0246 NV UP EI PL ZR NA PE NC
WR SS:1FFC = 46BA CFF0
              @:
46BA:0031 9A0000C846     CALL   @
>
```

The first two rows show you the contents of the CPU registers. The third row shows you the contents of the region of memory that will be altered (WRitten to) when the CALL instruction is executed. The fourth and fifth rows show you (1) that you have reached an address that corresponds to an unnamed entry in the symbol table, and (2) that the call is being made to another such address. The last line shows Periscope's command prompt, a greater than (>) sign.

Although this display will make long-time users of DOS DEBUG feel right at home, you will probably prefer using Periscope's "windowed" display instead. To switch to a windowed display, press *Ctrl-F10* (if you have a color monitor) or *Ctrl-F9* (if you have a monochrome monitor). Now you can see much more information at a glance:

```
46AA:0100  11 45 6E 74 65 72 20 74-77 6F 20 76 61 6C 75 65   .Enter two val>|0000
46AA:0110  73 3A 00 80 FF FF FF 7F-00 @@.0E 74 68 65 20 61   s:........the|0000
46AA:0120  6E 73 77 65 72 20 69 73-20 00 00 00 80 FF FF FF   answer is ....|0000
46AA:0130  7F 9A 00 00 C8 46 89 E5-BF 06 01 1E 57 BF 00 00   ....HF.e?...W?|0000
DO^ ─────────────────────────────────────────────────────────────────── |0000
AX=0000  BX=052E  CX=0552  DX=80D3  SP=2000  BP=2000  SI=00BA DI=0106      |0000
DS=4746  ES=4746  SS=476A  CS=46BA  IP=0038  FL=0246 NV UP EI PL ZR NA PE N|0000
R^__WR   SS:1FFC = 46BA CFF0 ──────────────────────────────────────────── |0000
              @:                                                           |0000
46BA:0031 9A0000C846     CALL    @                                        |0000
46BA:0036 89E5           MOV     BP,SP                                    |0000
A6:       Write('Enter two values:');                                    |0000
46BA:0038 BF0601         MOV     DI,0106              ; OUTPUT            |0000
46BA:003B 1E             PUSH    DS                                       |0000
46BA:003C 57             PUSH    DI                                       |0000
46BA:003D BF0000         MOV     DI,0000              ; A                 |0000
U^___ In C:\PERI\RUN.COM─────────────────────────────────────────────────|0000
```

>

The screen is now divided into five distinct sections, or windows. At the top of the screen is the Display window, used for examining memory; below it is the Registers window. To the right is the Stack window, which shows you the contents of the stack and, using the arrow now seen at the top, the location pointed to by the BP (Base Page) register. At the bottom of the screen is the Command window, where commands are entered and in many cases command output is displayed. In the middle of the screen is the Unassemble window. Here you can see a mixture of source code and machine code, and the instruction that is about to be executed is always highlighted by a reverse video bar.

Like most things in Periscope, the size and color of these windows can be changed at your discretion (consult the manual for details). Once you have the display configured to your liking, you can begin to experiment with some of the basic debugging commands. In the sections that follow, it is assumed that you will be using a windowed display while debugging and that you are using version 3.0 or greater of Periscope.

# Basic Periscope Commands

From Periscope's command prompt, you can get a complete list of the available commands by typing a question mark (?) followed by *Enter*. The following, however, are the ones you'll most likely need when you get started.

## The Trace (T) Command

The Trace command executes a specified number of machine language instructions, then stops. It allows you to single-step through your code slowly and carefully, and to monitor the results as you go.

This command takes the format

```
>t [<number>]
```

If no number is specified, a single instruction is executed.

**Useful tip:** There's no need to repeatedly press *T* and *Enter* while single-stepping. Once you have entered a command, you can repeat it simply by pressing the *F4* key.

## The Jump (J and JL) Commands

The Jump (J) command is somewhat like the Trace command, but it allows you to execute the next instruction in its entirety. For example, if the next instruction is a CALL to a procedure, entering *J* tells the debugger to execute the CALLed procedure, then stop at the instruction following the CALL. Jump can also be used to avoid stepping through interrupt (INT) calls, as well as instructions that tell the CPU to repeat a certain task, such as LOOP or REPZ MOVSB.

The Jump Line (JL) command can be used to jump from the current instruction to the next one that corresponds to a Turbo Pascal source-code line. It thus allows you to move rapidly through programs written in a high level language such as Pascal.

## The Go (G) Command

When you want to move even more rapidly to a particular point in your program, use the Go command. If you type *G* and press *Enter*, Periscope will execute your program until one of two things happens: the program ends or a breakpoint is encountered. Actually, there is a third event that could stop the execution of the program: You could press either the breakout switch (if you have one) or a special hotkey (if you have the auxiliary program PSKEY installed). PSKEY and Periscope's optional breakout switch, both very useful debugging aids, are beyond the scope of this chapter, so you'll need to consult the Periscope manual for more on their use.

The Go command has the following format:

```
>g [<address>] [...]
```

The *address* parameter(s) are optional, and you can specify as many as four of them at a time. If you do specify a parameter, Periscope will set a temporary breakpoint at the specified address, causing the execution of the program to stop if the instruction pointer (IP) ever points to that address. You can specify an address either as an offset within the current code segment or as a 32-bit pointer in *segment:offset* format. You can also specify an address by using a symbolic identifier. For example, the following command would set three temporary breakpoints:

```
>g 003D 46C8:0000 MyProc
```

Another way to specify an address is to refer to a line of source code. For example,

```
>g .A6
```

would set a temporary breakpoint at the address corresponding to line 6 of source file *A* (the first one listed in the MAP file, the second file is designated as *B*, and so on). Note that the period (.) in .A6 is optional, but by using it, you can clearly distinguish between line A6 and the hexadecimal offset A6 (00A6).

The Go command is useful both for skipping over sections of code that have been thoroughly debugged and for getting quickly to a particular procedure or line of source code.

## The Unassemble (U, US, UB) Commands

When using Periscope's windowed display, you can frequently locate a section of code that interests you by using the *PgUp* and *PgDn* keys to scroll through the Unassemble window. In some cases, however, it is faster and easier to use the Unassemble command to instruct Periscope to display the code at a particular address. For example, if the next instruction is a CALL to a procedure (call it *TheirProc*) in another unit, and you don't know whether you should bother to single-step through it, you could glance at it briefly by entering

```
>u TheirProc
```

The optional parameter to an Unassemble command can be a symbol, an offset, or an address in *segment:offset* format.

Two related commands are of particular interest to Turbo Pascal programmers. The Unassemble Source (US) command tells the debugger to display only source code in the Unassemble window whenever possible. The Unassemble Both (UB) command restores the display to its default state, in which case both source code and machine code are displayed.

### The Display (D, Dx) Commands

Periscope also has a host of Display commands that you can use to change both the contents and the format of the Display window. The most useful ones for Turbo Pascal programmers are Display Ascii (DA), Display Bytes (DB), Display Double words (DD, for pointers and long integers), Display unsigned Integer (DI), Display Number (DN, for signed integers), and Display Word (DW). Like the Unassemble commands, these have the format

```
>d [<address>]
```

where *address* can be specified either numerically or symbolically. The Display (D) command is generally used to change the contents of the Display window, where the Dx commands are used to change the format in which memory is displayed.

### The View (V) Command

The View command allows you to examine your source files while inside the debugger. The format for the View command is

```
>v filename.ext
```

When you give the View command, the specified file is displayed in the command window, and you can scroll through it using the cursor keys. This command is particularly useful when you want to glance at type or variable declarations, or at the interface section of a unit without disturbing the contents of the Unassemble window.

### The Enter (E) Command

The Enter command lets you make changes to memory while debugging. You might use it, for example, if you had determined that a particular routine would behave correctly if a pointer variable was set to **nil**, if a string variable was empty, or if a loop counter started at 1 rather than 0.

Using Enter, you could change the contents of the variable to test your theory.

The format of the Enter command looks like this:

```
>e  <address> [<list>]
```

where *address* points to the region of memory to be changed. The optional *list* parameter is used to specify the changes to be made. If you omit it, you can make changes in the interactive mode, a byte at a time.

## The Registers (R) Command

If the wrong value has already been loaded into a register, you can still change it using the Registers command. For example, if a variable that now equals 0, but should equal 1, has just been loaded into the AX register, you can enter

```
>r ax 1
```

to set the AX register to 1. You can also use the Registers command (carefully) to prevent certain instructions from being executed. For example, a near CALL that is about to be executed can be avoided by entering

```
>r ip ip+3
```

Finally, and less dangerously, you can use the Registers command without a parameter to reset the display in the Unassemble window to point to the instruction about to be executed.

## The Breakpoint (BC, BR, BM) Commands

Periscope has an impressive variety of commands for setting breakpoints, which come in two flavors: permanent and conditional.

Permanent breakpoints are usually set with the Breakpoint on Code (BC) command. For example:

```
>bc MyProc
```

would set a breakpoint at the start of the procedure named *MyProc*. Any time *MyProc* was called, the debugger would stop the execution of the program so that you could examine memory or single-step through the procedure. This command, like most of the earlier ones, takes an address as a parameter.

There are several conditional breakpoint commands, but the more common ones are Breakpoint on Register (BR) and Breakpoint on Memory (BM).

Unlike permanent breakpoints, conditional breakpoints occur only when a specified condition is met. For example:

```
>br cs ne cs
```

would tell the debugger to stop the program if CS does Not Equal CS—that is, if the value in the code segment (CS) register changes. Similarly,

```
>bm 0:0 0:3FC w
```

would tell the debugger to stop the execution of the program as soon as any change is made to the interrupt vector table at the bottom of memory (the *W* stands for Write, as opposed to *R* for Read).

The conditional breakpoint commands are powerful indeed, and so require a more complete explanation than can be given here. One final and important point should be made, however.

Conditional breakpoints generally require the debugger to monitor the execution of the program very carefully. Although the rewards can be great, the process is time-consuming. For that reason, Periscope requires you request this special treatment specifically by issuing a special command to watch for conditional breakpoints: either the Go Trace (GT) or the Go Monitor (GM) command (see the Periscope manual for details).

You have numerous options and tools to use in debugging your programming: syntax error handling, runtime error handling, range-checking, I/O error-checking, tracing, map files, and debuggers. The combination of these and the speed of Turbo Pascal create a powerful development environment for even the most serious programmer.

# 10

# The Turbo Pascal Menu Reference

This chapter is designed to help you quickly review all the menu commands available in the Turbo Pascal integrated environment. You'll learn how to select menu commands, then we'll discuss each menu item in detail.

## Menu Structure

Figure 10.1 shows the complete structure of Turbo Pascal's main menu and its successive pull-down menus.

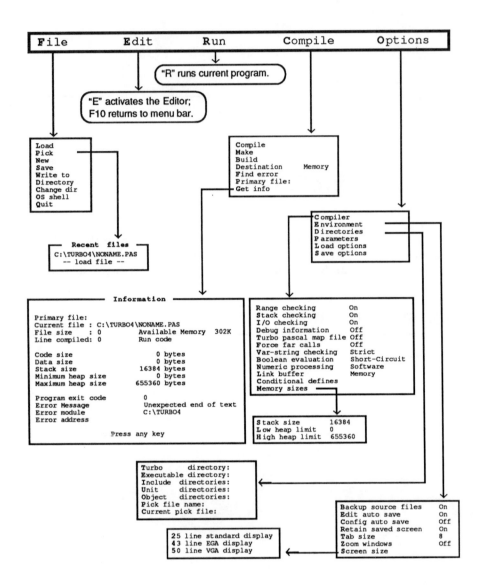

```
 File        Edit        Run        Compile        Options
```

"R" runs current program.

"E" activates the Editor;
F10 returns to menu bar.

```
Load
Pick
New
Save
Write to
Directory
Change dir
OS shell
Quit
```

```
Compile
Make
Build
Destination     Memory
Find error
Primary file:
Get info
```

```
Compiler
Environment
Directories
Parameters
Load options
Save options
```

```
 Recent files
C:\TURBO4\NONAME.PAS
 -- load file --
```

```
              Information
Primary file:
Current file : C:\TURBO4\NONAME.PAS
File size    : 0          Available Memory  302K
Line compiled: 0          Run code

Code size                  0 bytes
Data size                  0 bytes
Stack size             16384 bytes
Minimum heap size          0 bytes
Maximum heap size     655360 bytes

Program exit code          0
Error Message          Unexpected end of text
Error module           C:\TURBO4
Error address

              Press any key
```

```
Range checking          On
Stack checking          On
I/O checking            On
Debug information       Off
Turbo pascal map file   Off
Force far calls         Off
Var-string checking     Strict
Boolean evaluation      Short-Circuit
Numeric processing      Software
Link buffer             Memory
Conditional defines
Memory sizes
```

```
Stack size       16384
Low heap limit   0
High heap limit  655360
```

```
Turbo      directory:
Executable directory:
Include    directories:
Unit       directories:
Object     directories:
Pick file name:
Current pick file:
```

```
Backup source files   On
Edit auto save        On
Config auto save      Off
Retain saved screen   On
Tab size              8
Zoom windows          Off
Screen size
```

```
25 line standard display
43 line EGA display
50 line VGA display
```

Figure 10.1: Turbo Pascal's Menu Structure

Menu commands can be selected several ways. First, you can get to the main menu by pressing *F10*. If you're in the Edit window, you can get to the main menu by pressing *Ctrl-K D* or *Ctrl-K Q*. You can also press an *Alt* key and the first letter of the main menu item you'd like to get to; for example, *Alt-O* to get to the **O**ptions menu.

Once you're at the main menu, you can select an item by pressing the key corresponding to the first letter of the menu name: File, Edit, **R**un, Compile, and **O**ptions. File, Compile, and **O**ptions have several other items in their pull-down menus; **E**dit and **R**un have no other options. You can also use the *Up arrow* and *Down arrow* keys on your keyboard to move the highlight bar up and down the list of commands, pressing *Enter* when the bar is on the command you want. To close a menu, just press *Esc*.

Here's the five main menu selections:

**File**
Handles files (loading, saving, picking, creating, writing to disk), manipulates directories (listing, changing), quits the program, and invokes DOS.

**Edit**
Lets you create and edit source files in the built-in text editor.

**Run**
Automatically compiles, links, and runs your program.

**Compile**
Compiles and makes your programs into object and executable files, and more.

**Options**
Allows you to select compiler options (such as range-checking, debugging information, and memory sizes) and define an input string of parameters. Also records the Turbo, Executable, Include, Unit file and Object directories, saves compiler options, and loads options from the configuration file.

There are three general types of items on the Turbo Pascal menus:

■ **Commands** perform a task (running, compiling, storing options, and so on).

■ **Toggles** let you switch a Turbo Pascal feature on or off (**R**ange-checking, **E**dit auto save, and so on) or cycle through and select one of several options by repeatedly pressing the *Enter* key till you reach the item desired (such as **D**estination or **B**oolean evaluation).

■ **Settings** allow you to specify certain compile-time and runtime information to the compiler, such as directory locations, primary files, and so forth.

## The Bottom Line

Whether you're in one of the windows or one of the menus, the line at the bottom of the screen provides at-a-glance function-key help for your current position.

To see what other key combinations do in a different setting, hold down the *Alt* key for a few seconds. The bottom line changes to describe what function will be performed when you combine other keys with this key.

When you're in the main menu and the Edit window is active, the bottom line looks like this:

```
F1-Help  F2-Save  F3-Load  F5-Zoom  F6-Edit  F9-Make  F10-Main menu
```

When you hold down the *Alt* key, a summary of *Alt*-key combinations is displayed, like this:

```
Alt-F1-Last-Help  Alt-F3-Pick  Alt-F5-Saved Screen  Alt-F9-Compile  Alt-X-Exit
```

## The Edit Window

In this section, we describe the components of the Turbo Pascal Edit window and explain how to work in the window.

First off, to get into the Edit window, press *Enter* when positioned at the Edit option on the main menu (or press *E* from anywhere on the main menu). To get into the Edit window from anywhere in the system, including the Output window, just press *Alt-E*. (Remember, *Alt-E* is just a shortcut for *F10-E*.) Once you're in the Edit window, notice that there are double lines at the top of it, and its name is highlighted—that means it's the active window.

A new editor key, *Ctrl-F7*, expands the integrated environment's compiler directive settings into text and inserts them at the beginning of the current edit file. Try loading a file into the editor and pressing *Ctrl-F7*. If you haven't changed any of the default switch settings on the **O**ptions/**C**ompiler menu, the following text will be inserted at the top of the file in the editor:

```
{$R-,S+,I+,D+,T-,F-,V+,B-,N-,L+ }
{$M 16384,0,655360 }
```

These are all the options found on the **O**ptions/**C**ompiler and **M**emory sizes menus. In addition, any conditional defines from the **O**ptions/**C**ompiler/**C**onditional defines menu item would have been inserted as {$DEFINE *xxxx* } directives.

Besides the body of the Edit window, where you can see and edit several lines of your source file, the Turbo Pascal Edit screen has two information lines you should note: an Edit status line and the bottom line.

The status line at the top of the Edit window gives information about the file you are editing, where in the file the cursor is located, and which editing modes are activated:

```
Line n  Col n  Insert   Indent   Tab C:FILENAME.EXT
```

**Line n**          Cursor is on file line number *n*.

**Col n**           Cursor is on file column number *n*.

**Insert**          Insert mode is on; toggle Insert mode on and off with *Insert* or *Ctrl-V*.

**Indent**          Autoindent is on. Toggle it off and on with *Ctrl-O I*.

**Tab**             Tab mode is enabled. Toggle it on and off with *Ctrl-O T*.

**C:FILENAME.EXT** The drive (C:), name (FILENAME), and extension (.EXT) of the file you are editing.

The line at the bottom of the screen displays which hotkeys perform which action:

```
F1-Help  F2-Save  F3-Load  F5-Zoom  F6-Output  F9-Make  F10-Main Menu
```

To select one of these functions, press the listed key:

**F1-Help**         Opens a Help window that provides information about the Turbo Pascal editor commands.

**F2-Save**         Saves the file loaded in the Edit window.

**F3-Load**         Loads a new file into the Editor.

**F5-Zoom**         Makes the active window full screen. Toggle *F5* to get back to the split-screen environment.

**F6-Output**       In this case, *F6* takes you to the Output window; in general, *F6* switches between windows. Press it once more to make the Edit window active again.

**F9-Make**         Makes your .EXE file.

**F10-Main menu**   Invokes the main menu.

The editor uses a command structure similar to that of SideKick's NotePad and the orginal Turbo Pascal's editor; if you're unfamiliar with the editor these products use, Chapter 11 describes the editor commands in detail.

If you're entering code in the editor, you can press *Enter* to end a line (the editor has no wordwrap). The maximum line width is 249 characters; you'll get a beep if you try to type past that. (Note that the compiler only recognizes characters out to column 128.) The Edit window is 77 columns wide. If you type past column 77, the text you've already entered moves to the left as you type. The Edit window's status line gives the cursor's location in the file by line and column.

After you've entered your code into the Edit window, press *F10* to invoke the main menu. Your file will remain onscreen; you need only press *E* (for Edit) at the main menu to return to it, or *Alt-E* from anywhere.

# How to Work with Source Files in the Edit Window

When you invoke the Edit window before loading a particular file, the Turbo Pascal editor automatically names the file NONAME.PAS. At this point you have all the features of the editor at your fingertips. You can:

■ create a new source file either as NONAME.PAS or another file name

■ load and edit an existing file

■ pick a file from a list of edit files, and then load it into the Edit window

■ save the file viewed in the Edit window

■ write the file in the editor to a new file name

■ alternate between the Edit window and the Output window to find and correct runtime mistakes

While you are creating or editing a source file but before you have compiled and run it, you don't need the Output window. So you can press *F5* to zoom the Edit window to full screen. Press *F5* again to unzoom the Edit window (return to split-screen mode).

### Creating a New Source File

To create a new file, select one of the following methods:

■ If you have just entered Turbo Pascal and don't have an active pick file, you need only press *E* to create the file NONAME.PAS in the editor.

■ At the main menu, select **File/New**, then press *Enter*. This opens the Edit window with a file named NONAME.PAS.

■ At the main menu, select **File/Load**. The Load File Name prompt box opens; type in the name of your new source file. (Pressing the shortcut *F3* from within the Edit window will accomplish the same thing.)

*Turbo Pascal Owner's Handbook*

## Loading an Existing Source File

To load and edit an existing file, you can select two options: File/Load or File/Pick.

If you select File/Load at the main menu, you can

- Type in the name of the file you want to edit; paths are accepted—for example,

      C:\TP\TESTFILE.PAS

- Enter a mask in the Load File Name prompt box (using the DOS wildcards * and ?), and press *Enter*. Entering *.* will display all of the files in the current directory as well as any other directories. Directory names are followed by a backslash (\). Selecting a directory displays the files in that directory. Entering C:\*.PAS, for example, will bring up *only* the files with that extension in the root directory. You can change the wildcard mask by pressing *F4*. (For more on directories, look at Appendix G.)

- Press the *Up, Down, Left,* and *Right* arrow keys to highlight the file name you want to select. Then press *Enter* to load the selected file; you are placed in the Edit window. If you press *Enter* when you're positioned on a directory name, you'll get a new directory box.

Pick lets you quickly pick the name of a previously loaded file. So, if you select File/Pick or *Alt-F3* (see the discussion of the Pick option later in this chapter), you can

- Press *Alt-F* then *P* to bring up your pick list (or press the shortcut *Alt-F3*).
- Use the *Up* and *Down* arrow keys to move the selection bar to the file of your choice.

## Saving a Source File

In order to save a source file from anywhere in the system, press *F2*. If you're at the main menu, you can select File/Save.

## Writing an Output File

You can write the file in the editor to a new file or overwrite an existing file. You can write to the current (default) directory or specify a different drive and directory.

At the main menu, select File/**W**rite to. Then, in the New Name prompt box, enter the full path name of the new file name and press *Enter*.

      C:\DIR\SUBDIR\FILENAME.EXT

where C: (optional) is the drive; \DIR\SUBDIR\ represent optional directories; FILENAME.EXT is the name of the output file and its extension (the extension .PAS is assumed; append a period (.) at the end of your file name if you don't want an extension name).

Press *Esc* once to return to the main menu, twice to go back to the active window (the editor). You can also press *F6* or *Alt-E*.

If FILENAME.EXT already exists, the editor will verify that you want to overwrite the existing file before proceeding.

## *The Output Window*

The Output window contains program-generated output. At startup, it will display the last screen from DOS. You can scroll through this window using the cursor keys, as well as *Home*, *End*, *PgUp* and *PgDn*. When the Output window is active, the 25th line looks like this:

```
F1-Help  F2-Save  F3-Load  F5-Zoom  F6-Edit F9-Make  F10-Main menu
```

To use one of these features, press the desired key:

| | |
|---|---|
| **F1-Help** | Opens a Help window that offers info about the Output window. |
| **F2-Save** | Saves the file currently in the editor. |
| **F3-Load** | Loads a new file into the editor. |
| **F5-Zoom** | Expands the Output window to full screen. |
| **F6-Edit** | Makes the Edit window active. |
| **F9-Make** | Makes the .EXE file. |
| **F10-Main menu** | Invokes the main menu. |

# The File Menu

The File pull-down menu offers various choices for loading existing files, creating new files, and saving files. When you load a file, it is automatically placed in the editor. When you finish with a file, you can save it to any directory or file name. In addition, from this pull-down you can change to another directory, temporarily go to the DOS shell, or exit Turbo Pascal.

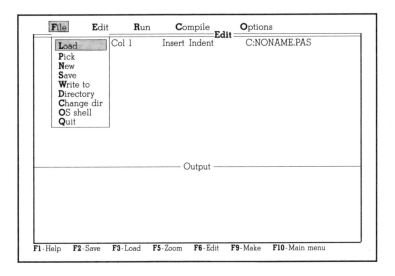

Figure 10.2: The File Menu

## Load

Loads a file. You can use DOS-style masks to get a listing of file choices, or you can load a specific file. Simply type in the name of the file you want to load.

You can move through the directory box by using first letter selection. Pressing the *B* key, for example, takes you to the first file name starting with *B*. Pressing *B* again takes you to the next file name, and so on. If there are no other file names beginning with the letter *B*, you will be taken back to the first one. If no file names start with the letter *B*, then the cursor will not move. Holding down the *Shift* key and pressing *B* will take you to the first subdirectory that begins with the letter *B*.

**Note:** If you enter an incorrect drive or directory, you'll get an error box onscreen. You'll get a verify box if you have an unsaved, modified file in the editor while you're trying to load another file. In either case, the hot keys are disabled until you press the key specified in the error or verify box.

## Pick

Lets you pick a file from a list of the previous eight files loaded into the Edit window. At the top of list, you'll find the file that is currently in the editor. This provides an easy way to reload the current file if you wish to abandon changes. The file selected is loaded into the Editor and the cursor is positioned at the location where you last edited that file. Note that the block marks and state is saved for each file, as are each of the four markers. If you select the "—load file—" item from the pick list, you'll get a Load File Name prompt box exactly as if you had selected File/Load or *F3*. *Alt-F3* is a short cut to get this list.

You can define the pick file name from the **O/D/P**ick file name menu item from within Turbo Pascal's installation program (TINST). This will have Turbo Pascal automatically save the current pick list when you exit Turbo Pascal and then reload that file upon reentering the program. For more information, see the **O/D/P**ick file name option.

### New
Specifies that the file is to be a new one. You are placed in the editor; by default, this file is called NONAME.PAS. (You can change this name later on when you save the file.)

### Save
Saves the file in the Editor to disk. If your file is named NONAME.PAS and you go to save it, the editor will ask if you want to rename it. From anywhere in the system, pressing *F2* will accomplish the same thing.

### Write to
Writes the file to a new name or overwrites an existing file. If a file by that name already exists, you'll be asked to verify the overwrite.

### Directory
Displays the directory and file set you want (to get the current directory, just press *Enter*).

You can move through the directory box by using first letter selection. Pressing the *B* key, for example, takes you to the first file name starting with *B*. Pressing *B* again takes you to the next file name, and so on. If there are no other file names beginning with the letter *B*, you will be taken back to the first one. If no file names start with the letter *B*, then the cursor will not move. Holding down the *Shift* key and pressing *B* will take you to the first subdirectory that begins with the letter *B*.

### Change dir
Displays the current directory and allows you to change to a specified drive and/or directory.

### OS shell

Leaves Turbo Pascal temporarily and takes you to the DOS prompt. To return to Turbo Pascal, type exit. This is useful when you want to run a DOS command without quitting Turbo Pascal.

### Quit

Quits Turbo Pascal and returns you to the DOS prompt to the currently active directory.

# The Edit Command

The Edit command invokes the built-in screen editor.

You can invoke the main menu from the editor by pressing *F10* (or *Alt* and the first letter of the main menu command you desire). Your source text remains displayed on the screen; you need only press *Esc* or *E* at the main menu to return to it (or *Alt-E* from anywhere).

# The Run Command

Run invokes the compiler if you have changed the file you're currently editing since the last time you compiled it. It then runs your program using the arguments given in **Options/Parameters**. After your program's finished running, you'll get a Press any key to return to Turbo Pascal message.

When the compiler is invoked because you have changed the edit file, it is the same as doing a **Make** (*F9*), followed by a **Run** (*Alt-R* or *F10 R*).

# The Compile Menu

Use the items on the Compile menu to Compile a program, to Make a program, to Build a program, to set the Destination of the object code (disk or memory), to Find a runtime error, to set a Primary file, or to Get information about the current source file.

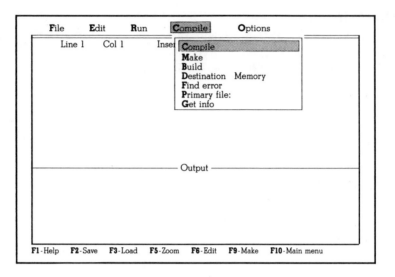

Figure 10.3: The Compile Menu

## Compile

This menu item is a command. The last file you loaded into the editor is compiled.

## Make

Invokes Turbo Pascal's Make sequence. If a primary file has been named, then that file is compiled; otherwise the last file loaded into the editor is compiled. Turbo Pascal checks all files upon which the file being compile depends. If the source file for a given unit has been modified since the .TPU (object code) file was created, then that unit is recompiled. If the interface for a given unit has been changed, then all other units that depend upon it are recompiled. If a unit links in an .OBJ file (external routines), and the .OBJ file is newer than the unit's .TPU file, then the unit is recompiled. If a unit includes an Include file and the Include file is newer than that unit's .TPU file, then the unit is recompiled.

## Build

Recompiles all your files regardless of whether they are out of date or not. This option is similar to **Make** except that it is unconditional; **Make** rebuilds only the files that aren't current.

## Destination

Use this option to specify whether the executable code will be saved to disk (as an .EXE file) or whether it will just be saved in memory (and thus lost when you exit from Turbo Pascal). Note that even if **Destination** is set to Memory, any units that are recompiled during a **M**ake or a **B**uild have their .TPU files updated on disk. If the code is being saved to disk, then the .EXE file name listed is derived from one of two names, in the following order:

- the **Primary** file name, or if none is specified
- the name of the last file you loaded into the Edit window.

## Find error

Finds the location of a runtime error. When a runtime error occurs, the address in memory of where it occurred is given in the format *seg:ofs*. When you return to Turbo Pascal, Turbo locates the error automatically for you. This command allows you to find the error again, given the *seg* and *ofs* values.

For this to work, you must turn on the **Debug** information menu item. When entering the error address, you must give it in hexadecimal, segment and offset notation. The format is *"xxxx:yyyy"*; for example, "2BE0:FFD4."

If runtime errors occur when running within the integrated environment, the default values for error address is set automatically. This allows you to re-find the error location after changing files. (Note that if you just move around in the same file, you can get back to the error location with the *Ctrl-Q W* command.)

When runtime errors occur under DOS, you should note the segment offset displayed on the screen. Then load the main program into the editor or specify it as the **Primary** file. Be sure to set the **Destination** to Disk. Then type in the segment offset value.

## Primary file

Use this option to specify which .PAS file will be compiled when you use **M**ake (*F9*) or **B**uild (*Alt-C B*).

## Get info

Brings up a window of information about the current .PAS file you're working with, including the size (in bytes and lines) of the source code, the size (in bytes of code and data) of the resulting .EXE (or .TPU) file, available memory, state of code, and error information.

When Turbo Pascal is compiling, a window pops up to display the compilation results. When compiling/making is complete, press any key to remove this compiling window. If an error occurs, you are automatically placed in the Edit window at the error.

# The Options Menu

The Options menu contains settings that determine how the integrated environment works. The settings affect things like compiler options, unit, object, and include directories, program runtime arguments, and so on.

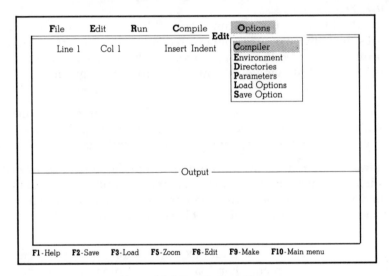

Figure 10.4: The Options Menu

### Compiler

These options allow you to specify different compiler options, including range-checking, stack-checking, I/O checking, and so on. These same options can also be specified directly in your source code using compiler directives (see Appendix C). Note that the first letter of each menu item corresponds to its equivalent compiler directive; for example, Range-checking corresponds to {$R}. (The only exception is compiler defines, which is /Dxxx.)

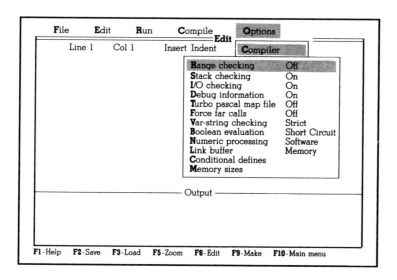

Figure 10.5: The Options/Compiler Menu

■ **Range-checking**: Allows you to enable or disable range-checking. When enabled, the compiler generates code to check that array and string subscripts are within bounds, and that assignments to scalar-type variables don't exceed the defined range. If the check fails, then the program halts with a runtime error. When disabled, no such checking is done. This is equivalent to the $R compiler directive.

■ **Stack checking**: Allows you to enable or disable stack checking. When enabled, the compiler generates code to check that space is available for local variables on the stack before each call to a procedure or function. If the check fails, then the program halts with a runtime error. When disabled, no such checking is done. This is equivalent to the $S compiler directive.

■ **I/O checking**: Allows you to enable or disable input/output (I/O) error checking. When enabled, the compiler generates code to check for I/O errors after every I/O call. If the check fails, then the program halts with a runtime error. When disabled, no such checking is done; however, the user can then test for I/O errors via the system function *IOResult*. This is equivalent to the $I compiler directive.

■ **Debug information**: Allows you to ask the compiler to generate debugging information for the program being compiled. If you are compiling to disk, the information is stored in the resulting .EXE or .TPU file. This allows the Compile/Find Error command to locate runtime errors in units previousy compiled. This must be on for the Compile/Find error item to work.

- **Turbo pascal map file**: Causes the compiler to generate a MAP file during the linking phase. the MAP file generated has a .TPM extension. This file is used by Find error when information is not in memory. You can also use this file with symbolic debuggers. TPMAP.EXE will convert the .TPM file to a MAP file.

- **Force far calls**: Allows you to force all procedure/function calls to be **far** calls. If not enabled, then the compiler will generate **near** calls for any procedures and functions within the file being compiled. This is equivalent to the $F compiler directive.

- **Var-string checking**: Allows you to choose between strict or relaxed string parameter error checking. With strict checking, the compiler compares the declared size of a **var**-type string parameter with the actual parameter being passed. If the declared size of the actual parameter is smaller than that of the formal parameter, then a compiler error occurs. With the relaxed option, no such checking is done. This is equivalent to the $V compiler directive.

- **Boolean evaluation**: Allows you to select between short-circuit and complete Boolean evaluation. With short-circuit evaluation, the compiler generates code to terminate evaluation of a Boolean expression as soon as possible; for example, in the expression **if** False **and** MyFunc..., the function *MyFunc* would never be called. With complete evaluation, all terms in a Boolean expression are evaluated. This is equivalent to the $B compiler directive.

- **Numeric processing**: Allows for two options—Hardware, which generates direct 8087 inline code and allows the use of IEEE floating-point types (single, double, extended, comp); and Software, which allows only the standard Turbo Pascal 6-byte real data type. This is equivalent to the $N compiler directive.

- **Link buffer**: Allows you to tell Turbo to use memory or disk for the link buffer. Using memory speeds things up, but you may run out of memory for large programs; using disk frees up memory but slows things down. This is equivalent to the $L compiler directive.

- **Conditional defines**: Defines symbols referenced in conditional compilation directives in your source code. Symbols are defined by typing in their name. Multiple symbols are separated by semicolons; for example, you may define the two symbols Test and Debug by entering Test;Debug.

When the compiler runs across a sequence like

```
{$IFDEF Test}
Writeln("x =",x:1);
{$ENDIF}
```

then the code for the *Writeln* will be generated. This is equivalent to defining symbols on the command line with the */Dxxx* directive under TPC.EXE.

■ **Memory sizes**: Lets you configure the memory map for the resulting code file. All three settings here can be specified in your source code using the *$M* compiler directive.

**Stack size**: Allows you to specify the size (in bytes) of the stack segment. The default size is 16K, the maximum size is 64K.

**Low heap limit**: Allows you to specify the minimum acceptable heap size (in bytes). The default minimum size is 0K. If you attempt to run your program and there is not enough heap space to satisfy the minimum requirement, then the program aborts with a runtime error.

**High heap limit**: Allows you to specify the maximum amount of memory (in bytes) to allocate to the heap. The default is 655360, which (on most systems) will allocate all available memory to the heap. This value must be greater than or equal to the smallest heap size.

## Environment

This menu's entries tell Turbo Pascal where to find the files it needs to compile, link, and provide Help. Some miscellaneous options permit you to tailor the Turbo Pascal working environment to suit your programming needs.

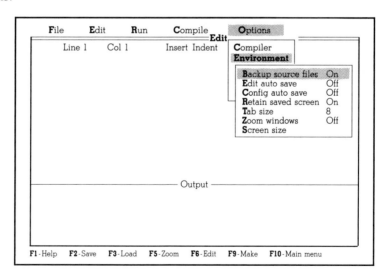

Figure 10.6: The Options/Environment Menu

- **Backup source files:** By default, Turbo Pascal automatically creates a backup of your source file when you do a Save. It saves the backup copy using the same file name and a .BAK extension. This activity can be turned off and on with this option.

- **Edit auto save:** Helps prevent loss of your source file by automatically saving your edit file (if it's been modified) when you use **Run** or **OS** shell.

- **Config auto save:** Helps prevent loss of options you have changed, such as compiler settings or environment settings. Whenever you exit, the current configuration file is updated if it has been changed.

- **Retain saved screen:** Tells the environment how long to save the last output from a **Run** or **OS** shell. When on, the saved screen will be kept the entire session. When off, the saved screen will be kept until the compiler needs to use the memory taken up by one saved screen.

- **Tab size:** Sets the hard tab size in the editor. The tab size can be set from 2 to 16. Note that Tab mode (*Ctrl-O T*) must be on for you to be able to use the *Tab* key to enter hard tabs.

- **Zoom windows:** **Z**oom *on* expands the Edit and Output windows to full screen. You can still switch between them, but only one window at a time will be visible. **Z**oom off returns to the split-screen environment containing both the Edit and Output windows.

- **Screen size:** Lets you choose between a 25-line standard display, a 43-line EGA display, and a 50-line VGA display. These options are only available on hardware that supports them.

## Directories

This menu lets you direct Turbo Pascal to the location of any directories listed, as well as to the pick file.

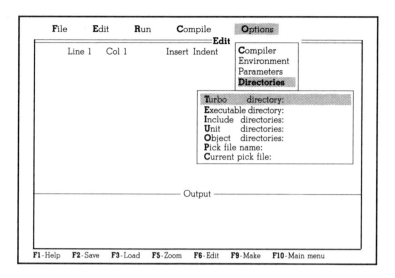

Figure 10.7: The Options/Directories Menu

- **Turbo directory:** This is used by the Turbo Pascal system to find the configuration file (.TP) and the help file (TURBO.HLP). For Turbo Pascal to find your default configuration file (TURBO.TP) at startup you must install this path using this command.

- **Executable directory:** .EXE files are stored here. If the entry is blank, the files are stored in the current directory.

- **Include directories:** Specifies the directories that contain your standard include files. Standard include files are those specified with the {$I filename} compiler directive. Multiple directories are separated by semicolons (;), like in the DOS path command.

- **Unit directories:** Specifies the directories that contain your Turbo Pascal unit files. Multiple directories are separated by semicolons (;), like in the DOS path command.

- **Object directories:** Specifies the directories that contain .OBJ files (assembly language routines). When Turbo Pascal encounters a {$L filename} directive, it looks first in the current directory, then in the directories specified here. Multiple directories are separated by semicolons (;), like in the DOS path command.

- **Pick file name:** Defines the name and location of a pick file. When this field is defined, a pick file will always be written. If it is not defined, then a pick file is written only if the Current pick file entry is non-blank. Since any name can be used, you must save the pick file name in your configuration file if it is not the default name of TURBO.PCK. For more information about this option, see the later section entitled "About the Pick File and the Pick List."

■ **Current pick file:** Shows the file name and location of the current pick file, if any. This is where the current pick list information will be stored if the pick file name changes or if you exit the integrated environment. This item is always disabled and is for informational purposes. For more information, see the later section entitled "About the Pick File and the Pick List."

### Parameters

This setting allows you to give your running programs command-line parameters (or arguments) exactly as if you had typed them on the DOS command line (redirection is not supported). It is only necessary to give the arguments here; the program name is omitted.

### Load Options

Loads a configuration file (the default file is TURBO.TP) previously saved with the **Save** options command.

### Save Options

Saves all your selected **Compiler, Environment,** and **Directories** options in a configuration file (the default file is TURBO.TP). On start-up, Turbo Pascal looks in the current directory for TURBO.TP; if the file's not found, then Turbo Pascal looks in the Turbo directory for the same file. If the file's not found there and you're running DOS 3.x, it will search the exec directory (or the directory where TURBO.EXE was started from).

## About the Pick List and Pick File

The pick list and pick file work together to save the state of your editing sessions. The pick list remembers what you do while you are in the integrated environment, and the pick file remembers after you have left the integrated environment or changed contexts with in it.

# The Pick List

The pick list is a pop-up menu located in the File menu. It provides a list of the eight most recent files that were loaded into the editor. Also, the first file in the list is the current file in the editor.

When you select File/Pick, the selection bar is placed on the second item in the menu; this would be the last file that was loaded into the editor. By selecting this file or scrolling down and selecting one of the other files on the menu, you will load that file into the editor. At this point, the editor will position the cursor where you were last. In addition, any markers and marked blocks will be as you left them.

The pick list is a handy way to move back and forth from one file to another. The hotkey *Alt-F3* takes you directly to the pick list, so pressing *Alt-F3 Enter* in succession swaps between two files. If the file you want is not on the pick list, you can select the last entry on the pick list menu, which is `"--load file--"` or press *F3* (Load file) to load that file.

# The Pick File

The pick file is used to store editor related information, including the contents of the pick list. For each entry in the pick list, its file name, file position, marked block, and markers are stored. In addition to information about each file, the pick file contains data on the state of the editor when you last exited. This includes the last search-and-replace strings and search options.

To create a pick file, you must define a pick file name. This is done by entering a file name in the **Pick** file name menu item found on the **Options/Directories** menu. When this field is defined the pick list is updated on disk when you exit the integrated environment.

# Loading a Pick File

If a pick file name is defined, the integrated environment will try to load it.

The pick file name can be defined in several ways. TINST—the Turbo Pascal integrated environment program—can be used to permanently install a pick file name into the TURBO.EXE file. A configuration file can be loaded that contains a pick file name. Or you can type in a pick file name. If a pick file name is defined but the integrated environment cannot find it, then an error message is issued.

If no pick file name is defined, then the integrated environment searches for the default pick file name, TURBO.PCK, first in the current directory, then in the Turbo directory, and if you are running under DOS 3.x, it will then search the executable directory.

Once a pick file is loaded, the integrated environment remembers the name and location of that file so that it can update that file when you exit after changing directories.

## Saving Pick Files

If a pick file has not been loaded and the Pick file name option is blank, then the integrated environment will not save a pick file to disk when you exit.

Usually, pick files are only saved on exit from the integrated environment. However, there are certain times when the current pick file is updated and a new pick file is started (or restarted).

Whenever you change the pick file name, the integrated environment will cause the current pick list to be written to the last pick file and then the newly named pick file will be in effect.

## Configuration Files and the Pick File

Since the pick file name is stored in the configuration file, it is possible to change pick files by loading a new configuration file. If the pick file name from the configuration file is different than the current pick file, then the current pick file is updated and the new pick file is loaded.

Note that two configuration files can easily use the same pick file; thus loading a configuration file with the same pick file name as the current one does not affect the pick file or the current pick list.

C H A P T E R

# 11

# Using the Editor

Turbo Pascal's built-in editor is specifically designed for creating program source text in the integrated environment. If you use the command-line version of the compiler, however, you'll be using another editor and can therefore skip this chapter.

The Turbo Pascal editor lets you enter up to 64K of text, 248 character lines, and any characters in the ASCII character set, extended character set, and control characters.

If you are familiar with WordStar, the version 3.0 Turbo Pascal editor, or the SideKick editor, you already know how to use the Turbo Pascal editor. At the end of this chapter, there's a summary of the few differences between Turbo Pascal's editor commands and the ever-familiar WordStar commands.

## Quick In, Quick Out

To invoke the editor in the integrated environment, choose Edit from Turbo Pascal's main menu by pressing *E* from anywhere on the main menu or by using the arrow keys to move to the Edit command and then pressing *Enter*. The Edit window becomes the "active" window; meaning the Edit window's title is highlighted and has a double line at the top, and the cursor is positioned in upper left-hand corner.

To enter text, you can type as though you were using a typewriter. To end a line, press the *Enter* key.

To invoke the main menu from within the editor, press *F10, Ctrl-K D,* or *Ctrl-K Q.* The data in the Edit window remains on screen, but the menu bar now becomes active. To get back to editing, press *E* again.

# The Edit Window Status Line

The status line at the top of the Edit window gives you information about the file you are editing: where in the file the cursor is located and which editing modes are activated:

```
Line n  Col n  Insert   Indent   Tab   C:FILENAME.TYP
```

Line n            Cursor is on file line number *n.*

Col n             Cursor is on file column number *n.*

Insert            Tells you that the editor is in Insert mode; characters entered on the keyboard are inserted at the cursor position, and text to the right of the cursor is moved further right.

                  Use the *Ins* key or *Ctrl-V* to toggle the editor between Insert mode and Overwrite mode.

                  In Overwrite mode, text entered at the keyboard overwrites characters under the cursor instead of inserting them before existing text.

Indent            Indicates the autoindent feature is on. You can toggle it off and on with the command *Ctrl-O I.*

Tab               Indicates whether or not you can insert tabs; toggle it on or off with *Ctrl-O T.*

C:FILENAME.EXT    Indicates the drive (C:), name (FILENAME), and extension (.EXT) of the file you are editing. If the file name and extension is NONAME.PAS, then you have not specified a file name yet. (NONAME.PAS is Turbo Pascal's default file name.)

# Editor Commands

The editor uses approximately 50 commands to move the cursor around, page through text, find and replace strings, and so on. These commands can be grouped into four main categories:

- cursor movement commands (basic and extended)
- insert and delete commands
- block commands
- miscellaneous commands

Table 11.1 summarizes the commands. Each entry in the table consists of a command definition, followed by the default keystrokes used to activate the command. The remainder of the chapter details each editor command.

Table 11.1: Summary of Editor Commands

### Basic Movement Commands

| | |
|---|---|
| Character left | *Ctrl-S* or *Left arrow* |
| Character right | *Ctrl-D* or *Right arrow* |
| Word left | *Ctrl-A* or *Ctrl-Left arrow* |
| Word right | *Ctrl-F* or *Ctrl-Right arrow* |
| Line up | *Ctrl-E* or *Up arrow* |
| Line down | *Ctrl-X* or *Down arrow* |
| Scroll up | *Ctrl-W* |
| Scroll down | *Ctrl-Z* |
| Page up | *Ctrl-R* or *PgUp* |
| Page down | *Ctrl-C* or *PgDn* |

### Extended Movement Commands

| | |
|---|---|
| Beginning of line | *Ctrl-Q S* or *Home* |
| End of line | *Ctrl-Q D* or *End* |
| Top of window | *Ctrl-Q E* or *Ctrl-Home* |
| Bottom of window | *Ctrl-Q X* or *Ctrl-End* |
| Top of file | *Ctrl-Q R* or *Ctrl-PgUp* |
| End of file | *Ctrl-Q C* or *Ctrl-PgDn* |
| Beginning of block | *Ctrl-Q B* |
| End of block | *Ctrl-Q K* |
| Last cursor position | *Ctrl-Q P* |
| Last error position | *Ctrl-Q W* |

### Insert and Delete Commands

| | |
|---|---|
| Insert mode on/off | *Ctrl-V* or *Ins* |
| Insert line | *Ctrl-N* |
| Delete line | *Ctrl-Y* |
| Delete to end of line | *Ctrl-Q Y* |
| Delete character left of cursor | *Ctrl-H* or *Backspace* |
| Delete character under cursor | *Ctrl-G* or *Del* |
| Delete word right of cursor | *Ctrl-T* |

## Block Commands

| | |
|---|---|
| Mark block-begin | *Ctrl-K B* or *F7* |
| Mark block-end | *Ctrl-K K* or *F8* |
| Mark single word | *Ctrl-K T* |
| Print block | *Ctrl-K P* |
| Copy block | *Ctrl-K C* |
| Delete block | *Ctrl-K Y* |
| Hide/display block | *Ctrl-K H* |
| Move block | *Ctrl-K V* |
| Read block from disk | *Ctrl-K R* |
| Write block to disk | *Ctrl-K W* |

## Miscellaneous Commands

| | |
|---|---|
| Abort operation | *Ctrl-U* |
| Autoindent on/off | *Ctrl-O I* or *Ctrl-Q I* |
| Control character prefix | *Ctrl-P* |
| Pair braces forward | *Ctrl-Q [* |
| Pair braces backward | *Ctrl-Q ]* |
| Find | *Ctrl-Q F* |
| Find and replace | *Ctrl-Q A* |
| Find place marker | *Ctrl-Q n* |
| Invoke main menu | *F10* |
| Load file | *F3* |
| Exit editor, no save | *Ctrl-K D* or *Ctrl-K Q* |
| Repeat last find | *Ctrl-L* |
| Restore line | *Ctrl-Q L* |
| Save and edit | *Ctrl-K S* or *F2* |
| Set place marker | *Ctrl-K n* |
| Tab | *Ctrl-I* or *Tab* |
| Tab mode | *Ctrl-O T* or *Ctrl-Q T* |
| Language help | *Ctrl-F1* |
| Insert compiler directives | *Ctrl-F7* |

# *Basic Movement Commands*

The editor uses control-key commands to move the cursor up, down, right, and left on the screen (you can also use the arrow keys). To control cursor movement in the part of your file currently onscreen, use the sequences shown in Table 11.2.

| When you press: | The cursor does this: |
|---|---|
| Ctrl-A or Ctrl-Left arrow | Moves to first letter in word to left of cursor |
| Ctrl-S | Moves to first position to left of cursor |
| Ctrl-D | Moves to first position to right of cursor |
| Ctrl-F or Ctrl-Right arrow | Moves to first letter in word to right of cursor |
| Ctrl-E or Ctrl-Up arrow | Moves up one line |
| Ctrl-R | Moves up one full screen |
| Ctrl-X or Ctrl-Down arrow | Moves down one line |
| Ctrl-C | Moves down one full screen |
| Ctrl-W | Scrolls screen down one line; cursor stays in line |
| Ctrl-Z | Scrolls screen up one line; cursor stays in line |

## *Extended Movement Commands*

The editor also provides six commands to move the cursor quickly to either ends of lines, to the beginning and end of the file, and to the last cursor position (see Table 11.3).

Table 11.3: Quick Movement Commands

| When you press: | The cursor does this: |
|---|---|
| Ctrl-Q S or Home | Moves to column one of the current line |
| Ctrl-Q D or End | Moves to the end of the current line |
| Ctrl-Q E or Ctrl-Home | Moves to the top of the screen |
| Ctrl-Q X or Ctrl-End | Moves to the bottom of the screen |
| Ctrl-Q R | Moves to the first character in the file |
| Ctrl-Q C | Moves to the last character in the file |

The *Ctrl-Q* prefix with a *B*, *K*, or *P* character allows you to jump to certain points in a document.

**Beginning of block**                                                  *Ctrl-K B*
Moves the cursor to the block-begin marker set with *Ctrl-K B*. The command works even if the block is not displayed (see "Hide/display block" under "Block Commands") or if the block-end marker is not set.

**End of block**                                                          *Ctrl-K K*
Moves the cursor to the block-end marker set with *Ctrl-K K*. The command works even if the block is not displayed (see "Hide/display block") or the block-begin marker is not set.

**Last cursor position**                                              *Ctrl-Q P*

Moves to the last position of the cursor before the last command. This command is particularly useful after a Find or Find/replace operation has been executed and you'd like to return to the last position before its execution.

**Last error position**                                              *Ctrl-Q W*

After the compiler has placed you in the editor with an error showing on the status line, you can later return to this position and redisplay the error by pressing *Ctrl-Q W*.

## Insert and Delete Commands

To write a program, you need to know more than just how to move the cursor around. You also need to be able to insert and delete text. The following commands insert and delete characters, words, and lines.

**Insert mode on/off**                                         *Ctrl-V or Ins*

When entering text, you can choose between two basic entry modes: Insert and Overwrite. You can switch between these modes with the Insert mode toggle, *Ctrl-V* or *Ins*. The current mode is displayed in the status line at the top of the screen.

Insert mode is the Turbo Pascal editor's default; this lets you insert new characters into old text. Text to the right of the cursor moves further right as you enter new text.

Use Overwrite mode to replace old text with new; any characters entered replace existing characters under the cursor.

**Delete character left of cursor**                     *Ctrl-H or Backspace*

Moves one character to the left and deletes the character positioned there. Any characters to the right of the cursor move one position to the left. You can use this command to remove line breaks.

**Delete character under cursor**                          *Ctrl-G or Del*

Deletes the character under the cursor and moves any characters to the right of the cursor one position to the left. You can use this command to remove line breaks.

**Delete word right of cursor**                                      *Ctrl-T*

Deletes the word to the right of the cursor. A word is defined as a sequence of characters delimited by one of the following characters:

$$space <> , ; . () [] ^ ' * + - / \$$$

This command works across line breaks, and can be used to remove them.

**Insert line**                                                          *Ctrl-N*

Inserts a line break at the cursor position.

**Delete line**                                                          *Ctrl-Y*

Deletes the line containing the cursor and moves any lines below it one line up. There's no way to restore a deleted line, so use this command with care.

**Delete to end of line**                                              *Ctrl-Q Y*

Deletes all text from the cursor position to the end of the line.

## Block Commands

The block commands also require a control-character command sequence. A block of text is any amount of text, from a single character to hundreds of lines, that has been surrounded with special block-marker characters. There can be only one block in a document at a time.

You mark a block by placing a block-begin marker before the first character and a block-end marker after the last character of the desired portion of text. Once marked, you can copy, move, or delete the block, or write it to a file.

**Mark block begin**                                              *Ctrl-K B* or *F7*

Marks the beginning of a block. The marker itself is not visible, and the block only becomes visible when the block-end marker is set. Marked text (a block) is displayed in a different intensity.

**Mark block end**                                                *Ctrl-K K* or *F8*

Marks the end of a block. The marker itself is invisible, and the block becomes visible only when the block-begin marker is also set.

**Mark single word**                                                   *Ctrl-K T*

Marks a single word as a block, replacing the block-begin/block-end sequence. If the cursor is placed within a word, then the word will be marked. If it is not within a word, then the word to the left of the cursor will be marked.

**Print block**                                                        *Ctrl-K P*

Prints the marked block.

**Copy block**                                                         *Ctrl-K C*

Copies a previously marked block to the current cursor position. The original block is unchanged, and the markers are placed around the new copy of the block. If no block is marked or the cursor is within the marked block, nothing happens.

**Delete block** *Ctrl-K Y*

Deletes a previously marked block. There is no provision to restore a deleted block, so be careful with this command.

**Hide/display block** *Ctrl-K H*

Causes the visual marking of a block to be alternately switched off and on. The block manipulation commands (copy, move, delete, and write to a file) work only when the block is displayed. Block-related cursor movements (jump to beginning/end of block) work whether the block is hidden or displayed.

**Move block** *Ctrl-K V*

Moves a previously marked block from its original position to the cursor position. The block disappears from its original position, and the markers remain around the block at its new position. If no block is marked, nothing happens.

**Read block from disk** *Ctrl-K R*

Reads a previously marked disk file into the current text at the cursor position, exactly as if it were a block. The text read is then marked as a block of different intensity.

When you issue this command, Turbo Pascal's editor prompts you for the name of the file to read. You can use DOS wildcards to select a file to read; a directory appears in a small window onscreen. The file specified can be any legal file name. If you don't specify a file type (.PAS, .TXT), the editor appends .PAS. To read a file without an extension, append a period to the file name.

**Write block to disk** *Ctrl-K W*

Writes a previously marked block to a file. The block is left unchanged in the current file, and the markers remain in place. If no block is marked, nothing happens.

When you issue this command, Turbo Pascal's editor prompts you for the name of the file to write to. To select a file to overwrite, use DOS wildcards; a directory appears in a small window onscreen. If the file specified already exists, the editor issues a warning and prompts for verification before overwriting the existing file. You can give the file any legal name (the default extension is .PAS). To write a file without an extension, append a period to the file name.

## Miscellaneous Editing Commands

This section describes commands that do not fall into any of the categories already covered.

**Abort operation** *Ctrl-U*

Lets you abort any command in progress whenever it pauses for input, such as when Find/replace asks `Replace Y/N?` or when you are entering a search string or a file name (block read and write).

**Autoindent on/off** *Ctrl-O I or Ctrl-Q I*

Provides automatic indenting of successive lines. When autoindent is active, the cursor does not return to column one when you press *Enter*; instead, it returns to the starting column of the line you just terminated.

When you want to change the indentation, use the space bar and *Left* arrow key to select the new column. When autoindent is on, the message `Indent` shows up in the status line; when off, the message disappears. Autoindent is on by default. (When Tab is on, it works the same way, but it will use tabs if possible when indenting.)

**Control character prefix** *Ctrl-P*

Allows you to enter control characters into the file by prefixing the desired control character with a *Ctrl-P*; that is, first press *Ctrl-P*, then press the desired control character. Control characters will appear as low-intensity capital letters on the screen (or inverse, depending on your screen setup).

**Go to error position** *Ctrl-Q W*

Displays the last error generated in the Edit window and places you in the editor at the point of error.

**Find** *Ctrl-Q F*

Lets you search for a string of up to 30 characters. When you enter this command, the status line is cleared, and the editor prompts you for a search string. Enter the string you are looking for and then press *Enter*.

The search string can contain any characters, including control characters. You enter control characters into the search string with the *Ctrl-P* prefix. For example, enter a *Ctrl-T* by holding down the *Ctrl* key as you press *P*, and then press *T*. You can include a line break in a search string by specifying *Ctrl-M J* carriage return/line feed). Note that *Ctrl-A* has a special meaning: It matches any character and can be used as a wildcard in search strings.

You can edit search strings with the Character left, Character right, Word left, and Word right commands. Word right recalls the previous search string, which you can then edit. To abort (quit) the search operation, use the Abort command (*Ctrl-U*).

When you specify the search string, Turbo Pascal's editor asks which search options you'd like to use. The following options are available:

B       Searches backward from the current cursor position toward the beginning of the text.

| G | Globally searches the entire text, irrespective of the current cursor position, stopping *only* at the last occurrence of the string. |
|---|---|
| L | Locally searches the marked block for the next occurrence of the string. |
| n | Where *n* equals a number, finds the *n*th occurrence of the search string, counted from the current cursor position. |
| U | Ignores uppercase/lowercase distinctions. |
| W | Searches for whole words only, skipping matching patterns embedded in other words. |

**Examples:**

| W | Searches for whole words only. The search string *term* will match *term*, for example, but not *terminal*. |
|---|---|
| BU | Searches backward and ignores uppercase/lowercase differences. *Block* matches both *blockhead* and *BLOCKADE*, and so on. |
| 125 | Finds the 125th occurrence of the search string. |

You can end the list of find options (if any) by pressing *Enter*; the search starts. If the text contains a target matching the search string, the editor positions the cursor on the target. The search operation can be repeated with the Repeat last find command (*Ctrl-L*).

### Find and replace                                              *Ctrl-Q A*
This operation works identically to the Find command except that you can replace the "found" string with any other string of up to 30 characters. Note that *Ctrl-A* has a special meaning: It matches any character and can be used as a wildcard in search strings.

After you specify the search string, the editor asks you to enter a replacement string. Enter up to 30 characters; control-character entry and editing is performed as stated in the Find command. If you press *Enter*, the editor replaces the target with nothing, effectively deleting it.

Your options are the same as those in the Find command, with the addition of the following:

| N | Replaces without asking; does not ask for confirmation of each occurrence of the search string. |
|---|---|
| n | Replaces the next *n* cases of the search string. When you're also using the G option, the search starts at the top of the file and ignores the *n*; otherwise it starts at the current cursor position. |
| L | Only replaces those strings local to a marked block. |

**Examples:**

> **N10** Finds the next ten occurrences of the search string and replaces each without asking.

> **GW** Finds and replaces whole words in the entire text, ignoring uppercase/lowercase. It prompts for a replacement string.

> **GNU** Finds (throughout the file) uppercase and lowercase small, antelope-like creatures and replaces them without asking.

Again, you can end the option list (if any) by pressing *Enter*; the Find/replace operation starts. When the editor finds the item (and if the *N* option is not specified), it then positions the cursor at one end of the item, and asks Replace (Y/N)? in the prompt line at the top of the screen. You can abort the Find/replace operation at this point with the Abort command (*Ctrl-U*). You can repeat the Find/replace operation with the Repeat last find command (*Ctrl-L*).

**Find place marker**                                                    *Ctrl-Q n*

Finds up to four place markers (0-3) in text; *n* is a user-determined number from 0-3. Move the cursor to any previously set marker by pressing *Ctrl-Q* and the marker number, *n*.

**Pair braces**                                              *Ctrl-Q [ or Ctrl-Q ]*

Moves the cursor to a matching {, [, (*, ", ', <, >, *), }, or ]. The cursor must be positioned on the character you want to match; in the case of (* or *), on the ( or ).

This command accounts for nested braces. If a match for the brace you are on cannot be found, then the cursor does not move. For (* *), { }, [ ], and < >, both *Ctrl-Q [* and *Ctrl-Q]* have the same effect. This is because the direction of the matching symbol can be determined. With " and ', the direction to search is determined by the key you select. Press *Ctrl-Q [* to find a match to the right; press *Ctrl-Q ]* to find a match to the left.

**Load file**                                                                  *F3*

Lets you edit an existing file or create a new file.

**Exit editor, no save**                                    *Ctrl-K D or Ctrl-K Q*

Quits the editor and returns you to the main menu. You can save the edited file on disk either explicitly with the main menu's **S**ave option under the File command or manually while in the editor (*Ctrl-K S or F2*).

**Repeat last find**                                                         *Ctrl-L*

Repeats the latest Find or Find/replace operation as if all information had been reentered.

**Restore line**                                                                          *Ctrl-Q L*

Lets you undo changes made to a line, as long as you have not left the line. The line is restored to its original state regardless of any changes you have made.

**Save file**                                                                        *Ctrl-K S* or *F2*

Saves the file and remains in the editor.

**Set place marker**                                                                      *Ctrl-K n*

You can mark up to four places in text; *n* is a user-determined number from 0-3. Press *Ctrl-K*, followed by a single digit *n* (0-3). After marking your location, you can work elsewhere in the file and then easily return to the marked location by using the *Ctrl-Q N* command.

**Tab**                                                                             *Ctrl-I* or *Tab*

Tabs default to eight columns apart in the Turbo Pascal editor. You can change the tab size in the **O**ptions/**E**nvironment menu.

**Tab mode**                                                                 *Ctrl-O T* or *Ctrl-Q T*

With Tab mode on, a tab is placed in the text using a fixed tab stop of 8. Toggle it off, and it spaces to the beginning of the first letter of each word in the previous line.

**Language help**                                                                        *Ctrl-F1*

While in the editor and with the cursor positioned on a constant, variable, procedure, function, or unit, pressing *Ctrl-F1* will bring up help on the specified item.

**Insert compiler directives**                                                           *Ctrl-F7*

If you haven't changed any of the default switch settings on the **O**ptions/**C**ompiler menu, pressing *Ctrl-F7* will insert the default compiler directives at the top of the file in the editor.

# The Turbo Pascal Editor versus WordStar

A few of the Turbo Pascal editor's commands are slightly different from WordStar. The Turbo Pascal editor contains only a subset of WordStar's commands, several features not found in WordStar have been added to enhance program source-code editing. These differences are discussed here, in alphabetical order.

**Autoindent**

The Turbo Pascal editor's *Ctrl-O I* command toggles the autoindent feature on and off.

### Cursor movement

Turbo Pascal's cursor movement controls—*Ctrl-S, Ctrl-D, Ctrl-E,* and *Ctrl-X*—move freely around on the screen without jumping to column one on empty lines. This does not mean that the screen is full of blanks, on the contrary, all trailing blanks are automatically removed. This way of moving the cursor is especially useful for program editing, for example, when matching indented statements.

### Delete to left

The WordStar sequence *Ctrl-Q Del* (delete from cursor position to beginning of line) is not supported.

### Mark word as block

Turbo Pascal allows you to mark a single word as a block using *Ctrl-K T.* This is more convenient than WordStar's two-step process of separately marking the beginning and the end of the word.

### Movement across line breaks

*Ctrl-S* and *Ctrl-D* do not work across line breaks. To move from one line to another you must use *Ctrl-E, Ctrl-X, Ctrl-A,* or *Ctrl-F.*

### Quit edit

Turbo Pascal's *Ctrl-K Q* does not resemble WordStar's *Ctrl-K Q* (quit edit) command. In Turbo Pascal, the changed text is not abandoned—it is left in memory, ready to be compiled and saved.

### Undo

Turbo Pascal's *Ctrl-Q L* command restores a line to its pre-edit contents as long as the cursor has not left the line.

### Updating disk file

Since editing in Turbo Pascal is done entirely in memory, the *Ctrl-K D* command does not change the file on disk as it does in WordStar. You must explicitly update the disk file with the Save option within the File menu or by using *Ctrl-K S* or *F2* within the editor.

# 12

# Command-Line Reference

For you die-hard hackers using custom editors and extended batch files—good news: Turbo Pascal 4.0 comes with a command-line version of the compiler so you can use the Turbo Pascal compiler without entering the integrated environment (TURBO.EXE). This version of the compiler—identical to the one in TURBO.EXE—is called TPC.EXE and is found on your distribution disk.

## Using the Compiler

Using TPC.EXE is easy; at the prompt, type

```
tpc [options] filename [options]
```

If *filename* does not have an extension, then TPC will assume .PAS. If you don't want the file you're compiling to have an extension, then append a period (.) to the end of *filename*. If you omit both *options* and *filename*, then TPC outputs a summary of its syntax and command-line options.

You can specify a number of options for TPC. An option consists of a slash (/) followed by one or two characters, either a letter or a dollar sign, followed by a letter. In some cases, the option is then followed by additional information, such as a path or a file name. Options can be given in any order and can come before and/or after the file name.

When you type the command, TPC compiles the file, links in the necessary runtime routines, and produces a file named *filename*.EXE. TPC has the same "smart" linker as TURBO, removing "dead" code and only linking in those routines actually needed. (If you compile a unit, it doesn't link, it produces a .TPU file.)

# Compiler Options

The integrated environment (TURBO) allows you to set various options using the menus. The command-line compiler (TPC) gives you access to most of those same options using the slash/command method described earlier. Alternately, you can precede options with a dash (-) instead of a slash (/). However, options that start with a dash must be separated from each other by blanks; those starting with a slash don't need to be separated but it's legal to do so.  So, for example, the following two command lines are equivalent and legal:

```
tpc -ic:\tp\include -xnames.dta sortname -$r- -$f+
tpc /ic:\tp\include/xnames.dta sortname /$r-/$f+
```

The first uses dashes, and so at least one blank separates options from each other; the second uses slashes, so no separation is needed.

Table 12.1 lists all the command-line options and gives their integrated environment equivalents.  In some cases, a single command-line option corresponds to two or three menu commands.

Table 12.1: Command-Line Options

| Command line | Menu selection |
| --- | --- |
| /$B+ | Options/Compiler/Boolean evaluation…Complete |
| /$B- | Options/Compiler/Boolean evaluation…Short Circuit |
| /$D+ | Options/Compiler/Debug information…On |
| /$D- | Options/Compiler/Debug information…Off |
| /$F+ | Options/Compiler/Force far calls…On |
| /$F- | Options/Compiler/Force far calls…Off |
| /$I+ | Options/Compiler/I/O checking…On |
| /$I- | Options/Compiler/I/O checking…Off |
| /$L+ | Options/Compiler/Link buffer...Memory |
| /$L- | Options/Compiler/Link buffer...Disk |
| /$Msss,min,max | Options/Compiler/Memory sizes |
| /$N+ | Options/Compiler/Numeric processing…Hardware |
| /$N- | Options/Compiler/Numeric processing…Software |
| /$R+ | Options/Compiler/Range checking…On |
| /$R- | Options/Compiler/Range checking…Off |
| /$S+ | Options/Compiler/Stack checking…On |
| /$S- | Options/Compiler/Stack checking…Off |
| /$T+ | Options/Compiler/Turbo pascal map file generation..On |
| /$T- | Options/Compiler/Turbo pascal map file generation..Off |
| /$V+ | Options/Compiler/Var-string checking…On |
| /$V- | Options/Compiler/Var-string checking…Off |

| Command line | Menu selection |
|---|---|
| /B | Compile/**Build** |
| /E*path* | **O**ptions/**D**irectories/**E**xecutable directory |
| /F*seg:ofs* | Compile/**F**ind error |
| /I*path* | **O**ptions/**D**irectories/**I**nclude directories |
| /M | Compile/**M**ake |
| /O*path* | **O**ptions/**D**irectories/**O**bject directories |
| /R*parms* | Compile/**D**estination...**M**emory |
| | **Run** |
| | **O**ptions/**P**arameters |
| | **Run** |
| /T*path* | **O**ptions/**D**irectories/**T**urbo directory |
| /U*path* | **O**ptions/**D**irectories/**U**nit directories |
| /X*parms* | Compile/**D**estination...**D**isk |
| | **O**ptions/**P**arameters |
| | **Run** |
| /D*defines* | **O**ptions/**C**ompiler/**C**onditional defines |
| /Q | (none) |

## *The Compiler Directive (/$) Command*

Turbo Pascal supports several compiler directives, some of which have been discussed in previous chapters, and all of which are described in Appendix C. These directives are usually embedded in the source code, taking one of the following forms:

```
{$directive+}
{$directive-}
{$directive info}
```

where *directive* is a single letter. These directives can also be specified on the command line, using the /$ or –$ option. Hence,

```
tpc mystuff /$r-
```

would compile MYSTUFF.PAS with range-checking turned off, while

```
tpc mystuff /$r+
```

would compile it with range-checking turned on. You can, of course, repeat this option in order to specify multiple compiler directives:

```
tpc mystuff /$r-/$i-/$v-/$f+
```

Remember, though, that if you use the dash instead of the slash, you must separate directives with at least one blank:

```
tpc mystuff -$r- -$i- -$v- -$f+
```

Alternately, TPC will allow you to put a list of directives (except for $M$),
separated by commas:

```
tpc mystuff /$r-,i-,v-,f+
```

Note that no dollar signs ($) are needed after the first one.

The one exception to this format is the memory allocation options ($M$). It
takes the format

```
/$mstack,heapmin,heapmax
```

where *stack* is the stack size, *heapmin* is the minimum heap size, and
*heapmax* is the maximum heap size. All three values are in bytes, and each
is a decimal number unless it is preceded by a dollar sign ($), in which case
it is assumed to be hexadecimal. So, for example, the following command
lines are equivalent:

```
tpc mystuff /$m16384,0,655360
tpc mystuff /$m$4000,$0,$A0000
```

Note that because of this format, you cannot use the $M$ option in a list of
directives separated by commas.

## Compiler Mode Options

A few options affect how the compiler itself functions. These are /M
(**Make**), /B (**Build**), /Q (**Quiet**), and /F (**Find error**). As with the other
options, you can use the dash format but must remember to separate the
options with at least one blank.

### The Make (/M) Option

Just like TURBO, TPC has a built-in MAKE utility to aid in project
maintenance. The /M option instructs TPC to check the dependencies of
the program you're compiling. If it makes use of any units, then TPC
searches for the .PAS file for each unit. If the unit is found, TPC checks the
time and date of its last modification against the time and date of the .TPU
file created. If the .PAS file has been more recently modified, then TPC
recompiles the unit. Units in TURBO.TPL are excluded from this process.

While recompiling the unit, TPC checks for any dependencies that it might
have on other units, and deals with those units in the same manner. The
result is that all units used by your program are brought up to date before
your program is compiled.

If you were applying this option to the previous example, the command would be

```
tpc mystuff /m
```

This option is the same as the **Compile/M**ake command within the integrated environment (TURBO.EXE).


## The Build All (/B) Option

What if you're unsure about what has been updated or what hasn't? Instead of relying upon the /*M* (**Make**) option to determine what needs to be updated, you can tell TPC to update *all* files (units) upon which your program depends. To do that, use the /*B* option. Note that you can't use /*M* and /*B* at the same time (and, in fact, it wouldn't make any sense).

If you were using this option in the previous example, the command would be

```
tpc mystuff /b
```

This option is the same as the **Compile/B**uild command within the integrated environment (TURBO.EXE).


## The Quiet Mode (/Q) Option

A quiet mode option has been added to the command-line compiler. With the default switches, TPC will display the file name and line number of the program module currently being compiled. It also displays the total time required at the end of the compilation. In quiet option,

```
TPC mystuff /Q
```

will suppress the printing of file names and line numbers during the compilation. Normally, TPC reports elapsed compilation time based on the IBM PC's internal timer. On generic MS-DOS machines using the /*Q* option, the current file name and line number is only updated when files are opened and closed, and the compiler does not calculate the elapsed time.


## The Find Error (/F) Option

This command is equivalent to the **Compile/F**ind error within TURBO. When you encounter a runtime error, you're given both the error code and the offset where it occurred. This option tells TPC to find where that error occurred, *provided* you've created a .TPM file with **D**ebug info (via the $*T* and $*D* compiler directives).

Suppose you have a file called TEST.PAS that contains the following program:

```
program Oops;
var
  i : integer;
begin
  i := 0;
  i := i div i;                          { Force a divide by zero error }
end.
```

Go ahead and compile this program using the command-line compiler, and at the same time have the compiler generate a Turbo Pascal Map file (.TPM):

```
tpc test /$t+
```

If you do a DIR TEST.*, DOS lists three files:

```
TEST.PAS   - your source code
TEST.EXE   - executable file
TEST.TPM   - Turbo Pascal Map for TEST.EXE
```

Now, run TEST and get a runtime error:

```
C:\ > test
Runtime error 200 at 0000:0010
```

Notice that you're given an error code (200) and the segment and offset (0000:0010 in hex) of the instruction pointer (IP) where the error occurred. How do you figure out which line in your source code caused the error? Since you already have a .TPM file, simply invoke the compiler, use the find runtime error option, and specify the segment and offset as reported in the error message:

```
C:\ >tpc test /f0000:0010
Turbo Pascal Version 4.0 Copyright (c) 1987 Borland International
TEST.PAS(6): Target address found.
    i := i DIV i;
         ^
```

Note that `test` refers to the .TPM file name. The compiler gives you the file name and line number, and points to the offending line in your source code.

If a .TPM file had not been present, here's what the screen would look like:

```
C:\ >tpc test /f0000:0010
Turbo Pascal Version 4.0 Copyright (c) 1987 Borland International
Error 133: Old or missing map file (TEST.TPM).
```

When a program is executed from disk and a runtime error occurs, a .TPM file must be present in order to find the location of the error in the source code. In that case, you would have to first re-compile TEST.PAS with the /$T+ option. Then you'd invoke TPC again and specify /f<*segment*>:<*offset*>, as done earlier.

The /$T directive determines whether a .TPM file is created. The /$D directive controls whether line number information is put into that .TPM file. It is possible to generate a .TPM file that contains only symbols and no line numbers by typing

```
C:\ >tpc test /$t+ /$d-
```

Then, when the now-familiar runtime error occurs, you'll have problems when trying to find its location using the /f option:

```
C:\ >tpc test /f0000:0010
Turbo Pascal Version 4.0 Copyright (c) 1987 Borland International
Error 125: Module has no debug information (OOPS).
```

Since no line numbers were placed in the file (you specified /$D-), the compiler can only provide the module name where the runtime error occurred (inside program OOPS).

By the way, you can also compile this program using the command- line compiler, and run it at the same time. Then, just like when we're running a program from inside the integrated environment, you don't need a .TPM file to find the runtime error:

```
1   C:\ >tpc test /r
2   Turbo Pascal Version 4.0 Copyright (c) 1987 Borland International
3   TEST.PAS(7)
4   7 lines, 0.1 seconds, 32 bytes code, 587 bytes data.
5   Runtime error 200 at 0000:0010.
6   TEST.PAS(6): Division by zero.
7       i := i DIV i;
8         ^
```

On line 1, you compile TEST.PAS and run it in memory (/r). Program execution begins on line 5—there's that darn runtime error again. Since you compiled to memory and ran, all the symbol and line number information is still available to the compiler. So, when a runtime error occurs, the compiler has all the information it needs to locate the error in the source code.

## Directory Options

TPC supports several options that are equivalent to commands in the Options/Directories menu in the integrated environment. These options allow you to specify the five directories used by TPC: executable, include, object, Turbo, and unit.

The first option tells TPC where to put the executable (.EXE) file it creates; the other four tell it where to search for certain types of files.

### The Executable Directory (/E) Option

This option lets you tell TPC where to put the .EXE and .TPM files it creates. It takes a path name as its argument:

```
tpc mystuff /ec:\tp\exec
```

If no such option is given, then TPC creates the .EXE and .TPM files in the current directory. This option is the same as the **O/D/E**xecutable directories command within TURBO.

### The Include Directories (/I) Option

In addition to units, Turbo Pascal supports include files, specified using the {$I *filename*} compiler directive. You can, in turn, specify a given directory (or directories) to be searched for any include files. For example, if your program has some include directives, and the files are located in C:\TPC\INCLUDE, then you could use the following option:

```
tpc mystuff /ic:\tp\include
```

TPC will search for those include files in C:\TPC\INCLUDE *after* searching the current directory. You can specify more than one path name by separating them with semicolons (;). The directories will then be searched in the order given. This option is identical to the **O/D/I**nclude directories command in TURBO. If multiple /*I* directives are given, the directories are concatenated together. Thus

```
tpc mystuff /ic:\tp\include;d:\move
```

is the same as

```
tpc mystuff /ic:\tp\include/id:\move
```

### The Object Directories (/O) Option

Turbo Pascal allows you to link in external assembly language routines, as explained in Chapters 5 and 26. The source code directive {$L} allows you to specify the .OBJ file name to link in. The /*O* compiler option tells TPC where to look for those files, much like the /*I* option.

For example, if your program used some assembly language routines that had already been assembled and whose .OBJ files were stored in C:\TPC\ASM, then you could say

```
tpc mystuff /oc:\tp\asm
```

If TPC didn't find any files requested by MYSTUFF.PAS in the current directory, it would look for them in that subdirectory. Like the $I option, you can specify multiple subdirectories by separating the path names with semicolons (;). This is identical to the O/D/Object directories command within TURBO.

If multiple /O directives are given, the directories are concatenated together. Thus

```
tpc mystuff /oc:\tp\include;d:\move
```

is the same as

```
tpc mystuff /oc:\tp\include/id:\move
```

## The Turbo Directory (/T) Option

TPC needs to find two files when it is executed: TPC.CFG, the configuration file; and TURBO.TPL, the resident library file. TPC automatically searches the current directory; if you're running under version 3.x (or later) of MS-DOS, then it also searches the directory containing TPC.EXE. The /T option lets you specify one other directory in which to search. For example, you could say

```
tpc mystuff /tc:\tp\bin
```

**Note:** If you want the /T option to affect the search for TPC.CFG, it must be the very first command-line argument. This is identical to the O/D/Turbo directory command within TURBO.

## The Unit Directories (/U) Option

When you compile a program that uses units, TPC first checks if the units are in TURBO.TPL (which is loaded along with TPC). If they aren't, then TPC searches for *unitname*.TPU in the current directory. With the /U option, you tell TPC what other locations to search for units. As with the previous options, you can specify more than one path name as long as you separate them with semicolons. For example, if you had units in two different directories, you might type something like this:

```
tpc mystuff /uc:\tp\units1;c:\tp\units2
```

This tells TPC to look in C:\TP\UNITS1 and C:\TP\UNITS2 for any units it doesn't find in TURBO.TPL and the current directory. This is identical to the **O/D/Unit** directories command within TURBO.

If multiple */IU* directives are given, the directories are concatenated together. Thus

```
tpc mystuff /uc:\tp\include;d:\move
```

is the same as

```
tpc mystuff /uc:\tp\include/ud:\move
```

## *Program Execution Options*

The last two options direct TPC to execute your program if it successfully compiles. You can tell it to either execute it in memory or to create an .EXE file and then execute it. In both cases, you can pass command-line parameters to the program if desired.

### *The Run In Memory (/R) Option*

Often when you're developing a program, you enter a modify-and-test cycle during which you make small, incremental changes and then view the effects. Since you're often debugging at the same time, you may not want to constantly produce .EXE files for all your test versions. TPC helps to support that cycle by accepting an option that tells it to compile your program to memory—keep it in RAM instead of creating an .EXE file on the disk—and then run it. For example, if you enter the command

```
tpc mystuff /r
```

then TPC will compile and execute MYSTUFF, but won't write any code out to disk. If a runtime error occurs, TPC automatically finds the runtime error, tells you the error number, address, and message, offending file name and line number, and then prints the source line on the screen.

Should your program require a parameter line, you can give one after the /R option, making sure to enclose it in double quotes:

```
tpc mystuff /r"file1 file2"
```

Everything after the /R and up to (but not including) the next option is passed to the program as the parameter line.

If you need to pass multiple parameters to a program, enclose *all* parameters in double quotes. You can embed slashes and dashes in your parameter line:

```
tpc mystuff /m /r"file1/x file2/x -2"
```

In this case, three parameters would be passed to program mystuff: *file1/x*, *file2/x*, and *–2*.

### *The eXecute (/X) Option*

TPC normally compiles your program, links in any units needed, creates an
.EXE file, and then halts. This option instructs TPC to execute the resulting
.EXE file:

```
tpc mystuff /x
```

Execution, of course, does not take place if an error has occurred during
compilation and linking. As with the */R* option, you can also specify a
parameter line:

```
tpc mystuff /x"file1 file2"
```

# The TPC.CFG File

You can set up a list of options in a configuration file called TPC.CFG,
which can be used in addition to the options entered on the command line.
Each line in TPC.CFG corresponds to an extra command-line argument
inserted before the actual command-line arguments. Thus, by creating a
TPC.CFG file, you can change the default setting of any command-line
option.

TPC allows you to enter the same command-line option several times,
ignoring all but the last occurrence. This way, even though you've changed
some settings with a TPC.CFG file, you can still override them on the
command line.

When TPC starts, it looks for TPC.CFG in the current directory. If it doesn't
find it there and if you are running DOS 3.*x*, it looks in the start directory
(where TPC.EXE resides). To force TPC to look in a specific list of
directories (in addition to the current directory), specify a */T* command-
line option as the first option on the command line.

If TPC.CFG contains a line that does not start with a slash (/) or a dash (-),
that line defines a default file name to compile. In that case, starting TPC
with an empty command line (or with a command line consisting of
command-line options only) will compile the default file name, instead of
displaying a syntax summary.

Here's an example TPC.CFG file, defining some of the directories:

```
/tc:\tpc\bin\turbo
/uc:\tpc\units
/oc:\tpc\asm
```

Now, if you type

```
tpc mystuff
```

at the system prompt, TPC acts as if you had typed in the following:

```
tpc /tc:\tpc\bin/turbo /uc:\tpc\units /uc:\tpc\asm mystuff
```

compiles MYSTUFF with the indicated directories specified.

You could also set up your configuration file with certain sets of options already given; for example, if you always wanted range-checking off and wanted the program to be executed after compilation, you could modify TPC.CFG to contain

```
/tc:\tpc\bin\turbo
/uc:\tpc\units
/oc:\tpc\asm
/$R-
/r
```

Then you could simply type

```
tpc mystuff
```

to generate the command line

```
tpc /tc:\tpc\bin/turbo /uc:\tpc\units /oc:\tpc\asm /$R- /r mystuff
```

C H A P T E R

# 13

# Tokens and Constants

*Tokens* are the smallest meaningful units of text in a Pascal program, and they are categorized as special symbols, identifiers, labels, numbers, and string constants.

A Pascal program is made up of tokens and separators, where a separator is either a blank or a comment. Two adjacent tokens must be separated by one or more separators if each token is a reserved word, an identifer, a label, or a number.

Separators cannot be part of tokens except in string constants.

## Special Symbols and Reserved Words

Turbo Pascal uses the following subsets of the ASCII character set:

- **Letters**—the English alphabet, *A* through *Z* and *a* through *z*.
- **Digits**—the Arabic numerals 0 through 9.
- **Hex digits**—the Arabic numerals 0 through 9, the letters *A* through *F*, and the letters *a* through *f*.
- **Blanks**—the space character (ASCII 32) and all ASCII control characters (ASCII 0 to 31), including the end-of-line or return character (ASCII 13).

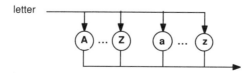

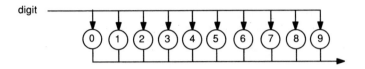

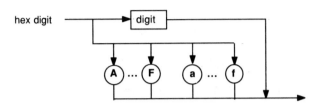

Special symbols and reserved words are characters that have one or more fixed meanings. These single characters are special symbols:

$$+ - * / = < > [ ] . , ( ) : ; \verb|^| @ \{ \} \$ \#$$

These character pairs are also special symbols:

$$<= >= := .. (* *) (. .)$$

Some special symbols are also operators. A left bracket ([) is equivalent to the character pair of left parentheses and a period ((.). Similarly, a right bracket (]) is equivalent to the character pair of a period and a right parentheses (.)).

Following are Turbo Pascal's reserved words:

| | | | | |
|---|---|---|---|---|
| absolute | end | inline | procedure | type |
| and | external | interface | program | unit |
| array | file | interrupt | record | until |
| begin | for | label | repeat | uses |
| case | forward | mod | set | var |
| const | function | nil | shl | while |
| div | goto | not | shr | with |
| do | if | of | string | xor |
| downto | implementation | or | then | |
| else | in | packed | to | |

Reserved words appear in lowercase **boldface** throughout this manual. Turbo Pascal isn't case sensitive, however, so you can use either uppercase or lowercase letters in your programs.

# Identifiers

Identifiers denote constants, types, variables, procedures, functions, units, programs, and fields in records. An identifier can be of any length, but only the first 63 characters are significant.

You'll notice that Turbo Pascal syntax is illustrated by diagrams. To read a syntax diagram, follow the arrows. Alternative paths are often possible; paths that begin at the left and end with an arrow on the right are valid. A path traverses boxes that hold the names of elements used to construct that portion of the syntax.

The names in rectangular boxes stand for actual constructions. Those in circular boxes—reserved words, operators, and punctuation—are the actual terms to be used in the program.

An identifier must begin with a letter and cannot contain spaces. Letters, digits, and underscore characters (ASCII $5F) are allowed after the first character. Like reserved words, identifiers are not case sensitive.

When several instances of the same identifier exist, you may need to qualify the identifier by a unit identifier in order to select a specific instance (units are described in Chapter 24). For example, to qualify the identifier *Ident* by the unit identifier *UnitName*, you would write *UnitName.Ident*. The combined identifier is called a *qualified identifier*.

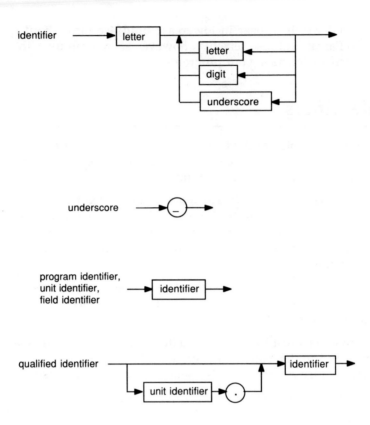

Here are some examples of identifiers:

```
Writeln
Exit
Real2String
System.MemAvail
Dos.Exec
Crt.Window
```

In this manual, standard and user-defined identifiers are *italicized* when they are referred to in text.

# Labels

A *label* is a digit sequence in the range 0 to 9999. Leading zeros are not significant. Labels are used with **goto** statements.

As an extension to standard Pascal, Turbo Pascal also allows identifiers to function as labels.

# Numbers

Ordinary decimal notation is used for numbers that are constants of type integer and real. A hexadecimal integer constant uses a dollar sign ($) as a prefix. Engineering notation (E or e, followed by an exponent) is read as "times ten to the power of" in real types. For example, 7E-2 means $7 \times 10^{-2}$; 12.25e+6 or 12.25e6 both mean $12.25 \times 10^{+6}$. Syntax diagrams for writing numbers follow.

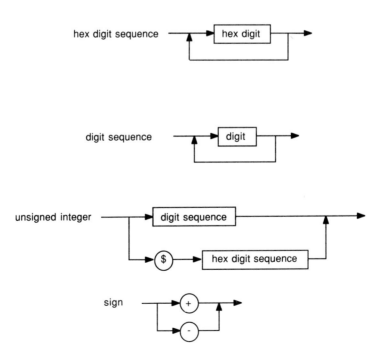

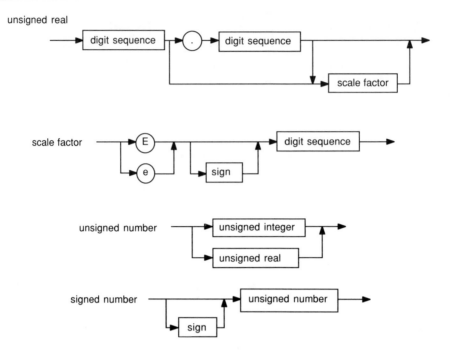

Numbers with decimals or exponents denote real-type constants. Other decimal numbers denote integer-type constants; they must be within the range –2147483648 to 2147483647.

Hexadecimal numbers denote integer-type constants; they must be within the range $00000000 to $FFFFFFFF. The resulting value's sign is implied by the hexademical notation.

# Character Strings

A character string is a sequence of zero or more characters from the extended ASCII character set (Appendix E), written on one line in the program and enclosed by apostrophes. A character string with nothing between the apostrophes is a *null string*. Two sequential apostrophes in a character string denote a single character, an apostrophe. The length attribute of a character string is the actual number of characters within the apostrophes.

As an extension to standard Pascal, Turbo Pascal allows control characters to be embedded in character strings. The # character followed by an unsigned integer constant in the range 0 to 255 denotes a character of the corresponding ASCII value. There must be no separators between the #

character and the integer constant. Likewise, if several control characters are part of a character string, there must be no separators between them.

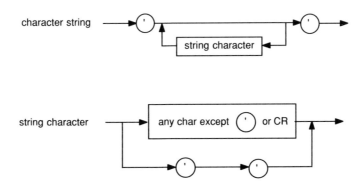

A character string of length zero (the null string) is compatible only with string types. A character string of length one is compatible with any char and string type. A character string of length *n*, where *n* is greater than or equal to 2, is compatible with any string type and with packed arrays of *n* characters.

Here are some examples of character strings:

```
'TURBO'      'You'll see'      ''''      ';'      ' '
#13#10       'Line 1'#13'Line2'      #7#7'Wake up!'#7#7
```

# Constant Declarations

A constant declaration declares an identifier that marks a constant within the block containing the declaration. A constant identifier cannot be included in its own declaration.

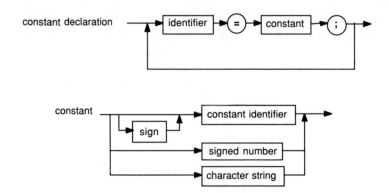

A constant identifier following a sign must denote a value of an integer or real type.

# Comments

The following constructs are comments and are ignored by the compiler:

```
{ Any text not containing right brace }
(* Any text not containing star/right parenthesis *)
```

A comment that contains a dollar sign ($) immediately after the opening { or (* is a compiler directive. A mnemonic of the compiler command follows the $ character. The compiler directives are summarized in Appendix C.

# Program Lines

Turbo Pascal program lines have a maximum length of 126 characters.

# 14

# Blocks, Locality, and Scope

A block is made up of declarations, which are written and combined in any order, and statements. Each block is part of a procedure declaration, a function declaration, or a program or unit. All identifiers and labels declared in the declaration part are local to the block.

## Syntax

The overall syntax of any block follows this format:

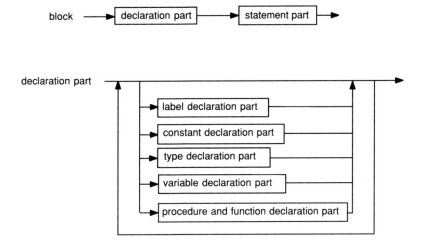

The *label declaration part* is where labels that mark statements in the corresponding statement part are declared. Each label must mark only one statement.

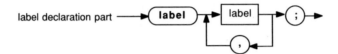

The digit sequence used for a label must be in the range 0 to 9999.

The *constant declaration part* consists of constant declarations local to the block.

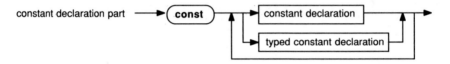

The *type declaration part* includes all type declarations to the block.

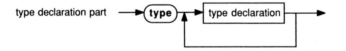

The *variable declaration part* is composed of variable declarations local to the block.

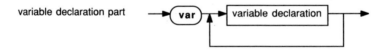

The *procedure and function declaration part* comprises procedure and function declarations local to the block.

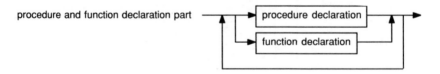

The *statement part* defines the statements or algorithmic actions to be executed by the block.

*Turbo Pascal Owner's Handbook*

statement part ⟶ compound statement ⟶

# Rules of Scope

The presence of an identifier or label in a declaration defines the identifier or label. Each time the identifier or label occurs again, it must be within the *scope* of this declaration. The scope of an identifier or label encompasses its declaration to the end of the current block, including all blocks enclosed by the current block; some exceptions follow.

- **Redeclaration in an enclosed block:** Suppose that *Exterior* is a block that encloses another block, *Interior*. If *Exterior* and *Interior* both have an identifier with the same name, for example, *j*, then *Interior* can only access the *j* it declared, and similarly Exterior can only access the *j* it declared.

- **Position of declaration within its block:** Identifiers and labels cannot be used until after they are declared. An identifier or label's declaration must come before any occurrence of that identifier or label in the program text, with one exception.

  The base type of a pointer type can be an identifier that has not yet been declared. However, the identifier must eventually be declared in the same type declaration part that the pointer type occurs in.

- **Redeclaration within a block:** An identifier or label can only be declared *once* in the outer level of a given block. The only exception to this is when it is declared within a contained block or is in a record's field list.

  A record field identifier is declared within a record type and is significant only in combination with a reference to a variable of that record type. So, you can redeclare a field identifier (with the same spelling) within the same block but not at the same level within the same record type. However, an identifier that has been declared can be redeclared as a field identifier in the same block.

# Scope of Interface and Standard Identifiers

Programs or units containing **uses** clauses have access to the identifiers belonging to the interface parts of the units in those **uses** clauses.

Each unit in a **uses** clause imposes a new scope that encloses the remaining units used and the entire program. The first unit in a **uses** clause represents the outermost scope, and the last unit represents the innermost scope. This implies that if two or more units declare the same identifier, an unqualified reference to the identifier will select the instance declared by the last unit in the **uses** clause. However, by writing a qualified identifier, every instance of the identifier can be selected.

The identifiers of Turbo Pascal's predefined constants, types, variables, procedures, and functions act as if they were declared in a block enclosing all used units and the entire program. In fact, these standard objects are defined in a unit called *System*, which is used by any program or unit before the units named in the **uses** clause. This suggests that any unit or program can redeclare the standard identifiers, but a specific reference can still be made through a qualified identifier, for example, *System.Integer* or *System.Writeln*.

*Turbo Pascal Owner's Handbook*

# 15

# Types

When you declare a variable, you must state its type. A variable's *type* circumscribes the set of values it can have and the operations that can be performed on it. A *type declaration* specifies the identifier that denotes a type.

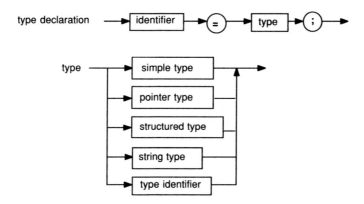

When an identifier occurs on the left side of a type declaration, it is declared as a type identifier for the block in which the type declaration occurs. A type identifier's scope does not include itself except for pointer types.

Following are the seven types of identifiers:

- simple type
- structured type
- pointer type

- ordinal type
- integer type
- real type
- string type

# Simple Types

Simple types define ordered sets of values.

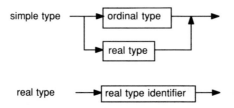

A type real identifier is one of the standard identifiers: real, single, double, extended, or comp. Refer to the sections entitled "Numbers" and "String Constants" in Chapter 13 to find out how to denote constant type integer and real values.

## *Ordinal Types*

Ordinal types are a subset of simple types. All simple types other than real types are ordinal types, which are set off by four characteristics:

- All possible values of a given ordinal type are an ordered set, and each possible value is associated with an *ordinality*, which is an integral value. Except for type intege values, the first value of every ordinal type has ordinality 0, the next has ordinality 1, and so on for each value in that ordinal type. An type integer value's ordinality is the value itself. In any ordinal type, each value other than the first has a predecessor, and each value other than the last has a successor based on the ordering of the type.
- The standard function *Ord* can be applied to any ordinal type value to return the ordinality of the value.
- The standard function *Pred* can be applied to any ordinal-type value to return the predecessor of the value. If applied to the first value in the ordinal type, *Pred* produces an error.

■ The standard function *Succ* can be applied to any ordinal-type value to return the successor of the value. If applied to the last value in the ordinal type, *Succ* produces an error.

The syntax of an ordinal type follows.

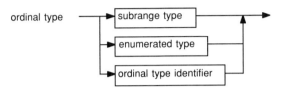

Turbo Pascal has seven predefined ordinal types: *integer, shortint, longint, byte, word, boolean*, and *char*. In addition, there are two other classes of user-defined ordinal types: enumerated types and subrange types.

## The Integer Type

There are five predefined integer types: *shortint, integer, longint, byte*, and *word*. Each type denotes a specific subset of the whole numbers, according to the following table:

Table 15.1: Predefined Integer Types

| Type | Range | Format |
|---|---|---|
| shortint | −128 .. 127 | Signed 8-bit |
| integer | −32768 .. 32767 | Signed 16-bit |
| longint | −2147483648 .. 2147483647 | Signed 32-bit |
| byte | 0 .. 255 | Unsigned 8-bit |
| word | 0 .. 65535 | Unsigned 16-bit |

Arithmetic operations with type integer operands use 8-bit, 16-bit, or 32-bit precision, according to the following rules:

- The type of an integer constant is the predefined integer type with the smallest range that includes the value of the integer constant.

- For a binary operator (an operator that takes two operands), both operands are converted to their common type before the operation. The *common type* is the predefined integer type with the smallest range that includes all possible values of both types. For instance, the common type of integer and byte is integer, and the common type of integer and word is longint. The operation is performed using the precision of the common type, and the result type is the common type.

- The expression on the right of an assignment statement is evaluated independently from the size or type of the variable on the left.

- Any byte-signed operand is converted to an intermediate word-signed operand that is compatible with both integer and word before any arithmetic operation is performed.

A type integer value can be explicitly converted to another integer type through typecasting. (Typecasting is described in Chapters 16 and 18.)

## The Boolean Type

Type boolean values are denoted by the predefined constant identifiers False and True. Because boolean is an enumerated type, these relationships hold:

- False < True
- *Ord*(False) = 0
- *Ord*(True) = 1
- *Succ*(False) = True
- *Pred*(True) = False

## The Char Type

This type's set of values are characters, ordered according to the extended ASCII character set (Appendix E). The function call *Ord(Ch)*, where *Ch* is a char value, returns *Ch*'s ordinality.

A string constant of length 1 can denote a constant char value. Any value of type char can be generated with the standard function *Chr*.

# The Enumerated Type

Enumerated types define ordered sets of values by enumerating the identifiers that denote these values. Their ordering follows the sequence in which the identifiers are enumerated.

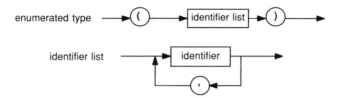

When an identifier occurs within the identifier list of an enumerated type, it is declared as a constant for the block in which the enumerated type is declared. This constant's type is the enumerated type being declared.

An enumerated constant's ordinality is determined by its position in the identifier list in which it is declared. The enumerated type in which it is declared becomes the constant's type. The first enumerated constant in a list has an ordinality of 0.

An example of an enumerated type follows:

```
suit = (club,diamond,heart,spade)
```

Given these declarations, *diamond* is a constant of type *suit*.

When the *Ord* function is applied to an enumerated type's value, *Ord* returns an integer that shows where the value falls with respect to the other values of the enumerated type. Given the preceding declarations, *Ord(club)* returns 0, *Ord(diamond)* returns 1, and so on.

# The Subrange Type

A subrange type is a range of values from an ordinal type called the *host type*. The definition of a subrange type specifies the least and the largest value in the subrange; its syntax follows:

Both constants must be of the same ordinal type. Subrange types of the form *a..b* require that *a* is less than or equal to *b*.

Examples of subrange types:

```
0..99
-128..127
club..heart
```

A variable of a subrange type has all the properties of variables of the host type, but its runtime value must be in the specified interval.

## The Real Type

A real type has a set of values that is a subset of real numbers, which can be represented in floating-point notation with a fixed number of digits. A value's floating-point notation normally comprises three values—$m$, $b$, and $e$—such that $m \times b^e = n$, where $b$ is always 2, and both $m$ and $e$ are integral values within the real type's range. These $m$ and $e$ values further prescribe the real type's range and precision.

There are five kinds of real types: *real*, *single*, *double*, *extended*, and *comp*. The single, double, extended, and comp types can only be operated on if you have an 8087 numeric coprocessor (explained later).

The real types differ in the range and precision of values they hold (see Table 15.2).

Table 15.2: Real Data Types

| Type | Range | Significant Digits | Size in Bytes |
|------|-------|--------------------|---------------|
| real | 2.9 X 10E-39 .. 1.7 X 10E38 | 11-12 | 6 |
| single | 1.5 X 10E-45 .. 3.4 X 10E38 | 7- 8 | 4 |
| double | 5.0 X 10E-324 .. 1.7 X 10E308 | 15-16 | 8 |
| extended | 1.9 X 10E-4951 .. 1.1 X 10E4932 | 19-20 | 10 |
| comp* | −2E+63+1..2E+63-1 | 19-20 | 8 |

* comp only holds integer values.

The comp type holds only integral values within the range $-2^{63}+1$ to $2^{63}-1$, which is approximately $-9.2 \times 10^{18}$ to $9.2 \times 10^{18}$.

Turbo Pascal supports two models of code generation for performing real-type operations: *software* floating point and *hardware* floating point. The appropriate model is selected through the $N compiler directive.

## Software Floating Point

In the $N- state, which is selected by default, the code generated performs all type real calculations in software by calling runtime library routines. For reasons of speed and code size, only operations on variables of type real are allowed in this state. Any attempt to compile statements that operate on the single, double, extended, and comp types generate an error.

## Hardware Floating Point

In the $N+ state, the code generated performs all type real calculations using the 8087 numeric coprocessor. This state permits the use of all five real types, but it requires the presence of an 8087 coprocessor at runtime and compile time.

For further details on hardware floating-point code generation, refer to Chapter 25, "Using the 8087 with Turbo Pascal."

# String Types

A type string value is a sequence of characters with a dynamic length attribute (depending on the actual character count during program execution) and a constant size attribute from 1 to 255. A string type declared without a size attribute is given the default size attribute 255. The length attribute's current value is returned by the standard function *Length*.

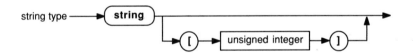

The ordering between any two string values is set by the ordering relationship of the character values in corresponding positions. In two strings of unequal length, each character in the longer string without a corresponding character in the shorter string takes on a higher or greater-than value; for example, 'Xs' is greater than 'X'. Null strings can only be equal to other null strings, and they hold the least string values.

Characters in a string can be accessed as components of an array, as described in "Arrays, Strings, and Indexes" in Chapter 16. Type string operators are described in "String Operators" and "Relational Operators" in Chapter 20. Type string standard procedures and functions are described in "String Procedures and Functions" in Chapter 25.

# Structured Types

A structured type, characterized by its structuring method and by its component type(s), holds more than one value. If a component type is structured, the resulting structured type has more than one level of structuring. A structured type can have unlimited levels of structuring.

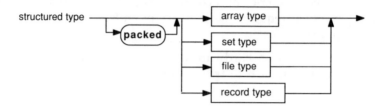

The word **packed** in a structured type's declaration tells the compiler to compress data storage, even at the cost of diminished access to a component of a variable of this type. The word **packed** has no effect in Turbo Pascal; instead packing occurs automatically whenever possible.

**Note:** The maximum permitted size of any structured type in Turbo Pascal is 65520 bytes.

## *Array Types*

Arrays have a fixed number of components of one type—the component type. In the following syntax diagram, the component type follows the word **of**.

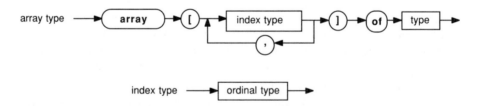

The index types, one for each dimension of the array, specify the number of elements. Valid index types are all ordinal types except longint and subranges of longint. The array can be indexed in each dimension by all values of the corresponding index type; the number of elements is therefore the number of values in each index type. The number of dimensions is unlimited.

The following is an example of an array type:

```
array[1..100] of real
```

If an array type's component type is also an array, you can treat the result as an array of arrays or as a single multidimensional array. For instance,

```
array[boolean] of array[1..10] of array[Size] of real
```

is interpreted the same way by the compiler as

```
array[boolean,1..10,Size] of real
```

You can also express

```
packed array[1..10] of packed array[1..8] of boolean
```

as

```
packed array[1..10,1..8] of boolean
```

You access an array's components by supplying the array's identifier with one or more indexes in brackets (see "Arrays, Strings, and Indexes" in Chapter 16).

An array type of the form

```
packed array[m..n] of char
```

where *m* is less than *n* is called a packed string type (the word **packed** may be omitted, because it has no effect in Turbo Pascal). A packed string type has certain properties not shared by other array types (see "Identical and Compatible Types" later in this chapter).

## *Record Types*

A record type comprises a set number of components, or fields, that can be of different types. The record type declaration specifies the type of each field and the identifier that names the field.

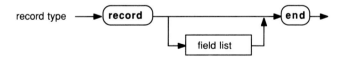

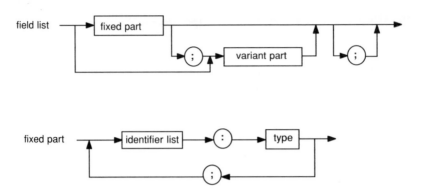

The fixed part of a record type sets out the list of fixed fields, giving an identifier and a type for each. Each field contains information that is always retrieved in the same way.

The following is an example of a record type:

```
record
  year:  integer;
  month: 1..12;
  day:   1..31;
end
```

The variant part shown in the syntax diagram of a record type declaration distributes memory space for more than one list of fields, so the information can be accessed in more ways than one. Each list of fields is a *variant*. The variants overlay the same space in memory, and all fields of all variants can be accessed at all times.

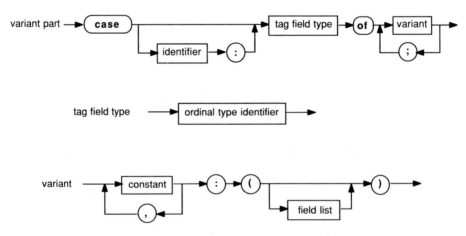

You can see from the diagram that each variant is identified by at least one constant. All constants must be distinct and of an ordinal type compatible with the tag-field type. Variant and fixed fields are accessed the same way.

An optional identifier, the tag-field identifier, can be placed in the variant part. If a tag-field identifier is present, it becomes the identifier of an additional fixed field—the tag field—of the record. The program can use the tag field's value to show which variant is active at a given time. Without a tag field, the program selects a variant by another criterion.

Some record types with variants follow.

```
record
  firstName,lastName : string[40];
  birthDate : Date;
  case citizen : boolean of
    True  : (birthPlace: string[40]);
    False : (country   : string[20];
             entryPort : string[20];
             entryDate : Date;
             exitDate  : Date);
end

record
  x,y : real;
  case kind : Figure of
    rectangle : (height,width: real);
    triangle : (size1,side2,angle: real);
    circle : (radius: real);
end
```

## *Set Types*

A set type's range of values is the power set of a particular ordinal type (the base type). Each possible value of a set type is a subset of the possible values of the base type.

A variable of a set type can hold from none to all values of the set.

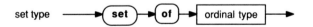

The base type must not have more than 256 possible values, and the ordinal values of the upper and lower bounds of the base type must be within the range 0 to 255. For these reasons, the base type of a set cannot be shortint, integer, longint, or word.

Set-type operators are described in the section entitled "Set Operators" in Chapter 18. "Set Constructors" in the same chapter shows how to construct set values.

Every set type can hold the value [ ], which is called the *empty set*.

## File Types

A file type consists of a linear sequence of components of the component type, which can be of any type except a file type or any structured type with a file-type component. The number of components is not set by the file-type declaration.

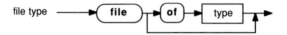

If the word **of** and the component type are omitted, the type denotes an untyped file. Untyped files are low-level I/O channels primarily used for direct access to any disk file regardless of its internal format.

The standard file type *Text* signifies a file containing characters organized into lines. Text files use special input/output procedures, which are discussed in Chapter 24.

# Pointer Types

A pointer type defines a set of values that point to dynamic variables of a specified type called the *base* type. A type pointer variable contains the memory address of a dynamic variable.

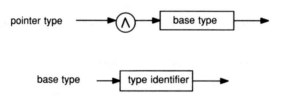

If the base type is an undeclared identifier, it must be declared in the same type declaration part as the pointer type.

You can assign a value to a pointer variable with the *New* procedure, the @ operator, or the *Ptr* function. The *New* procedure allocates a new memory area in the application heap for a dynamic variable and stores the address of that area in the pointer variable. The @ operator directs the pointer variable to the memory area containing any existing variable, including variables that already have identifiers. The *Ptr* function points the pointer variable to a specific memory address.

The reserved word **nil** denotes a pointer-valued constant that does not point to anything.

The predefined type pointer denotes an untyped pointer, that is, a pointer that does not point to any specific type. Variables of type Pointer cannot be dereferenced; writing the pointer symbol ^ after such a variable is an error. Like the value denoted by the word **nil**, values of type pointer are compatible with all other pointer types.

See Chapter 16's section entitled "Pointers and Dynamic Variables" for the syntax of referencing the dynamic variable pointed to by a pointer variable.

# Identical and Compatible Types

Two types may be the same, and this sameness (identity) is mandatory in some contexts. At other times, the two types need only be compatible or merely assignment-compatible. They are identical when they are declared with, or their definitions stem from, the same type identifier.

## Type Identity

Type identity is required only between actual and formal variable parameters in procedure and function calls.

Two types—say, *T1* and *T2*—are identical if one of the following is True: *T1* and *T2* are the same type identifier; *T1* is declared to be equivalent to a type identical to *T2*.

The second condition connotes that *T1* does not have to be declared directly to be equivalent to *T2*. The type declarations

```
T1 = integer;
T2 = T1;
T3 = integer;
T4 = T2;
```

result in *T1, T2, T3, T4*, and integer as identical types. The type declarations

```
T5 = set of integer;
T6 = set of integer;
```

don't make *T5* and *T6* identical, since **set of** *integer* is not a type identifier. Two variables declared in the same declaration, for example:

```
V1, V2: set of integer;
```

are of identical types—unless the declarations are separate. The declarations

```
V1: set of integer;
V2: set of integer;
V3: integer;
V4: integer;
```

mean *V3* and *V4* are of identical type, but not *V1* and *V2*.

## Type Compatibility

Compatibility between two types is sometimes required, such as in expressions or in relational operations. Type compatibility is important, however, as a precondition of assignment compatibility.

Type compatibility exists when at least one of the following conditions is True:

- Both types are the same.
- Both types are real types.
- Both types are integer types.
- One type is a subrange of the other.
- Both types are subranges of the same host type.
- Both types are set types with compatible base types.
- Both types are packed string types with an identical number of components.
- One type is a string type and the other is a string type, packed string type, or char type.
- One type is pointer and the other is any pointer type.

## Assignment Compatibility

Assignment compatibility is necessary when a value is assigned to something, such as in an assignment statement or in passing value parameters.

A value of type $T_2$ is assignment-compatible with a type $T_1$ (that is, $T_1 := T_2$ is allowed) if any of the following are True:

- $T_1$ and $T_2$ are identical types and neither is a file type or a structured type that contains a file-type component at any level of structuring.
- $T_1$ and $T_2$ are compatible ordinal types, and the values of type $T_2$ falls within the range of possible values of $T_1$.
- $T_1$ and $T_2$ are real types, and the value of type $T_2$ falls within the range of possible values of $T_1$.

- $T_1$ is a real type, and $T_2$ is an integer type.
- $T_1$ and $T_2$ are string types.
- $T_1$ is a string type, and $T_2$ is a char type.
- $T_1$ is a string type, and $T_2$ is a packed string type.
- $T_1$ and $T_2$ are compatible, packed string types.
- $T_1$ and $T_2$ are compatible set types, and all the members of the value of type $T_2$ fall within the range of possible values of $T_1$.
- $T_1$ and $T_2$ are compatible pointer types.

A compile or runtime error occurs when assignment compatibility is necessary and none of the items in the preceding list are True.

# The Type Declaration Part

Programs, procedures, and functions that declare types have a type declaration part. An example of this follows:

```
type
  Range       = integer;
  Number      = integer;
  Color       = (red,green,blue);
  TestIndex   = 1..100;
  TestValue   = -99..99;
  TestList    = array[TestIndex] of TestValue;
  TestListPtr = ^TestList;
  Date        = record
                    year: integer;
                    month: 1..12;
                    day: 1..31;
                end;
  MeasureData = record
                    when: Date;
                    count: TestIndex;
                    data: TestListPtr;
                end;
  MeasureList = array[1..50] of MeasureData;
  Name        = string[80];
  Sex         = (male,female);
  Person      = ^PersonData;
  PersonData  = record
                    name,firstName: Name;
                    age:            integer;
                    married:        boolean;
                    father,child,sibling: Person;
                      case s: Sex of
                        male:   (bearded: boolean);
                        female: (pregnant: boolean);
                end;
  People   = file of PersonData;
  IntFile  = file of integer
```

In the example, *Range*, *Number*, and integer are identical types. *TestIndex* is compatible and assignment-compatible with, but not identical to, the types *Number*, *Range*, and integer.

C  H  A  P  T  E  R

# 16

# Variables

## Variable Declarations

A variable declaration embodies a list of identifiers that designate new variables and their type.

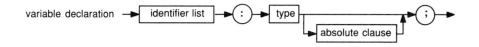

The type given for the variable(s) can be a type identifier previously declared in a **type** declaration part in the same block, in an enclosing block, or in a unit, or it can be a new type definition.

When an identifier is specified within the identifier list of a variable declaration, that identifier is a variable identifier for the block in which the declaration occurs. The variable can then be referred to throughout the block, unless the identifier is redeclared in an enclosed block. Redeclaration causes a new variable using the same identifier, without affecting the value of the original variable.

An example of a variable declaration part follows:

```
var
  X,Y,Z: real;
  I,J,K: integer;
  Digit: 0..9;
  C: Color;
  Done,Error: boolean;
  Operator: (plus, minus, times);
  Hue1,Hue2: set of Color;
```

```
Today: Date;
Results: MeasureList;
P1,P2: Person;
Matrix: array[1..10,1..10] of real;
```

Variables declared outside procedures and functions are called *global variables*, and reside in the *data segment*. Variables declared within procedures and functions are called *local variables*, and reside in the *stack segment*.

## *The Data Segment*

The maximum size of the data segment is 65520 bytes. When a program is linked (this happens automatically at the end of the compilation of a program), the global variables of all units used by the program, as well as the program's own global variables, are placed in the data segment.

If you need more than 65520 bytes of global data, you should allocate the larger structures as dynamic variables. For further details on this subject, see "Pointers and Dynamic Variables" later in this chapter.

## *The Stack Segment*

The size of the stack segment is set through a *$M* compiler directive—it can be anywhere from 1024 to 65520 bytes. The default stack segment size is 16384 bytes.

Each time a procedure or function is activated (called), it allocates a set of local variables on the stack. On exit, the local variables are disposed. At any time during the execution of a program, the total size of the local variables allocated by the active procedures and functions cannot exceed the size of the stack segment.

The *$S* compiler directive is used to include stack overflow checks in the code. In the default {$S+} state, code is generated to check for stack overflow at the beginning of each procedure and function. In the {$S-} state, no such checks are performed. A stack overflow may very well cause a system crash, so don't turn off stack checks unless you are absolutely sure that an overflow will never occur.

## Absolute Variables

Variables can be declared to reside at specific memory addresses, and are then called *absolute variables*. The declaration of such variables must include an **absolute** clause following the type:

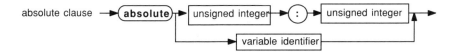

Note that the variable declaration's identifier list can only specify one identifier when an **absolute** clause is present.

The first form of the **absolute** clause specifies the segment and offset at which the variable is to reside:

```
CrtMode : byte absolute $0040:$0049;
```

The first constant specifies the segment base, and the second specifies the offset within that segment. Both constants must be within the range $0000 to $FFFF (0 to 65535).

The second form of the **absolute** clause is used to declare a variable "on top" of another variable, meaning it declares a variable that resides at the same memory address as another variable.

```
var
  Str: string[32];
  StrLen: byte absolute Str;
```

This declaration specifies that the variable *StrLen* should start at the same address as the variable *Str*, and because the first byte of a string variable contains the dynamic length of the string, *StrLen* will contain the length of *Str*.

# Variable References

A variable reference signifies one of the following:

- a variable
- a component of a structured- or string-type variable
- a dynamic variable pointed to by a pointer-type variable

The syntax for a variable reference is

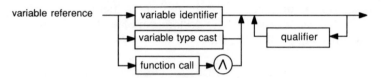

Note that the syntax for a variable reference allows a function call to a pointer function. The resulting pointer is then dereferenced to denote a dynamic variable.

# Qualifiers

A variable reference is a variable identifier with zero or more qualifiers that modify the meaning of the variable reference.

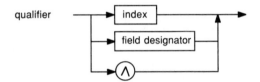

An array identifier with no qualifier, for example, references the entire array:

```
Results
```

An array identifier followed by an index denotes a specific component of the array—in this case a structured variable:

```
Results[Current+1]
```

With a component that is a record, the index can be followed by a field designator; here the variable access signifies a specific field within a specific array component.

```
Results[Current+1].data
```

The field designator in a pointer field can be followed by the pointer symbol (a ^) to differentiate between the pointer field and the dynamic variable it points to.

```
Results[Current+1].data^
```

If the variable being pointed to is an array, indexes can be added to denote components of this array.

```
Results[Current+1].data^[J]
```

## Arrays, Strings, and Indexes

A specific component of an array variable is denoted by a variable reference that refers to the array variable, followed by an index that specifies the component.

A specific character within a string variable is denoted by a variable reference that refers to the string variable, followed by an index that specifies the character position.

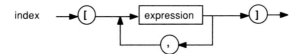

The index expressions select components in each corresponding dimension of the array. The number of expressions can't exceed the number of index types in the array declaration. Furthermore, each expression's type must be assignment-compatible with the corresponding index type.

When indexing a multidimensional array, multiple indexes or multiple expressions within an index can be used interchangeably. For example:

```
Matrix[I][J]
```

is the same as

```
Matrix[I,J]
```

You can index a string variable with a single index expression, whose value must be in the range 0..*n*, where *n* is the declared size of the string. This accesses one character of the string value, with the type char given to that character value.

The first character of a string variable (at index 0) contains the dynamic length of the string; that is, *Length(S)* is the same as *Ord(S[0])*. If a value is assigned to the length attribute, the compiler does not check whether this value is less than the declared size of the string. It is possible to index a string beyond its current dynamic length. The characters thus read are random, and assignments beyond the current length will not affect the actual value of the string variable.

## Records and Field Designators

A specific field of a record variable is denoted by a variable reference that refers to the record variable, followed by a field designator specifying the field.

Some examples of a field designator include:

```
Today.year
Results[1].count
Results[1].when.month
```

In a statement within a **with** statement, a field designator doesn't have to be preceded by a variable reference to its containing record.

## Pointers and Dynamic Variables

The value of a pointer variable is either **nil** or the address of a value that points to a dynamic variable.

The dynamic variable pointed to by a pointer variable is referenced by writing the pointer symbol (^) after the pointer variable.

You create dynamic variables and their pointer values with the standard procedures *New* and *GetMem*. You can use the @ operator and the standard function *Ptr* to create pointer values that are treated as pointers to dynamic variables.

**nil** does not point to any variable. The results are undefined if you access a dynamic variable when the pointer's value is **nil** or undefined.

Some examples of references to dynamic variables:

```
P1^
P1^.sibling^
Results[1].data^
```

# Variable Typecasts

A variable reference of one type can be changed into a variable reference of another type through a *variable typecast*.

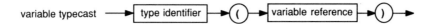

variable typecast → type identifier → ( → variable reference → ) →

When a variable typecast is applied to a variable reference, the variable reference is treated as an instance of the type specified by the type identifier. The size of the variable (the number of bytes occupied by the variable) must be the same as the size of the type denoted by the type identifier. A variable typecast can be followed by one or more qualifiers, as allowed by the specified type.

Some examples of variable typecasts follow:

```
type
  Point = record
            x,y: integer;
          end;
  List  = array[1..2] of integer;
var
  P: Point;
  L: longint;
  N: integer;
begin
  P := Point(L);
  N := Point(L).x;
  longint(P) := longint(P) + $00080008;
  List(P)[N] := 32;
end.
```

The built-in functions *Hi* and *Lo* return the high- and low-order bytes of a word or integer variable. To determine the high- and low-order words of a long integer variable, you should use a value typecast:

```
type
  WordRec = record                { used for typecast }
    Low, High : word;
end;

var
  L : longint;
begin
  L := $10000;                    { 65536 decimal }
  Writeln(WordRec(L).Low);        { 0 }
  Writeln(WordRec(L).High);       { 1 }
end.
```

Similarly, here's an inexpensive (code-wise) alternative to the *Seg* and *Ofs* functions:

```
type
  PtrRec = record                 { used for typecast }
    Ofs, Seg : word;
```

```
end;

var
  P : pointer;
begin
  P := Ptr($1234, $4567);
  Writeln(PtrRec(P).Ofs);        { $4567 }
  Writeln(PtrRec(P).Seg);        { $1234 }
end.
```

This generates less code and is faster than using the standard functions *Seg* and *Ofs*. Value typecasting is described in more detail in Chapter 18.

# 17

# Typed Constants

Typed constants can be compared to initialized variables—variables whose values are defined on entry to their block. Unlike an untyped constant (see the section entitled "Constant Declarations" in Chapter 13), the declaration of a typed constant specifies both the type and the value of the constant.

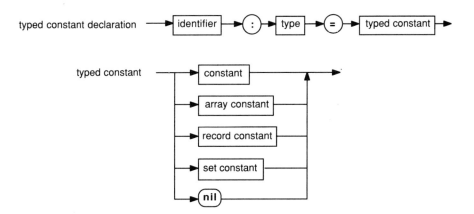

Typed constants can be used exactly like variables of the same type, and can appear on the left-hand side in an assignment statement. Note that typed constants are initialized *only once*—at the beginning of a program. Thus, for each entry to a procedure or function, the locally declared typed constants are not reinitialized.

# Simple-Type Constants

Declaring a typed constant as a simple type simply specifies the value of the constant:

```
const
  Maximum   : integer = 9999;
  Factor    : real = -0.1;
  Breakchar : char = #3;
```

Because a typed constant is actually a variable with a constant value, it cannot be interchanged with ordinary constants. For instance, it cannot be used in the declaration of other constants or types.

```
const
  Min : integer = 0;
  Max : integer = 99;
type
  Vector = array[Min..Max] of integer;
```

The *Vector* declaration is invalid, because *Min* and *Max* are typed constants.

# String-Type Constants

The declaration of a typed constant of a string type specifies the maximum length of the string and its initial value:

```
const
  Heading  : string[7] = 'Section';
  NewLine  : string[2] = #13#10;
  TrueStr  : string[5] = 'Yes';
  FalseStr : string[5] = 'No';
```

# Structured-Type Constants

The declaration of a structured-type constant specifies the value of each of the structure's components. Turbo Pascal supports the declaration of type array, record, set, and pointer constants; type file constants, and constants of array and record types that contain type file components are not allowed.

# Array-Type Constants

The declaration of an array-type constant specifies, enclosed in parentheses and separated by commas, the values of the components.

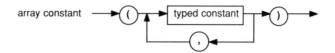

An example of an array-type constant follows:

```
type
  Status = (Active,Passive,Waiting);
  StatusMap = array[Status] of string[7];
const
  StatStr: StatusMap = ('Active','Passive','Waiting');
```

This example defines the array constant *StatStr*, which can be used to convert values of type *Status* into their corresponding string representations. The components of *StatStr* are

```
StatStr[Active]  = 'Active'
StatStr[Passive] = 'Passive'
StatStr[Waiting] = 'Waiting'
```

The component type of an array constant can be any type except a file type. Packed string-type constants (character arrays) can be specified both as single characters and as strings. The definition

```
const
  Digits: array[0..9] of char = ('0','1','2','3','4','5','6','7','8','9');
```

can be expressed more conveniently as

```
const
  Digits: array[0..9] of char = '0123456789';
```

Multidimensional array constants are defined by enclosing the constants of each dimension in separate sets of parentheses, separated by commas. The innermost constants correspond to the rightmost dimensions. The declaration

```
type
  Cube = array[0..1,0..1,0..1] of integer;
const
  Maze: Cube = (((0,1),(2,3)),((4,5),(6,7)));
```

provides an initialized array *Maze* with the following values:

```
Maze[0,0,0] = 0
```

```
Maze[0,0,1] = 1
Maze[0,1,0] = 2
Maze[0,1,1] = 3
Maze[1,0,0] = 4
Maze[1,0,1] = 5
Maze[1,1,0] = 6
Maze[1,1,1] = 7
```

## Record-Type Constants

The declaration of a record-type constant specifies the identifier and value of each field, enclosed in parentheses and separated by semicolons.

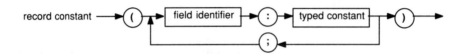

Some examples of record constants follow:

```
type
  Point  = record
             x,y: real;
           end;
  Vector = array[0..1] of Point;
  Month  = (Jan,Feb,Mar,Apr,May,Jun,Jly,Aug,Sep,Oct,Nov,Dec);
  Date   = record
             d: 1..31; m: Month; y: 1900..1999;
           end;
const
  Origin  : Point = (x: 0.0; y: 0.0);
  Line    : Vector = ((x: -3.1; y: 1.5),(x: 5.8; y: 3.0));
  SomeDay : Date = (d: 2; m: Dec; y: 1960);
```

The fields must be specified in the same order as they appear in the definition of the record type. If a record contains fields of file types, the constants of that record type cannot be declared. If a record contains a variant, only fields of the selected variant can be specified. If the variant contains a tag field, then its value must be specified.

## Set-Type Constants

The declaration of a set-type constant specifies zero or more member constants, enclosed in square brackets and separated by commas. A member constant is a constant, or a range consisting of two constants, separated by two periods.

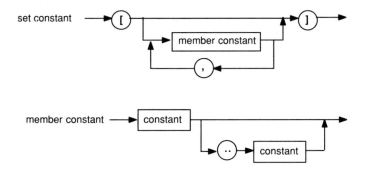

Some examples of set constants follow:

```
type
  Digits  = set of 0..9;
  Letters = set of 'A'..'Z';
const
  EvenDigits: Digits = [0,2,4,6,8];
  Vowels    : Letters = ['A','E','I','O','U','Y'];
  HexDigits : set of '0'..'z' = ['0'..'9','A'..'F','a'...f'];
```

# Pointer-Type Constants

The declaration of a pointer-type constant can only specify the value **nil**.
Some examples include

```
type
  NamePtr = ^NameRec;
  NameRec = record
              Next: NamePtr;
              Name: string[31];
            end;
const
  NameList: NamePtr = nil;
  NoName: NameRec = (Next: nil; Name: '');
```

# 18

# Expressions

Expressions are made up of *operators* and *operands*. Most Pascal operators are *binary*, that is, they take two operands; the rest are *unary* and take only one operand. Binary operators use the usual algebraic form, for example, *a* + *b*. A unary operator always precedes its operand, for example, *–b*.

In more complex expressions, rules of precedence clarify the order in which operations are performed (see Table 18.1).

Table 18.1: Precedence of Operators

| Operators | Precedence | Categories |
|---|---|---|
| @, not | first (high) | unary operators |
| *, /, div, mod, and, shl, shr | second | multiplying operators |
| +,-, or, xor | third | adding operators |
| =, <>, <, >, <=, >=, in | fourth (low) | relational operators |

There are three basic rules of precedence:

1. First, an operand between two operators of different precedence is bound to the operator with higher precedence.

2. Second, an operand between two equal operators is bound to the one on its left.

3. Third, expressions within parentheses are evaluated prior to being treated as a single operand.

Operations with equal precedence are normally performed from left to right, although the compiler may at times rearrange the operands to generate optimum code.

## Expression Syntax

The precedence rules follow from the syntax of expressions, which are built from factors, terms, and simple expressions.

A factor's syntax follows:

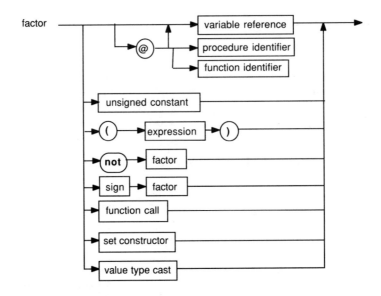

A function call activates a function and denotes the value returned by the function (see "Function Calls" later in this chapter). A set constructor denotes a value of a set type (see the section entitled "Set Constructors"). A value typecast changes the type of a value (see "Value Typecasts"). An unsigned constant has the following syntax:

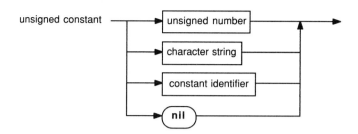

Some examples of factors include

```
X                         { Variable reference }
@X                       { Pointer to a variable }
15                         { Unsigned constant }
(X+Y+Z)                        { Subexpression }
Sin(X/2)                       { Function call }
['0..'9','A'..'Z']            { Set constructor }
not Done                 { Negation of a boolean }
char(Digit+48)                { Value typecast }
```

Terms apply the multiplying operators to factors:

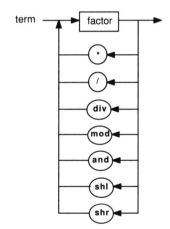

Here's some examples of terms:

```
X*Y
Z/(1-Z)
Done or Error
(X <= Y) and (Y < Z)
```

Simple expressions apply adding operators and signs to terms:

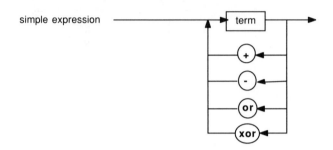

Here's some examples of simple expressions:

```
X+Y
-X
Hue1 + Hue2
I*J + 1
```

An expression applies the relational operators to simple expressions:

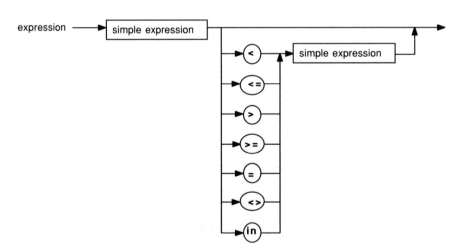

Here's some examples of expressions:

```
X = 1.5
Done <> Error
(I < J) = (J < K)
C in Hue1
```

# Operators

The operators are classified as arithmetic operators, logical operators, string operators, set operators, relational operators, and the @ operator.

## Arithmetic Operators

The following tables show the types of operands and results for binary and unary arithmetic operations.

Table 18.2: Binary Arithmetic Operations

| Operator | Operation | Operand Types | Result Type |
|---|---|---|---|
| + | addition | integer type<br>real type | integer type<br>real type |
| − | subtraction | integer type<br>real type | integer type<br>real type |
| * | multiplication | integer type<br>real type | integer type<br>real type |
| | division | integer type<br>real type | real type<br>real type |
| div | integer division | integer type | integer type |
| mod | remainder | integer type | integer type |

**Note:** The + operator is also used as a string or set operator, and the +, −, and * operators are also used as set operators.

Table 18.3: Unary Arithmetic Operations

| Operator | Operation | Operand Types | Result Type |
|---|---|---|---|
| + | sign identity | integer type<br>real type | integer type<br>real type |
| − | sign negation | integer type<br>real type | integer type<br>real type |

Any operand whose type is a subrange of an ordinal type is treated as if it were of the ordinal type.

If both operands of a +, −, *, **div**, or **mod** operator are of an integer type, the result type is of the common type of the two operands. (See the section "The Integer Type" in Chapter 15 for a definition of common types.)

If one or both operands of a +, −, or * operator are of a real type, the type of the result is real in the $N- state or extended in the $N+ state.

If the operand of the sign identity or sign negation operator is of an integer type, the result is of the same integer type. If the operator is of a real type, the type of the result is real or extended.

The value of $x/y$ is always of type real or extended regardless of the operand types. An error occurs if $y$ is zero.

The value of $i$ **div** $j$ is the mathematical quotient of $i/j$, rounded in the direction of zero to an integer-type value. An error occurs if $j$ is zero.

The **mod** operator returns the remainder obtained by dividing its two operands, that is,

```
i mod j = i - (i div j) * j
```

The sign of the result of **mod** is the same as the sign of $i$. An error occurs if $j$ is zero.


## *Logical Operators*

The types of operands and results for logical operations are shown in Table 18.4.

Table 18.4: Logical Operations

| Operator | Operation | Operand Types | Result Type |
|----------|-----------|---------------|-------------|
| **not** | Bitwise negation | integer type | integer type |
| **and** | Bitwise and | integer type | integer type |
| **or** | Bitwise or | integer type | integer type |
| **xor** | Bitwise xor | integer type | integer type |
| **shl** | Shift left | integer type | integer type |
| **shr** | Shift right | integer type | integer type |

**Note:** The **not** operator is a unary operator.

If the operand of the **not** operator is of an integer type, the result is of the same integer type.

If both operands of an **and**, **or**, or **xor** operator are of an integer type, the result type is the common type of the two operands.

The operations $i$ **shl** $j$ and $i$ **shr** $j$ shift the value of $i$ to the left or to the right by $j$ bits. The type of the result is the same as the type of $i$.

# Boolean Operators

The types of operands and results for boolean operations are shown in Table 18.5.

Table 18.5: Boolean Operations

| Operator | Operation | Operand Types | Result Type |
|----------|-----------|---------------|-------------|
| **not** | negation | boolean | boolean |
| **and** | logical and | boolean | boolean |
| **or** | logical or | boolean | boolean |
| **xor** | logical xor | boolean | boolean |

**Note:** The **not** operator is a unary operator.

Normal Boolean logic governs the results of these operations. For instance, *a* **and** *b* is True only if both *a* and *b* are True.

Turbo Pascal supports two different models of code generation for the **and** and **or** operators: complete evaluation and short-circuit (partial) evaluation.

Complete evaluation means that every operand of a Boolean expression, built from the **and** and **or** operators, is guaranteed to be evaluated, even when the result of the entire expression is already known. This model is convenient when one or more operands of an expression are functions with side effects that alter the meaning of the program.

Short-circuit evaluation guarantees strict left-to-right evaluation and that evaluation stops as soon as the result of the entire expression becomes evident. This model is convenient in most cases, since it guarantees minimum excution time, and usually minimum code size. Short-circuit evaluation also makes possible the evaluation of constructs that would not otherwise be legal; for instance:

```
while (I<=Length(S)) and (S[I]<>' ') do Inc(I);
while (P<>nil) and (P^.Value<>5) do P:=P^.Next;
```

In both cases, the second test is not evaluated if the first test is False.

The evaluation model is controlled through the $B compiler directive. The default state is {$B-} (unless changed using the **Options**/**Compiler** menu), and in this state, short-circuit evaluation code is generated. In the {$B+} state, complete evaluation code is generated.

Since standard Pascal does not specify which model should be used for Boolean expression evaluation, programs depending on either model being in effect are not truly portable. However, sacrificing portability is often worth gaining the execution speed and simplicity provided by the short-circuit model.

## String Operator

The types of operands and results for string operation are shown in Table 18.6.

Table 18.6: String Operation

| Operator | Operation | Operand Types | Result Type |
|----------|-----------|---------------|-------------|
| + | concatenation | string type, char type, or packed string type | string type |

Turbo Pascal allows the + operator to be used to concatenate two string operands. The result of the operation $s + t$, where $s$ and $t$ are of a string type, a char type, or a packed string type, is the concatenation of $s$ and $t$. The result is compatible with any string type (but not with char types and packed string types). If the resulting string is longer than 255 characters, it is truncated after character 255.

## Set Operators

The types of operands for set operations are shown in Table 18.7.

Table 18.7: Set Operations

| Operator | Operation | Operand Types |
|----------|-----------|---------------|
| + | union | compatible set types |
| − | difference | compatible set types |
| * | intersection | compatible set types |

The results of set operations conform to the rules of set logic:

■ An ordinal value $c$ is in $a + b$ only if $c$ is in $a$ or $b$.

■ An ordinal value $c$ is in $a − b$ only if $c$ is in $a$ and not in $b$.

■ An ordinal value $c$ is in $a * b$ only if $c$ is in both $a$ and $b$.

If the smallest ordinal value that is a member of the result of a set operation is *a* and the largest is *b*, then the type of the result is **set of** *a..b*.

## *Relational Operators*

The types of operands and results for relational operations are shown in Table 18.8.

Table 18.8: Relational Operations

| Operator Type | Operation | Operand Types | Result Type |
|---|---|---|---|
| = | equal | compatible simple, pointer, set, string, or packed string types | boolean |
| <> | not equal | compatible simple, pointer, set, string, or packed string types | boolean |
| < | less than | compatible simple, string, or packed string types | boolean |
| > | greater than | compatible simple, string, or packed string types | boolean |
| <= | less or equal | compatible simple, string, or packed string types | boolean |
| >= | greater or equal | compatible simple, string, or packed string types | boolean |
| <= | subset of | compatible set types | boolean |
| >= | superset of | compatible set types | boolean |
| in | member of | left operand: any ordinal type *t*; right operand: set whose base is compatible with *t*. | boolean |

## Comparing Simple Types

When the operands =, <>, <, >, >=, or <= are of simple types, they must be compatible types; however, if one operand is of a real type, the other can be of an integer type.

## Comparing Strings

The relational operators =, <>, <, >, >=, and <= compare strings according to the ordering of the extended ASCII character set. Any two string values can be compared, because all string values are compatible.

A char-type value is compatible with a string-type value, and when the two are compared, the char-type value is treated as a string-type value with length 1. When a packed string-type value with $n$ components is compared with a string-type value, it is treated as a string-type value with length $n$.

## Comparing Packed Strings

The relational operators =, <>, <, >, >=, and <= can also be used to compare two packed string-type values if both have the same number of components. If the number of components is $n$, then the operation corresponds to comparing two strings, each of length $n$.

## Comparing Pointers

The operators = and <> can be used on compatible pointer-type operands. Two pointers are equal only if they point to the same object.

**Note:** When comparing pointers, Turbo Pascal simply compares the segment and offset parts. Because of the segment mapping scheme of the 80×86 processors, two logically different pointers can in fact point to the same physical memory location. For instance, $0040:$0049 and $0000:$0449 are two pointers to the same physical address. Pointers returned by the standard procedures *New* and *GetMem* are always normalized (offset part in the range $0000 to $000F), and will therefore always compare correctly. When creating pointers with the *Ptr* standard function, special care must be taken if such pointers are to be compared.

## Comparing Sets

If *a* and *b* are set operands, their comparisons produce these results:

- *a* = *b* is True only if *a* and *b* contain exactly the same members; otherwise, *a* <> *b*.
- *a* <= *b* is True only if every member of *a* is also a member of *b*.
- *a* >= *b* is True only if every member of *b* is also a member of *a*.

## Testing Set Membership

The **in** operator returns True when the value of the ordinal type operand is a member of the set-type operand; otherwise, it returns False.

## *The @ Operator*

A pointer to a variable can be created with the @ operator. Table 18.9 shows the operand and result types.

Table 18.9: Pointer Operation

| Operator | Operation | Operand Types | Result Type |
|----------|-----------|---------------|-------------|
| @ | Pointer formation | Variable reference or procedure or function identifier | Pointer (same as **nil**) |

@ is a unary operator that takes a variable reference or a procedure or function identifier as its operand, and returns a pointer to the operand. The type of the value is the same as the type of **nil**, therefore it can be assigned to any pointer variable.

## @ with a Variable

The use of @ with an ordinary variable (not a parameter) is uncomplicated. Given the declarations

```
type
  TwoChar = array[0..1] of char;
var
  Int: integer;
  TwoCharPtr: ^TwoChar;
```

then the statement

```
TwoCharPtr := @Int;
```

causes *TwoCharPtr* to point to *Int*. *TwoCharPtr^* becomes a re-interpretation of the value of *Int*, as though it were an **array**[0..1] **of** char.

## @ with a Value Parameter

Applying @ to a formal value parameter results in a pointer to the stack location containing the actual value. Suppose *Foo* is a formal value parameter in a procedure and *FooPtr* is a pointer variable. If the procedure executes the statement

```
FooPtr := @Foo;
```

then *FooPtr^* references *Foo*'s value. However, *FooPtr^* does not reference *Foo* itself, rather it references the value that was taken from *Foo* and stored on the stack.

## @ with a Variable Parameter

Applying @ to a formal variable parameter results in a pointer to the actual parameter (the pointer is taken from the stack). Suppose *One* is a formal variable parameter of a procedure, *Two* is a variable passed to the procedure as *One*'s actual parameter, and *OnePtr* is a pointer variable. If the procedure executes the statement

```
OnePtr := @One;
```

then *OnePtr* is a pointer to *Two*, and *OnePtr^* is a reference to *Two* itself.

## @ with a Procedure or Function

You can apply @ to a procedure or a function to produce a pointer to its entry point. Turbo Pascal does not give you a mechanism for using such a pointer. The only use for a procedure pointer is to pass it to an assembly language routine or to use it in an **inline** statement.

# Function Calls

A function call activates the function specified by the function identifier. Any identifier declared to denote a function is a function identifier.

The function call must have a list of actual parameters if the corresponding function declaration contains a list of formal parameters. Each parameter takes the place of the corresponding formal parameter according to parameter rules set forth in Chapter 22.

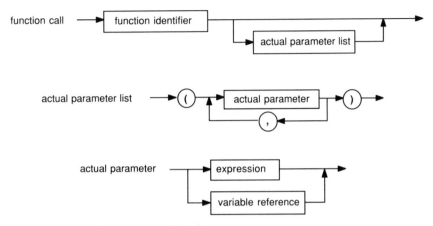

Some examples of function calls follow:

```
Sum(A,63)
Maximum(147,J)
Sin(X+Y)
Eof(F)
Volume(Radius,Height)
```

# Set Constructors

A set constructor denotes a set-type value, and is formed by writing expressions within brackets ([]). Each expression denotes a value of the set.

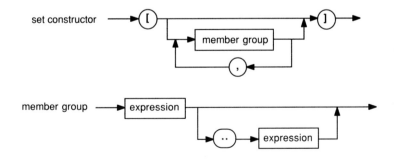

The notation [ ] denotes the empty set, which is assignment-compatible with every set type. Any member group *x..y* denotes as set members all values in the range *x..y*. If *x* is greater than *y*, then *x..y* does not denote any members and [*x..y*] denotes the empty set.

All expression values in member groups in a particular set constructor must be of the same ordinal type.

Some examples of set constructors follow:

```
[red, C, green]
[1, 5, 10..K mod 12, 23]
['A'..'Z', 'a'..'z', Chr(Digit+48)]
```

# Value Typecasts

The type of an expression can be changed to another type through a value typecast.

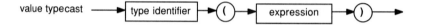

The expression type and the specified type must both be either ordinal types or pointer types. For ordinal types, the resulting value is obtained by converting the expression. The conversion may involve truncation or extension of the original value if the size of the specified type is different from that of the expression. In cases where the value is extended, the sign of the value is always preserved; that is, the value is sign-extended.

The syntax of a value typecast is almost identical to that of a variable typecast (see Chapter 16, "Variable Typecasts"). However, value typecasts operate on values not on variables, and can therefore not participate in variable references; that is, a value typecast may not be followed by qualifiers. In particular, value typecasts cannot appear on the left-hand side of an assignment statement.

Some examples of value typecasts include

```
integer('A')
char(48)
boolean(0)
Color(2)
Longint(@Buffer)
BytePtr(Ptr($40,$49))
```

# 19

# Statements

Statements describe algorithmic actions that can be executed. Labels can prefix statements, and these labels can be referenced by **goto** statements.

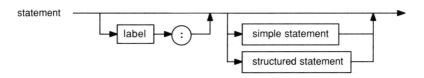

As you saw in Chapter 13, a label is either a digit sequence in the range 0 to 9999 or an identifier.

There are two main types of statements: simple statements and structured statements.

## Simple Statements

A *simple* statement is a statement that doesn't contain any other statements.

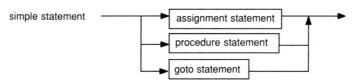

## Assignment Statements

Assignment statements either replace the current value of a variable with a new value specified by an expression or specify an expression whose value is to be returned by a function.

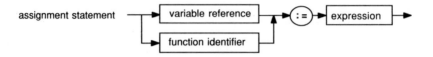

The expression must be assignment-compatible with the type of the variable or the result type of the function (see Chapter 15, "Type Compatibility").

Some examples of assignment statements follow:

```
X    := Y+Z;
Done := (I>=1) and (I<100);
Hue1 := [blue,Succ(C)];
I    := Sqr(J) - I*K;
```

## Procedure Statements

A **procedure** statement specifies the activation of the procedure denoted by the procedure identifier. If the corresponding procedure declaration contains a list of formal parameters, then the procedure statement must have a matching list of actual parameters (parameters listed in definitions are *formal* parameters; in the calling statement, they are *actual* parameters). The actual parameters are passed to the formal parameters as part of the call.

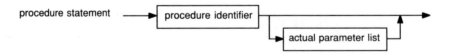

Some examples of procedure statements follow:

```
PrintHeading;
Transpose(A,N,M);
Find(Name,Address);
```

## Goto Statements

A **goto** statement transfers program execution to the statement prefixed by the label referenced in the **goto** statement. The syntax diagram of a **goto** statement follows:

The following rules should be observed when using **goto** statements:

- The label referenced by a **goto** statement must be in the same block as the **goto** statement. In other words, it is not possible to jump into or out of a procedure or function.

- Jumping into a structured statement from outside that structured statement (that is, jumping to a "deeper" level of nesting) can have undefined effects, although the compiler will not indicate an error.

# Structured Statements

Structured statements are constructs composed of other statements that are to be executed in sequence (compound and **with** statements), conditionally (conditional statements), or repeatedly (repetitive statements).

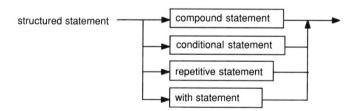

## Compound Statements

The compound statement specifies that its component statements are to be executed in the same sequence as they are written. The component statements are treated as one statement, crucial in contexts where the Pascal syntax only allows one statement. **begin** and **end** bracket the statements, which are separated by semicolons.

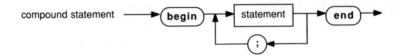

Here's an example of a compound statement:

```
begin
    Z := X;
    X := Y;
    Y := Z;
end;
```

## Conditional Statements

A conditional statement selects for execution a single one (or none) of its component statements.

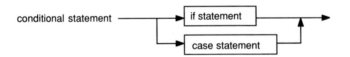

## If Statements

The syntax for an **if** statement reads like this:

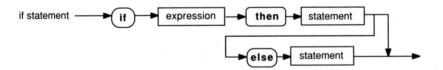

The expression must yield a result of the standard type boolean. If the expression produces the value True, then the statement following **then** is executed.

If the expression produces False and the **else** part is present, the statement following **else** is executed; if the **else** part is not present, nothing is executed.

The syntactic ambiguity arising from the construct

```
if e1 then if e2 then s1 else s2
```

is resolved by interpreting the construct as follows:

```
if e1 then
begin
  if e2 then
    s1
  else
    s2
end
```

In general, an **else** is associated with the closest **if** not already associated with an **else**.

Two examples of **if** statements follow:

```
if X < 1.5 then
  Z := X+Y
else
  Z := 1.5;


if P1 <> nil then
  P1 := P1^.father;
```

# Case Statements

The **case** statement consists of an expression (the selector) and a list of statements, each prefixed with one or more constants (called case constants) or with the word **else**. The selector must be of an ordinal type, and the ordinal values of the upper and lower bounds of that type must be within the range –32768 to 32767. Thus, string types and the integer types longInt and word are invalid selector types. All **case** constants must be unique and of an ordinal type compatible with the selector type.

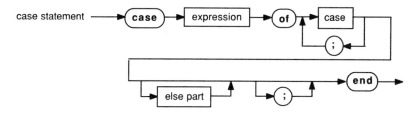

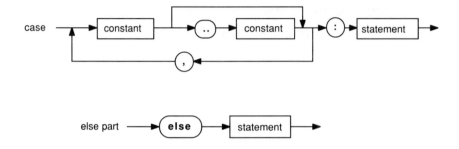

The **case** statement executes the statement prefixed by a **case** constant equal to the value of the selector or a **case** range containing the value of the selector. If no such **case** constant of the **case** range exists and an **else** part is present, the statement following **else** is executed. If there is no **else** part, nothing is executed.

Examples of **case** statements follow:

```
case Operator of
  plus:   X := X+Y;
  minus:  X := X-Y;
  times:  X := X*Y;
end;


case I of
  0,2,4,6,8: Writeln('Even digit');
  1,3,5,7,9: Writeln('Odd digit');
  10..100:   Writeln('Between 10 and 100');
else
  Writeln('Negative or greater than 100');
end;
```

## Repetitive Statements

Repetitive statements specify certain statements to be executed repeatedly.

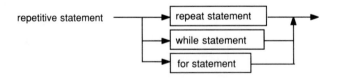

If the number of repetitions is known beforehand, the **for** statement is the appropriate construct. Otherwise, the **while** or **repeat** statement should be used.

# Repeat Statements

A **repeat** statement contains an expression that controls the repeated execution of a statement sequence within that **repeat** statement.

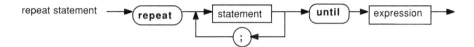

The expression must produce a result of type boolean. The statements between the symbols **repeat** and **until** are executed in sequence until, at the end of a sequence, the expression yields True. The sequence is executed at least once, because the expression is evaluated *after* the execution of each sequence.

Examples of **repeat** statements follow:

```
repeat
  K := I mod J;
  I := J;
  J := K;
until J = 0;


repeat
  Write('Enter value (0..9): ');
  Readln(I);
until (I >= 0) and (I <= 9);
```

# While Statements

A **while** statement contains an expression that controls the repeated execution of a statement (which can be a compound statement).

The expression controlling the repetition must be of type boolean. It is evaluated *before* the contained statement is executed. The contained statement is executed repeatedly as long as the expression is True. If the expression is False at the beginning, the statement is not executed at all.

Examples of **while** statements include:

```
while Data[I] <> X do I := I + 1;


while I > 0 do
begin
  if Odd(I) then Z := Z * X;
  I := I div 2;
  X := Sqr(X);
end;


while not Eof(InFile) do
begin
  Readln(InFile,Line);
  Process(Line);
end;
```

## For Statements

The **for** statement causes a statement (which can be a compound statement) to be repeatedly executed while a progression of values is assigned to a control variable.

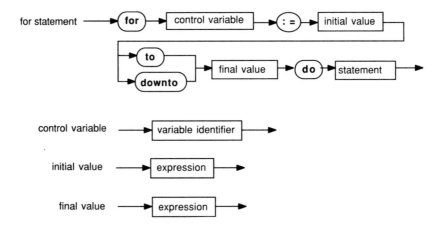

The control variable must be a variable identifier (without any qualifier) that signifies a variable declared to be local to the block containing the **for** statement. The control variable must be of an ordinal type. The initial and final values must be of a type assignment-compatible with the ordinal type.

When a **for** statement is entered, the initial and final values are determined once for the remainder of the execution of the **for** statement.

The statement contained by the **for** statement is executed once for every value in the range *initial value* to *final value*. The control variable always starts off at *initial value*. When a **for** statement uses **to**, the value of the control variable is incremented by one for each repetition. If *initial value* is greater than *final value*, the contained statement is not executed. When a **for** statement uses **downto**, the value of the control variable is decremented by one for each repetition. If *initial value* value is less than *final value*, the contained statement is not executed.

It's an error if the contained statement alters the value of the control variable. After a **for** statement is executed, the value of the control variable value is undefined, unless execution of the **for** statement was interrupted by a **goto** from the **for** statement.

With these restrictions in mind, the **for** statement

```
for V := Expr1 to Expr2 do Body;
```

is equivalent to

```
begin
  Temp1 := Expr1;
  Temp2 := Expr2;
  if Temp1 <= Temp2 then
  begin
    V := Temp1;
    Body;
    while V <> Temp2 do
    begin
      V := Succ(V);
      Body;
    end;
  end;
end;
```

and the **for** statement

```
for V := Expr1 downto Expr2 do Body;
```

is equivalent to

```
begin
  Temp1 := Expr1;
  Temp2 := Expr2;
  if Temp1 >= Temp2 then
  begin
    V := Temp1;
    Body;
    while V <> Temp2 do
    begin
      V := Pred(V);
      Body;
    end;
  end;
end;
```

where *Temp1* and *Temp2* are auxiliary variables of the host type of the variable *V* and don't occur elsewhere in the program.

Examples of **for** statements follow:

```
for I := 2 to 63 do
  if Data[I] > Max then Max := Data[I]


for I := 1 to 10 do
  for J := 1 to 10 do
  begin
    X := 0;
    for K := 1 to 10 do
      X := X + Mat1[I,K] * Mat2[K,J];
    Mat[I,J] := X;
  end;


for C := red to blue do Check(C);
```

## With Statements

The **with** statement is shorthand for referencing the fields of a record. Within a **with** statement, the fields of one or more specific record variables can be referenced using their field identifiers only. The syntax of a **with** statement follows:

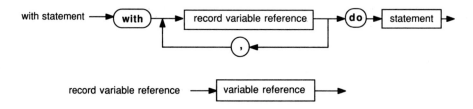

Following is an example of a **with** statement:

```
with Date do
  if month = 12 then
  begin
    month := 1;
    year  := year + 1
  end
  else
    month := month + 1;
```

This is equivalent to

```
if Date.month = 12 then
begin
  Date.month := 1;
  Date.year  := Date.year + 1
end
else
  Date.month := Date.month + 1;
```

Within a **with** statement, each variable reference is first checked as to whether it can be interpreted as a field of the record. If so, it is always interpreted as such, even if a variable with the same name is also accessible. Suppose the following declarations have been made:

```
type
  Point = record
            x,y: integer;
          end;
var
  x: Point;
  y: integer;
```

In this case, both *x* and *y* can refer to a variable or to a field of the record. In the statement

```
with x do
begin
  x := 10;
  y := 25;
end;
```

the *x* between **with** and **do** refers to the variable of type *Point*, but in the compound statement, *x* and *y* refer to *x.x* and *x.y*.

The statement

```
with V1,V2, ... Vn do s;
```

is equivalent to

```
with V1 do
  with V2 do
    ....
      with Vn do
        S;
```

In both cases, if *Vn* is a field of both *V1* and *V2*, it is interpreted as *V2.Vn*, not *V1.Vn*.

If the selection of a record variable involves indexing an array or dereferencing a pointer, these actions are executed once before the component statement is executed.

C     H     A     P     T     E     R

# 20

# Procedures and Functions

Procedures and functions allow you to nest additional blocks in the main program block. Each procedure or function declaration has a heading followed by a block. A procedure is activated by a procedure statement; a function is activated by the evaluation of an expression that contains its call and returns a value to that expression.

This chapter discusses the different types of procedure and function declarations and their parameters.

## Procedure Declarations

A procedure declaration associates an identifier with a block as a procedure; that procedure can then be activated by a procedure statement.

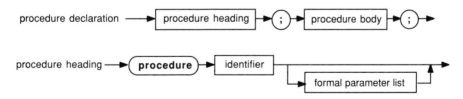

The procedure heading names the procedure's identifier and specifies the formal parameters (if any).

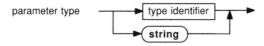

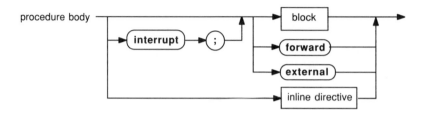

The syntax for a formal parameter list is shown in the section "Parameters" later in this chapter.

A procedure is activated by a procedure statement, which states the procedure's identifier and any actual parameters required. The statements to be executed on activation are noted in the statement part of the procedure's block. If the procedure's identifier is used in a procedure statement within the procedure's block, the procedure is executed recursively (it calls itself while executing).

Here's an example of a procedure declaration:

```
procedure NumString(N: integer; var S: string);
var
  V: integer;
begin
  V := Abs(N);
  S := '';
  repeat
    S := Chr(N mod 10 + Ord('0')) + S;
    N := N div 10;
  until N = 0;
  if N < 0 then S := '-' + S;
end;
```

A procedure declaration can optionally specify an **interrupt** directive before the block, and the procedure is then considered an interrupt procedure. Interrupt procedures are described in full in Chapter 26, "Inside Turbo Pascal." For now, note that interrupt procedures cannot be called from procedure statements, and that every interrupt procedure must specify a parameter list exactly like the following:

```
procedure MyInt(Flags,CS,IP,AX,BX,CX,DX,SI,DI,DS,ES,BP : word);
interrupt;
```

Instead of the block in a procedure or function declaration, you can write a **forward**, **external**, or **inline** declaration.

# Forward Declarations

A procedure declaration that specifies the directive **forward** instead of a block is a **forward** declaration. Somewhere after this declaration, the procedure must be defined by a *defining* declaration—a procedure declaration that uses the same procedure identifier but omits the formal parameter list and includes a block. The **forward** declaration and the defining declaration must appear in the same procedure and function declaration part. Other procedures and functions can be declared between them, and they can call the forward-declared procedure. Mutual recursion is thus possible.

The **forward** declaration and the defining declaration constitute a complete procedure declaration. The procedure is considered declared at the **forward** declaration.

An example of a **forward** declaration follows:

```
procedure Walter(m,n : integer); forward;

procedure Clara(x,y : real);
begin
  :
  Walter(4,5);
  :
end;

procedure Walter;
begin
  :
  Clara(8.3,2.4);
  :
end;
```

A procedure's defining declaration can be an **external** declaration; however, it cannot be an **inline** declaration or another **forward** declaration. Likewise, the defining declaration cannot specify an **interrupt** directive.

**Forward** declarations are not allowed in the interface part of a unit.

# External Declarations

**External** declarations allow you to interface with separately compiled procedures and functions written in assembly language. The **external** code must be linked with the Pascal program or unit through {$L *filename*} directives. For further details on linking with assembly language, refer to Chapter 26.

Examples of **external** procedure declarations follow:

```
procedure MoveWord(var source,dest; count: longInt); external;
procedure MoveLong(var source,dest; count: longInt); external;

procedure FillWord(var dest; data: integer; count: longInt); external;
procedure FillLong(var dest; data: longInt; count: longInt); external;

{$L BLOCK.OBJ}
```

You should use **external** procedures when you need to incorporate substantial amounts of assembly code. If you only require small amounts of code, use **inline** procedures instead.

## Inline Declarations

The **inline** directive permits you to write machine code instructions instead of the block. When a normal procedure is called, the compiler generates code that pushes the procedure's parameters onto the stack, and then generates a CALL instruction to call the procedure. When you "call" an **inline** procedure, the compiler generates code from the inline directive instead of the CALL. Thus, an **inline** procedure is "expanded" every time you refer to it, just like a macro in assembly language. Here's a short example of two **inline** procedures:

```
procedure DisableInterrupts; inline($FA);   { CLI }
procedure EnableInterrupts; inline($FB);   { STI }
```

Inline procedures are described in full in Chapter 26, "Inside Turbo Pascal."

# Function Declarations

A **function** declaration defines a part of the program that computes and returns a value.

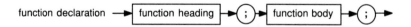

The **function** heading specifies the identifier for the function, the formal parameters (if any), and the function result type.

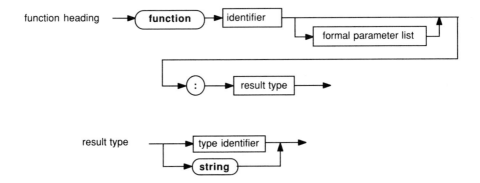

A function is activated by the evaluation of a **function** call. The **function** call gives the function's identifier and any actual parameters required by the function. A **function** call appears as an operand in an expression. When the expression is evaluated, the function is executed, and the value of the operand becomes the value returned by the function.

The statement part of the function's block specifies the statements to be executed upon activation of the function. The block should contain at least one assignment statement that assigns a value to the function identifier. The result of the function is the last value assigned. If no such assignment statement exists or if it is not executed, the value returned by the function is unspecified.

If the function's identifier is used in a function call within the function's block, the function is executed recursively.

Following are examples of **function** declarations:

```
function Max(a: Vector; n: integer): extended;
var
  x: extended;
  i: integer;
begin
  x := a[1];
  for i := 2 to n do
    if x < a[i] then x := a[i];
  Max := x;
end;

function Power(x: extended; y: integer): extended;
var
  z: extended;
  i: integer;
begin
  z := 1.0; i := y;
  while i > 0 do
```

```
begin
  if Odd(i) then z := z * x;
  i := i div 2;
  x := Sqr(x);
end;
Power := z;
end;
```

Like procedures, functions can be declared as **forward, external,** or **inline;** however, **interrupt** functions are not allowed.

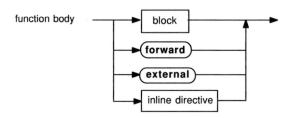

## Parameters

The declaration of a procedure or function specifies a formal parameter list. Each parameter declared in a formal parameter list is local to the procedure or function being declared, and can be referred to by its identifier in the block associated with the procedure or function.

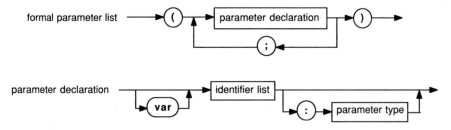

There are three kinds of parameters: *value, variable,* and *untyped variable.* They are characterized as follows:

- A parameter group without a preceding **var** and followed by a type is a list of value parameters.

- A parameter group preceded by **var** and followed by a type is a list of variable parameters.

- A parameter group preceded by **var** and not followed by a type is a list of untyped variable parameters.

# Value Parameters

A formal value parameter acts like a variable local to the procedure or function, except that it gets its initial value from the corresponding actual parameter upon activation of the procedure or function. Changes made to a formal value parameter do not affect the value of the actual parameter.

A value parameter's corresponding actual parameter in a procedure statement or function call must be an expression, and its value must not be of file type or of any structured type that contains a file type.

The actual parameter must be assignment-compatible with the type of the formal value parameter. If the parameter type is **string**, then the formal parameter is given a size attribute of 255.

# Variable Parameters

A variable parameter is employed when a value must be passed from a procedure or function to the caller. The corresponding actual parameter in a procedure statement or function call must be a variable reference. The formal variable parameter represents the actual variable during the activation of the procedure or function, so any changes to the value of the formal variable parameter are reflected in the actual parameter.

Within the procedure or function, any reference to the formal variable parameter accesses the actual parameter itself. The type of the actual parameter must be identical to the type of the formal variable parameter (you can bypass this restriction through untyped variable parameters). If the formal parameter type is **string**, it is given the length attribute 255, and the actual variable parameter must be a string type with a length attribute of 255.

File types can only be passed as variable parameters.

If referencing an actual variable parameter involves indexing an array or finding the object of a pointer, these actions are executed before the activation of the procedure or function.

# Untyped Variable Parameters

When a formal parameter is an untyped variable parameter, the corresponding actual parameter may be any variable reference, regardless of its type.

Within the procedure or function, the untyped variable parameter is typeless; that is, it is incompatible with variables of all other types, unless it is given a specific type through a variable typecast.

An example of untyped variable parameters follows:

```
function Equal(var source,dest; size: word): boolean;
type
  Bytes = array[0..MaxInt] of byte;
var
  N: integer;
begin
  N := 0;
  while (N<size) and (Bytes(dest)[N] <> Bytes(source)[N]) do Inc(N);
  Equal := N = size;
end;
```

This function can be used to compare any two variables of any size. For instance, given the declarations

```
type
  Vector = array[1..10] of integer;
  Point  = record
              x,y: integer;
            end;
var
  Vec1,Vec2: Vector;
  N: integer;
  P: Point;
```

then the function calls

```
    Equal(Vec1,Vec2,SizeOf(Vector))
    Equal(Vec1,Vec2,SizeOf(integer)*N)
    Equal(Vec[1],Vec1[6],SizeOf(integer)*5)
    Equal(Vec1[1],P,4)
```

compare *Vec1* to *Vec2*, compare the first *N* components of *Vec1* to the first *N* components of *Vec2*, compare the first five components of *Vec1* to the last five components of *Vec1*, and compare *Vec1[1]* to *P.x* and *Vec1[2]* to *P.y*.

# 21

# Programs and Units

## Program Syntax

A Turbo Pascal program takes the form of a procedure declaration except for its heading and an optional **uses** clause.

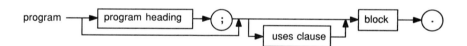

### *The Program Heading*

The program heading specifies the program's name and its parameters.

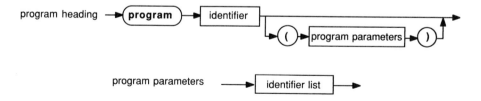

The program heading, if present, is purely decorative and is ignored by the compiler.

## The Uses Clause

The **uses** clause identifies all units used by the program, including units used directly and units used by those units.

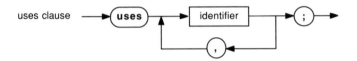

The *System* unit is always used automatically. *System* implements all low-level, runtime support routines to support such features as file I/O, string handling, floating point, dynamic memory allocation, and others.

Apart from *System*, Turbo Pascal implements many standard units, such as *Printer*, *Dos*, and *Crt*. These are not used automatically; you must include them in your **uses** clause, for instance,

```
uses Dos,Crt;                    { Can now access facilities in Dos and Crt }
```

The standard units are described in Chapter 24, "Standard Units."

To locate a unit specified in a **uses** clause, the compiler first checks the resident units—those units loaded into memory at startup from the TURBO.TPL file. If the unit is not among the resident units, the compiler assumes it must be on disk. The name of the file is assumed to be the unit name with extension .TPU. It is first searched for in the current directory, and then in the directories specified in the **O/D/U**nit directories menu or in a */U* directive on the TPC command line. For instance, the construct

```
uses Memory;
```

where *Memory* is not a resident unit, causes the compiler to look for the file MEMORY.TPU in the current directory, and then in each of the unit directories.

The {$U *filename*} directive allows you to override the compiler's file name selection. If a {$U *filename*} directive appears just before a unit name in a **uses** clause, the compiler uses that file name instead of the unit name. For instance, the construct

```
uses {$U MEM} Memory;
```

will cause the compiler to look for *Memory* in the file MEM.TPU. If the {$U *filename*} directive specifies a drive letter and/or a directory path, the unit is only searched for in that directory.

When the Compile/Make and Compile/Build commands compile the units specified in a **uses** clause, the source files are searched for in the same way as the .TPU files, and the name of a given unit's source file is assumed to be the unit name with extension .PAS. If you want a different extension, you can specify it in a {$U *filename*} directive. For example, the construct

```
uses {$U MEMORY.LIB} Memory;
```

will cause the compiler to look for *Memory*'s source text in the file MEMORY.LIB.

# Unit Syntax

Units are the basis of modular programming in Turbo Pascal. They are used to create libraries that you can include in various programs without making the source code available, and to divide large programs into logically related modules.

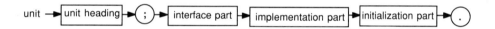

## *The Unit Heading*

The unit heading specifies the unit's name.

The unit name is used when referring to the unit in a **uses** clause. The name must be unique—two units with the same name cannot be used at the same time.

## *The Interface Part*

The interface part declares constants, types, variables, procedures, and functions that are *public*, that is, available to the host (the program or unit using the unit). The host can access these entities as if they were declared in a block that encloses the host.

interface part

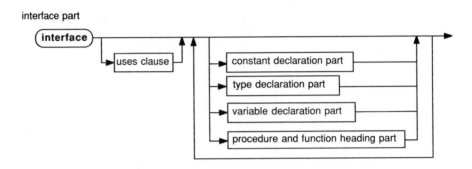

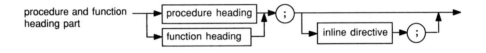

Unless a procedure or function is **inline**, the interface part only lists the procedure or function heading. The block of the procedure or function follows in the implementation part. **Note:** the procedure and function heading can be duplicated from the interface part. You don't have to specify the formal parameter list, but if you do, the compiler will issue a compile-time error if the interface and implementation declarations don't match.

## The Implementation Part

The implementation part defines the block of all public procedures and functions. In addition, it declares constants, types, variables, procedures, and functions that are *private*, that is, not available to the host.

implementation part

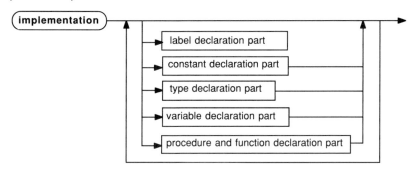

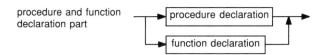

In effect, the procedure and function declarations in the interface part are like **forward** declarations, although the **forward** directive is not specified. Therefore, these procedures and functions can be defined and referenced in any sequence in the implementation part.

## *The Initialization Part*

The initialization part is the last part of a unit. It consists either of the reserved word **end** (in which case the unit has no initialization code) or of a statement part to be executed in order to initialize the unit.

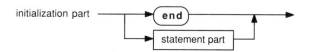

The initialization parts of units used by a program are executed in the same order that the units appear in the **uses** clause.

## Units that Use Other Units

The **uses** clause in the host need not name all units used directly or indirectly by the host. Consider the following example:

```
program Host;          unit Unit1;            unit Unit2;
uses Unit2;            interface              interface
const a = b;           const c = 1;           uses Unit1;
begin                  implementation         const b = c;
end.                   const d = 2;           implementation
                       end.                   end.
```

*Unit2* uses *Unit1*, so for *Host* to use *Unit2*, it first names *Unit1* in its **uses** clause. Because *Host* does not directly reference any identifiers in *Unit1*, it doesn't have to name *Unit1*.

The **uses** statement of program *Host* can be written in several ways:

**uses** Unit1, Unit2;   The identifiers in the interface sections of both units may be referenced in program *Host*.

**uses** Unit2;          Only the identifiers in the interface section of *Unit2* may be referenced in program *Host*.

In the second example, the compiler will recursively analyze unit dependencies and will correctly determine that *Unit2* is dependent on *Unit1*, and that program *Host* is dependent on both. Note that none of the identifiers declared in the interface section of *Unit1* are available to *Host* because it does not use *Unit1* explicitly.

When changes are made in the interface part of a unit, other units using the unit must be recompiled. However, if changes are only made to the implementation or the initialization part, other units that use the unit *need not* be recompiled. In the preceding example, if the interface part of *Unit1* is changed (for example, $c = 2$) *Unit2* must be recompiled; changing the implementation part (for example, $d = 1$) doesn't require the recompilation of *Unit2*.

When a unit is compiled, Turbo Pascal computes a *unit version number*, which is basically a checksum of the interface part. In the preceding example, when *Unit2* is compiled, the current version number of *Unit1* is saved in the compiled version of *Unit2*. When *Host* is compiled, the version number of *Unit1* is checked against the version number stored in *Unit2*. If the version numbers do not match, indicating that a change was made in the interface part of *Unit1* since *Unit2* was compiled, the compiler shows an error or recompiles *Unit2*, depending on the mode of compilation.

# 22

# Input and Output

This chapter briefly describes the standard (or built-in) input and output (I/O) procedures and functions of Turbo Pascal; for more detailed information, refer to Chapter 27.

## An Introduction to I/O

A Pascal file variable is any variable whose type is a file type. There are three classes of Pascal files: *typed*, *text*, and *untyped*. The syntax for writing file types is given in the section "Structured Types" in Chapter 15.

Before a file variable can be used, it must be associated with an external file through a call to the *Assign* procedure. An external file is typically a named disk file, but it can also be a device, such as the keyboard or the display. The external file stores the information written to the file or supplies the information read from the file.

Once the association with an external file is established, the file variable must be "opened" to prepare it for input and/or output. An existing file can be opened via the *Reset* procedure, and a new file can be created and opened via the *Rewrite* procedure. Text files opened with *Reset* are read-only, and text files opened with *Rewrite* and *Append* are write-only. Typed files and untyped files always allow both reading and writing regardless of whether they were opened with *Reset* or *Rewrite*.

The standard text-file variables *Input* and *Output* are opened automatically when program execution begins. *Input* is a read-only file associated with the keyboard and *Output* is a write-only file associated with the display.

Every file is a linear sequence of components, each of which has the component type (or record type) of the file. Each component has a component number. The first component of a file is considered to be component zero.

Files are normally accessed *sequentially*; that is, when a component is read using the standard procedure *Read* or written using the standard procedure *Write*, the current file position moves to the next numerically-ordered file component. However, typed files and untyped files can also be accessed randomly via the standard procedure *Seek*, which moves the current file position to a specified component. The standard functions *FilePos* and *FileSize* can be used to determine the current file position and the current file size.

When a program completes processing a file, the file must be closed using the standard procedure *Close*. After closing a file completely, its associated external file is updated. The file variable can then be associated with another external file.

By default, all calls to standard I/O procedures and functions are automatically checked for errors: If an error occurs, the program terminates displaying a runtime error message. This automatic checking can be turned on and off using the {$I+} and {$I-} compiler directives. When I/O checking is off—that is, when a procedure or function call is compiled in the {$I-} state—an I/O error does not cause the program to halt. To check the result of an I/O operation, you must instead call the standard function *IOResult*.

# Standard Procedures and Functions for All Files

Here's a summary of the procedures and functions you can use in all files.

## *Procedures*

| | |
|---|---|
| **Assign** | Assigns the name of an external file to a file variable. |
| **ChDir** | Changes the current directory. |
| **Close** | Closes an open file. |
| **Erase** | Erases an external file. |
| **GetDir** | Returns the current directory of a specified drive. |
| **MkDir** | Creates a subdirectory. |

| **Rename** | Renames an external file. |
|---|---|
| **Reset** | Opens an existing file. |
| **Rewrite** | Creates and opens a new file. |
| **RmDir** | Removes an empty subdirectory. |

## *Functions*

| **Eof** | Returns the end-of-file status of a file. |
|---|---|
| **IOResult** | Returns an integer value that is the status of the last I/O function performed. |

# Standard Procedures and Functions for Text Files

This section summarizes input and output using file variables of the standard type *Text*. Note that in Turbo Pascal the type *Text* is distinct from the type **file of** char.

When a text file is opened, the external file is interpreted in a special way: It is considered to represent a sequence of characters formatted into lines, where each line is terminated by an end-of-line marker (a carriage-return character, possibly followed by a line-feed character).

For text files, there are special forms of *Read* and *Write* that allow you to read and write values that are not of type char. Such values are automatically translated to and from their character representation. For example, *Read(f,i)*, where *i* is a type integer variable, will read a sequence of digits, interpret that sequence as a decimal integer, and store it in *i*.

As noted previously there are two standard text-file variables, *Input* and *Output*. The standard file variable *Input* is a read-only file associated with the operating system's standard input file (typically the keyboard), and the standard file variable *Output* is a write-only file associated with the operating system's standard output file (typically the display). *Input* and *Output* are automatically opened before a program begins execution, as if the following statements were executed:

```
Assign(Input,''); Reset(Input);
Assign(Output,''); Rewrite(Output);
```

Likewise, *Input* and *Output* are automatically closed after a program finishes executing.

**Note:** If a program uses the *Crt* standard unit, *Input* and *Output* will no longer by default refer to the standard input and standard output files. For further details, refer to the description of the *Crt* unit in Chapter 24, "Standard Units").

Some of the standard procedures and functions listed in this section need not have a file variable explicitly given as a parameter. If the file parameter is omitted, *Input* or *Output* will be assumed by default, depending on whether the procedure or function is input- or output-oriented. For instance, *Read(x)* corresponds to *Read(Input,x)* and *Write(x)* corresponds to *Write(Output,x)*.

If you do specify a file when calling one of the procedures or functions in this section, the file must have been associated with an external file using *Assign*, and opened using *Reset*, *Rewrite*, or *Append*. An error message is generated if you pass a file that was opened with *Reset* to an output-oriented procedure or function. Likewise, it's an error to pass a file that was opened with *Rewrite* or *Append* to an input-oriented procedure or function.

## *Procedures*

**Append**        Opens an existing file for appending.

**Flush**         Flushes the buffer of an output file.

**Read**          Reads one or more values from a text file into one or more variables.

**Readln**        Does what a *Read* does and then skips to the beginning of the next line in the file.

**SetTextBuf**    Assigns an I/O buffer to a text file.

**Write**         Writes one or more values to a text file.

**Writeln**       Does the same as a *Write*, and then writes an end-of-line marker to the file.

## *Functions*

**Eoln**          Returns the end-of-line status of a file.

**SeekEof**       Returns the end-of-file status of a file.

**SeekEoln**      Returns the end-of-line status of a file.

# Standard Procedures and Functions for Untyped Files

Untyped files are low-level I/O channels primarily used for direct access to any disk file regardless of type and structuring. An untyped file is declared with the word **file** and nothing more, for example:

```
var
  DataFile: file;
```

For untyped files, the *Reset* and *Rewrite* procedures allow an extra parameter to specify the record size used in data transfers.

For historical reasons, the default record size is 128 bytes. The preferred record size is 1, because that is the only value that correctly reflects the exact size of any file (no partial records are possible when the record size is 1).

Except for *Read* and *Write*, all typed file standard procedures and functions are also allowed on untyped files. Instead of *Read* and *Write*, two procedures called *BlockRead* and *BlockWrite* are used for high-speed data transfers.

**BlockRead**    Reads one or more records into a variable.

**BlockWrite**    Writes one or more records from a variable.

With the exception of text files, the following procedures and functions may be used on a file variable of any type:

**FilePos**    Returns the current file position of a file.

**FileSize**    Returns the current size of a file.

**Seek**    Moves the current position of a file to a specified component.

**Truncate**    Truncates the file size at the current file position.

# FileMode Variable

The *FileMode* variable defined by the *System* unit determines the access code to pass to DOS when typed and untyped files (not text files) are opened using the *Reset* procedure.

The default *FileMode* is 2, which allows both reading and writing. Assigning another value to *FileMode* causes all subsequent *Resets* to use that mode.

The range of valid *FileMode* values depends on the version of DOS in use. However, for all versions, the following modes are defined:

0:    Read only
1:    Write only
2:    Read/Write

DOS version 3.x defines additional modes, which are primarily concerned with file-sharing on networks. (For further details on these, please refer to your DOS Programmer's Reference manual.)

**Note:** New files created using *Rewrite* are always opened in Read/Write mode, corresponding to *FileMode* = 2.

# Devices in Turbo Pascal

Turbo Pascal and the DOS operating system regard external hardware, such as the keyboard, the display, and the printer, as *devices*. From the programmer's point of view, a device is treated as a file, and is operated on through the same standard procedures and functions as files.

Turbo Pascal supports two kinds of devices: DOS devices and text file devices.

## DOS Devices

DOS devices are implemented through reserved file names that have a special meaning attached to them. DOS devices are completely transparent—in fact, Turbo Pascal is not even aware when a file variable refers to a device instead of a disk file. For example, the program

```
var
  Lst: Text;
begin
  Assign(Lst,'LPT1'); Rewrite(Lst);
  Writeln(Lst,'Hello World...');
  Close(Lst);
end.
```

will write the string Hello World... on the printer, even though the syntax for doing so is exactly the same as for a disk file.

The devices implemented by DOS are used for obtaining or presenting legible input or output. Therefore, DOS devices are normally used only in connection with text files. On rare occasions, untyped files can also be useful for interfacing with DOS devices.

Each of the DOS devices is described in the next section. Other DOS implementations can provide additional devices, and still others cannot provide all the ones described here.

## The CON Device

CON refers to the CONsole device, in which output is sent to the display, and input is obtained from the keyboard. The *Input* and *Output* standard files and all files assigned an empty name refer to the CON device when input and/or output is not redirected.

Input from the CON device is line-oriented and uses the line-editing facilities described in the DOS manual. Characters are read from a line buffer, and when the buffer becomes empty, a new line is input.

An end-of-file character is generated by pressing *Ctrl-Z*, after which the *Eof* function will return True.

## The LPT1, LPT2, and LPT3 Devices

The line printer devices are the three possible printers you can use. If only one printer is connected, it is usually referred to as LPT1, for which the synonym PRN can also be used.

The line printer devices are output-only devices—an attempt to *Reset* a file assigned to one of these generates an immediate end-of-file.

**Note:** The standard unit *Printer* declares a text-file variable called *Lst*, and makes it refer to the LPT1 device. To easily write something on the printer from one of your programs, include *Printer* in the program's **uses** clause, and use *Write(Lst,...)* and *Writeln(Lst,...)* to produce your output.

## The COM1 and COM2 Devices

The communication port devices are the two serial communication ports. The synonym AUX can be used instead of COM1.

## The NUL Device

The null device ignores anything written to it, and generates an immediate end-of-file when read from. You should use this when you don't want to create a particular file, but the program requires an input or output file name.

## *Text-File Devices*

Text-file devices are used to implement devices unsupported by DOS or to make available another set of features other than those provided by a similar DOS device. A good example of a text file device is the CRT device implemented by the *Crt* standard unit. Its main function is to provide an interface to the display and the keyboard, just like the CON device in DOS. However, the CRT device is much faster and supports such invaluable features as color and windows (for further details on the CRT device, see Chapter 24, "Standard Units").

Contrary to DOS devices, text-file devices have no reserved file names; in fact, they have no file names at all. Instead, a file is associated with a text-file device through a customized *Assign* procedure. For instance, the *Crt* standard unit implements an *AssignCrt* procedure that associates text files with the CRT device.

In addition to the CRT device, Turbo Pascal allows you to write your own text file device drivers. A full description of this is given in the section "Writing Text File Device Drivers" in Chapter 26, "Inside Turbo Pascal."

# 23

# Standard Procedures and Functions

This chapter briefly describes all the standard (built-in) procedures and functions in Turbo Pascal, except for the I/O procedures and functions discussed in Chapter 22, "Input and Output." Additional procedures and functions are provided by the standard units described in Chapter 24, "Standard Units." For more detailed information, refer to Chapter 27, "Turbo Pascal Reference Lookup."

Standard procedures and functions are predeclared. Since all predeclared entities act as if they were declared in a block surrounding the program, no conflict arises from a declaration that redefines the same identifier within the program.

## Exit and Halt Procedures

**Exit**    Exits immediately from the current block.

**Halt**    Stops program execution and returns to the operating system.

## Dynamic Allocation Procedures and Functions

These procedures and functions are used to manage the heap—a memory area that occupies all or some of the free memory left when a program is executed. A complete discussion of the techniques used to manage the heap is given in the section "The Heap Manager" in Chapter 26, "Inside Turbo Pascal."

### Procedures

**Dispose**       Disposes a dynamic variable.

**FreeMem**       Disposes a dynamic variable of a given size.

**GetMem**        Creates a new dynamic variable of a given size and sets a pointer variable to point to it.

**Mark**          Records the state of the heap in a pointer variable.

**New**           Creates a new dynamic variable and sets a pointer variable to point to it.

**Release**       Returns the heap to a given state.

### Functions

**MaxAvail**      Returns the size of the largest contiguous free block in the heap, corresponding to the size of the largest dynamic variable that can be allocated at the time of the call to *MaxAvail*.

**MemAvail**      Returns the number of free bytes of heap storage available.

# Transfer Functions

The procedures *Pack* and *Unpack*, as defined in standard Pascal, are not implemented by Turbo Pascal.

**Chr**           Returns a character of a specified ordinal number.

**Ord**           Returns the ordinal number of an ordinal-type value.

**Round**         Rounds a type real value to a type longint value.

**Trunc**         Truncates a type real value to a type longint value.

# Arithmetic Functions

**Note:** When compiling in numeric processing mode, {$N+}, the return values of the floating-point routines in the *System* unit (*Sqrt, Pi, Sin*, and so on) are of type extended instead of real:

```
{$N+}
begin
  Writeln(Pi);                              { 3.14159265358979E+0000 }
```

```
end.
{$N-}
begin
  Writeln(Pi)                                    {   3.1415926536E+00 }
end.
```

**Abs**      Returns the absolute value of the argument.

**ArcTan**   Returns the arctangent of the argument.

**Cos**      Returns the cosine of the argument.

**Exp**      Returns the exponential of the argument.

**Frac**     Returns the fractional part of the argument.

**Int**      Returns the integer part of the argument.

**Ln**       Returns the natural logarithm of the argument.

**Pi**       Returns the value of *Pi* (3.1415926535897932385).

**Sin**      Returns the sine of the argument.

**Sqr**      Returns the square of the argument.

**Sqrt**     Returns the square root of the argument.

# Ordinal Procedures and Functions

### *Procedures*

**Dec**      Decrements a variable.

**Inc**      Increments a variable.

### *Functions*

**Odd**      Tests if the argument is an odd number.

**Pred**     Returns the predecessor of the argument.

**Succ**     Returns the successor of the argument.

# String Procedures and Functions

### Procedures

**Delete**    Deletes a substring from a string.

**Insert**    Inserts a substring into a string.

**Str**    Converts a numeric value to its string representation.

**Val**    Converts the string value to its numeric representation.

### Functions

**Concat**    Concatenates a sequence of strings.

**Copy**    Returns a substring of a string.

**Length**    Returns the dynamic length of a string.

**Pos**    Searches for a substring in a string.

# Pointer and Address Functions

**Addr**    Returns the address of a specified object.

**CSeg**    Returns the current value of the CS register.

**DSeg**    Returns the current value of the DS register.

**Ofs**    Returns the offset of a specified object.

**Ptr**    Converts a segment base and an offset address to a pointer-type value.

**Seg**    Returns the segment of a specified object.

**SPtr**    Returns the current value of the SP register.

**SSeg**    Returns the current value of the SS register.

# Miscellaneous Procedures and Functions

## *Procedures*

**FillChar**     Fills a specified number of contiguous bytes with a specified value.

**Move**     Copies a specified number of contiguous bytes from a source range to a destination range.

**Randomize**     Initializes the built-in random generator with a random value.

## *Functions*

**Hi**     Returns the high-order byte of the argument.

**Lo**     Returns the low-order byte of the argument.

**ParamCount**     Returns the number of parameters passed to the program on the command line.

**ParamStr**     Returns a specified command-line parameter.

**Random**     Returns a random number.

**SizeOf**     Returns the number of bytes occupied by the argument.

**Swap**     Swaps the high- and low-order bytes of the argument.

**UpCase**     Converts a character to uppercase.

# 24

# Standard Units

Chapters 20 and 23 described all the built-in procedures and functions of Turbo Pascal, which can be referred to without explicitly requesting them (as standard Pascal specifies). It's through Turbo Pascal's standard units, though, that you'll get the most programming power (see Chapter 27 for more information).

Standard units are no different from the units you can write yourself. The following standard units are available to you:

**Crt**       Exploits the full power of your PC's display and keyboard, including screen mode control, extended keyboard codes, color, windows, and sound.

**Dos**       Supports numerous DOS functions, including date-and-time control, directory search, and program execution.

**Graph3**    Implements Turbo Pascal 3.0 Turtlegraphics.

**Printer**   Allows you to easily access your printer.

**System**    Turbo Pascal's runtime library. This unit is automatically used by any unit or program.

**Turbo3**    Provides an even higher degree of compatibility with Turbo Pascal 3.0.

**Graph**     A powerful graphics package with device-independent graphics support for CGA, EGA, VGA, HERC, IBM 3270 PC, MCGA, and AT&T 6300.

To use one of the standard units, simply include its name in your **uses** clause, for instance:

```
uses Dos,Crt,Graph;
```

The standard units usually all reside in the TURBO.TPL library, which is automatically loaded when you start up Turbo Pascal. To save memory, you can move seldom-used units, such as *Turbo3* and *Graph3*, out of the TURBO.TPL file by using the TPUMOVER utility.

# Standard Unit Dependencies

Both the compatibility units, *Turbo3* and *Graph3*, depend on facilities made available by the *Crt* unit. So, when using *Turbo3* and *Graph3*, you must first specify *Crt* in your **uses** clause. Table 24.1 lists the standard units.

Table 24.1: Standard Units

| Unit | Uses |
|------|------|
| System | None |
| Printer | None |
| Dos | None |
| Crt | None |
| Graph | None |
| Turbo3 | Crt |
| Graph3 | Crt |

We purposefully didn't indicate in the table that all units use the *System* unit; that's because *System* is always used implicitly, and need never be specified in a **uses** clause.

# The System Unit

The *System* unit is, in fact, Turbo Pascal's runtime library. It implements low-level, runtime support routines for all built-in features, such as file I/O, string handling, floating point, and dynamic memory allocation. The *System* unit is used automatically by any unit or program, and need never be referred to in a **uses** clause.

The procedures and functions provided by *System* are described in Chapters 22, "Input and Output," and 23, "Standard Procedures and Functions." A number of predeclared variables are also available, including:

```
var
  Input     : text;
  Output    : text;
  PrefixSeg : word;
  HeapOrg   : pointer;
  HeapPtr   : pointer;
  FreePtr   : pointer;
  FreeMin   : word;
  HeapError : pointer;
  ExitProc  : pointer;
  RandSeed  : longint;
  FileMode  : byte;
```

*Input* and *Output* are the standard I/O files required by every Pascal implementation. By default, they refer to the standard input and output files in DOS. For further details, refer to Chapter 23.

*PrefixSeg* is a word variable containing the segment address of the Program Segment Prefix (PSP) created by DOS when the program was executed. For a complete description of the PSP, refer to your DOS manual.

*HeapOrg*, *HeapPtr*, *FreePtr*, *FreeMin*, and *HeapError* are used by the heap manager to implement Turbo Pascal's dynamic memory allocation routines. The heap manager is described in full in Chapter 26, "Inside Turbo Pascal."

The *ExitProc* pointer variable is used to implement exit procedures. This is also described in Chapter 26.

*RandSeed* stores the built-in random number generator's seed. By assigning a specific value to *RandSeed*, the *Random* function can be made to generate a specific sequence of random numbers over and over. This is useful in applications that deal with data encryption, statistics, and simulations.

The *FileMode* variable allows you to change the access mode in which typed files and untyped files are opened. For further details, refer to Chapter 22, "Input and Output."

The *System* unit "steals" several interrupt vectors. Before installing its own interrupt handling routines, *System* stores the old vectors in five global pointer variables:

```
  SaveInt00,           { $00 }
  SaveInt02,           { $02 }
  SaveInt23,           { $23 }
  SaveInt24,           { $24 }
  SaveInt75 : pointer; { $75 }
```

Note that the *System* unit contains an INT 24 handler for trapping critical errors. When running an .EXE program created by Turbo Pascal, a DOS critical error will be treated like any other I/O error: The program counter and an error number will display, and the program will terminate. Disk errors are detected by using {$I-} and checking *IOResult*. Here's a simple program that re-installs the original vector:

```
program Restore;
uses Dos;
begin
  SetIntVec($24, SaveInt24);                    { Restore original vector }
  ...
end.
```

Note that the original INT 24 vector is saved in a pointer variable in the *System* unit (SaveInt24).

# The Printer Unit

The *Printer* unit is a very small unit designed to make life easier when you're using the printer from within a program. *Printer* declares a text file called *Lst*, and associates it with the LPT1 device. Using *Printer* saves you the trouble of declaring, assigning, opening, and closing a text file yourself. Here's an example of a short program using *Printer*:

```
program HelloPrinter;
uses Printer;
begin
  Writeln(Lst,'Hello Printer...');
end.
```

# The Dos Unit

The *Dos* unit implements a number of very useful operating system and file-handling routines. None of the routines in the *Dos* unit are defined by standard Pascal, so they have been placed in their own module.

For a complete description of DOS operations, refer to the *IBM DOS Technical Manual*.

## Constants, Types, and Variables

Each of the constants, types, and variables defined by the *Dos* unit are briefly discussed in this section. For more detailed information, see the descriptions of the procedures and functions that depend on these objects in Chapter 27, "Turbo Pascal Reference Lookup."

## Flags Constants

The following constants are used to test individual flag bits in the Flags register after a call to *Intr* or *MsDos*:

```
const
  FCarry    = $0001;
  FParity   = $0004;
  FAuxiliary = $0010;
  FZero     = $0040;
  FSign     = $0080;
  FOverflow = $0800;
```

For instance, if *R* is a register's record, the tests

```
R.Flags and FCarry <> 0
R.Flags and FZero = 0
```

are True respectively if the Carry flag is set and if the Zero flag is clear.

## File Mode Constants

These constants are used by the file-handling procedures when opening and closing disk files. The mode fields of Turbo Pascal's file variables will contain one of the values specified below.

```
const
  fmClosed = $D7B0;
  fmInput  = $D7B1;
  fmOutput = $D7B2;
  fmInOut  = $D7B3;
```

## File Record Types

The record definitions used internally by Turbo Pascal are also declared in the *Dos* unit. *FileRec* is used for both typed and untyped files, while *TextRec* is the internal format of a variable of type text.

```
type
{ Typed and untyped files }
FileRec = record
            Handle: word;
            Mode: word;
            RecSize: word;
            Private: array[1..26] of byte;
            UserData: array[1..16] of byte;
            Name: array[0..79] of char;
          end;
```

```
{ Textfile record }
TextBuf = array[0..127] of char;
TextRec = record
            Handle   : word;
            Mode     : word;
            BufSize  : word;
            Private  : word;
            BufPos   : word;
            BufEnd   : word;
            BufPtr   : ^TextBuf;
            OpenFunc : pointer;
            InOutFunc : pointer;
            FlushFunc : pointer;
            CloseFunc : pointer;
            UserData : array[1..16] of Byte;
            Name     : array[0..79] of Char;
            Buffer   : TextBuf;
          end;
```

# File Attribute Constants

These constants are used to test, set, and clear file attribute bits in connection with the *GetFAttr*, *SetFAttr*, *FindFirst*, and *FindNext* procedures:

```
const
  ReadOnly  = $01;
  Hidden    = $02;
  SysFile   = $04;
  VolumeID  = $08;
  Directory = $10;
  Archive   = $20;
  AnyFile   = $3F;
```

The constants are additive, that is, the statement

```
  FindFirst('*.*', ReadOnly + Directory, S);
```

will locate all normal files as well as read-only files and subdirectories in the current directory. The *AnyFile* constant is simply the sum of all attributes.

# The Registers Type

Variables of type *Registers* are used by the *Intr* and *MsDos* procedures to specify the input register contents and examine the output register contents of a software interrupt.

```
type
  Registers = record
                case integer of
                  0: (AX,BX,CX,DX,BP,SI,DI,DS,ES,Flags: word);
                  1: (AL,AH,BL,BH,CL,CH,DL,DH: byte);
              end;
```

Notice the use of a variant record to map the 8-bit registers on top of their 16-bit equivalents.

# The DateTime Type

Variables of *DateTime* type are used in connection with the *UnpackTime* and *PackTime* procedures to examine and construct 4-byte, packed date-and-time values for the *GetFTime*, *SetFTime*, *FindFirst*, and *FindNext* procedures.

```
type
  DateTime = record
               Year,Month,Day,Hour,Min,Sec: integer;
             end;
```

Valid ranges are *Year* 1980..2099, *Month* 1..12, *Day* 1..31, *Hour* 0..23, *Min* 0..59, and *Sec* 0..59.

# The SearchRec Type

Variables of type *SearchRec* are used by the *FindFirst* and *FindNext* procedures to scan directories.

```
type
  SearchRec = record
                Fill: array[1..21] of byte;
                Attr: byte;
                Time: longint;
                Size: longint;
                Name: string[12];
              end;
```

The information for each file found by one of these procedures is reported back in a *SearchRec*. The *Attr* field contains the file's attributes (constructed from file attribute constants), *Time* contains its packed date and time (use *UnpackTime* to unpack), *Size* contains its size in bytes, and *Name* contains its name. The *Fill* field is reserved by DOS and should never be modified.

# The DosError Variable

*DosError* is used by many of the routines in the *Dos* unit to report errors.

```
var DosError: integer;
```

The values stored in *DosError* are DOS error codes. A value of 0 indicates no error; other possible error codes include:

2 = File not found
3 = Path not found
5 = Access denied
6 = Invalid handle
8 = Not enough memory
10 = Invalid environment
11 = Invalid format
18 = No more files

## Interrupt Support Procedures

Here's a brief listing of the interrupt support procedures:

| | |
|---|---|
| **GetIntVec** | Returns the address stored in a specified interrupt vector. |
| **Intr** | Executes a specified software interrupt. |
| **MsDos** | Executes a DOS function call. |
| **SetIntVec** | Sets a specified interrupt vector to a specified address. |

## Date and Time Procedures

| | |
|---|---|
| **GetDate** | Returns the current date set in the operating system. |
| **GetFTime** | Returns the date and time a file was last written. |
| **GetTime** | Returns the current time set in the operating system. |
| **PackTime** | Converts a *DateTime* record into a 4-byte, packed date-and-time character longint used by *SetFTime*. The fields of the *DateTime* record are not range-checked. |
| **SetDate** | Sets the current date in the operating system. |
| **SetFTime** | Sets the date and time a file was last written. |
| **SetTime** | Sets the current time in the operating system. |

| | |
|---|---|
| **UnpackTime** | Converts a 4-byte, packed date-and-time character longint returned by *GetFTime*, *FindFirst*, or *FindNext* into an unpacked *DateTime* record. |

## *Disk Status Functions*

| | |
|---|---|
| **DiskFree** | Returns the number of free bytes of a specified disk drive. |
| **DiskSize** | Returns the total size in bytes of a specified disk drive. |

## *File-Handling Procedures*

| | |
|---|---|
| **FindFirst** | Searches the specified (or current) directory for the first entry matching the specified file name and set of attributes. |
| **FindNext** | Returns the next entry that matches the name and attributes specified in a previous call to *FindFirst*. |
| **GetFAttr** | Returns the attributes of a file. |
| **SetFAttr** | Sets the attributes of a file. |

## *Process-Handling Procedures and Functions*

### *Procedures*

| | |
|---|---|
| **Execute** | Executes a specified program with a specified command line. |
| **Keep** | *Keep* (or Terminate Stay Resident) terminates the program and makes it stay in memory. |

### *Functions*

| | |
|---|---|
| **DosExitCode** | Returns the exit code of a subprocess. |

# The Crt Unit

The *Crt* unit implements a range of powerful routines that give you full control of your PC's features, such as screen mode control, extended keyboard codes, colors, windows, and sound. *Crt* can only be used in programs that run on IBM PCs, ATs, PS/2s, and true compatibles.

One of the major advantages to using *Crt* is the added speed and flexibility of screen output operations. Programs that do not use the *Crt* unit send their screen output through DOS, which adds a lot of overhead. With the *Crt* unit, output is sent directly to the BIOS or, for even faster operation, directly to video memory.

## *The Input and Output Files*

The initialization code of the *Crt* unit assigns the *Input* and *Output* standard text files to refer to the CRT instead of to DOS's standard input and output files. This corresponds to the following statements being executed at the beginning of a program:

```
AssignCrt(Input); Reset(Input);
AssignCrt(Output); Rewrite(Output);
```

This means that I/O redirection of the *Input* and *Output* files is no longer possible unless these files are explicitly assigned back to standard input and output by executing

```
Assign(Input,''); Reset(Input);
Assign(Output,''); Rewrite(Output);
```

## *Windows*

*Crt* supports a simple yet powerful form of windows. The *Window* procedure lets you define a window anywhere on the screen. When you write in such a window, the window behaves exactly as if you were using the entire screen, leaving the rest of the screen untouched. In other words, the screen outside the window is not accessible. Inside the window, lines can be inserted and deleted, the cursor wraps around at the right edge, and the text scrolls when the cursor reaches the bottom line.

All screen coordinates, except the ones used to define a window, are relative to the current window, and screen coordinates (1,1) correspond to the upper left corner of the screen.

The default window is the entire screen.

Screen modes for EGA (43 line) and VGA (50 line) are also supported (see the *TextMode* description in Chapter 27).

## Special Characters

When writing to *Output* or to a file that has been assigned to the CRT, the following control characters have special meanings:

**#7** Bell—emits a beep from the internal speaker.

**#8** Backspace—moves the cursor left one character. If the cursor is already at the left edge of the current window, nothing happens.

**#10** Line feed—moves the cursor one line down. If the cursor is already at the bottom of the current window, the window scrolls up one line.

**#13** Carriage return—returns the cursor to the left edge of the current window.

All other characters will appear on the screen when written.

## Line Input

When reading from *Input* or from a text file that has been assigned to *Crt*, text is input one line at a time. The line is stored in the text file's internal buffer, and when variables are read, this buffer is used as the input source. Whenever the buffer has been emptied, a new line is input.

When entering lines, the following editing keys are available:

| | |
|---|---|
| *BackSpace* | Deletes the last character entered. |
| *Esc* | Deletes the entire input line. |
| *Enter* | Terminates the input line and stores the end-of-line marker (carriage return/line feed) in the buffer. |
| *Ctrl-S* | Same as *BackSpace* |
| *Ctrl-D* | Recalls one character from the last input line. |
| *Ctrl-A* | Same as *Esc*. |
| *Ctrl-F* | Recalls the last input line. |
| *Ctrl-Z* | Terminates the input line and generates an end-of-file marker. |

*Ctrl-Z* will only generate an end-of-file marker if the *CheckEOF* variable has been set to True; it is False by default.

To test keyboard status and input single characters under program control, use the *KeyPressed* and *ReadKey* functions.

## Constants and Types

Each of the constants, types, and variables defined by the *Crt* unit are briefly discussed in this section.

## Crt Mode Constants

The following constants are used as parameters to the *TextMode* procedure:

```
const
  BW40 = 0;                          { 40x25 B/W on color adapter }
  BW80 = 2;                          { 80x25 B/W on color adapter }
  Mono = 7;                    { 80x25 B/W on monochrome adapter }
  C040  = 1;                       { 40x25 color on color adapter }
  C080  = 3;                       { 80x25 color on color adapter }
  Font8x8 = 256;                     { For EGA/VGA 43 and 50 line }
  C40 = C040;                            { For 3.0 compatibility }
  C80 = C080;                            { For 3.0 compatibility }
```

*BW40, C040, BW80,* and *C080* represent the four color text modes supported by the IBM PC Color/Graphics Adapter (CGA). The *Mono* constant represents the single black-and-white text mode supported by the IBM PC Monochrome Adapter. *Font8x8* represents EGA/VGA 43- and 50-line modes. The *C40* and *C80* constants are for 3.0 compatibility.

## Text Color Constants

The following constants are used in connection with the *TextColor* and *TextBackground* procedures:

```
const
  Black      = 0;
  Blue       = 1;
  Green      = 2;
  Cyan       = 3;
  Red        = 4;
  Magenta    = 5;
  Brown      = 6;
  LightGray  = 7;
```

```
DarkGray      = 8;
LightBlue     = 9;
LightGreen    = 10;
LightCyan     = 11;
LightRed      = 12;
LightMagenta  = 13;
Yellow        = 14;
White         = 15;
Blink         = 128;
```

Colors are represented by the numbers between 0 and 15; to easily identify each color, these constants can be used instead of numbers. In the color text modes, the foreground of each character is selectable from 16 colors, and the background from 8 colors. The foreground of each character can also be made to blink.

# Crt Variables

Here are the variables in *Crt*:

```
var
  CheckBreak  : boolean;
  CheckEof    : boolean;
  CheckSnow   : boolean;
  DirectVideo : boolean;
  LastMode    : word;
  TextAttr    : byte;
  WindMin     : word;
  WindMax     : word;
  SaveInt1B   : pointer;
```

## *CheckBreak*

Enables and disables checks for *Ctrl-Break*.

```
    var CheckBreak: boolean;
```

When *CheckBreak* is True, pressing *Ctrl-Break* will abort the program when it next writes to the display. When *CheckBreak* is False, pressing *Ctrl-Break* has no effect. *CheckBreak* is True by default. (At runtime, *Crt* stores the old Control-Break interrupt vector, $1B, in a global pointer variable called *SaveInt1B*.)

## *CheckEOF*

Enables and disables the end-of-file character:

```
var CheckEOF: boolean;
```

When *CheckEOF* is True, an end-of-file character is generated if you press *Ctrl-Z* while reading from a file assigned to the screen. When *CheckEOF* is False, pressing *Ctrl-Z* has no effect. *CheckEOF* is False by default.

## CheckSnow

Enables and disables "snow-checking" when storing characters directly in video memory.

```
var CheckSnow: boolean;
```

On most CGAs, interference will result if characters are stored in video memory outside the horizontal retrace intervals. This does not occur with Monochrome Adapters or EGAs.

When a color text mode is selected, *CheckSnow* is set to True, and direct video-memory writes will occur only during the horizontal retrace intervals. If you are running on a newer CGA, you may want to set *CheckSnow* to False at the beginning of your program and after each call to *TextMode*. This will disable snow-checking, resulting in significantly higher output speeds.

*CheckSnow* has no effect when *DirectVideo* is False.

## DirectVideo

Enables and disables direct memory access for *Write* and *Writeln* statements that output to the screen.

```
var DirectVideo: boolean;
```

When *DirectVideo* is True, *Write*s and *Writeln*s to files associated with the CRT will store characters directly in video memory instead of calling the BIOS to display them. When *DirectVideo* is False, all characters are written through BIOS calls, which is a significantly slower process.

*DirectVideo* always defaults to True. If, for some reason, you want characters displayed through BIOS calls, set *DirectVideo* to False at the beginning of your program and after each call to *TextMode*.

## LastMode

Each time *TextMode* is called, the current video mode is stored in *LastMode*. In addition, *LastMode* is initialized at program startup to the then-active video mode.

```
var LastMode: word;
```

## TextAttr

Stores the currently selected text attributes.

```
var TextAttr: byte;
```

The text attributes are normally set through calls to *TextColor* and *TextBackground*. However, you can also set them by directly storing a value in *TextAttr*. The color information is encoded in *TextAttr* as follows:

| 7 | 6 | 5 | 4 | 3 | 2 | 1 | 0 |
|---|---|---|---|---|---|---|---|
| B | b | b | b | f | f | f | f |

where *ffff* is the 4-bit foreground color, *bbb* is the 3-bit background color, and *B* is the blink-enable bit. If you use the color constants for creating *TextAttr* values, note that the background color can only be selected from the first 8 colors, and that it must be multiplied by 16 to get it into the correct bit positions. The following assignment selects blinking yellow characters on a blue background:

```
TextAttr := Yellow + Blue * 16 + Blink;
```

## WindMin and WindMax

Store the screen coordinates of the current window.

```
var WindMin, WindMax : word;
```

These variables are set by calls to the *Window* procedure. *WindMin* defines the upper left corner, and *WindMax* defines the lower right corner. The *X* coordinate is stored in the low byte, and the *Y* coordinate is stored in the high byte. For example, *Lo(WindMin)* produces the *X* coordinate of the left edge, and *Hi(WindMax)* produces the *Y* coordinate of the bottom edge. The upper left corner of the screen corresponds to (*X,Y*) = (0,0). Note, however, that for coordinates passed to *Window* and *GotoXY*, the upper left corner is at (1,1).

## Procedures

**AssignCrt**                    Associates a text file with the CRT.

| | |
|---|---|
| **ClrEol** | Clears all characters from the cursor position to the end of the line without moving the cursor. |
| **ClrScr** | Clears the screen and places the cursor in the upper left-hand corner. |
| **Delay** | Delays a specified number of milliseconds. |
| **DelLine** | Deletes the line containing the cursor and moves all lines below that line one line up. The bottom line is cleared. |
| **GotoXY** | Positions the cursor. $X$ is the horizontal position. $Y$ is the vertical position. |
| **HighVideo** | Selects high intensity characters. |
| **InsLine** | Inserts an empty line at the cursor position. |
| **LowVideo** | Selects low intensity characters. |
| **NoSound** | Turns off the internal speaker. |
| **Sound** | Starts the internal speaker. |
| **TextBackground** | Selects the background color. |
| **TextColor** | Selects the foreground character color. |
| **TextMode** | Selects a specific text mode. |
| **Window** | Defines a text window on the screen. |

## *Functions*

| | |
|---|---|
| **KeyPressed** | Returns True if a key has been pressed on the keyboard, and False otherwise. |
| **NormVideo** | Selects normal characters. |
| **ReadKey** | Reads a character from the keyboard. |
| **WhereX** | Returns the $X$-coordinate of the current cursor position, relative to the current window. $X$ is the horizontal position. |
| **WhereY** | Returns the $Y$-coordinate of the current cursor position, relative to the current window. $Y$ is the vertical position. |

# The Graph Unit

The *Graph* unit implements a complete library of more than 50 graphics routines that range from high-level calls, like *SetViewPort*, *Circle*, *Bar3D*, and *DrawPoly*, to bit-oriented routines, like *GetImage* and *PutImage*. Several fill and line styles are supported, and there are several fonts that may be magnified, justified, and oriented horizontally or vertically.

To compile a program that uses the *Graph* unit, you'll need your program's source code, the compiler, access to the standard units in TURBO.TPL and the *Graph* unit in GRAPH.TPU. To run a program that uses the *Graph* unit, in addition to your .EXE program, you'll need one or more of the graphics drivers (.BGI files, see below). In addition, if your program uses any stroked fonts, you'll need one or more font (.CHR) files as well.

(Pursuant to the terms of the license agreement, you can distribute the .CHR and .BGI files along with your programs.)

## *Drivers*

Graphics drivers are provided for the following graphics adapters (and true compatibles):

- CGA
- MCGA
- EGA
- VGA
- Hercules
- AT&T 400 line
- 3270 PC

Each driver contains code and data and is stored in a separate file on disk. At runtime, the *InitGraph* procedure identifies the graphics hardware, loads and initializes the appropriate graphics driver, puts the system into graphics mode, and then returns control to the calling routine. The *CloseGraph* procedure unloads the driver from memory and restores the previous video mode. You can switch back and forth between text and graphics modes using the *RestoreCrtMode* and *SetGraphMode* routines. To load the driver files yourself or link them into your .EXE, refer to *RegisterBGIdriver* in Chapter 27.

*Graph* supports computers with dual monitors. When *Graph* is initialized by calling *InitGraph*, the correct monitor will be selected for the graphics driver and mode requested. When terminating a graphics program, the previous video mode will be restored. If auto-detection of graphics hardware is requested on a dual monitor system, *InitGraph* will select the monitor and graphics card that will produce the highest quality graphics output.

| | |
|---|---|
| CGA.BGI | Driver for IBM CGA, MCGA |
| EGAVGA.BGI | Driver for IBM EGA, VGA |
| HERC.BGI | Driver for Hercules monochrome |
| ATT.BGI | Driver for AT&T 6300 (400 line) |
| PC3270.BGI | Driver for IBM 3270 PC |

## Coordinate System

By convention, the upper left corner of the graphics screen is (0,0). The *x* values, or columns, increment to the right. The *y* values, or rows, increment downward. Thus, in 320×200 mode on a CGA, the screen coordinates for each of the four corners with a specified point in the middle of the screen would look like this:

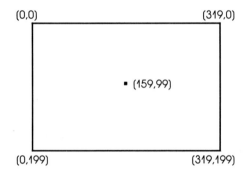

## Current Pointer

Many graphics systems support the notion of a current pointer (CP). The CP is similar in concept to a text mode cursor except that the CP is not visible.

```
Write('ABC');
```

In text mode, the preceding *Write* statement will leave the cursor in the column immediately following the letter C. If the C is written in column 80, then the cursor will wrap around to column 1 of the next line. If the C is written in column 80 on the 25th line, the entire screen will scroll up one line, and the cursor will be in column 1 of line 25.

```
MoveTo(0,0)
LineTo(20,20)
```

In graphics mode, the preceding *LineTo* statement will leave the CP at the last point referenced (20,20). The actual line output would be clipped to the current viewport if clipping is active. Note that the CP is never clipped.

The *MoveTo* command is the equivalent of *GoToXY*. It's only purpose is to move the CP. Only the commands that use the CP move the CP: *InitGraph*, *MoveTo*, *MoveRel*, *LineTo*, *LineRel*, *OutText*, *SetGraphMode*,* *GraphDefaults*,* *ClearDevice*,* *SetViewPort*,* and *ClearViewPort**. (The * indicates procedures that move the CP to (0,0).)

## *Text*

An 8×8 bit-mapped font and several "stroked" fonts are included for text output while in graphics mode. A bit-mapped character is defined by an 8×8 matrix of pixels. A stroked font is defined by a series of vectors that tell the graphics system how to draw the font.

The advantage to using a stroked font is apparent when you start to draw large characters. Since a stroked font is defined by vectors, it will still retain good resolution and quality when the font is enlarged.

When a bit-mapped font is enlarged, the matrix is multiplied by a scaling factor and as the scaling factors becomes larger, the characters' resolution becomes coarser. For small characters, the bit-mapped font should be sufficient, but for larger text you will want to select a "stroked" font.

The justification of graphics text is controlled by the *SetTextJustify* procedure. Scaling and font selection is done with the *SetTextStyle* procedure. Graphics text is output by calling either the *OutText* or *OutTextXY* procedures. Inquiries about the current text settings are made by calling the *GetTextSettings* procedure. The size of stroked fonts can be customized by the *SetUserCharSize* procedure.

Stroked fonts are each kept in a separate file on disk with a .CHR file extension. Font files can be loaded from disk automatically by the *Graph* unit at runtime (as described), or they can also be linked in or loaded by the user program and "registered" with the *Graph* unit.

A special utility, BINOBJ.EXE, is provided that converts a font file (or any binary data file, for that matter) to an .OBJ file that can be linked into a unit or program using the {$L} compiler directive. This makes it possible for a program to have all its font files built into the .EXE file. (Read the comments at the beginning of the GRLINK.PAS sample program Disk 3.)

## Figures and Styles

All kinds of support routines are provided for drawing and filling figures, including points, lines, circles, arcs, ellipses, rectangles, polygons, bars, 3-D bars, and pie slices. Use *SetLineStyle* to control whether lines are thick or thin, or whether they are solid, dotted, or built using your own pattern.

Use *SetFillStyle* and *SetFillPattern*, *FillPoly* and *FloodFill* to fill a region or a polygon with cross-hatching or other intricate patterns.

## Viewports and Bit Images

The *ViewPort* procedure makes all output commands operate in a rectangular region on the screen. Plots, lines, figures—all graphics output—are viewport-relative until the viewport is changed. Other routines are provided to clear a viewport and read the current viewport definitions. If clipping is active, all graphics output is clipped to the current port. Note that the CP is never clipped.

*GetPixel* and *PutPixel* are provided for reading and plotting pixels. *GetImage* and *PutImage* can be used to save and restore rectangular regions on the screen. They support the full complement of *BitBlt* operations (normal, **xor**, **or**, **and**, **not**).

## Paging and Colors

There are many other support routines, including support for multiple graphic pages (EGA, VGA, and Hercules only; especially useful for doing animation), palettes, colors, and so on.

## Error Handling

Internal errors in the *Graph* unit are returned by the function *GraphResult*. *GraphResult* returns an error code that reports the status of the last graphics operation. The following error return codes are defined:

- 0: No error
- –1: (BGI) graphics not installed (use *InitGraph*)
- –2: Graphics hardware not detected
- –3: Device driver file not found
- –4: Invalid device driver file

- −5: Not enough memory to load driver
- −6: Out of memory in scan fill
- −7: Out of memory in flood fill
- −8: Font file not found
- −9: Not enough memory to load font
- −10: Invalid graphics mode for selected driver
- −11: Graphics error
- −12: Graphics I/O error
- −13: Invalid font file
- −14: Invalid font number
- −15: Invalid device number

The following routines set *GraphResult*:

| | | |
|---|---|---|
| *Bar* | *InitGraph* | *SetGraphMode* |
| *Bar3D* | *PieSlice* | *SetLineStyle* |
| *ClearViewPort* | *RegisterBGIdriver* | *SetPalette* |
| *DetectGraph* | *RegisterBGIfont* | *SetTextJustify* |
| *DrawPoly* | *SetAllPalette* | *SetTextStyle* |
| *FillPoly* | *SetFillPattern* | *SetViewPort* |
| *FloodFill* | *SetFillStyle* | *ValidMode* |
| *ImageSize* | *SetGraphBufSize* | |

Note that *GraphResult* is reset to zero after it has been called. Therefore, the user should store the value of *GraphResult* into a temporary variable and then test it. The following return code constants are defined:

```
const
  { GraphResult error return codes }
  grOk               =    0;
  grNoInitGraph      =   -1;
  grNotDetected      =   -2;
  grFileNotFound     =   -3;
  grInvalidDriver    =   -4;
  grNoLoadMem        =   -5;
  grNoScanMem        =   -6;
  grNoFloodMem       =   -7;
  grFontNotFound     =   -8;
  grNoFontMem        =   -9;
  grInvalidMode      =  -10;
  grError            =  -11;
  grIOError          =  -12;
  grInvalidFont      =  -13;
  grInvalidFontNum   =  -14;
  grInvalidDeviceNum =  -15;
```

# Getting Started

Here's a simple graphics program:

```
1  program GraphTest;
2  uses
3    Graph;
4  var
5    GraphDriver : integer;
6    GraphMode   : integer;
7    ErrorCode   : integer;
8  begin
9    GraphDriver := Detect;                              { Set flag: do detection }
10   InitGraph(GraphDriver, GraphMode, 'C:\DRIVERS');
11   ErrorCode := GraphResult;
12   if ErrorCode <> grOk then                                           { Error? }
13   begin
14     Writeln('Graphics error: ', GraphErrorMsg(ErrorCode));
15     Writeln('Program aborted...');
16     Halt(1);
17   end;
18   Rectangle(0, 0, GetMaxX, GetMaxY);                 { Draw full screen box }
19   SetTextJustify(CenterText, CenterText);                    { Center text }
20   SetTextStyle(DefaultFont, HorizDir, 3);
21   OutTextXY(GetMaxX div 2, GetMaxY div 2,                { Center of screen }
22             'Borland Graphics Interface (BGI)');
23   Readln;
24   CloseGraph;
25 end. { GraphTest }
```

The program begins with a call to *InitGraph*, which autodetects the hardware and loads the appropriate graphics driver (located in C:\DRIVERS). If no graphics hardware is recognized or an error occurs during initialization, an error message is displayed and the program terminates. Otherwise, a box is drawn along the edge of the screen and text is displayed in the center of the screen.

**Note:** The AT&T 400 line card is not autodetected. You can still use the AT&T graphics driver by overriding autodection and passing *InitGraph* the AT&T driver code and a valid graphics mode. Replace lines 9 and 10 in the preceding example with the following three lines of code:

```
GraphDriver := ATT400;
GraphMode := ATT400Hi;
InitGraph(GraphDriver, GraphMode, 'C:\DRIVERS');
```

This instructs the graphics system to load the AT&T 400 line driver located in C:\DRIVERS and set the graphics mode to 640 by 400.

Here's another example that demonstrates how to switch back and forth between graphics and text modes:

```
1  program GraphTest;
2  uses
3    Graph;
4  var
5    GraphDriver : integer;
6    GraphMode   : integer;
7    ErrorCode   : integer;
8  begin
9    GraphDriver := Detect;                              { Set flag: do detection }
10   InitGraph(GraphDriver, GraphMode, 'C:\DRIVERS');
11   ErrorCode := GraphResult;
12   if ErrorCode <> grOk then                            { Error? }
13   begin
14     Writeln('Graphics error: ', GraphErrorMsg(ErrorCode));
15     Writeln('Program aborted...');
16     Halt(1);
17   end;
18   OutText('In Graphics mode. Press <RETURN>');
19   Readln;
20   RestoreCRTMode;
21   Write('Now in text mode. Press <RETURN>');
22   Readln;
23   SetGraphMode(GraphMode);
24   OutText('Back in Graphics mode. Press <RETURN>');
25   Readln;
26   CloseGraph;
27 end. { GraphTest }
```

Note that the *SetGraphMode* call on line 23 resets all the graphics parameters (palette, current pointer, foreground, and background colors, and so on) to the default values.

The call to *CloseGraph* restores the video mode that was detected initially by *InitGraph* and frees the heap memory that was used to hold the graphics driver.

# User-Written Heap Management Routines

Two heap management routines are used by the *Graph* unit: *GraphGetMem* and *GraphFreeMem*. *GraphGetMem* allocates memory for graphics device drivers, stroked fonts, and a scan buffer. *GraphFreeMem* deallocates the memory allocated to the drivers. The standard routines take the following form:

```
procedure GraphGetMem(var P : pointer; Size : word);
{ Allocate memory for graphics }

procedure GraphFreeMem(var P : pointer; Size : word);
{ Deallocate memory for graphics }
```

Two pointers are defined by *Graph* that by default point to the two standard routines described here. The pointers are defined as follows:

```
var
  GraphGetMemPtr  : pointer;          { Pointer to memory allocation routine }
  GraphFreeMemPtr : pointer           { Pointer to memory deallocation routine }
```

The heap management routines referenced by *GraphGetMemPtr* and *GraphFreeMemPtr* are called by the *Graph* unit to allocate and deallocate memory for three different purposes:

- a multi-purpose graphics buffer whose size can be set by a call to *SetGraphBufSize* (default = 4K)
- a device driver that is loaded by *InitGraph* (*.BGI files)
- a stroked font file that is loaded by *SetTextStyle* (*.CHR files)

The graphics buffer is always allocated on the heap. The device driver is allocated on the heap unless your program loads or links one in and calls *RegisterBGIdriver*, and the font file is allocated on the heap when you select a stroked font using *SetTextStyle*—unless your program loads or links one in and calls *RegisterBGIfont*.

Upon initialization of the *Graph* unit, these pointers point to the standard graphics allocation and deallocation routines that are defined in the implementation section of the *Graph* unit. You can insert you own memory management routines by assigning these pointers the address of your own routines. The user-defined routines must have the same parameter lists as the standard routines and must be *far* procedures. The following is an example of user-defined allocation and deallocation routines; notice the use of *MyExitProc* to automatically call *CloseGraph* when the program terminates:

```
program UserHeapManagement;
{ Illustrates how the user can steal the heap }
{ management routines used by the Graph unit. }
uses
  Graph;
var
  GraphDriver, GraphMode : integer;
  ErrorCode              : integer;        { Used to store GraphResult return code }
  PreGraphExitProc       : pointer;             { Used to save original exit proc }

{$F+}  { User routines must be far call model }

procedure MyGetMem(var P : pointer; Size : word);
{ Allocate memory for graphics device drivers, fonts, and scan buffer }
begin
  GetMem(P, Size)
end; { MyGetMem }

procedure MyFreeMem(var P : pointer; Size : word);
```

```
{ Deallocate memory for graphics device drivers, fonts, and scan buffer }
begin
  if P <> Nil then                                { Don't free Nil pointers! }
  begin
    FreeMem(P, Size);
    P := Nil;
  end;
end; { MyFreeMem }

procedure MyExitProc;
{ Always gets called when program terminates }
begin
  ExitProc := PreGraphExitProc;                   { Restore original exit proc }
  CloseGraph;                                     { Do heap clean up }
end; { MyExitProc }
{$F-}
begin
  { Install clean-up routine }
  PreGraphExitProc := ExitProc;
  ExitProc := @MyExitProc;

  GraphGetMemPtr := @MyGetMem;                     { Steal memory allocation }
  GraphFreeMemPtr := @MyFreeMem;                   { Steal memory deallocation }

  GraphDriver := Detect;
  InitGraph(GraphDriver, GraphMode, '');
  ErrorCode := GraphResult;
  if ErrorCode <> grOk then
  begin
    Writeln('Graphics error: ', GraphErrorMsg(ErrorCode));
    Readln;
    Halt(1);
  end;
  Line(0, 0, GetMaxX, GetMaxY);
  OutTextXY(1, 1, 'Press <Return>:');
  Readln;
end.  { UserHeapManagment }
```

# Graph Interface Section: Constants, Types, and Variables

There are many useful constant and type declarations in the *Graph* unit. Here is an excerpt from the interface section of GRAPH.TPU for your reference:

```
const
  { GraphResult error return codes }
  grOk             =   0;
  grNoInitGraph    =  -1;
  grNotDetected    =  -2;
  grFileNotFound   =  -3;
  grInvalidDriver  =  -4;
  grNoLoadMem      =  -5;
  grNoScanMem      =  -6;
```

```
grNoFloodMem       = -7;
grFontNotFound     = -8;
grNoFontMem        = -9;
grInvalidMode      = -10;
grError            = -11;                        { Generic error }
grIOerror          = -12;
grInvalidFont      = -13;
grInvalidFontNum   = -14;
grInvalidDeviceNum = -15;


{ Define graphics drivers }
Detect   = 0;                              { Requests autodetection }
CGA      = 1;
MCGA     = 2;
EGA      = 3;
EGA64    = 4;
EGAMono  = 5;
RESERVED = 6;
HercMono = 7;
ATT400   = 8;
VGA      = 9;
PC3270   = 10;


{ Graphics modes for each driver }
CGAC0     = 0;      { 320x200 palette 0: LightGreen, LightRed, Yellow; 1 page }
CGAC1     = 1;      { 320x200 palette 1: LightCyan, LightMagenta, White; 1 page }
CGAC2     = 2;             { 320x200 palette 2: Green, Red, Brown; 1 page }
CGAC3     = 3;       { 320x200 palette 3: Cyan, Magenta, LightGray; 1 page }
CGAHi     = 4;                                   { 640x200 1 page }
MCGAC0    = 0;      { 320x200 palette 0: LightGreen, LightRed, Yellow; 1 page }
MCGAC1    = 1;      { 320x200 palette 1: LightCyan, LightMagenta, White; 1 page }
MCGAC2    = 2;             { 320x200 palette 2: Green, Red, Brown; 1 page }
MCGAC3    = 3;       { 320x200 palette 3: Cyan, Magenta, LightGray; 1 page }
MCGAMed   = 4;                                   { 640x200 1 page }
MCGAHi    = 5;                                   { 640x480 1 page }
EGALo     = 0;                          { 640x200 16 color 4 page }
EGAHi     = 1;                          { 640x350 16 color 2 page }
EGA64Lo   = 0;                          { 640x200 16 color 1 page }
EGA64Hi   = 1;                           { 640x350 4 color 1 page }
EGAMonoHi = 3;           { 640x350 64K on card, 1 page; 256K on card, 2 page }
HercMonoHi = 0;                                  { 720x348 2 page }
ATT400C0  = 0;      { 320x200 palette 0: LightGreen, LightRed, Yellow; 1 page }
ATT400C1  = 1;      { 320x200 palette 1: LightCyan, LightMagenta, White; 1 page }
ATT400C2  = 2;             { 320x200 palette 2: Green, Red, Brown; 1 page }
ATT400C3  = 3;       { 320x200 palette 3: Cyan, Magenta, LightGray; 1 page }
ATT400Med = 4;                                   { 640x200 1 page }
ATT400Hi  = 5;                                   { 640x400 1 page }
VGALo     = 0;                          { 640x200 16 color 4 page }
VGAMed    = 1;                          { 640x350 16 color 2 page }
VGAHi     = 2;                          { 640x480 16 color 1 page }
PC3270Hi  = 0;                                   { 720x350 1 page }

{ Colors for SetPalette and SetAllPalette }
Black     = 0;
Blue      = 1;
Green     = 2;
Cyan      = 3;
Red       = 4;
```

```
Magenta      = 5;
Brown        = 6;
LightGray    = 7;
DarkGray     = 8;
LightBlue    = 9;
LightGreen   = 10;
LightCyan    = 11;
LightRed     = 12;
LightMagenta = 13;
Yellow       = 14;
White        = 15;

{ Line styles and widths for Get/SetLineStyle }
SolidLn   = 0;
DottedLn  = 1;
CenterLn  = 2;
DashedLn  = 3;
UserBitLn = 4;                                    { User-defined line style }

NormWidth  = 1;
ThickWidth = 3;

{ Set/GetTextStyle constants }
DefaultFont   = 0;                                 { 8x8 bit-mapped font }
TriplexFont   = 1;                                    { "Stroked" fonts }
SmallFont     = 2;
SansSerifFont = 3;
GothicFont    = 4;

HorizDir = 0;                                             { Left to right }
VertDir  = 1;                                            { Bottom to top }

UserCharSize = 0;                            { User-defined character size }

{ Clipping constants }
ClipOn  = True;
ClipOff = False;

{ Bar3D constants }
TopOn  = True;
TopOff = False;

{ Fill patterns for Get/SetFillStyle }
EmptyFill      = 0;                      { Fills area in background color }
SolidFill      = 1;                      { Fills area in solid fill color }
LineFill       = 2;                                       { --- fill }
LtSlashFill    = 3;                                       { /// fill }
SlashFill      = 4;                      { /// fill with thick lines }
BkSlashFill    = 5;                      { \\\ fill with thick lines }
LtBkSlashFill  = 6;                                       { \\\ fill }
HatchFill      = 7;                                { Light hatch fill }
XHatchFill     = 8;                          { Heavy cross hatch fill }
InterleaveFill = 9;                            { Interleaving line fill }
WideDotFill    = 10;                           { Widely spaced dot fill }
CloseDotFill   = 11;                          { Closely spaced dot fill }
UserFill       = 12;                               { User-defined fill }
```

```
{ BitBlt operators for PutImage }
NormalPut    = 0;                                              { MOV }
XORPut       = 1;                                              { XOR }
OrPut        = 2;                                              { OR  }
AndPut       = 3;                                              { AND }
NotPut       = 4;                                              { NOT }

{ Horizontal and vertical justification for SetTextJustify }
LeftText   = 0;
CenterText = 1;                          { CenterText = 1; already defined above }
RightText  = 2;

BottomText = 0;
TopText    = 2;

const
  MaxColors = 15;
type
  PaletteType = record
                  Size   : byte;
                  Colors : array[0..MaxColors] of shortint;
                end;

  LineSettingsType = record
                       LineStyle : word;
                       Pattern   : word;
                       Thickness : word;
                     end;

  TextSettingsType = record
                       Font      : word;
                       Direction : word;
                       CharSize  : word;
                       Horiz     : word;
                       Vert      : word;
                     end;

  FillSettingsType = record                          { Predefined fill style }
                       Pattern : word;
                       Color   : word;
                     end;

  FillPatternType = array[1..8] of byte;              { User-defined fill style }
  PointType = record
                X, Y : integer;
              end;

  ViewPortType = record
                   x1, y1, x2, y2 : integer;
                   Clip           : boolean;
                 end;

  ArcCoordsType = record
                    X, Y           : integer;
                    Xstart, Ystart : integer;
                    Xend, Yend     : integer;
                  end;
```

```
var
  GraphGetMemPtr  : pointer;                    { Allows user to steal heap allocation }
  GraphFreeMemPtr : pointer;                    { Allows user to steal heap deallocation }

{ *** High-level error handling *** }
function GraphErrorMsg(ErrorCode : integer) : string;
function GraphResult : integer;

{ *** Detection, initialization, and CRT mode routines *** }
procedure DetectGraph(var GraphDriver, GraphMode : integer);
procedure InitGraph(var GraphDriver : integer;
                    var GraphMode   : integer;
                        PathToDriver : string);
function RegisterBGIfont(font : pointer) : integer;
function RegisterBGIdriver(driver : pointer) : integer;
procedure SetGraphBufSize(BufSize : word);
procedure GetModeRange(GraphDriver : integer; var LoMode, HiMode : integer);
procedure SetGraphMode(Mode : integer);
function GetGraphMode : integer;
procedure GraphDefaults;
procedure RestoreCrtMode;
procedure CloseGraph;
function GetX : integer;
function GetY : integer;
function GetMaxX : integer;
function GetMaxY : integer;

{ *** Screen, viewport, page routines *** }
procedure ClearDevice;
procedure SetViewPort(x1, y1, x2, y2 : integer; Clip : boolean);
procedure GetViewSettings(var ViewPort : ViewPortType);
procedure ClearViewPort;
procedure SetVisualPage(Page : word);
procedure SetActivePage(Page : word);

{ *** Point-oriented routines *** }
procedure PutPixel(X, Y : integer; Pixel : word);
function GetPixel(X, Y : integer) : word;

{ *** Line-oriented routines *** }
procedure LineTo(X, Y : integer);
procedure LineRel(Dx, Dy : integer);
procedure MoveTo(X, Y : integer);
procedure MoveRel(Dx, Dy : integer);
procedure Line(x1, y1, x2, y2 : integer);
procedure GetLineSettings(var LineInfo : LineSettingsType);
procedure SetLineStyle(LineStyle : word;
                       Pattern   : word;
                       Thickness : word);

{ *** Polygon, fills and figures *** }
procedure Rectangle(x1, y1, x2, y2 : integer);
procedure Bar(x1, y1, x2, y2 : integer);
procedure Bar3D(x1, y1, x2, y2 : integer; Depth : word; Top : boolean);
procedure DrawPoly(NumPoints : word; var PolyPoints);
procedure FillPoly(NumPoints : word; var PolyPoints);
procedure GetFillSettings(var FillInfo : FillSettingsType);
procedure GetFillPattern(var FillPattern : FillPatternType);
```

```
procedure SetFillStyle(Pattern : word; Color : word);
procedure SetFillPattern(Pattern : FillPatternType; Color : word);
procedure FloodFill(X, Y : integer; Border : word);

{ *** Arc, circle, and other curves *** }
procedure Arc(X, Y : integer; StAngle, EndAngle, Radius : word);
procedure GetArcCoords(var ArcCoords : ArcCoordsType);
procedure Circle(X, Y : integer; Radius : word);
procedure Ellipse(X, Y : integer;
                  StAngle, EndAngle : word;
                  XRadius, YRadius  : word);
procedure GetAspectRatio(var Xasp, Yasp : word);
procedure PieSlice(X, Y : integer; StAngle, EndAngle, Radius : word);

{ *** Color and palette routines *** }
procedure SetBkColor(Color : word);
procedure SetColor(Color : word);
function GetBkColor : word;
function GetColor : word;
procedure SetAllPalette(var Palette);
procedure SetPalette(ColorNum : word; Color : shortint);
procedure GetPalette(var Palette : PaletteType);
function GetMaxColor : word;

{ *** Bit-image routines *** }
function  ImageSize(x1, y1, x2, y2 : integer) : word;
procedure GetImage(x1, y1, x2, y2 : integer; var BitMap);
procedure PutImage(X, Y : integer; var BitMap; BitBlt : word);

{ *** Text routines *** }
procedure GetTextSettings(var TextInfo : TextSettingsType);
procedure OutText(TextString : string);
procedure OutTextXY(X, Y : integer; TextString : string);
procedure SetTextJustify(Horiz, Vert : word);
procedure SetTextStyle(Font, Direction : word; CharSize : word);
procedure SetUserCharSize(MultX, DivX, MultY, DivY : word);
function  TextHeight(TextString : string) : word;
function  TextWidth(TextString : string) : word;
```

## Procedures

| | |
|---|---|
| **Arc** | Draws a circular arc from start angle to end angle, using $(x,y)$ as the center point. |
| **Bar** | Draws a bar using the current fill style and color. |
| **Bar3D** | Draws a 3-D bar using the current fill style and color. |
| **Circle** | Draws a circle using $(x,y)$ as the center point. |
| **ClearDevice** | Clears the currently selected output device and homes the current pointer. |

| | |
|---|---|
| **ClearViewPort** | Clears the current viewport. |
| **CloseGraph** | Shuts down the graphics system. |
| **DetectGraph** | Checks the hardware and determines which graphics driver and mode to use. |
| **DrawPoly** | Draws the outline of a polygon using the current line style and color. |
| **Ellipse** | Draws an elliptical arc from start angle to end angle, using $(X,Y)$ as the center point. |
| **FillPoly** | Fills a polygon, using the scan converter. |
| **FloodFill** | Fills a bounded region using the current fill pattern and fill color. |
| **GetArcCoords** | Allows the user to inquire about the coordinates of the last *Arc* command. |
| **GetAspectRatio** | Returns the effective resolution of the graphics screen from which the aspect ratio (*Xasp:Yasp*) can be computed. |
| **GetFillPattern** | Returns the last fill pattern set by a call to *SetFillPattern*. |
| **GetFillSettings** | Allows the user to inquire about the current fill pattern and color as set by *SetFillStyle* or *SetFillPattern*. |
| **GetImage** | Saves a bit image of the specified region into a buffer. |
| **GetLineSettings** | Returns the current line style, line pattern, and line thickness as set by *SetLineStyle*. |
| **GetModeRange** | Returns the lowest and highest valid graphics mode for a given driver. |
| **GetPalette** | Returns the current palette and its size. |
| **GetTextSettings** | Returns the current text font, direction, size, and justification as set by *SetTextStyle* and *SetTextJustify*. |
| **GetViewSettings** | Allows the user to inquire about the current viewport and clipping parameters. |
| **GraphDefaults** | Homes the current pointer (CP) and resets the graphics system. |

| | |
|---|---|
| **InitGraph** | Initializes the graphics system and puts the hardware into graphics mode. |
| **Line** | Draws a line from the (*x1*, *y1*) to (*x2*, *y2*). |
| **LineRel** | Draws a line to a point that is a relative distance from the current pointer (CP). |
| **LineTo** | Draws a line from the current pointer to (*x,y*). |
| **MoveRel** | Moves the current pointer (CP) a relative distance from its current position. |
| **MoveTo** | Moves the current graphics pointer (CP) to (*x,y*). |
| **OutText** | Sends a string to the output device at the current pointer. |
| **OutTextXY** | Sends a string to the output device. |
| **PieSlice** | Draws and fills a pie slice, using (*X,Y*) as the center point and drawing from start angle to end angle. |
| **PutImage** | Puts a bit image onto the screen. |
| **PutPixel** | Plots a pixel at *x,y*. |
| **Rectangle** | Draws a rectangle using the current line style and color. |
| **RestoreCrtMode** | Restores the original screen mode before graphics is initialized. |
| **SetActivePage** | Set the active page for graphics output. |
| **SetAllPalette** | Changes all palette colors as specified. |
| **SetBkColor** | Sets the current background color using the palette. |
| **SetColor** | Sets the current drawing color using the palette. |
| **SetFillPattern** | Selects a user-defined fill pattern. |
| **SetFillStyle** | Sets the fill pattern and color. |
| **SetGraphBufSize** | Allows you to change the size of the buffer used for scan and flood fills. |
| **SetGraphMode** | Sets the system to graphics mode and clears the screen. |
| **SetLineStyle** | Sets the current line width and style. |
| **SetPalette** | Changes one palette color as specified by *ColorNum* and *Color*. |

| | |
|---|---|
| **SetTextJustify** | Sets text justification values used by *OutText* and *OutTextXY*. |
| **SetTextStyle** | Sets the current text font, style, and character magnification factor. |
| **SetUserCharSize** | Lets you change the character width and height for stroked fonts. |
| **SetViewPort** | Sets the current output viewport or window for graphics output. |
| **SetVisualPage** | Sets the visual graphics page number. |

## Functions

| | |
|---|---|
| **GetBkColor** | Returns the current background color. |
| **GetColor** | Returns the current drawing color. |
| **GetGraphMode** | Returns the current graphics mode. |
| **GetMaxColor** | Returns the highest color that can be passed to *SetColor*. |
| **GetMaxX** | Returns the rightmost column (*x* resolution) of the current graphics driver and mode. |
| **GetMaxY** | Returns the bottommost row (*y* resolution) of the current graphics driver and mode. |
| **GetPixel** | Gets the pixel value at *X,Y*. |
| **GetX** | Returns the *X* coordinate of the current position (CP). |
| **GetY** | Returns the *Y* coordinate of the current position (CP). |
| **GraphErrorMsg** | Returns an error message string for the specified *ErrorCode*. |
| **GraphResult** | Returns an error code for the last graphics operation. |
| **ImageSize** | Returns the number of bytes required to store a rectangular region of the screen. |
| **RegisterBGIdriver** | Registers a valid BGI driver with the graphics system. |
| **RegisterBGIfont** | Registers a valid BFI font with the graphics system. |

| **TextHeight** | Returns the height of a string in pixels. |
| **TextWidth** | Returns the width of a string in pixels. |

For a detailed description of each procedure or function, refer to Chapter 27.

# The Turbo3 Unit

Every routine in this unit is duplicated or improved upon in other standard units. The *Turbo3* unit is provided for backward compatibility only. By using *Turbo3*, you gain more 3.0-compatibility, but lose direct access to important new features built into some of the standard routines duplicated here. (Note that you can still call these standard routines by using the unit override syntax; for example, *Turbo3*'s *MemAvail* calls the *System.MemAvail* function even if you are using the *Turbo3* unit in your program. For more information about referring to routines with the same name in other units, look at Chapter 4, "Units and Related Mysteries.")

**Note:** The routines that follow are *not* described in Chapter 27, the lookup section. For more detailed information about *Turbo3* routines, refer to your Turbo Pascal 3.0 reference manual.

## *Interface Section*

Here's a look at the **interface** section of the *Turbo3* unit:

```
unit Turbo3;
interface
uses Crt;
var
  Kbd    : Text;
  CBreak : boolean absolute CheckBreak;

function MemAvail: integer;
function MaxAvail: integer;
function LongFileSize(var F): real;
function LongFilePos(var F): real;
procedure LongSeek(var F; Pos: real);
procedure HighVideo;
procedure NormVideo;
procedure LowVideo;
function IOResult : integer;
```

As you can see, there are two global variables, five functions, and four procedures declared in the *Turbo3* unit.

# Kbd

This is provided for 3.0 programs that read from the keyboard device; for example, *Read(Kbd, CharVar)*. Note that there is now a function in the *Crt* unit called *ReadKey* that should be used in place of *Read(Kbd, CharVar)*. Here are two programs that read a character and report whether an extended key was typed (*F1, F2, Left arrow*, and so on):

In version 3.0:

```
program TestKbd;
uses Crt, Turbo3;
var
  c : char;
begin
  Read(Kbd, c);
  if (c = #27) and KeyPressed then
  begin
    Read(Kbd, c);
    Writeln('Extended key: ', c);
  end
  else
    Writeln(c);
end.
```

Notice that the *Kbd* device handler converts extended keys from (null + character) to (ESC + second character). Since *Esc* (#27) is a perfectly valid key to enter from the keyboard, a call to *KeyPressed* must be made to determine whether the #27 is the first key from an extended key or an actual *Esc* typed on the keyboard. If an *Esc* is typed, followed quickly by another character before the program detected the *Esc*, the two keys would be mistaken as an extended keystroke.

In version 4.0:

```
program TestReadKey;
uses Crt;
var
  c : char;

begin
  c := ReadKey;
  if (c = #0) then
    Writeln('Extended key: ', ReadKey);
  else
    Writeln(c);
end.
```

The code in 4.0 is smaller (and faster), and contains none of the ambiguity about the leading character of an extended keystroke. (It is impossible to generate a null character from the keyboard except when using the extended keys.)

# Cbreak

*Cbreak* has been renamed to *CheckBreak* in version 4.0. Backward compatibility is achieved by giving *Cbreak* the same address as *CheckBreak*, which is declared in the *Crt* unit. The statement *Cbreak* := *False* turns off Control-Break checking; *Cbreak* := *True* turns it back on.

## *Procedures*

| | |
|---|---|
| **LongSeek** | Moves the current position of a file to a specified component. Uses a real number parameter to specify the component number. |
| **HighVideo** | Sets the video attribute to yellow on black (color systems) or white on black (black and white, mono systems). |
| **NormVideo** | Same as *HighVideo*. Sets the video attribute to yellow on black (color systems) or white on black (black and white, mono systems). |
| **LowVideo** | Sets the video attribute to *LightGray* on black. |

## *Functions*

| | |
|---|---|
| **MemAvail** | Returns the number of free paragraphs of heap storage available. |
| **MaxAvail** | Returns the size of the largest contiguous free block in the heap (in paragraphs). |
| **LongFileSize** | Returns the size of the file. The value returned is a real number. |
| **LongFilePos** | Returns the current file position of a file. The value returned is a real number. |
| **IOResult** | *IOResult* returns an integer value that is the status of the last I/O operation performed. The *Turbo3 IOResult* function returns 3.0-compatible return codes wherever possible. |

# The Graph3 Unit

The *Graph3* unit is a direct implementation of the turtlegraphics driver provided by Turbo Pascal 3.0. In Turbo Pascal 3.0, the turtlegraphics driver was made up of two files, GRAPH.P and GRAPH.BIN that supported the IBM CGA and compatibles. GRAPH.P actually defines the external machine code routines contained in GRAPH.BIN.

*Graph3* combines GRAPH.P and GRAPH.BIN into a single unit, still retaining the same functionality. The only modification you need to make to a Turbo Pascal 3.0 program that uses the turtlegraphics driver is to remove the {$I GRAPH.P} compiler directive, replacing it with a reference to *Crt* and *Graph3* in your program's **uses** clause.

**Note:** The routines that follow are *not* described in Chapter 27, the lookup section. For more detailed information about *Graph3]* routines, refer to your Turbo Pascal 3.0 reference manual.

Here are *Graph3*'s constants:

```
const
  North = 0;
  East  = 90;
  South = 180;
  West  = 270;
```

## *Procedures*

| | |
|---|---|
| **Arc** | Draws an arc using the given parameters. |
| **Back** | Moves the turtle backward by the given distance. (Turtlegraphics) |
| **Circle** | Draws a circle. |
| **ClearScreen** | Clears the active window and homes the turtle. (Turtlegraphics) |
| **ColorTable** | Defines a color translation table that lets the current color of any given point determine the new color of that point when it is redrawn. |
| **Draw** | Draws a line between the specified endpoints and in the specified color. |
| **FillPattern** | Fills a rectangular area with the current pattern using the specified color. |
| **FillScreen** | Fills the entire active window with the indicated color. |
| **FillShape** | Fills an area of any shape with the specified color. |
| **Forwd** | Moves the turtle forward by the given distance. (Turtlegraphics) |

| | |
|---|---|
| **GetDotColor** | Returns the color value of the dot at the indicated location. |
| **GetPic** | Copies the contents of an area on the screen into a buffer; the contents can later be restored using *PutPic*. |
| **GraphBackground** | Sets background color of screen. |
| **GraphColorMode** | Sets you in 320x200 color graphics mode. |
| **GraphMode** | Sets you in 320x200 black-and-white graphics mode. |
| **GraphWindow** | Lets you define an area of the screen as the active window in any of the graphics modes. |
| **Heading** | Returns the current heading of the turtle. (Turtlegraphics) |
| **HideTurtle** | Hides the turtle. (Turtlegraphics) |
| **HiRes** | Sets screen in 640x200 high-resolution graphics mode. |
| **HiResColor** | Selects the color used for drawing in high-resolution graphics. |
| **Home** | Puts the turtle in its home position. (Turtlegraphics) |
| **NoWrap** | Disables "wrapping" for the turtle. (Turtlegraphics) |
| **Palette** | Activates the color palette specified. |
| **Pattern** | Defines an 8x8 pattern to be used by *FillPattern*. |
| **PenDown** | Puts the turtle's pen "down" so that any movement of the turtle results in drawing. (Turtlegraphics) |
| **PenUp** | Puts the turtle's pen "up" so that the turtle can be moved without drawing. (Turtlegraphics) |
| **Plot** | Plots a point at the specified coordinates and in the specified color. |
| **PutPic** | Copies the contents of a buffer. |
| **SetHeading** | Turns the turtle to the specified angle. (Turtlegraphics) |

| | |
|---|---|
| **SetPenColor** | Sets the color used for the turtle's pen. (Turtlegraphics) |
| **SetPosition** | Moves the turtle to the given coordinates without drawing a line. (Turtlegraphics) |
| **ShowTurtle** | Makes the turtle visible. (Turtlegraphics) |
| **TurnLeft** | Turns the turtle's heading to the left (counter-clockwise). (Turtlegraphics) |
| **TurnRight** | Turns the turtle's heading to the right (clockwise). (Turtlegraphics) |
| **TurtleWindow** | Defines an area of the screen as the active turtle graphics screen. (Turtlegraphics) |
| **TurtleThere** | Tests if the turtle is visible and in the active window. (Turtlegraphics) |
| **TurtleDelay** | Sets a delay between each step of the turtle. (Turtlegraphics) |
| **Wrap** | Forces wraparound when the turtle attempts to move past the boundaries of the active window. (Turtlegraphics) |
| **XCor** | Returns the current $X$-coordinate of the turtle. (Turtlegraphics) |
| **YCor** | Returns the current $Y$-coordinate of the turtle. (Turtlegraphics) |

C  H  A  P  T  E  R

# 25

# Using the 8087

There are two kinds of numbers you can work with in Turbo Pascal: integers (shortint, integer, longint, byte, word) and reals (real, single, double, extended, comp). Reals are also known as floating-point numbers. The 8086 processor is designed to easily handle integer values, but it takes considerably more time and effort to handle reals. The 8086 family of processors has a corresponding family of math coprocessors, the 8087s.

The 8087 is a special hardware numeric processor that can be installed in your PC. It executes floating-point instructions very quickly, so if you use floating point a lot, you'll probably want a coprocessor.

Turbo Pascal is designed to provide optimal floating-point performance whether or not you have an 8087.

- For programs running on any PC, with or without an 8087, Turbo Pascal provides the real type and an associated library of software routines that handle floating-point operations. The real type occupies 6 bytes of memory, providing a range of $2.9 \times 10^{-39}$ to $1.7 \times 10^{38}$ with 11 to 12 significant digits. The software floating-point library is optimized for speed and size, trading in some of the fancier features provided by the 8087 processor.

- If you're only writing programs for systems that have a math coprocessor, you can instruct Turbo Pascal to produce code that uses the 8087 chip. This gives you access to four additional real types (single, double, extended, and comp), and an extended floating-point range of 1.9 × 10E-4951 .. 1.1 × 10E4932 with 19 to 20 significant digits.

You can switch between the two different models of floating-point code generation with the $N compiler directives or with the O/C/Numeric processing menu item. {$N-} indicates software floating point (the default), and {$N+} indicates hardware floating point.

The remainder of this chapter discusses special issues concerning Turbo Pascal programs that use the 8087 coprocessor.

# The 8087 Data Types

For programs that use the 8087, Turbo Pascal provides four new real types in addition to the type real.

- The single type is the smallest format you can use with floating-point numbers. It occupies 4 bytes of memory, providing a range of $1.5 \times 10^{-45}$ to $3.4 \times 10^{38}$ with 7 to 8 significant digits.

- The double type occupies 8 bytes of memory, providing a range of $5.0 \times 10^{-324}$ to $1.7 \times 10^{308}$ with 15 to 16 significant digits.

- The extended type is the largest floating-point type supported by the 8087. It occupies 10 bytes of memory, providing a range of $1.9 \times 10E\text{-}4951$ to $1.1 \times 10E4932$ with 19 to 20 significant digits. Any arithmetic involving real-type values is performed with the range and precision of the extended type.

- The comp type stores integral values in 8 bytes, providing a range of $-2^{63}+1$ to $2^{63}-1$, which is approximately $-9.2 \times 10^{18}$ to $9.2 \times 10^{18}$. Comp may be compared to a double-precision longint, but it is considered a real type because arithmetic done with comp uses the 8087 coprocessor. Comp is well suited for representing monetary values as integral values of cents or mils (thousands) in business applications.

Whether or not you have an 8087, the 6-byte real type is always available, so you need not modify your source code when switching to the 8087, and you can still read data files generated by programs that use software floating point.

Note, however, that hardware floating-point calculations on variables of type real are slightly slower than on other types. This is because the 8087 cannot directly process the real format—instead, calls must be made to library routines to convert real values to extended before operating on them. If you are concerned with optimum speed and never need to run on a system without an 8087, you may want to use the single, double, extended, and comp types exclusively.

# Extended Range Arithmetic

The extended type is the basis of all floating-point computations with the 8087. Turbo Pascal uses the extended format to store all non-integer numeric constants and evaluates all non-integer numeric expressions to extended. The entire right side of the following assignment, for instance, will be computed in extended before being converted to the type on the left side:

```
var
  X,A,B,C : real;
begin
  X := (B + Sqrt(B * B - A * C)) / A;
end;
```

With no special effort by the programmer, Turbo Pascal performs computations using the precision and range of the extended type. The added precision means smaller round-off errors, and the additional range means overflow and underflow are less common, so that programs work more often.

You can go beyond Turbo Pascal's automatic *extended* capabilities. For example, you can declare variables used for intermediate results to be of type extended. The following example computes a sum of products:

```
var
  Sum : single;
  X,Y : array[1..100] of single;
  I   : integer;
  T   : extended;                          { For intermediate results }
begin
  T := 0.0;
  for I := 1 to 100 do T := T + X[I] * Y[I];
  Sum := T;
end;
```

Had *T* been declared single, the assignment to *T* would have caused a round-off error at the limit of single precision at each loop entry. But because *T* is extended, all round-off errors are at the limit of extended precision, except for the one resulting from the assignment of *T* to *Sum*. Fewer round-off errors mean more accurate results.

You can also declare formal value parameters and function results to be of type extended. This avoids unnecessary conversions between numeric types, which can result in loss of accuracy. For example:

```
function Area(Radius: extended): extended;
begin
  Area := Pi * Radius * Radius;
end;
```

## Comparing Reals

Because real-type values are approximations, the results of comparing values of different real types are not always as expected. For example, if $X$ is a variable of type single and $Y$ is a variable of type double, then the following statements will output False:

```
X := 1/3;
Y := 1/3;
Writeln(X = Y);
```

The reason is that $X$ is accurate only to 7 to 8 digits, where $Y$ is accurate to 15 to 16 digits, and when both are converted to extended, they will differ after 7 to 8 digits. Likewise, the statements

```
X := 1/3;
Writeln(X = 1/3);
```

will output False, since the result of 1/3 in the *Writeln* statement is calculated with 20 significant digits.

## The 8087 Evaluation Stack

The 8087 coprocessor has an internal evaluation stack that can be up to eight levels deep. Accessing a value on the 8087 stack is much faster than accessing a variable in memory; so to achieve the best possible performance, Turbo Pascal uses the 8087's stack for storing temporary results and passing parameters to procedures and functions.

The implication of using the 8087 stack for parameter transfers is that a procedure or function cannot have more than eight value parameters of the 8087 types (single, double, extended, or comp). The compiler will not give an error if you attempt to declare more, but the program will terminate with a runtime error when you call the subprogram. There are no limits to the number of parameters of type real you can have, and likewise, you can declare any number of **var** parameters.

**Note:** As part of its entry code, a procedure or function stores any 8087-type value parameters in temporary locations allocated on the 8086 stack.

The parameters only occupy 8087 stack space during the call, not during execution of the procedure or function.

In theory, very complicated real-type expressions can cause an 8087 stack overflow. However, this is not likely to occur, since it would require the expression to generate more than eight temporary results.

A more tangible danger lies in nested function calls. If such constructs are not coded correctly, they can very well cause an 8087 stack overflow.

Assuming function *Test* is an *extended* function that takes three extended value parameters, then the construct

```
X := Test(A,B,Test(C,D,Test(E,F,Test(X,Y,Z))));
```

will cause an 8087 stack overflow. This is because at the innermost call to *Test,* six floating-point values have already been pushed on the 8087 stack, leaving room for only two more. The correct construct in this case is

```
X := Test(X,Y,Z);
X := Test(E,F,X);
X := Test(C,D,X);
X := Test(A,B,X);
```

A corresponding situation can arise in functions that execute recursively. Consider the following procedure that calculates Fibonacci numbers using recursion:

```
function Fib(N: integer): extended;
begin
  if N = 0 then Fib := 0.0 else
  if N = 1 then Fib := 1.0 else
  Fib := Fib(N-1) + Fib(N-2);
end;
```

A call to this version of *Fib* will cause an 8087 stack overflow for values of *N* larger than 8. The reason is that the calculation of the last assignment requires a temporary on the 8087 stack to store the result of *Fib(N-1)*. Each recursive invocation allocates one such temporary, causing an overflow the ninth time. The correct construct is this case is

```
function Fib(N: integer): extended;
var
  F1,F2: extended;

begin
  if N = 0 then
    Fib := 0.0
  else
    if N = 1 then
      Fib := 1.0
```

```
    else
    begin
      F1 := Fib(N-1); F2 := Fib(N-2);
      Fib := F1 + F2;
    end;
end;
```

The temporary results are now stored in variables allocated on the 8086 stack. (The 8086 stack can of course also overflow, but this would typically require significantly more recursive calls.)

# Writing Reals with the 8087

In the {$N+} state, the *Write* and *Writeln* standard procedures output four digits, not two, for the exponent in a floating-point decimal string to provide for the extended numeric range. Likewise, the *Str* standard procedure returns a four-digit exponent when floating-point format is selected.

# Units Using the 8087

Units that use the 8087 can only be used by other units or programs that are compiled in the {$N+} state.

The fact that a unit uses the 8087 is determined by whether it contains 8087 instructions—not by the state of the $N compiler directive at the time of its compilation. This makes the compiler more forgiving in cases where you accidentally compile a unit (that doesn't use the 8087) in the {$N+} state.

Note that the use of 8087 instructions from object code linked in from .OBJ files is not detected. If you link with an .OBJ file that uses the math coprocessor, the .OBJ must do its own initialization and error-checking.

# 26

# Inside Turbo Pascal

In this chapter, we provide technical information for advanced Turbo Pascal programmers. We'll cover such topics as memory maps, the heap manager, internal data formats, calling conventions, and more.

Figure 26.1 (on page 336) depicts the memory map of a Turbo Pascal program.

The Program Segment Prefix (PSP) is a 256-byte area built by MS-DOS when the .EXE file is loaded. The segment address of PSP is stored in the predeclared word variable *PrefixSeg*.

Each module (which includes the main program and each unit) has its own code segment. The main program occupies the first code segment; the code segments that follow it are occupied by the units (in reverse order from how they are listed in the **uses** clause), and the last code segment is occupied by the runtime library (the *System* unit). The size of a single code segment cannot exceed 64K, but the total size of the code is limited only by the available memory.

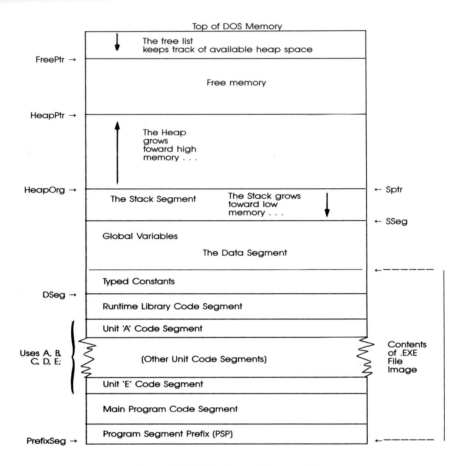

Figure 26.1: Turbo Pascal Memory Map

The data segment (addressed through DS) contains all typed constants followed by all global variables. The DS register is never changed during program execution. The size of the data segment cannot exceed 64K.

On entry to the program, the stack segment register (SS) and the stack pointer (SP) are loaded so that SS:SP points to the first byte past the stack segment. The SS register is never changed during program execution, but SP can move downward until it reaches the bottom of the segment. The size of the stack segment cannot exceed 64K; the default size is 16K, but this can be changed with a $M compiler directive.

The heap stores *dynamic variables,* that is, variables allocated through calls to the *New* and *GetMem* standard procedures. It occupies all or some of the free memory left when a program is executed. The actual size of the heap depends on the minimum and maximum heap values, which can be set with the $M compiler directive. Its size is guaranteed to be at least the minimum heap size and never more than the maximum heap size. If the minimum amount of memory is not available, the program will not execute. The default heap minimum is 0 bytes, and the default heap maximum is 640 Kb; this means that by default the heap will occupy all remaining memory.

As you might expect, the heap manager (which is part of Turbo Pascal's runtime library) manages the heap. It is described in detail in the following section.

# The Heap Manager

The heap is a stack-like structure that grows from low memory in the heap segment. The bottom of the heap is stored in the variable *HeapOrg*, and the top of the heap, corresponding to the bottom of free memory, is stored in the variable *HeapPtr*. Each time a dynamic variable is allocated on the heap (via *New* or *GetMem*), the heap manager moves *HeapPtr* upward by the size of the variable, in effect stacking the dynamic variables on top of each other.

*HeapPtr* is always normalized after each operation, thus forcing the offset part into the range $0000 to $000F. The maximum size of a single variable that can be allocated on the heap is 65521 bytes (corresponding to $10000 minus $000F), since every variable must be completely contained in a single segment.

## Disposal Methods

The dynamic variables stored on the heap are disposed of in one of two ways: (1) through *Dispose* or *FreeMem* or (2) through *Mark* and *Release*. The simplest scheme is that of *Mark* and *Release*; for example, if the following statements are executed:

```
New(Ptr1);
New(Ptr2);
Mark(P);
New(Ptr3);
New(Ptr4);
New(Ptr5);
```

the layout of the heap will then look like Figure 26.2.

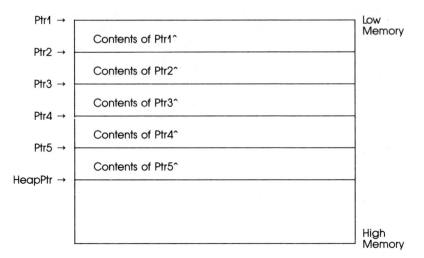

Figure 26.2: Disposal Method Using Mark and Release

The *Mark(P)* statement marks the state of the heap just before *Ptr3* is allocated (by storing the current *HeapPtr* in *P*). If the statement *Release(P)* is executed, the heap layout becomes like that of Figure 26.3, effectively disposing of all pointers allocated since the call to *Mark*.

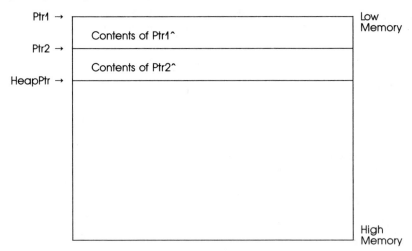

Figure 26.3: Heap Layout with Release(P) Executed

**Note:** Executing *Release(HeapOrg)* completely disposes of the entire heap because *HeapOrg* points to the bottom of the heap.

For applications that dispose of pointers in exactly the reverse order of allocation, the *Mark* and *Release* procedures are very efficient. Yet most

*Turbo Pascal Owner's Handbook*

programs tend to allocate and dispose of pointers in a more random manner, requiring the more-sophisticated management technique implemented by *Dispose* and *FreeMem*. These procedures allow an application to dispose of any pointer at any time.

When a dynamic variable that is not the topmost variable on the heap is disposed of through *Dispose* or *FreeMem*, the heap becomes fragmented. Assuming that the same statement sequence has been executed, then after executing *Dispose(Ptr3)*, a "hole" is created in the middle of the heap (see Figure 26.4).

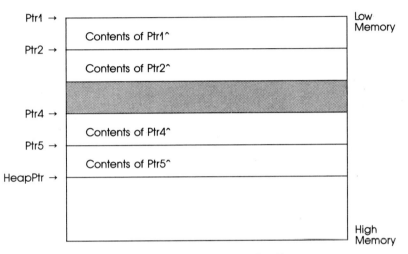

Figure 26.4: Creating a "Hole" in the Heap

If at this time *New(Ptr3)* has been executed, it would again occupy the same memory area. On the other hand, executing *Dispose(Ptr4)* enlarges the free block, since *Ptr3* and *Ptr4* were neighboring blocks (see Figure 26.5).

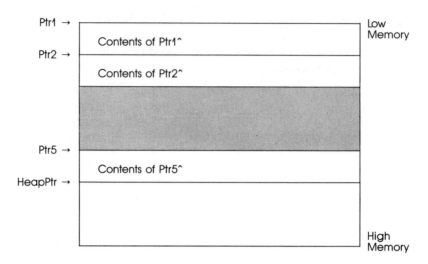

Figure 26.5: Enlarging the Free Block

Finally, executing *Dispose(Ptr5)* first creates an even bigger free block, and then lowers *HeapPtr*. This, in effect, releases the free block, since the last valid pointer is now *Ptr2* (see Figure 26.6).

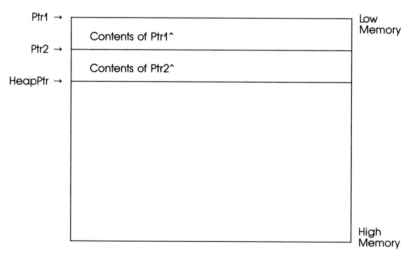

Figure 26.6: Releasing the Free Block

The heap is now in the same state as it would be after executing *Release(P)*, as shown in Figure 26.2. However, the free blocks created and destroyed in the process were tracked for possible reuse.

# The Free List

The addresses and sizes of the free blocks generated by *Dispose* and *FreeMem* operations are kept on a *free list*, which grows downward from high memory in the heap segment. Whenever a dynamic variable is allocated, the free list is checked before the heap is expanded. If a free block of adequate size (greater than or equal to the size of the requested block size) exists, it is used.

**Note:** The *Release* procedure always clears the free list, thus causing the heap manager to "forget" about any free blocks that might exist below the heap pointer. If you mix calls to *Mark* and *Release* with calls to *Dispose* and *FreeMem*, you must ensure that no such free blocks exist.

The free list pointer is stored in a variable called *FreePtr*. Although declared to be of type *pointer*, *FreePtr* is actually a pointer to an array of free-list records, as indicated by the *FreeListP* type:

```
type
   FreeRec   = record
                  OrgPtr,EndPtr: pointer;
               end;
   FreeList  = array[0..8190] of FreeRec;
   FreeListP = ^FreeList;
```

The *OrgPtr* and *EndPtr* fields of each record define the origin and end of each free block. (*EndPtr* is in fact a pointer to the first byte after the block.) Both are normalized pointers. The number of entries in the *FreeList* array is calculated from

```
FreeCount = (8192 - Ofs(FreePtr^) div 8) mod 8192
```

This means that there can be up to 8191 entries in the free list. When the offset part of *FreePtr* is 0, the free list is empty. *FreePtr* can be compared to the stack pointer in the sense that it grows downward, and that all bytes from *FreePtr* to the end of the heap segment are part of the "free stack."

**Note:** Trying to dispose of a pointer when the free list is full causes a runtime error. However, a full free list is a highly unlikely situation—it would reqire 8191 completely noncontiguous blocks to be disposed of and not reused.

*FreePtr* also serves to mark the top of free memory in the heap (the bottom of which is pointed to by *HeapPtr*). Note, though, that when the offset part of *FreePtr* is 0, $1000 must be added to the segment part to produce the true top-of-heap pointer. (In fact, the segment part of *FreePtr* always contains the segment address of top-of-memory minus $1000.)

When disposing of a range of noncontiguous pointers, the free list grows (expands downward) to make room for an entry for each block. As long as there is enough room between *HeapPtr* and *FreePtr*, this presents no problem. However, when the heap is almost full, there may not be enough room to cater to the larger free list, in which case a runtime error will occur.

In particular, imagine that the free list is empty and that the heap is almost full. In that situation, disposing of a range of pointers other than the topmost pointer will cause a block expansion of the free list.

To prevent, or foresee, such problems, the heap manager provides a word variable *FreeMin* that can be set to control the minimum allowable size of the memory region between *HeapPtr* and *FreePtr*. You cannot use *New* or *GetMem* to allocate a variable that would make the size of that region less than *FreeMin*. Likewise, *MemAvail* and *MaxAvail* will subtract *FreeMin* from the size of that region before returning their results.

The value stored in *FreeMin* is in bytes. To ensure room for a specific number of free-list entries, multiply that number by 8 and store it in *FreeMin*.

A final note on the free list concerns a potential problem with "granularity." The granularity of Turbo Pascal's heap manager is 1 byte; that is, if you allocate 1 byte, it will only occupy that 1 byte. In most situations, and especially when using *Mark* and *Release* or when not disposing of anything at all, this guarantees optimum use of the memory available. However, it can also be deceiving.

When randomly allocating and disposing of a lot of blocks of differing sizes, such as line records in a text-processing program, a number of very small free blocks can result and possibly cause the free list to overflow. As an example, assume a block of 50 bytes is allocated and disposed of, thus becoming an entry on the free list. If the next allocation request is for a block of 49 bytes, that block will be reused, leaving a 1-byte free block entry on the free list. Until one of the neighboring blocks are disposed of (thereby merging the 1-byte block into a bigger block), the 1-byte block is very unlikely to become re-allocated. Thus, it will occupy a free-list entry for a long time, if not for the program's duration.

If a free list overflow occurs because of this, you can introduce a "resolution factor" to round upward the size specified by each call to *GetMem* and *FreeMem* to a factor of some number. In general, the higher the number, the less likely unusable free blocks will occur. To do this you would write your own *GetMem* and *FreeMem* routines that would modify the *Size* parameter and then call *System.GetMem* or *System.FreeMem*:

```
procedure GetMem(var P : pointer; Size : word);
begin
  System.GetMem(P, (Size + 15) and $FFF0);                    { 16 byte blocks }
end;

procedure FreeMem(var P : pointer; Size : word);
begin
  System.FreeMem(P, (Size + 15) and $FFF0);                   { 16 byte blocks }
end;
```

## *The Heap Error Function*

The *HeapError* variable allows you to install a heap error function, which gets called whenever the heap manager cannot complete an allocation request. *HeapError* is a pointer that points to a function with the following header:

```
{$F+} function HeapFunc(Size: word): integer; {$F-}
```

Note that the {$F+} compiler directive forces the heap error function to use the far call model.

The heap error function is installed by assigning its address to the *HeapError* variable:

```
HeapError:=@HeapFunc;
```

The heap error function gets called whenever a call to *New* or *GetMem* cannot complete the request. The *Size* parameter contains the size of the block that could not be allocated, and the heap error function should attempt to free a block of at least that size.

Depending on its success, the heap error function should return 0, 1, or 2. A return of 0 indicates failure, causing a runtime error to occur immediately. A return of 1 also indicates failure, but instead of a runtime error, it causes *New* or *GetMem* to return a **nil** pointer. Finally, a return of 2 indicates success and causes a retry (which could also cause another call to the heap error function).

The standard heap error function always returns 0, thus causing a runtime error whenever a call to *New* or *GetMem* cannot be completed. However, for many applications, the simple heap error function that follows is more appropriate:

```
{$F+} function HeapFunc(Size: word) integer; {$F-}
begin
  HeapFunc:=1;
end;
```

When installed, this function causes *New* or *GetMem* to return **nil** when they cannot complete the request, instead of aborting the program.

# Internal Data Formats

## Integer Types

The format selected to represent an integer-type variable depends on its minimum and maximum bounds:

- If both bounds are within the range −128..127 (shortint), the variable is stored as a signed byte.
- If both bounds are within the range 0..255 (byte), the variable is stored as an unsigned byte.
- If both bounds are within the range −32768..32767 (integer), the variable is stored as a signed word.
- If both bounds are within the range 0..65535 (word), the variable is stored.
- Otherwise, the variable is stored as a signed double word (longint).

## Char Types

A char, or a subrange of a char type, is stored as an unsigned byte.

## Boolean Types

A boolean type is stored as a byte that can assume the value of 0 (False) or 1 (True).

## Enumerated Types

An enumerated type is stored as an unsigned byte if the enumeration has 256 or fewer values; otherwise, it is stored as an unsigned word.

## Floating-Point Types

The floating-point types (real, single, double, extended, and comp) store the binary representations of a sign (+ or −), an *exponent*, and a *significand*. A represented number has the value

$$+/-\ \text{significand} \times 2^{\text{exponent}}$$

where the significand has a single bit to the left of the binary decimal point (that is, 0 <= significand < 2).

**Note:** In the figures that follow, *msb* means most significant bit, and *lsb* means least significant bit. The left-most items are stored at the highest addresses. For example, for a real-type value, *e* is stored in the first byte, *f* in the following five bytes, and *s* in the most significant bit of the last byte.

## The Real Type

A 6-byte (48-bit) *Real* number is divided into three fields:

The value *v* of the number is determined by

```
if 0 < e <= 255, then v = (-1)ˢ * 2^(e-129) * (1.f).
if e = 0, then v = 0.
```

$$\text{if } 0 < e <= 255,\ \text{then } v = (-1)^s * 2^{(e-129)} * (1.f).$$
$$\text{if } e = 0,\ \text{then } v = 0.$$

**Note:** The real type cannot store denormals, NaNs, and infinities. Denormals become zero when stored in a real, and NaNs and infinities produce an overflow error if an attempt is made to store them in a real.

## The Single Type

A 4-byte (32-bit) *Single* number is divided into three fields:

The value *v* of the number is determined by

$$\text{if } 0 < e < 255,\qquad \text{then } v = (-1)^s * 2^{(e-127)} * (1.f).$$

```
if e = 0   and f <> 0, then v = (-1)^s * 2^(-126) * (0.f).
if e = 0   and f = 0,  then v = (-1)^s * 0.
if e = 255 and f = 0,  then v = (-1)^s * Inf.
if e = 255 and f <> 0, then v is a NaN.
```

## The Double Type

An 8-byte (64-bit) *Double* number is divided into three fields:

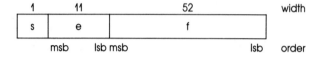

The value $v$ of the number is determined by

```
if 0 < e < 2047,      then v = (-1)^s * 2^(e-1023) * (1.f).
if e = 0    and f <> 0, then v = (-1)^s * 2^(-1022) * (0.f).
if e = 0    and f = 0,  then v = (-1)^s * 0.
if e = 2047 and f = 0,  then v = (-1)^s * Inf.
if e = 2047 and f <> 0, then v is a NaN.
```

## The Extended Type

A 10-byte (80-bit) *Extended* number is divided into four fields:

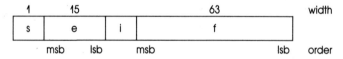

The value $v$ of the number is determined by

```
if 0 <= e < 32767,     then v = (-1)^s * 2^(e-16383) * (i.f).
if e = 32767 and f = 0,  then v = (-1)^s * Inf.
if e = 32767 and f <> 0, then v is a NaN.
```

## The Comp Type

An 8-byte (64-bit) *Comp* number is divided into two fields:

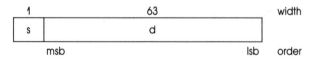

The value $v$ of the number is determined by

```
if s = 1 and d = 0, then v is a NaN
```

Otherwise, $v$ is the two's complement 64-bit value.

## Pointer Types

A pointer type is stored as a double word, with the offset part in the low word and the segment part in the high word. The pointer value **nil** is stored as a double-word zero.

## String Types

A string occupies as many bytes as its maximum length plus one. The first byte contains the current dynamic length of the string, and the following bytes contain the characters of the string. The length byte and the characters are considered unsigned values. Maximum string length is 255 characters plus a length byte (**string[255]**).

## Set Types

A set is a bit array, where each bit indicates whether an element is in the set or not. The maximum number of elements in a set is 256, so a set never occupies more than 32 bytes. The number of bytes occupied by a particular set is calculated as

```
ByteSize = (Max div 8) - (Min div 8) + 1
```

where *Min* and *Max* are the lower and upper bounds of the base type of that set. The byte number of a specific element $E$ is

```
ByteNumber = (E div 8) - (Min div 8)
```

and the bit number within that byte is

```
BitNumber = E mod 8
```

where $E$ denotes the ordinal value of the element.

## Array Types

An array is stored as a contiguous sequence of variables of the component type of the array. The components with the lowest indexes are stored at the lowest memory addresses. A multidimensional array is stored with the right-most dimension increasing first.

## Record Types

The fields of a record are stored as a contiguous sequence of variables. The first field is stored at the lowest memory address. If the record contains variant parts, then each variant starts at the same memory address.

## File Types

File types are represented as records. Typed files and untyped files occupy 128 bytes, which are laid out as follows:

```
type
  FileRec = record
              Handle   : word;
              Mode     : word;
              RecSize  : word;
              Private  : array[1..26] of byte;
              UserData : array[1..16] of byte;
              Name     : array[0..79] of char;
            end;
```

Text files occupy 256 bytes, which are laid out as follows:

```
type
  CharBuf = array[0..127] of char;
  TextRec = record
              Handle   : word;
              Mode     : word;
              BufSize  : word;
              Private  : word;
              BufPos   : word;
              BufEnd   : word;
              BufPtr   : ^CharBuf;
              OpenFunc : pointer;
              InOutFunc: pointer;
              FlushFunc: pointer;
              CloseFunc: pointer;
              UserData : array[1..16] of byte;
              Name     : array[0..79] of char;
              Buffer   : CharBuf;
            end;
```

*Handle* contains the file's handle (when open) as returned by MS-DOS.

The *Mode* field can assume one of the following "magic" values:

```
const
  fmClosed = $D7B0;
  fmInput  = $D7B1;
  fmOutput = $D7B2;
  fmInOut  = $D7B3;
```

*fmClosed* indicates that the file is closed. *fmInput* and *fmOutput* indicate that the file is a text file that has been reset (*fmInput*) or rewritten (*fmOutput*). *fmInOut* indicates that the file variable is a typed or an untyped file that has been reset or rewritten. Any other value indicates that the file variable has not been assigned (and thereby not initialized).

The *UserData* field is never accessed by Turbo Pascal, and is free for user-written routines to store data in.

*Name* contains the file name, which is a sequence of characters terminated by a null character (#0).

For typed files and untyped files, *RecSize* contains the record length in bytes, and the *Private* field is unused but reserved.

For text files, *BufPtr* is a pointer to a buffer of *BufSize* bytes, *BufPos* is the index of the next character in the buffer to read or write, and *BufEnd* is a count of valid characters in the buffer. *OpenFunc*, *InOutFunc*, *FlushFunc*, and *CloseFunc* are pointers to the I/O routines that control the file. The upcoming section entitled "Text File Device Drivers" provides information on that subject.

# Calling Conventions

Parameters are transferred to procedures and functions via the stack. Before calling a procedure or function, the parameters are pushed onto the stack in their order of declaration. Before returning, the procedure or function removes all parameters from the stack.

The skeleton code for a procedure or function call looks like this:

```
PUSH    Param1
PUSH    Param2
:
PUSH    ParamX
CALL    ProcOrFunc
```

Parameters are passed either by *reference* or by *value*. When a parameter is passed by reference, a pointer that points to the actual storage location is pushed onto the stack. When a parameter is passed by value, the actual value is pushed onto the stack.

## Variable Parameters

Variable parameters (**var** parameters) are always passed by reference—a pointer points to the actual storage location.

## Value Parameters

Value parameters are passed by value or by reference depending on the type and size of the parameter. In general, if the value parameter occupies 1, 2, or 4 bytes, the value is pushed directly onto the stack. Otherwise a pointer to the value is pushed, and the procedure or function then copies the value into a local storage location.

**Note:** The 8086 does not support byte-sized PUSH and POP instructions, so byte-sized parameters are always transferred onto the stack as words. The low-order byte of the word contains the value, and the high-order byte is unused (and undefined).

An integer type or parameter is passed as a byte, a word, or a double word, using the same format as an integer-type variable. (For double words, the high-order word is pushed before the low-order word so that the low-order word ends up at the lowest address.)

A char-type parameter is passed as an unsigned byte.

A boolean-type parameter is passed as a byte with the value 0 or 1.

An enumerated-type parameter is passed as an unsigned byte if the enumeration has 256 or fewer values; otherwise it is passed as an unsigned word.

A real-type parameter (type real) is passed as 6 bytes on the stack, thus being an exception to the rule that only 1, 2, and 4 byte values are passed directly on the stack.

An 8087-type parameter (type single, double, extended, or comp) is **not** passed on the 8086 stack. Instead, 8087-type parameters are pushed in order of appearance onto the internal stack of the 8087 numeric co-processor. This limits to eight the allowable number of 8087-type value parameters of a procedure or function (the 8087 stack is only eight levels deep).

A pointer-type parameter is passed as a double word (the segment part is pushed before the offset part so that the offset part ends up at the lowest address).

A string-type parameter is passed as a pointer to the value.

A set-type parameter is passed as a pointer to an "unpacked" set that occupies 32 bytes.

Arrays and records with 1, 2, or 4 bytes are passed directly onto the stack. Other arrays and records are passed as pointers to the value.

## Function Results

Ordinal-type function results (integer, char, boolean, and enumeration types) are returned in the CPU registers: Bytes are returned in AL, words are returned in AX, and double words are returned in DX:AX (high-order word in DX, low-order word in AX).

Real-type function results (type real) are returned in the DX:BX:AX registers (high-order word in DX, middle word in BX, low-order word in AX).

8087-type function results (type single, double, extended, and comp) are returned in the 8087 coprocessor's top-of-stack register (ST(0)).

Pointer-type function results are returned in DX:AX (segment part in DX, offset part in AX).

For a string-type function result, the caller pushes a pointer to a temporary storage location before pushing any parameters, and the function returns a string value in that temporary location. The function must not remove the pointer.

## Near and Far Calls

The 8086 CPU supports two kinds of call and return instructions: *near* and *far*. The near instructions transfer control to another location within the same code segment, and the far instructions allow a change of code segment.

A near CALL instruction pushes a 16-bit return address (offset only) onto the stack, and a far CALL instruction pushes a 32-bit return address (both segment and offset). The corresponding RET instructions pop only an offset or both an offset and a segment.

Turbo Pascal will automatically select the correct call model based on the procedure's declaration. Procedures declared in the **interface** section of a unit are far—they can be called from other units. Procedures declared in a program or in the **implementation** section of a unit are near—they can only be called from within that program or unit.

For some specific purposes, a procedure may be required to be far; for instance, exit procedures, text file device drivers, and other features that involve procedure pointers. The *$F* compiler directive forces the far model into effect. Procedures and functions compiled in the {$F+} state are always far; Turbo Pascal automatically selects the correct model in the {$F-} state. The default state is {$F-}.

A procedure or function is said to be nested when it is declared within another procedure or function. Nested procedures and functions always use the near call model regardless of the setting of the {$F} compiler switch, since they are only "visible" within a specific procedure or function in the same code segment.

When calling a nested procedure or function, the compiler generates a PUSH BP instruction just before the CALL, in effect passing the caller's BP as an additional parameter. Once the called procedure has set up its own BP, the caller's BP is accessible as a word stored at [BP+4]. Using this "link" at [BP+4], the called procedure can access the local variables in the caller's stack frame. If the caller itself is also a nested procedure, it also has a link at [BP+4], and so on. The following demonstrates how to access local variables from an **inline** statement in a nested procedure:

```
procedure A;
var IntA: Integer;
procedure B;
var IntB: Integer;
procedure C;
var IntC: Integer;

begin inline(
  $8B/$46/<IntC/            { MOV AX,IntC[BP] ;AX = IntA }
  $8B/$5E/$04/              { MOV BX,[BP+4] ;BX = B's stack frame }
  $36/$8B/$47/<IntB/        { MOV AX,SS:IntB[BX] ;AX = IntB }
  $8B/$5E/$04/              { MOV BX,[BP+4] ;BX = B's stack frame }
  $36/$8B/$5F/$04/          { MOV BX,SS:[BX+4] ;BX = C's stack frame }
  $36/$8B/$47/<IntA);       { MOV AX,SS:IntA[BX] ;AX = IntA }
end;  {C}
begin {B}
end;  {B}
begin {A}
end;  {A}
```

**Note:** Nested procedures and functions cannot be declared with the external directive.

## Entry and Exit Code

Each Pascal procedure and function begins and ends with standard entry and exit code that creates and removes its activation.

The standard entry code is

```
PUSH  BP                                              ;Save BP
MOV   BP,SP                                 ;Set up stack frame
SUB   SP,LocalSize                      ;Allocate local variables
```

where *LocalSize* is the size of the local variables. The SUB instruction is only present if *LocalSize* is not 0. If the procedure's call model is near, the parameters start at BP + 4; if it is far, they start at BP + 6.

The standard exit code is

```
MOV   SP,BP                              ;De-allocate local variables
POP   BP                                              ;Restore BP
RET   ParamSize                    ;Remove parameters and return
```

where *ParamSize* is the size of the parameters. The RET instruction is either a near or a far return, depending on the procedure's call model.

## Register-Saving Conventions

Procedures and functions should preserve the BP, SP, SS, and DS registers. All other registers may be modified.

# Linking with Assembly Language

Procedures and functions written in assembly language can be linked with Turbo Pascal programs or units using the $L compiler directive. The assembly language source file must be assembled into an object file (extension .OBJ) using an assembler. Multiple object files can be linked with a program or unit through multiple $L directives.

Procedures and functions written in assembly language must be declared as **external** in the Pascal program or unit, for example,

```
function LoCase(Ch: char): char; external;
```

In the corresponding assembly language source file, all procedures and functions must appear in a segment named CODE, and the names of the external procedures and functions must appear in PUBLIC directives. (CSEG is also accepted as a segment name in place of CODE.)

You must ensure that an assembly language procedure or function matches its Pascal definition with respect to call model (near or far), number of parameters, types of parameters, and result type.

An assembly language source file can declare variables in a segment named DATA. Such variables are private to the assembly language source file and cannot be referenced from the Pascal program or unit. However, they reside in the same segment as the Pascal globals, and can be accessed through the DS segment register. (DSEG is also accepted as a segment name in place of DATA.)

All procedures, functions, and variables declared in the Pascal program or unit, and the ones declared in the **interface** section of the used units, can be referenced from the assembly language source file through EXTRN directives. Again, it is up to you to supply the correct type in the EXTRN definition.

When an object file appears in a $L directive, Turbo Pascal converts the file from the Intel relocatable object module format (.OBJ) to its own internal relocatable format. This conversion is possible only if certain rules are observed:

- All procedures and functions must be placed in a segment named CODE, and all private variables must be placed in a segment named DATA. All other segments are ignored, and so are GROUP directives. The segment definitions can specify BYTE or WORD alignment; when linked, they are always word-aligned. The segment definitions can optionally specify PUBLIC (which is ignored), but they should not specify a class name. (CSEG is also accepted as a segment name in place of CODE, and DSEG is accepted as a segment name in place of DATA.)

- When declaring variables in the DATA or DSEG segment, always use a question mark (?) to specify the value, for instance:

```
Count   DW  ?
Buffer  DB  128 DUP(?)
```

Turbo Pascal ignores any request to create initialized variables in the DATA or DSEG segment.

- When referring to EXTRN procedures and functions, do not specify an offset. For example, the following construct is not allowed:

```
EXTRN   MyProc : NEAR
CALL    MyProc + 8
```

Note that this restriction does not apply to EXTRN variables.

■ Byte-sized references to EXTRN symbols are not allowed. For example, this means that the HIGH and LOW operators cannot be used with EXTRN symbols.

## Examples of Assembly Language Routines

The following code is an example of a unit that implements two assembly language string-handling routines. The *UpperCase* function converts all characters in a string to uppercase, and the *StringOf* function returns a string of characters of a specified length.

```
unit Strings;
interface
function UpperCase(S: string): string;
function StringOf(Ch: char; Count: byte): string;
implementation
{$L STRS}
function UpperCase; external;
function StringOf; external;
end.
```

The assembly language file that implements the *UpperCase* and *StringOf* routines is shown next. It must be assembled into a file called STRS.OBJ before the *Strings* unit can be compiled. Note that the routines use the far call model because they are declared in the **interface** section of the unit.

```
CODE    SEGMENT BYTE PUBLIC

        ASSUME  CS:CODE

        PUBLIC  UpperCase,StringOf              ;Make them known

; function UpperCase(S: string): string

UpperRes        EQU     DWORD PTR [BP+10]
UpperStr        EQU     DWORD PTR [BP+6]

UpperCase       PROC FAR

        PUSH    BP                              ;Save BP
        MOV     BP,SP                  ;Set up stack frame
        PUSH    DS                              ;Save DS
        LDS     SI,UpperStr            ;Load string address
        LES     DI,UpperRes            ;Load result address
        CLD                            ;Forward string-ops
        LODSB                          ;Load string length
        STOSB                              ;Copy to result
        MOV     CL,AL                  ;String length to CX
        XOR     CH,CH
        JCXZ    U3                     ;Skip if empty string
```

```
U1:      LODSB                                              ;Load character
         CMP     AL,'a'                              ;Skip if not 'a'..'z'
         JB      U2
         CMP     AL,'z'
         JA      U2
         SUB     AL,'a'-'A'                           ;Convert to uppercase
U2:      STOSB                                             ;Store in result
         LOOP    U1                                 ;Loop for all characters
U3:      POP     DS                                            ;Restore DS
         POP     BP                                            ;Restore BP
         RET     4                          ;Remove parameter and return

UpperCase        ENDP

; function StringOf(Ch: char; Count: byte): string

StrOfRes         EQU     DWORD PTR [BP+10]
StrOfchar        EQU     BYTE PTR [BP+8]
StrOfCount       EQU     BYTE PTR [BP+6]

StringOf         PROC FAR

         PUSH    BP                                               ;Save BP
         MOV     BP,SP                                   ;Set up stack frame
         LES     DI,StrOfRes                          ;Load result address
         MOV     AL,StrOfCount                                ;Load count
         CLD                                         ;Forward string-ops
         STOSB                                             ;Store length
         MOV     CL,AL                                        ;Count to CX
         XOR     CH,CH
         MOV     AL,StrOfChar                            ;Load character
         REP     STOSB                          ;Store string of characters
         POP                                                  ;Restore BP
         RET     4                         ;Remove parameters and return

StringOf         ENDP

CODE     ENDS

         END
```

The next example shows how an assembly language routine can refer to
Pascal routines and variables. The Numbers program reads up to 100
integer values, and then calls an assembly language procedure to check the
range of each of these values. If a value is out of range, the assembly
language procedure calls a Pascal procedure to print it.

```
program Numbers;
{$L CHECK}
var
  Data: array[1..100] of integer;
  Count,I: integer;

procedure RangeError(N: integer);
begin
  Writeln('Range error: ',N);
```

```
end;

procedure CheckRange(Min,Max: integer); external;
begin
  Count := 0;
  while not Eof and (Count<100) do
  begin
    Count := Count+1; Readln(Data[Count]);
  end;
  CheckRange(-10,10);
end.
```

The assembly language file that implements the *CheckRange* procedure is
shown next. It must be assembled into a file called CHECK.OBJ before the
NUMBERS program can be compiled. Note that the procedure uses the
near call model because it is declared in a program.

```
DATA     SEGMENT WORD PUBLIC

         EXTRN    Data:WORD,Count:WORD                  ;Pascal variables

DATA     ENDS

CODE     SEGMENT BYTE PUBLIC

         ASSUME   CS:CODE,DS:DATA

         EXTRN    RangeError:NEAR              ;Implemented in Pascal

         PUBLIC   CheckRange                   ;Implemented here

CheckRange      PROC    NEAR

         MOV     BX,SP                    ;Get parameters pointer
         MOV     AX,SS:[BX+4]                     ;Load Min
         MOV     DX,SS:[BX+2]                     ;Load Max
         XOR     BX,BX                     ;Clear Data index
         MOV     CX,Count                       ;Load Count
         JCXZ    SD4                          ;Skip if zero
SD1:     CMP     Data[BX],AX                    ;Too small?
         JL      SD2                            ;Yes, jump
         CMP     Data[BX],DX                    ;Too large?
         JLE     SD3                             ;No, jump
SD2:     PUSH    AX                         ;Save registers
         PUSH    BX
         PUSH    CX
         PUSH    DX
         PUSH    Data[BX]           ;Pass offending value to Pascal
         CALL    RangeError                ;Call Pascal procedure
         POP     DX                         ;Restore registers
         POP     CX
         POP     BX
         POP     AX
SD3:     INC     BX                       ;Point to next element
         INC     BX
         LOOP    SD1                          ;Loop for each item
```

```
SD4:    RET     4                              ;Clean stack and return

CheckRange      ENDP

CODE    ENDS

        END
```

# Inline Machine Code

For very short assembly language subroutines, Turbo Pascal's **inline** statements and directives are very convenient. They allow you to insert machine code instructions directly into the program or unit text instead of through an object file.

## *Inline Statements*

An **inline** statement consists of the reserved word **inline** followed by one or more inline elements, separated by slashes and enclosed in parentheses:

```
inline(10/$2345/Count+1/Data-Offset);
```

Here's the syntax of an inline statement:

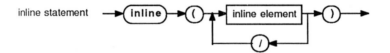

Each inline element consists of an optional size specifier, < or >, and a constant or a variable identifier, followed by zero or more offset specifiers (see the syntax that follows). An offset specifier consists of a + or a − followed by a constant.

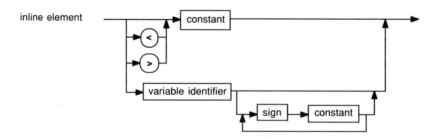

Each inline element generates 1 byte or one word of code. The value is computed from the value of the first constant or the offset of the variable identifier, to which is added or subtracted the value of each of the constants that follow it.

An inline element generates 1 byte of code if it consists of constants only and if its value is within the 8-bit range (0..255). If the value is outside the 8-bit range or if the inline element refers to a variable, one word of code is generated (least-significant byte first).

The < and > operators can be used to override the automatic size selection we described earlier. If an inline element starts with a < operator, only the least-significant byte of the value is coded, even if it is a 16-bit value. If an inline element starts with a > operator, a word is always coded, even though the most-significant byte is 0. For example, the statement

```
inline(<$1234/>$44);
```

generates 3 bytes of code: $34,$44,$00.

The value of a variable identifier in an inline element is the offset address of the variable within its base segment. The base segment of global variables—variables declared at the outermost level in a program or a unit—and typed constants is the data segment, which is accessible through the DS register. The base segment of local variables—variables declared within the current subprogram—is the stack segment. In this case the variable offset is relative to the BP register, which automatically causes the stack segment to be selected.

**Note:** Registers BP, SP, SS, and DS must be preserved by **inline** statements; all other registers can be modified.

The following example of an **inline** statement generates machine code for storing a specified number of words of data in a specified variable. When called, procedure *FillWord* stores *Count* words of the value *Data* in memory, starting at the first byte occupied by *Dest*.

```
procedure FillWord(var Dest,Count,Data: word);
begin
  inline(
    $C4/$BE/Dest/                  { LES DI,Dest[BP] }
    $8B/$8E/Count/                 { MOV CX,Count[BP] }
    $8B/$86/Data/                  { MOV AX,Data[BP] }
    $FC/                           { CLD }
    $F3/$AB);                      { REP STOSW }
end;
```

**Inline** statements can be freely mixed with other statements throughout the statement part of a block.

# Inline Directives

Inline directives let you write procedures and functions that expand into a given sequence of machine code instructions whenever they are called. These are comparable to macros in assembly language. The syntax for an inline directive is the same as that of an inline statement:

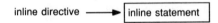

When a normal procedure or function is called (including one that contains **inline** statements), the compiler generates code that pushes the parameters (if any) onto the stack, and then generates a CALL instruction to call the procedure or function. However, when you call an inline procedure or function, the compiler generates code from the inline directive instead of the CALL. Here's a short example of two inline procedures:

```
procedure DisableInterrupts; inline($FA);                          { CLI }
procedure EnableInterrupts; inline($FB);                           { STI }
```

When *DisableInterrupts* is called, it generates 1 byte of code—a CLI instruction.

Procedures and functions declared with inline directives can have parameters; however, the parameters cannot be referred to symbolically in the inline directive (other variables can, though). Also, because such procedures and functions are in fact macros, there is no automatic entry and exit code, nor should there be any return instruction.

The following function multiplies two integer values, producing a longint result:

```
function LongMul(X,Y : integer): longint;
inline(
  $58/                                         { POP AX ;Pop Y }
  $5A/                                         { POP DX ;Pop X }
  $F7/$EA);                                    { IMUL DX ;DX : AX = X*Y }
```

Note the lack of entry and exit code and the missing return instruction. These are not required, because the 4 bytes are inserted into the instruction stream when *LongMul* is called.

Inline directives are intended for very short (less than 10 bytes) procedures and functions only.

Because of the macro-like nature of inline procedures and functions, they cannot be used as arguments to the @ operator and the *Addr*, *Ofs*, and *Seg* functions.

# Direct Memory and Port Access

## The Mem, MemW, and MemL Arrays

Turbo Pascal implements three predefined arrays, *Mem*, *MemW*, and *MemL*, which are used to directly access memory. Each component of *Mem* is a byte, each component of *MemW* is a word, and each component of *MemL* is a longint.

The *Mem* arrays use a special syntax for indexes: Two expressions of the integer-type word, separated by a colon, are used to specify the segment base and offset of the memory location to access. Some examples include

```
Mem[$0040:$0049] := 7;
Data := MemW[Seg(V):Ofs(V)];
MemLong := MemL[64:3*4];
```

The first statement stores the value 7 in the byte at $0040:$0049. The second statement moves the word value stored in the first 2 bytes of the variable *V* into the variable *Data*. The third statement moves the longint value stored at $0040:$000C into the variable *MemLong*.

## The Port and PortW Arrays

For access to the 80x86 CPU data ports, Turbo Pascal implements two predefined arrays, *Port* and *PortW*. Both are one-dimensional arrays, and each element represents a data port, whose port address corresponds to its index. The index type is the integer-type word. Components of the *Port* array are of type byte, and components of the *PortW* array are of type word.

When a value is assigned to a component of *Port* or *PortW*, the value is output to the selected port. When a component of *Port* or *PortW* is referenced in an expression, its value is input from the selected port. Some examples include:

```
Port[$20] := $20;
Port[Base] := Port[Base] xor Mask;
while Port[$B2] and $80 = 0 do                           { Wait };
```

Use of the *Port* and *PortW* arrays is restricted to assignment and reference in expressions only, that is, components of *Port* and *PortW* cannot be used as variable parameters. Furthermore, references to the entire *Port* or *PortW* array (reference without index) are not allowed.

# Interrupt Handling

The Turbo Pascal runtime library and the code generated by the compiler are fully interruptible. Also, most of the runtime library is reentrant, which allows you to write interrupt service routines in Turbo Pascal.

## *Writing Interrupt Procedures*

Interrupt procedures are declared with the **interrupt** directive. Every interrupt procedure must specify the following procedure header (or a subset of it, as explained later):

```
procedure IntHandler(Flags,CS,IP,AX,BX,CX,DX,SI,DI,DS,ES,BP: word);
interrupt;
begin
   :
   :
end;
```

As you can see, all the registers are passed as pseudo-parameters so you can use and modify them in your code. You can omit some or all of the parameters, starting with *Flags* and moving towards *BP*. It is an error to declare more parameters than are listed in the preceding example or to omit a specific parameter without also omitting the ones before it (although no error is reported). For example:

```
procedure IntHandler(DI,ES,BP : word);
procedure IntHandler(SI,DI,DS,ES,BP : word);
```

On entry, an interrupt procedure automatically saves all registers (regardless of the procedure header) and initializes the DS register:

```
PUSH    AX
PUSH    BX
PUSH    CX
PUSH    DX
PUSH    SI
PUSH    DI
PUSH    DS
PUSH    ES
PUSH    BP
MOV     BP,SP
SUB     SP,LocalSize
MOV     AX,SEG DATA
MOV     DS,AX
```

Notice the lack of a STI instruction to enable further interrupts. You should code this yourself (if required) using an inline statement. The exit code restores the registers and executes an interrupt-return instruction:

```
MOV     SP,BP
POP     BP
POP     ES
POP     DS
POP     DI
POP     SI
POP     DX
POP     CX
POP     BX
POP     AX
IRET
```

An interrupt procedure can modify its parameters. Changing the declared parameters will modify the corresponding register when the interrupt handler returns. This can be useful when you are using an interrupt handler as a user service, much like the DOS INT 21H services.

Interrupt procedures that handle hardware-generated interrupts should refrain from using any of Turbo Pascal's input and output or dynamic memory allocation routines, because they are not reentrant. Likewise, no DOS functions can be used, because DOS is not reentrant.

# Text File Device Drivers

As mentioned in Chapter 8, Turbo Pascal allows you to define your own text file device drivers. A *text file device driver* is a set of four functions that completely implement an interface between Turbo Pascal's file system and some device.

The four functions that define each device driver are *Open*, *InOut*, *Flush*, and *Close*. The function header of each function is

```
function DeviceFunc(var F: TextRec): integer;
```

where *TextRec* is the text file record type defined in the earlier section, "File Types." Each function must be compiled in the {$F+} state to force it to use the far call model. The return value of a device interface function becomes the value returned by *IOResult*. The return value of 0 indicates a successful operation.

To associate the device interface functions with a specific file, you must write a customized *Assign* procedure (like the *AssignCrt* procedure in the *Crt* unit). The *Assign* procedure must assign the addresses of the four device interface functions to the four function pointers in the text file variable. In addition, it should store the *fmClosed* "magic" constant in the *Mode* field, store the size of the text file buffer in *BufSize*, store a pointer to the text file buffer in *BufPtr*, and clear the *Name* string.

Assuming, for example, that the four device interface functions are called *DevOpen*, *DevInOut*, *DevFlush*, and *DevClose*, the *Assign* procedure might look like this:

```
procedure AssignDev(var F: Text);
begin
  with TextRec(F) do
  begin
    Mode       := fmClosed;
    BufSize    := SizeOf(Buffer);
    BufPtr     := @Buffer;
    OpenFunc   := @DevOpen;
    InOutFunc  := @DevInOut;
    FlushFunc  := @DevFlush;
    CloseFunc  := @DevClose;
    Name[0]    := #0;
  end;
end;
```

The device interface functions can use the *UserData* field in the file record to store private information. This field is not modified by the Turbo Pascal file system at any time.

## *The Open Function*

The *Open* function is called by the *Reset*, *Rewrite*, and *Append* standard procedures to open a text file associated with a device. On entry, the *Mode* field contains *fmInput*, *fmOutput*, or *fmInOut* to indicate whether the *Open* function was called from *Reset*, *Rewrite*, or *Append*.

The *Open* function prepares the file for input or output, according to the *Mode* value. If *Mode* specified *fmInOut* (indicating that *Open* was called from *Append*), it must be changed to *fmOutput* before *Open* returns.

*Open* is always called before any of the other device interface functions. For that reason, *Assign* only initializes the *OpenFunc* field, leaving initialization of the remaining vectors up to *Open*. Based on *Mode*, *Open* can then install pointers to either input- or output-oriented functions. This saves the *InOut*, *Flush*, and *Close* functions from determining the current mode.

## The InOut Function

The *InOut* function is called by the *Read, Readln, Write, Writeln, Page, Eof, Eoln, SeekEof, SeekEoln,* and *Close* standard procedures and functions whenever input or output from the device is required.

When *Mode* is *fmInput*, the *InOut* function reads up to *BufSize* characters into *BufPtr^*, and returns the number of characters read in *BufEnd*. In addition, it stores 0 in *BufPos*. If the *InOut* function returns 0 in *BufEnd* as a result of an input request, *Eof* becomes True for the file.

When *Mode* is *fmOutput*, the *InOut* function writes *BufPos* characters from *BufPtr^*, and returns 0 in *BufPos*.

## The Flush Function

The *Flush* function is called at the end of each *Read, Readln, Write,* and *Writeln*. It can optionally flush the text file buffer.

If *Mode* is *fmInput*, the *Flush* function can store 0 in *BufPos* and *BufEnd* to flush the remaining (un-read) characters in the buffer. This feature is seldom used.

If *Mode* is *fmOutput*, the *Flush* function can write the contents of the buffer, exactly like the *InOut* function, which ensures that text written to the device appears on the device immediately. If *Flush* does nothing, the text will not appear on the device until the buffer becomes full or the file is closed.

## The Close Function

The *Close* function is called by the *Close* standard procedure to close a text file associated with a device. (The *Reset, Rewrite,* and *Append* procedures also call *Close* if the file they are opening is already open.) If *Mode* is *fmOutput*, then before calling *Close*, Turbo Pascal's file system calls *InOut* to ensure that all characters have been written to the device.

## Examples of Text File Device Drivers

The following unit implements a text file device driver for the communication ports (serial ports) of an IBM PC:

```
unit AuxInOut;
interface
uses Dos;
```

```
procedure AssignAux(var F: Text; Port,Params: word);
implementation
{$R-,S-}
type
  AuxRec = record
             Port,Params: word;
             Unused: array[1..12] of byte;
           end;

procedure AuxInit(Port,Params: word);
inline(
  $58/                                    { POP AX    ;Pop parameters }
  $5A/                                    { POP DX    ;Pop port number }
  $B4/$00/                                { MOV AH,0 ;Code for initialize }
  $CD/$14);                               { INT 14H  ;Call BIOS }

function AuxInChar(Port: word): char;
inline(
  $5A/                                    { POP DX    ;Pop port number }
  $B4/$02/                                { MOV AH,2 ;Code for input }
  $CD/$14);                               { INT 14H  ;Call BIOS }

procedure AuxOutChar(Port: word; Ch: char);
inline(
  $58/                                    { POP AX    ;Pop character }
  $5A/                                    { POP DX    ;Pop port number }
  $B4/$01/                                { MOV AH,1 ;Code for output }
  $CD/$14);                               { INT 14H  ;Call BIOS }

function AuxInReady(Port: word): boolean;
inline(
  $5A/                                    { POP DX     ;Pop port number }
  $B4/$03/                                { MOV AH,3   ;Code for status }
  $CD/$14/                                { INT 14H    ;Call BIOS }
  $88/$E0/                         { MOV AL,AH  ;Get line status in AH }
  $24/$01);                        { AND AL,1   ;Isolate Data Ready bit }

{$F+}

function AuxInput(var F: TextRec): integer;
var
  P: word;
begin
  with F,AuxRec(UserData) do
  begin
    P := 0;
    while AuxInReady(Port) and (P<BufSize) do
    begin
      BufPtr^[P] := AuxInChar(Port); Inc(P);
    end;
    BufPos := 0; Bufend := P;
  end;
  AuxInput := 0;
end;

function AuxOutput(var F: TextRec): integer;
var
  P: word;
```

```pascal
begin
  with F,AuxRec(UserData) do
  begin
    P := 0;
    while P<BufPos do
    begin
      AuxOutChar(Port,BufPtr^[P]); Inc(P);
    end;
    BufPos := 0;
  end;
  AuxOutput := 0;
end;

function AuxIgnore(var F: TextRec): integer;
begin
  AuxIgnore := 0;
end;

function AuxOpen(var F: TextRec): integer;
begin
  with F,AuxRec(UserData) do
  begin
    AuxInit(Port,Params);
    if Mode=fmInput then
    begin
      InOutFunc := @AuxInput;
      FlushFunc := @AuxIgnore;
    end else
    begin
      Mode := fmOutput;
      InOutFunc := @AuxOutput;
      FlushFunc := @AuxOutput;
    end;
    CloseFunc := @AuxIgnore;
  end;
  AuxOpen := 0;
end;

{$F-}

procedure AssignAux;
begin
  with TextRec(F) do
  begin
    Handle := $FFFF;
    Mode := fmClosed;
    BufSize := Sizeof(Buffer);
    BufPtr := @Buffer;
    OpenFunc := @AuxOpen;
    AuxRec(UserData).Port := Port;
    AuxRec(UserData).Params := Params;
    Name[0] := #0;
  end;
end;
end.
```

The *TextRec* record is defined in the *Dos* unit. The first two words of the 16-byte *UserData* array are used for storing the communications port number and parameter byte. The remaining 12 bytes are not used. Note that the *AuxRec* record is used only for typecasting.

The *AuxInit* procedure initializes a specified communications port according to a specified parameter byte. The *AuxInChar* function reads a character from the specified port. The *AuxOutChar* procedure outputs a character to the specified port. The *AuxInReady* function returns True if a character is ready to be read from the specified port. Notice the use of inline directives to implement these procedures and functions. For further details on the communication ports, refer to the *IBM PC Technical Reference Manual*.

*AssignAux* initializes a specified text file variable to refer to a specified communication port with a specified parameter byte. Port numbers 0 and 1 correspond to COM1 and COM2. The parameter byte is described in the *IBM PC Technical Reference Manual*.

*AuxOpen* initializes the selected communication port and sets up the function pointers according to the *Mode* field. Note that for output, *FlushFunc* is set to the same address as *InOutFunc*, causing the text file buffer to be flushed after each *Write* or *Writeln*.

*AuxInput* inputs up to *BufSize* characters from the selected port, and *AuxOutput* outputs the contents of the buffer to the selected port.

*AuxIgnore* is used in those cases where no special action is required, such as for *Close* and for *Flush* (when in input mode).

The following short program uses the *AuxInOut* unit to write a string to one of the communication ports. Through the *AssignAux* procedure, the Com1 file is associated with the COM1 port using 1200 baud, no parity, 1 stop bit, and 8 data bits:

```
program TestAux;
uses AuxInOut;
var
  Com1: Text;
begin
  AssignAux(Com1,0,$83);
  Rewrite(Com1);
  Writeln(Com1,'Device Drivers are fun!');
  Close(Com1);
end.
```

# Exit Procedures

By installing an exit procedure, you can gain control over a program's termination process. This is useful when you want to make sure specific actions are carried out before a program terminates; a typical example is updating and closing files.

The *ExitProc* pointer variable allows you to install an exit procedure. The exit procedure always gets called as a part of a program's termination, whether it is a normal termination, a termination through a call to *Halt*, or a termination due to a runtime error.

An exit procedure takes no parameters, and must be compiled in the {$F+} state to force it to use the far call model.

When implemented properly, an exit procedure actually becomes part of a chain of exit procedures. This chain makes it possible for units as well as programs to install exit procedures. Some units install an exit procedure as part of their initialization code, and then rely on that specific procedure to be called to clean up after the unit; for instance, to close files or to restore interrupt vectors. The procedures on the exit chain get executed in reverse order of installation. This ensures that the exit code of one unit does not get executed before the exit code of any units that depend upon it.

To keep the exit chain intact, you must save the current contents of *ExitProc* before changing it to the address of your own exit procedure. Furthermore, just before returning, your exit procedure must re-install the saved value of *ExitProc*. The following program demonstrates a skeleton method of implementing an exit procedure:

```
program Testexit;
var
  ExitSave: pointer;

{$F+}
procedure MyExit; {$F-}
begin
  :
  :
  ExitProc := ExitSave;
end;
begin
  ExitSave := ExitProc;
  ExitProc := @MyExit;
  :
  :
end.
```

On entry, the program saves the contents of *ExitProc* in *ExitSave*, and then installs the *MyExit* exit procedure. After having been called as part of the termination process and just before returning, *MyExit* re-installs the previous exit procedure.

The termination routine in the runtime library keeps calling exit procedures until *ExitProc* becomes nil. To avoid infinite loops, *ExitProc* is set to nil before every call, so the next exit procedure is called only if the current exit procedure assigns an address to *ExitProc*. If an error occurs in an exit procedure, the exit procedure will not yet have assigned a new value to *ExitProc*, since this is done just before it returns.

An exit procedure may learn the cause of termination by examining the *ExitCode* integer variable and the *ErrorAddr* pointer variable.

In case of normal termination, *ExitCode* is zero and *ErrorAddr* is nil. In case of termination through a call to *Halt*, *ExitCode* contains the value passed to *Halt* and *ErrorAddr* is nil. Finally, in case of termination due to a runtime error, *ExitCode* contains the error code and *ErrorAddr* contains the address of the statement in error.

The last exit procedure (the one installed by the runtime library) closes the *Input* and *Output* files, and restores the interrupt vectors that were captured by Turbo Pascal. In addition, if *ErrorAddr* is not nil, it outputs a runtime error message.

If you wish to present runtime error messages yourself, install an exit procedure that examines *ErrorAddr* and outputs a message if it is not nil. In addition, before returning, make sure to set *ErrorAddr* to nil, so that the error is not reported again by other exit procedures.

Once the runtime library has called all exit procedures, it returns to DOS, passing as a return code the value stored in *ExitCode*.

# Automatic Optimizations

Turbo Pascal performs several different types of code optimizations, ranging from constant folding and short-circuit Boolean expression evaluation all the way up to smart linking. Here are some of the types of optimizations performed.

## Constant Folding

If the operand(s) of an operator are constants of an ordinal type, Turbo Pascal evaluates the expression at compile time. For example, *X := 3 + 4 * 2* produces the exact same code as *X := 11*.

Likewise, if the operand of an *Abs*, *Sqr*, *Succ*, *Pred*, *Odd*, *Lo*, *Hi*, or *Swap* function call is a constant of an ordinal type, the function is evaluated at compile time.

If an array index expression is a constant, the address of the component is evaluated at compile time. For example, accessing *Data[5,5]* is just as efficient as accessing a simple variable.

## *Constant Merging*

Using the same string constant two or more times in a statement part generates only one copy of the constant. For example, two or more *Write('Done')* statements in the same statement part will reference the same copy of the string constant *'Done'*.

## *Short-Circuit Evaluation*

Turbo Pascal implements short-circuit Boolean evaluation, which means that evaluation of a Boolean expression stops as soon as the result of the entire expression becomes evident. This guarantees minimum execution time, and usually minimum code size. Short-circuit evaluation also makes possible the evaluation of constructs that would not otherwise be legal; for instance:

```
while (I<=Length(S)) and (S[I]<>' ') do Inc(I);
while (P<>nil) and (P^.Value<>5) do P:=P^.Next;
```

In both cases, the second test is not evaluated if the first test is False.

The opposite of short-circuit evaluation is complete evaluation, which is selected through a {$B+} compiler directive. In this state, every operand of a Boolean expression is guaranteed to be evaluated.

## *Order of Evaluation*

As permitted by the Pascal standards, operands of an expression are frequently evaluated differently from the left to right order in which they are written. For example, the statement

```
I:=F(J) div G(J);
```

where *F* and *G* are functions of type integer, causes *G* to be evaluated before *F*, since this enables the compiler to produce better code. Because of this, it is important that an expression never depend on any specific order of evaluation of the embedded functions. Referring to the previous example, if *F* must be called before *G*, use a temporary variable:

```
T:=F(J); I:=T div G(J);
```

**Note**: As an exception to this rule, when short-circuit evaluation is enabled (the {$B-} state), boolean operands grouped with **and** or **or** are *always* evaluated from left to right.

## Range-Checking

Assignment of a constant to a variable and use of a constant as a value parameter is range-checked at compile time; no runtime range-check code is generated. For example, X:=999, where X is of type *Byte*, causes a compile-time error.

## Shift instead of Multiply

The operation X * C, where C is a constant and a power of 2, is coded using a Shl instruction.

Likewise, when the size of an array's components is a power of 2, a Shl instruction (not a Mul instruction) is used to scale the index expression.

## Dead Code Removal

Statements that are known never to execute do not generate any code. For example, these constructs don't generate any code:

```
if False then statement
while False do statement
```

## Smart Linking

The linker automatically removes unused code on a per-procedure basis; that is, procedures and functions that are part of a compilation but never get called are removed in the .EXE file.

# 27

# Turbo Pascal Reference Lookup

This chapter describes all the procedures and functions of Turbo Pascal 4.0. For your convenience, they're arranged alphabetically. Here's a sample layout so you can easily understand the format of the lookup; note that only the relevant items are listed in each entry.

## Sample procedure      What unit it occupies

| | |
|---|---|
| **Function** | What it does |
| **Declaration** | How it's declared; italicized items are user-defined |
| **Result type** | What it returns if it's a function |
| **Remarks** | General information about the procedure or function |
| **Restrictions** | Things to be aware of |
| **Differences** | From 3.0 |
| **See also** | Related procedures/functions, etc. |
| **Example** | Sample program or code fragment |

**Note:** When compiling in numeric processing mode, {$N+}, the return values of the floating point routines in the *System* unit (*Sqrt, Pi, Sin*, and so on) are of type extended instead of real.

# Abs function

| | |
|---|---|
| **Function** | Returns the absolute value of the argument. |
| **Declaration** | `Abs(x)` |
| **Result type** | Same type as parameter. |
| **Remarks** | $x$ is an integer-type or real-type expression. The result, of the same type as $x$, is the absolute value of $x$. |
| **Example** | |

```
var
  r: real;
  i: integer;

begin
  r := Abs(-2.3);      { 2.3 }
  i := Abs(-157);      { 157 }
end.
```

# Addr function

| | |
|---|---|
| **Function** | Returns the address of a specified object. |
| **Declaration** | `Addr(x)` |
| **Result type** | pointer |
| **Remarks** | $x$ is any variable, or a procedure or function identifier. The result is a pointer that points to $x$. Like **nil**, the result of *Addr* is assignment compatible with all pointer types. |
| | **Note:** The @ operator produces the same result as *Addr*. |
| **See also** | *Ptr* |
| **Example** | |

```
var p: pointer;
begin
  p := Addr(p);          { Now points to itself }
end.
```

# Append procedure

| | |
|---|---|
| **Function** | Opens an existing file for appending. |

| | |
|---|---|
| **Declaration** | Append(**var** f: text) |
| **Remarks** | *f* is a text-file variable that must have been associated with an external file using *Assign*. |

*Append* opens the existing external file with the name assigned to *f*. It is an error if there is no existing external file of the given name. If *f* was already open, it is first closed and then re-opened. The current file position is set to the end of the file.

If a *Ctrl-Z* (ASCII 26) is present in the last 128-byte block of the file, the current file position is set to overwrite the first *Ctrl-Z* in the block. In this way, text can be appended to a file that terminates with a *Ctrl-Z*.

If *f* was assigned an empty name, such as *Assign(f,'')*, then, after the call to *Append*, *f* will refer to the standard output file (standard handle number 1).

After a call to *Append*, *f* becomes write-only, and *Eof(f)* is always True.

With {$I-}, *IOResult* will return a 0 if the operation was successful; otherwise, it will return a nonzero error code.

| | |
|---|---|
| **See also** | *Reset, Rewrite* |
| **Example** | |

```
var f: text;
begin
  Assign(f, 'TEST.TXT');
  Rewrite(f);                           { Create new file }
  Writeln(f, 'original text');
  Close(f);                   { Close file, save changes }
  Append(f);                    { Add more text onto end }
  Writeln(f, 'appended text');
  Close(f);                   { Close file, save changes }
end.
```

---

# Arc procedure                                    Graph

---

| | |
|---|---|
| **Function** | Draws a circular arc around start angle to end angle, using (*x,y*) as the center point. |
| **Declaration** | Arc(X, Y: integer; StAngle, EndAngle, Radius: word) |

| | |
|---|---|
| **Remarks** | Draws a circular arc around $(x,y)$, with a radius of *Radius*. The *Arc* travels from *StAngle* to *EndAngle* and is drawn in the current drawing color. |
| | Each graphics driver contains an aspect ratio that is used by *Circle*, *Arc*, and *PieSlice*. A start angle of 0 and an end angle of 360 will draw a complete circle. The angles for *Arc*, *Ellipse*, and *PieSlice* are counterclockwise with 0 degrees at 3 o'clock, 90 degrees at 12 o'clock, and so on. Information about the last call to *Arc* can be retrieved with a call to *GetArcCoords*. |
| **Restrictions** | Must be in graphics mode. |
| **See also** | *Circle, Ellipse, GetArcCoords, GetAspectRatio, PieSlice* |
| **Example** | |

```
uses Graph;
var
  Gd, Gm: integer;
  Radius: integer;

begin
  Gd := Detect;
  InitGraph(Gd, Gm, '');
  if GraphResult <> grOk then
    Halt(1);
  for Radius := 1 to 5 do
    Arc(100, 100, 0, 90, Radius*10);
  Readln;
  CloseGraph;
end.
```

# ArcTan function

| | |
|---|---|
| **Function** | Returns the arctangent of the argument. |
| **Declaration** | `ArcTan(x: real)` |
| **Result type** | real |
| **Remarks** | $x$ is a real-type expression. The result is the principal value, in radians, of the arctangent of $x$. |
| **Example** | |

```
var r: real;
begin
  r := ArcTan(Pi);
end.
```

# Assign procedure

**Function**   Assigns the name of an external file to a file variable.

**Declaration**   `Assign(f; name: string)`

**Remarks**   *f* is a file variable of any file type, and *name* is a string-type expression. All further operations on *f* will operate on the external file with the file name *name*.

After a call to *Assign*, the association between *f* and the external file continues to exist until another *Assign* is done on *f*.

A file name consists of a path of zero or more directory names separated by backslashes, followed by the actual file name:

`Drive:\DirName\...\DirName\FileName`

If the path begins with a backslash, it starts in the root directory; otherwise, it starts in the current directory.

*Drive* is a disk drive identifier (*A-Z*). If *Drive* and the colon are omitted, the default drive is used. *\DirName\...\DirName* is the root directory and sub-directory path to the file name. *FileName* consists of a name of up to eight characters, optionally followed by a period and an extension of up to three characters.

The maximum length of the entire file name is 79 characters.

**Restrictions**   *Assign* must never be used on an open file.

A special case arises when *name* is an empty string; that is, when *Length(name)* is zero. In that case, *f* becomes associated with the standard input or standard output file. These special files allow a program to utilize the I/O redirection feature of the DOS operating system. If assigned an empty name, then after a call to *Reset(f)*, *f* will refer to the standard input file, and after a call to *Rewrite(f)*, *f* will refer to the standard output file.

**Example**
```
{ Try redirecting this program from DOS
  to PRN, disk file, etc. }
var f: text;
begin
```

```
    Assign(f, '');                          { Standard output }
    Rewrite(f);
    Writeln(f, 'standard output...');
    Close(f);
end.
```

# AssignCrt procedure                                  Crt

**Function**        Associates a text file with the CRT.

**Declaration**     `AssignCrt(var f: Text)`

**Remarks**         *AssignCrt* works exactly like the *Assign* standard pro-
                    cedure except that no file name is specified. Instead, the
                    text file is associated with the CRT.

                    This allows faster output (and input) than would
                    normally be possible using standard output (or input).

**Example**
```
uses Crt;
var f: text;

begin
  Write('Output to screen or printer [S, P]? ');
  if UpCase(ReadKey) = 'P' then
    Assign(f, 'PRN')                        { Output to printer }
  else
    AssignCrt(f);                           { Output to screen, use
                                              fast CRT write routines }
  Rewrite(f);
  Writeln(f, 'Fast output via CRT routines...');
  Close(f);
end.
```

# Bar procedure                                        Graph

**Function**        Draws a bar using the current fill style and color.

**Declaration**     `Bar(x1, y1, x2, y2: integer)`

**Remarks**         Draws a filled-in rectangle (used in bar charts, for
                    example). Uses the pattern and color defined by
                    *SetFillStyle* or *SetFillPattern*. To draw an outlined bar, call
                    *Bar3D* with a depth of zero.

**Restrictions**    Must be in graphics mode.

| | |
|---|---|
| **See also** | *Bar3D, GraphResult, SetFillStyle, SetFillPattern, SetLineStyle* |
| **Example** | |

```pascal
uses Graph;
var
  Gd, Gm  : integer;
  I, Width: integer;

begin
  Gd := Detect;
  InitGraph(Gd, Gm, '');
  if GraphResult <> grOk then
    Halt(1);
  Width := 10;
  for I := 1 to 5 do
    Bar(I*Width, I*10, Succ(I)*Width, 200);
  Readln;
  CloseGraph;
end.
```

# Bar3D procedure                                          Graph

| | |
|---|---|
| **Function** | Draws a 3-D bar using the current fill style and color. |
| **Declaration** | `Bar3D(x1, y1, x2, y2: integer; Depth: word; Top: boolean)` |
| **Remarks** | Draws a filled-in, three-dimensional bar. Uses the pattern and color defined by *SetFillStyle* or *SetFillPattern*. The 3-D outline of the bar is drawn in the current line style and color as set by *SetLineStyle* and *SetColor*. *Depth* is the number of pixels deep of the 3-D outline. If *Top* is True, a 3-D top is put on the bar; if *Top* is False, no top is put on the bar (making it possible to stack several bars on top one another). |
| | A typical depth could be calculated by taking 25% of the width of the bar: |

```pascal
Bar3d(x1,y1,x2,y2,(x2-x1+1) div 4, TopOn);
```

The following constants are defined:

```pascal
const
  TopOn  = True;
  TopOff = False;
```

| | |
|---|---|
| **Restrictions** | Must be in graphics mode. |
| **See also** | *Bar, GraphResult, SetFillStyle, SetFillPattern, SetLineStyle* |

```
uses Graph;
var
  Gd, Gm: integer;
  y0, y1, y2, x1, x2: integer;

begin
  Gd := Detect;
  InitGraph(Gd, Gm, '');
  if GraphResult <> grOk then
    Halt(1);
  y0 := 10;
  y1 := 60;
  y2 := 110;
  x1 := 10;
  x2 := 50;
  Bar3D(x1, y0, x2, y1, 10, TopOn);
  Bar3D(x1, y1, x2, y2, 10, TopOff);
  Readln;
  CloseGraph;
end.
```

# BlockRead procedure

**Function**    Reads one or more records into a variable.

**Declaration**    
```
BlockRead(var f: file; var buf; count: word
          [; var result: word ])
```

**Remarks**    *f* is an untyped file variable, *buf* is any variable, *count* is an expression of type word, and *result* is a variable of type word.

*BlockRead* reads *count* or less records from the file *f* into memory, starting at the first byte occupied by *buf*. The actual number of complete records read (less than or equal to *count*) is returned in the optional parameter *result*. If *result* is not specified, an I/O error will occur if the number read is not equal to *count*.

The entire block transferred occupies at most *count* * *recsize* bytes, where *recsize* is the record size specified when the file was opened (or 128 if it was omitted). It's an error if *count* * *recsize* is greater than 65535 (64 Kb).

*result* is an optional parameter. Here is how it works: If the entire block was transferred, *result* will be equal to *count* on return. Otherwise, if *result* is less than *count*, the end of the file was reached before the transfer was completed. In that case, if the file's record size is greater than one, *result* returns the number of complete records read; that is, a possible last partial record is not included in *result*.

The current file position is advanced by *result* records as an effect of the *BlockRead*.

With {$I-}, *IOResult* will return a 0 if the operation was successful; otherwise, it will return a nonzero error code.

| | |
|---|---|
| **Restrictions** | File must be open. |
| **Differences** | 3.0 read partial records; 4.0 discards them. |
| **See also** | *BlockWrite* |
| **Example** | |

```
program CopyFile;
{ Simple, fast file copy program with NO error-checking }
var
  FromF, ToF: file;
  NumRead, NumWritten: word;
  buf: array[1..2048] of char;

begin
  Assign(FromF, ParamStr(1));              { Open input file }
  Reset(FromF, 1);                         { Record size = 1 }
  Assign(ToF, ParamStr(2));                { Open output file }
  Rewrite(ToF, 1);                         { Record size = 1 }
  Writeln('Copying ', FileSize(FromF), ' bytes...');
  repeat
    BlockRead(FromF,buf,SizeOf(buf),NumRead);
    BlockWrite(ToF,buf,NumRead,NumWritten);
  until (NumRead = 0) or (NumWritten <> NumRead);
  Close(FromF);
  Close(ToF);
end.
```

# BlockWrite procedure

| | |
|---|---|
| **Function** | Writes one or more records from a variable. |
| **Declaration** | BlockWrite(BlockWrite(**var** f: **file**; **var** buf; count: word<br>[; **var** result: word ]) |
| **Remarks** | *f* is an untyped file variable, *buf* is any variable, *count* is an expression of type word, and *result* is a variable of type word. |

*BlockWrite* writes *count* or less records to the file *f* from memory, starting at the first byte occupied by *buf*. The actual number of complete records written (less than or equal to *count*) is returned in the optional parameter *result*. If *result* is not specified, an I/O error will occur if the number written is not equal to *count*.

The entire block transferred occupies at most *count* * *recsize* bytes, where *recsize* is the record size specified when the file was opened (or 128 if it was omitted). It is an error if *count* * *recsize* is greater than 65535 (64K).

*result* is an optional parameter. Here is how it works: If the entire block was transferred, *result* will be equal to *count* on return. Otherwise, if *result* is less than *count*, the disk became full before the transfer was completed. In that case, if the file's record size is greater than one, *result* returns the number of complete records written; that is, it's possible a remaining partial record is not included in *result*.

The current file position is advanced by *result* records as an effect of the *BlockWrite*.

With {$I-}, *IOResult* will return a 0 if the operation was successful; otherwise, it will return a nonzero error code.

| | |
|---|---|
| **Restrictions** | File must be open. |
| **Differences** | 3.0 read partial records; 4.0 discards them. |
| **See also** | *BlockRead* |
| **Example** | See example for *BlockRead*. |

# ChDir procedure

| | |
|---|---|
| **Function** | Changes the current directory. |
| **Declaration** | ChDir(s: **string**) |
| **Remarks** | *s* is a string-type expression. The current directory is changed to a path specified by *s*. If *s* specifies a drive letter, the current drive is also changed. |
| | With {$I-}, *IOResult* will return a 0 if the operation was successful; otherwise, it will return a nonzero error code. |

| See also | *GetDir, RmDir, MkDir* |
|---|---|
| Example | |

```
begin
  {$I-}
  { Get directory name from command line }
  ChDir(ParamStr(1));
  if IOResult <> 0 then
    Writeln('Cannot find directory');
end.
```

# Chr function

| Function | Returns a character with a specified ordinal number. |
|---|---|
| Declaration | `Chr(x: byte)` |
| Result type | char |
| Remarks | *x* is an integer-type expression. The result is the character with an ordinal value (ASCII value) of *x*. |
| See also | *Ord* |
| Example | |

```
uses Printer;
begin
  Writeln(Lst, Chr(12));          { Send form feed to printer }
end.
```

# Circle procedure                                            Graph

| Function | Draws a circle using (*X,Y*) as the center point. |
|---|---|
| Declaration | `Circle(X, Y: integer; Radius: word)` |
| Remarks | The circle is drawn in the current color set by *SetColor*. Each graphics driver contains an aspect ratio that is used by *Circle, Arc,* and *PieSlice* to make circles. |
| Restrictions | Must be in graphics mode. |
| See also | *Arc, Ellipse, GetArcCoords, GetAspectRatio, PieSlice* |
| Example | |

```
uses Graph;
var
  Gd, Gm: integer;
  Radius: integer;

begin
  Gd := Detect;
```

```
        InitGraph(Gd, Gm, '');
        if GraphResult <> grOk then
          Halt(1);
        for Radius := 1 to 5 do
          Circle(100, 100, Radius*10);
        Readln;
        CloseGraph;
      end.
```

# ClearDevice procedure                     Graph

**Function**        Clears the graphics screen and prepares it for output.

**Declaration**     `ClearDevice`

**Remarks**         *ClearDevice* moves the current pointer to (0,0) and clears
                    the screen using the background color set by *SetBkColor*
                    and prepares it for output.

**Restrictions**    Must be in graphics mode.

**See also**        *ClearViewPort, CloseGraph, InitGraph, RestoreCrtMode,*
                    *SetGraphMode, GraphDefaults*

**Example**
```
uses Crt, Graph;
var
  Gd, Gm: integer;

begin
  Gd := Detect;
  InitGraph(Gd, Gm, '');
  if GraphResult <> grOk then
    Halt(1);
  Randomize;
  repeat
    LineTo(Random(200), Random(200));
  until KeyPressed;
  ClearDevice;
  Readln;
  CloseGraph;
end.
```

# ClearViewPort procedure                   Graph

**Function**        Clears the current viewport.

**Declaration**     `ClearViewPort`

| | |
|---|---|
| **Remarks** | Sets the fill color to the background color (*Palette*[0]), calls *Bar*, and moves the current pointer to (0,0). |
| **Restrictions** | Must be in graphics mode. |
| **See also** | *SetViewPort, GetViewSettings, Bar* |
| **Example** | |

```
uses Graph;
var
  Gd, Gm: integer;

begin
  Gd := Detect;
  InitGraph(Gd, Gm, '');
  if GraphResult <> grOk then
    Halt(1);
  Rectangle(19, 19, GetMaxX-19, GetMaxY-19);
  SetViewPort(20, 20, GetMaxX-20, GetMaxY-20, ClipOn);
  OutTextXY(0, 0, '<RETURN> clears viewport:');
  Readln;
  ClearViewPort;
  OutTextXY(0, 0, '<RETURN> to quit:');
  Readln;
  CloseGraph;
end.
```

# Close procedure

| | |
|---|---|
| **Function** | Closes an open file. |
| **Declaration** | Close(f) |
| **Remarks** | *f* is a file variable of any file type that was previously opened with *Reset, Rewrite,* or *Append.* The external file associated with *f* is completely updated and then closed, and its DOS file handle is freed for reuse. |
| | With {$I-}, *IOResult* will return a 0 if the operation was successful; otherwise, it will return a nonzero error code. |
| **See also** | *Append, Assign, Reset, Rewrite* |
| **Example** | |

```
var f: file;
begin
  Assign(f, '\AUTOEXEC.BAT');                    { Open file }
  Reset(f, 1);
  Writeln('File size = ', FileSize(f));
  Close(f);                                      { Close file }
end.
```

# CloseGraph procedure                                          Graph

**Function**        Shuts down the graphics system.

**Declaration**     `CloseGraph`

**Remarks**         *CloseGraph* restores the original screen mode before
                    graphics was initialized and frees the memory allocated
                    on the heap for the graphics scan buffer. *CloseGraph* also
                    deallocates driver and font memory buffers if they were
                    allocated by calls to *GraphGetMem* and *GraphFreeMem*.

**Restrictions**    Must be in graphics mode.

**See also**        *InitGraph, RestoreCrtMode*

**Example**
```
uses Graph;
var
  Gd, Gm: integer;

begin
  Gd := Detect;
  InitGraph(Gd, Gm, '');
  if GraphResult <> grOk then
    Halt(1);
  Line(0, 0, GetMaxX, GetMaxY);
  Readln;
  CloseGraph;                            { Shut down graphics }
end.
```

# ClrEol procedure                                                Crt

**Function**        Clears all characters from the cursor position to the end
                    of the line without moving the cursor.

**Declaration**     `ClrEol`

**Remarks**         All character positions are set to blanks with the
                    currently defined text attributes. Thus, if *TextBackground*
                    is not black, the column from the cursor to the right
                    edge of the screen becomes the background color.

                    This procedure is window-relative:
```
Window(1,1,60,20);
ClrScr;
```

will clear from the current cursor position (1,1) to the right edge of the active window (60,1).

**See also**    *ClrScr, Window*

**Example**
```
uses Crt;
begin
  TextBackground(LightGray);
  ClrEol;  { Changes cleared columns to LightGray background }
end.
```

# ClrScr procedure                                            Crt

**Function**    Clears the screen and places the cursor in the upper left-hand corner.

**Declaration**    ClrScr

**Remarks**    All character positions are set to blanks with the currently defined text attributes. Thus, if *TextBackground* is not black, the entire screen becomes the background color. This also applies to characters cleared by *ClrEol*, *InsLine*, and *DelLine*, as well as empty lines created by scrolling.

This procedure is window-relative:
```
Window(1,1,60,20);
ClrScr;
```
will clear a $60 \times 20$ rectangle beginning at (1,1).

**See also**    *ClrEol, Window*

**Example**
```
uses Crt;
begin
  TextBackground(LightGray);
  ClrScr;   { Changes entire screen to LightGray background }
end.
```

# Concat function

**Function**    Concatenates a sequence of strings.

**Declaration**    Concat(s1 [ , s2, ..., sn ]: ; **string**)

**Result type**    string

| Remarks | Each parameter is a string-type expression. The result is the concatenation of all the string parameters. If the resulting string is longer than 255 characters, it is truncated after the 255th character. |
|---|---|

Example

```
var s: string;
begin
  s := Concat('ABC', 'DEF');                    { 'ABCDEF' }
end.
```

# Copy function

| Function | Returns a substring of a string. |
|---|---|
| Declaration | Copy(s: **string**; index: integer; count: integer) |
| Result type | string |
| Remarks | *s* is a string-type expression. *index* and *count* are integer-type expressions. *Copy* returns a string containing *count* characters starting with the *index*th character in *s*. If *index* is larger than the length of *s*, an empty string is returned. If *count* specifies more characters than remain starting at the *index*th position, only the remainder of the string is returned. |

Example

```
var s: string;
begin
  s := 'ABCDEF';
  s := Copy(s, 2, 3)                            { 'BCD' }
end.
```

# Cos function

| Function | Returns the cosine of the argument. |
|---|---|
| Declaration | Cos(x: real) |
| Result type | real |
| Remarks | *x* is a real-type expression. The result is the cosine of *x*. *x* is assumed to represent an angle in radians. |

Example

```
var r: real;
begin
  r := Cos(Pi);
```

```
end.
```

# CSeg function

| | |
|---|---|
| **Function** | Returns the current value of the CS register. |
| **Declaration** | `CSeg` |
| **Result type** | word |
| **Remarks** | The result of type word is the segment address of the code segment within which *CSeg* was called. |
| **See also** | *DSeg, Sseg* |

# Dec procedure

| | |
|---|---|
| **Function** | Decrements a variable. |
| **Declaration** | `Dec(var x [ ; n: longint ])` |
| **Remarks** | $x$ is an ordinal-type variable, and $n$ is an integer-type expression. $x$ is decremented by 1, or by $n$ if $n$ is specified; that is, $Dec(x)$ corresponds to $x := x\text{-}1$, and $Dec(x,n)$ corresponds to $x := x\text{-}n$. |
| | *Dec* generates optimized code and is especially useful in a tight loop. |
| **See also** | *Inc, Pred, Succ* |
| **Example** | |

```
var
  IntVar: integer;
  LongintVar: longint;

begin
  Dec(IntVar);                    { IntVar := IntVar - 1 }
  Dec(LongintVar, 5);      { LongintVar := LongintVar - 5 }
end.
```

# Delay procedure                                     Crt

| | |
|---|---|
| **Function** | Delays a specified number of milliseconds. |
| **Declaration** | `Delay(ms: word)` |

| **Remarks** | *ms* specifies the number of milliseconds to wait. |
|---|---|
| | *Delay* is an approximation, so the delay period will not last exactly *ms* milliseconds. |

# Delete procedure

| **Function** | Deletes a substring from a string. |
|---|---|
| **Declaration** | Delete(**var** s: **string**;<br>　　　index: integer; count: integer) |
| **Remarks** | *s* is a string-type variable. *index* and *count* are integer-type expressions. *Delete* deletes *count* characters from *s* starting at the *index*th position. If *index* is larger than the length of *s*, no characters are deleted. If *count* specifies more characters than remain starting at the *index*th position, the remainder of the string is deleted. |
| **See also** | *Insert, Copy, Concat, Pos* |

# DelLine procedure                                                  Crt

| **Function** | Deletes the line containing the cursor. |
|---|---|
| **Declaration** | DelLine |
| **Remarks** | The line containing the cursor is deleted, and all lines below are moved one line up (using the BIOS scroll routine). A new line is added at the bottom. |
| | All character positions are set to blanks with the currently defined text attributes. Thus, if *TextBackground* is not black, the new line becomes the background color. |
| | This procedure is window-relative: |

```
Window(1,1,60,20);
DelLine;
```

will delete the first line in the window, which is the tenth line on the screen.

| **See also** | *Insline, Window* |
|---|---|

# DetectGraph procedure                    Graph

**Function**        Checks the hardware and determines which graphics driver and mode to use.

**Declaration**     DetectGraph(**var** GraphDriver, GraphMode: integer)

**Remarks**         Returns the detected driver and mode value that can be passed to *InitGraph*, which will then load the correct driver. If no graphics hardware was detected, the *GraphDriver* parameter and *GraphResult* will return a value of –2 (*grNotDetected*).

The following constants are defined:

```
const
  Detect    =  0;               { Request autodetection }
  CGA       =  1;
  MCGA      =  2;
  EGA       =  3;
  EGA64     =  4;
  EGAMono   =  5;
  RESERVED  =  6;
  HercMono  =  7;
  ATT400    =  8;
  VGA       =  9;
  PC3270    = 10;
```

Unless instructed otherwise, *InitGraph* calls *DetectGraph*, finds and loads the correct driver, and initializes the graphics system. The only reason to call *DetectGraph* directly is to override the driver that *DetectGraph* recommends. The example that follows identifies the system as a 64K or 256K EGA, and loads the CGA driver instead. Note that when you pass *InitGraph* a *Graph-Driver* other than *Detect*, you must also pass in a valid *GraphMode* for the driver requested.

**See also**        *InitGraph, GraphResult*

**Example**
```
uses Graph;
var
  GraphDriver, GraphMode: integer;

begin
  DetectGraph(GraphDriver, GraphMode);
  if (GraphDriver = EGA) or
     (GraphDriver = EGA64) then
  begin
    GraphDriver := CGA;
```

```
      GraphMode := CGAHi;
   end;
   InitGraph(GraphDriver,GraphMode,'');
   if GraphResult <> grOk then
      Halt(1);
   Line(0, 0, GetMaxX, GetMaxY);
   Readln;
   CloseGraph;
end.
```

# DiskFree function                                           Dos

| | |
|---|---|
| **Function** | Returns the number of free bytes of a specified disk drive. |
| **Declaration** | `DiskFree(Drive: word)` |
| **Result type** | longint |
| **Remarks** | A *Drive* of 0 indicates the default drive, 1 indicates drive *A*, 2 indicates *B*, and so on. *DiskFree* returns −1 if the drive number is invalid. |
| **See also** | *DiskSize, GetDir* |
| **Example** | ```
uses Dos;
begin
   Writeln(DiskFree(0) div 1024, ' k-bytes ');
end.
``` |

# DiskSize function                                           Dos

| | |
|---|---|
| **Function** | Returns the total size in bytes of a specified disk drive. |
| **Declaration** | `DiskSize(Drive: word)` |
| **Result type** | longint |
| **Remarks** | A *Drive* of 0 indicates the default drive, 1 indicates drive *A*, 2 indicates *B*, and so on. *DiskSize* returns −1 if the drive number is invalid. |
| **See also** | *DiskFree, GetDir* |
```

| Example | `uses Dos;`<br>`begin`<br>  `Writeln(DiskSize(0) div 1024, ' k-bytes ');`<br>`end.` |

# Dispose procedure

| | |
|---|---|
| **Function** | Disposes a dynamic variable. |
| **Declaration** | `Dispose(var p: pointer)` |
| **Remarks** | *p* is a pointer variable of any pointer type that was previously assigned by the *New* procedure or was assigned a meaningful value by an assignment statement. *Dispose* destroys the variable referenced by *p* and returns its memory region to the heap. After a call to *Dispose*, the value of *p* becomes undefined, and it is an error to subsequently reference *p*^. |
| **Restrictions** | If *p* does not point to a memory region in the heap, a runtime error occurs. |
| **See also** | *Release, FreeMem* |
| **Example** | `type`<br>  `Str18 = string[18];`<br>`var`<br>  `p: ^Str18;`<br><br>`begin`<br>  `New(p);`<br>  `p^ := 'Now you see it...';`<br>  `Dispose(p);`        `{ Now you don't... }`<br>`end.` |

# DosExitCode function        Dos

| | |
|---|---|
| **Function** | Returns the exit code of a subprocess. |
| **Declaration** | `DosExitCode` |
| **Result type** | word |
| **Remarks** | The low byte is the code sent by the terminating process. The high byte is 0 for normal termination, 1 if terminated by *Ctrl-C*, 2 if terminated due to a device error, or 3 if terminated by the *Keep* procedure. |

# DrawPoly procedure                                     Graph

**Function**        Draws the outline of a polygon using the current line
                    style and color.

**Declaration**     DrawPoly(NumPoints: word; **var** PolyPoints)

**Remarks**         *PolyPoints* is an untyped parameter that contains the
                    coordinates of each intersection in the polygon.
                    *NumPoints* specifies the number of coordinates in
                    *PolyPoints*. A coordinate consists of two words, an *x* and
                    a *y* value.

                    *DrawPoly* uses the current line style and color.

                    Note that in order to draw a closed figure with *n*
                    vertices, you must pass *N* + 1 coordinates to *DrawPoly*,
                    and where *PolyPoints[n+1]* = *PolyPoints[1]* (see the
                    example that follows). In order to draw a triangle, for
                    example, four coordinates must be passed to *DrawPoly*.

**Restrictions**    Must be in graphics mode.

**See also**        *FillPoly, GetLineSettings, SetColor, SetLineStyle,*
                    *GraphResult*

**Example**
```
uses Graph;
const
  Triangle: array[1..4] of PointType = ((x:  50; y: 100),
                                        (x: 100; y: 100),
                                        (x: 150; y: 150),
                                        (x:  50; y: 100));
var
  Gd, Gm: integer;

begin
  Gd := Detect;
  InitGraph(Gd, Gm, '');
  if GraphResult <> grOk then
    Halt(1);
  DrawPoly(SizeOf(Triangle)
    div SizeOf(PointType),Triangle);   { 4 }
  Readln;
  CloseGraph;
end.
```

# DSeg function

**Function**                    Returns the current value of the DS register.

**Declaration**           DSeg

**Result type**          word

**Remarks**              The result of type word is the segment address of the data segment.

**See also**             *CSeg, Sseg*

# Ellipse procedure           Graph

**Function**           Draws an elliptical arc from start angle to end angle, using $(X,Y)$ as the center point.

**Declaration**         

```
Ellipse(X, Y: integer; StAngle, EndAngle: word;
        XRadius, YRadius: word)
```

**Remarks**           Draws an elliptical arc using $(X,Y)$ as a center point, and *XRadius* and *YRadius* as the horizontal and vertical axes. The ellipse travels from *StAngle* to *EndAngle* and is drawn in the current color.

A start angle of 0 and an end angle of 360 will draw a complete oval. The angles for *Arc, Ellipse,* and *PieSlice* are counterclockwise with 0 degrees at 3 o'clock, 90 degrees at 12 o'clock, and so on. Information about the last call to *Ellipse* can be retrieved with a call to *GetArcCoords*.

**Restrictions**     Must be in graphics mode.

**See also**         *Circle, Arc, PieSlice, GetArcCoords, GetAspectRatio*

**Example**

```
uses Graph;
var
  Gd, Gm: integer;
begin
  Gd := Detect;
  InitGraph(Gd, Gm, '');
  if GraphResult <> grOk then
    Halt(1);
  Ellipse(100,100,0,360,30,50);
  Ellipse(100,100,0,180,50,30);
```

```
      Readln;
      CloseGraph;
    end.
```

# Eof function (text files)

**Function**      Returns the end-of-file status of a text file.

**Declaration**   Eof [ (**var** f: text) ]

**Result type**   boolean

**Remarks**       *f*, if specified, is a text-file variable. If *f* is omitted, the
                  standard file variable *Input* is assumed. *Eof(f)* returns
                  True if the current file position is beyond the last
                  character of the file or if the file contains no components;
                  otherwise, *Eof(f)* returns False.

                  With {$I-}, *IOResult* will return a 0 if the operation was
                  successful; otherwise, it will return a nonzero error code.

**See also**      *Eoln*

**Example**
```
      var
        f : text;
        ch: char;
      begin
        { Get file to read from command line }
        Assign(f, ParamStr(1));
        Reset(f);
        while not Eof(f) do
        begin
          Read(f,ch);
          Write(ch);                          { Dump text file }
        end;
      end.
```

# Eof function (typed, untyped files)

**Function**      Returns the end-of-file status of a typed or untyped file.

**Declaration**   Eof(f)

**Result type**   boolean

**Remarks**       *f* is a file variable. *Eof(f)* returns True if the current file
                  position is beyond the last component of the file or if the

file contains no components; otherwise, *Eof(f)* returns False.

With {$I-}, *IOResult* will return a 0 if the operation was successful; otherwise, it will return a nonzero error code.

# Eoln function

| | |
|---|---|
| **Function** | Returns the end-of-line status of a file. |
| **Declaration** | `Eoln [ (var f: text) ]` |
| **Result type** | boolean |
| **Remarks** | *f*, if specified, is a text-file variable. If *f* is omitted, the standard file variable *Input* is assumed. *Eoln(f)* returns True if the current file position is at an end-of-line marker or if *Eof(f)* is True; otherwise, *Eoln(f)* returns False. |

When checking *Eoln* on standard input that has not been redirected, the following program will wait for a carriage return to be entered before returning from the call to *Eoln*:

```
begin
   Writeln(Eoln);          { This call causes the program }
                           { to wait for keyboard input }
end.
```

With {$I-}, *IOResult* will return a 0 if the operation was successful; otherwise, it will return a nonzero error code.

| | |
|---|---|
| **See also** | *Eof* |

# Erase procedure

| | |
|---|---|
| **Function** | Erases an external file. |
| **Declaration** | `Erase(f)` |
| **Remarks** | *f* is a file variable of any file type. The external file associated with *f* is erased. |

With {$I-}, *IOResult* will return a 0 if the operation was successful; otherwise, it will return a nonzero error code.

| Restrictions | *Erase* must never be used on an open file. |
| --- | --- |
| See also | *Rename* |
| Example | |

```
var
  f :  file;
  ch: char;

begin
  { Get file to delete from command line }
  Assign(f, ParamStr(1));
  {$I-}
  Reset(f);
  {$I+}
  if IOResult <> 0 then
    Writeln('Cannot find ', ParamStr(1))
  else
  begin
    Close(f);
    Write('Erase ', ParamStr(1), '? ');
    Readln(ch);
    if UpCase(ch) = 'Y' then
    Erase(f);
  end;
end.
```

# Exec procedure                                    Dos

| Function | Executes a specified program with a specified command line. |
| --- | --- |
| Declaration | Exec(Path, CmdLine: **string**) |
| Remarks | The program name is given by the *Path* parameter, and the command line is given by *CmdLine*. To execute a DOS internal command, run COMMAND.COM; for instance, |

```
Exec('\COMMAND.COM','/C DIR *.PAS');
```

The /C in front of the command is a requirement of COMMAND.COM (but not of other applications). Errors are reported in *DosError*; possible error codes are 2, 8, 10, and 11. The exit code of any child process is reported by the *DosExitCode* function.

*Exec* does not change the memory allocation state before executing the program. Therefore, when compiling a program that uses *Exec,* be sure to specify a maximum heap size; otherwise, there won't be enough memory (*DosError* = 8).

**See also**     *DosExitCode*

**Example**

```
{$M $4000,0,0 }     { 16K stack, no heap required or reserved }
uses Dos;
var
  ProgramName, CmdLine: string;

begin
  Write('Program to Exec (include full path): ');
  Readln(ProgramName);
  Write('Command line to pass to ', ProgramName, ': ');
  Readln(CmdLine);
  Writeln('About to Exec...');
  Exec(ProgramName, CmdLine);
  Writeln('...back from Exec');
  if DosError <> 0 then                        { Error? }
    Writeln('Dos error #', DosError)
  else
    Writeln('Exec successful.',
            'Child process exit code = ',
            'DosExitCode);
end.
```

# Exit procedure

**Function**       Exits immediately from the current block.

**Declaration**    `Exit`

**Remarks**        When *Exit* is executed in a subroutine (procedure or function), it causes the subroutine to return. When it is executed in the statement part of a program, it causes the program to terminate. A call to *Exit* is analagous to a **goto** statement addressing a label just before the **end** of a block.

**See also**       *Halt*

**Example**

```
uses Crt;
procedure WasteTime;
begin
  repeat
    if KeyPressed then Exit;
    Write('Xx');
```

```
      until False;
    end;
    begin
      WasteTime;
    end.
```

# Exp function

| | |
|---|---|
| **Function** | Returns the exponential of the argument. |
| **Declaration** | `Exp(x: real)` |
| **Result type** | real |
| **Remarks** | $x$ is a real-type expression. The result is the exponential of $x$; that is, the value $e$ raised to the power of $x$, where $e$ is the base of the natural logarithms. |
| **See also** | *Ln* |

# FilePos function

| | |
|---|---|
| **Function** | Returns the current file position of a file. |
| **Declaration** | `FilePos(f)` |
| **Result type** | longint |
| **Remarks** | $f$ is a file variable. If the current file position is at the beginning of the file, *FilePos(f)* returns 0. If the current file position is at the end of the file—that is, if *Eof(f)* is True—*FilePos(f)* is equal to *FileSize(f)*. |
| | With {$I-}, *IOResult* will return a 0 if the operation was successful; otherwise, it will return a nonzero error code. |
| **Restrictions** | Cannot be used on a text file. File must be open. |
| **Differences** | The result type in 3.0 was an integer. |
| **See also** | *FileSize, Seek* |

# FileSize function

| | |
|---|---|
| **Function** | Returns the current size of a file. |

| | |
|---|---|
| **Declaration** | `FileSize(f)` |
| **Result type** | longint |
| **Remarks** | *f* is a file variable. *FileSize(f)* returns the number of components in *f*. If the file is empty, *FileSize(f)* returns 0. |
| | With {$I-}, *IOResult* will return a 0 if the operation was successful; otherwise, it will return a nonzero error code. |
| **Restrictions** | Cannot be used on a text file. File must be open. |
| **Differences** | The result type in 3.0 was an integer. |
| **See also** | *FilePos* |
| **Example** | |

```
var
  f: file of byte;

begin
  { Get file name from command line }
  Assign(f, ParamStr(1));
  Reset(f);
  Writeln('File size in bytes: ', FileSize(f));
  Close(f);
end.
```

# FillChar procedure

| | |
|---|---|
| **Function** | Fills a specified number of contiguous bytes with a specified value. |
| **Declaration** | `FillChar(var x; count: word; ch: char)` |
| **Remarks** | *x* is a variable reference of any type. *count* is an expression of type word. *ch* is an ordinal-type expression. *FillChar* writes the value of *ch* into *count* contiguous bytes of memory, starting at the first byte occupied by *x*. No range-checking is performed, so be careful. |
| | Whenever possible, use the *SizeOf* function to specify the count parameter when using *FillChar* on strings. Remember to set the length byte after the fill. |
| **See also** | *Move* |

```
var s: string[80];
begin
  { Set a string to all spaces }
  FillChar(s, SizeOf(s), ' ');
  s[0] := #80;                              { Set length byte }
end.
```

# FillPoly procedure                     Graph

**Function**        Draws and fills a polygon using the scan converter.

**Declaration**     `FillPoly(NumPoints: word; var PolyPoints)`

**Remarks**         *PolyPoints* is an untyped parameter that contains the
coordinates of each intersection in the polygon.
*NumPoints* specifies the number of coordinates in
*PolyPoints*. A coordinate consists of two words, an *x* and
a *y* value.

*FillPoly* calculates all the horizontal intersections, and
then fills the polygon using the current fill style and
color defined by *SetFillStyle* or *SetFillPattern*. The outline
of the polygon is drawn in the current line style and
color as set by *SetLineStyle*.

If an error occurs while filling the polygon, *GraphResult*
will return a value of –6 (*grNoScanMem*).

**Restrictions**    Must be in graphics mode.

**See also**        *DrawPoly, GetFillSettings, SetFillStyle, SetFillPattern,
GetLineSettings, SetLineStyle, GraphResult*

**Example**
```
uses Graph;
const
  Triangle : array[1..3] of PointType = ((x:  50; y: 100),
                                         (x: 100; y: 100),
                                         (x: 150; y: 150));
var
  Gd, Gm : integer;
begin
  Gd := Detect;
  InitGraph(Gd, Gm, '');
  if GraphResult <> grOk then
    Halt(1);
  FillPoly(SizeOf(Triangle) div SizeOf(PointType), Triangle);
                                                            { 3 }
```

```
      Readln;
      CloseGraph;
   end.
```

# FindFirst procedure                                    Dos

**Function**        Searches the specified (or current) directory for the first
                    entry matching the specified file name and set of
                    attributes.

**Declaration**     FindFirst(Path: **string**; Attr: word;
                              **var** S: SearchRec)

**Remarks**         *Path* is the directory mask (for example, * . *). The *Attr*
                    parameter specifies the special files to include (in
                    addition to all normal files). Here are the file attributes
                    as they are declared in the *Dos* unit:

```
const
   { File attribute constants }
   ReadOnly  = $01;
   Hidden    = $02;
   SysFile   = $04;
   VolumeID  = $08;
   Directory = $10;
   Archive   = $20;
   AnyFile   = $3F;
```

                    The result of the directory search is returned in the
                    specified search record. *SearchRec* is declared in the *Dos*
                    unit:

```
type
   { Search record used by FindFirst and FindNext }
   SearchRec = record
                  Fill: array[1..21] of byte;
                  Attr: byte;
                  Time: longint;
                  Size: longint;
                  Name: string[12];
               end;
```

                    Errors are reported in *DosError*; possible error codes are
                    2 (Directory Not Found) and 18 (No More Files).

**See also**        *FindNext*

```
uses Dos;
var
  DirInfo: SearchRec;

begin
  FindFirst('*.PAS', Archive, DirInfo);   { Same as DIR *.PAS }
  while DosError = 0 do
  begin
    Writeln(DirInfo.Name);
    FindNext(DirInfo);
  end;
end.
```

# FindNext procedure                                      Dos

**Function**      Returns the next entry that matches the name and attributes specified in a previous call to *FindFirst*.

**Declaration**   FindNext(**var** S: SearchRec)

**Remarks**       *S* must be the same one Passed to *FindFirst* (*SearchRec* is declared in *Dos* unit; see *FindFirst*). Errors are reported in *DosError*; the only possible error code is 18, which indicates no more files.

**See also**      *FindFirst*

**Example**       See *FindFirst* example

# FloodFill procedure                                    Graph

**Function**      Fills a bounded region with the current fill pattern.

**Declaration**   FloodFill(x, y: integer; Border: word);

**Remarks**       This procedure is called to fill an enclosed area on bitmap devices. (*x,y*) is a seed within the enclosed area to be filled. The current fill pattern, as set by *SetFillStyle* or *SetFillPattern*, is used to flood the area bounded by *Border* color. If the seed point is within an enclosed area, then the inside will be filled. If the seed is outside the enclosed area, then the exterior will be filled.

If an error occurs while flooding a region, *GraphResult* will return a value of –7 (*grNoFloodMem*).

Note that *FloodFill* stops after two blank lines have been output. This can occur with a sparse fill pattern and a small polygon. In the following program, the rectangle is not completely filled:

```
program StopFill;
uses Graph;
var
  Driver, Mode: integer;
begin
  Driver := Detect;
  InitGraph(Driver, Mode, 'c:\bgi');
  if GraphResult <> grOk then
    Halt(1);
  SetFillStyle(LtSlashFill, GetMaxColor);
  Rectangle(0, 0, 8, 20);
  FloodFill(1, 1, GetMaxColor);
  Readln;
  CloseGraph;
end.
```

In this case, using a denser fill pattern like *SlashFill* will completely fill the figure.

**Restrictions**     Use *FillPoly* instead of *FloodFill* whenever possible so that you can maintain code compatibility with future versions. Must be in graphics mode.

**See also**     *SetFillStyle, SetFillPattern*

**Example**
```
uses Graph;
var
  Gd, Gm: integer;
begin
  Gd := Detect;
  InitGraph(Gd, Gm, '');
  if GraphResult <> grOk then
    Halt(1);
  SetColor(GetMaxColor);
  Circle(50, 50, 20);
  FloodFill(50,50,GetMaxColor);
  Readln;
  CloseGraph;
end.
```

# Flush procedure

| | |
|---|---|
| **Function** | Flushes the buffer of a text file open for output. |
| **Declaration** | `Flush(var f: text)` |
| **Remarks** | *f* is a text-file variable. |

When a text file has been opened for output using *Rewrite* or *Append*, a call to *Flush* will empty the file's buffer. This guarantees that all characters written to the file at that time have actually been written to the external file. *Flush* has no effect on files opened for input.

With {$I-}, *IOResult* will return a 0 if the operation was successful; otherwise, it will return a nonzero error code.

# Frac function

| | |
|---|---|
| **Function** | Returns the fractional part of the argument. |
| **Declaration** | `Frac(x: real)` |
| **Result type** | real |
| **Remarks** | *x* is a real-type expression. The result is the fractional part of *x*, that is, $Frac(x) = x - Int(x)$. |
| **See also** | *Int* |
| **Example** | |

```
var r: real;
begin
  r := Frac(123.456);   { 0.456 }
end.
```

# FreeMem procedure

| | |
|---|---|
| **Function** | Disposes a dynamic variable of a given size. |
| **Declaration** | `FreeMem(var p: pointer; size: word)` |
| **Remarks** | *p* is a pointer variable of any pointer type that was previously assigned by the *GetMem* procedure or was assigned a meaningful value by an assignment |

statement. *Size* is an expression of type word, specifying the size in bytes of the dynamic variable to dispose; it must be *exactly* the number of bytes previously allocated to that variable by *GetMem*. *FreeMem* destroys the variable referenced by *p* and returns its memory region to the heap. If *p* does not point to a memory region in the heap, a runtime error occurs. After a call to *FreeMem*, the value of *p* becomes undefined, and it is an error to subsequently reference *p^*.

**Differences**     In 3.0, *size* was an integer.

**See also**     *Dispose, GetMem, Release*

# GetArcCoords procedure                     Graph

**Function**     Allows the user to inquire about the coordinates of the last *Arc* command.

**Declaration**     GetArcCoords(**var** ArcCoords: ArcCoordsType)

**Remarks**     *GetArcCoords* returns a variable of type *ArcCoordsType*. *ArcCoordsType* is predeclared as follows:

```
type
  ArcCoordsType = record
                    X, Y
                    Xstart, Ystart, Xend, Yend: integer;
                  end;
```

*GetArcCoords* returns a variable containing the center point (*X,Y*), the starting position (*Xstart,Ystart*), and the ending position (*Xend,Yend*) of the last *Arc* command. These values are useful if you need to connect a line to the end of an *Arc*.

**Restrictions**     Must be in graphics mode.

**See also**     *Arc, Ellipse, PieSlice, PieSliceXY*

**Example**
```
uses Graph;
var
  Gd, Gm : integer;
  ArcCoords : ArcCoordsType;

begin
  Gd := Detect;
  InitGraph(Gd, Gm, '');
  if GraphResult <> grOk then
```

```
  Halt(1);
Arc(100,100,0,270,30);
GetArcCoords(ArcCoords);
with ArcCoords do
  Line(Xstart, Ystart, Xend, Yend);
Readln;
CloseGraph;
end.
```

# GetAspectRatio procedure                   Graph

**Function**        Returns the effective resolution of the graphics screen
                    from which the aspect ratio (*Xasp:Yasp*) can be com-
                    puted.

**Declaration**     GetAspectRatio(**var** Xasp, Yasp: word)

**Remarks**         Each driver and graphics mode has an aspect ratio
                    associated with it (maximum *y* resolution divided by
                    maximum *x* resolution). This ratio can be computed by
                    making a call to *GetAspectRatio* and then dividing the
                    *Xasp* parameter by the *Yasp* parameter. This ratio is used
                    to make circles, arcs, and pie slices round.

**Restrictions**    Must be in graphics mode.

**See also**        *Arc, Circle, GetMaxX, GetMaxY, PieSlice*

**Example**
```
uses Graph;
var
  Gd, Gm : integer;
  Xasp, Yasp : word;
  XSideLength, YSideLength : integer;

begin
  Gd := Detect;
  InitGraph(Gd, Gm, '');
  if GraphResult <> grOk then
    Halt(1);
  GetAspectRatio(Xasp, Yasp);
  XSideLength := 20;

  { Adjust Y length for aspect ratio }
  YSideLength := Round((Xasp/Yasp) * XSideLength);
```

```
{ Draw a "square" rectangle on the screen }
Rectangle(0, 0, XSideLength, YSideLength);
Readln;
CloseGraph;
end.
```

# GetBkColor function                    Graph

**Function**        Returns the index into the palette of the current background color.

**Declaration**     `GetBkColor`

**Result type**     word

**Remarks**         Background colors can range from 0 to 15, depending on the current graphics driver and current graphics mode.

*GetBkColor* will return 0 if the 0th palette entry is changed by a call to *SetPalette* or *SetAllPalette*.

**Restrictions**    Must be in graphics mode.

**See also**        *GetColor, GetPalette, InitGraph, SetAllPalette, SetBkColor, SetColor, SetPalette*

**Example**
```
uses Crt, Graph;
var
  Gd, Gm: integer;
  Color: word;
  Pal: PaletteType;

begin
  Gd := Detect;
  InitGraph(Gd, Gm, '');
  if GraphResult <> grOk then
    Halt(1);
  Randomize;
  GetPalette(Pal);
  if Pal.Size <> 1 then
    begin
      repeat                              { Cycle through colors }
        Color := Succ(GetBkColor);
        if Color > Pal.Size-1 then
          Color := 0;
        SetBkColor(Color);
        LineTo(Random(GetMaxX), Random(GetMaxY));
      until KeyPressed;
```

```
      end
    else
      Line(0, 0, GetMaxX, GetMaxY);
    Readln;
    CloseGraph;
  end.
```

# GetColor function                              Graph

**Function**        Returns the color value passed to the previous
                    successful call to *SetColor*.

**Declaration**     GetColor

**Result type**     word

**Remarks**         Drawing colors can range from 0 to 15, depending on
                    the current graphics driver and current graphics mode.

**Restrictions**    Must be in graphics mode.

**See also**        *GetBkColor, GetPalette, SetAllPalette, SetColor, SetPalette*

**Example**
```
uses Graph;
var
  Gd, Gm: integer;
  Color: word;
  Pal: PaletteType;

begin
  Gd := Detect;
  InitGraph(Gd, Gm, '');
  if GraphResult <> grOk then
    Halt(1);
  Randomize;
  GetPalette(Pal);
  repeat
    Color := Succ(GetColor);
    if Color > Pal.Size-1 then
      Color := 0;
    SetColor(Color);
    LineTo(Random(GetMaxX), Random(GetMaxY));
  until KeyPressed;
  CloseGraph;
end.
```

# GetDate procedure                                          Dos

| | |
|---|---|
| **Function** | Returns the current date set in the operating system. |
| **Declaration** | GetDate(**var** Year, Month, Day, DayofWeek: word) |
| **Remarks** | Ranges of the values returned are *Year* 1980..2099, *Month* 1..12, *Day* 1..31, and *DayOfWeek* 0..6 (where 0 corresponds to Sunday). |
| **See also** | *SetDate, GetTime, SetTime* |

# GetDir procedure

| | |
|---|---|
| **Function** | Returns the current directory of a specified drive. |
| **Declaration** | GetDir(d: byte; **var** s: **string**) |
| **Remarks** | *d* is an integer-type expression, and *s* is a string-type variable. The current directory of the drive specified by *d* is returned in *s*. *d* = 0 indicates the current drive, 1 indicates drive *A*, 2 indicates drive *B*, and so on. |
| | With {$I-}, *IOResult* will return a 0 if the operation was successful; otherwise, it will return a nonzero error code. |
| **See also** | *ChDir, MkDir, RmDir* |

# GetFAttr procedure                                         Dos

| | |
|---|---|
| **Function** | Returns the attributes of a file. |
| **Declaration** | GetFAttr(**var** f; **var** Attr: word); |
| **Remarks** | *F* must be a file variable (typed, untyped, or text file) that has been assigned but not opened. The attributes are examined by **and**ing them with the file attribute masks defined as constants in the *Dos* unit: |

```
const
  { File attribute constants }
  ReadOnly = $01;
  Hidden   = $02;
  SysFile  = $04;
  VolumeID = $08;
```

```
                      Directory = $10;
                      Archive   = $20;
                      AnyFile    = $3F;
```

Errors are reported in *DosError*; possible error codes are 3 (Invalid Path) and 5 (File Access Denied).

**Restrictions**   *f* cannot be open.

**See also**   *SetFAttr, GetFTime, SetFTime*

**Example**
```
uses Dos;
var
  f: file;
  attr: word;

begin
  { Get file name from command line }
  Assign(f, ParamStr(1));
  GetFAttr(f, attr);
  Writeln(ParamStr(1));
  if DosError <> 0 then
    Writeln('Dos error code = ', DosError)
  else
  begin
    Write('Attribute = ', attr, 'to:'to);
    { Determine file attribute type
      using flags in Dos unit }
    if attr and ReadOnly <> 0 then
      Writeln('read only file');
    if attr and Hidden <> 0 then
      Writeln('hidden file');
    if attr and SysFile <> 0 then
      Writeln('system file');
    if attr and VolumeID <> 0 then
      Writeln('volume ID');
    if attr and Directory <> 0 then
      Writeln('directory name');
    if attr and Archive <> 0 then
      Writeln('archive (normal file)');
  end; { else }
end.
```

# GetFillPattern procedure          Graph

**Function**   Returns the last fill pattern and color set by a previous call to *SetFillPattern*.

**Declaration**   `GetFillPattern(var FillPattern: FillPatternType);`

| Remarks | *FillPatternType* is declared in the *Graph* unit: |
|---|---|

```
type
   FillPatternType = array[1..8] of byte;
```

If no user call has been made to *SetFillPattern*, *GetFillPattern* will return an array filled with *$FF*.

| Restrictions | Must be in graphics mode. |
|---|---|
| See also | *SetFillPattern, GetFillSettings* |

# GetFillSettings procedure         Graph

| Function | Returns the last fill pattern and color set by a previous call to *SetFillPattern*. |
|---|---|
| Declaration | GetFillSettings(**var** FillInfo: FillSettingsType) |
| Remarks | *GetFillSettings* returns a variable of type *FillSettingsType*. *FillSettingsType* is predeclared as follows: |

```
type
   FillSettingsType = record
                         Pattern: word;
                         Color: word;
                      end;
```

The *Pattern* field reports the current fill pattern selected. The *Color* field reports the current fill color selected. Both the fill pattern and color can be changed by calling the *SetFillStyle* or *SetFillPattern* procedure. If *Pattern* is equal to *UserFill*, use *GetFillPattern* to get the user-defined fill pattern that is selected.

| Restrictions | Must be in graphics mode. |
|---|---|
| See also | *SetFillStyle, GetFillPattern, SetFillPattern* |
| Example | |

```
uses Graph;
var
  Gd, Gm  : integer;
  FillInfo: FillSettingsType;

begin
  Gd := Detect;
  InitGraph(Gd, Gm, '');
  if GraphResult <> grOk then
    Halt(1);
  GetFillSettings(FillInfo);      { Save fill style and color }
```

```
        Bar(0, 0, 50, 50);
        SetFillStyle(XHatchFill, GetMaxColor);        { New style }
        Bar(50, 0, 100, 50);
        with FillInfo do
          SetFillStyle(Pattern, Color);   { Restore old fill style }
        Bar(100, 0, 150, 50);
        Readln;
        CloseGraph;
    end.
```

# GetFTime procedure                                     Dos

| | |
|---|---|
| **Function** | Returns the date and time a file was last written. |
| **Declaration** | `GetFTime(`**`var`** `f;` **`var`** `Time: longint);` |
| **Remarks** | *f* must be a file variable (typed, untyped, or text file) that has been assigned and opened. The time returned in the *Time* parameter may be unpacked through a call to *UnpackTime*. Errors are reported in *DosError*; the only possible error code is 6 (Invalid File Handle). |
| **Restrictions** | *f* must be open. |
| **See also** | *SetFTime, PackTime, UnPackTime* |

# GetGraphMode function                                Graph

| | |
|---|---|
| **Function** | Returns the current graphics mode. |
| **Declaration** | `GetGraphMode` |
| **Result type** | integer |
| **Remarks** | *GetGraphMode* returns the current graphics mode set by *InitGraph* or *SetGraphMode*. The *Mode* value is an integer from 0 to 5, depending on the current driver. |
| | The following mode constants are defined: |

| Graphics Driver | Graphics Modes | Value | Column x Row | Palette | Pages |
|---|---|---|---|---|---|
| CGA | CGAC0 | 0 | 320x200 | C0 | 1 |
| | CGAC1 | 1 | 320x200 | C1 | 1 |
| | CGAC2 | 2 | 320x200 | C2 | 1 |
| | CGAC3 | 3 | 320x200 | C3 | 1 |
| | CGAHi | 4 | 640x200 | 2 color | 1 |
| MCGA | MCGAC0 | 0 | 320x200 | C0 | 1 |
| | MCGAC1 | 1 | 320x200 | C1 | 1 |
| | MCGAC2 | 2 | 320x200 | C2 | 1 |
| | MCGAC3 | 3 | 320x200 | C3 | 1 |
| | MCGAMed | 4 | 640x200 | 2 color | 1 |
| | MCGAHi | 5 | 640x480 | 2 color | 1 |
| EGA | EGALo | 0 | 640x200 | 16 color | 4 |
| | EGAHi | 1 | 640x350 | 16 color | 2 |
| EGA64 | EGA64Lo | 0 | 640x200 | 16 color | 1 |
| | EGA64Hi | 1 | 640x350 | 4 color | 1 |
| EGA-MONO | EGAMonoHi | 3 | 640x350 | 2 color | 1* |
| | EGAMonoHi | 3 | 640x350 | 2 color | 2** |
| HERC | HercMonoHi | 0 | 720x348 | 2 color | 2 |
| ATT400 | ATT400C0 | 0 | 320x200 | C0 | 1 |
| | ATT400C1 | 1 | 320x200 | C1 | 1 |
| | ATT400C2 | 2 | 320x200 | C2 | 1 |
| | ATT400C3 | 3 | 320x200 | C3 | 1 |
| | ATT400Med | 4 | 640x200 | 2 color | 1 |
| | ATT400Hi | 5 | 640x400 | 2 color | 1 |
| VGA | VGALo | 0 | 640x200 | 16 color | 2 |
| | VGAMed | 1 | 640x350 | 16 color | 2 |
| | VGAHi | 2 | 640x480 | 16 color | 1 |
| PC3270 | PC3270Hi | 0 | 720x350 | 2 color | 1 |

\* 64K on EGAMono card
\*\* 256K on EGAMono card

**Restrictions**  Must be in graphics mode.

**See also**  *ClearDevice, DetectGraph, InitGraph, RestoreCrtMode, SetGraphMode*

**Example**
```
uses Graph;
var
  Gd, Gm: integer;
```

```
    Mode  : integer;

begin
  Gd := Detect;
  InitGraph(Gd, Gm, '');
  if GraphResult <> grOk then
    Halt(1);
  OutText('<RETURN> to leave graphics:');
  Readln;
  RestoreCRTMode;
  Writeln('Now in text mode');
  Write('<RETURN> to enter graphics mode:');
  Readln;
  SetGraphMode(GetGraphMode);
  OutTextXY(0, 0, 'Back in graphics mode');
  OutTextXY(0, TextHeight('H'), '<RETURN> to quit:');
  Readln;
  CloseGraph;
end.
```

# GetImage procedure                 Graph

**Function**        Saves a bit image of the specified region into a buffer.

**Declaration**     `GetImage(x1, y1, x2, y2: integer; var BitMap);`

**Remarks**         *x1, y1, x2,* and *y2* define a rectangular region on the
                    screen. *BitMap* is an untyped parameter that must be
                    greater than or equal to 4 plus the amount of area
                    defined by the region. The first two words of *BitMap* are
                    reserved for the width and height of the region.

                    The remaining part of *BitMap* is used to save the bit
                    image itself. Use the *ImageSize* function to determine the
                    size requirements of *BitMap.*

**Restrictions**    Must be in graphics mode. The memory required to save
                    the region must be less than 64K.

**See also**        *ImageSize, PutImage*

**Example**
```
uses Graph;
var
  Gd, Gm : integer;
  P      : pointer;
  Size   : word;

begin
  Gd := Detect;
```

```
    InitGraph(Gd, Gm, '');
    if GraphResult <> grOk then
      Halt(1);
    Bar(0, 0, GetMaxX, GetMaxY);
    Size := ImageSize(10,20,30,40);
    GetMem(P, Size);                { Allocate memory on heap }
    GetImage(10,20,30,40,P^);
    Readln;
    ClearDevice;
    PutImage(100, 100, P^, NormalPut);
    Readln;
    CloseGraph;
  end.
```

# GetIntVec procedure                                        Dos

| | |
|---|---|
| **Function** | Returns the address stored in a specified interrupt vector. |
| **Declaration** | GetIntVec(IntNo: byte; **var** Vector: pointer) |
| **Remarks** | *IntNo* specifies the interrupt vector number (0..255), and the address is returned in *Vector*. |
| **See also** | *SetIntVec* |

# GetLineSettings procedure                              Graph

| | |
|---|---|
| **Function** | Returns the current line style, line pattern, and line thickness as set by *SetLineStyle*. |
| **Declaration** | GetLineSettings(**var** LineInfo: LineSettingsType) |
| **Remarks** | The following type and constants are defined: |

```
type
  LineSettingsType = record
                       LineStyle: word;
                       Pattern: word;
                       Thickness: word;
                     end;

const
  { Line styles }
  SolidLn    = 0;
  DottedLn   = 1;
  CenterLn   = 2;
```

```
                    DashedLn   = 3;
                    UserBitLn  = 4;                    { User-defined line style }

                    { Line widths }
                    NormWidth  = 1;
                    ThickWidth = 3;
```

**Restrictions**    Must be in graphics mode.

**See also**        *SetLineStyle*

**Example**
```
uses Graph;
var
  Gd, Gm  : integer;
  OldStyle: LineSettingsType;

begin
  Gd := Detect;
  InitGraph(Gd, Gm, '');
  if GraphResult <> grOk then
    Halt(1);
  Line(0, 0, 100, 0);
  GetLineSettings(OldStyle);
  SetLineStyle(DottedLn, 0, ThickWidth);        { New style }
  Line(0, 10, 100, 10);
  with OldStyle do                      { Restore old line style }
    SetLineStyle(LineStyle, Pattern, Thickness);
  Line(0, 20, 100, 20);
  Readln;
  CloseGraph;
end.
```

# GetMaxColor function                          Graph

**Function**        Returns the highest color that can be passed to the
                    *SetColor* procedure.

**Declaration**     `GetMaxColor : word;`

**Remarks**         As an example, on a 256K EGA, *GetMaxColor* will always
                    return 15, which means that any call to *SetColor* with a
                    value from 0..15 is valid. On a CGA in high-resolution
                    mode or on a Hercules monochrome adapter,
                    *GetMaxColor* returns a value of 1 because these adapters
                    only support draw colors of 0 or 1.

**Restrictions**    Must be in graphics mode.

**See also**        *SetColor*

# GetMaxX function                                        Graph

**Function**        Returns the right-most column (*x* resolution) of the
                    current graphics driver and mode.

**Declaration**     GetMaxX

**Result type**     integer

**Remarks**         Returns the maximum *x* value for the current graphics
                    driver and mode. On a CGA in 320×200 mode; for
                    example, *GetMaxX* will return 319.

                    *GetMaxX* and *GetMaxY* are invaluable for centering,
                    determining the boundries of a region on the screen, and
                    so on.

**Restrictions**    Must be in graphics mode.

**See also**        *GetMaxY, GetX, GetY, MoveTo*

**Example**
```
uses Graph;
var
  Gd, Gm: integer;

begin
  Gd := Detect;
  InitGraph(Gd, Gm, '');
  if GraphResult <> grOk then
    Halt(1);
  Rectangle(0,0,GetMaxX,GetMaxY);    { Draw a full-screen box }
  Readln;
  CloseGraph;
end.
```

# GetMaxY function                                        Graph

**Function**        Returns the bottom-most row (*y* resolution) of the
                    current graphics driver and mode.

**Declaration**     GetMaxY

**Result type**     integer

**Remarks**         Returns the maximum *y* value for the current graphics
                    driver and mode. On a CGA in 320×200 mode; for
                    example, *GetMaxY* will return 199.

*GetMaxX* and *GetMaxY* are invaluable for centering, determining the boundaries of a region on the screen, and so on.

**Restrictions**   Must be in graphics mode.

**See also**   *GetMaxX, GetX, GetY, MoveTo*

**Example**
```
uses Graph;
var
  Gd, Gm: integer;

begin
  Gd := Detect;
  InitGraph(Gd, Gm, '');
  if GraphResult <> grOk then
    Halt(1);
  Rectangle(0,0,GetMaxX,GetMaxY);    { Draw a full-screen box }
  Readln;
  CloseGraph;
end.
```

# GetMem procedure

**Function**   Creates a new dynamic variable of the specified size, and puts the address of the block in a pointer variable.

**Declaration**   GetMem(**var** p: pointer; size: word)

**Remarks**   *p* is a pointer variable of any pointer type. *Size* is an expression of type word specifying the size in bytes of the dynamic variable to allocate. The newly created variable can be referenced as *p^*.

If there isn't enough free space in the heap to allocate the new variable, a runtime error occurs. (It is possible to avoid a runtime error; see "The HeapError Function" in Chapter 26.)

**Restrictions**   The largest block that can be allocated on the heap at one time is 65521 bytes (64Kb-$F). If the heap is not fragmented, for example at the beginning of a program, successive calls to *GetMem* will return neighboring blocks of memory.

**Differences**   In 3.0, *size* was an integer.

**See also**   *New, FreeMem*

# GetModeRange procedure                    Graph

**Function**        Returns the lowest and highest valid graphics mode for
                    a given driver.

**Declaration**     GetModeRange(GraphDriver     : integer;
                              **var** LoMode, HiMode: integer);

**Remarks**         The output from the following program:

```
uses Graph;
var
  Lowest, Highest : integer;

begin
  GetModeRange(EGA64, Lowest, Highest);
  Write('Lowest = ', Lowest);
  Write(' Highest = ', Highest);
end.
```

will be *Lowest* = 0 and *Highest* = 1.

If the value of *GraphDriver* is invalid, the return parameters are set to –1.

**See also**        *SetGraphMode, InitGraph, DetectGraph*

# GetPalette procedure                      Graph

**Function**        Returns the current palette and its size.

**Declaration**     GetPalette(**var** Palette: PaletteType)

**Remarks**         Returns the current palette and its size in a variable of
                    type *PaletteType*. *PaletteType* is predefined as follows:

```
const
  MaxColors = 15;
type
  PaletteType = record
                  Size: byte;
                  Colors: array[0..MaxColors] of shortint;
                end;
```

The size field reports the number of colors in the palette
for the current driver in the current mode. *Colors*
contains the actual colors 0..*Size*-1.

| | |
|---|---|
| **Restrictions** | Must be in graphics mode. |
| **See also** | *SetPalette, SetAllPalette* |
| **Example** | |

```pascal
uses Graph;
var
  Gd, Gm : integer;
  Color  : word;
  Palette: PaletteType;

begin
  Gd := Detect;
  InitGraph(Gd, Gm, '');
  if GraphResult <> grOk then
    Halt(1);
  GetPalette(Palette);
  if Palette.Size <> 1 then
    for Color := 0 to Pred(Palette.Size) do
    begin
      SetColor(Color);
      Line(0, Color*5, 100, Color*5);
    end
  else
    Line(0, 0, 100, 0);
  Readln;
  CloseGraph;
end.
```

# GetPixel function                                      Graph

| | |
|---|---|
| **Function** | Gets the pixel value at *X,Y*. |
| **Declaration** | `GetPixel(X,Y: integer)` |
| **Result type** | word |
| **Remarks** | Gets the pixel color at (*X,Y*). |
| **Restrictions** | Must be in graphics mode. |
| **See also** | *PutPixel, GetImage, PutImage* |
| **Example** | |

```pascal
uses Graph;
var
  Gd, Gm    : integer;
  PixelColor: word;

begin
  Gd := Detect;
  InitGraph(Gd, Gm, '');
```

```
      if GraphResult <> grOk then
        Halt(1);
      PixelColor := GetPixel(10,10);
      if PixelColor = 0 then
        PutPixel(10, 10, GetMaxColor);
      Readln;
      CloseGraph;
    end.
```

# GetTextSettings procedure               Graph

**Function**        Returns the current text font, direction, size, and
                    justification as set by *SetTextStyle* and *SetTextJustify*.

**Declaration**     GetTextSettings(**var** TextInfo: TextSettingsType)

**Remarks**         The following type and constants are defined:

```
type
  TextSettingsType = record
                       Font: word;
                       Direction: word;
                       CharSize: word;
                       Horiz: word;
                       Vert: word;
                     end;

const
  DefaultFont    = 0;                    { 8x8 bit mapped font }
  TriplexFont    = 1;                       { "Stroked" fonts }
  SmallFont      = 2;
  SansSerifFont  = 3;
  GothicFont     = 4;
  HorizDir       = 0;                       { Left to right }
  VertDir        = 1;                       { Bottom to top }
```

**Restrictions**    Must be in graphics mode.

**See also**        *InitGraph, SetTextJustify, SetTextStyle, TextHeight,
                    TextWidth*

**Example**         ```
uses Graph;
var
  Gd, Gm  : integer;
  OldStyle: TextSettingsType;

begin
  Gd := Detect;
```
```

```
        InitGraph(Gd, Gm, '');
        if GraphResult <> grOk then
          Halt(1);
        GetTextSettings(OldStyle);
        OutTextXY(0, 0, 'Old text style');
        SetTextJustify(LeftText, CenterText);
        SetTextStyle(TriplexFont, VertDir, 4);
        OutTextXY(GetMaxX div 2, GetMaxY div 2, 'New Style');
        with OldStyle do
        begin                             { Restore old text style }
          SetTextJustify(Horiz, Vert);
          SetTextStyle(Font, Direction, CharSize);
        end;
        OutTextXY(0, TextHeight('H'), 'Old style again');
        Readln;
        CloseGraph;
      end.
```

# GetTime procedure                                        Dos

**Function**      Returns the current time set in the operating system.

**Declaration**   `GetTime(var Hour, Minute, Second, Sec100: word)`

**Remarks**       Ranges of the values returned are *Hour* 0..23, *Minute*
                  0..59, *Second* 0..59, and *Sec*100 (hundredths of seconds)
                  0..99.

**See also**      *SetTime, GetDate, SetDate*

# GetViewSettings procedure                            Graph

**Function**      Returns the current viewport and clipping settings, as
                  set by *SetViewPort*.

**Declaration**   `GetViewSettings(var ViewPort: ViewPortType)`

**Remarks**       *GetViewSettings* returns a variable of type *ViewPortType*.
                  *ViewPortType* is predeclared as follows:

```
      type
        ViewPortType = record
                         x1, y1, x2, y2: integer;
                         Clip: boolean;
                       end;
```

The points (*x1*, *y1*) and (*x2*, *y2*) are the dimensions of the active viewport and are given in absolute screen coordinates. *Clip* is a Boolean variable that controls whether clipping is active.

**Restrictions**  Must be in graphics mode.

**See also**  *SetViewPort*

**Example**
```
uses Graph;
var
  Gd, Gm  : integer;
  ViewPort: ViewPortType;

begin
  Gd := Detect;
  InitGraph(Gd, Gm, '');
  if GraphResult <> grOk then
    Halt(1);
  GetViewSettings(ViewPort);
  with ViewPort do
  begin
    Rectangle(0, 0, x2-x1, y2-y1);
    if Clip then
      OutText('Clipping is active.')
    else
      OutText('No clipping today.');
  end;
  Readln;
  CloseGraph;
end.
```

# GetX function                                    Graph

**Function**  Returns the *X* coordinate of the current position (CP).

**Declaration**  GetX

**Result type**  integer

**Remarks**  *GetX* is viewport-relative. In the following example:

1  `SetViewPort(0,0,GetMaxX,GetMaxY,True);`
2  `MoveTo(5,5);`
3  `SetViewPort(10,10,100,100,True);`
4  `MoveTo(5,5);`

■ Line 1 moves CP to absolute (0,0), and *GetX* would also return a value of 0.

- Line 2 moves CP to absolute (5,5), and *GetX* would also return a value of 5.

- Line 3 moves CP to absolute (10,10), but *GetX* would return a value of 0.

- Line 4 moves CP to absolute (15,15), but *GetX* would return a value of 5.

**Restrictions**    Must be in graphics mode.

**See also**    *GetViewSettings, GetY, InitGraph, MoveTo, SetViewPort*

**Example**

```
uses Graph;
var
  Gd, Gm: integer;
  X, Y: integer;

begin
  Gd := Detect;
  InitGraph(Gd, Gm, '');
  if GraphResult <> grOk then
    Halt(1);
  OutText('Starting here. ');
  X := GetX;
  Y := GetY;
  OutTextXY(20, 10, 'Now over here...');
  OutTextXY(X, Y, 'Now back over here.');
  Readln;
  CloseGraph;
end.
```

# GetY function      Graph

**Function**    Returns the *Y* coordinate of the current position (CP).

**Declaration**    `GetY`

**Result type**    integer

**Remarks**    *GetY* is viewport-relative. In the following example:

```
1   SetViewPort(0,0,GetMaxX,GetMaxY,True);
2   MoveTo(5,5);
3   SetViewPort(10,10,100,100,True);
4   MoveTo(5,5);
```

- Line 1 moves CP to absolute (0,0), and *GetY* would also return a value of 0.

- Line 2 moves CP to absolute (5,5), and *GetY* would also return a value of 5.
- Line 3 moves CP to absolute (10,10), but *GetY* would return a value of 0.
- Line 4 moves CP to absolute (15,15), but *GetY* would return a value of 5.

**Restrictions**  Must be in graphics mode.

**See also**  *GetViewSettings, GetX, InitGraph, MoveTo, SetViewPort*

**Example**
```
uses Graph;
var
  Gd, Gm: integer;
  X, Y: integer;
begin
  Gd := Detect;
  InitGraph(Gd, Gm, '');
  if GraphResult <> grOk then
    Halt(1);
  OutText('Starting here. ');
  X := GetX;
  Y := GetY;
  OutTextXY(20, 10, 'Now over here...');
  OutTextXY(X, Y, 'Now back over here.');
  Readln;
  CloseGraph;
end.
```

# GotoXY procedure                                           Crt

**Function**  Positions the cursor.

**Declaration**  `GotoXY(X, Y: byte)`

**Remarks**  The cursor is moved to the position within the current window specified by *X* and *Y* (*X* is the column, *Y* is the row). The upper left corner is (1,1).

This procedure is window-relative:

```
Window(1,10,60,20);
GotoXY(1,1);
```

and will move the cursor to the upper left corner of the active window (absolute coordinates (1,10)).

**Restrictions**    If the coordinates are in any way invalid, the call to *GotoXY* is ignored.

**See also**    *Window, WhereX, WhereY*

# GraphDefaults procedure        Graph

**Function**    Resets the graphics settings.

**Declaration**    `GraphDefaults;`

**Remarks**    Homes the current pointer (CP) and resets the graphics system to the default values for

- viewport
- palette
- draw and background colors
- line style and line pattern
- fill style, fill color, and fill pattern
- active font, text style, text justification, and user char size

**Restrictions**    Must be in graphics mode.

**See also**    *InitGraph*

# GraphErrorMsg function        Graph

**Function**    Returns an error message string for the specified *ErrorCode*.

**Declaration**    `GraphErrorMsg(ErrorCode: integer)`

**Result type**    string

**Remarks**    This function returns a string containing an error message that corresponds with the error codes in the graphics system. This makes it easy for a user program to display a descriptive error message ("Device driver not found" instead of "error code –3").

**See also**    *GraphResult*

**Example**
```
uses Graph;
var
  GraphDriver, GraphMode: integer;
  ErrorCode: integer;
```

```
begin
  GraphDriver := Detect;
  InitGraph(GraphDriver, GraphMode, '');
  ErrorCode := GraphResult;
  if ErrorCode <> grOk then
  begin
    Writeln('Graphics error: ', GraphErrorMsg(ErrorCode));
    Readln;
    Halt(1);
  end;
  Line(0, 0, GetMaxX, GetMaxY);
  Readln;
  CloseGraph;
end.
```

# GraphResult function                          Graph

| | |
|---|---|
| **Function** | Returns an error code for the last graphics operation. |
| **Declaration** | `GraphResult` |
| **Result type** | integer |
| **Remarks** | Returns an error code for the last graphics operation. The following error return codes are defined: |

| Error Code | Graphics Error Constant | Corresponding Error Message String |
|---|---|---|
| 0 | grOk | No error |
| −1 | grNoInitGraph | (BGI) graphics not installed (use *InitGraph*) |
| −2 | grNotDetected | Graphics hardware not detected |
| −3 | grFileNotFound | Device driver file not found |
| −4 | grInvalidDriver | Invalid device driver file |
| −5 | grNoLoadMem | Not enough memory to load driver |
| −6 | grNoScanMem | Out of memory in scan fill |
| −7 | grNoFloodMem | Out of memory in flood fill |
| −8 | grFontNotFound | Font file not found |
| −9 | grNoFontMem | Not enough memory to load font |
| −10 | grInvalidMode | Invalid graphics mode for selected driver |
| −11 | grError | Graphics error |
| −12 | grIOerror | Graphics I/O error |
| −13 | grInvalidFont | Invalid font file |
| −14 | grInvalidFontNum | Invalid font number |
| −15 | grInvalidDeviceNum | Invalid device number |

The following routines set *GraphResult*:

| | | |
|---|---|---|
| *DetectGraph* | *SetAllPattern* | *SetPalette* |
| *ImageSize* | *SetFillStyle* | *SetTextJustify* |
| *InitGraph* | *SetGraphBufSize* | *SetTextStyle* |
| *RegisterBGIdriver* | *SetGraphMode* | *SetViewPort* |
| *RegisterBGIfont* | *SetLineStyle* | |

Note that *GraphResult* is reset to zero after it has been called (similar to *IOResult*). Therefore, the user should store the value of *GraphResult* into a temporary variable and then test it.

**Restrictions**    A string function, *GraphErrorMsg*, is provided that returns a string that corresponds with each error code.

**See also**    *GraphErrorMsg*

**Example**
```
uses Graph;
var
  ErrorCode: integer;
  GrDriver, GrMode: integer;
```

```
begin
  GrDriver := Detect;
  InitGraph(GrDriver, GrMode, '');
  ErrorCode := GraphResult;                   { Check for errors }
  if ErrorCode <> grOk then
  begin
    Writeln('Graphics error:');
    Writeln(GraphErrorMsg(ErrorCode));
    Writeln('Program aborted...');
    Halt(1);
  end;

  { Do some graphics... }
  ClearDevice;
  Rectangle(0, 0, GetMaxX, GetMaxY);
  Readln;
  CloseGraph;
end.
```

# Halt procedure

**Function**      Stops program execution and returns to the operating system.

**Declaration**   `Halt [ ( exitcode: word ) ]`

**Remarks**       *exitcode* is an optional expression of type word that specifies the exit code of the program. *Halt* without a parameter corresponds to *Halt(0)*. The exit code can be examined by a parent process using the *DosExitCode* function in the *Dos* unit or through an *ERRORLEVEL* test in a DOS batch file.

Note that *Halt* will initiate execution of any unit *Exit* procedures (see Chapter 26).

**See also**      *Exit*

# Hi function

**Function**      Returns the high-order byte of the argument.

**Declaration**   `Hi(x)`

**Result type**   byte

| Remarks | *x* is an expression of type integer or word. *Hi* returns the high-order byte of *x* as an unsigned value. |
|---|---|
| See also | *Lo, Swap* |
| Example | |

```
var w: word;
begin
  w := Hi($1234);   { $12 }
end;
```

# HighVideo procedure                                    Crt

| Function | Selects high-intensity characters. |
|---|---|
| Declaration | `HighVideo` |
| Remarks | There is a byte variable in *Crt—TextAttr*—that is used to hold the current video attribute. *HighVideo* sets the high intensity bit of *TextAttr*'s foreground color, thus mapping colors 0-7 onto colors 8-15. |
| Differences | In 3.0, *HighVideo* always selected yellow on black (white on black in mono and BW80 video modes). |
| See also | *NormVideo, LowVideo, TextColor, TextBackground* |
| Example | |

```
uses Crt;
begin
  TextAttr := LightGray;
  HighVideo;                              { Color is now white }
end.
```

# ImageSize function                                   Graph

| Function | Returns the number of bytes required to store a rectangular region of the screen. |
|---|---|
| Declaration | `ImageSize(x1, y1, x2, y2: integer)` |
| Result type | word |
| Remarks | *x1, y1, x2,* and *y2* define a rectangular region on the screen. *ImageSize* determines the number of bytes necessary for *GetImage* to save the specified region of the screen. The image size includes space for two word variables that store the width and height of the region. |

If the memory required to save the region is greater than or equal to 64K, a value of 0 is returned and *GraphResult* will return –11 (*grError*).

**Restrictions**    Must be in graphics mode.

**See also**    *GetImage, PutImage*

**Example**
```
uses Graph;
var
  Gd, Gm: integer;
  P: pointer;
  Size: word;

begin
  Gd := Detect;
  InitGraph(Gd, Gm, '');
  if GraphResult <> grOk then
    Halt(1);
  Bar(0, 0, GetMaxX, GetMaxY);
  Size := ImageSize(10,20,30,40);
  GetMem(P, Size);                    { Allocate memory on heap }
  GetImage(10,20,30,40,P^);
  Readln;
  ClearDevice;
  PutImage(100, 100, P^, NormalPut);
  Readln;
  CloseGraph;
end.
```

# Inc procedure

**Function**    Increments a variable.

**Declaration**    `Inc(var x [ ; n: longint ] )`

**Remarks**    *x* is an ordinal-type variable, and *n* is an integer-type expression. *x* is incremented by 1, or by *n* if *n* is specified; that is, *Inc(x)* corresponds to *x := x+1*, and *Inc(x,n)* corresponds to *x := x+n*.

*Inc* generates optimized code and is especially useful for use in tight loops.

**See also**    *Dec, Pred*

**Example**
```
var
  IntVar: integer;
  LongintVar: longint;
```

```
begin
  Inc(IntVar);                    { IntVar := IntVar + 1 }
  Inc(LongintVar, 5);      { LongintVar := LongintVar + 5 }
end.
```

# InitGraph procedure                          Graph

**Function**         Initializes the graphics system and puts the hardware into graphics mode.

**Declaration**
```
InitGraph(var GraphDriver: integer;
          var GraphMode: integer; DriverPath: string)
```

**Remarks**          Both *GraphDriver* and *GraphMode* are **var** parameters.

If *GraphDriver* is equal to *Detect (0)*, a call is made to *DetectGraph*, the appropriate graphics driver is initialized, and a graphics mode is selected.

If *GraphDriver* is not equal to 0, the value of *GraphDriver* is assumed to be a driver number; that driver is selected, and the system is put into the mode specified by *GraphMode*. Note that if you override autodetection in this manner, you must supply a valid *GraphMode* parameter for the driver requested.

*DriverPath* specifies the directory path where the graphics drivers can be found. If *DriverPath* is null, the driver files must be in the current directory.

Normally, *InitGraph* loads a graphics driver by allocating memory for the driver (through *GraphGetMem*), then loads the appropriate .BGI file from disk. As an alternative to this dynamic loading scheme, you can link a graphics driver file (or several of them) directly into your executable program file. You do this by first converting the .BGI file to an .OBJ file (using the BINOBJ utility), then placing calls to *RegisterBGIdriver* in your source code (before the call to *InitGraph*) to register the graphics driver(s). When you build your program, you must link the .OBJ files for the registered drivers. You can also load a BGI driver onto the heap and then register it using *RegisterBGIdriver*.

If memory for the graphics driver is allocated on the heap using *GraphGetMem*, that memory is released when a call is made to *CloseGraph*.

After calling *InitGraph*, *GraphDriver* will be set to the current graphics driver, and *GraphMode* will be set to the current graphics mode.

If an error occurred, both *GraphDriver* and *GraphResult* (a function) will return one of the following values:

| | |
|---|---|
| –2 | Cannot detect a graphics card |
| –3 | Cannot find driver file |
| –4 | Invalid driver |
| –5 | Insufficient memory to load driver |
| –10 | Invalid graphics mode for selected driver |
| –15 | Invalid device number |

*InitGraph* resets all graphics settings to their defaults (current pointer, palette, color, viewport, etc.).

Several useful constants are defined for each graphics driver supported:

| Error Code | Graphics Error Constant | Corresponding Error Message String |
|---|---|---|
| 0 | grOk | No error |
| –1 | grNoInitGraph | (BGI) graphics not installed (use *InitGraph*) |
| –2 | grNotDetected | Graphics hardware not detected |
| –3 | grFileNotFound | Device driver file not found |
| –4 | grInvalidDriver | Invalid device driver file |
| –5 | grNoLoadMem | Not enough memory to load driver |
| –6 | grNoScanMem | Out of memory in scan fill |
| –7 | grNoFloodMem | Out of memory in flood fill |
| –8 | grFontNotFound | Font file not found |
| –9 | grNoFontMem | Not enough memory to load font |
| –10 | grInvalidMode | Invalid graphics mode for selected driver |
| –11 | grError | Graphics error |
| –12 | grIOerror | Graphics I/O error |
| –13 | grInvalidFont | Invalid font file |
| –14 | grInvalidFontNum | Invalid font number |
| –15 | grInvalidDeviceNum | Invalid device number |

| Restrictions | Must be in graphics mode. |
| --- | --- |
| See also | *CloseGraph, DetectGraph, RestoreCrtMode, SetGraphMode, GraphResult, SetGraphBufSize, RegisterBGIdriver, RegisterBGIfont, GraphDefaults* |
| Example | |

```
uses Graph;
var
  grDriver: integer;
  grMode  : integer;
  ErrCode : integer;

begin
  grDriver := Detect;
  InitGraph(grDriver,grMode,'');
  ErrCode := GraphResult;
  if ErrCode = grOk then
    begin  { Do graphics }
      Line(0, 0, GetMaxX, GetMaxY);
      Readln;
      CloseGraph;
    end
  else
    Writeln('Graphics error:', GraphErrorMsg(ErrCode));
end.
```

# Insert procedure

| Function | Inserts a substring into a string. |
| --- | --- |
| Declaration | Insert(source: **string**; **var** s: **string**; index: integer) |
| Remarks | *source* is a string-type expression. *s* is a string-type variable of any length. *index* is an integer-type expression. *Insert* inserts *source* into *s* at the *index*th position. If the resulting string is longer than 255 characters, it is truncated after the 255th character. |
| See also | *Delete, Copy, ConCat, Pos* |
| Example | |

```
var
  s: string;
begin
  s := 'Honest Lincoln';
  Insert('Abe ', s, 8);              { ' Honest Abe Lincoln ' }
end.
```

# InsLine procedure                                     Crt

**Function**        Inserts an empty line at the cursor position.

**Declaration**     InsLine

**Remarks**         All lines below the inserted line are moved down one line, and the bottom line scrolls off the screen (using the BIOS scroll routine).

All character positions are set to blanks with the currently defined text attributes. Thus, if *TextBackground* is not black, the new line becomes the background color.

This procedure is window-relative:

```
Window(1,10,60,20);
InsLine;
```

and will insert a line 60 columns wide at absolute coordinates (1,10).

**See also**        *DelLine, Window*

# Int function

**Function**        Returns the integer part of the argument.

**Declaration**     Int(x: real)

**Result type**     real

**Remarks**         *x* is a real-type expression. The result is the integer part of *x*, that is, *x* rounded toward zero.

**See also**        *Frac*

**Example**
```
var r: real;
begin
  r := Int(123.456);    { 123.0 }
end.
```

# Intr procedure                                     Dos

**Function**        Executes a specified software interrupt.

| Declaration | `Intr(IntNo: byte; `**`var`**` Regs: Registers)` |
|---|---|
| Remarks | *IntNo* is the software interrupt number (0..255). *Registers* is a record defined in DOS: |

```
type
  Registers = record
                case integer of
                  0: (AX,BX,CX,DX,BP,SI,DI,DS,ES,
                      Flags: word);
                  1: (AL,AH,BL,BH,CL,CH,DL,DH: byte);
              end;
```

Before executing the specified software interrupt, *Intr* loads the 8086 CPU's AX, BX, CX, DX, BP, SI, DI, DS, and ES registers from the *Regs* record. When the interrupt completes, the contents of the AX, BX, CX, DX, BP, SI, DI, DS, ES, and Flags registers are stored back into the *Regs* record.

For details on writing interrupt procedures, refer to the section "Interrupt Handling" in Chapter 26, "Inside Turbo Pascal."

| Restrictions | Software interrupts that depend on specific values in SP or SS on entry, or modify SP and SS on exit, cannot be executed using this procedure. |
|---|---|
| Differences | In 3.0, the *Registers* variable passed to *Intr* was a user-defined type. In 4.0, the *Registers* variable must be of type *Registers* defined in the *Dos* unit. |
| See also | *MsDos* |

# IOResult function

| Function | Returns an integer value that is the status of the last I/O operation performed. |
|---|---|
| Declaration | `IOResult` |
| Result type | word |
| Remarks | I/O checking must be off—{$*I-*}—in order to trap I/O errors using *IOResult*. If an I/O error occurs and I/O checking is off, all subsequent I/O operations are ignored until a call is made to *IOResult*. A call to *IOResult* clears its internal error flag. |

The codes returned are summarized in Appendix I, "Error Messages and Codes." A value of 0 reflects a successful I/O operation.

**Differences**   In 3.0, return codes were mapped differently.

**Example**

```pascal
var f: file of byte;
begin
  { Get file name command line }
  Assign(f, ParamStr(1));
  {$I-}
  Reset(f);
  {$I+}
  if IOResult = 0 then
    Writeln('File size in bytes: ', FileSize(f))
  else
    Writeln('File not found');
end.
```

# Keep procedure                                              Dos

**Function**      *Keep* (or Terminate Stay Resident) terminates the program and makes it stay in memory.

**Declaration**   Keep(ExitCode: word)

**Remarks**       The entire program stays in memory—including data segment, stack segment, and heap—so be sure to specify a maximum size for the heap using the $M$ compiler directive. The *ExitCode* corresponds to the one passed to the *Halt* standard procedure.

**Restrictions**  Use with care! **T**erminate **S**tay **R**esident (TSR) programs are complex and *no* other support for them is provided. Refer to the MS-DOS technical documentation for more information.

**See also**      *DosExitCode*

# KeyPressed function                                         Crt

**Function**      Returns True if a key has been pressed on the keyboard; False otherwise.

**Declaration**   KeyPressed

| | |
|---|---|
| **Result type** | boolean |
| **Remarks** | The character (or characters) is left in the keyboard buffer. *KeyPressed* does not detect shift keys like *Shift*, *Alt*, *NumLock*, and so on. |
| **Differences** | In 3.0, break-checking {$C-} had to be off. 4.0 has no such restriction. |
| **See also** | *ReadKey* |
| **Example** | |

```
uses Crt;
begin
  repeat
    Write('Xx');       { Fill the screen until a key is typed }
  until KeyPressed;
end.
```

# Length function

| | |
|---|---|
| **Function** | Returns the dynamic length of a string. |
| **Declaration** | Length(s: **string**) |
| **Result type** | integer |
| **Remarks** | *s* is a string-type expression. The result is the length of *s*. |
| **Example** | |

```
var f: text; s: string;
begin
  Assign(f, 'gary.pas');
  Reset(f);
  Readln(f, s);
  Writeln('"', s, '"')
  Writeln('length = ', length(s));
end.
```

# Line procedure                                    Graph

| | |
|---|---|
| **Function** | Draws a line from the (*x1*, *y1*) to (*x2*, *y2*). |
| **Declaration** | Line(x1, y1, x2, y2: integer) |
| **Remarks** | Draws a line in the style and thickness defined by *SetLineStyle* and uses the color set by *SetColor*. |
| | Note that |

```
    MoveTo(100,100);
    LineTo(200,200);
```

is equivalent to

```
    Line(100,100,200,200);
    MoveTo(200,200);
```

Use *LineTo* when the current pointer is at one endpoint of the line. If you want the current pointer updated automatically when the line is drawn, use *LineRel* to draw a line a relative distance from the CP. Note that *Line* doesn't update the current pointer.

**Restrictions**  Must be in graphics mode.

**See also**  *LineTo, LineRel, GetLineStyle, SetLineStyle*

**Example**
```
uses Crt, Graph;
var
  Gd, Gm: integer;

begin
  Gd := Detect;
  InitGraph(Gd, Gm, '');
  if GraphResult <> grOk then
    Halt(1);
  Randomize;
  repeat
    Line(Random(200),Random(200),Random(200),Random(200));
  until KeyPressed;
  Readln;
  CloseGraph;
end.
```

# LineRel procedure                          Graph

**Function**  Draws a line to a point that is a relative distance from the current pointer (CP).

**Declaration**  `LineRel(Dx, Dy: integer);`

**Remarks**  *LineRel* will draw a line from the current pointer to a point that is a relative (*Dx,Dy*) distance from the current pointer. The current line style and pattern, as set by *SetLineStyle*, are used for drawing the line and uses the color set by *SetColor*. Relative move and line commands are useful for drawing a shape on the screen whose starting point can be changed to draw the same shape in a different location on the screen.

The current pointer is set to the last point drawn by *LineRel.*

**Restrictions**     Must be in graphics mode.

**See also**     *Line, LineTo, MoveRel, SetLineStyle, GetLineStyle*

**Example**
```
uses Graph;
var
  Gd, Gm: integer;

begin
  Gd := Detect;
  InitGraph(Gd, Gm, '');
  if GraphResult <> grOk then
    Halt(1);
  MoveTo(1,2);
  LineRel(100, 100);                { Draw to the point (101,102) }
  Readln;
  CloseGraph;
end.
```

# LineTo procedure                                    Graph

**Function**     Draws a line from the current pointer to $(x,y)$.

**Declaration**     `LineTo(x, y: integer)`

**Remarks**     Draws a line in the style and thickness defined by *SetLineStyle* and uses the color set by *SetColor.*

Note that

```
MoveTo(100,100);
LineTo(200,200);
```

is equivalent to

```
Line(100,100,200,200);
```

The first method is slower and uses more code. Use *LineTo* only when the current pointer is at one endpoint of the line. Use *LineRel* to draw a line a relative distance from the CP. Note that the second method doesn't change the value of the current pointer.

*LineTo* moves the current pointer to $(x,y)$.

| | |
|---|---|
| **Restrictions** | Must be in graphics mode. |
| **See also** | *Line, LineRel, MoveTo, MoveRel, SetLineStyle, GetLineStyle* |
| **Example** | |

```pascal
uses Crt, Graph;
var
  Gd, Gm: integer;

begin
  Gd := Detect;
  InitGraph(Gd, Gm, '');
  if GraphResult <> grOk then
    Halt(1);
  Randomize;
  repeat
    LineTo(Random(200),Random(200));
  until KeyPressed;
  Readln;
  CloseGraph;
end.
```

# Ln function

| | |
|---|---|
| **Function** | Returns the natural logarithm of the argument. |
| **Declaration** | `Ln(x: real)` |
| **Result type** | real |
| **Remarks** | *x* is a real-type expression. The result is the natural logarithm of *x*. |
| **See Also** | *Exp* |

# Lo function

| | |
|---|---|
| **Function** | Returns the low-order byte of the argument. |
| **Declaration** | `Lo(x)` |
| **Result type** | byte |
| **Remarks** | *x* is an expression of type integer or word. *Lo* returns the low-order byte of *x* as an unsigned value. |
| **See also** | *Hi, Swap* |

Example

```
var w: word;
begin
  w := Lo($1234);   { $34 }
end.
```

# LowVideo procedure                                      Crt

| | |
|---|---|
| **Function** | Selects low intensity characters. |
| **Declaration** | LowVideo |
| **Remarks** | There is a byte variable in *Crt—TextAttr*—that is used to hold the current video attribute. *LowVideo* clears the high-intensity bit of *TextAttr*'s foreground color, thus mapping colors 8-15 onto colors 0-7. |
| **Differences** | In 3.0, *LowVideo* always selected *LightGray* on black. |
| **See also** | *HighVideo, NormVideo, TextColor, TextBackground* |
| **Example** | |

```
uses Crt;
begin
  TextAttr := White;
  LowVideo;                         { Color is now light gray }
end.
```

# Mark procedure

| | |
|---|---|
| **Function** | Records the state of the heap in a pointer variable. |
| **Declaration** | Mark(**var** p: pointer) |
| **Remarks** | *p* is a pointer variable of any pointer type. The current value of the heap pointer is recorded in *p*, and can later be used as an argument to *Release*. |
| **Restrictions** | *Mark* and *Release* cannot be used interchangeably with *Dispose* and *FreeMem* unless certain rules are observed. For a complete discussion of this topic, refer to the section entitled "The Heap Manager" in Chapter 26. |
| **See also** | *Release, FreeMem, Dispose* |

# MaxAvail function

**Function**     Returns the size of the largest contiguous free block in the heap, corresponding to the size of the largest dynamic variable that can be allocated at that time.

**Declaration**  MaxAvail

**Result type**  longint

**Remarks**      This number is calculated by comparing the sizes of all free blocks below the heap pointer to the size of free memory above the heap pointer. To find the total amount of free memory on the heap, call *MemAvail*. Your program can specify minimum and maximum heap requirements using the {$M} compiler directive (see Appendix C).

**Differences**  In 3.0, the returned value was an integer that represented the size of the largest free block in paragraphs.

**See also**     *MemAvail*

**Example**
```
type
  FriendRec = record
                Name: string[30];
                Age : byte;
              end;
var
  p: pointer;

begin
  if MaxAvail < SizeOf(FriendRec) then
    Writeln('Not enough memory')
  else
  begin
    { Allocate memory on heap }
    GetMem(p, SizeOf(FriendRec));
    :
    :
  end;
end.
```

# MemAvail function

**Function**     Returns the sum of all free blocks in the heap.

| | |
|---|---|
| **Declaration** | `MemAvail` |
| **Result type** | longint |
| **Remarks** | This number is calculated by adding the sizes of all free blocks below the heap pointer to the size of free memory above the heap pointer. Note that unless *Dispose* and *FreeMem* were never called, a block of storage the size of the returned value is unlikely to be available due to fragmentation of the heap. To find the largest free block, call *MaxAvail*. Your program can specify minimum and maximum heap requirements using the {$M} compiler directive (see Appendix C). |
| **Differences** | In 3.0, the returned value was an integer that represented the number of free paragraphs. |
| **See also** | *MaxAvail* |
| **Example** | |

```
begin
  Writeln(MemAvail, ' bytes available');
  Writeln('Largest block contains ', MaxAvail, ' bytes');
end.
```

# MkDir procedure

| | |
|---|---|
| **Function** | Creates a subdirectory. |
| **Declaration** | `MkDir(s: string)` |
| **Remarks** | *s* is a string-type expression. A new subdirectory with the path specified by *s* is created. The last item in the path cannot be an existing file name. |
| | With {$I-}, *IOResult* will return a 0 if the operation was successful; otherwise, it will return a nonzero error code. |
| **See also** | *RmDir, ChDir, GetDir* |
| **Example** | |

```
begin
  {$I-}
  { Get directory name from command line }
  MkDir(ParamStr(1));
  if IOResult <> 0 then
    Writeln('Cannot create directory')
  else
    Writeln('New directory created');
end.
```

# Move procedure

**Function**        Copies a specified number of contiguous bytes from a source range to a destination range.

**Declaration**     `Move(`**`var`**` source, dest; count: word)`

**Remarks**         *source* and *dest* are variable references of any type. *count* is an expression of type word. *Move* copies a block of *count* bytes from the first byte occupied by *source* to the first byte occupied by *dest*. No checking is performed, so be careful with this procedure.

**Note:** When *source* and *dest* are in the same segment, that is, when the segment parts of their addresses are equal, *Move* automatically detects and compensates for any overlap. Intrasegment overlaps never occur on statically and dynamically allocated variables (unless they are deliberately forced), and they are therefore not detected.

Whenever possible, use the *SizeOf* function to determine the *count*.

**See also**        *FillChar*

**Example**
```
var
  a: array[1..4] of char;
  b: longint;

begin
  Move(a, b, SizeOf(a));                    { SizeOf = safety! }
end.
```

# MoveRel procedure                                      Graph

**Function**        Moves the current pointer (CP) a relative distance from its current location.

**Declaration**     `MoveRel(Dx, Dy: integer)`

**Remarks**         *MoveRel* moves the current pointer (CP) to a point that is a relative (*Dx,Dy*) distance from the current pointer. Relative move and line commands are useful for drawing a shape on the screen whose starting point can be changed to draw the same shape in a different location on the screen.

| **Restrictions** | Must be in graphics mode. |
|---|---|
| **See also** | *LineRel, LineTo, MoveTo* |

**Example**
```
uses Graph;
var
  Gd, Gm: integer;

begin
  Gd := Detect;
  InitGraph(Gd, Gm, '');
  if GraphResult <> grOk then
    Halt(1);
  MoveTo(1,2);
  MoveRel(10,10);                    { Move to the point (11, 12) }
  PutPixel(GetX, GetY, GetMaxColor);
  Readln;
  CloseGraph;
end.
```

# MoveTo procedure                                      Graph

| **Function** | Moves the current pointer (CP) to $(x,y)$. |
|---|---|
| **Declaration** | `MoveTo(x, y: integer)` |
| **Remarks** | The CP is similar to a text mode cursor except that the CP is not visible. The following routines move the CP: |

|  |  |
|---|---|
| *ClearDevice* | *MoveRel* |
| *ClearViewPort* | *MoveTo* |
| *GraphDefaults* | *OutText* |
| *InitGraph* | *SetGraphMode* |
| *LineRel* | *SetViewPort* |
| *LineTo* | |

If a viewport is active, the CP will be viewport-relative (the $x$ and $y$ values will be added to the viewport's $x1$ and $y1$ values). The CP is never clipped at the current viewport's boundaries.

| **See also** | *GetMaxX, GetMaxY, GetX, GetY, MoveRel* |
|---|---|

**Example**
```
uses Graph;
var
  Gd, Gm: integer;

begin
  Gd := Detect;
```

```
    InitGraph(Gd, Gm, '');
    if GraphResult <> grOk then
      Halt(1);
    MoveTo(0,0);                    { Upper left corner of viewport }
    LineTo(GetMaxX, GetMaxY);
    Readln;
    CloseGraph;
end.
```

# MsDos procedure                                          Dos

**Function**       Executes a DOS function call.

**Declaration**    MsDos(**var** Regs: Registers);

**Remarks**        The effect of a call to *MsDos* is the same as a call to *Intr*
                   with an *IntNo* of $21. *Registers* is a record declared in the
                   *Dos* unit:

```
type
   Registers = record
                   case integer of
                      0: (AX,BX,CX,DX,BP,SI,DI,DS,ES,
                           Flags: word);
                      1: (AL,AH,BL,BH,CL,CH,DL,DH: byte);
                   end;
```

**Restrictions**   Software interrupts that depend on specific calls in SP or
                   SS on entry or modify SP and SS on exit cannot be
                   executed using this procedure.

**Differences**    In 3.0, no type-checking was performed on the *Registers*
                   parameter.

**See also**       *Intr*

# New procedure

**Function**       Creates a new dynamic variable and sets a pointer
                   variable to point to it.

**Declaration**    New(**var** p: pointer)

**Remarks**        *p* is a pointer variable of any pointer type. The size of the
                   allocated memory block corresponds to the size of the
                   type that *p* points to. The newly created variable can be

referenced as *p^*. If there isn't enough free space in the heap to allocate the new variable, a runtime error occurs. (It is possible to avoid a runtime error in this case; see "The HeapError Function" in Chapter 26.)

**See also**    *GetMem, Dispose*

# NormVideo procedure                                    Crt

**Function**     Selects the original text attribute read from the cursor location at startup.

**Declaration**  NormVideo

**Remarks**      There is a byte variable in *Crt—TextAttr*—that is used to hold the current video attribute. *NormVideo* restores *TextAttr* to the value it had when the program was started.

**Differences**  In 3.0, *NormVideo* and *HighVideo* were identical; see *HighVideo*.

**See also**     *HighVideo, LowVideo, TextColor, TextBackground*

# NoSound procedure                                      Crt

**Function**     Turns off the internal speaker.

**Declaration**  NoSound

**Remarks**      The following program fragment emits a 440-hertz tone for half a second:

```
Sound(440); Delay(500); NoSound;
```

**See also**     *Sound*

# Odd function

**Function**     Tests if the argument is an odd number.

**Declaration**  Odd(x: longint)

**Result type**  boolean

**Remarks**     *x* is a longint-type expression. The result is True if *x* is an odd number, and False if *x* is an even number.

# Ofs function

**Function**     Returns the offset of a specified object.

**Declaration**     `Ofs(x)`

**Result type**     word

**Remarks**     *x* is any variable, or a procedure or function identifier. The result of type word is the offset part of the address of *x*.

**See also**     *Seg, Addr*

# Ord function

**Function**     Returns the ordinal number of an ordinal-type value.

**Declaration**     `Ord(x)`

**Result type**     longint

**Remarks**     *x* is an ordinal-type expression. The result is of type longint and its value is the ordinality of *x*.

**See also**     *Chr*

# OutText procedure                                           Graph

**Function**     Sends a string to the output device at the current pointer.

**Declaration**     `OutText(TextString: `**`string`**`)`

**Remarks**     *TextString* is output at the current pointer using the current justification settings. *TextString* is always truncated at the viewport border if it is too long. If one of the stroked fonts is active, *TextString* is truncated at the screen boundary if it is too long. If the default (bit-mapped) font is active and the string is too long to fit on the screen, no text is displayed.

*OutText* uses the font set by *SetTextStyle*. In order to maintain code compatibility when using several fonts, use the *TextWidth* and *TextHeight* calls to determine the dimensions of the string.

*OutText* uses the output options set by *SetTextJustify* (justify, center, rotate 90 degrees, and so on).

The current pointer (CP) is only updated by *OutText* if the direction is horizontal, and the horizontal justification is left. Text output direction is set by *SetTextStyle* (horizontal or vertical); text justification is set by *SetTextJustify* (CP at the left of the string, centered around CP, or CP at the right of the string—written above CP, below CP, or centered around CP). In the following example, block #1 outputs *ABCDEF* and moves CP (text is both horizontally output and left-justified); block #2 outputs *ABC* with *DEF* written right on top of it because text is right-justified; similarly, block #3 outputs *ABC* with *DEF* written right on top of it because text is written vertically.

```
program CPupdate;
uses Graph;
var
   Driver, Mode: integer;

begin
   Driver := Detect;
   InitGraph(Driver, Mode, '');
   if GraphResult < 0 then
     Halt(1);

   { #1 }
   MoveTo(0, 0);
   SetTextStyle(DefaultFont, HorizDir, 1);      { CharSize = 1 }
   SetTextJustify(LeftText, TopText);
   OutText('ABC');                              { CP is updated
                                                }
   OutText('DEF');                              { CP is updated
                                                }

   { #2 }
   MoveTo(100, 50);
   SetTextStyle(DefaultFont, HorizDir, 1);      { CharSize = 1 }
   SetTextJustify(RightText, TopText);
   OutText('ABC');                              { CP is updated
                                                }
   OutText('DEF');                              { CP is updated
                                                }
```

```
{ #3 }
MoveTo(100, 100);
SetTextStyle(DefaultFont, VertDir, 1);         { CharSize = 1 }
SetTextJustify(LeftText, TopText);
OutText('ABC');                                 { CP is NOT updated }
OutText('DEF');                                 { CP is NOT updated }
Readln;
CloseGraph;
end.
```

The CP is never updated by *OutTextXY*.

The default font (8×8 bit-mapped) is not clipped at the screen edge. Instead, if any part of the string would go off the screen, no text is output. For example, the following statements would have no effect:

```
SetViewPort(0, 0, GetMaxX, GetMaxY, ClipOn);
SetTextJustify(LeftText, TopText);
OutTextXY(-5, 0);                              { -5,0 not on screen }
OutTextXY(GetMaxX - 1, 0, 'ABC');                 { Part of 'A', }
                                            { All of 'BC' off screen }
```

The "stroked" fonts are clipped at the screen edge, however.

**Restrictions**   Must be in graphics mode.

**See also**   *OutTextXY, SetTextStyle, SetTextJustify, GetTextSettings, TextHeight, TextWidth, SetUserCharSize*

**Example**
```
uses Graph;
var
  Gd, Gm: integer;

begin
  Gd := Detect;
  InitGraph(Gd, Gm, '');
  if GraphResult <> grOk then
    Halt(1);
  OutText('Easy to use');
  Readln;
  CloseGraph;
end.
```

# OutTextXY procedure                         Graph

**Function**   Sends a string to the output device.

| Declaration | `OutTextXY(X,Y: integer; TextString: string)` |
|---|---|
| **Remarks** | *TextString* is output at *(X,Y)*. *TextString* is always truncated at the viewport border if it is too long. If one of the stroked fonts is active, *TextString* is truncated at the screen boundary if it is too long. If the default (bit-mapped) font is active and the string is too long to fit on the screen, no text is displayed.

Use *OutText* to output text at the current pointer; use *OutTextXY* to output text elsewhere on the screen.

*OutTextXY* uses the font set by *SetTextStyle*. In order to maintain code compatibility when using several fonts, use the *TextWidth* and *TextHeight* calls to determine the dimensions of the string.

*OutTextXY* uses the output options set by *SetTextJustify* (justify, center, rotate 90 degrees, and so forth). |
| **Restrictions** | Must be in graphics mode. |
| **See also** | *OutText, SetTextStyle, SetTextJustify, GetTextSetting, TextHeight, TextWidth, SetUserCharSize* |
| **Example** | |

```
uses Graph;
var
  Gd, Gm: integer;

begin
  Gd := Detect;
  InitGraph(Gd, Gm, '');
  if GraphResult <> grOk then
    Halt(1);
  MoveTo(0, 0);
  OutText('Inefficient');
  Readln;
  OutTextXY(GetX, GetY, 'Also inefficient');
  Readln;
  ClearDevice;
  OutTextXY(0, 0, 'Perfect!');              { Replaces above }
  Readln;
  CloseGraph;
end.
```

# PackTime procedure                                    Dos

**Function**       Converts a *DateTime* record into a 4-byte, packed date-and-time longint used by *SetFTime*.

**Declaration**    `PackTime(`**`var`**` DT: DateTime; `**`var`**` Time: longint)`

**Remarks**        *DateTime* is a record declared in the *Dos* unit:

```
DateTime = record
              Year, Month, Day, Hour,
              Min, Sec: word
           end;
```

The fields of the *DateTime* record are not range-checked.

**See also**       *UnpackTime, GetFTime, SetFTime, GetFTime, SetTime*

# ParamCount function

**Function**       Returns the number of parameters passed to the program on the command line.

**Declaration**    `ParamCount`

**Result type**    word

**Remarks**        Blanks and tabs serve as separators.

**See also**       *ParamStr*

**Example**
```
begin
  if ParamCount < 1 then
    Writeln('No parameters on command line')
  else
    Writeln(ParamCount, ' parameter(s)');
end.
```

# ParamStr function

**Function**       Returns a specified command-line parameter.

**Declaration**    `ParamStr(index)`

**Result type**    string

| Remarks | *index* is an expression of type word. *ParamStr* returns the *index*th parameter from the command line, or an empty string if *index* is zero or greater than *ParamCount*. |
|---|---|
| See also | *ParamCount* |

**Example**

```
var i: word;
begin
  for i := 1 to ParamCount do
    Writeln(ParamStr(i));
end.
```

# Pi function

| Function | Returns the value of Pi (3.1415926535897932385). |
|---|---|
| Declaration | Pi |
| Result type | real |
| Remarks | Precision varies, depending on whether the compiler is in 8087 (80287, 80387) or software-only mode. |
| Differences | In 3.0, *Pi* was a constant. |

# PieSlice procedure          Graph

| Function | Draws and fills a pie slice, using (*X,Y*) as the center point and drawing from start angle to end angle. |
|---|---|
| Declaration | PieSlice(x, y: integer; StAngle, EndAngle, Radius: word) |
| Remarks | The pie slice is outlined using the current color, and filled using the pattern and color defined by *SetFillStyle* or *SetFillPattern*. |
| | Each graphics driver contains an aspect ratio that is used by *Circle*, *Arc*, and *PieSlice*. A start angle of 0 and an end angle of 360 will draw and fill a complete circle. The angles for *Arc*, *Ellipse*, and *PieSlice* are counterclockwise with 0 degrees at 3 o'clock, 90 degrees at 12 o'clock, and so on. |
| | If an error occurs while filling the pie slice, *GraphResult* will return a value of –6 (*grNoScanMem*). |
| Restrictions | Must be in graphics mode. |

**See also**    *Arc, Circle, Ellipse, GetArcCoords, GetAspectRatio,*
*SetFillStyle, SetFillPattern, SetGraphBufSize*

**Example**
```
uses Graph;
const
  Radius = 30;
var
  Gd, Gm: integer;

begin
  Gd := Detect;
  InitGraph(Gd, Gm, '');
  if GraphResult <> grOk then
    Halt(1);
  PieSlice(100, 100, 0, 270, Radius);
  Readln;
  CloseGraph;
end.
```

# Pos function

**Function**       Searches for a substring in a string.

**Declaration**    `Pos(substr, s: string)`

**Result type**    byte

**Remarks**        *substr* and *s* are string-type expressions. *Pos* searches for
*substr* within *s,* and returns an integer value that is the
index of the first character of *substr* within *s.* If *substr* is
not found, *Pos* returns zero.

**Example**
```
var s: string;
begin
  s := '   123.5';
  { Convert spaces to zeroes }
  while Pos(' ', s) > 0 do
    s[Pos(' ', s)] := '0';
end.
```

# Pred function

**Function**       Returns the predecessor of the argument.

**Declaration**    `Pred(x)`

**Result type**    Same type as parameter.

| | |
|---|---|
| **Remarks** | *x* is an ordinal-type expression. The result, of the same type as *x*, is the predecessor of *x*. |
| **See also** | *Succ, Dec, Inc* |

# Ptr function

| | |
|---|---|
| **Function** | Converts a segment base and an offset address to a pointer-type value. |
| **Declaration** | `Ptr(seg, ofs: word)` |
| **Result type** | pointer |
| **Remarks** | *seg* and *ofs* are expressions of type word. The result is a pointer that points to the address given by *seg* and *ofs*. Like **nil**, the result of *Ptr* is assignment compatible with all pointer types. |
| | The function result may be dereferenced: |

```
if Ptr($40, $49)^ = 7 then
  Writeln('Video mode = mono');
```

| | |
|---|---|
| **See also** | *Addr* |
| **Example** | |

```
var p: ^byte;
begin
  p := Ptr($40, $49);
  Writeln('Current video mode is ', p^);
end.
```

# PutImage procedure                           Graph

| | |
|---|---|
| **Function** | Puts a bit image onto the screen. |
| **Declaration** | `PutImage(x, y: integer; var BitMap; BitBlt: word)` |
| **Remarks** | (*x,y*) is the upper left corner of a rectangular region on the screen. *BitMap* is an untyped parameter that contains the height and width of the region, and the bit image that will be put onto the screen. *BitBlt* specifies which binary operator will be used to put the bit image onto the screen. |

The following constants are defined:

```
const
  NormalPut  = 0;     { MOV }
  XORPut     = 1;     { XOR }
  OrPut      = 2;     { OR  }
  AndPut     = 3;     { AND }
  NotPut     = 4;     { NOT }
```

Each constant corresponds to a binary operation. For example, *PutImage(x,y,BitMap,NormalPut)* puts the image stored in *BitMap* at (*x,y*) using the assembly language MOV instruction for each byte in the image.

Similarly, *PutImage(x,y,BitMap,XORPut)* puts the image stored in *BitMap* at (*x,y*) using the assembly language XOR instruction for each byte in the image. This is an often-used animation technique for "dragging" an image around the screen.

*PutImage(x,y,Bitmap,NotPut)* inverts the bits in *BitMap* and then puts the image stored in *BitMap* at (*x, y*) using the assembly language MOV for each byte in the image. Thus, the image appears in inverse video of the original *BitMap*.

Note that *PutImage* is never clipped to the viewport boundary. Moreover—with one exception—it is not actually clipped at the screen edge either. Instead, if any part of the image would go off the screen, no image is output. In the following example, the first image would be output, but the middle three *PutImage* statements would have no effect:

```
program NoClip;
uses graph;
var
  Driver, Mode: integer;
  p: pointer;

begin
  Driver := Detect;
  InitGraph(Driver, Mode, '');
  if GraphResult < 0 then
    Halt(1);
  SetViewPort(0, 0, GetMaxX, GetMaxY, clipon);
  GetMem(p, ImageSize(0, 0, 99, 49));
  PieSlice(50, 25, 0, 360, 45);
  GetImage(0, 0, 99, 49, p^);      { Width = 100, height = 50 }
```

```
    ClearDevice;
    PutImage(GetMaxX - 99, 0,                    { Will barely fit }
            p^, NormalPut);
    PutImage(GetMaxX - 98, 0,              { x + height > GetMaxX }
            p^, NormalPut);
    PutImage(-1, 0,                        { -1,0 not on screen }
            p^, NormalPut);
    PutImage(0, -1,                        { 0,-1 not on screen }
            p^, NormalPut);
    PutImage(0, GetMaxY - 30,             { Will output 31 "lines" }
            p^, NormalPut);
    Readln;
    CloseGraph;
end.
```

In the last *PutImage* statement, the height is clipped at the lower screen edge, and a partial image is displayed. This is the only time any clipping is performed on *PutImage* output.

**Restrictions**    Must be in graphics mode.

**See also**    *GetImage, ImageSize*

**Example**
```
uses Graph;
var
  Gd, Gm: integer;
  P: pointer;
  Size: word;

begin
  Gd := Detect;
  InitGraph(Gd, Gm, '');
  if GraphResult <> grOk then
    Halt(1);
  Bar(0, 0, GetMaxX, GetMaxY);
  Size := ImageSize(10,20,30,40);
  GetMem(P, Size);                    { Allocate memory on heap }
  GetImage(10,20,30,40,P^);
  Readln;
  ClearDevice;
  PutImage(100, 100, P^, NormalPut);
  Readln;
  CloseGraph;
end.
```

# PutPixel procedure                                Graph

**Function**       Plots a pixel at *x,y*.

**Declaration**    `PutPixel(x, y: integer; Pixel: word)`

**Remarks**        Plots a point in the color defined by *Pixel* at *(x,y)*.

**Restrictions**   Must be in graphics mode.

**See also**       *GetImage, GetPixel, PutImage*

**Example**
```
uses Crt, Graph;
var
  Gd, Gm: integer;
  Color : word;

begin
  Gd := Detect;
  InitGraph(Gd, Gm, '');
  if GraphResult <> grOk then
    Halt(1);
  Color := GetMaxColor;
  Randomize;
  repeat
    PutPixel(Random(100),Random(100),Color);   { Plot "stars" }
    Delay(10);
  until KeyPressed;
  Readln;
  CloseGraph;
end.
```

# Random function

**Function**       Returns a random number.

**Declaration**    `Random [ ( range: word) ]`

**Result type**    real or word, depending on the parameter

**Remarks**        If *range* is not specified, the result is a *Real* random number within the range equals $x < 1$. If *range* is specified, it must be an expression of type integer, and the result is a word random number within the range equals $x < range$. If *range* equals 0, a value of 0 will be returned.

The *Random* number generator should be initialized by making a call to *Randomize*.

**See also**    *Randomize*

**Example**
```
uses Crt;
begin
  Randomize;
  repeat
    { Write text in random colors }
    TextAttr := Random(256);
    Write('!');
  until KeyPressed;
end.
```

# Randomize procedure

**Function**    Initializes the built-in random generator with a random value.

**Declaration**    `Randomize`

**Remarks**    The random value is obtained from the system clock.

**Note:** The random-number generator's seed is stored in a predeclared longint variable called *RandSeed*. By assigning a specific value to *RandSeed*, a specific sequence of random numbers can be generated over and over. This is particularly useful in applications that use data encryption.

**See also**    *Random*

# Read procedure (text files)

**Function**    Reads one or more values from a text file into one or more variables.

**Declaration**    `Read( [ var f: text; ] v1 [, v2,...,vn ] )`

**Remarks**    *f*, if specified, is a text-file variable. If *f* is omitted, the standard file variable *Input* is assumed. Each *v* is a variable of type char, integer, real, or string.

With a type char variable, *Read* reads one character from the file and assigns that character to the variable. If *Eof(f)* was True before *Read* was executed, the value *Chr(26)* (a *Ctrl-Z* character) is assigned to the variable. If *Eoln(f)* was True, the value *Chr(13)* (a carriage-return character) is assigned to the variable. The next *Read* will start with the next character in the file.

With a type integer variable, *Read* expects a sequence of characters that form a signed number, according to the syntax shown in the section "Numbers" in Chapter 13, "Tokens and Constants." Any blanks, tabs, or end-of-line markers preceding the numeric string are skipped. Reading ceases at the first blank, tab, or end-of-line marker following the numeric string or if *Eof(f)* becomes True. If the numeric string does not conform to the expected format, an I/O error occurs; otherwise, the value is assigned to the variable. If *Eof(f)* was True before *Read* was executed or if *Eof(f)* becomes True while skipping initial blanks, tabs, and end-of-line markers, the value 0 is assigned to the variable. The next *Read* will start with the blank, tab, or end-of-line marker that terminated the numeric string.

With a type real variable, *Read* expects a sequence of characters that form a signed whole number, according to the syntax shown in the section "Numbers" in Chapter 13, "Tokens and Constants" (except that hexadecimal notation is not allowed). Any blanks, tabs, or end-of-line markers preceding the numeric string are skipped. Reading ceases at the first blank, tab, or end-of-line marker following the numeric string or if *Eof(f)* becomes True. If the numeric string does not conform to the expected format, an I/O error occurs; otherwise, the value is assigned to the variable. If *Eof(f)* was True before *Read* was executed, or if *Eof(f)* becomes True while skipping initial blanks, tabs, and end-of-line markers, the value 0 is assigned to the variable. The next *Read* will start with the blank, tab, or end-of-line marker that terminated the numeric string.

With a type string variable, *Read* reads all characters up to, but not including, the next end-of-line marker or until *Eof(f)* becomes True. The resulting character string is assigned to the variable. If the resulting string is longer than the maximum length of the string variable, it is truncated. The next *Read* will start with the end-of-line marker that terminated the string.

With {$I-}, *IOResult* will return a 0 if the operation was successful; otherwise, it will return a nonzero error code.

**Restrictions**  *Read* with a type string variable does not skip to the next line after reading. For this reason, you cannot use successive *Read* calls to read a sequence of strings, since you will never get past the first line; after the first *Read*, each subsequent *Read* will see the end-of-line marker and return a zero-length string. Instead, use multiple *Readln* calls to read successive string values.

**Differences**  See Appendix A.

**See also**  *Readln, ReadKey*

## Read procedure (typed files)

**Function**  Reads a file component into a variable.

**Declaration**  Read(f , v1 [, v2,...,vn ] )

**Remarks**  *f* is a file variable of any type except text, and each *v* is a variable of the same type as the component type of *f*. For each variable read, the current file position is advanced to the next component. It's an error to attempt to read from a file when the current file position is at the end of the file, that is, when *Eof(f)* is True.

With {$I-}, *IOResult* will return a 0 if the operation was successful; otherwise, it will return a nonzero error code.

**Restrictions**  File must be open.

**See also**  *Write*

## ReadKey function                                                    Crt

**Function**  Reads a character from the keyboard.

**Declaration**  ReadKey

**Result type**  char

**Remarks**  The character read is not echoed to the screen. If *KeyPressed* was True before the call to *ReadKey*, the character is returned immediately. Otherwise, *ReadKey* waits for a key to be typed.

The special keys on the PC keyboard generate extended scan codes. (The extended scan codes are summarized in Appendix E.) Special keys are the function keys, the cursor control keys, *Alt* keys, and so on. When a special key is pressed, *ReadKey* first returns a null character (#0), and then returns the extended scan code. Null characters cannot be generated in any other way, so you are guaranteed the next character will be an extended scan code.

The following program fragment reads a character or an extended scan code into a variable called *Ch* and sets a Boolean variable called *FuncKey* to True if the character is a special key:

```
Ch := ReadKey;
if Ch <> #0 then FuncKey := False else
begin
  FuncKey := True;
  Ch := ReadKey;
end;
```

The *CheckBreak* variable controls whether *Ctrl-Break* should abort the program or be returned like any other key. When *CheckBreak* is False, *ReadKey* returns a *Ctrl-C* (#3) for *Ctrl-Break*.

**See also**          *KeyPressed*

# Readln procedure

**Function**          Executes the *Read* procedure then skips to the next line of the file.

**Declaration**       Readln( [ **var** f: text; ] v1 [, v2,...,vn ] )

**Remarks**           *Readln* is an extension to *Read*, as it is defined on text files. After executing the *Read*, *Readln* skips to the beginning of the next line of the file.

*Readln(f)* with no parameters causes the current file position to advance to the beginning of the next line (if there is one; otherwise, it goes to the end of the file).

*Readln* with no parameter list altogether corresponds to *Readln(Input)*.

With {$I-}, *IOResult* will return a 0 if the operation was successful; otherwise, it will return a nonzero error code.

**Restrictions**    Works only on text files, including standard input. File must be open for input.

**See also**    *Read*

# Rectangle procedure                          Graph

**Function**       Draws a rectangle using the current line style and color.

**Declaration**    `Rectangle(x1, y1, x2, y2: integer)`

**Remarks**        *(x1, y1)* define the upper left corner of the rectangle, and *(x2, y2)* define the lower right corner (0 <= x1 < x2 <= *GetMaxX*, and 0 <= y1 < y2 <= *GetMaxY*).

The rectangle will be drawn in the current line style and color, as set by *SetLineStyle* and *SetColor*.

**Restrictions**   Must be in graphics mode.

**See also**       *Bar, Bar3D, SetLineStyle, SetColor*

**Example**
```
uses Crt, Graph;
var
  GraphDriver, GraphMode: integer;
  x1, y1, x2, y2: integer;

begin
  GraphDriver := Detect;
  InitGraph(GraphDriver,GraphMode,'');
  if GraphResult<> grOk then
    Halt(1);
  Randomize;
  repeat
    x1 := Random(GetMaxX);
    y1 := Random(GetMaxY);
    x2 := Random(GetMaxX-x1) + x1;
    y2 := Random(GetMaxY-y1) + y1;
    Rectangle(x1, y1, x2, y2);
  until KeyPressed;
  CloseGraph;
end.
```

# RegisterBGIdriver function      Graph

**Function**

Registers a user-loaded or linked-in BGI driver with the graphics system.

**Declaration**

`RegisterBGIdriver(driver: pointer) : integer;`

**Remarks**

If an error occurs, the return value is less than 0; otherwise, the internal driver number is returned. This routine enables a user to load a driver file and "register" the driver by passing its memory location to *RegisterBGIdriver*. When that driver is used by *InitGraph*, the registered driver will be used (instead of being loaded from disk by the *Graph* unit). A user-registered driver can be loaded from disk onto the heap, or converted to an .OBJ file (using BINOBJ.EXE) and linked into the .EXE.

*grInvalidDriver* is a possible error return, where the error code equals –4 and the driver header is not recognized.

The following program loads the CGA driver onto the heap, registers it with the graphics system, and calls *InitGraph*:

```
program LoadDriv;
uses Graph;
var
  Driver, Mode: integer;
  DriverF: file;
  DriverP: pointer;

begin
  { Open driver file, read into memory, register it }
  Assign(DriverF, 'CGA.BGI');
  Reset(DriverF, 1);
  GetMem(DriverP, FileSize(DriverF));
  BlockRead(DriverF, DriverP^, FileSIze(DriverF));
  if RegisterBGIdriver(DriverP) < 0 then
  begin
    Writeln('Error registering driver: ',
            GraphErrorMsg(GraphResult));
    Halt(1);
  end;

  { Init graphics }
  Driver := CGA;
  Mode := CGAHi;
```

```
InitGraph(Driver, Mode, '');
if GraphResult < 0 then
  Halt(1);
OutText('Driver loaded by user program');
Readln;
CloseGraph;
end.
```

The program begins by loading the CGA driver file from disk and registering it with the *Graph* unit. Then a call is made to *InitGraph* to initialize the graphics system. You may wish to incorporate one or more driver files directly into your .EXE file. In this way, the graphics drivers that your program needs will be built-in and only the .EXE will be needed in order to run. The process for incorporating a driver file into your .EXE is straightforward:

1. Run BINOBJ on the driver file(s).
2. Link the resulting .OBJ file(s) into your program.
3. Register the linked-in driver file(s) before calling *InitGraph*.

For a detailed explanation and example of the preceding, refer to the comments at the top of the GRLINK.PAS example program on Disk 3. Documentation on the BINOBJ utility is contained in a file named BINOBJ.DOC on Disk 2.

It is also possible to register font files; refer to the description of *RegisterBGIfont*.

**Restrictions**   Note that the driver must be registered *before* the call to *InitGraph*. If a call is made to *RegisterBGIdriver* once graphics have been activated, a value of –11 (*grError*) will be returned.

**See also**   *InitGraph*

# RegisterBGIfont function                          Graph

**Function**   Registers a user-loaded or linked-in BGI font with the graphics system.

**Declaration**   `RegisterBGIfont(font: pointer) : integer;`

**Remarks**     The return value is less than 0 if an error occurs; otherwise, the internal font number is returned. This routine enables a user to load a font file and "register" the font by passing its memory location to *RegisterBGIfont*. When that font is selected with a call to *SetTextStyle*, the registered font will be used (instead of being loaded from disk by the *Graph* unit). A user-registered font can be loaded from disk onto the heap, or converted to an .OBJ file (using BINOBJ.EXE) and linked into the .EXE.

Here are some possible error returns:

| Error Code | Error Identifier | Comments |
|---|---|---|
| –11 | grError | There is no room in the font table to register another font. (The font table holds up to 10 fonts, and only 4 are provided, so this error should not occur.) |
| –13 | grInvalidFont | The font header is not recognized. |
| –14 | grInvalidFontNum | The font number in the font header is not recognized. |

The following program loads the triplex font onto the heap, registers it with the graphics system, and then alternates between using triplex and another stroked font that *Graph* loads from disk (*SansSerifFont*):

```
program LoadFont;
uses Graph;
var
  Driver, Mode: integer;
  FontF: file;
  FontP: pointer;

begin
  { Open font file, read into memory, register it }
  Assign(FontF, 'TRIP.CHR');
  Reset(FontF, 1);
  GetMem(FontP, FileSize(FontF));
  BlockRead(FontF, FontP^, FileSize(FontF));
  if RegisterBGIfont(FontP) < 0 then
```

```
begin
  Writeln('Error registering font: ',
        GraphErrorMsg(GraphResult));
  Halt(1);
end;

{ Init graphics }
Driver := Detect;
InitGraph(Driver, Mode, '..\');
if GraphResult < 0 then
  Halt(1);
Readln;

{ Select registered font }
SetTextStyle(TriplexFont, HorizDir, 4);
OutText('Triplex loaded by user program');
MoveTo(0, TextHeight('a'));
Readln;

{ Select font that must be loaded from disk }
SetTextStyle(SansSerifFont, HorizDir, 4);
OutText('Your disk should be spinning...');
MoveTo(0, GetY + TextHeight('a'));
Readln;

{ Re-select registered font (already in memory) }
SetTextStyle(TriplexFont, HorizDir, 4);
OutText('Back to Triplex');
Readln;
CloseGraph;
end.
```

The program begins by loading the triplex font file from disk and registering it with the *Graph* unit. Then a call to *InitGraph* is made to initialize the graphics system. Watch the disk drive indicator and press *Enter*. Because the triplex font is already loaded into memory and registered, *Graph* does not have to load it from disk (and therefore your disk drive should not spin). Next, the program will activate the sans serif font by loading it from disk (it is unregistered). Press *Enter* again and watch the drive spin. Finally, the triplex font is selected again. Since it is in memory and already registered, the drive will not spin when you press *Enter*.

There are several reasons to load and register font files. First, *Graph* only keeps one stroked font in memory at a time. If you have a program that needs to quickly alternate between stroked fonts, you may want to load and register the fonts yourself at the beginning of your program. Then *Graph* will not load and unload the fonts each time a call to *SetTextStyle* is made.

Second, you may wish to incorporate the font files directly into your .EXE file. This way, the font files that your program needs will be built-in, and only the .EXE and driver files will be needed in order to run. The process for incorporating a font file into your .EXE is straightforward:

1. Run BINOBJ on the font file(s).
2. Link the resulting .OBJ file(s) into your program.
3. Register the linked-in font file(s) before calling *InitGraph*.

For a detailed explanation and example of the preceding, refer to the comments at the top of the GRLINK.PAS example program on Disk 3. Documentation on the BINOBJ utility is contained in a file named BINOBJ.DOC on Disk 2.

Note that the default (8×8 bit-mapped) font is built into GRAPH.TPU, and thus is always in memory. Once a stroked font has been loaded, your program can alternate between the default font and the stroked font without having to reload either one of them.

It is also possible to register driver files; refer to the description of *RegisterBGIdriver*.

**See also**          *SetTextStyle*

# Release procedure

**Function**          Returns the heap to a given state.

**Declaration**       `Release(var p: pointer)`

**Remarks**           *p* is a pointer variable of any pointer type that was previously assigned by the *Mark* procedure. *Release* disposes all dynamic variables that were allocated by *New* or *GetMem* since *p* was assigned by *Mark*.

**Restrictions**      *Mark* and *Release* cannot be used interchangeably with *Dispose* and *FreeMem* unless certain rules are observed.

For a complete discussion of this topic, refer to the section entitled "The Heap Manager" in Chapter 26.

**See also**      *Mark, Dispose, FreeMem*

# Rename procedure

**Function**        Renames an external file.

**Declaration**     Rename(f; newname: **string**)

**Remarks**         *f* is a file variable of any file type. *newname* is a string-type expression. The external file associated with *f* is renamed to *newname*. Further operations on *f* will operate on the external file with the new name.

With {$I-}, *IOResult* will return 0 if the operation was successful; otherwise, it will return a nonzero error code.

**Restrictions**    *Rename* must never be used on an open file.

**See also**        *Erase*

# Reset procedure

**Function**        Opens an existing file.

**Declaration**     Reset(f [ : **file**; recsize: word ] )

**Remarks**         *f* is a file variable of any file type, which must have been associated with an external file using *Assign*. *recsize* is an optional expression of type word, which can only be specified if *f* is an untyped file.

*Reset* opens the existing external file with the name assigned to *f*. It's an error if no existing external file of the given name exists. If *f* was already open, it is first closed and then re-opened. The current file position is set to the beginning of the file.

If *f* was assigned an empty name, such as *Assign(f,")*, then after the call to *Reset*, *f* will refer to the standard input file (standard handle number 0).

If *f* is a text file, *f* becomes read-only. After a call to *Reset*, *Eof(f)* is True if the file is empty; otherwise, *Eof(f)* is False.

If *f* is an untyped file, *recsize* specifies the record size to be used in data transfers. If *recsize* is omitted, a default record size of 128 bytes is assumed.

With {*$I-*}, *IOResult* will return a 0 if the operation was successful; otherwise, it will return a nonzero error code.

**Differences**  In 3.0, an empty file name was invalid.

**See also**  *Rewrite, Append, Assign*

**Example**
```
function FileExists(FileName: string): boolean;
{ Boolean function that returns True if the file exists;
  otherwise, it returns False. Closes the file if it exists. }
var
  f: file;

begin
  {$I-}
  Assign(f, FileName);
  Reset(f);
  Close(f);
  {$I+}
  FileExists := (IOResult = 0) and (FileName <> '');
end;  { FileExists }

begin
  if FileExists(ParamStr(1)) then { Get file name from command
                                                           line }
    Writeln('File exists')
  else
    Writeln('File not found');
end.
```

# RestoreCrtMode procedure            Graph

**Function**  Restores the screen mode to its original state before graphics was initialized.

**Declaration**  `RestoreCrtMode`

**Remarks**  Restores the original video mode detected by *InitGraph*. Can be used in conjunction with *SetGraphMode* to switch back and forth between text and graphics modes.

**Restrictions**  Must be in graphics mode.

**See also**  *DetectGraph, InitGraph, SetGraphMode*

```
uses Graph;
var
  Gd, Gm: integer;
  Mode  : integer;

begin
  Gd := Detect;
  InitGraph(Gd, Gm, '');
  if GraphResult <> grOk then
    Halt(1);
  OutText('<RETURN> to leave graphics:');
  Readln;
  RestoreCRTMode;
  Writeln('Now in text mode');
  Write('<RETURN> to enter graphics mode:');
  Readln;
  SetGraphMode(GetGraphMode);
  OutTextXY(0, 0, 'Back in graphics mode');
  OutTextXY(0, TextHeight('H'), '<RETURN> to quit:');
  Readln;
  CloseGraph;
end.
```

# Rewrite procedure

**Function**      Creates and opens a new file.

**Declaration**   `Rewrite(f [ : file; recsize: word ] )`

**Remarks**       *f* is a file variable of any file type, which must have been associated with an external file using *Assign*. *recsize* is an optional expression of type word, which can only be specified if *f* is an untyped file.

*Rewrite* creates a new external file with the name assigned to *f*. If an external file with the same name already exists, it is deleted and a new empty file is created in its place. If *f* was already open, it is first closed and then re-created. The current file position is set to the beginning of the empty file.

If *f* was assigned an empty name, such as *Assign(f,'')*, then after the call to *Rewrite*, *f* will refer to the standard output file (standard handle number 1).

If *f* is a text file, *f* becomes write-only. After a call to *Rewrite, Eof(f)* is always True.

If *f* is an untyped file, *recsize* specifies the record size to be used in data transfers. If *recsize* is omitted, a default record size of 128 bytes is assumed.

With {*$I-*}, *IOResult* will return a 0 if the operation was successful; otherwise, it will return a nonzero error code.

**Differences**    In 3.0, an empty file name was invalid.

**See also**    *Reset, Append, Assign*

**Example**
```
var f: text;
begin
  Assign(f, 'NEWFILE.$$$');
  Rewrite(f);
  Writeln(f,'Just created file with this text in it...');
  Close(f);
end.
```

# RmDir procedure

**Function**    Removes an empty subdirectory.

**Declaration**    RmDir(s: **string**)

**Remarks**    *s* is a string-type expression. The subdirectory with the path specified by *s* is removed. If the path does not exist, is non-empty, or is the currently logged directory, an I/O error will occur.

With {*$I-*}, *IOResult* will return a 0 if the operation was successful; otherwise, it will return a nonzero error code.

**See also**    *MkDir, ChDir, GetDir*

**Example**
```
begin
  {$I-}
  { Get directory name from command line }
  RmDir(ParamStr(1));
  if IOResult <> 0 then
    Writeln('Cannot remove directory')
  else
    Writeln('directory removed');
end.
```

# Round function

| | |
|---|---|
| **Function** | Rounds a real-type value to an integer-type value. |
| **Declaration** | `Round(x: real)` |
| **Result type** | longint |
| **Remarks** | *x* is a real-type expression. *Round* returns a longint value that is the value of *x* rounded to the nearest whole number. If *x* is exactly halfway between two whole numbers, the result is the number with the greatest absolute magnitude. A runtime error occurs if the rounded value of *x* is not within the longint range. |
| **Differences** | In 3.0, *Round* returned an integer value. |
| **See also** | *Trunc, Int* |

# Seek procedure

| | |
|---|---|
| **Function** | Moves the current position of a file to a specified component. |
| **Declaration** | `Seek(f; n: longint)` |
| **Remarks** | *f* is any file variable type except text, and *n* is an expression of type longint. The current file position of *f* is moved to component number *n*. The number of the first component of a file is 0. In order to expand a file, it is possible to seek one component beyond the last component; that is, the statement *Seek(f,FileSize(f))* moves the current file position to the end of the file. |
| | With {$I-}, *IOResult* will return a 0 if the operation was successful; otherwise, it will return a nonzero error code. |
| **Restrictions** | Cannot be used on text files. File must be open. |
| **Differences** | In 3.0, *n* was an integer; *LongSeek* took a real number value for *n*. |
| **See also** | *FilePos* |

# SeekEof function

**Function**  Returns the end-of-file status of a file.

**Declaration**  SeekEof [ (**var** f: text) ]

**Result type**  boolean

**Remarks**  *SeekEof* corresponds to *Eof* except that it skips all blanks, tabs, and end-of-line markers before returning the end-of-file status. This is useful when reading numeric values from a text file.

With {$I-}, *IOResult* will return a 0 if the operation was successful; otherwise, it will return a nonzero error code.

**Restrictions**  Can only be used on text files. File must be open.

**See also**  *Eof, SeekEoln*

# SeekEoln function

**Function**  Returns the end-of-line status of a file.

**Declaration**  SeekEoln [ (**var** f: text) ]

**Result type**  boolean

**Remarks**  *SeekEoln* corresponds to *Eoln* except that it skips all blanks and tabs before returning the end-of-line status. This is useful when reading numeric values from a text file.

With {$I-}, *IOResult* will return a 0 if the operation was successful; otherwise, it will return a nonzero error code.

**Restrictions**  Can only be used on text files. File must be open.

**See also**  *Eoln, SeekEof*

# Seg function

**Function**  Returns the segment of a specified object.

**Declaration**  Seg(x)

**Result type**  word

| Remarks | $x$ is any variable, or a procedure or function identifier. The result, of type word, is the segment part of the address of $x$. |
|---|---|
| See also | *Ofs, Addr* |

# SetActivePage procedure                          Graph

| Function | Set the active page for graphics output. |
|---|---|
| Declaration | SetActivePage(Page: word) |
| Remarks | Makes *Page* the active graphics page. All graphics output will now be directed to *Page*. |

Multiple pages are only supported by the EGA (256K), VGA, and Hercules graphics cards. With multiple graphics pages, a program can direct graphics output to an off-screen page, then quickly display the off-screen image by changing the visual page with the *SetVisualPage* procedure. This technique is especially useful for animation.

| Restrictions | Must be in graphics mode. |
|---|---|
| See also | *SetVisualPage* |
| Example | |

```
uses Graph;
var
  Gd, Gm: integer;

begin
  Gd := Detect;
  InitGraph(Gd, Gm, '');
  if GraphResult <> grOk then
    Halt(1);
  if (Gd=HercMono) or (Gd=EGA) or
     (Gd=EGA64) or (Gd=VGA) then
    begin
      SetVisualPage(0);
      SetActivePage(1);
      Rectangle(10, 20, 30, 40);
      SetVisualPage(1);
    end
  else
    OutText('No paging supported.');
  Readln;
  CloseGraph;
```

```
   end.
```

# SetAllPalette procedure        Graph

**Function**       Changes all palette colors as specified.

**Declaration**    SetAllPalette(**var** Palette)

**Remarks**        *Palette* is an untyped parameter. The first byte is the length of the palette. The next *n* bytes will replace the current palette colors. Each color may range from –1 to 15. A value of –1 will not change the previous entry's value.

Note that valid colors depend on the current graphics driver and current graphics mode.

If invalid input is passed to *SetAllPalette*, *GraphResult* will return a value of –11 (*grError*), and no changes to the palette settings will occur.

Changes made to the palette are seen immediately on the screen. In the example listed here, several lines are drawn on the screen, then the palette is changed. Each time a palette color is changed, all occurrences of that color on the screen will be changed to the new color value.

The following types and constants are defined:

```
const
  Black        =  0;
  Blue         =  1;
  Green        =  2;
  Cyan         =  3;
  Red          =  4;
  Magenta      =  5;
  Brown        =  6;
  LightGray    =  7;
  DarkGray     =  8;
  LightBlue    =  9;
  LightGreen   = 10;
  LightCyan    = 11;
  LightRed     = 12;
  LightMagenta = 13;
  Yellow       = 14;
  White        = 15;
  MaxColors    = 15;
```

```
type
  PaletteType  = record
                   Size: byte;
                   Colors: array[0...MaxColors] of shortint;
                 end;
```

**Restrictions**   Must be in graphics mode.

**See also**   *GetBkColor, GetColor, GetPalette, SetBkColor, SetColor, SetPalette, GraphResult*

**Example**

```
uses Graph;
var
  Gd, Gm : integer;
  Palette: PaletteType;

begin
  Gd := Detect;
  InitGraph(Gd, Gm, '');
  if GraphResult <> grOk then
    Halt(1);
  Line(0, 0, GetMaxX, GetMaxY);
  with Palette do
  begin
    Size       := 4;
    Colors[0] := 5;
    Colors[1] := 3;
    Colors[2] := 1;
    Colors[3] := 2;
    SetAllPalette(Palette);
  end;
  Readln;
  CloseGraph;
end.
```

# SetBkColor procedure                          Graph

**Function**   Sets the current background color using the palette.

**Declaration**   SetBkColor(Color: word)

**Remarks**   Background colors may range from 0 to 15, depending on the current graphics driver and current graphics mode. On a CGA, *SetBkColor* sets the flood overscan color.

*SetBkColor(N)* makes the *N*th color in the palette the new background color. The only exception is *setBkColor(0)*, which always sets the background color to black.

**Restrictions**     Must be in graphics mode.

**See also**     *GetBkColor, GetColor, GetPalette, SetAllPalette, SetColor, SetPalette*

**Example**
```
uses Crt, Graph;
var
  GraphDriver, GraphMode: integer;
  Palette: PaletteType;

begin
  GraphDriver := Detect;
  InitGraph(GraphDriver,GraphMode,'');
  Randomize;
  if GraphResult <> grOk then
    Halt(1);
  GetPalette(Palette);
  repeat
    if Palette.Size <> 1 then
      SetBkColor(Random(Palette.Size));
    LineTo(Random(GetMaxX),Random(GetMaxY));
  until KeyPressed;
  CloseGraph;
end.
```

# SetColor procedure                          Graph

**Function**     Sets the current drawing color using the palette.

**Declaration**     `SetColor(Color: word)`

**Remarks**     *SetColor(5)* makes the fifth color in the palette the current drawing color. Drawing colors may range from 0 to 15, depending on the current graphics driver and current graphics mode.

*GetMaxColor* returns the highest valid color for the current driver and mode.

**Restrictions**     Must be in graphics mode.

**See also**     *GetBkColor, GetColor, GetPalette, SetAllPalette, SetBkColor, SetPalette, GraphResult, GetMaxColor*

```
uses Crt, Graph;
var
  GraphDriver, GraphMode: integer;

begin
  GraphDriver := Detect;
  InitGraph(GraphDriver, GraphMode, '');
  if GraphResult <> grOk then
    Halt(1);
  Randomize;
  repeat
    SetColor(Random(GetMaxColor)+1);
    LineTo(Random(GetMaxX),Random(GetMaxY));
  until KeyPressed;
end.
```

# SetDate procedure                               Dos

**Function**      Sets the current date in the operating system.

**Declaration**   SetDate(Year, Month, Day, DayofWeek: word)

**Remarks**       Valid parameter ranges are *Year* 1980..2099, *Month* 1..12, and *Day* 1..31. If the date is invalid, the request is ignored.

**See also**      *GetDate, GetTime, SetTime*

# SetFAttr procedure                              Dos

**Function**      Sets the attributes of a file.

**Declaration**   SetFAttr(**var** f; Attr: word)

**Remarks**       *f* must be a file variable (typed, untyped, or text file) that has been assigned but not opened. The attribute value is formed by adding the appropriate attribute masks defined as constants in the *Dos* unit.

```
const
  { File attribute constants }
  ReadOnly  = $01;
  Hidden    = $02;
  SysFile   = $04;
  VolumeID  = $08;
  Directory = $10;
```

```
        Archive  = $20;
        AnyFile  = $3F;
```

Errors are reported in *DosError*; possible error codes are 3 (Invalid Path) and 5 (File Access Denied).

**Restrictions**    *f* cannot be open.

**See also**    *GetFAttr, GetFTime, SetFTime*

**Example**
```
uses Dos;
var
  f: file;

begin
  Assign(f, 'C:\AUTOEXEC.BAT');
  SetFAttr(f, Hidden);                            {Uh-oh}
  Readln;
  SetFAttr(f, Archive);                           { Whew!}
end.
```

# SetFillPattern procedure                        Graph

**Function**    Selects a user-defined fill pattern.

**Declaration**    `SetFillPattern(Pattern: FillPatternType; Color: word)`

**Remarks**    Sets the pattern and color for all filling done by *FillPoly*, *FloodFill*, *Bar*, *Bar3D*, and *PieSlice* to the bit pattern specified in *Pattern* and the color specified by *Color*. If invalid input is passed to *SetFillPattern*, *GraphResult* will return a value of −11 (*grError*), and the current fill settings will be unchanged. *FillPatternType* is predefined as follows:

```
type
  FillPatternType = array[1..8] of byte;
```

The fill pattern is based on the underlying byte values contained in the *Pattern* array. The pattern array is 8 bytes long with each byte corresponding to 8 pixels in the pattern. Whenever a bit in a pattern byte is valued at 1, a pixel will be plotted. For example, the following pattern represents a checkerboard (50 % gray scale):

| Binary | | Hex | |
|---|---|---|---|
| 10101010 | = | $AA | (1st byte) |
| 01010101 | = | $55 | (2nd byte) |
| 10101010 | = | $AA | (3rd byte) |
| 01010101 | = | $55 | (4th byte) |
| 10101010 | = | $AA | (5th byte) |
| 01010101 | = | $55 | (6th byte) |
| 10101010 | = | $AA | (7th byte) |
| 01010101 | = | $55 | (8th byte) |

User-defined fill patterns enable you to create patterns different from the predefined fill patterns that can be selected with the *SetFillStyle* procedure. Whenever you select a new fill pattern with *SetFillPattern* or *SetFillStyle*, all fill operations will use that fill pattern.

**Restrictions**      Must be in graphics mode.

**See also**      *GraphResult*

**Example**
```
uses Graph;
const
  Gray50: FillPatternType = ($AA,$55,$AA,$55,
                             $AA,$55,$AA,$55);
var
  Gd, Gm: integer;

begin
  Gd := Detect;
  InitGraph(Gd, Gm, '');
  if GraphResult <> grOk then
    Halt(1);
  SetFillPattern(Gray50, White);
  Bar(0, 0, 100, 100);      { Draw a bar in a 50% gray scale }
  Readln;
  CloseGraph;
end.
```

# SetFillStyle procedure                    Graph

**Function**      Sets the fill pattern and color.

**Declaration**      SetFillStyle(Pattern: word; Color: word)

| Remarks | Sets the pattern and color for all filling done by *FillPoly*, *Bar*, *Bar3D*, and *PieSlice*. A variety of fill patterns are available. The default pattern is solid, and the default color is the maximum color in the palette. If invalid input is passed to *SetFillStyle*, *GraphResult* will return a value of –11 (*grError*), and the current fill settings will be unchanged. The following constants are defined: |

```
const
  { Fill patterns for Get/SetFillStyle: }
  EmptyFill     = 0;    { Fills area in background color }
  SolidFill     = 1;    { Fills area in solid fill color }
  LineFill      = 2;                        { --- fill }
  LtSlashFill   = 3;                        { /// fill }
  SlashFill     = 4;         { /// fill with thick lines }
  BkSlashFill   = 5;         { \\\ fill with thick lines }
  LtBkSlashFill = 6;                        { \\\ fill }
  HatchFill     = 7;               { Light hatch fill }
  XHatchFill    = 8;          { Heavy cross hatch fill }
  InterleaveFill = 9;         { Interleaving line fill }
  WideDotFill   = 10;         { Widely spaced dot fill }
  CloseDotFill  = 11;         { Closely spaced dot fill }
```

| Restrictions | Must be in graphics mode. |

| See also | *Bar*, *Bar3D*, *FillPoly*, *GetFillSettings*, *PieSlice*, *GetMaxColor*, *GraphResult* |

| Example | |

```
SetFillStyle(SolidFill,0);
Bar(x1, y1, x2, y2);
SetFillStyle(XHatchFill,1);
Bar(x1, y1, x2, y2);
```

# SetFTime procedure                                      Dos

| Function | Sets the date and time a file was last written. |

| Declaration | SetFTime(**var** f; Time: longint) |

| Remarks | *F* must be a file variable (typed, untyped, or text file) that has been assigned and opened. The *Time* parameter can be created through a call to *PackTime*. Errors are reported in *DosError*; the only possible error code is 6 (Invalid File Handle). |

| Restrictions | *f* must be open. |

See also      *GetFTime, PackTime, UnpackTime*

# SetGraphBufSize procedure     Graph

**Function**     Allows you to change the size of the buffer used for scan and flood fills.

**Declaration**     `SetGraphBufSize(BufSize: word);`

**Remarks**     The internal buffer size is set to *BufSize*, and a buffer is allocated on the heap when a call is made to *InitGraph*.

The default buffer size is 4K, which is large enough to fill a polygon with about 650 vertices. Under rare circumstances, enlarging the buffer may be necessary in order to avoid a buffer overflow.

**Restrictions**     Note that once a call to *InitGraph* has been made, calls to *SetGraphBufSize* are ignored.

**See also**     *FloodFill, FillPoly*

# SetGraphMode procedure     Graph

**Function**     Sets the system to graphics mode and clears the screen.

**Declaration**     `SetGraphMode(Mode: integer)`

**Remarks**     *Mode* must be a valid mode for the current device driver. *SetGraphMode* is used to select a graphics mode different than the default one set by *InitGraph*.

*SetGraphMode* can also be used in conjunction with *RestoreCrtMode* to switch back and forth between text and graphics modes.

*SetGraphMode* resets all graphics settings to their defaults (current pointer, palette, color, viewport, and so forth).

*GetModeRange* returns the lowest and highest valid modes for the current driver.

If an attempt is made to select an invalid mode for the current device driver, *GraphResult* will return a value of −10 (*grInvalidMode*).

The following constants are defined:

| Graphics Driver | Graphics Modes | Value | Column x Row | Palette | Pages |
|---|---|---|---|---|---|
| CGA | CGAC0 | 0 | 320x200 | C0 | 1 |
| | CGAC1 | 1 | 320x200 | C1 | 1 |
| | CGAC2 | 2 | 320x200 | C2 | 1 |
| | CGAC3 | 3 | 320x200 | C3 | 1 |
| | CGAHi | 4 | 640x200 | 2 color | 1 |
| MCGA | MCGAC0 | 0 | 320x200 | C0 | 1 |
| | MCGAC1 | 1 | 320x200 | C1 | 1 |
| | MCGAC2 | 2 | 320x200 | C2 | 1 |
| | MCGAC3 | 3 | 320x200 | C3 | 1 |
| | MCGAMed | 4 | 640x200 | 2 color | 1 |
| | MCGAHi | 5 | 640x480 | 2 color | 1 |
| EGA | EGALo | 0 | 640x200 | 16 color | 4 |
| | EGAHi | 1 | 640x350 | 16 color | 2 |
| EGA64 | EGA64Lo | 0 | 640x200 | 16 color | 1 |
| | EGA64Hi | 1 | 640x350 | 4 color | 1 |
| EGA- | EGAMonoHi | 3 | 640x350 | 2 color | 1* |
| MONO | EGAMonoHi | 3 | 640x350 | 2 color | 2** |
| HERC | HercMonoHi | 0 | 720x348 | 2 color | 2 |
| ATT400 | ATT400C0 | 0 | 320x200 | C0 | 1 |
| | ATT400C1 | 1 | 320x200 | C1 | 1 |
| | ATT400C2 | 2 | 320x200 | C2 | 1 |
| | ATT400C3 | 3 | 320x200 | C3 | 1 |
| | ATT400Med | 4 | 640x200 | 2 color | 1 |
| | ATT400Hi | 5 | 640x400 | 2 color | 1 |
| VGA | VGALo | 0 | 640x200 | 16 color | 2 |
| | VGAMed | 1 | 640x350 | 16 color | 2 |
| | VGAHi | 2 | 640x480 | 16 color | 1 |
| PC3270 | PC3270Hi | 0 | 720x350 | 2 color | 1 |

*   64K on EGAMono card
** 256K on EGAMono card

**Restrictions**   A successful call to *InitGraph* must have been made before calling this routine.

**See also**   *ClearDevice, DetectGraph, GetGraphMode, InitGraph, RestoreCrtMode, GraphResult, GetModeRange*

Example

```
uses Graph;
var
  GraphDriver: integer;
  GraphMode  : integer;
  LowMode    : integer;
  HighMode   : integer;

begin
  GraphDriver := Detect;
  InitGraph(GraphDriver, GraphMode, '');
  if GraphResult <> grOk then
    Halt(1);
  GetModeRange(GraphDriver, LowMode, HighMode);
  SetGraphMode(LowMode);          { Select low-resolution mode }
  Line(0, 0, GetMaxX, GetMaxY);
  Readln;
  CloseGraph;
end.
```

# SetIntVec procedure                                      Dos

**Function**      Sets a specified interrupt vector to a specified address.

**Declaration**   `SetIntVec(IntNo: byte; Vector: pointer)`

**Remarks**       *IntNo* specifies the interrupt vector number (0..255), and
                  *Vector* specifies the address. *Vector* is often constructed
                  with the @ operator to produce the address of an
                  interrupt procedure. Assuming *Int1BSave* is a variable of
                  type pointer, and *Int1BHandler* is an interrupt procedure
                  identifier, the following statement sequence installs a
                  new interrupt $1*B* handler and later restores the original
                  handler:

```
GetIntVec($1B, Int1BSave);
SetIntVec($1B, @Int1BHandler);
  :
  :
SetIntVec($1B, Int1BSave);
```

**See also**      *GetIntVec*

# SetLineStyle procedure                                 Graph

**Function**      Sets the current line width and style.

**Declaration**     SetLineStyle(LineStyle: word; Pattern: word; Thickness: word)

**Remarks**     Affects all lines drawn by *Line, LineTo, Rectangle, DrawPoly, Arc, Circle,* etc. Lines can be drawn solid, dotted, centerline, or dashed. If invalid input is passed to *SetLineStyle, GraphResult* will return a value of −11 (*grError*), and the current line settings will be unchanged. The following constants are declared:

```
const
  SolidLn   = 0;
  DottedLn  = 1;
  CenterLn  = 2;
  DashedLn  = 3;
  UserBitLn = 4;                { User-defined line style }
  NormWidth = 1;
  ThickWidth = 3;
```

*LineStyle* is a value from *SolidLn* to *UserBitLn*(0..4), *Pattern* is ignored unless *LineStyle* equals *UserBitLn,* and *Thickness* is *NormWidth* or *ThickWidth.* When *LineStyle* equals *UserBitLn,* the line is output using the 16-bit pattern defined by the *Pattern* parameter. For example, if *Pattern* = $AAAA, then the 16-bit pattern looks like this:

```
1010101010101010                         { NormWidth }

1010101010101010                         { ThickWidth }
1010101010101010
1010101010101010
```

**Restrictions**     Must be in graphics mode.

**See also**     *GetLineSettings, Line, LineRel, LineTo, GraphResult*

**Example**
```
uses Graph;
var
  Gd, Gm: integer;
  x1, y1, x2, y2: integer;

begin
  Gd := Detect;
  InitGraph(Gd, Gm, '');
  if GraphResult <> grOk then
    Halt(1);
  x1 := 10;
  y1 := 10;
  x2 := 200;
  y2 := 150;
  SetLineStyle(DottedLn, 0, NormWidth);
  Rectangle(x1, y1, x2, y2);
```

```
    SetLineStyle(UserBitLn, $C3, ThickWidth);
    Rectangle(Pred(x1), Pred(y1), Succ(x2), Succ(y2));
    Readln;
    CloseGraph;
end.
```

## SetPalette procedure                              Graph

**Function**          Changes one palette color as specified by *ColorNum* and
                      *Color*.

**Declaration**       SetPalette(ColorNum: word; Color: shortint)

**Remarks**           Changes the *ColorNum* entry in the palette to *Color*.
                      *SetPalette(0,LightCyan)* makes the first color in the palette
                      light cyan. *ColorNum* may range from 0 to 15, depending
                      on the current graphics driver and current graphics
                      mode. If invalid input is passed to *SetPalette*, *GraphResult*
                      will return a value of –11 (*grError*), and the palette will
                      be unchanged.

                      Changes made to the palette are seen immediately on
                      the screen. In the example here, several lines are drawn
                      on the screen, then the palette is changed randomly.
                      Each time a palette color is changed, all occurrences of
                      that color on the screen will be changed to the new color
                      value.

                      The following constants are defined:

```
const
  Black        =  0;
  Blue         =  1;
  Green        =  2;
  Cyan         =  3;
  Red          =  4;
  Magenta      =  5;
  Brown        =  6;
  LightGray    =  7;
  DarkGray     =  8;
  LightBlue    =  9;
  LightGreen   = 10;
  LightCyan    = 11;
  LightRed     = 12;
  LightMagenta = 13;
  Yellow       = 14;
  White        = 15;
```

| | |
|---|---|
| **Restrictions** | Must be in graphics mode. |
| **See also** | *GetBkColor, GetColor, GetPalette, SetAllPalette, SetBkColor, SetColor, GraphResult* |
| **Example** | |

```
uses Crt, Graph;
var
  GraphDriver, GraphMode: integer;
  Color: word;
  Palette: PaletteType;

begin
  GraphDriver := Detect;
  InitGraph(GraphDriver, GraphMode, '');
  if GraphResult <> grOk then
    Halt(1);
  GetPalette(Palette);
  if Palette.Size <> 1 then
    begin
      for Color := 0 to Pred(Palette.Size) do
      begin
        SetColor(Color);
        Line(0, Color*5, 100, Color*5);
      end;
      Randomize;
      repeat
        SetPalette(Random(Palette.Size),Random(Palette.Size));
      until KeyPressed;
    end
  else
    Line(0, 0, 100, 0);
  Readln;
  CloseGraph;
end.
```

# SetTextBuf procedure

| | |
|---|---|
| **Function** | Assigns an I/O buffer to a text file. |
| **Declaration** | SetTextBuf(**var** f: text; **var** buf [ ; size: word ] ) |
| **Remarks** | *f* is a text-file variable, *buf* is any variable, and *Size* is an optional expression of type word. |

Each text-file variable has an internal 128-byte buffer that, by default, is used to buffer *Read* and *Write* operations. This buffer is adequate for most applications. However, heavily I/O-bound programs, such as applications that copy or convert text files, will benefit from a larger buffer, because it reduces disk head movement and file system overhead.

*SetTextBuf* changes the text file *f* to use the buffer specified by *buf* instead of *f*'s internal buffer. *Size* specifies the size of the buffer in bytes. If *Size* is omitted, *SizeOf(buf)* is assumed; that is, by default, the entire memory region occupied by *buf* is used as a buffer. The new buffer remains in effect until *f* is next passed to *Assign*.

**Restrictions**     *SetTextBuf* should never be applied to an open file, although it can be called immediately after *Reset*, *Rewrite*, and *Append*. Calling *SetTextBuf* on an open file once I/O operations has taken place can cause loss of data because of the change of buffer.

Turbo Pascal doesn't ensure that the buffer exists for the entire duration of I/O operations on the file. In particular, a common error is to install a local variable as a buffer, and then use the file outside the procedure that declared the buffer.

**Differences**     Alternative to 3.0's syntax: **var** f:text[2048].

**Example**
```
var
  f  : text;
  ch : char;
  buf: array[1..10240] of char;              { 10K buffer }
begin
  { Get file to read from command line }
  Assign(f, ParamStr(1));
  { Bigger buffer for faster reads }
  SetTextBuf(f, buf);
  Reset(f);
  { Dump text file onto screen }
  while not Eof(f) do
  begin
    Read(f, ch);
    Write(ch);
  end;
end.
```

# SetTextJustify procedure           Graph

**Function**
     Sets text justification values used by *OutText* and *OutTextXY*.

**Declaration**
     `SetTextJustify(Horiz, Vert: word)`

**Remarks**
     Text output after a *SetTextJustify* will be justified around the current pointer in the manner specified. Given the following:

```
SetTextJustify(CenterText, CenterText);
OutTextXY(100, 100, 'ABC');
```

The point(100,100) will appear in the middle of the letter *B*. The default justification settings can be restored by *SetTextJustify(LeftText, TopText)*. If invalid input is passed to *SetTextJustify*, *GraphResult* will return a value of –11 (*grError*), and the current text justification settings will be unchanged.

The following constants are defined:

```
const
  { Horizontal justification }
  LeftText   = 0;
  CenterText = 1;
  RightText  = 2;

  { Vertical justification }
  BottomText = 0;
  CenterText = 1;                        { Not declared twice }
  TopText    = 2;
```

**Restrictions**
     Must be in graphics mode.

**See also**
     *SetLineStyle, GetTextSettings, TextHeight, TextWidth, OutText, OutTextXY, SetUserCharSize, GraphResult*

**Example**
```
uses Graph;
var
  Gd, Gm: integer;

begin
  Gd := Detect;
  InitGraph(Gd, Gm, '');
  if GraphResult <> grOk then
    Halt(1);
  { Center text onscreen }
```

```
SetTextJustify(CenterText, CenterText);
OutTextXY(Succ(GetMaxX)
   div 2, Succ(GetMaxY)
   div 2, 'Easily Centered');
Readln;
CloseGraph;
end.
```

# SetTextStyle procedure                    Graph

**Function**       Sets the current text font, style, and character magnification factor.

**Declaration**
```
SetTextStyle(Font: word; Direction: word;
             CharSize: word)
```

**Remarks**        Affects all text output by *OutText* and *OutTextXY*. One 8×8 bit-mapped font and several "stroked" fonts are available. Font directions supported are normal (left to right) and vertical (90 degrees to normal text, starts at the bottom and goes up). The size of each character can be magnified using the *CharSize* factor. A *CharSize* value of one will display the 8×8 bit-mapped font in an 8×8 pixel rectangle on the screen, a *CharSize* value equal to 2 will display the 8×8 bit-mapped font in a 16×16 pixel rectangle and so on (up to a limit of 10 times the normal size). Always use *TextHeight* and *TextWidth* to determine the actual dimensions of the text.

The normal size values for text are 1 for the default font and 4 for a stroked font. These are the values that should be passed as the *CharSize* parameter to *SetTextStyle*. *SetUserCharSzie* can be used to customize the dimensions of stroked font text.

Normally, stroked fonts are loaded from disk onto the heap when a call is made to *SetTextStyle*. However, you can load the fonts yourself or link them directly to your .EXE file. In either case, use *RegisterBGIfont* to register the font with the *Graph* unit.

When "stroked" fonts are loaded from disk, errors can occur when trying to load them. If an error occurs, *GraphResult* will return one of the following values:

| | |
|---|---|
| –8 | Font file not found |
| –9 | Not enough memory to load the font selected |
| –11 | Graphics error |
| –12 | Graphics I/O error |
| –13 | Invalid font file |
| –14 | Invalid font number |

The following type and constants are declared:

```
const
  { Set/GetTextStyle constants }
  DefaultFont   = 0;                      { 8x8 bit mapped font }
  TriplexFont   = 1;                         { "Stroked" fonts }
  SmallFont     = 2;
  SansSerifFont = 3;
  GothicFont    = 4;

  HorizDir  = 0;                              { Left to right }
  VertDir   = 1;                              { Bottom to top }
```

**Restrictions**   Must be in graphics mode.

**See also**   *SetTextJustify, GetTextSettings, OutText, OutTextXY, TextHeight, TextWidth, Registerbgifont, GraphResult, SetUserCharSize*

**Example**
```
uses Graph;
var
  Gd, Gm : integer;
  Y, Size: integer;

begin
  Gd := Detect;
  InitGraph(Gd, Gm, '');
  if GraphResult <> grOk then
    Halt(1);
  Y := 0;
  for Size := 1 to 4 do
  begin
    SetTextStyle(DefaultFont, HorizDir, Size);
    OutTextXY(0, Y, 'Size = ' + Chr(Size+48));
    Inc(Y, TextHeight('H') + 1);
  end;
  Readln;
  CloseGraph;
end.
```

# SetTime procedure          Dos

**Function**      Sets the current time in the operating system.

**Declaration**    `SetTime(Hour, Minute, Second, Sec100: word)`

**Remarks**       Valid parameter ranges are *Hour* 0..23, *Minute* 0..59, *Second* 0..59, and *Sec*100 (hundredths of seconds) 0-99. If the time is not valid, the request is ignored.

**See also**      *GetTime, GetDate, SetDate*

# SetUserCharSize procedure      Graph

**Function**      Allows the user to vary the character width and height for stroked fonts.

**Declaration**    `SetUserCharSize(MultX, DivX, MultY, DivY: byte);`

**Remarks**       *MultX:DivX* is the ratio multiplied by the normal width for the active font; *MultY:DivY* is the ratio multiplied by the normal height for the active font. In order to make text twice as wide, for example, use a *MultX* value of 2, and set *DivX* equal to 1 (2 **div** 1 = 2). The following program shows how to change the height and width of text:

```
program CharSize;
uses Graph;
var
  Driver, Mode, Err: integer;

begin
  Driver := Detect;
  InitGraph(Driver, Mode, '');
  Err := GraphResult;
  if Err < 0 then
  begin
    Writeln('Graphics error: ', GraphErrorMsg(Err));
    Halt(1);
  end;

  { Showoff }
  SetTextStyle(TriplexFont, Horizdir, 4);
  OutText('Norm');
  SetUserCharSize(1, 3, 1, 2);
  SetTextStyle(TriplexFont, Horizdir, UserCharSize);
```

```
OutText('Short ');
SetUserCharSize(3, 1, 1, 1);
SetTextStyle(TriplexFont, Horizdir, UserCharSize);
OutText('Wide');
Readln;
CloseGraph;
end.
```

Note that *SetUserCharSize* is called, followed immediately by a call to *SetTextStyle*.

**Restrictions**    Must be in graphics mode.

**See also**    *SetTextStyle, OutText, OutTextXY, TextHeight, TextWidth*

---

# SetViewPort procedure                    Graph

---

**Function**    Sets the current output viewport or window for graphics output.

**Declaration**    `SetViewPort(x1, y1, x2, y2: integer; Clip: boolean);`

**Remarks**    *(x1, y1)* define the upper left corner of the viewport, and *(x2, y2)* define the lower right corner ($0 <= x1 < x2$ and $0 <= y1 < y2$). The upper left corner of a viewport is (0,0).

The Boolean variable *Clip* determines whether drawings are clipped at the current viewport boundaries. *SetViewPort(0, 0, GetMaxX, GetMaxY, True)* always sets the viewport to the entire graphics screen. If invalid input is parsed to *SetViewPort*, *GraphResult* will return –11 (*grError*), and the current view settings will be unchanged. The following constants are defined:

```
const
  ClipOn  = True;
  ClipOff = False;
```

All graphics commands (for example, *GetX, OutText, Rectangle, MoveTo*, and so on) are viewport-relative. In the example, note that *MoveTo* moves the current pointer to (5,5) *inside* the viewport (the absolute coordinates would be (15,25)).

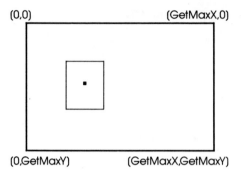

(0,0)　　　　　　　　　　　　　　　　(GetMaxX,0)

(0,GetMaxY)　　　　　　(GetMaxX,GetMaxY)

If the Boolean variable *Clip* is set to True when a call to *SetViewPort* is made, all drawings will be clipped to the current viewport. Note that the "current pointer" is never clipped. The following will not draw the complete line requested because the line will be clipped to the current viewport:

```
SetViewPort(10, 10, 20, 20, ClipOn);
Line(0, 5, 15, 5);
```

The line would start at absolute coordinates (10,15) and terminate at absolute coordinates (25,15) if no clipping was performed. But since clipping was performed, the actual line that would be drawn would start at absolute coordinates (10,15) and terminate at coordinates (20,15).

*InitGraph, GraphDefaults,* and *SetGraphMode* all reset the viewport to the entire graphics screen. The current viewport settings are available by calling the procedure *GetViewSettings,* which accepts a parameter of the following global type:

```
type
   ViewPortType = record
                       x1, y1, x2, y2: integer;
                       Clip: boolean;
                   end;
```

*SetViewPort* moves the current pointer to (0,0).

**Restrictions**　　Must be in graphics mode.

**See also**　　*ClearViewPort, GetViewSettings, GraphResult*

**Example**
```
uses Graph;
var
  Gd, Gm: integer;
```

```
begin
  Gd := Detect;
  InitGraph(Gd, Gm, '');
  if GraphResult <> grOk then
    Halt(1);
  if (Gd = HercMono)
    or (Gd = EGA) or (Gd = EGA64) or (Gd = VGA) then
    begin
      SetVisualPage(0);
      SetActivePage(1);
      Rectangle(10, 20, 30, 40);
      SetVisualPage(1);
    end
  else
    OutText('No paging supported.');
  Readln;
  CloseGraph;
end.
```

# SetVisualPage procedure                    Graph

| | |
|---|---|
| **Function** | Sets the visual graphics page number. |
| **Declaration** | `SetVisualPage(Page: word)` |
| **Remarks** | Makes *Page* the visual graphics page. |
| | Multiple pages are only supported by the EGA (256K), VGA, and Hercules graphics cards. With multiple graphics pages, a program can direct graphics output to an off-screen page, then quickly display the off-screen image by changing the visual page with the *SetVisualPage* procedure. This technique is especially useful for animation. |
| **Restrictions** | Must be in graphics mode. |
| **See also** | *SetActivePage* |
| **Example** | |

```
uses Graph;
var
  Gd, Gm: integer;

begin
  Gd := Detect;
  InitGraph(Gd, Gm, '');
  if GraphResult <> grOk then
    Halt(1);
  if (Gd = HercMono)
```

```
         or (Gd = EGA) or (Gd = EGA64) or (Gd = VGA) then
         begin
           SetVisualPage(0);
           SetActivePage(1);
           Rectangle(10, 20, 30, 40);
           SetVisualPage(1);
         end
       else
         OutText('No paging supported.');
       Readln;
       CloseGraph;
     end.
```

# Sin function

| | |
|---|---|
| **Function** | Returns the sine of the argument. |
| **Declaration** | `Sin(x: real)` |
| **Result type** | real |
| **Remarks** | $x$ is a real-type expression. The result is the sine of $x$. $x$ is assumed to represent an angle in radians. |
| **Example** | |

```
var
  r: real;

begin
  r := Sin(Pi);
end.
```

# SizeOf function

| | |
|---|---|
| **Function** | Returns the number of bytes occupied by the argument. |
| **Declaration** | `SizeOf(x)` |
| **Result type** | word |
| **Remarks** | $x$ is either a variable reference or a type identifier. *SizeOf* returns the number of bytes of memory occupied by $x$. |

*SizeOf* should always be used when passing values to *FillChar, Move, GetMem,* and so on:

```
FillChar(s, SizeOf(s), 0);
GetMem(p, SizeOf(RecordType));
```

**Example**

```
type
  CustRec = record
              Name  : string[30];
              Phone : string[14];
            end;
var
  p: ^CustRec;

begin
  GetMem(p, SizeOf(CustRec));
end.
```

# Sound procedure                                    Crt

| | |
|---|---|
| **Function** | Starts the internal speaker. |
| **Declaration** | Sound(Hz: word) |
| **Remarks** | *Hz* specifies the frequency of the emitted sound in hertz. The speaker continues until explicitly turned off by a call to *NoSound*. |
| **See also** | *NoSound* |

**Example**

```
uses Crt;
begin
  Sound(220);                              { Beep }
  Delay(200);                              { Pause }
  NoSound;                                 { Relief! }
end.
```

# SPtr function

| | |
|---|---|
| **Function** | Returns the current value of the SP register. |
| **Declaration** | SPtr |
| **Result type** | word |
| **Remarks** | The result, of type word, is the offset of the stack pointer within the stack segment. |
| **See also** | *Sseg* |

# Sqr function

| | |
|---|---|
| **Function** | Returns the square of the argument. |
| **Declaration** | Sqr(x) |
| **Result type** | Same type as parameter. |
| **Remarks** | *x* is an integer-type or real-type expression. The result, of the same type as *x*, is the square of *x*, or *x* * *x*. |

# Sqrt function

| | |
|---|---|
| **Function** | Returns the square root of the argument. |
| **Declaration** | Sqrt(x: real) |
| **Result type** | real |
| **Remarks** | *x* is a real-type expression. The result is the square root of *x*. |

# SSeg function

| | |
|---|---|
| **Function** | Returns the current value of the SS register. |
| **Declaration** | SSeg |
| **Result type** | word |
| **Remarks** | The result, of type word, is the segment address of the stack segment. |
| **See also** | *SPtr, CSeg, DSeg* |

# Str procedure

| | |
|---|---|
| **Function** | Converts a numeric value to its string representation. |
| **Declaration** | Str(x [ : width [ : decimals ] ]; **var** s: **string**) |
| **Remarks** | *x* is an integer-type or real-type expression. *width* and *decimals* are integer-type expressions. *s* is a string-type variable. *Str* converts *x* to its string representation, |

according to the *width* and *decimals* formatting parameters. The effect is exactly the same as a call to the *Write* standard procedure with the same parameters, except that the resulting string is stored in *s* instead of being written to a text file.

**See also**    *Val, Write*

**Example**

```
function IntToStr(i: longint): string;
{ Convert any integer type to a string }
var
  s: string[11];

begin
  Str(i, s);
  IntToStr := s;
end;

begin
  Writeln(IntToStr(-5322));
end.
```

# Succ function

**Function**    Returns the successor of the argument.

**Declaration**    Succ(x)

**Result type**    Same type as parameter.

**Remarks**    *x* is an ordinal-type expression. The result, of the same type as *x*, is the successor of *x*.

**See also**    *Pred, Inc*

# Swap function

**Function**    Swaps the high- and low-order bytes of the argument.

**Declaration**    Swap(x)

**Result type**    Same type as parameter.

**Remarks**    *x* is an expression of type integer or word.

**See also**    *Hi, Lo*

**Example**

```
var
  x: word;
```

```
begin
  x := Swap($1234);   { $3412 }
end.
```

# TextBackground procedure                      Crt

**Function**        Selects the background color.

**Declaration**     `TextBackground(Color: byte);`

**Remarks**         *Color* is an integer expression in the range 0..7, corres-
                    ponding to one of the first eight color constants:

```
const
  { Foreground and background color constants }
  Black     = 0;
  Blue      = 1;
  Green     = 2;
  Cyan      = 3;
  Red       = 4;
  Magenta   = 5;
  Brown     = 6;
  LightGray = 7;
```

There is a byte variable in *Crt—TextAttr*—that is used to
hold the current video attribute. *TextBackground* sets bits
4-6 of *TextAttr* to *Color*.

The background of all characters subsequently written
will be in the specified color.

**See also**        *TextColor, HighVideo, NormVideo, LowVideo*

# TextColor procedure                           Crt

**Function**        Selects the foreground character color.

**Declaration**     `TextColor(Color:  byte)`

**Remarks**         *Color* is an integer expression in the range 0..15, corres-
                    ponding to one of the color constants defined in *Crt*:

```
const
  { Foreground and background color constants }
  Black     = 0;
  Blue      = 1;
```

```
Green        = 2;
Cyan         = 3;
Red          = 4;
Magenta      = 5;
Brown        = 6;
LightGray    = 7;
DarkGray     = 8;
LightBlue    = 9;
LightGreen   = 10;
LightCyan    = 11;
LightRed     = 12;
LightMagenta = 13;
Yellow       = 14;
White        = 15;
```

There is a byte variable in *Crt*—*TextAttr*—that is used to hold the current video attribute. *TextColor* sets bits 0-3 to *Color*. If *Color* is greater than 15, the blink bit (bit 7) is also set; otherwise, it is cleared.

You can make characters blink by adding 128 to the color value. The *Blink* constant is defined for that purpose; in fact, for compatibility with Turbo Pascal 3.0, any *Color* value above 15 causes the characters to blink. The foregound of all characters subsequently written will be in the specified color.

**Differences**    In 3.0, *Blink* was equal to 16.

**See also**    *TextBackground, HighVideo, NormVideo, LowVideo*

**Example**

```
TextColor(Green);                    { Selects green characters }
TextColor(LightRed+Blink);                   { Selects blinking
                                           light-red characters }

TextColor(14);                      { Selects yellow characters }
```

# TextHeight function          Graph

**Function**    Returns the height of a string in pixels.

**Declaration**    `TextHeight(TextString: `**`string`**`)`

**Result type**    word

**Remarks**    Takes the current font size and multiplication factor, and determines the height of *TextString* in pixels. This is useful for adjusting the spacing between lines, computing viewport heights, sizing a title to make it fit on a graph or in a box, and more.

For example, with the 8×8 bit-mapped font and a multiplication factor of 1 (set by *SetTextStyle*), the string *Turbo* is 8 pixels high.

It is important to use *TextHeight* to compute the height of strings, instead of doing the computation manually. In that way, no source code modifications have to be made when different fonts are selected.

**Restrictions**     Must be in graphics mode.

**See also**     *OutText, OutTextXY, SetTextStyle, TextWidth, SetUserCharSize*

**Example**
```
uses Graph;
var
  Gd, Gm : integer;
  Y, Size: integer;

begin
  Gd := Detect;
  InitGraph(Gd, Gm, '');
  if GraphResult <> grOk then
    Halt(1);
  Y := 0;
  for Size := 1 to 5 do
  begin
    SetTextStyle(DefaultFont, HorizDir, Size);
    OutTextXY(0, Y, 'Turbo Graphics');
    Inc(Y, TextHeight('Turbo Graphics'));
  end;
  Readln;
  CloseGraph;
end.
```

# TextMode procedure                               Crt

**Function**     Selects a specific text mode.

**Declaration**     TextMode(Mode: word)

**Remarks**     The following constants are defined:

```
const
  { CRT modes }
  BW40 = 0;                    { 40x25 B/W on color adapter }
```

```
BW80   =  2;                { 80x25 B/W on color adapter }
Mono   =  7;                { 80x25 B/W on monochrome adapter }
CO40   =  1;                { 40x25 color on color adapter }
CO80   =  3;                { 80x25 color on color adapter }
Font8x8 = 256;              { For EGA/VGA 43 and 50 line }
C40 = CO40;                 { For 3.0 compatibility }
C80 = CO80;                 { For 3.0 compatibility }
```

Other values cause *TextMode* to assume C80.

When *TextMode* is called, the current window is reset to the entire screen, *DirectVideo* is set to True, *CheckSnow* is set to True if a color mode was selected, the current text attribute is reset to normal corresponding to a call to *NormVideo*, and the current video is stored in *LastMode*. In addition, *LastMode* is initialized at program startup to the then active video mode.

Specifying *TextMode(LastMode)* causes the last active text mode to be re-selected. This is useful when you want to return to text mode after using a graphics package, such as *Graph* or *Graph3*.

The following call to *TextMode*:

```
TextMode(c80 + Font8x8)
```

will reset the display into 43 lines and 80 columns on an EGA, or 50 lines and 80 columns on a VGA with a color monitor. *TextMode(Lo(LastMode))* always turns off 43- or 50-line mode and resets the display (although it leaves the video mode unchanged); while

$TextMode(Lo(LastMode) + Font8 \times 8)$

will keep the video mode the same, but reset the display into 43 or 50 lines.

If your system is in 43- or 50-line mode when you load a Turbo Pascal program, the mode will be preserved by the *Crt* startup code, and the window variable that keeps track of the maximum number of lines on the screen (*WindMax*) will be initialized correctly.

Here's how to write a "well-behaved" program that will restore the video mode to its original state:

```
program Video;
uses Crt;
```

```
var
  OrigMode: integer;

begin
  OrigMode := LastMode;           { Remember original mode }
  ...
  TextMode(OrigMode);
end.
```

Note that *TextMode* does not support graphics modes, and therefore *TextMode(OrigMode)* will only restore those modes supported by *TextMode*.

**Differences**    In 3.0, a call to *TextMode* with no parameters is now done by calling *TextMode(Last)*.

**See also**    *RestoreCrt*

---

# TextWidth function      Graph

---

**Function**    Returns the width of a string in pixels.

**Declaration**    `TextWidth(TextString: string)`

**Result type**    word

**Remarks**    Takes the string length, current font size, and multiplication factor, and determines the width of *TextString* in pixels. This is useful for computing viewport widths, sizing a title to make it fit on a graph or in a box, and so on.

For example, with the 8×8 bit-mapped font and a multiplication factor of 1 (set by *SetTextStyle*), the string *Turbo* is 40 pixels wide.

It is important to use *TextWidth* to compute the width of strings, instead of doing the computation manually. In that way, no source code modifications have to be made when different fonts are selected.

**Restrictions**    Must be in graphics mode.

**See also**    *OutText, OutTextXY, SetTextStyle, TextHeight, SetUserCharSize*

**Example**
```
uses Graph;
var
  Gd, Gm: integer;
```

```
      Row   : integer;
      Title : string;
      Size  : integer;
    begin
      Gd := Detect;
      InitGraph(Gd, Gm, '');
      if GraphResult <> grOk then
        Halt(1);
      Row := 0;
      Title := 'Turbo Graphics';
      Size := 1;
      while TextWidth(Title) < GetMaxX do
      begin
        OutTextXY(0, Row, Title);
        Inc(Row, TextHeight('M'));
        Inc(Size);
        SetTextStyle(DefaultFont, HorizDir, Size);
      end;
      Readln;
      CloseGraph;
    end.
```

# Trunc function

| | |
|---|---|
| **Function** | Truncates a real-type value to an integer-type value. |
| **Declaration** | `Trunc(x: real)` |
| **Result type** | longint |
| **Remarks** | *x* is a real-type expression. *Trunc* returns a longint value that is the value of *x* rounded toward zero. |
| **Restrictions** | A runtime error occurs if the truncated value of *x* is not within the longint range. |
| **Differences** | In 3.0, the result type was an integer. |
| **See also** | *Round, Int* |

# Truncate procedure

| | |
|---|---|
| **Function** | Truncates the file size at the current file position. |
| **Declaration** | `Truncate(f)` |

| | |
|---|---|
| **Remarks** | *f* is a file variable of any type. All records past *f* are deleted and the current file position also becomes end-of-file (*Eof(f)* is True). |
| | If I/O checking is off, the *IOResult* function will return a nonzero value if an error occurs. |
| **Restrictions** | *f* must be open. *Truncate* does not work on text files. |
| **See also** | *Seek, Reset* |

# UnpackTime procedure                                Dos

| | |
|---|---|
| **Function** | Converts a 4-byte, packed date-and-time longint returned by *GetFTime, FindFirst,* or *FindNext* into an unpacked *DateTime* record. |
| **Declaration** | UnpackTime(Time: longint; **var** DT: DateTime) |
| **Remarks** | *DateTime* is a record declared in the *Dos* unit: |

```
DateTime = record
             Year, Month, Day, Hour,
             Min, Sec: word
           end;
```

| | |
|---|---|
| | The fields of the *Time* record are not range-checked. |
| **See also** | *PackTime, GetFTime, SetFTime, GetTime, SetTime* |

# UpCase function

| | |
|---|---|
| **Function** | Converts a character to uppercase. |
| **Declaration** | UpCase(ch: char) |
| **Result type** | char |
| **Remarks** | *ch* is an expression of type char. The result of type char is *ch* converted to uppercase. Character values not in the range *a..z* are unaffected. |

# Val procedure

| | |
|---|---|
| **Function** | Converts the string value to its numeric representation. |

| **Declaration** | `Val(s: ` **`string`** `; ` **`var`** ` v: NumType; ` **`var`** ` code: integer);` |
|---|---|

**Remarks**

*s* is a string-type expression. *v* is an integer-type or real-type variable. *NumType* is any numeric type. *code* is a variable of type integer. *s* must be a sequence of characters that form a signed whole number according to the syntax shown in the section "Numbers" in Chapter 13. *Val* converts *s* to its numeric representation and stores the result in *v*. If the string is somehow invalid, the index of the offending character is stored in *code*; otherwise, *code* is set to zero.

The standard procedure *Val*, which converts a string's contents to a numeric variable, performs range-checking differently depending on the state of {$R} and the type of the parameter *V*:

```
Val(s: string; var V; var Code: integer);
```

With range-checking on, {$R+}, an out-of-range value always generates a runtime error. With range-checking off, {$R-}, the values for an out-of-range value vary depending upon the data type of *V*. If *V* is a real or longint type, the value of *V* is undefined and *Code* returns a nonzero value. For any other numeric type, *Code* returns a value of zero, and *V* will contain the results of an overflow calculation (assuming the string value is within the long integer range).

Therefore, you should pass *Val* a longint variable and perform range-checking before making an assignment of the returned value:

```
{$R-}
Val('65536', LongIntVar, Code)
if (Code <> 0) or
   (LongIntVar < 0) or (LongIntVar > 65535) then
   ...                                            { Error }
else
   WordVar := LongIntVar;
```

In this example, *LongIntVar* would be set to 65536, and *Code* would equal 0. Because 65536 is out of range for a word variable, an error would be reported.

In addition, *Val* has been modified to ignore leading spaces.

**Restrictions**

Leading spaces must be deleted.

*Str*

**Example**

```
var i, code: integer;
begin
  { Get text from command line }
  Val(ParamStr(1), i, code);
  { Error during conversion to integer? }
  if code <> 0 then
    Writeln('Error at position: ', code)
  else
    Writeln('Value = ', i);
end.
```

# WhereX function                                    Crt

| | |
|---|---|
| **Function** | Returns the X-coordinate of the current cursor position, relative to the current window. |
| **Declaration** | WhereX |
| **Result type** | byte |
| **See also** | *WhereY, GotoXY, Window* |

# WhereY function                                    Crt

| | |
|---|---|
| **Function** | Returns the Y-coordinate of the current cursor position, relative to the current window. |
| **Declaration** | WhereY |
| **Result type** | byte |
| **See also** | *WhereX, GotoXY, Window* |

# Window procedure                                   Crt

| | |
|---|---|
| **Function** | Defines a text window on the screen. |
| **Declaration** | Window(X1, Y1, X2, Y2: byte) |
| **Remarks** | X1 and Y1 are the coordinates of the upper left corner of the window, and X2 and Y2 are the coordinates of the lower right corner. The upper left corner of the screen corresponds to (1,1). The minimum size of a text |

window is one column by one line. If the coordinates are in any way invalid, the call to *Window* is ignored.

The default window is (1,1,80,25) in 80-column modes, and (1,1,40,25) in 40-column modes, corresponding to the entire screen.

All screen coordinates (except the window coordinates themselves) are relative to the current window. For instance, *GotoXY*(1,1) will always position the cursor in the upper left corner of the current window.

Many *Crt* procedures and functions are window-relative, including *ClrEol*, *ClrScr*, *DelLine*, *GotoXY*, *Insline*, *WhereX*, *WhereY*, *Read*, *Readln*, *Write*, *Writeln*.

*WindMin* and *WindMax* store the current window definition (refer to Chapter 24).

**Example**

```
uses Crt;
var
  x, y: byte;

begin
  TextBackground(Black);                    { Clear screen }
  ClrScr;
  repeat
    x := Succ(Random(80));                  { Draw random windows }
    y := Succ(Random(25));
    Window(x, y, x + Random(10), y + Random(8));
    TextBackground(Random(16));             { In random colors }
    ClrScr;
  until KeyPressed;
end.
```

# Write procedure (text files)

**Function**      Writes one or more values to a text file.

**Declaration**   Write( [ **var** f: text; ] v1 [, v2,...,vn ] )

**Remarks**       *f*, if specified, is a text-file variable. If *f* is omitted, the standard file variable *Output* is assumed. Each *p* is a write parameter. Each write parameter includes an output expression whose value is to be written to the file. A write parameter can also contain the specifications of a field width and a number of decimal places.

Each output expression must be of a type char, integer, real, string, packed string, or boolean.

A write parameter has the form

```
OutExpr [ : MinWidth [ : DecPlaces ] ]
```

where *OutExpr* is an output expression. *MinWidth* and *DecPlaces* are type integer expressions.

*MinWidth* specifies the minimum field width, which must be greater than 0. Exactly *MinWidth* characters are written (using leading blanks if necessary) except when *OutExpr* has a value that must be represented in more than *MinWidth* characters. In that case, enough characters are written to represent the value of *OutExpr*. Likewise, if *MinWidth* is omitted, then the necessary number of characters are written to represent the value of *OutExpr*.

*DecPlaces* specifies the number of decimal places in a fixed-point representation of a type real value. It can be specified only if *OutExpr* is of type real, and if *MinWidth* is also specified. When *MinWidth* is specified, it must be greater than or equal to 0.

**Write with a type char value:** If *MinWidth* is omitted, the character value of *OutExpr* is written to the file. Otherwise, *MinWidth* −1 blanks followed by the character value of *OutExpr* is written.

**Write with a type integer value:** If *MinWidth* is omitted, the decimal representation of *OutExpr* is written to the file with no preceding blanks. If *MinWidth* is specified and its value is larger than the length of the decimal string, enough blanks are written before the decimal string to make the field width *MinWidth*.

**Write with a type real value:** If *OutExpr* has a type real value, its decimal representation is written to the file. The format of the representation depends on the presence or absence of *DecPlaces*.

If *DecPlaces* is omitted (or if it is present, but has a negative value), a floating-point decimal string is written. If *MinWidth* is also omitted, a default *MinWidth* of 17 is assumed; otherwise, if *MinWidth* is less than 8, it is assumed to be 8. The format of the floating-point string is

```
[  | - ] <digit> . <decimals> E [ + | - ] <exponent>
```

The components of the output string are shown in Table 27.1:

Table 27.1: Components of the Output String

| | |
|---|---|
| [  | – ] | " " or "-", according to the sign of *OutExpr* |
| <digit> | Single digit, "0" only if *OutExpr* is 0 |
| <decimals> | Digit string of *MinWidth*-7 (but at most 10) digits |
| E | Uppercase [E] character |
| [ + | – ] | According to sign of exponent |
| <exponent> | Two-digit decimal exponent |

If *DecPlaces* is present, a fixed-point decimal string is written. If *DecPlaces* is larger than 11, it is assumed to be 11. The format of the fixed-point string follows:

```
[ <blanks> ] [ - ] <digits> [ . <decimals> ]
```

The components of the fixed-point string are shown in Table 27.2:

Table 27.2: Components of the Fixed-Point String

| | |
|---|---|
| [ <blanks> ] | Blanks to satisfy *MinWidth* |
| [ – ] | If *OutExpr* is negative |
| <digits> | At least one digit, but no leading zeros |
| [ . <decimals> ] | Decimals if *DecPlaces* > 0 |

**Write with a string-type value:** If *MinWidth* is omitted, the string value of *OutExpr* is written to the file with no leading blanks. If *MinWidth* is specified, and its value is larger than the length of *OutExpr*, enough blanks are written before the decimal string to make the field width *MinWidth*.

**Write with a packed string type value:** If *OutExpr* is of packed string type, the effect is the same as writing a string whose length is the number of elements in the packed string type.

**Write with a Boolean value:** If *OutExpr* is of type boolean, the effect is the same as writing the strings True or False, depending on the value of *OutExpr*.

With {$I-}, *IOResult* will return a 0 if the operation was successful; otherwise, it will return a nonzero error code.

**Restrictions**        File must be open for output.

**Differences**        See Appendix A

**See also**        *Writeln*

# Write procedure (typed files)

**Function**        Writes a variable into a file component.

**Declaration**        `Write(f, v1 [, v2,...,vn ] )`

**Remarks**        *f* is a file variable, and each *v* is a variable of the same type as the component type of *f*. For each variable written, the current file position is advanced to the next component. If the current file position is at the end of the file—that is, if *Eof(f)* is True—the file is expanded.

With {$I-}, *IOResult* will return a 0 if the operation was successful; otherwise, it will return a nonzero error code.

**See also**        *Writeln*

# Writeln procedure

**Function**        Executes the *Write* procedure, then outputs an end-of-line marker to the file.

**Declaration**        `Writeln( [ var f: text; ] v1 [, v2,...,vn ] )`

**Remarks**        *Writeln* procedure is an extension to the *Write* procedure, as it is defined for text files. After executing the Write, *Writeln* writes an end-of-line marker (carriage-return/line-feed) to the file.

*Writeln(f)* with no parameters writes an end-of-line marker to the file. (*Writeln* with no parameter list altogether corresponds to *Writeln(Output)*.)

**Restrictions**        File must be open for output.

**Differences**      See Appendix A.

**See also**          *Write*

# A

# Differences Between Version 3.0 and 4.0

This appendix lists the differences between version 3.0 of Turbo Pascal and version 4.0. Despite the many changes to the compiler and the introduction of many powerful features, version 4.0 is highly compatible with previous releases. As you will see by reading through this section, most of the differences are small, resulting from the introduction of some of the new features.

Where appropriate, we've made suggestions how to make any conversion necessary. Also consult Chapter 8 for more information on converting from version 3.0 to version 4.0.

## Program Declarations

In version 3.0, the program name (the identifier given in the **program** statement) could be the same as another identifier in the program. In version 4.0, the program name must be unique—there cannot be a label, constant, data type, variable, procedure, or function, unit with the same name. That's because you can now refer to any identifier declared in your program as *progname.identifier*. This lets you resolve ambiguities in case you use a unit that also declares something named *identifier*. In that situation, you can refer to the unit's item as *unitname.identifier* (see Chapter 4).

In version 3.0, all Pascal items (constants, data types, variables, procedures, functions) had to be compiled at the same time and were located either in your source file or in an include file. In version 4.0, you can collect a group of constants, data types, variables, procedures and functions, compile them separately into a unit, and then use them in a series of programs. (See Chapter 4 for more details on units.)

In version 3.0, you could not have a program with more than 64K of code, and the compiler produced a .COM file. To get around this, you had to use chaining and/or overlays. In version 4.0, your code size is limited only by the operating system (and your computer), since each unit itself can have up to 64K of code. Because of this, neither chaining nor overlays are supported in version 4.0. If you have been using chaining, you can either use the *Exec* procedure (found in the *Dos* unit), or you can convert your .CHN files to units. If you've been using overlays, you should break your program into several sections and make each section a unit.

## Compiler Directives

In version 3.0, you could embed a set of compiler directives in your code to set (or clear) certain options. In version 4.0, that set has been modified. Here is a list of the current compiler directives; see Appendix C for more details:

| Directive | Description | Default |
|---|---|---|
| $B+/- | Boolean evaluation (+=complete,-=short) | $B- |
| $D+/- | Debug information (+=on,-=off) | $D+ |
| $F+/- | Force far calls (+= all far,-=as needed | $F- |
| $I+/- | I/O error checking (+=on, -=off) | $I+ |
| $I file | Include file | |
| $L+/- | Link buffer location (+=memory,-=disk) | $L+ |
| $L file | Link object file | |
| $M s,l,h | Memory allocation (stack,minheap,maxheap)16K,0,655360 | |
| $N+/- | Numeric coprocessor (+=8087,-=software) | $N- |
| $R+/- | Range-checking(+=on,-=off) | $R+ |
| $S+/- | Stack overflow checking (+=on,-=off) | $S+ |
| $T+/- | .TPM file generation (+=on,-=off) | $T- |
| $U file | Unit file name | |
| $V+/- | Var-string checking (+=on,-=off) | $V+ |

In version 3.0, the include option ({$I *filename*}) could be placed anywhere, and could simply contain executable statements. In version 4.0, the include option cannot be placed within a **begin/end** pair; if *filename* contains executable statements, they must be within a complete procedure or function or the file must contain the entire main body of the program, including **begin/end**.

In version 3.0, the include option ({$I *filename*}) did not require a space between $I and *filename*. In version 4.0, you must have a space after the $I.

In version 3.0, you could not nest include files; that is, if your program had the directive {$I *mystuff.pas*}, then MYSTUFF.PAS could not have any $I (include) directives. In version 4.0, you can nest include files and units up to eight levels deep.

# Predeclared Identifiers

In version 3.0, all predefined constants, data types, variables, procedures, and functions were always available. In version 4.0, many of those predefined items are now located in one of the standard units (*Dos, Crt, Printer, Graph, Turbo3, Graph3*). In order to use those items, your program must have a **uses** statement listing the units to be used. For example,

```
uses Crt, Dos;
```

Here's a list of the 4.0 units with their items that were predeclared in version 3.0:

| 4.0 | 3.0 |
| --- | --- |
| *Dos* | *MsDos, Intr, Exec* (*Execute* in 3.0) |
| *Crt* | *KeyPressed, TextMode, Window, GotoXY, WhereX, WhereY, ClrScr, CrlEol, InsLine, DelLine, TextColor, TextBackground, LowVideo, NormVideo, Delay, Sound, NoSound,* and all the text mode and text color constants |
| *Printer* | *Lst* |
| *Turbo3* | *Kbd, CBreak, LongFileSize, LongFilePos, LongSeek* |
| *Graph3* | All the basic, advanced, and turtlegraphics routines |

In version 3.0, the following predefined items were available: *CrtExit, CrtInit, Aux, Con, Trm, Usr, ConInPtr, ConOutPtr, ConStPtr, LstOutPtr, UsrInPtr, UsrOutPtr, ErrorPtr*. In version 4.0, you can now write powerful I/O drivers (see Chapter 26).

In version 3.0, *CBreak* was an undocumented Boolean variable that let you enable or disable checking for program interruption via *Ctrl-Break*. In version 4.0, it is documented and has been renamed *CheckBreak*; *CBreak* is still available in the *Turbo3* unit.

In version 3.0, the *Execute* procedure was passed a file variable. In version 4.0, it has been renamed *Exec* (found in the *Dos* unit), and you pass it a program name and a command line (parameters).

In version 3.0, the predefined file variables *Aux, Con, Kbd, Lst, Trm,* and *Usr* were all available. In version 4.0, none of them are predefined; however, *Lst* is available by using the unit *Printer*, and *Kbd* is available in the unit *Turbo3*. By using the *Dos* unit, you can write your own device drivers; see Chapter 26 for more details.

In version 3.0, the functions *MemAvail* and *MaxAvail* were of type integer and returned the number of paragraphs (16-byte chunks) free. In version 4.0, those functions are of type longint and return the number of bytes free. Note that the original versions are available in the unit *Turbo3*.

In version 3.0, the *FileSize, FilePos,* and *FileSeek* functions returned a value of type integer. In version 4.0, they return a value of type longint and can return values up to 2,147,483,647.

In version 3.0, *MemW* returned an integer value. In version 4.0, it returns a value of type word.

In version 3.0, the *LongFile* functions (*LongFileSize, LongFilePos, LongSeek*) returned a value of type real. In version 4.0, these functions are available only through the *Turbo3* unit, and they return a value of type real.

In version 3.0, the procedures *MsDos* and *Intr* both had an untyped parameter; you had to declare the appropriate register data structure and pass it in. In version 4.0, *MsDos* and *Intr* both require a parameter of type *Registers*, which is also defined in the *Dos* unit.

In version 3.0, the procedure *Intr* took a constant of type integer as its first parameter. In version 4.0, it accepts any expression (constant, variable, and so on), but the value must be of type byte.

In version 3.0, the function *IOResult* returned error codes specific to Turbo Pascal. In version 4.0, *IOResult* returns standard MS-DOS error codes. (*Turbo3* contains an *IOResult* function that maps 4.0 error codes to 3.0 values wherever possible.)

In version 3.0, if you had several successive I/O errors and then called *IOResult*, it would return the error code corresponding to the first I/O error. In version 4.0, it returns the code corresponding to the last (most recent) I/O error.

In version 3.0, the procedure *Seek* took a parameter of type integer for the record number. In version 4.0, that parameter is now of type longint.

In version 3.0, you could call *TextMode* without any parameters; this would restore the text mode to the last active mode before graphics. In version 4.0, *TextMode* must always have a parameter; however, there is now the predefined text mode constant *Last*, which sets the text mode to the last active mode before graphics:

```
TextMode(LastMode);
```

# Programming Changes

In version 3.0, the *Addr* function returned the address of any variable. Even though *Addr* is supported in 4.0, you should now use the @ operator instead, so that *Ptr := Addr(Item)* becomes *Ptr := @Item*.

In version 3.0, assignment was allowed between types that were identical but defined separately:

```
var
  A: ^integer;
  B: ^integer;

begin
  ...
  A := B;
  ...
```

In version 4.0, stricter type-checking is enforced, and the preceding code would produce a compiler error. For variables to be assignment-compatible, they must either be declared together, like so:

```
var
  A,B: ^integer;
```

or they must be of the same defined data type:

```
type
  IntPtr = ^integer;
var
  A: IntPtr;
  B: IntPtr;
```

In version 3.0, you could use a string variable of length 1 as a case selector in a **case** statement. In version 4.0, you no longer can, though you can use the individual characters.

In version 3.0, the type char was compatible with a string of length 1:

```
var
  Ch: char;
  S: string[10];
begin
  S  := 'a';
  Ch := S;
  ...
```

You could also use the function *Copy* in a similar fashion:

```
S  := 'abc';
Ch := Copy(S,2,1);
```

In version 4.0, neither is allowed. You can, however, still assign *Ch* to *S*, and you can always assign *S[1]* to *Ch*.

In version 3.0, you could call the procedure *Close* on a file that was already closed with no results. In version 4.0, it produces an I/O error, which you can handle by disabling I/O error checking (via the {$I-} option) and testing the value returned by *IOResult*.

In version 3.0, you could use *CSeg* and *DSeg* in **absolute** statements:

```
var
  Parameters: string[127] absolute CSeg: $80;
```

In version 4.0, neither *CSeg* nor *DSeg* is allowed in **absolute** statements.

In version 3.0, there were no restrictions on where the control variable used in a **for** loop was declared. In version 4.0, the control variable must either be a global variable or, if the **for** loop is in a procedure or function, local to that procedure or function. The following code now results in a compiler error:

```
procedure Outer;
var
  I: integer;

procedure Inner;
begin
  for I := 1 to 10 do                            { I is declared in Outer }
    Writeln(I)
end;  { of proc Inner }

begin  { main body of Outer }
  Inner
end;  { of proc Outer }
```

In version 3.0, you could not assign –32768 directly to an integer variable; instead, you had to use the hex constant $8000. In version 4.0, you can now assign –32768 directly; the hex constant $8000 (which now equals +32768) is of type word and cannot be assigned to variables of type integer. You can also assign $FFFF8000 to an integer variable.

In version 3.0, you could declare labels in the **label** section without using the labels in your program. In version 4.0, if you declare a label and then don't use it, you'll get a compiler error. In that case, you need to either use the label in your code or remove it from the **label** declarations.

In version 3.0, you could (optionally) set the buffer size on a text file when you declared it:

```
var
  F: text[4096];                          { Buffer size of 4096 bytes }
```

In version 4.0, you now declare the text buffer as a data structure and assign it to the text file using the *SetTextBuf* procedure:

```
var
  F  : text;
  Buf: array[0..4095] of char;

begin
  Assign(F,'MyFile.TXT');
  SetTextBuf(F,Buf);
  Reset(F);
  ...
```

In version 3.0, you could use *Read(Kbd,Ch)* to do a direct, unechoed read from the keyboard. In version 4.0, the function *ReadKey* performs the same task and allows you to easily detect special keys (function keys, keypad keys, and so on):

```
  Ch := ReadKey;
  if Ch = #0 then                           { Special key }
  begin
    Ch := ReadKey;                          { Read again }
    ...                            { Handle special key }
  end
  else ...;                        { Handle regular key }
```

(*Kbd* is still supported in the *Turbo3* unit; however, we strongly recommend that you switch to using *ReadKey*.)

In version 3.0, certain versions of the compiler supported the BCD (binary-coded decimal) data type. In version 4.0, you have no such data type. Consider using the longint (a 4-byte integer) type instead; if you have an 8087 math coprocessor, you can set the {$N+} compiler option and use the comp data type (an 8-byte integer). A sample program contained on the distribution disks demonstrates how to convert your BCD data for use with 4.0 data types (see the README file on the disk).

In version 3.0, if you had the following code:

```
var
  I: integer;
```

```
begin
  I := 30;
  Write('Enter I:  '); Readln(I);
  ...
```

and pressed *Enter* when asked to enter I, the program would continue and would leave *I* with a value of 30. In version 4.0, your program won't continue until you enter an integer value.

In version 3.0, typed constants resided in the code segment (CS). In version 4.0, they reside in the data segment.

# Other Additions and Improvements

In version 3.0, you had to use the *Move* function to copy data from one data structure to another if the structures were not assignment-compatible:

```
type
  Buffer = array[0..5] of byte;
var
  BufPtr: ^Buffer;
  X     : real;

begin
  New(BufPtr);
  ...
  Move(BufPtr^,X,SizeOf(X));
```

The exception was for ordinal data types (char, byte, integer, boolean, enumerated types), in which case you use retyping (typecasting):

```
  IntVar   := byte('a');
  MonthVar := Month(3);
```

In version 4.0, typecasting has been extended to all types, with the requirement that the source and destination be exactly the same size:

```
type
  Buffer = array[0..5] of byte;
var
  BufPtr: ^Buffer;
  X: real;

begin
  New(BufPtr);
  ...
  X := real(BufPtr^);
```

In version 3.0, you were limited to the integer types byte (0..255, 1 byte) and integer (-32768..32767, 2 bytes). In version 4.0, you also have the types shortint (-128..127, 1 byte), word (0..65535, 2 bytes), and longint (-2147483648..2147483647, 4 bytes).

In version 3.0, you were limited to the floating-point type real. In version 4.0, if you have an 8087 math coprocessor in your machine, you can set the {$N+} option and use three additional floating-point data types: single (4 bytes), double (8 bytes), and extended (10 bytes). You can also use the 8-byte integer type, comp.

In version 3.0, you had to give an explicit length to any string variable you declared; you also had to define your own type if you wanted to pass strings as parameters:

```
type
  BigStr = string[255];
var
  Name: string[20];
  S    : BigStr;
...
procedure Whatever(T : BigStr);
...
```

In version 4.0, you can now declare a variable to be of type **string**, which is equivalent to **string**[255]; you can declare formal parameters to be of type **string**:

```
var
  S: string;
  ...
procedure Whatever(T: string);
  ...
```

In version 3.0, all terms in a Boolean expression were evaluated, even if one term already ensured that the expression was True or False. Because of that, you couldn't write

```
if (B = 0) or (A/B = X) then ...
```

since the second term would be evaluated even if B = 0, which would produce a runtime error. In version 4.0, such expressions can be *short-circuited*. If *B = 0*, then the entire expression is True, and the expression *(A/B = X)* isn't evaluated. If desired, you can force version 4.0 to evaluate all terms by using the {$B+} option.

In version 3.0, you used *ErrorPtr* to set up your own error handler. In version 4.0, *ErrorPtr* no longer exists; instead, you can handle both abnormal and normal termination of your program through *ExitProc* (see Chapter 26 for more details).

In version 3.0, you had to use assembly language coding to create an interrupt handler. In version 4.0, you can write interrupt handlers in Pascal by declaring procedures to be of type **interrupt**.

In version 3.0, you had the predefined identifiers *Mem* and *MemW* for direct memory access. In version 4.0, you also have *MemL*, which maps an array of type longint onto memory.

In version 3.0, you could embed machine code within procedures and functions (or the main body of your program) using the **inline** statement. In version 4.0, you can also declare entire short procedures and functions to be of type **inline**; the machine code is then directly inserted (much like macro expansion) everywhere the procedure or function is called.

In version 3.0, external assembly language routines had to be in .BIN format and were declared in your program as offsets to the first routine in the file. In version 4.0, those routines can be in .OBJ format (produced by an assembler) and are simply declared external, with a {$L *files*} directive listing the .OBJ files to be linked in.

In version 3.0, all procedure and function calls were near calls, which meant all code had to be in the same segment. In version 4.0, the compiler automatically generates near or far calls as needed, and you can force all calls to be far using the {$F+} option.

In version 3.0, there were no provisions to aid debugging of executable files. In version 4.0, you can set {$D+} and {$T+} directives to support symbolic debugging (Periscope, and so forth). See Chapter 9 for more information.

# B

# Comparing Turbo Pascal 4.0 with ANSI Pascal

This appendix compares Turbo Pascal to ANSI Pascal as defined by ANSI/IEEE770X3.97-1983 in the book *American National Standard Pascal Computer Programming Language* (ISBN 0-471-88944-X, published by The Institute of Electrical and Electronics Engineers in New York).

## Exceptions to ANSI Pascal Requirements

Turbo Pascal complies with the requirements of ANSI/IEEE770X3.97-1983 with the following exceptions:

- In ANSI Pascal, an identifier can be of any length and all characters are significant. In Turbo Pascal, an identifier can be of any length, but only the first 63 characters are significant.

- In ANSI Pascal, the @ symbol is an alternative for the ^ symbol. In Turbo Pascal, the @ symbol is an operator, which is never treated identically with the ^ symbol.

- In ANSI Pascal, a comment can begin with { and end with *), or begin with (* and end with }. In Turbo Pascal, comments must begin and end with the same set of symbols.

- In ANSI Pascal, each possible value of the tag type in a variant part must appear once. In Turbo Pascal, this requirement is not enforced.

- In ANSI Pascal, the component type of a file type cannot be a structured type having a component of a file type. In Turbo Pascal, this requirement is not enforced.

- In ANSI Pascal, a file variable has an associated buffer variable, which is referenced by writing the ^ symbol after the file variable. In Turbo Pascal, a file variable does not have an associated buffer variable, and writing the ^ symbol after a file variable is an error.

- In ANSI Pascal, the statement part of a function must contain at least one assignment to the function identifier. In Turbo Pascal, this requirement is not enforced.

- In ANSI Pascal, a field that is the selector of a variant part cannot be an actual variable parameter. In Turbo Pascal, this requirement is not enforced.

- In ANSI Pascal, procedures and functions allow procedural and functional parameters; these parameters are not allowed in Turbo Pascal.

- In ANSI Pascal, the standard procedures *Reset* and *Rewrite* do not require pre-initialization of file variables. In Turbo Pascal, file variables must be assigned the name of an external file using the *Assign* procedure before they are passed to *Reset* or *Rewrite*.

- ANSI Pascal defines the standard procedures *Get* and *Put*, which are used to read from and write to files. These procedures are not defined in Turbo Pascal.

- In ANSI Pascal, the syntax *New(p,c1,...,cn)* creates a dynamic variable with a specific active variant. In Turbo Pascal, this syntax is not allowed.

- In ANSI Pascal, the syntax *Dispose(q,k1,...,km)* removes a dynamic variable with a specific active variant. In Turbo Pascal, this syntax is not allowed.

- ANSI Pascal defines the standard procedures *Pack* and *Unpack*, which are used to "pack" and "unpack" packed variables. These procedures are not defined in Turbo Pascal.

- In ANSI Pascal, the term $i$ **mod** $j$ always computes a positive value, and it is an error if $j$ is zero or negative. In Turbo Pascal, $i$ **mod** $j$ is computed as $i - (i$ **div** $j) * j$, and it is not an error if $j$ is negative.

- In ANSI Pascal, a **goto** statement within a block can refer to a label in an enclosing block. In Turbo Pascal, this is an error.

- In ANSI Pascal, it is an error if the value of the selector in a **case** statement is not equal to any of the case constants. In Turbo Pascal, this is not an error; instead, the **case** statement is ignored unless it contains an **else** clause.

- In ANSI Pascal, statements that *threaten* the control variable of a **for** statement are not allowed. In Turbo Pascal, this requirement is not enforced.

- In ANSI Pascal, a *Read* from a text file with a char-type variable assigns a blank to the variable if *Eoln* was True before the *Read*. In Turbo Pascal, a carriage return character (ASCII 13) is assigned to the variable in this situation.

■ In ANSI Pascal, a *Read* from a text file with an integer-type or real-type variable ceases as soon as the next character in the file is not part of a signed integer or a signed number. In Turbo Pascal, reading ceases when the next character in the file is a blank or a control character (including the end-of-line marker).

■ In ANSI Pascal, a *Write* to a text file with a packed string-type value causes the string to be truncated if the specified field width is less than the length of the string. In Turbo Pascal, the string is always written in full, even if it is longer than the specified field width.

**Note**: Turbo Pascal is unable to detect whether a program violates any of the exceptions listed here.

# Extensions to ANSI Pascal

The following Turbo Pascal features are extensions to Pascal as specified by ANSI/IEEE770X3.97-1983.

■ The following are reserved words in Turbo Pascal:

| | | |
|---|---|---|
| **absolute** | **interface** | **string** |
| **external** | **interrupt** | **unit** |
| **implementation** | **shl** | **uses** |
| **inline** | **shr** | **xor** |

■ An identifier can contain underscore characters (_) after the first character.

■ Integer constants can be written in hexadecimal notation; such constants are prefixed by a $.

■ Identifiers can serve as labels.

■ String constants are compatible with the Turbo Pascal string types, and can contain control characters and other nonprintable characters.

■ Label, constant, type, variable, procedure, and function declarations can occur any number of times in any order in a block.

■ Turbo Pascal implements the additional integer types shortint, longint, byte, and word, and the additional real types single, double, extended, and comp.

■ Turbo Pascal implements string types, which differ from the packed string types defined by ANSI Pascal in that they include a dynamic-length attribute that can vary during execution.

- The type compatibility rules are extended to make char types and packed string types compatible with string types.
- Variables can be declared at absolute memory addresses using an **absolute** clause.
- A variable reference can contain a call to a pointer-type function, the result of which is then dereferenced to denote a dynamic variable.
- String-type variables can be indexed as arrays to access individual characters in a string.
- The type of a variable reference can be changed to another type through a variable typecast.
- Turbo Pascal implements typed constants, which can be used to declare initialized variables of all types except file types.
- Turbo Pascal implements three new logical operators: **xor**, **shl**, and **shr**.
- The **not**, **and**, **or**, and **xor** operators can be used with integer-type operands to perform bitwise logical operations.
- The + operator can be used to concatenate strings.
- The relational operators can be used to compare strings.
- Turbo Pascal implements the @ operator, which is used to obtain the address of a variable or a procedure or function.
- The type of an expression can be changed to another type through a value typecast.
- The **case** statement allows constant ranges in **case** label lists, and provides an optional **else** part.
- Procedures and functions can be declared with **external**, **inline**, and **interrupt** directives to support assembly language subroutines, inline machine code, and interrupt procedures.
- A variable parameter can be untyped (typeless), in which case any variable reference can serve as the actual parameter.
- Turbo Pascal implements units to facilitate modular programming and separate compilation.
- Turbo Pascal implements the following file-handling procedures and functions, which are not available in ANSI Pascal:

| | | | |
|---|---|---|---|
| *Append* | *Close* | *Flush* | *RmDir* |
| *BlockRead* | *Erase* | *GetDir* | *Seek* |
| *BlockWrite* | *FilePos* | *MkDir* | *SeekEof* |
| *ChDir* | *FileSize* | *Rename* | *SeekEoln* |

- String-type values can be input and output with the *Read*, *Readln*, *Write*, and *Writeln* standard procedures.

■ Turbo Pascal implements the following standard procedures and functions, which are not found in ANSI Pascal:

| | | | |
|---|---|---|---|
| Addr | FreeMem | MaxAvail | Randomize |
| CSeg | GetMem | MemAvail | Release |
| Concat | Halt | Move | SPtr |
| Copy | Hi | Ofs | SSeg |
| DSeg | Inc | ParamCount | Seg |
| Dec | Insert | ParamStr | SizeOf |
| Delete | Int | Pi | Str |
| Exit | Length | Pos | Swap |
| FillChar | Lo | Ptr | UpCase |
| Frac | Mark | Random | Val |

■ Turbo Pascal implements further standard constants, types, variables, procedures, and functions through standard units.

**Note**: Turbo Pascal is unable to detect whether a program uses any of the extensions listed here.

# Implementation-Dependent Features

The effect of using an implementation-dependent feature of Pascal, as defined by ANSI/IEEE770X3.97-1983, is unspecified. Programs should not depend on any specific path being taken in cases where an implementation-dependent feature is being used. Implementation-dependent features include

■ the order of evaluation of index expressions in a variable reference

■ the order of evaluation of expressions in a set constructor

■ the order of evaluation of operands of a binary operator

■ the order of evaluation of actual parameters in a function call

■ the order of evaluation of the left and right sides of an assignment

■ the order of evaluation of actual parameters in a procedure statement

■ the effect of reading a text file to which the procedure *Page* was applied during its creation

■ the binding of variables denoted by the program parameters to entities external to the program

# Treatment of Errors

This section lists those errors from Appendix D of the ANSI Pascal Standard that are not automatically detected by Turbo Pascal. The numbers referred to here are the numbers used in the ANSI Pascal Standard. Errors 6, 19-22, and 25-31 are not detected because they are not applicable to Turbo Pascal.

2. If $t$ is a tag field in a variant part and $f$ is a field within the active variant of that variant part, it is an error to alter the value of $t$ while a reference to $f$ exists. This error is not detected.

3. If $p$ is a pointer variable, it is an error to reference $p^\wedge$ if $p$ is **nil**. This error is not detected.

4. If $p$ is a pointer variable, it is an error to reference $p^\wedge$ if $p$ is undefined. This error is not detected.

5. If $p$ is a pointer variable, it is an error to alter the value of $p$ while a reference to $p^\wedge$ exists. This error is not detected.

42. The function call *Eoln(f)* is an error if *Eof(f)* is True. In Turbo Pascal this is not an error, and *Eoln(f)* is True when *Eof(f)* is True.

43. It is an error to reference a variable in an expression if the value of that variable is undefined. This error is not detected.

46. A term of the form $i$ **mod** $j$ is an error if $j$ is zero or negative. In Turbo Pascal, it is not an error if $j$ is negative.

48. It is an error if a function does not assign a result value to the function identifier. This error is not detected.

51. It is an error if the value of the selector in a **case** statement is not equal to any of the case constants. In Turbo Pascal, this is not an error; instead, the **case** statement is ignored unless it contains an **else** clause.

# C

# Compiler Directives

Some of the Turbo Pascal compiler's features are controlled through *compiler directives*. A compiler directive is introduced as a comment with a special syntax. Turbo Pascal allows compiler directives wherever comments are allowed.

You can put compiler directives in your source code, in the command line for the command-line compiler (use the format /$<*directive*> instead of {*directive*}), in the command-line configuration file, or in the integrated environment (through the Options/Compiler menu items).

A compiler directive starts with a $ as the first character after the opening comment delimiter. The $ is immediately followed by a name (one or more letters) that designates the particular directive. There are three types of directives:

- **Switch directives**. These directives turn particular compiler features on or off by specifying + or – immediately after the directive name.
- **Parameter directives**. These directives specify parameters that affect the compilation, such as file names and memory sizes.
- **Conditional directives**. These directives control conditional compilation of parts of the source text, based on user-definable conditional symbols.

All directives, except switch directives, must have at least one blank between the directive name and the parameters. Here are some examples of compiler directives:

```
{$B+}
{$R- Turn off range-checking}
{$I TYPES.INC}
{$U C:\UNITS\MEM}
```

```
{$M 65520,8192,655360}
{$DEFINE Debug}
{$IFDEF Debug}
{$ENDIF}
```

# Switch Directives

Switch directives are either *global* or *local*. Global directives affect the entire compilation, whereas local directives affect only the part of the compilation that extends from the directive until the next occurrence of the same directive.

Global directives must appear before the declaration part of the program or the unit being compiled, that is, before the first **uses**, **label**, **const**, **type**, **procedure**, **function**, or **begin** keyword. Local directives, on the other hand, can appear anywhere in the program or unit.

Multiple switch directives can be grouped in a single compiler directive comment by separating them with commas; for example:

```
{$B+,R-,S-}
```

There can be no spaces between the directives in this case.

## Boolean Evaluation

**Syntax:** {$B+} or {$B-}

**Default:** {$B-}

**Type:** Local

**Menu equivalent:** Options/Compiler/Boolean evaluation

This directive switches between the two different models of code generation for the **and** and **or** Boolean operators.

In the {$B+} state, the compiler generates code for complete Boolean expression evaluation. This means that every operand of a Boolean expression, built from the **and** and **or** operators, is guaranteed to be evaluated, even when the result of the entire expression is already known.

In the {$B-} state, the compiler generates code for short-circuit Boolean expression evaluation, which means that evaluation stops as soon as the result of the entire expression becomes evident. For further details, refer to the section "Boolean Operators" in Chapter 18.

## Debug Information

**Syntax:** {$D+} or {$D-}

**Default:** {$D+}

**Type:** Global

**Menu equivalent:** Options/Compiler/Debug information

This switch enables or disables the generation of debug information. Debug information consists of a line number table for each procedure, which maps object code addresses into source text line numbers.

When a runtime error occurs in a program or unit that was compiled with the option **D**ebug information on, Turbo Pascal uses that information to locate the statement in the source text that caused the error.

For units, the debug information is recorded in the .TPU file, along with the unit's object code and symbols. For programs, when compiling to memory, it is kept in memory for later use. When compiling to disk, it is recorded in the .TPM file, provided .TPM file generation is enabled through a {$T+} directive. Debug information increases the size of .TPU and .TPM files, and takes up additional room when compiling to memory, but it does not affect the size or speed of the executable program.

The TPMAP.EXE utility converts debug information in a .TPM file to a line-number table in the resulting .MAP file. A number of symbolic debuggers can use the line-number information to display source code lines.


## Force Far Calls

**Syntax:** {$F+} or {$F-}

**Default:** {$F-}

**Type:** Local

**Menu equivalent:** Options/Compiler/Force far calls

This switch controls which call model to use for subsequently compiled procedures and functions. Procedures and functions compiled in the {$F+} state always use the far call model. In the {$F-} state, Turbo Pascal automatically selects the appropriate model: far if the procedure or function is declared in the **interface** section of a unit; near otherwise.

The {$F} (force far calls) compiler directive has no effect on a nested procedure. The nested procedure is always of near model.

The near and far call models are described in full in Chapter 26, "Inside Turbo Pascal."

## Input/Output Checking

**Syntax:** {$I+} or {$I-}

**Default:** {$I+}

**Type:** Local

**Menu equivalent:** Options/Compiler/I/O checking

This switch enables or disables the automatic code generation that checks the result of a call to an I/O procedure. I/O procedures are described in Chapter 22, "Input and Output." If an I/O procedure returns a nonzero I/O result when this switch is on, the program terminates, displaying a runtime error message. When this switch is off, you must check for I/O errors by using the *IOResult* function.

## Link Buffer

**Syntax:** {$L+} or {$L-}

**Default:** {$L+}

**Type:** Global

**Menu equivalent:** Options/Compiler/Link buffer

This directive enables or disables buffering in memory when linking .TPU files at the end of compiling a program to disk.

Turbo Pascal's built-in linker is a two-pass linker. In the first pass through the .TPU files, the linker marks every procedure that gets called by other procedures. In the second pass, it generates the .EXE file by extracting the marked procedures from the .TPU files. In the {$L+} state, the .TPU files are kept in memory between two passes; in the {$L-} state, they are reread during the second pass. {$L+} is faster than {$L-} but requires more memory, so for very large programs you'll have to turn link buffering off.

## Numeric Processing

**Syntax:** {$N+} or {$N-}

**Default:** {$N-}

**Type:** Global

**Menu equivalent:** Options/Compiler/Numeric processing

This directive switches between the two different models of floating-point code generation supported by Turbo Pascal. In the {$N-} state, code is generated to perform all real-type calculations in software by calling runtime library routines. In the {$N+} state, code is generated to perform all real-type calculations using the 8087 numeric coprocessor.

For further details on floating-point code generation, refer to Chapter 25, "Using the 8087."

# Range-Checking

**Syntax:** {$R+} or {$R-}

**Default:** {$R-}

**Type:** Local

**Menu equivalent:** Options/Compiler/Range checking

This switch enables or disables the generation of range-checking code. In the {$R+} state, all array and string-indexing expressions are checked to be within the defined bounds, and all assignments to scalar and subrange variables are checked to be within range. If a range-check fails, the program terminates, displaying a runtime error message. Enabling range-checking slows down your program and makes it larger. Use this option when debugging, then turn it off once the program is bug-free.

# Stack Overflow Checking

**Syntax:** {$S+} or {$S-}

**Default:** {$S+}

**Type:** Local

**Menu equivalent:** Options/Compiler/Stack checking

This switch enables or disables the generation of stack-overflow-checking code. In the {$S+} state, the compiler generates code at the beginning of each procedure or function, which checks whether there is sufficient stack space for the local variables. When there is not enough stack space, a call to a procedure or function compiled with {$S+} causes the program to terminate, displaying a runtime error message. In the {$S-} state, such a call is most likely to cause a system crash.

# TPM File Generation

**Syntax:** { $T+} or { $T-}

**Default:** { $T-}

**Type:** Global

**Menu equivalent:** Options/Compiler/Turbo pascal map file

This switch enables or disables the generation of a .TPM file when compiling a program to disk.

A program's .TPM file is used by the Compile/Find error menu command to locate the statement in the source text that caused a runtime error in the program's .EXE file. This requires, however, that the program (and the units it uses) be compiled in the {$D+} state, otherwise the .TPM file will not contain all the necessary debug information. If some units weren't compiled with {$D+}, the compiler will report the unit name, but not position the source text.

The TPMAP.EXE utility converts .TPM files to .MAP files, which can be processed by most symbolic debuggers.

**Note:** The $T directive has no effect when compiling a unit or when compiling a program to memory.

# Var-String Checking

**Syntax:** { $V+} or { $V-}

**Default:** { $V+}

**Type:** Local

**Menu equivalent:** Options/Compiler/Var-string checking

This directive controls type-checking on strings passed as variable parameters. In the {$V+} state, strict type-checking is performed, requiring the formal and actual parameters to be of *identical* string types. In the {$V-} state, any string type variable is allowed as an actual parameter, even if the declared maximum length is not the same as that of the formal parameter.

# Parameter Directives

## Include File

**Syntax**: `{$I filename}`

**Type**: Local

**Menu equivalent:** Options/Directories/Include directories  This directive instructs the compiler to include the named file in the compilation. In effect, the file is inserted in the compiled text right after the {$I *filename*} directive. The default extension for *filename* is .PAS. If *filename* does not specify a directory, then, in addition to searching for the file in the current directory, Turbo Pascal searches in the directories specified in the Options/Directories/Include directories menu, or in the directories specified in the /I option on the TPC command line.

Turbo Pascal allows, at most, five input files to be open at any given time. This means that include files can be nested up to eight levels deep.

There is one restriction to the use of include files: An include file cannot be specified in the middle of a statement part. In fact, all statements between the **begin** and **end** of a statement part must reside in the same source file.

## Link Object File

**Syntax**: `{$L filename}`

**Type**: Local

**Menu equivalent:** Options/Directories/Object directories

This directive instructs the compiler to link the named file with the program or unit being compiled. The $L is used to link with code written in assembly language for subprograms declared to be **external**. The named file must be an Intel relocatable object file (.OBJ file). The default extension for *filename* is .OBJ. If *filename* does not specify a directory, then, in addition to searching for the file in the current directory, Turbo Pascal searches in the directories specified in the Options/Directories/Object directories menu, or in the directories specified in the /O option on the TPC command line.

For further details about linking with assembly language, refer to Chapter 26, "Inside Turbo Pascal."

## Memory Allocation Sizes

**Syntax:** `{$M stacksize,heapmin,heapmax}`

**Default:** `{$M 16384,0,655360}`

**Type:** Global

**Menu equivalent:** Options/Compiler/Memory sizes

This directive specifies a program's memory allocation parameters. *stacksize* must be an integer number in the range 1024 to 65520, which specifies the size of the stack segment. *heapmin* must be in the range 0 to 655360, and *heapmax* must be in the range *heapmin* to 655360. *heapmin* and *heapmax* specify the minimum and maximum sizes of the heap, respectively.

The stack segment and the heap are further discussed in Chapter 16, "Variables," and Chapter 26, "Inside Turbo Pascal."

**Note:** The $M directive has no effect when used in a unit.

## Unit File Name

**Syntax:** `{$U filename}`

**Type:** Local

**Menu equivalent:** Options/Directories/Unit directories

This directive allows you to specify the file name of a unit's source file and .TPU file in cases where the unit name and its file name differ. The {$U *filename*} directive has no effect unless it appears just before a unit name in a **uses** clause.

For further details on the effect of a {$U *filename*} in a **uses** clause, refer to Chapter 21, "Programs and Units."

# Conditional Compilation

Turbo-Pascal's conditional compilation directives allow you to produce different code from the same source text, based on conditional symbols.

There are two basic conditional compilation constructs, which closely resemble Pascal's **if** statement. The first construct

```
{$IFxxx} ... {$ENDIF}
```

causes the source text between {$IF*xxx*} and {$ENDIF} to be compiled only if the condition specified in {$IF*xxx*} is True; if the condition is False, the source text between the two directives is ignored.

The second conditional compilation construct

```
{$IFxxx} ... {$ELSE} ... {$ENDIF}
```

causes either the source text between {$IF*xxx*} and {$ELSE} or the source text between {$ELSE} and {$ENDIF} to be compiled, based on the condition specified by the {$IF*xxx*}.

Here are some examples of conditional compilation constructs:

```
{$IFDEF Debug}
  Writeln('X = ',X);
{$ENDIF}

{$IFDEF CPU87}
  {$N+}
  type
    real = double;
{$ELSE}
  {$N-}
  type
    single = real;
    double = real;
    extended = real;
    comp = real;
{$ENDIF}
```

Conditional compilation constructs can be nested to a level of 16. For every {$IF*xxx*}, the corresponding {$ENDIF} must be found within the same source file—which means there must be an equal number of {$IF*xxx*}'s and {$ENDIF}'s in every source file.

## *Conditional Symbols*

Conditional compilation is based on the evaluation of conditional symbols. Conditional symbols are defined and undefined (forgotten) using the directives

```
{$DEFINE name}
{$UNDEF name}
```

You can also use the /D switch in the command-line compiler or the menu selection **O/C/Conditional defines** from within the integrated environment.

Conditional symbols are best compared to Boolean variables: They are either True (defined) or False (undefined). The {$DEFINE} directive sets a given symbol to True, and the {$UNDEF} directive sets it to False.

Conditional symbols follow the exact same rules as Pascal identifiers: They must start with a letter, followed by any combination of letters, digits, and underscores. They can be of any length, but only the first 63 characters are significant.

**Note**: Conditional symbols and Pascal identifiers have no correlation whatsoever. Conditional symbols cannot be referenced in the actual program, and the program's identifiers cannot be referenced in conditional directives. For example, the construct

```
const
  Debug = True;
begin
  {$IFDEF Debug}
    Writeln('Debug is on');
  {$ENDIF}
end;
```

will *not* compile the *Writeln* statement. Likewise, the construct

```
{$DEFINE Debug}
begin
  if Debug then
    Writeln('Debug is on');
end;
```

will result in an unknown identifier error in the **if** statement.

Turbo Pascal defines the following standard conditional symbols:

**VER40**     Always defined, indicating that this is version 4.0 of Turbo Pascal. Future versions will instead define their corresponding version symbol, for instance, VER41 for version 4.1.

**MSDOS**     Always defined, indicating that the operating system is MS-DOS or PC-DOS. Versions of Turbo Pascal for other operating systems will instead define a symbolic name for that particular operating system.

**CPU86**     Always defined, indicating that the CPU belongs to the 80x86 family of processors. Versions of Turbo Pascal for other CPUs will instead define a symbolic name for that particular CPU.

**CPU87**     Defined if an 8087 numeric coprocessor is present at compile time. If the construct

```
{$IFDEF CPU87} {$N+} {$ELSE} {$N-} {$ENDIF}
```

appears at the beginning of a compilation, Turbo Pascal will automatically select the appropriate model of floating-point code generation for that particular computer.

Other conditional symbols can be defined before a compilation using the **O/C/Conditional defines** menu, or the */D* command-line option if you are using TPC.

## The DEFINE Directive

**Syntax**: {$DEFINE name}

Defines a conditional symbol of the given name. The symbol is known for the remainder of the compilation or until it appears in an {$UNDEF *name*} directive. The {$DEFINE *name*} directive has no effect if *name* is already defined.

## The UNDEF Directive

**Syntax**: {$UNDEF name}

Undefines a previously defined conditional symbol. The symbol is forgotten for the remainder of the compilation or until it reappears in a {$DEFINE *name*} directive. The {$UNDEF *name*} directive has no effect if *name* is already undefined.

## The IFDEF Directive

**Syntax**: {$IFDEF name}

Compiles the source text that follows it if *name* is defined.

## The IFNDEF Directive

**Syntax**: {$IFNDEF symbol}

Compiles the source text that follows it if *name* is not defined.

## The IFOPT Directive

**Syntax**: `{$IFOPT switch}`

Compiles the source text that follows it if *switch* is currently in the specified state. *switch* consists of the name of a switch option, followed by a + or a −. For example, the construct

```
{$IFOPT N+}
  type real = extended;
{$ENDIF}
```

will compile the type declaration if the $N$ option is currently active.

## The ELSE Directive

**Syntax**: `{$ELSE}`

Switches between compiling and ignoring the source text delimited by the last {$IF*xxx*} and the next {$ENDIF}.

## The ENDIF Directive

**Syntax**: `{$ENDIF}`

Ends the conditional compilation initiated by the last {$IF*xxx*} directive.

# D

# The Turbo Pascal Utilities

This appendix describes in detail the three stand-alone utility programs
that come with Turbo Pascal: MAKE, TOUCH, and GREP.

## The Stand-Alone MAKE Utility

This section contains complete documentation for creating makefiles and
using MAKE.

### Creating Makefiles

A makefile contains the definitions and relationships needed to help MAKE
keep your program(s) up-to-date. You can create as many makefiles as you
want and name them whatever you want. If you don't specify a makefile
when you run MAKE (using the *–f* option), then MAKE looks for a file with
the default name MAKEFILE.

You create a makefile with any ASCII text editor, such as Turbo Pascal's
built-in interactive editor. All rules, definitions, and directives end with a
carriage return; if a line is too long, you can continue it to the next line by
placing a backslash (\) as the last character on the line.

Whitespace—spaces and tabs—is used to separate adjacent identifiers (such
as dependencies) and to indent commands within a rule.

Creating a makefile is almost like writing a program—with definitions,
commands, and directives. Here's a list of the constructs allowed in a
makefile:

- comments
- explicit rules
- implicit rules
- macro definitions
- directives: file inclusion, conditional execution, error detection, macro undefinition

Let's look at each of these in more detail.

# Comments

Comments begin with a number sign (#); the rest of the line following the # is ignored by MAKE. Comments can be placed anywhere and never have to start in a particular column.

A backslash (\) will *not* continue a comment onto the next line; instead, you must use a # on each line. In fact, you cannot use a backslash as a continuation character in a line that has a comment. That's because if the backslash precedes the #, it is no longer the last character on the line; if it follows the #, it is part of the comment itself.

Here are some examples of comments in a makefile:

```
# makefile for GETSTARS.EXE
# does complete project maintenance
# implicit rule
.asm.obj                          #.OBJ files depend on >ASM files
  masm $*.asm,$*.obj;             # command to create them
# unconditional rule
getstars.exe:                         # always create GETSTARS.EXE
  tpc getstars /m                     # command to create it
# dependencies
slib2.obj: slib2.asm              # uses the implicit rule above
slib1.obj: slib1.asm              # recast as an explicit rule
  masm slib1.asm,slib1.obj;
# end of makefile
```

# Explicit Rules

Explicit rules take the form

```
    target [target ... ]: [source source ... ]
       [command]
       [command]
       ...
```

where *target* is the file to be updated, *source* is a file upon which *target* depends, and *command* is any valid MS-DOS command (including invocation of .BAT files and execution of .COM and .EXE files).

Explicit rules define one or more target names, zero or more source files, and an optional list of commands to be performed. Target and source file names listed in explicit rules can contain normal MS-DOS drive and directory specifications, but they cannot contain wildcards.

Syntax here is important. *target* must be at the start of a line (in column 1), and each *command* must be indented (preceded by at least one space character or tab). As mentioned before, the backslash (\) can be used as a continuation character if the list of source files or a given command is too long for one line. Finally, both the source files and the commands are optional; it is possible to have an explicit rule consisting only of *target* [*target* ...] followed by a colon.

The idea behind an explicit rule is that the command or commands listed will create or update *target*, usually using the *source* files. When MAKE encounters an explicit rule, it first checks to see if any of the *source* files are target files elsewhere in the makefile. If so, those rules are evaluated first.

Once all the *source* files have been created or updated based on other explicit (or implicit) rules, MAKE checks to see if *target* exists. If not, each *command* is invoked in the order given. If *target* does exist, its time and date of last modification are compared against the time and date for each *source*. If any *source* has been modified more recently than *target*, the list of commands is executed.

A given file name can occur on the left side of an explicit rule only once in a given execution of MAKE.

Each command line in an explicit rule begins with whitespace. MAKE considers all lines following an explicit rule to be part of the command list for that rule, up to the next line that begins in column 1 (without any preceding whitespace) or up to the end of the file. Blank lines are ignored.

An explicit rule, with no command lines following it, is treated a little differently than an explicit rule with command lines.

- If an explicit rule exists for a target with commands, the only files that the target depends on are the ones listed in the explicit rule.
- If an explicit rule has no commands, the targets depend on the files given in the explicit rule, and they also depend on any file that matches an implicit rule for the target(s).

Here is a makefile with examples of explicit rules:

```
myutil.obj: myutil.asm
  masm myutil.asm,myutil.obj;

myapp.exe:  myapp.pas myglobal.tpu myutils.tpu
  tpc myapp /Tc:\tp4\bin

myglobal.tpu: myglobal.pas
  tpc myglobal /Tc:\tp4\bin

myutils.tpu: myutils.pas myglobal.tpu myutil.obj
  tpc myutils /Tc:\tp4\bin
```

- The first explicit rule states that MYUTIL.OBJ depends upon MYUTIL.ASM, and that MYUTIL.OBJ is created by executing the given MASM command. (The /T plus path name in all these examples will be explained later.)

- The second rule states that MYAPP.EXE depends upon MYAPP.PAS, MYGLOBAL.TPU, and MYUTILS.TPU, and is created by the given TPC command.

- The third rule states that MYGLOBAL.TPU depends upon MYGLOBAL.PAS, and is created by the given TPC command.

- The last rule states that MYUTILS.TPU depends upon MYUTILS.PAS, MYGLOBAL.TPU, and MYUTIL.OBJ, and is created by the given TPC command.

- If you reorder the rules so that the one for MYAPP.EXE comes first, followed by the others, MAKE will recompile (or reassemble) only the files that it has to in order to correctly update everything. This is because MAKE with no target on the command line will try to execute the first explicit rule it finds in the makefile.

- In practice, you would usually omit the last two explicit rules and simply append a /M directive to the command under the explicit rule for MYAPP.EXE. You will need to add, however, all the source dependencies from MYGLOBAL.TPU and MYUTILS.TPU to the source for MYAPP.EXE.

## Implicit Rules

MAKE also allows you to define *implicit* rules, which are generalizations of explicit rules. What does that mean? Here's an example to illustrate the relationship between the two types. Consider this explicit rule from the previous sample program:

```
myutil.obj: myutil.asm
  masm myutil.asm,myutil.obj;
```

This rule is a common one, because it follows a general principle: An .OBJ file is dependent on the .ASM file with the same file name and is created by executing MASM. In fact, you might have a makefile where you have several (or even several dozen) explicit rules following this same format.

By redefining the explicit rule as an implicit rule, you can eliminate all the explicit rules of the same form. As an implicit rule, it would look like this:

```
.asm.obj:
   masm $*.asm,$*.obj;
```

This rule means, "any file ending with .OBJ depends on the file with the same name that ends in .ASM, and the .OBJ file is created using the command `masm $*.asm,$*.obj`, where *$\** represents the file's name with no extension." (The symbol *$\** is a special macro and is discussed in the next section.)

The syntax for an implicit rule follows:

```
.source_extension.target_extension:
   {command}
   {command}
   . . .
```

Note the commands are optional and must be indented. The *source_extension* (which must begin in column 1) is the extension of the source file, that is, it applies to any file having the format

```
fname.source_extension
```

Likewise, the *target_extension* refers to the the file

```
fname.target_extension
```

where *fname* is the same for both files. In other words, this implicit rule replaces all explicit rules having the format

```
fname.target_extension:fname.source_extension
   [command]
   [command]
   . . .
```

for any *fname*.

Implicit rules are used if no explicit rule for a given target can be found or if an explicit rule with no commands exists for the target.

The extension of the file name in question is used to determine which implicit rule to use. The implicit rule is applied if a file is found with the same name as the target, but with the mentioned source extension. For example, suppose you had a makefile (named MAKEFILE) whose contents were

```
.asm.obj:
  masm $*.asm,$*.obj;
```

If you had an assembly language routine named RATIO.ASM that you wanted to compile to RATIO.OBJ, you could use the command

```
make ratio.obj
```

MAKE would take RATIO.OBJ to be the target. Since there is no explicit rule for creating RATIO.OBJ, MAKE applies the implicit rule and generates the command

```
masm ratio.asm,ratio.obj;
```

which, of course, does the step necessary to create RATIO.OBJ.

Implicit rules are also used if an explicit rule is given with no commands. Suppose, as mentioned before, you had the following implicit rule at the start of your makefile:

```
.pas.tpu:
  tpc $<
```

You could then rewrite the last two explicit rules as follows:

```
myglobal.tpu: myglobal.pas
myutils.tpu: myutils.pas myglobal.tpu myutil.obj
```

Since you don't have explicit information on how to create these .TPU files, MAKE applies the implicit rule defined earlier.

Several implicit rules can be written with the same target extension, but only one such rule can apply at a time. If more than one implicit rule exists for a given target extension, each rule is checked in the order the rules appear in the makefile, until all applicable rules are checked.

MAKE uses the first implicit rule that it discovers for a file with the source extension. Even if the commands of that rule fail, no more implicit rules are checked.

All lines following an implicit rule are considered to be part of the command list for the rule, up to the next line that begins without whitespace or to the end of the file. Blank lines are ignored. The syntax for a command line is provided later in this appendix.

Unlike explicit rules, MAKE does not know the full file name with an implicit rule. For that reason, special macros are provided with MAKE that allow you to include the name of the file being built by the rule. (For details, see the discussion of macro definitions later in this appendix.)

Here are some examples of implicit rules:

```
.pas.exe:
  tpc $<

.pas.tpu:
  tpc $<

.asm.obj:
  masm $* /mx;
```

In the first example, the target files are .EXE files and their source files are .PAS files. This example has one command line in the command list (command-line syntax is covered later). Likewise, the second implicit rule creates .TPU files from .PAS files.

The last example directs MAKE to assemble a given file from its .ASM source file, using MASM with the /mx option.

## Command Lists

We've talked about both explicit and implicit rules, and how they can have lists of commands. Let's talk about those commands and your options in setting them up.

Commands in a command list must be indented—that is, preceded by at least one space character or tab—and take the form

```
[ prefix ... ] command_body
```

Each command line in a command list consists of an (optional) list of prefixes, followed by a single command body.

The prefixes allowed in a command modify the treatment of these commands by MAKE. The prefix is either the at (@) sign or a hyphen (-) followed immediately by a number.

@    Keeps MAKE from displaying the command before executing it. The display is hidden even if the –s option was not given on the MAKE command line. This prefix applies only to the command on which it appears.

*–num*    Affects how MAKE treats exit codes. If a number (*num*) is provided, then MAKE will abort processing only if the exit status exceeds the number given. In this example, MAKE will abort only if the exit status exceeds 4:

```
-4 myprog sample.x
```

If no *–num* prefix is given, MAKE checks the exit status for the command. If the status is nonzero, MAKE will stop and delete the current target file.

> – With a hyphen but no number, MAKE will not check the exit status at all. Regardless of what the exit status was, MAKE will continue.

The *command body* is treated exactly as if it were entered as a line to COMMAND.COM, with the exception that redirection and pipes are not supported. MAKE executes the following built-in commands by invoking a copy of COMMAND.COM to perform them:

| | | | | |
|---|---|---|---|---|
| break | cd | chdir | cls | copy |
| md | mkdir | path | prompt | ren |
| rename | set | time | type | ver |
| verify | vol | | | |

MAKE searches for any other command name using the MS-DOS search algorithm:

- The current directory is searched first, followed by each directory in the path.
- In each directory, first a file with the extension .COM is checked, then an .EXE file, and finally a .BAT.
- If a .BAT file is found, a copy of COMMAND.COM is invoked to execute the batch file.

Obviously, if an extension is supplied in the command line, MAKE searches only for that extension.

This command will cause COMMAND.COM to execute the change-directory command:

```
cd c:\include
```

This command will be searched for using the full search algorithm:

```
tpc myprog.pas /$B+,R+,I+
```

This command will be searched for using only the .COM extension:

```
myprog.com geo.xyz
```

This command will be executed using the explicit file name provided:

```
c:\myprogs\fil.exe -r
```

## Macros

Often certain commands, file names, or options are used again and again in your makefile. In an example earlier in this appendix, all the TPC commands used the switch */Tc:\tp4\bin*, which means that the files TPC.CFG and TURBO.TPL are in the subdirectory C:\TP4\BIN. Suppose you wanted to switch to another subdirectory for those files; what would you do? You could go through and modify all the /T options, inserting the appropriate path name. Or, you could define a macro.

A *macro* is a name that represents some string of characters (letters and digits). A *macro definition* gives a macro name and the expansion text; thereafter, when MAKE encounters the macro name, it replaces the name with the expansion text.

Suppose you defined the following macro at the start of your makefile:

```
TURBO=c:\tp4\bin
```

You've defined the macro *TURBO*, which is equivalent to the string *c:\tp4\bin*. You could now rewrite the makefile as follows:

```
TURBO=c:\tp4\bin
myapp.exe:  myapp.pas myglobal.tpu myutils.tpu
  tpc myapp /T$(TURBO)

myutils.tpu: myutils.pas myglobal.tpu myutil.obj
  tpc myutils /T$(TURBO)

myglobal.tpu: myglobal.pas
  tpc myglobal /T$(TURBO)

myutil.obj: myutil.asm
  masm myutil.asm,myutil.obj;
```

Everywhere the Turbo directory is specified, you use the macro invocation *$(TURBO)*. When you run MAKE, *$(TURBO)* is replaced with its expansion text, *m*. The result is the same set of commands you had before.

So what have you gained? Flexibility. By changing the first line to

```
TURBO=c:\tp4\project
```

you've changed all the commands to use the configuration and library files in a different subdirectory. In fact, if you leave out the first line altogether, you can specify which subdirectory you want each time you run MAKE, using the *–D* (Define) option:

```
make -DTURBO=c:\tp4\project
```

This tells MAKE to treat *TURBO* as a macro with the expansion text *c:\tp4\project*.

Macro definitions take the form

*macro_name=expansion text*

where *macro_name* is the name of a macro made up of a string of letters and digits with no whitespace in it, though you can have whitespace between *macro_name* and the equal sign (=). *expansion text* is any arbitrary string containing letters, digits, whitespace, and punctuation; it is ended by a carriage return.

If *macro_name* has previously been defined, either by a macro definition in the makefile or by the *–D* option on the MAKE command line, the new definition replaces the old.

Case is significant in macros; that is, the macros names *turbo*, *Turbo*, and *TURBO* are all considered to be different.

Macros are invoked in your makefile with the format

```
$(macro_name)
```

The parentheses are required for all invocation, even if the macro name is just one character, with the exception of three special predefined macros that we'll talk about in just a minute. This construct—*$(macro_name)*—is known as a *macro invocation*.

When MAKE encounters a macro invocation, it replaces the invocation with the macro's expansion text. If the macro is not defined, MAKE replaces it with the null string.

**Macros in macros:** Macro cannot be invoked on the left (*macro_name*) side of a macro definition. They can be used on the right (*expansion text*) side, but they are not expanded until the macro being defined is invoked. In other words, when a macro invocation is expanded, any macros embedded in its expansion text are also expanded.

**Macros in rules:** Macro invocations are expanded immediately in rule lines.

**Macros in directives:** Macro invocations are expanded immediately in *!if* and *!elif* directives. If the macro being invoked in an *!if* or *!elif* directive is not currently defined, it is expanded to the value 0 (False).

**Macros in commands:** Macro invocations in commands are expanded when the command is executed.

MAKE comes with several special predefined macros built-in: *$d*, *$\**, *$<*, *$:*, *$.*, and *$&*. The first is a defined test macro, used in the conditional directives *!if* and *!elif*; the others are file name macros, used in explicit and implicit rules. The various file name macros work in similar ways, expanding to some variation of the full path name of the file being built. In addition, the current SET environment strings are automatically loaded as macros, and the macro __MAKE__ is defined to be 1 (one).

## Defined Test Macro ($d)

This macro expands to 1 if the given macro name is defined, or to 0 if it is not. The content of the macro's expansion text does not matter. This special macro is allowed only in *!if* and *!elif* directives. For example, if you wanted to modify your makefile so that it would use a particular Turbo Pascal directory if you didn't specify one, you could put this at the start of your makefile:

```
!if !$d(TURBO)              # if TURBO is not defined
TURBO=c:\tp4\bin            # define it to C:\TP4\BIN
!endif
```

If you invoke MAKE with the command line

```
make -DTURBO=c:\tp4\project
```

then *TURBO* is defined as *c:\tp4\project*. If, however, you just invoke MAKE by itself

```
make
```

then *TURBO* is defined as `c:\tp4\bin`, your "default" subdirectory.

## Base File Name Macro ($*)

This macro is allowed in the commands for an explicit or an implicit rule. The macro expands to the file name being built, excluding any extension, like this:

```
File name is A:\P\TESTFILE.PAS
$* expands to A:\P\TESTFILE
```

For example, you could modify the explicit MYAPP.EXE rule already given to look like this:

```
myapp.exe:  myapp.pas myglobal.tpu myutils.tpu
  tpc $* /T$(TURBO)
```

When the command in this rule is executed, the macro $* is replaced by the target file name (without an extension), *myapp*. This macro is very useful for implicit rules. For example, an implicit rule for TPC might look like this (assuming that the macro *TURBO* has been or will be defined):

```
.pas.exe:
  tpc $* /T$(TURBO)
```

### Full File Name Macro ($<)

The full file name macro ($<) is also used in the commands for an explicit or implicit rule. In an explicit rule, $< expands to the full target file name (including extension), like this:

```
File name is A:\P\TESTFILE.PAS
$< expands to A:\P\TESTFILE.PAS
```

For example, the rule

```
starlib.tpu: starlib.pas
  copy $< \oldtpus
  tpc $* /T$(TURBO)
```

will copy STARLIB.TPU to the directory \OLDTPUS before compiling STARLIB.PAS.

In an implicit rule, $< takes on the file name plus the source extension. For example, the previous implicit rule

```
.asm.obj:
  masm $*.asm,$*.obj;
```

can be rewritten as

```
.asm.obj:
  masm $<,$*.obj;
```

### File Name Path Macro ($:)

This macro expands to the path name (without the file name), like this:

```
File name is A:\P\TESTFILE.PAS
$: expands to A:\P\
```

### File Name and Extension Macro ($.)

This macro expands to the file name, with extension, like this:

```
File name is A:\P\TESTFILE.PAS
$. expands to TESTFILE.PAS
```

### File Name Only Macro ($&)

This macro expands to the file name only, without path or extension, like this:

```
File name is A:\P\TESTFILE.PAS
$& expands to TESTFILE
```

## Directives

The version of MAKE bundled with Turbo Pascal allows something that other versions of MAKE don't: conditional directives similiar to those allowed for Turbo Pascal. You can use these directives to include other makefiles, to make the rules and commands conditional, to print out error messages, and to "undefine" macros.

Directives in a makefile begin with an exclamation point (!). Here is the complete list of MAKE directives:

```
!include
!if
!else
!elif
!endif
!error
!undef
```

A *file-inclusion directive* (*!include*) specifies a file to be included into the makefile for interpretation at the point of the directive. It takes the following form:

```
!include "filename"
```

or

```
!include <filename>
```

These directives can be nested arbitrarily deep. If an include directive attempts to include a file that has already been included in some outer level of nesting (so that a nesting loop is about to start), the inner include directive is rejected as an error.

How do you use this directive? Suppose you created the file PATH.MAC so it contained the following:

```
!if !$d(TURBO)
TURBO=c:\tp4\bin
!endif
```

You could then make use of this conditional macro definition in any makefile by including the directive

```
!include "PATH.MAC"
```

When MAKE encounters the *!include* directive, it opens the specified file and reads the contents as if they were in the makefile itself.

*Conditional directives* (*!if*, *!elif*, *!else*, and *!endif*) give a programmer a measure of flexibility in constructing makefiles. Rules and macros can be "conditionalized" so that a command-line macro definition (using the *–D* option) can enable or disable sections of the makefile.

The format of these directives parallels, but is more extensive than, the conditional directives allowed by Turbo Pascal:

```
!if expression
  [ lines ]
!endif

!if expression
  [ lines ]
!else
  [ lines ]
!endif

!if expression
  [ lines ]
!elif expression
  [ lines ]
!endif
```

**Note:** *[ lines ]* can be any of the following:

```
macro_definition
explicit_rule
implicit_rule
include_directive
if_group
error_directive
undef_directive
```

The conditional directives form a group, with at least an !if directive beginning the group and an !endif directive closing the group.

■ One *!else* directive can appear in the group.

■ *!elif* directives can appear between the *!if* and any *!else* directives.

■ Rules, macros, and other directives can appear between the various conditional directives in any number. Note that complete rules, with their commands, cannot be split across conditional directives.

■ Conditional directive groups can be nested arbitrarily deep.

Any rules, commands, or directives must be complete within a single source file.

Any *!if* directives must have matching *!endif* directives within the same source file. Thus the following include file is illegal regardless of what is contained in any file that might include it, because it does not have a matching *!endif* directive:

```
!if $(FILE_COUNT) > 5
some rules
!else
other rules
<end-of-file>
```

The expression allowed in an *!if* or an *!elif* directive uses a syntax similar to that found in the C programming language. The expression is evaluated as a simple 32-bit signed integer expression.

Numbers can be entered as decimal, octal, or hexadecimal constants. For example, these are legal constants in an expression:

```
4536                                                    # decimal constant
0677                              # octal constant (note the leading zero)
0x23aF                                              # hexadecimal constant
```

and any of the following unary operators:

| | |
|---|---|
| – | negation |
| ~ | bit complement |
| ! | logical not |

An expression can use any of the following binary operators:

| | |
|---|---|
| + | addition |
| – | subtraction |
| * | multiplication |
| / | division |
| % | remainder |
| » | right shift |
| « | left shift |
| & | bitwise and |
| \| | bitwise or |
| ^ | bitwise exclusive or |
| && | logical and |
| \|\| | logical or |
| > | greater than |
| < | less than |
| >= | greater than or equal to |
| <= | less than or equal to |
| == | equality |
| != | inequality |

An expression can contain the following ternary operator:

? :    The operand before the ? is treated as a test.

If the value of that operand is nonzero, then the second operand (the part between the ? and the colon) is the result. If the value of the first operand is zero, the value of the result is the value of the third operand (the part after the :).

Parentheses can be used to group operands in an expression. In the absence of parentheses, binary operators are grouped according to the same precedence given in the C language.

As in C, grouping is from left to right for operators of equal precedence, except for the ternary operator (? :), which is right to left.

Macros can be invoked within an expression, and the special macro $d() is recognized. After all macros have been expanded, the expression must have proper syntax. Any words in the expanded expression are treated as errors.

The *error directive* (*!error*) causes MAKE to stop and print a fatal diagnostic containing the text after *!error*. It takes the format

```
!error any_text
```

This directive is designed to be included in conditional directives to allow a user-defined abort condition. For example, you could insert the following code in front of the first explicit rule:

```
!if !$d(TURBO)
# if TURBO is not defined
!error TURBO not defined
!endif
```

If you reach this spot without having defined *TURBO*, then MAKE will stop with this error message:

```
Fatal makefile 5: Error directive: TURBO not defined
```

The *undefine directive* (*!undef*) causes any definition for the named macro to be forgotten. If the macro is currently undefined, this directive has no effect. The syntax is

```
!undef macro_name
```

## Using MAKE

You now know a lot about how to write makefiles; now's the time to learn how to use them with MAKE. The simplest way to use MAKE is to type the command

```
make
```

at the MS-DOS prompt. MAKE then looks for MAKEFILE; if it can't find it, it looks for MAKEFILE.MAK; if it can't find that, it halts with an error message.

What if you want to use a file with a name other than MAKEFILE or MAKEFILE.MAK? You give MAKE the file (*-f*) option, like this:

```
make -fstars.mak
```

The general syntax for MAKE is

```
make option option ... target target ...
```

where *option* is a MAKE option (discussed later) and *target* is the name of a target file to be handled by explicit rules.

Here are the syntax rules:

- The word *make* is followed by a space, then a list of make options.
- Each make option must be separated from its adjacent options by a space. Options can be placed in any order, and any number of these options can be entered (as long as there is room in the command line).
- After the list of make options comes a space, then an optional list of targets.
- Each target must also be separated from its adjacent targets by a space. MAKE evaluates the target files in the order listed, recompiling their constituents as necessary.

If the command line does not include any target names, MAKE uses the first target file mentioned in an explicit rule. If one or more targets are mentioned on the command line, they will be built as necessary.

Here are some more examples of MAKE command lines:

```
make -n -fstars.mak
make -s
make -Iinclude -DTURBO=c:\tp4\project
```

MAKE will stop if any command it has executed is aborted via a *Ctrl-Break*. Thus, a *Ctrl-C* will stop the currently executing command and MAKE as well.

## The BUILTINS.MAK File

When using MAKE, you will often find that there are macros and rules (usually implicit ones) that you use again and again. You've got three ways of handling them. First, you can put them in each and every makefile you create. Second, you can put them all in one file and use the *!include* directive in each makefile you create. Third, you can put them all in a file named BUILTINS.MAK.

Each time you run MAKE, it looks for a file named BUILTINS.MAK; if it finds the file, MAKE reads it in before handling MAKEFILE (or whichever makefile you want it to process).

The BUILTINS.MAK file is intended for any rules (usually implicit rules) or macros that will be commonly used in files anywhere on your computer.

There is no requirement that any BUILTINS.MAK file exist. If MAKE finds a BUILTINS.MAK file, it interprets that file first. If MAKE cannot find a BUILTINS.MAK file, it proceeds directly to interpreting MAKEFILE (or whatever makefile you specify).

## How MAKE Searches for Files

MAKE will search for BUILTINS.MAK in the current directory or in the exec directory if your computer is running under DOS 3.x. You should place this file in the same directory as the MAKE.EXE file.

MAKE always searches for the makefile in the current directory only. This file contains the rules for the particular executable program file being built. The two files have identical syntax rules.

MAKE also searches for any *!include* files in the current directory. If you use the *–I* (Include) option, it will also search in the specified directory.

## MAKE Command-Line Options

We've alluded to several of MAKE's command-line options; now we'll present a complete list of them. Note that case (upper or lower) **is** significant; the option *–d* is not a valid substitute for *–D*.

**–D***identifier*    Defines the named identifier to the string consisting of the single character 1.

**–D***iden=string*   Defines the named identifier *iden* to the string after the equal sign. The string cannot contain any spaces or tabs.

| | |
|---|---|
| **–I**_directory_ | MAKE will search for include files in the indicated directory (as well as in the current directory). |
| **–U**_identifier_ | Undefines any previous definitions of the named identifier. |
| **–s** | Normally, MAKE prints each command as it is about to be executed. With the –s option, no commands are printed before execution. |
| **–n** | Causes MAKE to print the commands, but not actually perform them. This is useful for debugging a makefile. |
| **–f**_filename_ | Uses _filename_ as the MAKE file. If _filename_ does not exist and no extension is given, tries _filename_.MAK. |
| **–?** or **–h** | Prints help message. |

# MAKE Error Messages

MAKE diagnostic messages fall into two classes: fatals and errors. When a fatal error occurs, execution immediately stops. You must take appropriate action and then restart the execution. Errors will indicate some sort of syntax or semantic error in the source makefile. MAKE will complete interpreting the makefile and then stop.

## *Fatals*

### Don't know how to make XXXXXXXX

This message is issued when MAKE encounters a nonexistent file name in the build sequence, and no rule exists that would allow the file name to be built.

### Error directive: XXXX

This message is issued when MAKE processes an #*error* directive in the source file. The text of the directive is displayed in the message.

### Incorrect command line argument: XXX

This error occurs if MAKE is executed with incorrect command-line arguments.

### Not enough memory

This error occurs when the total working storage has been exhausted. You should try this on a machine with more memory. If you already have 640K in your machine, you may have to simplify the source file.

**Unable to execute command**

This message is issued after attempting to execute a command. It could be caused because the command file could not be found, or because it was misspelled. A less likely possibility is that the command exists but is somehow corrupted.

**Unable to open makefile**

This message is issued when the current directory does not contain a file named MAKEFILE.

## Errors

**Bad file name format in include statement**

Include file names must be surrounded by quotes or angle brackets. The file name was missing the opening quote or angle bracket.

**Bad undef statement syntax**

An *!undef* statement must contain a single identifier and nothing else as the body of the statement.

**Character constant too long**

Character constants can be only one or two characters long.

**Command arguments too long**

The arguments to a command executed by MAKE were more than 127 characters—a limit imposed by MS-DOS.

**Command syntax error**

This message occurs if

- the first rule line of the makefile contained any leading whitespace.
- an implicit rule did not consist of *.ext.ext:*.
- an explicit rule did not contain a name before the : character.
- a macro definition did not contain a name before the = character.

**Division by zero**

A divide or remainder in an *!if* statement has a zero divisor.

**Expression syntax error in *!if* statement**

The expression in an *!if* statement is badly formed—it contains a mismatched parenthesis, an extra or missing operator, or a missing or extra constant.

**File name too long**

The file name given in an *!include* directive was too long for MAKE to process. File path names in MS-DOS must be no more than 78 characters long.

**Illegal character in constant expression X**

MAKE encountered some character not allowed in a constant expression. If the character is a letter, this indicates a (probably) misspelled identifier.

**Illegal octal digit**

An octal constant was found containing a digit of 8 or 9.

**Macro expansion too long**

A macro cannot expand to more than 4096 characters. This error often occurs if a macro recursively expands itself. A macro cannot legally expand to itself.

**Misplaced elif statement**

An *!elif* directive was encountered without any matching *!if* directive.

**Misplaced else statement**

An *!else* directive was encountered without any matching *!if* directive.

**Misplaced endif statement**

An *!endif* directive was encountered without any matching *!if* directive.

**No file name ending**

The file name in an include statement was missing the correct closing quote or angle bracket.

**Redefinition of target XXXXXXXX**

The named file occurs on the left-hand side of more than one explicit rule.

**Unable to open include file XXXXXXXXX.XXX**

The named file could not be found. This could also be caused if an include file included itself. Check whether the named file exists.

**Unexpected end of file in conditional started on line #**

The source file ended before MAKE encountered an *!endif*. The *!endif* was either missing or misspelled.

**Unknown preprocessor statement**

A ! character was encountered at the beginning of a line, and the statement name following was not *error, undef, if, elif, include, else,* or *endif.*

# The TOUCH Utility

There are times when you want to force a particular target file to be recompiled or rebuilt, even though no changes have been made to its sources. One way to do this is to use the TOUCH utility included with

Turbo Pascal. TOUCH changes the date and time of one or more files to the current date and time, making it "newer" than the files that depend on it.

To force a target file to be rebuilt, "touch" one of the files that target depends on. To touch a file (or files), enter

```
touch filename [ filename ... ]
```

at the DOS prompt. TOUCH will then update the file's creation date(s).

Once you do this, you can invoke MAKE to rebuild the touched target file(s). (You can use the DOS wildcards * and ? with TOUCH.)

# The GREP Utility

Also included on your Turbo Pascal disks is a stand-alone utility program called GREP. This is a powerful search utility that can look for text in several files at once. For example, if you have forgotten what program you defined a procedure called *SetUpMyModem*, you could use GREP to search the contents of all the .PAS files in your directory to look for the string *SetUpMyModem*.

The command-line syntax for GREP follows:

```
GREP [options] searchstring file[s]
```

where *options* consists of one or more single characters preceded by a hyphen; *searchstring* definds the pattern to search for.

## *The GREP Switches*

Each individual switch character can be followed by the symbol "+" to turn the option on, or by another hyphen (-) to turn the option off. The default is + (that is, *–r* means the same thing as *–r+*). Here is a list of the option characters used with GREP:

–r  The text defined by *searchstring* is treated as a regular expression instead of a literal string.

–l  Only the name of each file containing a match is printed. After a match is found, the file name is printed and processing immediately moves on to the next file.

–c  Only a count of matching lines is printed. For each file that contains at least one matching line, the file name and a count of the number of matching lines is printed. Matching lines are not printed.

−n  Each matching line that is printed is preceded by its line number.

−v  Only non-matching lines are printed. Only lines that *do not* contain the search string are considered to be matching lines.

−i  Ignore uppercase/lowercase differences (case folding). All letters *a-z* are treated identically to the corresponding letters *A-Z* in all situations.

−d  Search subdirectories. For each file set specified on the command line, all files that match the wildcard file specification are searched in the directory specified *and* all subdirectories below the specified directory. If a file-set is given without a path, it is assumed to be the current directory.

−z  Verbose. The file name of every file searched is printed. Each matching line is preceded by its line number. A count of matching lines in each file is given, even if it's zero.

−w  Write Options. Combine the options given on the command line with the default options and write these to a new .COM file as the new defaults. This option allows you to tailor the default option settings to your own taste.

Several of these options are in direct conflict with each other. In these cases, the following order applies (the first one is the one that takes precedence):

*−z  −l  −c  −n*

Each occurrence of an option overrides the previous definition. The default setting for each option can be installed.

## *How to Search in GREP*

The search string can be enclosed in quotation marks to prevent spaces and tabs from being treated as delimiters. Matches will not cross line boundaries. When the *−r* switch is used, the search string is treated as a regular expression (as opposed to a literal expression) and the following symbols take on special meanings:

^   A circumflex at the start of the expression matches the start of a line.

\$   A dollar sign at the end of the expression matches the end of a line.

.   A period matches any character.

*   An expression followed by an asterisk wildcard matches zero or more occurrences of that expression: *fo\** matches *f, fo, foo*, etc.

+      An expression followed by a plus sign matches one or more occurrences of that expression: *fo+* matches *fo, foo*, etc., but not *f*.

[]     A string enclosed in brackets matches any character in that string, but no others. If the first character in the string is a circumflex (^), the expression matches any character except the characters in the string. For example, *[xyz]* matches *x, y*, and *z*, while *[^xyz]* matches *a* and *b*, but not *x* or *y*. A range of characters can be specified by two characters separated by a hyphen (-). These can be combined to form expressions like *[a-bd-z?]* to match any letter except *c*, and *?*.

       **Note:** Four characters (*$, +, *,* and *.)* do not have any special meaning when used in a set. The character ^ is only treated specially if it immediately follows the beginning of the set (that is, immediately after the *[*).

\      The backslash "escape character" tells GREP to seach for the literal character that follows it. For example, \. matches a period instead of any character.

Any ordinary character not mentioned in this list matches that character. A concatenation of regular expressions is a regular expression.

## Examples of Using GREP

The following examples assume all options default to off.

---

### grep main( *.pas

| | |
|---|---|
| **Matches:** | `main()` |
| | `mymain(` |
| **Does not match:** | `mymainfunc()` |
| | `MAIN(i: integer);` |
| **Searches:** | *.pas in current directory |
| **Note:** | By default, search is case-sensitive. |

### grep –r [^a-z]main\ *( *.pas

| | |
|---|---|
| **Matches:** | `main(i:integer)` |
| | `main(i,j:integer)` |
| | `if (main ()) halt;` |
| **Does not match:** | `mymain()` |

```
                    MAIN(i:integer);
```

**Searches:**        *.pas in current directory

**Note:**            Since spaces and tabs are normally considered to be
                     command-line delimiters, you must quote them if you
                     wish to include them as part of a regular expression. In
                     this case, the space after *main* was quoted using the
                     backslash escape character. You could also accomplish
                     this by placing the space or the entire regular expression
                     in double quotes (").

# grep –ri [a-c]:\\data\.fil *.pas *.inc

**Matches:**         ```
                     A:\data.fil
                     c:\Data.Fil
                     B:\DATA.FIL
                     ```

**Does not match:**  ```
                     d:\data.fil
                     a:data.fil
                     Writeln("c:\\data.fil");
                     ```

**Searches:**        *.pas and *.inc in current directory

**Note:**            If you wish to search for the characters "\" and ".", you
                     must quote them by placing the backslash (\) escape
                     character immediately in front of them.

# grep –ri [^a-z]word[^a-z] *.doc

**Matches:**         ```
                     every new word must be on a new line.
                     MY WORD!
                     word--smallest unit of speech.
                     In the beginning there was the WORD, and the WORD
                     ```

**Does not match:**  ```
                     Each file has at least 2000 words.
                     He misspells toward as toword.
                     ```

**Searches:**        *.doc in the current directory

**Note:**            This format basically defines a word search.

# grep "search string with spaces" *.doc *.asm
# a:\work\myfile.*

**Matches:**         ```
                     This is a search string with spaces in it.
                     ```

**Does not match:**  ```
                     THIS IS A SEARCH STRING WITH SPACES IN IT.
                     This is a search string with many spaces in it.
                     ```

| | |
|---|---|
| **Searches:** | *.doc and *.asm in the current directory, and myfile.* in a directory called \work on drive A: |
| **Note:** | Example of how to search for a string with embedded spaces. |

## grep –rd "[ ,.:?'\"]"$ \*.doc

| | |
|---|---|
| **Matches:** | ```
He said hi to me.
Where are you going?
Happening in anticipation of a unique situation,
Examples include the following:
"Many men smoke, but fu man chu."
``` |
| **Does not match:** | ```
He said "Hi" to me
Where are you going? I'm headed to the beach this
``` |
| **Searches:** | *.doc in the root directory and all its subdirectories on the current drive |
| **Note:** | Searches for ,.:?' and " at the end of a line. Notice that the double quote within the range has an escape character in front of it so it is treated as a normal character instead of the ending quote for the string. Also, notice the $ character appears outside of the quoted string, which demonstrates how regular expressions can be concatenated together to form a longer expression. |

## grep –ild " the " \*.doc
## grep –i –l –d " the " \*.doc
## grep –il –d " the " \*.doc

| | |
|---|---|
| **Matches:** | ```
Anyway, this is the time we have
do you think? The main reason we are
``` |
| **Does not match:** | ```
He said "Hi" to me just when I
Where are you going? I'll bet you're headed to
``` |
| **Searches:** | *.doc in the root directory and all its subdirectories on the current drive |
| **Note:** | Ignores case and prints the names of any files that contain at least one match. The examples show the different ways of specifying multiple switches. |

# The BINOBJ Utility

A utility program BINOBJ.EXE has been added that converts any file to an .OBJ file so it can be linked into a Turbo Pascal program as a "procedure." This is useful if you have a binary data file that must reside in the code segment or is too large to make into a typed constant array. For example, you can use BINOBJ with the *Graph* unit to link the graphics driver or font files directly into your .EXE file. Then, to use your graph program, you need only have the .EXE file (see the example GRLINK.PAS on Disk 2).

BINOBJ takes three parameters:

```
BINOBJ  <source[.BIN]>  <destination[.OBJ]>  <public name>
```

*source* is the binary file to convert; *destination* is the name of the .OBJ to be produced; and *public name* is the name of the procedure as it will be declared in your Turbo Pascal program.

The following example, the procedure *ShowScreen*, takes a pointer as a parameter and moves 4000 bytes of data to screen memory. The file called MENU.DTA contains the image of the main menu screen (80 * 25 * 2 = 4000 bytes).

Here's a simple (no error-checking) version of MYPROG.PAS:

```pascal
program MyProg;

procedure ShowScreen(var ScreenData : pointer);
{ Display a screenful of data--no error-checking! }
var
  ScreenSegment: word;

begin
  if (Lo(LastMode) = 7) then          { Mono? }
    ScreenSegment := $B000
  else
    ScreenSegment := $B800;
  Move(ScreenData^,                   { From pointer }
      Ptr(ScreenSegment, 0)^,         { To video memory }
      4000);                          { 80 * 25 * 2 }
end;

var
  MenuP : pointer;
  MenuF : file;

begin
  Assign(MenuF, 'MENU.DTA');          { Open screen data file }
  Reset(MenuF, 1);
  GetMem(MenuP, 4000);                { Allocate buffer on heap }
  BlockRead(MenuF, MenuP^, 4000);     { Read screen data }
  Close(MenuF);
  ShowScreen(MenuP);                  { Display screen }
end.
```

The screen data file (MENU.DTA) is opened and then read into a buffer on the heap. Both MYPROG.EXE and MENU.DTA must be present at runtime for this program to work. You can use BINOBJ to convert MENU.DTA to an .OBJ file (MENUDTA.OBJ) and tell it to associate the data with a procedure called *MenuData*. Then you can declare the fake external procedure *MenuData*, which actually contains the screen data. Once you link in the .OBJ file with the {$L} compiler directive, *MenuData* will be 4000 bytes long and contain your screen data. First, run BINOBJ on MENU.DTA:

```
binobj MENU.DTA MENUDTA MenuData
```

The first parameter, MENU.DTA, shows a familiar file of screen data; the second, MENUDTA, is the name of the .OBJ file to be created (since you didn't specify an extension, .OBJ will be added). The last parameter, *MenuData*, is the name of the external procedure as it will be declared in your progam. Now that you've converted MENU.DTA to an .OBJ file, here's what the new MYPROG.PAS looks like:

```
program MyProg;

procedure ShowScreen(ScreenData : pointer);
{ Display a screenful of data--no error checking! }
var
  ScreenSegment: word;
begin
  if (Lo(LastMode) = 7) then                          { Mono? }
    ScreenSegment := $B000
  else
    ScreenSegment := $B800;
  Move(ScreenData^,                            { From pointer }
      Ptr(ScreenSegment, 0)^,               { To video memory }
      4000);                                   { 80 * 25 * 2 }
end;

procedure MenuData; external;
{$L MENUDTA.OBJ }
begin
  ShowScreen(@MenuData);                       { Display screen }
end.
```

Notice that *ShowScreen* didn't change at all, and that the ADDRESS of your procedure is passed using the @ operator.

The advantage of linking the screen data into the .EXE is apparent: You don't need any support files in order to run the program. In addition, you have the luxury of referring to your screen by name (*MenuData*). The disadvantages are that (1) every time you modify the screen data file, you must reconvert it to an .OBJ file and recompile MYPROG and (2) you have to have a separate .OBJ file (and **external** procedure) for each screen you want to display.

BINOBJ is especially useful when the binary file you wish to link in is fairly stable. One of the sample graphics programs uses BINOBJ to build two units that contain the driver and font files; refer to the extensive comment at the beginning of GRLINK.PAS on Disk 2.

*Turbo Pascal Owner's Handbook*

# E

# Reference Materials

This chapter is devoted to certain reference materials, including an ASCII table, keyboard scan codes, and extended codes.

## ASCII Codes

The **A**merican **S**tandard **C**ode for **I**nformation **I**nterchange (ASCII) is a code that translates alphabetic and numeric characters and symbols and control instructions into 7-bit binary code. Table E.1 shows both printable characters and control characters.

| DEC | HEX | CHAR | DEC | HEX | CHAR | DEC | HEX | CHAR | DEC | HEX | CHAR |
|---|---|---|---|---|---|---|---|---|---|---|---|
| 0 | 0 |  | 32 | 20 |  | 64 | 40 | @ | 96 | 60 | ` |
| 1 | 1 | ☺ | 33 | 21 | ! | 65 | 41 | A | 97 | 61 | a |
| 2 | 2 | ● | 34 | 22 | " | 66 | 42 | B | 98 | 62 | b |
| 3 | 3 | ♥ | 35 | 23 | # | 67 | 43 | C | 99 | 63 | c |
| 4 | 4 | ♦ | 36 | 24 | $ | 68 | 44 | D | 100 | 64 | d |
| 5 | 5 | ♣ | 37 | 25 | % | 69 | 45 | E | 101 | 65 | e |
| 6 | 6 | ♠ | 38 | 26 | & | 70 | 46 | F | 102 | 66 | f |
| 7 | 7 | ● | 39 | 27 | ' | 71 | 47 | G | 103 | 67 | g |
| 8 | 8 | ◘ | 40 | 28 | ( | 72 | 48 | H | 104 | 68 | h |
| 9 | 9 | ○ | 41 | 29 | ) | 73 | 49 | I | 105 | 69 | i |
| 10 | A | ◎ | 42 | 2A | * | 74 | 4A | J | 106 | 6A | j |
| 11 | B | ♂ | 43 | 2B | + | 75 | 4B | K | 107 | 6B | k |
| 12 | C | ♀ | 44 | 2C | , | 76 | 4C | L | 108 | 6C | l |
| 13 | D | ♪ | 45 | 2D | - | 77 | 4D | M | 109 | 6D | m |
| 14 | E | ♫ | 46 | 2E | . | 78 | 4E | N | 110 | 6E | n |
| 15 | F | ¤ | 47 | 2F | / | 79 | 4F | O | 111 | 6F | o |
| 16 | 10 | ► | 48 | 30 | 0 | 80 | 50 | P | 112 | 70 | p |
| 17 | 11 | ◄ | 49 | 31 | 1 | 81 | 51 | Q | 113 | 71 | q |
| 18 | 12 | ↕ | 50 | 32 | 2 | 82 | 52 | R | 114 | 72 | r |
| 19 | 13 | ‼ | 51 | 33 | 3 | 83 | 53 | S | 115 | 73 | s |
| 20 | 14 | ¶ | 52 | 34 | 4 | 84 | 54 | T | 116 | 74 | t |
| 21 | 15 | § | 53 | 35 | 5 | 85 | 55 | U | 117 | 75 | u |
| 22 | 16 | ■ | 54 | 36 | 6 | 86 | 56 | V | 118 | 76 | v |
| 23 | 17 | ↨ | 55 | 37 | 7 | 87 | 57 | W | 119 | 77 | w |
| 24 | 18 | ↑ | 56 | 38 | 8 | 88 | 58 | X | 120 | 78 | x |
| 25 | 19 | ↓ | 57 | 39 | 9 | 89 | 59 | Y | 121 | 79 | y |
| 26 | 1A | → | 58 | 3A | : | 90 | 5A | Z | 122 | 7A | z |
| 27 | 1B | ← | 59 | 3B | ; | 91 | 5B | [ | 123 | 7B | { |
| 28 | 1C | ∟ | 60 | 3C | < | 92 | 5C | \ | 124 | 7C | \| |
| 29 | 1D | ↔ | 61 | 3D | = | 93 | 5D | ] | 125 | 7D | } |
| 30 | 1E | ▲ | 62 | 3E | > | 94 | 5E | ^ | 126 | 7E | ~ |
| 31 | 1F | ▼ | 63 | 3F | ? | 95 | 5F | _ | 127 | 7F | ⌂ |

| DEC | HEX | CHAR | DEC | HEX | CHAR | DEC | HEX | CHAR | DEC | HEX | CHAR |
|-----|-----|------|-----|-----|------|-----|-----|------|-----|-----|------|
| 128 | 80 | Ç | 160 | A0 | á | 192 | C0 | └ | 224 | E0 | α |
| 129 | 81 | ü | 161 | A1 | í | 193 | C1 | ┴ | 225 | E1 | β |
| 130 | 82 | é | 162 | A2 | ó | 194 | C2 | ┬ | 226 | E2 | Γ |
| 131 | 83 | â | 163 | A3 | ú | 195 | C3 | ├ | 227 | E3 | π |
| 132 | 84 | ä | 164 | A4 | ñ | 196 | C4 | ─ | 228 | E4 | Σ |
| 133 | 85 | à | 165 | A5 | Ñ | 197 | C5 | ┼ | 229 | E5 | σ |
| 134 | 86 | å | 166 | A6 | ª | 198 | C6 | ╞ | 230 | E6 | μ |
| 135 | 87 | ç | 167 | A7 | º | 199 | C7 | ╟ | 231 | E7 | τ |
| 136 | 88 | ê | 168 | A8 | ¿ | 200 | C8 | ╚ | 232 | E8 | Φ |
| 137 | 89 | ë | 169 | A9 | ⌐ | 201 | C9 | ╔ | 233 | E9 | θ |
| 138 | 8A | è | 170 | AA | ¬ | 202 | CA | ╩ | 234 | EA | Ω |
| 139 | 8B | ï | 171 | AB | ½ | 203 | CB | ╦ | 235 | EB | δ |
| 140 | 8C | î | 172 | AC | ¼ | 204 | CC | ╠ | 236 | EC | ∞ |
| 141 | 8D | ì | 173 | AD | ¡ | 205 | CD | ═ | 237 | ED | ø |
| 142 | 8E | Ä | 174 | AE | « | 206 | CE | ╬ | 238 | EE | ∈ |
| 143 | 8F | Å | 175 | AF | » | 207 | CF | ╧ | 239 | EF | ∩ |
| 144 | 90 | É | 176 | B0 | ░ | 208 | D0 | ╨ | 240 | F0 | ≡ |
| 145 | 91 | æ | 177 | B1 | ▒ | 209 | D1 | ╤ | 241 | F1 | ± |
| 146 | 92 | Æ | 178 | B2 | ▓ | 210 | D2 | ╥ | 242 | F2 | ≥ |
| 147 | 93 | ô | 179 | B3 | │ | 211 | D3 | ╙ | 243 | F3 | ≤ |
| 148 | 94 | ö | 180 | B4 | ┤ | 212 | D4 | ╘ | 244 | F4 | ⌠ |
| 149 | 95 | ò | 181 | B5 | ╡ | 213 | D5 | ╒ | 245 | F5 | ⌡ |
| 150 | 96 | û | 182 | B6 | ╢ | 214 | D6 | ╓ | 246 | F6 | ÷ |
| 151 | 97 | ù | 183 | B7 | ╖ | 215 | D7 | ╫ | 247 | F7 | ≈ |
| 152 | 98 | ÿ | 184 | B8 | ╕ | 216 | D8 | ╪ | 248 | F8 | ° |
| 153 | 99 | Ö | 185 | B9 | ╣ | 217 | D9 | ┘ | 249 | F9 | • |
| 154 | 9A | Ü | 186 | BA | ║ | 218 | DA | ┌ | 250 | FA | · |
| 155 | 9B | ¢ | 187 | BB | ╗ | 219 | DB | █ | 251 | FB | √ |
| 156 | 9C | £ | 188 | BC | ╝ | 220 | DC | ▄ | 252 | FC | ⁿ |
| 157 | 9D | ¥ | 189 | BD | ╜ | 221 | DD | ▌ | 253 | FD | ² |
| 158 | 9E | ₧ | 190 | BE | ╛ | 222 | DE | ▐ | 254 | FE | ■ |
| 159 | 9F | ƒ | 191 | BF | ┐ | 223 | DF | ▀ | 255 | FF | |

# Extended Key Codes

Extended key codes are returned by those keys or key combinations that cannot be represented by the standard ASCII codes listed in Table E.1. (See *ReadKey* in Chapter 27 for a description about how to determine if an extended key has been pressed.)

Table E.2 shows the second code and what it means.

Table E.2: Extended Key Codes

| Second Code | Meaning |
|---|---|
| 3 | *NUL* (null character) |
| 15 | *Shift Tab (—<vv)* |
| 16-25 | *Alt-Q / W / E / R / T / Y / U / I / O / P* |
| 30-38 | *Alt-A / S / D / F / G / H / I / J / K / L* |
| 44-50 | *Alt-Z / X / C / V / B / N / M* |
| 59-68 | Keys *F1-F10* (disabled as softkeys) |
| 71 | *Home* |
| 72 | *Up arrow* |
| 73 | *PgUp* |
| 75 | *Left arrow* |
| 77 | *Right arrow* |
| 79 | *End* |
| 80 | *Down arrow* |
| 81 | *PgDn* |
| 82 | *Ins* |
| 83 | *Del* |
| 84-93 | *F11-F20 (Shift-F1 to Shift-F10)* |
| 94-103 | *F21-F30 (Ctrl-F1 through F10)* |
| 104-113 | *F31-F40 (Alt-F1 through F10)* |
| 114 | *Ctrl-PrtSc* |
| 115 | *Ctrl-Left arrow* |
| 116 | *Ctrl-Right arrow* |
| 117 | *Ctrl-End* |
| 118 | *Ctrl-PgDn* |
| 119 | *Ctrl-Home* |
| 120-131 | *Alt-1 / 2 / 3 / 4 / 5 / 6 / 7 / 8 / 9 / 0 / - / =* |
| 132 | *Ctrl-PgUp* |
| 133 | *F11* |
| 134 | *F12* |
| 135 | *Shift-F11* |
| 136 | *Shift-F12* |
| 137 | *Ctrl-F11* |
| 138 | *Ctrl-F12* |
| 139 | *Alt-F11* |
| 140 | *Alt-F12* |

# Keyboard Scan Codes

Keyboard scan codes are the codes returned from the keys on the IBM PC keyboard, as they are seen by Turbo Pascal. These keys are useful when you're working at the assembly language level. Note that the keyboard scan codes displayed in Table E.3 on page 584 are in hexadecimal values.

| Key | Scan Code in Hex | Key | Scan Code in Hex |
|---|---|---|---|
| Esc | 01 | Left/Right arrow | 0F |
| !1 | 02 | Q | 10 |
| @2 | 03 | W | 11 |
| #3 | 04 | E | 12 |
| $4 | 05 | R | 13 |
| %5 | 06 | T | 14 |
| ^6 | 07 | Y | 15 |
| &7 | 08 | U | 16 |
| *8 | 09 | I | 17 |
| (9 | 0A | O | 18 |
| )0 | 0B | P | 19 |
| _- | 0C | {[ | 1A |
| += | 0D | }] | 1B |
| Backspace | 0E | Return | 1C |
| Ctrl | 1D | \|\ | 2B |
| A | 1E | Z | 2C |
| S | 1F | X | 2D |
| D | 20 | C | 2E |
| F | 21 | V | 2F |
| G | 22 | B | 30 |
| H | 23 | N | 31 |
| J | 24 | M | 32 |
| K | 25 | <, | 33 |
| L | 26 | >. | 34 |
| :; | 27 | ?/ | 35 |
| "' | 28 | RightShift | 36 |
| ~' | 29 | PrtSc* | 37 |
| LeftShift | 2A | Alt | 38 |
| SpaceBar | 39 | 7Home | 47 |
| Caps Lock | 3A | 8Up arrow | 48 |
| F1 | 3B | 9Pg Up | 49 |
| F2 | 3C | Minus sign | 4A |
| F3 | 3D | 4Left arrow | 4B |
| F4 | 3E | 5 | 4C |
| F5 | 3F | 6Right arrow | 4D |
| F6 | 40 | + | 4E |
| F7 | 41 | 1End | 4F |
| F8 | 42 | 2Down arrow | 50 |
| F9 | 43 | 3PgDn | 51 |
| F10 | 44 | 0Ins | 52 |
| F11 | D9 | Del | 53 |
| F12 | DA | Num Lock | 45 |
| Scroll Lock | 46 | | |

# F

# Customizing Turbo Pascal

This appendix explains how to customize Turbo Pascal and install your customizations in the TURBO.EXE file.

## What Is TINST?

TINST is the Turbo Pascal installation program that you can use to customize TURBO.EXE (the integrated environment version of Turbo Pascal). Through TINST, you can change various default settings in the Turbo Pascal operating environment, such as the screen size, editing commands, menu colors, and default directories. It directly modifies certain default values within your copy of TURBO.EXE.

With TINST, you can do any of the following:

- set up paths to the directories where your include files, unit files, configuration files, Help files, Pick file, and executable files are located
- customize the Editor command keys
- set up Turbo Pascal's editor defaults and onscreen appearance
- set up the default video display mode
- change screen colors
- resize Turbo Pascal's Edit and Output windows
- change the defaults of any of the settings accessible through the Options/Compiler menu or the Options/Compiler/Memory sizes menu
- change the defaults of any of the settings accessible through the Options/Environment menu or the Options/Environment/Screen size menu

- change the destination setting (menu equivalent: **Compile/Destination**)
- determine the primary file (menu equivalent: **Compile/Primary** file)

Turbo Pascal comes ready to run; there is no installation *per se*. You can copy the files from the distribution disks to your working floppies (or hard disk) as described in Chapter 1, then run Turbo Pascal.

You will need to also run TINST if you want to do any of the following:

- automatically load a configuration file (TURBO.TP) that does not reside in the current directory
- change Turbo Pascal's default menu colors
- force the display mode or snow checking

If you want to store path names (to all the different directories you use when running Turbo Pascal) directly in TURBO.EXE, you'll need to use one of the menu options (off of **Options/Directories**) from within the TINST program.

You can use the **Editor commands** option to reconfigure (customize) the interactive editor's keystrokes to your liking.

The **Environment** option is for setting various defaults for the default editing modes and the appearance of the Turbo Pascal integrated environment.

With **Display** mode, you can specify the video display mode that Turbo Pascal will operate in, and whether your display is a "snowy" video adapter.

You can customize the colors of almost every part of Turbo Pascal's integrated environment through the **Set colors** option.

The **Resize windows** option allows you to change the sizes of the Edit and Output windows.

# Running TINST

1. To get started, type `tinst` *Enter* at the DOS prompt. TURBO.EXE must be in the same directory as TINST; if it isn't, you must add the path name of TURBO.EXE to the command invoking TINST.

   **Note:** TINST comes up in black and white by default. If you have a color monitor and want to run TINST in color rather than black and white, type `tinst /c` *Enter* at the DOS prompt.

Note that you can use one version of TINST to customize several different copies of Turbo Pascal on your system. These various copies of TURBO.EXE can have different executable program names. Simply invoke TINST and give a (relative or absolute) path name to the copy of TURBO.EXE you're customizing; for example,

```
tinst c:\turbo00\tp00.exe
tinst ..\..\bwtp.exe
tinst /c c:\borland\colortp.exe
```

In this way, you can customize the different copies of Turbo Pascal on your system to use different editor command keys, different menu colors, and so on, if you're so inclined.

2. From the main TINST installation menu, you can select Compile, Options, Editor commands, Display mode, Set colors, Resize windows, or Quit/save. You can either press the highlighted capital letter of a given option, or use the *Up* and *Down* arrow keys to move to your selection and then press *Enter*. For instance, press *S* to Set the colors of the Turbo Pascal integrated environment.

3. In general, pressing *Esc* (more than once if necessary) will return you from a submenu to the main installation menu.

## *The Turbo Pascal Directories Option*

With the **Directories** option, you can specify a path to each of the TURBO.EXE default directories. These are the directories Turbo Pascal searches when looking for an alternate configuration file, the Help file, and the object, include, and unit files, along with the directory where it will place your executable program.

When you select **Options/Directories**, TINST brings up a menu with the following items:

- **Turbo directory**
- **Executable directory**
- **Include directories**
- **Unit directories**
- **Object directories**
- **Pick file name**

## Object directories, Include directories, and Unit directories

You can enter multiple directories in Include directories and Unit directories. You must separate these "ganged" directory path names with a semicolon ( ; ), and can enter a maximum of 127 characters with either menu item. You can enter absolute or relative path names.

For example, if you have three directories of include files, you could enter the following in the Include directories pop-up input window:

```
c:\turbo\include;c:myincld;a:..\..\include2
```

If, in addition, you have divided your unit files among four different directories, and want Turbo Pascal to search each of those directories when looking for units, you could enter the following in the Unit directories pop-up input window:

```
c:\turbo\startups;c:\turbo\stdunits;c:..\myunits2;a:newunits3
```

## Executable directory and Turbo directory

The Executable directory and Turbo directory menu items each take one (absolute or relative) directory path name; each item accepts a maximum of 64 characters.

The Turbo directory is where Turbo Pascal will look for the Help files, the default pick file, and TURBO.TP (the default configuration file) if they aren't located in the current directory.

For example, you could type the following path name at the Turbo directory menu item:

```
c:\turbo\cfgsnhlp
```

Then, if Turbo Pascal can't find the configuration and Help files in the current directory, it will look for them in the directory called TURBO\CFGSNHLP (off the root directory of the C drive).

## Pick file name

When you select this menu item, an input window pops up. Type in the path name of the Pick file you want Turbo Pascal to load or create. The default Pick file name is TURBO.PCK.

After typing a path name (or names) for any of the Environment menu items, press *Enter* to accept, then press *Esc* to return to the main TINST installation menu. When you exit the program, TINST prompts whether you want to save the changes. Once you save the Turbo directory paths, the locations are written to disk and become part of TURBO.EXE's default settings.

## The Editor Commands Option

Turbo Pascal's interactive editor provides many editing functions, including commands for

- cursor movement
- text insertion and deletion
- block and file manipulation
- string search (plus search-and-replace)

These editing commands are assigned to certain keys (or key combinations), which are explained in detail in Chapter 11.

When you select Editor commands from TINST's main installation menu, the Install Editor screen comes up, displaying three columns of text:

- The left-hand column describes all the functions available in Turbo Pascal's interactive editor.
- The middle column lists the *Primary* keystrokes; what keys or special key combinations you press to invoke a particular editor command.
- The right-hand column lists the *Secondary* keystrokes; these are optional alternate keystrokes you can also press to invoke the same editor command.

**Note:** Secondary keystrokes always take precedence over primary keystrokes.

The bottom lines of text in the Install Editor screen summarize the keys you use to select entries in the Primary and Secondary columns.

| Key | Legend | What It Does |
|-----|--------|--------------|
| *Left, Right, Up,* and *Down Arrow* keys | Select | Selects the editor command you want to re-key |
| *PgUp* and *PgDn* | Page | Scrolls up or down one full screen page |
| *Enter* | Modify | Enters the keystroke-modifying mode |
| *R* | Restore factory defaults | Resets all editor commands to the factory default keystrokes |
| *Esc* | Exit | Leaves the Install Editor screen and returns to the main TINST installation menu |
| *F4* | Key Modes | Toggles between the three flavors of keystroke combinations |

After you press *Enter* to enter the modify mode, a pop-up window appears on screen, listing the currently defined keystrokes for the selected command. The bottom lines of text in the Install Editor screen summarize the keys you use to change those keystrokes.

| Key | Legend | What It Does |
| --- | --- | --- |
| *Backspace* | Backspace | Deletes keystroke to left of cursor |
| *Enter* | Accept | Accepts newly defined keystrokes for selected editor command |
| *Esc* | Abandon changes | Abandons changes to the current selection, restoring the command's original keystrokes, and returns to the Install Editor screen (ready to select another editor command) |
| *F2* | Restore | Abandons changes to current selection, restoring the command's original keystrokes, but keeps the current command selected for redefinition |
| *F3* | Clear | Clears the current selection's keystroke definition, but keeps the current command selected for redefinition |
| *F4* | Key Modes | Toggles between the three flavors of keystroke combinations: WordStar-like, Ignore case, and Verbatim |

**Note:** To enter the keys *F2, F3, F4,* or the backquote (') character, as part of an editor command key sequence, first press the backquote key, then the appropriate function key.

Keystroke combinations come in three flavors: WordStar-like, **I**gnore case, and **V**erbatim. These are listed on the bottom line of the screen; the highlighted one is the current selection.

## WordStar-Like Selection

All commands must begin with a special key or a control key. Subsequent characters can be any key.

If you type a letter (or one of these five characters: [,], \, ^, –) in this mode, it will automatically be entered as a control-character combination. For example:

- Typing *a* or *A* or *Ctrl-A* will yield < *Ctrl A* >
- Typing *y* or *Y* or *Ctrl-y* will yield < *Ctrl Y* >
- Typing *[* will yield <*Ctrl [*>

In the Turbo Pascal editor, you must then explicitly press the special key or *Ctrl* key when entering the first keystroke of a command-key sequence, but for the subsequent keystrokes of that command you can use a lowercase, uppercase, or control key.

For example, if you customize an editor command to be < *Ctrl A* > < *Ctrl B* > < *Ctrl C* > in WordStar-like mode, you can type any of the following in the Turbo Pascal editor to activate that command:

- < *Ctrl A* > < *Ctrl B* > < *Ctrl C* >
- < *Ctrl A* > < *Ctrl B* > < *C* >
- < *Ctrl A* > < *Ctrl B* > < *c* >
- < *Ctrl A* > < *B* > < *Ctrl C* >
- < *Ctrl A* > < *B* > < *C* >
- < *Ctrl A* > < *B* > < *c* >
- < *Ctrl A* > < *b* > < *Ctrl C* >
- < *Ctrl A* > < *b* > < *C* >
- < *Ctrl A* > < *b* > < *c* >

In WordStar-like keystrokes, any letter you type is converted to a control-uppercase-letter combination. Five other characters are also converted to control-character combinations:

- left square bracket ([)
- backslash (\)
- right square bracket (])
- caret (^, also known as *Shift 6*)
- minus (-)

## Ignore Case Selection

In Ignore case keystrokes, the only character conversions are from lowercase to uppercase (letters only). All commands must begin with a special key or a control key. Subsequent characters can be any key. In this mode all alpha (letter) keys you enter are converted to their uppercase equivalents. When you type a letter in this mode, it is *not* automatically entered as a control-character combination; if a keystroke is to be a control-letter combination, you must hold down the *Ctrl* key while typing the letter. For example:

- Typing *a* or *A* will yield *A* (if this is the first keystroke, you'll get an error message)
- Typing *Ctrl y* or *Ctrl Y* will yield *< Ctrl Y >*
- Typing *Ctrl [* will yield *< Ctrl [ >*

In **I**gnore case keystrokes, the only character conversions are from lowercase to uppercase (letters only).

### Verbatim Selection

These keystrokes must always explicitly begin with a character that is a special key or control key. If you type a letter in this mode, it will be entered exactly as you type it.

- Typing *a* will yield *a* (if this is the first keystroke, you'll get an error message)
- Typing *A* will yield *A* (if this is the first keystroke, you'll get an error message)
- Typing *Ctrl Y* will yield *< Ctrl Y >*
- Typing *Ctrl y* will yield *< Ctrl y >*
- Typing *Ctrl [* will yield *< Ctrl [ >*

In Verbatim keystrokes, what you enter in the Install Editor screen for a command's keystroke sequence is exactly what you must type in the Turbo Pascal editor when you want to invoke that command. If, for example, you enter *< Ctrl A > b* and *< Crtl H > B* as the Verbatim primary and secondary keystroke sequences for some editor command, you will only be able to type those keys to invoke the command. Using the same letters but in different cases—*< Ctrl A > B* and *< Ctrl H > b*—won't work.

## Allowed Keystrokes

Although TINST provides you with lots of flexibility for customizing the Turbo Pascal editor commands to your own taste, there are a few rules governing the keystroke sequences you can define. Some of the rules apply to any keystroke definition, while others only come into effect in certain keystroke modes.

## *Global Rules*

1. You can enter a maximum of six keystrokes for any given editor command. Certain key combinations are equivalent to two keystrokes, such as *Alt* (*any valid key*), the cursor-movement keys (*Up arrow, PgDn, Del,* etc.) and all function keys or function key combinations (*F4, Shift-F7, Alt-F8,* etc.).

2. The first keystroke must be a character that is non-alphanumeric, non-punctuation; in other words, it must be a control key or a special key.

3. To enter the *Esc* key as a command keystroke, type *Ctrl[.*

4. To enter the *Backspace* key as a command keystroke, type *Ctrl H.*

5. To enter the *Enter* key as a command keystroke, type *Ctrl M.*

6. The Turbo Pascal predefined Help function keys (*F1* and *Alt F2*) can't be reassigned as Turbo Pascal editor command keys. Any other function key can, however. If you enter a hotkey as part of an editor command key sequence, TINST will issue a warning that you are overriding a hotkey in the editor and will verify whether you want to override that key.

## Turbo Pascal Editor Keystrokes

| Command name | Primary | Secondary |
|---|---|---|
| New Line | * \<CtrlM\> | • \<CtrlM\> |
| Cursor Left | * \<CtrlS\> | • \<Lft\> |
| Cursor Right | * \<CtrlD\> | • \<Rgt\> |
| Word Left | * \<CtrlA\> | • \<CtrlLft\> |
| Word Right | * \<CtrlF\> | • \<CtrlRgt\> |
| Cursor Up | * \<CtrlE\> | • \<Up\> |
| Cursor Down | * \<CtrlX\> | • \<Dn\> |
| Scroll Up | * \<CtrlW\> | • |
| Scroll Down | * \<CtrlZ\> | • |

| Command name | Primary | Secondary |
|---|---|---|
| Page Up | * \<CtrlR> | • \<PgUp> |
| Page Down | * \<CtrlC> | • \<PgDn> |
| Left of Line | * \<CtrlQ>\<CtrlS> | • \<Home> |
| Right of Line | * \<CtrlQ>\<CtrlD> | • \<End> |
| Top of Screen | * \<CtrlQ>\<CtrlE> | • \<CtrlHome> |
| Bottom of Screen | * \<CtrlQ>\<CtrlX> | • \<CtrlEnd> |
| Top of File | * \<CtrlQ>\<CtrlR> | • \<CtrlPgUp> |
| Bottom of File | * \<CtrlQ>\<CtrlC> | • \<CtrlPgDn> |
| Move to error | * \<CtrlQ>\<CtrlW> | • |
| Move to Block Begin | * \<CtrlQ>\<CtrlB> | • |
| Move to Block End | * \<CtrlQ>\<CtrlK> | • |
| Move to Block End | * \<CtrlQ>\<CtrlK> | • |
| Move to Previous Pos | * \<CtrlQ>\<CtrlP> | • |
| Move to Marker 0 | * \<CtrlQ>0 | • |
| Move to Marker 1 | * \<CtrlQ>1 | • |
| Move to Marker 2 | * \<CtrlQ>2 | • |
| Move to Marker 3 | * \<CtrlQ>3 | • |
| Toggle Insert | * \<CtrlV> | • \<Ins> |
| Insert Line | * \<CtrlN> | • |
| Delete Line | * \<CtrlY> | • |
| Delete to End of Line | * \<CtrlQ>\<CtrlY> | • |
| Delete Word | * \<CtrlT> | • |
| Delete Char | * \<CtrlG> | • \<Del> |
| Delete Char Left | * \<CtrlBkSp> | • \<CtrlH> |
| Set Block Begin | * \<CtrlK>\<CtrlB> | • |
| Set Block End | * \<CtrlK>\<CtrlK> | • |
| Mark Word | * \<CtrlK>\<CtrlT> | • |
| Hide Block | * \<CtrlK>\<CtrlH> | • |
| Set Marker 0 | * \<CtrlK>0 | • |
| Set Marker 1 | * \<CtrlK>1 | • |
| Set Marker 2 | * \<CtrlK>2 | • |
| Set Marker 3 | * \<CtrlK>3 | • |
| Copy Block | * \<CtrlK>\<CtrlC> | • |
| Move Block | * \<CtrlK>\<CtrlV> | • |
| Delete Block | * \<CtrlK>\<CtrlY> | • |
| Read Block | * \<CtrlK>\<CtrlR> | • |
| Write Block | * \<CtrlK>\<CtrlW> | • |
| Print Block | * \<CtrlK>\<CtrlP> | • |
| Exit Editor | * \<CtrlK>\<CtrlD> | • \<CtrlK>\<CtrlQ> |
| Tab | * \<CtrlI> | • |
| Toggle Autoindent | * \<CtrlO>\<CtrlI> | •\<CtrlQ>\<CtrlI> |
| Toggle Tabs | * \<CtrlO>\<CtrlT> | •\<CtrlQ>\<CtrlT> |
| Restore Line | * \<CtrlQ>\<CtrlL> | • |
| Find String | * \<CtrlQ>\<CtrlF> | • |
| Find and Replace | * \<CtrlQ>\<CtrlA> | • |

```
Command name              Primary                Secondary
------------              -------                ---------
Search Again           * <CtrlL>                  •
Insert Control Char    * <CtrlP>                  •
Save file              * <CtrlK><CtrlS>           •
Match pair             * <CtrlQ><Ctrl[>           •
Match pair backward    * <CtrlQ><Ctrl]>           •
```

## *The Options/Environment Option*

You can install several editor default modes of operation with this option. The items on the menu, and their significance, are described here.

First, take a look at the bottom status line for directions on how to select these options: Either use the arrow keys to move the selection bar to the option and then press *Enter*, or press the key that corresponds to the highlighted capital letter of the option.

You can change the operating environment defaults to suit your preferences (and your monitor) then save them as part of Turbo Pascal. Of course, you'll still be able to change these settings from inside Turbo Pascal's editor.

**Note:** Any option you install with TINST that also appears as a menu-settable option in TURBO.EXE will be overridden whenever you load a configuration file that contains a different setting for that option.

**Backup source files** (default = on)
With **B**ackup source files on, Turbo Pascal automatically creates a backup of your source file when you do a **File/Save**. It uses the same file name, and adds a .BAK extension: the backup file for FILENAME, FILENAME.C or FILENAME.XYZ would be FILENAME.BAK. With **B**ackup source files off, no .BAK file is created.

**Edit auto save** (default = on)
With **E**dit auto save on, Turbo Pascal automatically saves the file in the editor (if it's been modified since last saved) whenever you use **R**un (or *Alt-R*) or **OS** shell. This helps prevent the loss of your source files in the event of some calamity. With **E**dit auto save off, no such automatic saving occurs.

**Config auto save** (default = on)
With **C**onfig auto save on, Turbo Pascal automatically saves the configuration file (if it's been modified since last saved) whenever you use **R**un (or *Alt-R*), **File/OS** shell, or **File/Quit** (or *Alt X*). Which file it saves the current (recently modified) configuration to depends on three sets of factors.

**Zoom state** (default = off)
With Zoom state on, Turbo Pascal starts up with the Edit window occupying the full screen; when you switch to the Output window, it will also be full-screen. With Zoom state off, the Edit window occupies the top portion of the screen, above the Output window. (You can resize the windows with the Resize windows option from the main installation menu.)

**Insert mode** (default = on)
With Insert mode on, the editor inserts anything you enter from the keyboard at the cursor position, and pushes existing text to the right of the cursor even further right. Toggling Insert mode off allows you to overwrite text at the cursor.

**Autoindent mode** (default = on)
With Autoindent mode on, the cursor returns to the starting column of the previous line when you press *Enter*. When autoindent mode is toggled off, the cursor always returns to column one.

**Use tabs** (default = off)
With Use tabs on, when you press the *Tab* key, the editor places a tab character (^I) in the text using the tab size specified with **Tab size**. With Use tabs off, when you press the *Tab* key, the editor inserts enough space characters to align the cursor with the first letter of each word in the previous line.

**Screen size**
When you select Screen size, a menu pops up. The items in this menu allow you to set the Turbo Pascal integrated environment display to one of three sizes (25-, 43-, or 50-line). The available sizes depend on your hardware: 25-line mode is always available; 43-line mode is for systems with an EGA, while 50-line mode is for PS/2 or other VGA-equipped systems.

## *The Display Mode Option*

Normally, Turbo Pascal will correctly detect your system's video mode. You should only change the Display mode option if

- you want to select a mode other than the current video mode
- you have a Color/Graphics Adapter that doesn't "snow"
- you think Turbo Pascal is incorrectly detecting your hardware
- your system has a composite screen, which acts like a CGA with only one color—for this situation, select Black and white

Press *D* to select **Display** mode from the installation menu. A pop-up menu will appear; from this menu you can select the screen mode Turbo Pascal will use during operation. Your options include **Default**, **Color**, **Black and white**, or **Monochrome**.

**Default**

By default, Turbo Pascal always operates in the mode that is active when you load it.

**Color**

Turbo Pascal uses 80-column color mode no matter what mode is active when you load TURBO.EXE, and switches back to the previously active mode when you exit.

**Black and white**

Turbo Pascal uses 80-column black and white mode characters no matter what mode is active, and switches back to the previously active mode when you exit. This is required for composite monitors.

**Monochrome**

Turbo Pascal uses monochrome mode if you're currently in monochrome mode, and switches back to the previously active mode when you exit.

When you select one of the first three options, the program conducts a video test on your screen; look at the bottom status line for instructions about what to do.

When you press any key, a window comes up with the query

```
Was there Snow on the screen?
```

You can choose

- Yes, the screen was "snowy"
- No, always turn off snow checking
- Maybe, always check the hardware

Look to the status line for more about **Maybe**. Press *Esc* to return to the main installation menu.

## *The Color Customization Option*

Pressing *C* from the main installation menu allows you to make extensive changes to the Colors of your version of Turbo Pascal. After pressing *C*, you will see a menu with these options:

- Customize colors

- Default color set
- Turquoise color set
- Magenta color set

Because there are nearly 50 different screen items that you can color-customize, you will probably find it easier to choose a *preset* set of colors. Three preset color sets are on disk.

Press *D*, *T*, or *M*, and scroll through the colors for the Turbo Pascal screen items using the *PgUp* and *PgDn* keys. If you don't like any of the preset color sets, you can design your own.

To make custom colors, press *C* to **C**ustomize colors. Now you have a choice of 12 items that can be color-customized in Turbo Pascal; some of these are text items, some are screen lines and boxes. Choose one of these items by pressing a letter *A* through *L*.

Once you choose a screen item to color-customize, you will see a pop-up menu and a viewport. The viewport is an example of the screen item you chose, while the pop-up menu displays the components of that selection. The viewport also reflects the change in colors as you scroll through the color palette.

For example, if you chose **H** to customize the colors of Turbo Pascal's error boxes, you would see a new pop-up menu with the four different parts of an error box: **T**itle, **B**order, **N**ormal text, and **H**ighlighted text.

You must now select one of the components from the pop-up menu. Type the appropriate highlighted letter, and you're treated to a color palette for the item you chose. Using the arrow keys, select a color to your liking from the palette. Watch the viewport to see how that item looks in that color. Press *Enter* to record your selection.

Repeat this procedure for every screen item you want to color-customize. When you are finished, press *Esc* until you are back at the main installation menu.

**Note:** Turbo Pascal maintains three internal color tables: color, black and white, and monochrome. TINST only allows you to change one of these three color sets at a time, based upon your current video mode. So, for example, if you wanted to change to the black and white color table, you must set your video mode to BW80 at the DOS prompt and then load TINST.

## *The Resize Windows Option*

This option allows you to change the respective sizes of Turbo Pascal's Edit and Output windows. Press *R* to choose **Resize** windows from the main installation menu.

Using the *Up arrow* and *Down arrow* keys, you can move the bar dividing the Edit window from the Output window. Neither window can be smaller than three lines. When you have resized the windows to your liking, press *Enter*. You can discard your changes and return to the Installation menu by pressing *Esc*.

**Note:** If you are running Turbo Pascal in 43- or 50-line mode, the ratio of the lines in 25-line mode will be used.

# Quitting the Program

Once you have finished making all desired changes, select **Quit/save** at the main installation menu. The message

```
Save changes to TURBO.EXE? (Y/N)
```

will appear at the bottom of the screen.

- ■ If you press *Y* (for **Yes**), all the changes you have made will be permanently installed into Turbo Pascal. (Of course, you can always run TINST again if you want to change them.)
- ■ If you press *N* (for **No**), your changes will be ignored and you will be returned to the operating system prompt without changing Turbo Pascal's defaults or startup appearance. If you press *Esc*, you'll be returned to the menu.

If you decide you want to restore the original Turbo Pascal factory defaults, simply copy TURBO.EXE from your master disk onto your work disk. You can also restore the Editor commands by selecting the **E** option at the main menu, then press *R* (for restore factory defaults) and *Esc*.

# G

# A DOS Primer

If you are new to computers or to DOS, you may have trouble understanding certain terms used in this manual. This appendix provides you with a brief overview of the following DOS concepts and functions:

- what DOS is and does
- the proper way to load a program
- directories, subdirectories, and the path command
- using AUTOEXEC.BAT files

This information is by no means a complete explanation of the DOS operating system. If you need more details, please refer to the MS-DOS or PC-DOS user's manual that came with your computer system.

Turbo Pascal runs under the MS-DOS or PC-DOS operating system, version 2.0 or later.

## What Is DOS?

DOS is shorthand for Disk Operating System. MS-DOS is Microsoft's version of DOS, while PC-DOS is IBM's rendition. DOS is the traffic coordinator, manager, and operator for the transactions that occur between the parts of the computer system and the computer system and you. DOS operates in the background, taking care of may of the menial computer tasks you wouldn't want to have to think about—for instance, the flow of characters between your keyboard and the computer, between the computer and your printer, and between your disk(s) and internal memory (RAM).

Other transactions are initiated by entering commands on the DOS command line; in other words, immediately after the DOS prompt. Your DOS prompt probably looks like one of the following:

```
A>
B>
C>
```

The capital letter refers to the active disk drive (the one DOS and you are using right now). For instance, if the prompt is *A>*, it means you are working with the files on drive *A*, and that commands you give DOS will refer to that drive. When you want to switch to another disk, making it the active disk, all you do is type the letter of the disk, followed by a colon and press *Enter*. For instance, to switch to drive *B*, just type

```
B: Enter
```

There are a few commands you will use often with DOS, if you haven't already, such as

| | |
|---|---|
| DEL or ERASE | To erase a file |
| DIR | To see a list of files on the logged disk |
| COPY | To copy files from one disk to another |
| TURBO | To load Turbo Pascal |

DOS doesn't care whether you type in uppercase or lowercase letters, or a combination of both, so you can enter your commands however you like.

We'll assume you know how to use the first three commands listed; if you don't, refer to your DOS manual. Next, we will explain the proper way to load a program like Turbo Pascal, which is the last command—*TURBO*.

# How to Load a Program

On your distribution disk, you'll find the main Turbo Pascal program under the file name TURBO.EXE. This program file is necessary for all functions, so you always need it when you start the program. A file name with the extension, or "last name," .COM or .EXE is a program file you can load and run (use, start) by typing its first name at the DOS prompt. To start Turbo Pascal, you simply type TURBO and press *Enter*, and Turbo Pascal will be loaded into your computer's memory.

There's one thing you need to remember about loading Turbo Pascal and other similar programs: *You must be logged onto the disk and directory where the program is located in order to load it*; unless you have set up a DOS path (described shortly), DOS won't know where to find the program.

For instance, if your distribution disk with the TURBO.EXE program is in drive *A* but the prompt you see on your screen is *B>*, DOS won't know what you're talking about if you type TURBO and press *Enter*. Instead of starting Turbo Pascal, it will give you the message Bad command or file name.

It's as if you were shuffling through the "Pet Records" file in your file cabinet looking for information about your home finances. You're in the wrong place. So if you happen to get that DOS message, simply switch to drive *A* by typing *A:* and then press *Enter*. Then type TURBO and press *Enter* to load Turbo Pascal.

You can set up a "path" to the Turbo Pascal files so that DOS can find them, using the DOS *path* command. See the section titled "The AUTOEXEC.BAT File" for more information.

# Directories

A *directory* is a convenient way to organize your floppy or hard disk files. Directories allow you to subdivide your disk into sections, much the way you might put groups of manila file folders into separate file boxes. For instance, you might want to put all your file folders having to do with finance—a bank statement file, an income tax file, or the like—into a box labeled "Finances."

On your computer, it would be convenient to make a directory to hold all your Turbo Pascal files, another for your SideKick files, another for your letters, and so on. That way, when you type DIR on the DOS command line, you don't have to wade through hundreds of file names looking for the file you want. You'll get a listing of only the files on the directory you're currently logged onto.

Although you can make directories on either floppy or hard disks, they are used most often on hard disks. Because hard disks can hold a greater volume of data, there is a greater need for organization and compartmentalization.

When you're at the DOS level, rather than in Turbo Pascal or another program, you can tell DOS to create directories, move files around between directories, and display which files are in a particular directory.

In the examples that follow, we assume you are using a hard disk system, and that you are logged onto the hard disk so that the prompt you see on your screen is C>. If you want to create directories on your floppy disks, substitute *A* or *B* for *C* in the example.

To make a directory for your Turbo Pascal files, do the following:

1. At the *C*> prompt, type `MKDIR Turbo` and press *Enter*. The MKDIR command tells DOS to make a directory called TURBO.

2. Type `CHDIR TURBO` and press *Enter*. The CHDIR command tells DOS to move you into the TURBO directory.

3. Now, put the Turbo Pascal disk you want to copy *from* into one of your floppy drives—let's say *A* for this example—and type `COPY A:*.*` *Enter*. (The asterisks are *wildcards* that stand for all files.) The COPY command tells DOS to copy all files on the *A* drive to the TURBO directory on the *C* drive. As each file on the disk is copied, you will see it listed on the screen.

That's all there is to it. Treat a directory the same way you would a disk drive: To load Turbo Pascal, you must be in the TURBO directory before typing TURBO and pressing *Enter* or DOS won't be able to find the program.

# Subdirectories

If you are someone who really likes organization, you can subdivide your directories into subdirectories. You can create as many directories and subdirectories as you like—just don't forget where you put your files!

A subdirectory is created the same way as a directory. To create a subdirectory from the TURBO directory (for instance, for storing your unit files), do the following:

1. Be sure you are in the TURBO directory.
2. Type MKDIR UNITS *Enter*.
3. Type CHDIR UNITS. You are now in the UNITS subdirectory.
4. Copy your unit files to the new subdirectory.

# Where Am I? The $p $g Prompt

You've probably noticed when you change directories that you still see the *C*> prompt; there is no evidence of the directory or subdirectory you are currently in. This can be confusing, especially if you leave your computer for a while. It's easy to forget where you were when you left.

DOS gives you an easy way to find out. Just type

```
prompt=$p $g
```

and from now on (until you turn your computer off or reboot), the prompt will show you exactly where you are. Try it. If you are still in the UNITS subdirectory, your DOS prompt will look like

```
C:\TURBO\UNITS >
```

# The AUTOEXEC.BAT File

To avoid typing the prompt command (discussed in the previous section) to see where you are every time you turn on your computer, you can set up an AUTOEXEC.BAT file to do it for you. The AUTOEXEC.BAT file is a useful tool to set your computer to do things automatically when it starts up. There are many more things it can do, but rather than go into great detail here, we suggest referring to your DOS manual for more information. We will show you how to create an AUTOEXEC.BAT file that will automatically change your prompt so you know where you are in your directory structure, set a *path* to the TURBO directory, and then load Turbo Pascal.

The DOS *path* command tells your computer where to look for commands it doesn't recognize. DOS only recognizes programs in the current (logged) directory, unless there is a path to the directory containing pertinent programs or files.

In the following example, we will set a path to the TURBO directory.

If you have an AUTOEXEC.BAT file in your root (main) directory, your computer will do everything in that file when you first turn your computer on. (The root directory is where you see the *C>* or *C:\* prompt, with no directory names following it.)

Here's how to create an AUTOEXEC.BAT file.

1. Type CHDIR \ to get to the root directory.
2. Type COPY CON AUTOEXEC.BAT *Enter*. This tells DOS to copy whatever you type next into a file called AUTOEXEC.BAT.
3. Type
   ```
   PROMPT=$P $G Enter
   PATH=C:\TURBO
   CHDIR TURBO
   Ctrl-Z Enter
   ```
   The *Ctrl-Z* sequence saves your commands in the AUTOEXEC.BAT file.

To test your new AUTOEXEC.BAT file, reboot your computer by holding down the *Ctrl* and *Alt* keys and then pressing *Del*. You should see C:\TURBO>.

# Changing Directories

How do you get from one directory to another? It depends on where you want to go. The basic DOS command for changing directories is CHDIR. Use it like this:

- **To move from one directory to another**: For example, to change from the TURBO directory to one called SPRINT, type the following from the TURBO directory:

    `C:\TURBO> CHDIR \SPRINT` *Enter*

    Notice the backslash (\) before the directory name. Whenever you are moving from one directory to another unrelated directory, type the name of the directory, preceded by a backslash.

- **To move from a directory to its subdirectory**: For example, to move from the TURBO directory to the UNITS subdirectory, type the following from the TP directory:

    `C:\TP> CHDIR UNITS` *Enter*

    In this case, you did not need the backslash, because the UNITS directory is a direct offshoot of the TP directory. In fact, DOS would have misunderstood what you meant if you had used the backslash—DOS would have thought that UNITS was a directory off the main (root) directory.

- **To move from a subdirectory to its parent directory**: For example, to move from the UNITS subdirectory to the TP directory, type the following from the UNITS subdirectory:

    `C:\TP\UNITS> CHDIR ..` *Enter*

    DOS will move you back to the TP directory. Any time you want to move back to the parent directory, use a space followed by two periods after the CHDIR command.

- **To move to the root directory**: The *root directory* is the original directory. It is the parent (or grandparent) of all directories (and subdirectories). When you are in the root directory, you'll see this prompt: C:\ >.

    To move to the root directory from any other directory, simply type

    `CHDIR \` *Enter*

    The backslash without a directory name signals DOS that you want to return to the root directory.

This appendix has presented only a quick look at DOS and some of its functions. Once you're familiar with the information given here, you may want to study your DOS manual and discover all the other things you can do with your computer's operating system. There are many DOS functions not mentioned here that can simplify and enhance your computer use.

# H

# Glossary

Here are some quick glossary ideas. Enjoy.

**absolute variable**  A variable declared to exist at a fixed location in memory rather than letting the compiler determine its location.

**ANSI**  The acronym for the the American National Standards Institute, the organization that, among other things, describes the elements of so-called standard Pascal.

**ASCII character set**  The American Standard Code for Information Interchange's standard set of numbers to represent the characters and control signals used by computers.

**actual parameter**  A variable, expression, or constant that is substituted for a formal parameter in a procedure or function call.

**address**  A specific location in memory.

**algorithm**  A set of rules that defines the solution to a problem.

**allocate**  To reserve memory space for a particular purpose, usually from the heap.

**array**  A sequential group of identical data elements that are arranged in a single data structure and are accessible by an index.

**argument**  An alternative name for a parameter (see actual parameter).

**assignment operator**  The symbol :=, which gives a value to a variable or function of the same type.

**assignment statement**  A statement that assigns a specific value to an identifier.

**assembler**  A program that converts assembly-language programs into machine language.

**assembly language**  The first language level above machine language. Assembly language is specific to the microprocessor it is running on. The major difference between assembly language and machine language is that assembly language provides mnemonics, making it easier to read and write.

**base type**  The type of values in an array.

**binary**  Base 2; a method of representing numbers using only two digits, 0 and 1.

**bit**  A binary digit with a value of either 0 or 1. The smallest unit of data in a computer.

**block**  The associated declaration and statement parts of a program or subprogram.

**body**  The instructions pertaining to a program or a subprogram (a procedure or function).

**boolean**  A data type that can have a value of True or False.

**braces**  The characters { and }, used to delimit comments; sometimes called curly brackets.

**brackets**  The characters [ and ]; sometimes called square brackets.

**buffer**  An area of memory allocated as temporary storage.

**bug**  An error in a program. Syntax errors refer to incorrect use of the rules of the programming language; logic errors refer to incorrect strategy in the program to accomplish the intended result.

**build**  The process of recompiling all the units used by a program.

**byte**  A sequence of 8 bits.

**call**  To cause a subprogram (procedure or function) to execute by referring to its name.

**case label**  A constant, or list of constants, that label a component statement in a **case** statement.

**case selector**  An expression whose result is used to select which component statement of a **case** statement will be executed.

**central processing unit (CPU)**  The "brain" of a computer system, which interprets and executes instructions and controls the other components of the system.

**chaining** The passing of control from one program to another.

**char** A Pascal type that represents a single character.

**code** Instructions to a computer. Code is made up of algorithms.

**code segment** A portion of a compiled program up to 32767 bytes in length.

**comment** An explanatory statement in the source code enclosed by the symbols (* *) or { }.

**compiler** A program that translates a program written in a high-level language into machine language.

**compiler directive** An instruction to the compiler that is embedded within the program; for example, {$R+} turns on range-checking.

**compound statement** A series of statements surrounded by a matching set of the reserved words **begin** and **end**.

**concatenate** The joining of two or more strings.

**constant** A fixed value in a program.

**control character** A special nonprinting character in the ASCII character set designed originally to control a printing device or communications link.

**control structure** A statement that manages the flow of execution of a program.

**crash** A sudden computer failure due to a hardware problem or program error.

**data segment** The segment in memory where the static global variables are stored.

**data structures** Areas of related items in memory, represented as arrays, records, or linked lists.

**debugger** A special program that provides capabilities to start and stop execution of a program at will, as well as analyze values that the program is manipulating.

**debugging** Thr process of finding and removing bugs from programs.

**decimal** A method of representing numbers using base 10 notation, where legal digits range from 0 to 9.

**declare** The act of explicitly defining the name and type of an identifier in a program.

**dereferencing** The act of accessing a value pointed to by a pointer variable (rather than the pointer variable itself).

**definition part** The part of a program where constants, labels, and structured types are defined.

**delimiter** A boundary marker that can be a word, a character, or a symbol.

**directory** A work area on a disk or a listing of files (or directories) on a disk.

**documentation** A written explanation of a computer program. Documentation can vary from manuals hundreds of pages long to a one-line comment embedded in the program itself.

**dynamic** Something that varies while the program is running.

**dynamic allocation** The allocation and deallocation of memory from the heap at runtime.

**dynamic variable** A variable on the heap.

**element** One of the items in an array.

**enumerated type** A user-defined scalar type that consists of an arbitrary list of identifiers.

**evaluate** To compute the value of an expression.

**expression** Part of a statement that represents a value or can be used to calculate a value.

**extension** Any addition to the standard definition of a language. Also, the optional three-character ending (following the period) in a standard DOS file name.

**execute** To carry out the program's instructions.

**external** A file of one or more subprograms that have been written in assembly language and assembled to native executable code.

**field list** The field name and type definition of a record.

**field width** The number of place holders in an output statement.

**file** A collection of data that can be stored on and retrieved from a disk.

**file pointer** A pointer that tracks where the next object will be retrieved from within a file.

**file variable** An identifier in a program that represents a file.

**fixed-point notation** The representation of real numbers without decimal points.

**flag** A variable, usually of type integer or boolean, that changes value to indicate that an event has taken place.

**floating-point notation** The representation of real numbers using decimal points.

**formal parameter** An identifier in a procedure or function declaration heading that represents the arguments that will be passed to the subprogram when it is called.

**forward declaration** The declaration of a procedure or function and its parameters in advance of the actual definition of the subroutine.

**function** A subroutine that computes and returns a value.

**global variable** A variable declared in the main program block that can be accessed from anywhere within the program.

**high-level language** A programming language that more closely resembles human language than machine language. Pascal is a high-level language.

**heap** An area of memory reserved for the dynamic allocation of variables.

**hexadecimal** A method of representing numbers using base 16 notation, where legal digits range from 0 to 9 and *A* to *F*.

**identifier** A user-defined name for a specific item (a constant, type, variable, procedure, function, unit, program, and field). It must begin with a letter and cannot contain spaces.

**implementation** The particular embodiment of a programming language. Turbo Pascal is an implementation of standard Pascal for IBM-compatible computers.

**increment** To increase the value of a variable.

**index** A position within a list of elements.

**index type** The type of indexes in an array.

**initialize** The process of giving a known initial value to a variable or data structure.

**input** The information a program receives from some external device, such as a keyboard.

**integer** A numeric variable that is a whole number from –32768 to +32767.

**interactive** A program that communicates with a user through some I/O device.

**interrupt** The temporary halting of a program in order to process an event of higher priority.

**interpreter**  A program that sequentially interprets each statement in a program into machine code and then immediately executes it.

**I/O**  Short for Input/Output. The process of receiving or sending data.

**I/O error**  An error that occurs while trying to input or output data.

**I/O redirection**  The DOS ability to direct input/output to access devices other than the default DOS devices.

**iteration**  The process of repetition or looping.

**keyword**  A reserved word in Pascal. In this manual, keywords are shown in boldface type (for example, **begin, end, nil**).

**label**  An identifier that marks a place in the program text for a **goto** statement. Labels have digit sequences whose values range from 0 to 9999.

**level**  The depth of nesting prcedures or control structures.

**linked list**  A dynamic data structure that is made up of elements, each of which point to the next element in the list through a pointer variable.

**literal**  An unnamed constant in a program.

**local identifier**  An identifier declared within a procedure or a function.

**local variable**  A variable declared within a procedure or a function.

**long word**  A location in memory occupying 4 adjacent bytes; the storage required for a variable of type longint.

**loop**  A set of statements that are executed repeatedly.

**main procedure**  The program part enclosed by the outermost **begin** and **end**.

**machine language**  A language consisting of strings of 0s and 1s that the computer interprets as instructions; compare the glossary entry for "assembly language."

**main program**  The **begin/end** block terminated by a period that appears at the end of a program; also called the *statement part*.

**make**  The process of recompiling only those units whose source code has been modified since the last compile. A program that manages this process.

**memory**  The space within the computer for holding information and running programs.

**module**  A self-contained routine or group of routines.

**nesting**  The placement of one unit within another.

**nil pointer**  A pointer having the special value nil; a nil pointer doesn't point to anything.

**node**  An individual element of a tree or list.

**object code**  The output of a compiler.

**offset**  An index within a segment.

**operand**  An argument that is combined with one or more operands and operators to form an expression.

**operating system**  A program that manages all operations and resources of the computer.

**operator**  A symbol, such as +, that is used to form expressions.

**operator hierarchy**  The rules that determine the order in which operators in an expression are evaluated.

**ordinal type**  An ordered range of values; same as scalar type.

**output**  The result of running a program. Output can be sent to a printer, displayed on screen, or written to disk.

**overflow**  The condition that results when an operation produces a value that is more positive or negative than the computer can represent, given the allocated space for the value or expression.

**parameter**  A variable or value that is passed to a procedure or function.

**parameter list**  The list of value and variable parameters declared in the heading of a procedure or function declaration.

**Pascal, Blaise**  A French mathematician and philosopher (1623-66) who built a mechanical adding machine, considered to be an early predecessor to calculators and computers.

**pass**  To use as a parameter.

**pointer**  A variable that points to a specific memory location.

**pop**  The removal of the topmost element from a stack.

**port**  An I/O device that can be accessed through the CPU's data bus.

**precedence**  The order in which operators are executed.

**predefined identifier**  A constant, type, file, logical device, procedure, or function that is available to the programmer without having to be defined or declared.

**procedure**  A subprogram that can be called from various parts of a larger program.

**procedure call**  The invocation of a procedure.

**program**  A set of instructions for a computer to carry out.

**prompt**  A string printed by a program to signal to the user that input is desired and (sometimes) what kind of input is expected.

**push**  The addition of an element to the top of a stack.

**random access**  Directly accessing an element of a data structure without sequentially searching the entire structure for the element.

**random-access memory (RAM)**  Memory devices that can be read from and written to.

**range-checking**  A Turbo Pascal feature that checks a value to make sure it is within the legal range defined.

**read-only memory (ROM)**  The memory device from which data can be read but not written.

**real number**  A number represented by decimal point and/or scientific notation.

**record**  A structured data type referenced by one identifier that consists of several different fields.

**recursion**  A programming technique in which a subprogram calls itself.

**relational operator**  The operators =, <>, <, >, <=, >=, and **in**, all of which are used to form Boolean expressions.

**reserved word**  An identifier reserved by the compiler. A word whose use and meaning is reserved for use only by the program. You cannot redefine the meaning of a reserved word.

**result**  The value returned by a procedure, function, or program.

**runtime**  During the execution of a program.

**scalar type**  Any Pascal type consisting of ordered components (for example, integer, char, longint, enumerated types, and so forth).

**scientific notation**  A description of a number that uses a number between 1 and 10 (called the mantissa) multiplied by a power of 10 (called the exponent). Because computers cannot easily display exponents on the screen, scientific notation on computers is usually written using an *E*, as in 24E15—which means 24 multiplied by 10 to the 15th power.

**scope**  The visibility of an identifier within a program.

**segment**  On 8088-based machines, RAM is divided into several segments, or parts, each made up of 64K of memory.

**separate compilation** The ability to break a large program into several discrete modules, compile each module separately, then link them into a large, executable (.EXE) file.

**separator** A blank or a comment.

**sequential access** The ordered access of each element of a data structure, starting at the first element of the structure.

**set** An unordered group of elements, all of the same scalar type.

**set operator** The symbols +, −, *, =, <=, >=, <>, and **in**, all of which return set-type results when used with set-type operands.

**simple type** A type that contains only a single value.

**source code** The input to a compiler.

**stack** A data structure in which the last element stored is the first to be removed.

**stack overflow** An error condition that occurs when the amount of space allocated to the computer's stack is used up.

**stack segment** The segment in memory allocated as the program's stack.

**statement** The simplest unit in a program; statements are separated by semicolons.

**static variable** A variable with a lifetime that exists the entire length of the program. Memory for static variables is allocated in the data segment (or area).

**string** A sequence of characters that can be treated as a single unit.

**structured type** One of the predefined types (array, set, record, file, or string) that are composed of structured data elements.

**subprogram** A procedure or function within a program; a subroutine.

**subrange** A continuous range of any scalar type.

**subscript** An identifier used to access a particular element of an array.

**syntax error** An error caused by violating the rules of a programming language.

**terminal** An I/O device for communication between a human being and a computer.

**tracing** Manually stepping through each statement in a program in order to understand the program's behavior—an important debugging technique.

**transfer function** A function that converts a value of one type to a value of another type.

**tree** A dynamic data structure in which a node (branch of a tree) may point to one or more other nodes.

**type definition** The specification of a non-predefined type. Defines the set of values a variable can have and the operations that can be performed on it.

**typed constant** A variable with a value that is defined at compile time but can be modified at runtime. (Think of it as a preinitialized variable.)

**type conversion** The reformulation of a value in another form, for example, the conversion of integer values to real.

**type coercion** Technique also known as typecasting in which one variable is forced to be read as another type.

**underlying type** The scalar type corresponding to a particular subrange.

**unit** A program module that makes it possible to do separate compilation. A unit can contain code, data, type and/or constant declarations. A unit can use other units, and is broken into interface (public) and implementation (private) sections.

**untyped parameter** A formal parameter that allows the actual parameter to be of any type.

**value parameter** A procedure or function parameter that is passed by value; that is, the value of the parameter is passed and cannot be changed.

**vanilla** Programmer's lingo for standard or basic.

**variable declaration** A declaration that consists of the variable and its associated type.

**variable parameter** A procedure or function parameter that is passed by reference; that is, the address of the parameter is passed so that the value of the parameter can be accessed and modified.

**variant record** A record in which some fields share the same area in memory.

**word** A location in memory occupying 2 adjacent bytes; the storage required for a variable of type integer.

A     P     P     E     N     D     I     X

# I

# Error Messages and Codes

## Compiler Error Messages

The following lists the possible error messages you can get from the compiler during program development. Whenever possible, the compiler will display additional diagnostic information in the form of an identifier or a file name, for example:

```
Error 15: File not found (WINDOW.TPU).
```

When an error is detected, Turbo Pascal (in the integrated environment) automatically loads the source file and places the cursor at the error. The command-line compiler displays the error message and number and the source line, and uses a caret (^) to indicate where the error occurred. Note, however, that some errors are not detected until a little later in the source text. For example, a type mismatch in an assignment statement cannot be detected until the entire expression after the := has been evaluated. In such cases, look for the error to the left of or above the cursor.

**1 Out of memory.**

This error occurs when the compiler has run out of memory. There are a number of possible solutions to this problem:

■ If Compile/Destination is set to Memory, set it to Disk in the integrated environment.

■ If Options/Compiler/Link buffer in the integrated environment is set to Memory, set it to Disk. Alternatively, place a {$L-} directive at the beginning of your program. Use /$L- option to link to disk in the command-line compiler.

- If you are using any memory-resident utilities, such as SideKick and SuperKey, remove them from memory.

- If you are using TURBO.EXE, try use TPC.EXE instead—it takes up less memory.

If none of these suggestions help, your program or unit may simply be too large to compile in the amount of memory available, and you may have to break it into two or more smaller units.

## 2  Identifier expected.

An identifier was expected at this point. You may be trying to redeclare a reserved word.

## 3  Unknown identifier.

This identifier has not been declared.

## 4  Duplicate identifier.

The identifier has already been used within the current block.

## 5  Syntax error.

An illegal character was found in the source text. You may have forgotten the quotes around a string constant.

## 6  Error in real constant.

The syntax of real-type constants is defined in Chapter 13, "Tokens and Constants."

## 7  Error in integer constant.

The syntax of integer-type constants is defined in Chapter 13, "Tokens and Constants." Note that whole real numbers outside the maximum integer range must be followed by a decimal point and a zero; for example, 12345678912.0.

## 8  String constant exceeds line.

You have most likely forgotten the ending quote in a string constant.

### 9  Too many nested files.

The compiler allows no more than five nested source files. Most likely you have more than four nested include files.

### 10  Unexpected end of file. You might have gotten this error message because of one of the following:

- Your source file ends before the final **end** of the main statement part. Most likely, your **begin**s and **end**s are unbalanced.
- An include file ends in the middle of a statement part. Every statement part must be entirely contained in one file.
- You didn't close a comment.

### 11  Line too long.

The maximum line length is 126 characters.

### 12  Type identifier expected.

The identifier does not denote a type as it should.

### 13  Too many open files.

If this error occurs, your CONFIG.SYS file does not include a FILES=*xx* entry or the entry specifies too few files. Increase the number to some suitable value, for instance, 20.

### 14  Invalid file name.

The file name is invalid or specifies a nonexistent path.

### 15  File not found.

The file could not be found in the current directory or in any of the search directories that apply to this type of file.

### 16  Disk full.

Delete some files or use a new disk.

**17 Invalid compiler directive.**

The compiler directive letter is unknown, one of the compiler directive parameters is invalid, or you are using a global compiler directive when compilation of the body of the program has begun.

**18 Too many files.**

There are too many files involved in the compilation of the program or unit. Try not to use that many files, for instance, by merging include files or making the file names shorter.

**19 Undefined type in pointer definition.**

The type was referenced in a pointer-type declaration previously, but it was never declared.

**20 Variable identifier expected.**

The identifier does not denote a variable as it should.

**21 Error in type.**

This symbol cannot start a type definition.

**22 Structure too large.**

The maximum allowable size of a structured type is 65520 bytes.

**23 Set base type out of range.**

The base type of a set must be a subrange with bounds in the range 0..255 or an enumerated type with no more than 256 possible values.

**24 File components may not be files.**

**file of file** constructs are not allowed.

**25 Invalid string length.**

The declared maximum length of a string must be in the range 1..255.

**26 Type mismatch.**

This is due to

- incompatible types of the variable and the expression in an assignment statement
- incompatible types of the actual and formal parameter in a call to a procedure or function
- an expression type that is incompatible with index type in array indexing
- incompatible types of operands in an expression

**27 Invalid subrange base type.**

All ordinal types are valid base types.

**28 Lower bound greater than upper bound.**

The declaration of a subrange type specifies a lower bound greater than the upper bound.

**29 Ordinal type expected.**

Real types, string types, structured types, and pointer types are not allowed here.

**30 Integer constant expected.**

**31 Constant expected.**

**32 Integer or real constant expected.**

**33 Type identifier expected.**

The identifier does not denote a type as it should.

**34 Invalid function result type.**

Valid function result types are all simple types, string types, and pointer types.

**35 Label identifier expected.**

The identifier does not denote a label as it should.

**36 BEGIN expected.**

**37 END expected.**

**38 Integer expression expected.**

The preceding expression must be of an integer type.

**39 Ordinal expression expected.**

The preceding expression must be of an ordinal type.

**40 Boolean expression expected.**

The preceding expression must be of type boolean.

**41 Operand types do not match operator.**

The operator cannot be applied to operands of this type, for example, '*A*' div '2'.

**42 Error in expression.**

This symbol cannot participate in an expression in the way it does. You may have forgotten to write an operator between two operands.

**43 Illegal assignment.**

- Files and untyped variables cannot be assigned values.
- A function identifier can only be assigned values within the statement part of the function.

**44 Field identifier expected.**

The identifier does not denote a field in the preceding record variable.

**45 Object file too large.**

Turbo Pascal cannot link in .OBJ files larger than 64K.

### 46 Undefined external.

The **external** procedure or function did not have a matching PUBLIC definition in an object file. Make sure you have specified all object files in {*$L filename*} directives, and check the spelling of the procedure or function identifier in the .ASM file.

### 47 Invalid object file record.

The .OBJ file contains an invalid object record; make sure the file is in fact an .OBJ file.

### 48 Code segment too large.

The maximum size of the code of a program or unit is 65520 bytes. If you are compiling a program, move some procedures or functions into a unit. If you are compiling a unit, break it into two or more units.

### 49 Data segment too large.

The maximum size of a program's data segment is 65520 bytes, including data declared by the used units. If you need more global data than this, declare the larger structures as pointers, and allocate them dynamically using the *New* procedure.

### 50 DO expected.

### 51 Invalid PUBLIC definition.

■ The identifier was made public through a PUBLIC directive in assembly language, but is has no matching **external** declaration in the Pascal program or unit.

■ Two or more PUBLIC directives in assembly language define the same identifier.

■ The .OBJ file defines PUBLIC symbols that do not reside in the CODE segment.

### 52 Invalid EXTRN definition.

■ The identifier was referred to through an EXTRN directive in assembly language, but it is not declared in the Pascal program or unit, nor in the interface part of any of the used units.

■ The identifier denotes an **absolute** variable.

■ The identifier denotes an **inline** procedure or function.

**53  Too many EXTRN definitions.**

Turbo Pascal cannot handle .OBJ files with more than 256 EXTRN definitions.

**54  OF expected.**

**55  INTERFACE expected.**

**56  Invalid relocatable reference.**

- The .OBJ file contains data and relocatable references in segments other than CODE. For example, you are attempting to declare initialized variables in the DATA segment.
- The .OBJ file contains byte-sized references to relocatable symbols. This error occurs if you use the HIGH and LOW operators with relocatable symbols or if you refer to relocatable symbols in DB directives.
- An operand refers to a relocatable symbol that was not defined in the CODE segment or in the DATA segment.
- An operand refers to an EXTRN procedure or function with an offset, for example, *CALL SortProc+8*.

**57  THEN expected.**

**58  TO or DOWNTO expected.**

**59  Undefined forward.**

- The procedure or function was declared in the **interface** part of a unit, but its definition never occurred in the **implementation** part.
- The procedure or function was declared with **forward**, but its definition was never found.

**60  Too many procedures.**

Turbo Pascal does not allow more than 512 procedures or functions per module. If you are compiling a program, move some procedures or functions into a unit. If you are compiling a unit, break it into two or more units.

### 61  Invalid typecast.

■ The sizes of the variable reference and the destination type differ in a variable typecast.

■ You are attempting to typecast an expression where only a variable reference is allowed.

### 62  Division by zero.

The preceding operand attempts to divide by zero.

### 63  Invalid file type.

The file type is not supported by the file-handling procedure; for example, *readln* with a typed file or *Seek* with a text file.

### 64  Cannot Read or Write variables of this type.

■ *Read* and *Readln* can input variables of char, integer, real, and string types.

■ *Write* and *Writeln* can output variables of char, integer, real, string, and boolean types.

### 65  Pointer variable expected.

The preceding variable must be of a pointer type.

### 66  String variable expected.

The preceding variable must be of a string type.

### 67  String expression expected.

The preceding expression must be of a string type.

### 68  Circular unit reference.

Two units are not allowed to use each other:

```
unit U1;        unit U2;
uses U2;        uses U1;
  ...             ...
```

In this example, doing a Make on either unit will generate error 68.

**69 Unit name mismatch.**

The name of the unit found in the .TPU file does not match the name specified in the **uses** clause.

**70 Unit version mismatch.**

One or more of the units used by this unit have been changed since the unit was compiled. Use **Compile/Make** or **Compile/Build** in the integrated environment and */M* or */B* options in the command-line compiler to automatically compile units that need recompilation.

**71 Duplicate unit name.**

You have already named this unit in the **uses** clause.

**72 Unit file format error.**

The .TPU file is somehow invalid; make sure it is in fact a .TPU file.

**73 Implementation expected.**

**74 Constant and case types do not match.**

The type of the **case** constant is incompatible with the **case** statement's selector expression.

**75 Record variable expected.**

The preceding variable must be of a record type.

**76 Constant out of range.**

- You are trying to index an array with an out-of-range constant.
- You are trying to assign an out-of-range constant to a variable.
- You are trying to pass an out-of-range constant as a parameter to a procedure or function.

**77 File variable expected.**

The preceding variable must be of a file type.

**78 Pointer expression expected.**

The preceding expression must be of a pointer type.

### 79 Integer or real expression expected.

The preceding expression must be of an integer or a real type.

### 80 Label not within current block.

A **goto** statement cannot reference a label outside the current block.

### 81 Label already defined.

The label already marks a statement.

### 82 Undefined label in preceding statement part.

The label was declared and referenced in the preceding statement part, but it was never defined.

### 83 Invalid @ argument.

Valid arguments are variable references and procedure or function identifiers.

### 84 UNIT expected.

### 85 ";" expected.

### 86 ":" expected.

### 87 "," expected.

### 88 "(" expected.

### 89 ")" expected.

### 90 "=" expected.

### 91 ":=" expected.

### 92 "[" or "(." expected.

### 93 "]" or ".)" expected.

**94 "." expected.**

**95 ".." expected.**

**96 Too many variables.**

■ The total size of the global variables declared within a program or unit cannot exceed 64K.

■ The total size of the local variables declared within a procedure or function cannot exceed 64 Kb.

**97 Invalid FOR control variable.**

The **for** statement control variable must be a simple variable defined in the declaration part of the current subprogram.

**98 Integer variable expected.**

The preceding variable must be of an integer type.

**99 Files are not allowed here.**

A typed constant cannot be of a file type.

**100 String length mismatch.**

The length of the string constant does not match the number of components in the character array.

**101 Invalid ordering of fields.**

The fields of a record-type constant must be written in the order of declaration.

**102 String constant expected.**

**103 Integer or real variable expected.**

The preceding variable must be of an integer or real type.

**104 Ordinal variable expected.**

The preceding variable must be of an ordinal type.

## 105 INLINE error.

The < operator is not allowed in conjunction with relocatable references to variables—such references are always word-sized.

## 106 Character expression expected.

The preceding expression must be of a char type.

## 107 Too many relocation items.

The size of the relocation table part of the .EXE file exceeds 64K, which is Turbo Pascal's upper limit. If you encounter this error, your program is simply too big for Turbo Pascal's linker to handle. It is probably also too big for DOS to execute. You will have to split the program into a "main" part that executes two or more "subprogram" parts using the *Exec* procedure in the *Dos* unit.

## 108 Not enough memory to run program.

There is not enough memory to run the program from within the TURBO environment. If you are using any memory-resident utilities, such as SideKick and SuperKey, remove them from memory. If that doesn't help, compile the program to disk, and exit TURBO to execute.

## 109 Cannot find EXE file.

For some reason, the .EXE file previously generated by the compiler has disappeared.

## 110 Cannot run a unit.

You cannot run a unit. To test a unit, write a program that uses the unit.

## 111 Compilation aborted.

The compilation was aborted by *Ctrl-Break.*

## 112 CASE constant out of range.

For integer type **case** statements, the constants must be within the range $-32768..32767$.

## 113 Error in statement.

This symbol cannot start a statement.

### 114  Cannot call an interrupt procedure.

You cannot directly call an interrupt procedure.

### 115  Must have an 8087 to compile this.

The compiler requires an 8087 coprocessor to compile programs and units in the {$N+} state.

### 116  Must be in 8087 mode to compile this.

This construct can only be compiled in the {$N+} state. Operations on the 8087 real types, single, double, extended, and comp, are not allowed in the {$N-} state.

### 117  Target address not found.

The Compile/Find error command in the integrated environment or the /F option in the command-line version could not locate a statement that corresponds to the specified address.

### 118  Include files are not allowed here.

Every statement part must be entirely contained in one file.

### 119  TPM file format error.

The .TPM file is somehow invalid; make sure it is in fact a .TPM file.

### 120  NIL expected.

### 121  Invalid qualifier.

■ You are trying to index a variable that is not an array.

■ You are trying to specify fields in a variable that is not a record.

■ You are trying to dereference a variable that is not a pointer.

### 122  Invalid variable reference.

The preceding construct follows the syntax of a variable reference, but it does not denote a memory location. Most likely, you are calling a pointer function, but forgetting to dereference the result.

### 123 Too many symbols.

The program or unit declares more than 64K of symbols. If you are compiling with {$D+}, try turning it off—note, however, that this will prevent you from finding runtime errors in that module. Otherwise, you could try moving some declarations into a separate unit.

### 124 Statement part too large.

Turbo Pascal limits the size of a statement part to about 24K. If you encounter this error, move sections of the statement part into one or more procedures. In any case, with a statement part of that size, it's worth the effort to clarify the structure of your program.

### 125 Module has no debug information

A runtime error occurred in a module (program or unit) that has no debug information, and for that reason Turbo Pascal cannot show you the corresponding statement. Recompile the module with **D**ebug info on, and use **C**ompile/**F**ind error to locate the error in the integrated environment or the /F option in the command-line compiler.

### 126 Files must be var parameters

You are attempting to declare a file type value parameter. File type parameters must be **var** parameters.

### 127 Too many conditional symbols

There is not enough room to define further conditional symbols. Try to eliminate some symbols, or shorten some of the symbolic names.

### 128 Misplaced conditional directive

The compiler encountered an {$ELSE} or {$ENDIF} directive without a matching {$IFDEF}, {$IFNDEF}, or {$IFOPT} directive.

### 129 ENDIF directive missing

The source file ended within a conditional compilation construct. There must be an equal number of {$IF*xxx*}s and {$ENDIF}s in a source file.

### 130 Error in initial conditional defines

The initial conditional symbols specified in **O/C/**Conditional defines or in a */D* directive are invalid. Turbo Pascal expects zero or more identifiers separated by blanks, commas, or semicolons.

### 131 Header does not match previous definition

- The procedure or function header specified in the **interface** part does not match this header.
- The procedure or function header specified in the **forward** declaration does not match this header.

### 132 Critical disk error

A critical error occurred during compilation (for example, drive not ready error).

### 133 Old map file

The .TPM file is older than the corresponding .EXE file. This indicates that the last time you compiled your program, a .TPM file was not produced. For example, if TEST.TPM is older than TEST.EXE, you must recompile TEST.PAS with the {$T} compiler directive in order to find a runtime error.

# Runtime Errors

Certain errors at runtime cause the program to display an error message and terminate:

```
Runtime error nnn at xxxx:yyyy
```

where *nnn* is the runtime error number, and *xxxx:yyyy* is the runtime error address (segment and offset).

The runtime errors are divided into four categories: DOS errors 1-99; I/O errors, 100-149; critical errors, 150-199; and fatal errors, 200-255.

## *DOS Errors*

### 2 File not found.

Reported by *Reset*, *Append*, *Rename*, or *Erase* if the name assigned to the file variable does not specify an existing file.

### 3 Path not found.

- Reported by *Reset*, *Rewrite*, *Append*, *Rename*, or *Erase* if the name assigned to the file variable is invalid or specifies an unexisting subdirectory.
- Reported by *ChDir*, *MkDir*, or *RmDir* if the path is invalid or speficies an unexisting subdirectory.

### 4 Too many open files.

Reported by *Reset*, *Rewrite*, or *Append* if the program has too many open files. DOS never allows more than 15 open files per process. If you get this error with less than 15 open files, it may indicate that the CONFIG.SYS file does not include a FILES=$xx$ entry or that the entry specifies too few files. Increase the number to some suitable value, for instance, 20.

### 5 File access denied.

- Reported by *Reset* or *Append* if *FileMode* allows writing and the name assigned to the file variable specifies a directory or a read-only file.
- Reported by *Rewrite* if the directory is full or if the name assigned to the file variable specifies a directory or an existing read-only file.
- Reported by *Rename* if the name assigned to the file variable specifies a directory or if the new name specifies an existing file.
- Reported by *Erase* if the name assigned to the file variable specifies a directory or a read-only file.
- Reported by *MkDir* if a file with the same name exists in the parent directory, if there is no room in the parent directory, or if the path specifies a device.
- Reported by *RmDir* if the directory isn't empty, if the path doesn't specify a directory, or if the path specifies the root directory.
- Reported by *Read* or *BlockRead* on a typed or untyped file if the file is not open for reading.
- Reported by *Write* or *BlockWrite* on a typed or untyped file if the file is not open for writing.

### 6 Invalid file handle.

This error is reported if an invalid file handle is passed to a DOS system call. It should never occur; if it does, it is an indication that the file variable is somehow trashed.

### 12 Invalid file access code.

Reported by *Reset* or *Append* on a typed or untyped file if the value of *FileMode* is invalid.

### 15 Invalid drive number.

Reported by *GetDir* if the drive number is invalid.

### 16 Cannot remove current directory.

Reported by *RmDir* if the path specifies the current directory.

### 17 Cannot rename across drives.

Reported by *Rename* if both names are not on the same drive.

## *I/O Errors*

These errors cause termination if the particular statement was compiled in the {$I+} state. In the {$I-} state, the program continues to execute, and the error is reported by the *IOResult* function.

### 100 Disk read error.

Reported by *Read* on a typed file if you attempt to read past the end of the file.

### 101 Disk write error.

Reported by *Close, Write, Writeln, Flush*, or *Page* if the disk becomes full.

### 102 File not assigned.

Reported by *Reset, Rewrite, Append, Rename*, and *Erase* if the file variable has not been assigned a name through a call to *Assign*.

### 103 File not open.

Reported by *Close, Read, Write, Seek, Eof, FilePos, FileSize, Flush, BlockRead*, or *BlockWrite* if the file is not open.

### 104 File not open for input.

Reported by *Read, Readln, Eof, Eoln, SeekEof*, or *SeekEoln* on a text file if the file is not open for input.

**105  File not open for output.**

Reported by *Write*, *Writeln*, and *Page* on a text file if the file is not open for output.

**106  Invalid numeric format.**

Reported by *Read* or *Readln* if a numeric value read from a text file does not conform to the proper numeric format.

## Critical Errors

**150  Disk is write-protected.**

**151  Unknown unit.**

**152  Drive not ready.**

**153  Unknown command.**

**154  CRC error in data.**

**155  Bad drive request structure length.**

**156  Disk seek error.**

**157  Unknown media type.**

**158  Sector not found.**

**159  Printer out of paper.**

**160  Device write fault.**

**161  Device read fault.**

**162  Hardware failure.**

Refer to your DOS programmer's reference manual for more information about critical errors.

# Fatal Errors

These errors always immediately terminate the program.

**200 Division by zero.**

**201 Range check error.**

This error is reported by statements compiled in the {$R+} state when one of the following situations arise:

- The index expression of an array qualifier was out of range.
- An attempt was made to assign an out of range value to a variable.
- An attempt was made to pass an out of range value as a parameter to a procedure or function.

**202 Stack overflow error.**

This error is reported on entry to a procedure or function compiled in the {$S+} state when there is not enough stack space to allocate the subprogram's local variables. Increase the size of the stack by using the $M compiler directive.

**203 Heap overflow error.**

This error is reported by *New* or *GetMem* when there is not enough free space in the heap to allocate a block of the requested size. For a complete discussion of the heap manager, refer to Chapter 26, "Inside Turbo Pascal."

**204 Invalid pointer operation.**

This error is reported by *Dispose* or *FreeMem* if the pointer is **nil** or points to a location outside the heap, or if the free list cannot be expanded.

**205 Floating point overflow.**

A floating-point operation produced an overflow.

## 206  Floating point underflow

A floating-point operation produced an underflow. This error is only reported if you are using the 8087 numeric coprocessor with a control word that unmasks underflow exceptions. By default, an underflow causes a result of zero to be returned.

## 207  Invalid floating point operation

■ The real value passed to *Trunc* or *Round* could not be converted to an integer within the longint range (-2147483648 to 2147483647).

■ The argument passed to the *Sqrt* function was negative.

■ The argument passed to the *Ln* function was zero or negative.

■ An 8087 stack overflow occurred. For further details on correctly programming the 8087, refer to Chapter 25.

# Borland
# Software

**BORLAND**
*I N T E R N A T I O N A L*

4585 Scotts Valley Drive, Scotts Valley, CA 95066

Available at better dealers nationwide.
To order by credit card, call (800) 255-8008; CA (800) 742-1133;
CANADA (800) 237-1136.

# QUATTRO™

## THE PROFESSIONAL SPREADSHEET

*Borland's super graphic new generation spreadsheet: Twice the power at half the price! Ten types of presentation-quality graphs. Compatible with 1-2-3®, dBASE®, Paradox® and other spreadsheets and databases.*

Quattro, Borland's new generation professional spreadsheet, proves there are better and faster ways to get your work done—whether it's graphics, recalculations, macros, or search and sort.

### Presentation-quality graphics

Quattro has excellent built-in graphics capabilities that help you create a wide variety of graphs. Bar graphs, line graphs, pie charts, XY graphs, area charts—you can create up to 10 types of graphs, and print them directly from the spreadsheet or store them for future use.

### Smarter recalculation

When a formula needs to be recalculated, Quattro uses "intelligent recalc" to recalculate only those formulas whose elements have changed. This makes Quattro smarter and faster than other spreadsheets.

### Greater macro capability

You can create macros instantly by *recording* your actions and storing them in the spreadsheet. The number of macros is limited only by memory. A built-in macro debugging environment makes it easy to find and correct problem areas. Quattro also includes a set of over 40 macro commands which make up a programming language.

*Suggested retail price $195.00 (not copy protected)*

### Direct compatibility

Quattro can directly load and use data files created with other spreadsheet and database programs like 1-2-3, dBASE, and Paradox. Quattro can read and even write WKS, WK1, and WKE files. You can also import ASCII and other text files into the spreadsheet.

### Easy installation

Quattro can detect most computers and screen types, so it's always ready to load and run!

Plus, like all other Borland products, Quattro is *not copy protected!*

### Technical Features

- Understands your 1-2-3 macros
- 100 built-in financial and statistical functions
- Menu Builder add-in for customizing menus
- Supports 8087/80287 math coprocessors
- Supports EGA, CGA, and VGA graphics adapters
- Pop-up menus
- Shortcuts to menu commands
- Context-sensitive online help
- Three types of choice lists: @functions and syntax, macro commands, and existing block names
- Pointing lets you specify a block of cells using arrow keys
- Search (or Query) lets you find specific records or cells
- Lets you arrange/rearrange data in alphabetical, numerical, or chronological order
- Supports Expanded Memory Specification to create spreadsheets larger than 640K
- Supports PostScript™ printers and typesetters

Minimum system requirements: For the IBM PS/2™ and the IBM® and Compaq® families of personal computers and all 100% compatibles. PC-DOS (MS-DOS®) 2.0 or later. Two floppies or a hard disk. 384K.

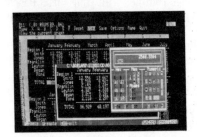

# SUPERKEY® THE PRODUCTIVITY BOOSTER

## RAM-resident
## Increased productivity for IBM®PCs or compatibles

### SuperKey's simple macros are electronic shortcuts to success. By letting you reduce a lengthy paragraph into a single keystroke of your choice, SuperKey eliminates repetition.

### SuperKey turns 1,000 keystrokes into 1!

SuperKey can record lengthy keystroke sequences and play them back at the touch of a single key. Instantly. Like magic.

In fact, with SuperKey's simple macros, you can turn "Dear Customer: Thank you for your inquiry. We are pleased to let you know that shipment will be made within 24 hours. Sincerely," into the one keystroke of your choice!

### SuperKey keeps your confidential files—confidential!

Without encryption, your files are open secrets. Anyone can walk up to your PC and read your confidential files (tax returns, business plans, customer lists, personal letters, etc.).

With SuperKey you can encrypt any file, *even* while running another program. As long as you keep the password secret, only *you* can decode your file correctly. SuperKey also implements the U.S. government Data Encryption Standard (DES).

- ☑ RAM resident—accepts new macro files even while running other programs
- ☑ Pull-down menus
- ☑ Superfast file encryption
- ☑ Choice of two encryption schemes
- ☑ On-line context-sensitive help
- ☑ One-finger mode reduces key commands to single keystroke
- ☑ Screen OFF/ON blanks out and restores screen to protect against "burn in"
- ☑ Partial or complete reorganization of keyboard
- ☑ Keyboard buffer increases 16 character keyboard "type-ahead" buffer to 128 characters
- ☑ Real-time delay causes macro playback to pause for specified interval
- ☑ Transparent display macros allow creation of menus on top of application programs
- ☑ Data entry and format control using "fixed" or "variable" fields
- ☑ Command stack recalls last 256 characters entered

### Suggested Retail Price: $99.95 (not copy protected)

**Minimum system configuration:** IBM PC, XT, AT, PCjr, and true compatibles. PC-DOS (MS-DOS) 2.0 or greater. 128K RAM. One disk drive.

BOR 0062C

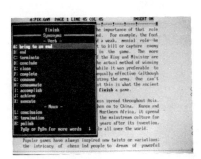

# REFLEX: THE WORKSHOP™

*Includes 22 "instant templates" covering a broad range of business applications (listed below). Also shows you how to customize databases, graphs, crosstabs, and reports. It's an invaluable analytical tool and an important addition to another one of our best sellers, Reflex: The Database Manager.*

## Fast-start tutorial examples:

Learn Reflex® as you work with practical business applications. The Reflex Workshop Disk supplies databases and reports large enough to illustrate the power and variety of Reflex features. Instructions in each Reflex Workshop chapter take you through a step-by-step analysis of sample data. You then follow simple steps to adapt the files to your own needs.

## 22 practical business applications:

Workshop's 22 "instant templates" give you a wide range of analytical tools:

### Administration
- Scheduling Appointments
- Planning Conference Facilities
- Managing a Project
- Creating a Mailing System
- Managing Employment Applications

### Sales and Marketing
- Researching Store Check Inventory
- Tracking Sales Leads
- Summarizing Sales Trends
- Analyzing Trends

### Production and Operations
- Summarizing Repair Turnaround

- Tracking Manufacturing Quality Assurance
- Analyzing Product Costs

### Accounting and Financial Planning
- Tracking Petty Cash
- Entering Purchase Orders
- Organizing Outgoing Purchase Orders
- Analyzing Accounts Receivable
- Maintaining Letters of Credit
- Reporting Business Expenses
- Managing Debits and Credits
- Examining Leased Inventory Trends
- Tracking Fixed Assets
- Planning-Commercial Real Estate Investment

Whether you're a newcomer learning Reflex basics or an experienced "power user" looking for tips, Reflex: The Workshop will help you quickly become an expert database analyst.

**Minimum system configuration: IBM PC, AT, and XT, and true compatibles. PC-DOS (MS-DOS) 2.0 or greater. 384K RAM minimum. Requires Reflex: The Database Manager, and IBM Color Graphics Adapter, Hercules Monochrome Graphics Card or equivalent.**

 **BORLAND**
INTERNATIONAL

*Suggested Retail Price: $69.95
(not copy protected)*

# TURBO PROLOG ™

## the natural language of Artificial Intelligence

### Turbo Prolog brings fifth-generation supercomputer power to your IBM®PC!

## Turbo Prolog takes programming into a new, natural, and logical environment

With Turbo Prolog, because of its natural, logical approach, both people new to programming *and* professional programmers can build powerful applications such as expert systems, customized knowledge bases, natural language interfaces, and smart information management systems.

Turbo Prolog is a *declarative* language which uses deductive reasoning to solve programming problems.

Turbo Prolog provides a fully integrated programming environment like Borland's Turbo Pascal,® the *de facto* worldwide standard.

## You get the complete Turbo Prolog programming system

You get the 200-page manual you're holding, software that includes the lightning-fast Turbo Prolog six-pass compiler and interactive editor, and the free GeoBase natural query language database, which includes commented source code on disk, ready to compile. (GeoBase is a complete database designed and developed around U.S. geography. You can modify it or use it "as is.")

## Turbo Prolog's development system includes:

- ☐ A complete Prolog compiler that is a variation of the Clocksin and Mellish Edinburgh standard Prolog.
- ☐ A full-screen interactive editor.
- ☐ Support for both graphic and text windows.
- ☐ All the tools that let you build your own expert systems and **AI** applications with unprecedented ease.

**Minimum system configuration:** IBM PC, XT, AT, Portable, 3270, PCjr and true compatibles. PC-DOS (MS-DOS) 2.0 or later. 384K RAM minimum.

*Suggested Retail Price: $99.95*
*(not copy protected)*

# TURBO PROLOG™ TOOLBOX

## Enhances Turbo Prolog with more than 80 tools and over 8,000 lines of source code

### Turbo Prolog, the natural language of Artificial Intelligence, is the most popular AI package in the world with more than 100,000 users. Our new Turbo Prolog Toolbox extends its possibilities.

The Turbo Prolog Toolbox enhances Turbo Prolog—our 5th-generation computer programming language that brings supercomputer power to your IBM PC and compatibles—with its more than 80 tools and over 8,000 lines of source code that can be incorporated into your programs, quite easily.

---

**Turbo Prolog Toolbox features include:**

- ☑ Business graphics generation: boxes, circles, ellipses, bar charts, pie charts, scaled graphics
- ☑ Complete communications package: supports XModem protocol
- ☑ File transfers from Reflex,® dBASE III,® Lotus 1-2-3,® Symphony®
- ☑ A unique parser generator: construct your own compiler or query language
- ☑ Sophisticated user-interface design tools
- ☑ 40 example programs
- ☑ Easy-to-use screen editor: design your screen layout and I/O
- ☑ Calculated fields definition
- ☑ Over 8,000 lines of source code you can incorporate into your own programs

---

*Suggested Retail Price: $99.95 (not copy protected)*

**Minimum system configuration:** IBM PC, XT, AT or true compatibles. PC-DOS (MS-DOS) 2.0 or later. Requires Turbo Prolog 1.10 or higher. Dual-floppy disk drive or hard disk. 512K.

**BORLAND** INTERNATIONAL

# TURBO BASIC®

## The high-speed BASIC you've been waiting for!

*You probably know us for our Turbo Pascal® and Turbo Prolog.® Well, we've done it again! We've created Turbo Basic, because BASIC doesn't have to be slow.*

### If BASIC taught you how to walk, Turbo Basic will teach you how to run!

With Turbo Basic, your only speed is "Full Speed Ahead"! Turbo Basic is a complete development environment with an *amazingly fast compiler,* an *interactive editor* and a *trace debugging system*. And because Turbo Basic is also compatible with BASICA, chances are that you already know how to use Turbo Basic.

### Turbo Basic ends the basic confusion

There's now one standard: Turbo Basic. And because Turbo Basic is a Borland product, the price is right, the quality is there, and the power is at your fingertips. Turbo Basic is part of the fast-growing Borland family of programming languages we call the "Turbo Family." And hundreds of thousands of users are already using Borland's languages. So, welcome to a whole new generation of smart PC users!

### Free spreadsheet included with source code!

Yes, we've included MicroCalc,™ our sample spreadsheet, complete with source code. So you can get started right away with a "real program." You can compile and run it "as is," or modify it.

---

### A technical look at Turbo Basic

- ☑ Full recursion supported
- ☑ Standard IEEE floating-point format
- ☑ Floating-point support, with full 8087 coprocessor integration. Software emulation if no 8087 present
- ☑ Program size limited only by available memory (no 64K limitation)
- ☑ EGA, CGA, MCGA and VGA support
- ☑ Full integration of the compiler, editor, and executable program, with separate windows for editing, messages, tracing, and execution
- ☑ Compile and run-time errors place you in source code where error occurred
- ☑ Access to local, static and global variables
- ☑ New long integer (32-bit) data type
- ☑ Full 80-bit precision
- ☑ Pull-down menus
- ☑ Full window management

---

### Suggested Retail Price: $99.95 (not copy protected)

**Minimum system configuration:** IBM PC, AT, XT, PS/2 or true compatibles. 320K. One floppy drive. PC-DOS (MS-DOS) 2.0 or later.

**BORLAND**
INTERNATIONAL

Turbo Basic, Turbo Prolog and Turbo Pascal are registered trademarks and MicroCalc is a trademark of Borland International, Inc. Other brand and product names are trademarks or registered trademarks of their respective holders.
Copyright 1987 Borland International

BOR 0265B

# TURBO BASIC®
# DATABASE TOOLBOX™

**With the Turbo Basic Database Toolbox you can build your own powerful, professional-quality database programs. And like all other Borland Toolboxes, it's advanced enough for professional programmers yet easy enough for beginners.**

### Three ready-to-use modules

The Toolbox enhances your programming with three problem-solving modules:

***Turbo Access*** quickly locates, inserts, or deletes records in a database using B+ trees—the fastest method for finding and retrieving database information. (Source code is included.)

***Turbo Sort*** uses the *Quicksort* method to sort data on single items or on multiple keys. Features virtual memory management for sorting large data files. (Commented source code is on disk.)

***TRAINER*** is a demonstration program that graphically displays how B+ trees work. You can key in sample records and see a visual index of B+ trees being built.

### Free sample database

Included is a free sample database with source code. Just compile it, and it's ready to go to work for you—you can use it as is or customize it. You can search the database by keywords or numbers, update records, or add and delete them, as needed.

### Saves you time and money

If you're a professional programmer writing software for databases or other applications where search-and-sort capabilities are important, we can save you time and money. Instead of writing the same tedious but essential routines over and over again, you can simply include any of the Toolbox's modules in your own compiled programs.

---

### Technical Features

- ☑ Maximum number of files open: 15 files, or 7 data sets
- ☑ Maximum file size: 32 Mb
- ☑ Maximum record size: 32K
- ☑ Maximum number of records: +2 billion
- ☑ Maximum field size: 32K
- ☑ Maximum key size: 128 bytes
- ☑ Maximum number of keys: +2 billion

---

**Suggested Retail Price: $99.95   (not copy protected)**

**Minimum system requirements:** For the IBM PS/2 and the IBM® and Compaq® families of personal computers and all 100% compatibles, running Turbo Basic 1.0. PC-DOS (MS-DOS®) 2.0 or later. Memory: 640K.

# TURBO BASIC®
# EDITOR TOOLBOX™

*With Turbo Basic we gave you the fastest BASIC around. Now the Turbo Basic Editor Toolbox will help you build your own superfast editor to incorporate into your Turbo Basic programs. We provide all the editing routines. You plug in the features you want!*

### Two sample editors with source code

To demonstrate the tremendous power of the Toolbox, we've included two sample editors with complete source code:

***FirstEd.*** A complete editor with windows, block commands, and memory-mapped screen routines, all ready to include in your programs.

***MicroStar™:*** A full-blown text editor with a pull-down menu user interface and all the standard features you'd expect in any word processor. Plus features other word processors can't begin to match:

- ☑ RAM-based editor for superfast editing
- ☑ View and edit up to eight windows at a time
- ☑ Support for line, stream, and column block mode
- ☑ Instant paging, scrolling, and text display
- ☑ Up to eight hidden buffers at a time to edit, swap, and call text from

- ☑ Multitasking to let you print in the "background"
- ☑ Keyboard installation for customizing command keys
- ☑ Custom designing of colors for text, windows, menus, and status line
- ☑ Support for DOS functions like Copy file, Delete file, Change directory, and Change logged drive

### Build the word processor of your choice!

We give you easy-to-install modules. Use them to build yourself a full-screen editor with pull-down menus, and make it work as fast as most word processors—without having to spend hundreds of dollars!

Source code for everything in the Toolbox is provided. Use any of its features in your own Turbo Basic programs or in programs you develop for others. You don't even have to pay royalties!

***Suggested Retail Price: $99.95 (not copy protected)***

**Minimum system requirements:** For the IBM PS/2™ and the IBM® and Compaq® families of personal computers and all 100% compatibles running Turbo Basic 1.0. PC-DOS (MS-DOS®) 2.0 or greater. Memory: 640K.

# TURBO C®

## A complete interactive development environment

**With Turbo C, you can expect what only Borland delivers: Quality, Speed, Power and Price. And with its compilation speed of more than 7000 lines a minute, Turbo C makes everything else look like an exercise in slow motion.**

### Turbo C: The C compiler for both amateurs and professionals

If you're just beginning and you've "kinda wanted to learn C," now's your chance to do it the easy way. Turbo C's got everything to get you going. If you're already programming in C, switching to Turbo C will considerably increase your productivity and help make your programs both smaller and faster.

### Turbo C: a complete interactive development environment

Like Turbo Pascal® and Turbo Prolog,™ Turbo C comes with an interactive editor that will show you syntax errors right in your source code. Developing, debugging, and running a Turbo C program is a snap!

---

#### Technical Specifications

☑ Compiler: One-pass compiler generating native in-line code, linkable object modules and assembler. The object module format is compatible with the PC-DOS linker. Supports small, medium, compact, large, and huge memory model libraries. Can mix models with near and far pointers. Includes floating point emulator (utilizes 8087/80287 if installed).

☑ Interactive Editor: The system includes a powerful, interactive full-screen text editor. If the compiler detects an error, the editor automatically positions the cursor appropriately in the source code.

☑ Development Environment: A powerful "Make" is included so that managing Turbo C program development is easy. Borland's fast "Turbo Linker" is also included. Also includes pull-down menus and windows. Can run from the environment or generate an executable file.

☑ Links with relocatable object modules created using Borland's Turbo Prolog into a single program.

☑ ANSI C compatible.

☑ Start-up routine source code included.

☑ Both command line and integrated environment versions included.

---

#### "Sieve" benchmark (25 iterations)

|  | Turbo C | Microsoft® C | Lattice C |
|---|---|---|---|
| Compile time | **3.89** | 16.37 | 13.90 |
| Compile and link time | **9.94** | 29.06 | 27.79 |
| Execution time | **5.77** | 9.51 | 13.79 |
| Object code size | **274** | 297 | 301 |
| Price | **$99.95** | $450.00 | $500.00 |

Benchmark run on a 6 Mhz IBM AT using Turbo C version 1.0 and the Turbo Linker version 1.0; Microsoft C version 4.0 and the MS overlay linker version 3.51; Lattice C version 3.1 and the MS object linker version 3.05.

---

**Suggested Retail Price: $99.95\* (not copy protected)**  \*Introductory offer good through July 1, 1987.

**Minimum system configuration:** IBM PC, XT, AT and true compatibles. PC-DOS (MS-DOS) 2.0 or later. One floppy drive. 320K.

**BORLAND**
INTERNATIONAL

# EUREKA: THE SOLVER™

## The solution to your most complex equations—in seconds!

If you're a scientist, engineer, financial analyst, student, teacher, or any other professional working with equations, Eureka: The Solver can do your Algebra, Trigonometry and Calculus problems in a snap.

Eureka also handles maximization and minimization problems, plots functions, generates reports, and saves an incredible amount of time. Even if you're not a computer specialist, Eureka can help you solve your real-world mathematical problems fast, without having to learn numerical approximation techniques. Using Borland's famous pull-down menu design and context-sensitive help screens, Eureka is easy to learn and easy to use—as simple as a hand-held calculator.

### $X + exp(X) = 10$ solved instantly instead of eventually!

Imagine you have to "solve for X," where $X + exp(X) = 10$, and you don't have Eureka: The Solver. What you do have is a problem, because it's going to take a lot of time guessing at "X." With Eureka, there's no guessing, no dancing in the dark—you get the right answer, right now. (PS: $X = 2.0705799$, and Eureka solved that one in .4 of a second!)

### How to use Eureka: The Solver

It's easy.
1. Enter your equation into the full-screen editor
2. Select the "Solve" command
3. Look at the answer
4. You're done

You can then tell Eureka to
- Evaluate your solution
- Plot a graph
- Generate a report, then send the output to your printer, disk file or screen
- Or all of the above

---

#### Some of Eureka's key features
You can key in:
- ☑ A formula or formulas
- ☑ A series of equations—and solve for all variables
- ☑ Constraints (like X has to be $<$ or $= 2$)
- ☑ A function to plot
- ☑ Unit conversions
- ☑ Maximization and minimization problems
- ☑ Interest Rate/Present Value calculations
- ☑ Variables we call "What happens?," like "What happens if I change this variable to 21 and that variable to 27?"

#### Eureka: The Solver includes
- ☑ A full-screen editor
- ☑ Pull-down menus
- ☑ Context-sensitive Help
- ☑ On-screen calculator
- ☑ Automatic 8087 math co-processor chip support
- ☑ Powerful financial functions
- ☑ Built-in and user-defined math and financial functions
- ☑ Ability to generate reports complete with plots and lists
- ☑ Polynomial finder
- ☑ Inequality solutions

---

**Minimum system configuration:** IBM PC, AT, XT, PS/2, Portable, 3270 and true compatibles. PC-DOS (MS-DOS) 2.0 and later. 384K.

*Suggested Retail Price: $167.00*
*(not copy protected)*

# SIDEKICK® THE DESKTOP ORGANIZER Release 2.0
### Macintosh™

## The most complete and comprehensive collection of desk accessories available for your Macintosh!

Thousands of users already know that SideKick is the best collection of desk accessories available for the Macintosh. With our new Release 2.0, the best just got better.

We've just added two powerful high-performance tools to SideKick—Outlook™: The Outliner and MacPlan™: The Spreadsheet. They work in perfect harmony with each other and *while* you run other programs!

### Outlook: The Outliner

- It's the desk accessory with more power than a stand-alone outliner
- A great desktop publishing tool, Outlook lets you incorporate both text and graphics into your outlines
- Works hand-in-hand with MacPlan
- Allows you to work on several outlines at the same time

### MacPlan: The Spreadsheet

- Integrates spreadsheets and graphs
- Does both formulas and straight numbers
- Graph types include bar charts, stacked bar charts, pie charts and line graphs
- Includes 12 example templates free!
- Pastes graphics and data right into Outlook creating professional memos and reports, complete with headers and footers.

---

**SideKick: The Desktop Organizer, Release 2.0 now includes**

- ☑ Outlook: The Outliner
- ☑ MacPlan: The Spreadsheet
- ☑ Mini word processor
- ☑ Calendar
- ☑ PhoneLog
- ☑ Analog clock
- ☑ Alarm system
- ☑ Calculator
- ☑ Report generator
- ☑ Telecommunications (new version now supports XModem file transfer protocol)

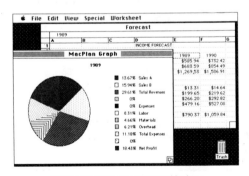

*MacPlan does both spreadsheets and business graphs. Paste them into your Outlook files and generate professional reports.*

## Suggested Retail Price: $99.95 (not copy protected)

**Minimum system configurations:** Macintosh 512K or Macintosh Plus with one disk drive. One 800K or two 400K drives are recommended. With one 400K drive, a limited number of desk accessories will be installable per disk.

# TURBO PASCAL® MACINTOSH™

## The ultimate Pascal development environment

### Borland's new Turbo Pascal for the Mac is so incredibly fast that it can compile 1,420 lines of source code in the 7.1 seconds it took you to read this!

And reading the rest of this takes about *5 minutes*, which is plenty of time for Turbo Pascal for the Mac to compile at least *60,000 more lines* of source code!

### Turbo Pascal for the Mac does both Windows and "Units"

The *separate* compilation of routines offered by Turbo Pascal for the Mac creates modules called "Units," which can be linked to any Turbo Pascal program. This "modular pathway" gives you "pieces" which can then be integrated into larger programs. You get a more efficient use of memory and a reduction in the time it takes to develop large programs.

### Turbo Pascal for the Mac is so compatible with Lisa® that they should be living together

Routines from Macintosh Programmer's Workshop Pascal and Inside Macintosh can be compiled and run with only the subtlest changes. Turbo Pascal for the Mac is also compatible with the Hierarchical File System of the Macintosh.

---

### The 27-second Guide to Turbo Pascal for the Mac

- Compilation speed of more than 12,000 lines per minute
- "Unit" structure lets you create programs in modular form
- Multiple editing windows—up to 8 at once
- Compilation options include compiling to disk or memory, or compile and run
- No need to switch between programs to compile or run a program
- Streamlined development and debugging
- Compatibility with Macintosh Programmer's
- Workshop Pascal (with minimal changes)
- Compatibility with Hierarchical File System of your Mac
- Ability to define default volume and folder names used in compiler directives
- Search and change features in the editor speed up and simplify alteration of routines
- Ability to use all available Macintosh memory without limit
- "Units" included to call all the routines provided by Macintosh Toolbox

---

### Suggested Retail Price: $99.95* (not copy protected)

*Introductory price expires July 1, 1987

**Minimum system configuration:** Macintosh 512K or Macintosh Plus with one disk drive.

**3 MacWinners from Borland!**
First there was SideKick for the Mac, then Reflex for the Mac, and now Turbo Pascal for the Mac"!

# TURBO PASCAL® TUTOR

*From the folks who created Turbo Pascal. Borland's new Turbo Pascal Tutor is everything you need to start programming in Turbo Pascal on the Macintosh!™ It takes you from the bare basics to advanced programming in a simple, easy-to-understand fashion.*

No gimmicks. It's all here.

The manual, the Tutor application, and 30 sample programs provide a step-by-step tutorial in three phases: programming in Pascal, programming on the Macintosh, and programming in Turbo Pascal on the Macintosh. Here's how the manual is set up:

### Turbo Pascal for the Absolute Novice

delivers the basics—a concise history of Pascal, key terminology, your first program.

### A Programmer's Guide to Turbo Pascal

covers Pascal specifics—program structure, procedures and functions, arrays, strings, and so on. We've also included Turbo Typist, a textbook sample program.

### Advanced Programming

takes you a step higher into stacks, queues, binary trees, linked structures, writing large programs, and more.

### Using the Power of the Macintosh

discusses the revolutionary hardware and software features of this machine. It introduces the 600-plus utility routines in the Apple Toolbox.

### Programming the Macintosh in Turbo Pascal

shows you how to create true Macintosh programs that use graphics, pull-down menus, dialog boxes, and so on. Finally, MacTypist, a complete stand-alone application featuring animated graphics, builds on Turbo Typist and demonstrates what you can do with all the knowledge you've just acquired.

The disk contains the source code for all the sample programs, including Turbo Typist, MacTypist, and Turbo Tutor. The Tutor's split screen lets you run a procedure and view its source code simultaneously. After running it, you can take a test on the procedure. If you're stuck for an answer, a Hint option steers you in the right direction.

---

## Macintosh topics included are

- ☑ memory management
- ☑ resources and resource files
- ☑ QuickDraw
- ☑ events
- ☑ windows
- ☑ controls
- ☑ menus
- ☑ desk accessory support
- ☑ dialogs
- ☑ File Manager
- ☑ debugging

---

**Suggested Retail Price: $69.95**

**Minimum system requirements:** Any Macintosh with at least 512K of RAM. Requires Turbo Pascal.

## BORLAND
### INTERNATIONAL

# EUREKA: THE SOLVER™

**If you're a scientist, engineer, financial analyst, student, teacher, or any other professional working with equations, Eureka: The Solver can do your Algebra, Trigonometry and Calculus problems in a snap.**

Eureka also handles maximization and minimization problems, plots functions, generates reports, and saves an incredible amount of time. Even if you're not a computer specialist, Eureka can help you solve your real-world mathematical problems fast, without having to learn numerical approximation techniques. Eureka is easy to learn and easy to use—as simple as a hand-held calculator.

### $X + exp(X) = 10$ solved instantly instead of eventually!

Imagine you have to solve for X, where $X + exp(X) = 10$, and you don't have Eureka: The Solver. What you do have is a problem, because it's going to take a lot of time guessing at X. With Eureka, there's no guessing, no dancing in the dark— you get the right answer, right now. (PS: $X = 2.0705799$, and Eureka solved that one in less than 5 seconds!)

### How to use Eureka: The Solver
It's easy.
1. Enter your equation into a problem text window
2. Select the "Solve" command
3. Look at the answer
4. You're done

You can then tell Eureka to:
- Verify the solutions
- Draw a graph
- Zoom in on interesting areas of the graph
- Generate a report and send the output to your printer or disk file
- Or all of the above

---

### Some of Eureka's key features
You can key in:
- ☑ A formula or formulas
- ☑ A series of equations—and solve for all variables
- ☑ Constraints (like X must be $<$ or $= 2$)
- ☑ Functions to plot
- ☑ Unit conversions
- ☑ Maximization and minimization problems
- ☑ Interest Rate/Present Value calculations
- ☑ Variables we call "What happens?," like "What happens if I change this variable to 21 and that variable to 27?"

### Eureka: The Solver includes:
- ☑ Calculator+ desk accessory
- ☑ Powerful financial functions
- ☑ Built-in and user-defined functions
- ☑ Reports: generate and save them as MacWrite™ files—complete with graphs and lists—or as Text Only files
- ☑ Polynomial root finder
- ☑ Inequality constraints
- ☑ Logging: keep an up-to-the-minute record of your work
- ☑ Macintosh™ text editor
- ☑ On-screen Help system

---

**Suggested Retail Price: $195.00 (not copy protected)**

**Minimum system configuration:** Macintosh 512K, Macintosh Plus, SE, or II with one 800K disk drive or two 400K disk drives.

Eureka: The Solver is a trademark of Borland International, Inc. Macintosh is a trademark of McIntosh Laboratory, Inc. licensed to Apple Computer, Inc. Copyright 1987 Borland International

BOR 0415

# TURBO PASCAL TOOLBOX™
# NUMERICAL METHODS

**Turbo Pascal Numerical Methods Toolbox for the Macintosh implements the latest high-level mathematical methods to solve common scientific and engineering problems. Fast.**

So every time you need to calculate an integral, work with Fourier transforms, or incorporate any of the classical numerical analysis tools into your programs, you don't have to reinvent the wheel, because the Numerical Methods Toolbox is a complete collection of Turbo Pascal routines and programs that gives you applied state-of-the-art math tools. It also includes two graphics demo programs that use least-square and Fast Fourier Transform routines to give you the picture along with the numbers.

The Turbo Pascal Numerical Methods Toolbox is a must if you're involved with any type of scientific or engineering computing on the Macintosh. Because it comes with complete source code, you have total control of your application at all times.

## What Numerical Methods Toolbox will do for you:

- Find solutions to equations
- Interpolations
- Calculus: numerical derivatives and integrals
- Matrix operations: inversions, determinants, and eigenvalues

- Differential equations
- Least-squares approximations
- Fourier transforms
- Graphics

---

### *Five free ways to look at Least-Squares Fit!*

As well as a free demo of Fast Fourier Transforms, you also get the Least-Squares Fit in five different forms—which gives you five different methods of fitting curves to a collection of data points. You instantly get the picture! The five different forms are

1. Power
2. Exponential
3. Logarithm

4. 5-term Fourier
5. 5-term Poynomial

They're all ready to compile and run as is.

---

## Suggested Retail Price: $99.95 (not copy protected)

**Minimum system requirements:** Macintosh 512K, Macintosh Plus, SE, or II, with one 800K disk drive (or two 400K).

All Borland products are trademarks or registered trademarks of Borland International, Inc. or Borland/Analytica, Inc. Macintosh is a trademark licensed to Apple Computer, Inc. Copyright 1987 Borland International A Borland *Turbo Toolbox* product

BOR 0419

# Borland
# Software
# ORDER TODAY

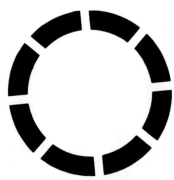

# Index

# C

# G

# L

Labels, 197, 527
  declaration part, 202
Language help
  online, 176
Large programs, 631
  managing, 85-98
Last text mode constant, 525
$L compiler directive, 63, 84, 158,
  161, 353, 522, 530, 540
Length function, 118, 286, 440
Libraries
  files, 4
  program, 12
  routines, 120
Line input, Crt, 299
Line numbers, in .MAP files, 539
Line procedure, 320, 440
LineRel procedure, 320, 441
Line settings, 417
LineTo procedure, 320, 442
Link
  assembly language, 353
  buffer, 158, 540
  $L directive, 63
  object file, 543
Ln function, 285, 443
Loading
  options, 151, 162
  pick files, 163
  programs in DOS, 602
  Turbo Pascal, 25
Load options, 151, 162
Lo function, 287, 443
Logical operators, 48, 240
LongFile functions (3.0), 112, 524
LongFilePos function, 108, 115, 324,
  523
LongFileSize function, 108, 115, 324,
  523-524
Longint data type, 40, 76, 207
LongSeek function, 108, 115, 324, 524
Loops
  defined, 39
  for, 55
  repeat..until, 54

  while, 53
Low heap limit setting, 159
LowVideo procedure, 112, 116, 304,
  324, 444, 523
LPT devices, 281, 292
LST:, 112
Lst function, 117, 292, 523
LstOutPtr, 523

# M

Machine code, 32, 358-361
Macros
  inline, 360-361
  makefile, 556-561
Main screen, integrated environment,
  20
Make command, 3, 32, 34, 88, 154,
  182
MAKE utility, 13, 89-91
  command-line options, 89-91, 549,
    566
  error messages, 567-569
  syntax, 565
  using, 565
Makefiles, creating, 549
.MAP files, 4, 132-142, 539, 542
  menu option, 158
Mark procedure, 284, 337-338, 444
MASM assembler, 84
Math coprocessor, 40, 76, 94, 96, 119,
  329-334, 350, 526-527, 540
  data types, 76
  error messages, 632
  evaluation stack, 332
  menu option, 158
  mode, 632
  $N+ directive, 76, 119
MaxAvail function, 108, 112, 115, 121,
  284, 324, 342, 445, 523
MaxInt, 39
$M compiler directive, 121, 159, 182,
  336, 438, 445-446, 522
Mem array, 361, 530
MemAvail function, 108, 112, 115,
  121, 284, 322, 324, 342, 445, 523
MemL array, 361, 530

# V